MEDIEVAL CHILDREN

MEDIEVAL CHILDREN

Nicholas Orme

Yale University Press
New Haven and London

For Verity

Designed by Adam Freudenheim

Set in Baskerville by Best-Set Typesetter Ltd., Hong Kong

Printed in China through World Print, Ltd.

Library of Congress Cataloging-in-Publication Data

Orme, Nicholas.
    Medieval children / Nicholas Orme.
        p. cm.
    Includes bibliographical references and index
    ISBN 0-300-08541-9 (alk. paper)
        1. Children—England—History. 2. England—Social Conditions—1066–1485.
        3. Social history—Medieval, 500–1500. I. Title.

    HQ792.G7 O74 2001
    305.23'0942'0902–dc21

                                                                        2001026172

A catalogue record for this book is available from the British Library

10 9 8 7 6 5 4 3 2 1

CONTENTS

LIST OF ILLUSTRATIONS

ACKNOWLEDGEMENTS

The author and publishers are grateful for permission to reproduce illustrations as follows:

Her Majesty Queen Elizabeth II (46; 72).
The Bibliographical Society (5; 20; 25; 37; 91; 103; 107).
The Team Rector and Churchwardens, Doddiscombsleigh Church (11; 78; 79; 80).
The Dean and Chapter of Exeter Cathedral (24; 41; 59; 105).
Glasgow University Library (89).
The British Library, London (31; 45; 74; 77; 85; 86; 93; 95; 98; 122).
The Guildhall Library, London (32).
The Museum of London (2; 27; 62; 63; 64).
The National Gallery, London (30).
The Victoria and Albert Museum, London (97).
The John Rylands University Library, Manchester (3; 54).
The Rare Book and Manuscript Library, Columbia University, New York (90).
The Pierpont Morgan Library, New York (47).
The Master and Fellows of Balliol College, Oxford (17; 92).
The Bodleian Library, Oxford (4; 6; 7; 9; 12; 18; 21; 23; 33; 34; 35; 38; 43; 44; 48; 49; 52; 53; 57; 61; 65; 67; 68; 69; 70; 73; 76; 82; 83; 88; 99; 100; 101; 104; 106; 111; 112; 113; 114; 115; 118; 120; 123; 124).
The Rector and Fellows of Lincoln College, Oxford (51).
The President and Fellows of Magdalen College, Oxford (56; 87).
The Warden and Fellows of New College, Oxford (40).
The President and Fellows of Trinity College, Oxford (22).
The Master and Fellows of University College, Oxford (116).
Mr A. G. Swift (81).
Biblioteca Marciana, Venice (1; 28).
Kunsthistorisches Museum, Vienna (58)

PREFACE

This book has been long in the making, and my first thanks must go to the publishers for their patience during the process: in particular to Mr Adam Freudenheim for his care and courtesy as designer and editor. The University of Exeter, my colleagues in the Department of History, the British Academy, the Leverhulme Trust, and the Nuffield Foundation generously enabled me to take periods of study leave for research and writing. Magdalen College and St John's College, Oxford, provided much appreciated hospitality. Two leading experts on medieval childhood, Mme Danièle Alexandre-Bidon and Professor Shulamith Shahar, kindly shared information and advice, as did Mrs Iona Opie, the foremost British authority on the history of childhood. Dr Roger Bowers gave me valuable assistance in the field of music, and my colleague Dr John Critchley made perceptive comments on the whole of the book. I am most grateful for help on other subjects to Dr W. R. J. Barron, Miss Marian Campbell, Dr Michael Clanchy, Professor Helen Cooper, Dr Julia Crick, Dr A. I. Doyle, Mr Geoff Egan, Mrs A. Fitzsimons, Professor Anne Hudson, Dr Anthony Musson, Professor Derek Pearsall, Pamela Lady Wedgwood (Dr Pamela Tudor-Craig), and Dr Edward Wilson. The photography in the book is much indebted to Miss Madeleine Midgley, Mr A. G. Swift, and Mr Andrew Teed, and the text to the assistance of the staff of the archives and libraries listed in the bibliography. Without having been a parent, however, I could never have written this book at all, and it owes more than I can say to my wife Rona and my daughter Verity, to whom it is dedicated.

Introduction

1   A domestic scene from an early sixteenth-century Flemish manuscript. Artists had long taken a special interest in children and their pursuits.

WHAT IS CHILDHOOD? The question is not easy to answer, despite the fact that we have all been children ourselves. To start with, childhood lacks clear boundaries. In one sense it begins at birth, yet a baby takes a year or so to become a recognisable child that walks and talks. Its exit point is even less defined. The *Oxford English Dictionary* ends it at puberty, but puberty varies in age by gender and from child to child. A young person is not fully grown in body until well after puberty, and in knowledge and experience often much later. Our laws do not agree when childhood stops; they dole out adulthood in spoonfuls, one at a time. During the last hundred years, the ages of fourteen, fifteen, sixteen, seventeen, eighteen, and twenty-one have all been fixed as thresholds when a child may stay alone at home, leave school, do full-time work, marry, drive a vehicle, join the armed forces, suffer capital punishment, or vote in elections. Nor have these thresholds stayed constant; some have been raised and others lowered.

The span of childhood too, however defined, enfolds an enormous range of development. How can the same word apply to a baby or toddler at one end and an adolescent at the other? True, all children share features which distinguish them from adults. Even at puberty, they are smaller, less experienced, and under a measure of control. They go to school, not to work, and are clothed, eat, play, and read in ways that differ in certain respects from their elders. Yet the old and the young have things in common as well. The clothes, food, games, and reading of children may imitate those of their parents, or be identical except in scale. Adults treat children as juniors and as equals. When we tell a child to improve its table manners, for example, we relate to it both as a child (since adults rarely say this to each other) and as an adult (since we wish it to act like one). Modern society counts children and adults together for some purposes, notably in reckoning populations, and one might argue that the two groups share more of their leisure today than they did a century ago. Separate recreations for fathers, mothers, and children have been eroded by ones that are taken together.

The words we use for children and young people reflect these complexities. Sometimes we are specific, when we talk of a 'baby', 'infant', and 'toddler', or an 'adolescent', 'teenager', and 'youth'. 'Child', on the other hand, is less clear-cut. Teenagers cry 'we are not children' while their parents still think that they are. The media apply the word 'child' to victims and to the vulnerable well into the teens, long after the age at which in other circumstances they refer to 'students' or 'young people'. Parents may talk of 'kids' of any age, while children apply the term (or have done) to those who are younger than themselves. As for the words 'boy' and 'girl', they can be used of anyone from a baby to an adolescent paper boy or stable girl, and adults as well as children may spend an evening out with 'the boys' or 'the girls'.

We are wise to remind ourselves of the anomalies of modern childhood, because it is often held that childhood in the past was less distinct from adulthood than is the case today. When I talk about medieval children to people who are not historians of the subject, their most frequent response is to ask if such children were regarded as small adults, or to assert that this was so. The view seems widely established in popular thought. Our minds recall stories of children

working in mines and factories down to the mid nineteenth century, and imagine
that childhood hardly existed up to those times, except in a physical sense. That,
of course, is to overlook the classes of society which did not labour in this way,
and the earlier societies where such labour was absent. Then there is the evidence
of paintings which confronts us in stately homes and art galleries. Royal and noble
children appear dressed like their elders, and we assume that such children lived
and were treated as adults. That, in turn, is to ignore the purpose of such paintings to show royal and noble status, and to forget how many modern children
wear suits, dresses, sportswear, and informal clothes that are modelled on those
of adults.

The popular view may also owe something to historical writers of the 1960s
and 70s, who sought to show that childhood in the middle ages was impoverished
and disregarded by modern standards. The leading exponents of this view
included the historians Philippe Ariès, Lloyd de Mause, and Lawrence Stone, of
whom Ariès is probably the best known.[1] In his book *L'Enfant et la vie familiale sous
l'Ancien régime* (1960), translated into English as *Centuries of Childhood* (1962), he
argued that childhood was not a distinct cultural period, nor recognised as one
by adults, until the sixteenth or seventeenth centuries.[2] His book centred on
France (and to some extent England) in the early modern period, rather than the
middle ages, but it sought to emphasise the difference between the two eras. The
book's English blurb claimed that 'before the seventeenth century, a child was
regarded as a small and inadequate adult. The concept of "the childish" as something distinct from adults is a creation of the modern world.' Ariès's own words
were more careful than this, modifying the proposition with 'it seems' and 'as if',
and pointing to contrasts between childhood in the seventeenth century and in
the present day. Nevertheless, he believed that medieval children lived very dissimilar lives from their early-modern successors.[3]

He thought that this arose for three reasons. Many children died young, all
lived closely together with adults, and most were sent away from home in youth
to school or to service in other people's houses. The result, he concluded, was
that children were less distinct as a group than was so later on. Ariès conceded
that medieval fathers and mothers might care for their children and love them,
but he felt that the relationship was usually more detached and less sympathetic.

2 Toy cooking utensils of the late medieval and Tudor
period, manufactured for children and found in London.

Adults were not so interested in childhood or aware of it as a separate state: 'in medieval society the idea of childhood did not exist'.[4] He also claimed that children enjoyed less of a separate culture than in later times: notably with regard to their dress, which he too regarded as adult in nature. A casual reader of the book might assume that its author came to these conclusions from detailed study. In fact, the book made little use of medieval sources other than painting, sculpture, and a few (mainly literary) records of the fifteenth century.

Ariès's views have been influential, especially among those who are not medieval historians. They mirror the popular assumptions mentioned above, not to mention the ancient instinct to set a boundary between 'medieval' and 'modern' times. Since Ariès wrote, however, a good deal of research has been done on medieval childhood. In terms of general surveys, Shulamith Shahar has published *Childhood in the Middle Ages* (1990), covering western Europe, as have Pierre Riché and Danièle Alexandre-Bidon in *L'Enfance au Moyen Age* (1994). In England particularly, Sally Crawford has given an account of *Childhood in Anglo-Saxon England* (2000). More specialised studies include a number of books and articles by the present author, since 1973, on medieval schools and schoolbooks, the history of royal and noble children, and children's culture and religion.[5] Barbara Hanawalt's book *The Ties that Bound* (1986) has explored the lives of children outside school, especially in the countryside, through its pioneering analysis of records of coroners' inquests. So has *The Rescue of the Innocents* by Ronald Finucane (1997), a similar survey of miracle records. Mention should also be made of the work of Iona and Peter Opie on children's games and folklore. Although this is based chiefly on post-medieval evidence, it has provided a large body of comparable material, instructively arranged and analyzed.[6]

None of the scholars mentioned above has found material to support the assertions of Ariès; all, in different ways, have rebutted them. They have gathered copious evidence to show that adults regarded childhood as a distinct phase or phases of life, that parents treated children like children as well as like adults, that they did so with care and sympathy, and that children had cultural activities and possessions of their own. This book reaches similar conclusions. Medieval people, especially (but not only) after the twelfth century, had concepts of what childhood was, and when it began and ended. The arrival of children in the world was a notable event, and their upbringing and education were taken seriously. The

Church and the common (secular) law regarded children as equal to adults for some purposes. Equally, both branches of authority accepted that children were not yet adults and required separate treatment. Adults provided culture for children by means of toys (Fig. 2), games, and literature, but children created their own as well. They spent time by themselves, talking and playing away from their elders, sometimes against their elders' conventions and wishes.

Let us explore these matters in more detail, beginning with the words applied to children in medieval times. There was a rich vocabulary of these, sometimes specific, sometimes ambiguous, like their successors today.[7] In the former category came words which normally implied a definite age: 'baby', 'infant', and 'faunt' (a variant of 'infant') for the very young, and 'damsel', 'stripling', and 'youth' for those who were older. The ambiguous words included 'child' and 'bairn' for children of either sex, and words for each of the sexes – 'boy', 'groom', 'knave', and 'lad' for young males, and 'girl', 'lass', 'maid', and 'wench' for young females. All these words could be used to mean a baby, a child, an adolescent, or a young adult. Even 'baby' might be applied to children older than infants, and 'child' was especially flexible. Although it could encompass boys and girls, it often implied boys in particular, and in some literary works it denoted a boy as old as a squire or a young knight in his late teens. Equally, it might signify girlishness, as when the shepherd in *The Winter's Tale* finds the abandoned Perdita and asks 'a boy or a child?'[8] Contrariwise, Jesus is described as a 'wenchel', the earlier form of 'wench', and more than one chaste knight as a 'maid', while 'girl' first meant a child of either sex.

Context may have made these words more precise than they appear in dictionaries based on the whole of medieval literature. For there were certainly notions of childhood, enshrined both in words and in writings. Medieval people believed that human life progressed through a series of stages, each with its own characteristics: 'the ages of man'.[9] This belief was inherited from classical writers: not in a single form but in several versions, current alongside each other. Writers divided life into three, four, five, six, seven, or twelve periods. Those who thought of it as falling into three parts ignored childhood altogether, envisaging youth (typified by a young adult), maturity, and old age. This is the pattern presented by Chaucer in his portraits of the Squire, the Knight, and the Franklin in *The Canterbury Tales*. Four-fold schemes might or might not include children. Byrhtferth's eleventh-century encyclopaedia, the *Manual*, talks of childhood, adolescence, maturity, and age, but most medieval writers called the first of these ages 'adolescence' and symbolised it by a young man like the Squire.[10]

Schemes of six and seven ages, on the other hand, mentioned childhood uniformly, and were very well known. They occur in the influential Latin dictionary, *Liber Etymologiarum*, by Isidore of Seville (d. 636); in the chief encyclopaedia read in England during the later middle ages, *De Proprietatibus Rerum* (Fig. 3); and, most famously, in Jacques's speech on the ages of man in Shakespeare's *As You Like It*.[11] In these analyses, infancy became an age of its own, lasting from growth in the womb or birth until the age of seven. Childhood (typified for Jacques by a schoolboy) followed from seven to fourteen, and adolescence (by a

3 The Ages of Man, from the 1495 edition of Bartholomew's famous encyclopaedia. They include (top left) a baby, a boy on a primitive hobby horse, and a youth with a bow.

lover) from fourteen to twenty-eight. There were words for these stages in Latin, *infantia*, *pueritia*, and *adolescentia*, and these made their way into English in about 1400, though they remained for a long time scholarly rather than popular ones. Two pairs of them, 'infant' and 'infancy', 'adolescent' and 'adolescence', proved their worth and are still with us, but 'puerice' and 'puerility', denoting the age from seven to fourteen, never became common and were usually expressed by 'childhood'.

Childhood, then, was a concept – both as a single period from birth to puberty and as one divided into infancy and childhood, with adolescence as a further stage before adulthood. Nor were these merely perceptions of scholars or poets. Childhood was recognised in medieval England for religious and legal purposes. The Church made a clear distinction between adults and children, at least by about 1200. Adults could (or should) confess to a priest, receive holy communion, pay tithes and Church dues, get married fully and permanently, and be

4   Boys imitating their elders, playing at the quintain, from the fourteenth century English *Romance of Alexander*.

anointed if they were sick. Children could not do these things, or did not need to, until puberty when they reached sexual and mental maturity.[12] The English common law took a similar view. It identified a number of ages of majority, varying from twelve to twenty-one, at which young people acquired the right to administer their own affairs and property, and the duty of shouldering adult responsibilities.[13] The English Parliament, when making laws about work and taxation, laid down the ages at which these laws should apply to children.[14]

There were many practical ways, too, in which children formed a separate group or groups within society, and were understood to do so by adults. They required special beds, food, and clothes – different in scale and sometimes in kind from those of their elders. They called for special care and special people to provide it: the midwife, the godparent, and sometimes the nurse. They were given toys which, by at least 1300, might be manufactured and purchased for them. They needed schools and schoolteachers to teach them, and these schools, by the thirteenth century, were distinct from universities for young adults. In schools, there were alphabet tablets and schoolbooks for children's use, often with sympathy for their capabilities and interests. In churches, there were fonts to baptise them, and a sacrament of confirmation to follow their baptisms. Adults helped to create a special culture for children in these respects, and children added to it with their own language, play, and calendar customs.[15]

That is not to deny that children partook of adult life, as they have always done. Children are brought up to be adults, not as pet-animals. From earliest times, they have been encouraged to accustom themselves to their elders' timetables, food, speech, skills, knowledge, and behaviour. Medieval religion and law grouped children and adults together for some purposes. Both had to belong to the Church; both enjoyed access to many of its resources, including churches, shrines, and miraculous healing. Children who died by mischance were subject, like adults, to coroners' inquests, and all baptised children, like adults, had funerals and burials in churchyards. Their souls too qualified for salvation and passage to heaven. Some of the rhymes and songs used by children were adult ones, and so were some of their games (Fig. 4). There were also certain respects in which

5 Ploughman, boy, and oxen, from John Fitzherbert's *New Tract for Husbandmen* (*c.* 1530). The fact that adults and children were often together did not prevent them having different lives and interests.

children were treated more like adults than is the case today. This is especially apparent in lower ages of majority (as low as twelve for some purposes). Even below that age, it was possible to marry and to enter a monastery, though neither practice was common. But the sum of the evidence does not support the view that children were merely small adults, different in this respect from children today.

So it cannot be over-emphasised that there is nothing to be said for Ariès's view of childhood in the middle ages, nor indeed of a major shift in its history during the sixteenth and seventeenth centuries, as opposed to changes of detail. The main difference, as one proceeds through the centuries, is the survival of evidence. The later one goes, the more one learns about childhood. Medieval people probably wrote less on the subject than their successors, and much of what they wrote has disappeared. But we can hardly blame them for a lack of interest in childhood merely because they did not write about it. Fewer people could write, and their reasons for writing had less to do with children. When it was relevant to refer to them, in coroners' records or accounts of miracles, adults did so with the same care and consistency that they gave to themselves. As we have argued already, there was a recognition of childhood by the Church and the common law, and by society through its concept of the ages of man – a concept whose existence Ariès knew and admitted. As for the factors which he believed made childhood different, they existed but without the effects he supposed. True, many children died but there is no reason to assume that this caused parents to sorrow less, to remember them less, and to cherish the survivors less than would be the case today. Evidence shows that some parents did all these things, and about most parents we know nothing at all.

Similar points can be made about children's spatial lives. Their close proximity to adults in the home did not prevent them being alone or with their contemporaries, especially out of doors. Married men and women lived just as closely together, yet no one would say that there was not a culture peculiar to men (both singly and in groups) or likewise to women. Many children indeed left home to study or word, but this most often happened when they approached their teens. During the first ten or twelve years of life, they were usually at home, able to bond with their parents. When they left, their departure did not prevent both sides retaining emotional ties or keeping in touch by messages or letters. As for the view that medieval children had no culture of their own, the evidence now available shows the reverse. They wore clothes, had toys, chanted rhymes, played games, and read literature invented by themselves or designed especially for them. Even when these clothes, rhymes, and games were similar to those of adults, they could still be used separately by children and in distinctive ways. Ariès's views were mistaken: not simply in detail but in substance. It is time to lay them to rest.

The present book is the first attempt to explore these topics in England throughout most of the medieval centuries, in greater detail than is possible in a review of western Europe. It encompasses childhood from birth till about the mid teens, and uses 'children' loosely in this sense. Some attention has also been given to adolescence specifically, from about twelve to twenty-one, especially in the fields of religion, literature, and growing up. The chronological range of the book extends from the seventh century to the middle of the sixteenth, but the depth is greatest in the high and later middle ages (from 1100 to 1550), from which most evidence survives. One topic is largely ignored, that of formal public education in schools, on the grounds that it is a large and complex one that has been covered elsewhere by the present author and other writers. An exception has been made in favour of the process of learning to read, because this is a subject little explored in books about schools. Reading was probably learnt at home as well as at school, and has greater claims to inclusion in a study of child-hood as a whole.

The word 'medieval' is used to indicate the whole span of time from the Anglo-Saxon period to the early sixteenth century, and the people who lived in that era. This is done only in cases where ideas, practices, or institutions existed widely across society throughout the period. For example, the baptism of children at or near birth may be described as a 'medieval' practice. Otherwise, it is not my intention to suggest that the period was a static one, or that everyone believed or did the same at any single time. On the contrary, the medieval era witnessed great social and cultural changes, and its people often differed in their views and activities, one from another and even personally within their own lifespans. Quotations from written sources are translated, when in Latin, and modernised, when in Middle English. Editorial additions are shown in square brackets. Turning Middle into Modern English alters the flavour of the original, and sometimes dictates replacing old words with new ones, but those who wish to consult the original texts may easily locate them from the references.

If authors may express a hope for their works, mine is to reveal the richness of the material about medieval English children. Far from being a ghostly or peripheral presence in writings, art, and archaeology, they are a prominent and well-recorded group of the population. From birth to adolescence, through family life, relationships with others, recreations, work, religion, and the law, to disease, death, and the after-life, they have generated far more material than can be handled, even briefly, within one pair of covers. And, as the reader will by now have realised, I believe them to have been ourselves, five hundred or a thousand years ago.

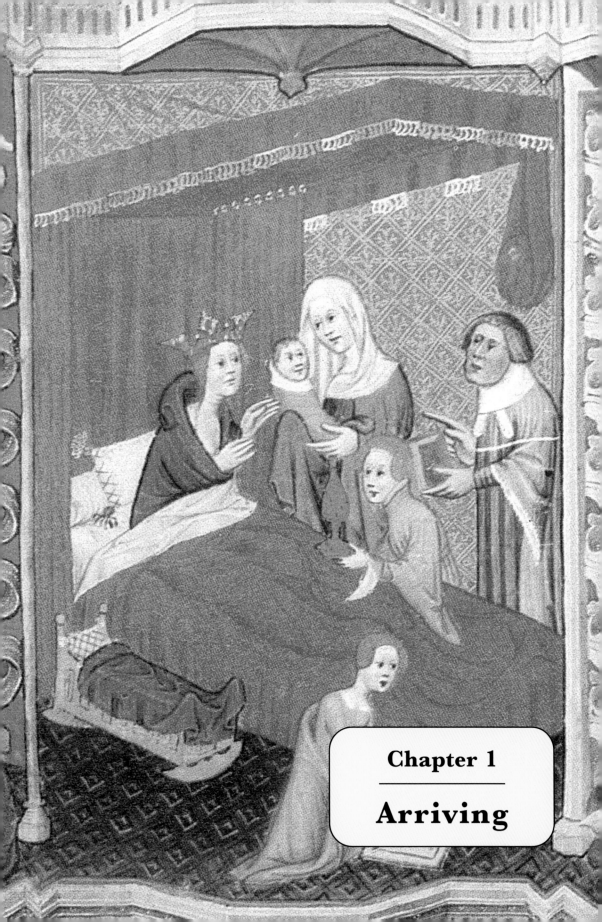

Chapter 1

Arriving

BIRTH

ONCE A YEAR, the world unites in praise of birth and babyhood. Christmas celebrates the story that God was born like the rest of us, as a tiny child. Yet the story as told today, by carols, Christmas cards, and Nativity plays, is more of a frame than a picture. We hear about the prelude to the birth, as Mary and Joseph travel to the inn. We encounter the sequel: the angels and the shepherds. But what went on between? How did Mary give birth? Who assisted her, and what did Joseph do? The gospel accounts do not tell us, because they expect us to know. Medieval people thought that they knew, and showed what they thought in their drama. In the great play cycle of York, Joseph leaves to get light and fuel, Mary stands modestly between the ox and ass, and when he returns the baby has been born.[1] In the cycles of Chester and 'N-Town', the latter of which was acted in East Anglia (perhaps at Norwich), Joseph goes away to find two midwives. When they arrive, the birth has taken place. The midwives, Salome and Zelomye (or Tebell), are astonished to find that Mary shows no signs of her delivery; she is still a virgin.[2]

These versions of the Christmas story grew out of two beliefs. One was theological. Not only was Mary's conception of Jesus a unique and miraculous event, but so was her pregnancy and delivery. Her baby did not grow in her womb like a normal child, and she did not suffer the labour of an ordinary mother; even her maidenhood remained unbroken. The other belief was rooted in everyday life. People assumed that men in ancient Palestine, like men in medieval England, were not allowed to be present when women gave birth. The only proper attendants were other women – midwives, neighbours, or servants. Men may have helped with births in emergencies or in remote places, but even this was irregular. In the much-read medieval romance of *Bevis of Hampton*, Bevis and his wife Josian are travelling with one servant through a forest when she goes into labour. They take her to an empty lodge and Bevis prepares to assist, but she dismisses him abruptly:

> For God's love go hence away . . .
> And let me work, and Our Lady;
> Shall never woman's privity [*private parts*]
> To man be showed for me.[3]

She gives birth alone to twin boys – a piece of fiction, but a reflection of popular views and customs.

Before birth, there was pregnancy about which medieval people thought that they knew a good deal. Their notions of human development were based on ancient science, going back to Greece and the Near East in pre-Christian times.[4] One of their chief authorities was Aristotle. He believed that the human embryo,

---

6   The flight into Egypt. To medieval Christians, everything about the baby Jesus was miraculous: his conception, his growth in the womb, his birth, and his preservation from King Herod.

after conception, developed in three stages matching the three kinds of life in the world. At first, the embryonic matter was like a vegetable, with the power merely to feed itself and grow. Next, it added the characteristics of an animal: the ability to feel, desire, and move. Eventually, it became recognisably human in shape and gained a rational or intellectual soul.[5] A male embryo acquired this final shape and soul at about forty days. A female embryo grew more slowly, and took about three months to do so. For Aristotle, a soul was merely the life-force possessed by a living thing, so that the early embryo had a vegetable soul, then an animal one, and finally that of a human being. He and other ancient writers therefore made a distinction between the pre-human embryo, which was not human in appearance or soul, and the developing foetus which was. They regarded the latter as human and the former as not human, and imposed different penalties on those who injured a foetus or its mother before and after this point.

More detailed accounts of the timetable of embryonic development were pro-duced by classical writers on medicine like Hippocrates and Galen, and these were well established in western Europe by the time of St Augustine, in about AD 400. Augustine considered that the male embryo grew to human shape in four stages. During the first six days, its matter consisted of a milky fluid. This was converted to blood in nine days and consolidated into flesh in a further twelve. The last stage, in which the flesh acquired the shape and members of a human, took another eighteen; a total of forty-five days. Augustine saw a Christian paral-lel here. In the Gospel of John, Jesus compared his body to the Temple in Jerusalem, a Temple that had taken forty-six years to build.[6] On the assumption that the Virgin Mary conceived him on 25 March (the feast of the Annunciation of her pregnancy by the Archangel Gabriel) and gave birth on 25 December, his time in her womb lasted exactly 276 days: six times forty-six, a significant number.[7] True, Jesus was not a typical man. He was believed to have been unique in possessing his whole shape and organs from the moment of his incarnation by the Holy Spirit in the Virgin Mary. After all, he could not have gone through a period (like other human beings) when he was merely vegetative and animal. Some medieval pictures of the incarnation of Jesus showed him passing from the Spirit to the Virgin in the form of a tiny, complete man, needing only to grow. But his time in the womb seemed to confirm the fact that forty-six days was the perfect period for an embryo to gain human characteristics.

Christianity laid a stronger emphasis on the human soul and its immortality than Aristotle had done. This did not change the earlier distinction between the pre-human embryo and the human foetus, but reinforced it. Medieval Christians came to believe that God put the soul into the foetus when it took human shape, at about forty-six days for a male and ninety for a female; until that point, the embryo was not human and had neither human life nor human soul. This was universally held to be so in the middle ages: by popes like Innocent III and theologians like Thomas Aquinas, Roger Bacon, and Giles of Rome.[8] It was only in the late nineteenth century that the Catholic Church began to assert that the human soul existed from the moment of conception, with all that this implies for the treatment of embryos. Lawyers took the same view as theologians: both canon

7   The thirteenth-century English friar Bartholomew. His encyclopaedia is a mine of information on all matters, including conception and birth.

lawyers of the Church and common lawyers of the English legal system. Thomas of Chobham, writing his manual for confessors in 1216, observed that it was worse to destroy a formed foetus than an unformed one. The law of Moses, he believed, imposed a fine for the latter but the death penalty for the former.[9] Later in the thirteenth century, the great English lawyer Henry Bracton defined the killing of an unborn child in a similar way. It counted as homicide only if the foetus was already formed and 'animated', possessing a soul.[10]

The scientific understanding of the embryo in late-medieval England was a similar one, based on Aristotle, Augustine, and their counterparts. A good place to read about it is the encyclopaedia of the Franciscan friar Bartholomew the Englishman, or Bartholomew Glanville as he is sometimes known (Fig. 7). His work, *De Proprietatibus Rerum*, 'On the Properties of Things', was probably written on the continent in about the 1240s, and is a survey of creation, beginning with God and traversing mankind, animals, plants, geography, and geology. It was widely read in its original Latin form down to the sixteenth century, and reached a large lay public through translations into English, French, Dutch, and Spanish. The English version was produced by John Trevisa for Lord Berkeley in 1398, and was still in sufficient demand to be published when printing began. Wynkyn de Worde brought out an edition in 1495 and other printers did so in 1535 and 1582.[11] This kept it as a main source of popular information on human generation and birth until Shakespeare's time.

Following Aristotle, Bartholomew wrote that a child was formed by the father's seed together with matter contributed by the mother (he does not use the word 'egg').[12] If the resulting embryo grew on the woman's right side, it became a male; if on the left side, a female. The relative virtue or power of the father's seed and the mother's matter determined the child's characteristics. If the father's was dominant, the child inherited his attributes, and so on. The account of the growth of the male embryo resembles that of Augustine, except in ascribing seven days to the first stage of development. This enabled the perfect period of growth to be calculated as that of Jesus: forty-six days. Bartholomew, like Aristotle, was careful to point out that human beings grew at different rates, rather than in one standard way. Those who were born early also achieved their basic shape early on, as quickly as thirty days from conception rather than the ideal forty-six. Babies developed their members one by one, not equally and all together.

Time in the womb varied from eight to ten months. Girls took longer to grow than boys, because the elements that formed a boy were hotter, as were its surroundings in the womb. Only with the formation of a human figure, however, did the embryo take human life and soul – for Bartholomew as for other medieval writers. By the eighth month, the ability of the child to move in the womb showed its wish to be born. Sometimes, this moving enfeebled it and was the explanation why some babies, when born, did not live long. Much could be learnt about a forthcoming child from the condition of its mother's breasts. Firm breasts pre-saged a healthy child, drooping ones a feeble child, and small or lean breasts a still-birth or premature baby. The expression of milk by the nipples was a further sign of weakness. If the right breast was larger than the left, the child would be a boy, and if the left was greater, a girl.[13]

Reading Bartholomew reminds us that birth in the middle ages was a haz-ardous process. It was recognised as such, and there was a craving for reassurance about the outcome. Churches owned relics which, they promised, would ensure a safe delivery. Many of these were girdles or belts, perhaps because they symbol-ised undoing and could be laid on or around a woman's abdomen before she gave birth or while she did so. Canterbury Cathedral lent St Anselm's belt to women in childbirth by the early twelfth century.[14] A holier girdle still, that of the Virgin Mary, reposed at Westminster Abbey and was loaned to pregnant ladies in the royal family. It was dispatched to Gascony for Henry III's queen Eleanor of Provence, to Knaresborough (Yorks.) for Edward I's daughter Elizabeth, and was probably the same as 'Our Lady girdle' which a monk brought to Queen Elizabeth of York in 1502.[15] Other religious houses claimed relics of similar virtue. There was a second girdle of the Virgin at Bruton Abbey (Som.), part of a third at Dale Abbey (Derbs.), a lace of her smock, girdles of St Ælred, St Bernard, and St Francis, the chains of St Peter, and (at Burton-on-Trent, Staffs.) the staff of St Modwenna for pregnant women to lean on. Even parish churches made such claims, as Kelham (Notts.) did with the finger of St Stephen.[16]

Women unable to reach a relic, or to have one brought to them, turned to other forms of supernatural aid. One of these, by the later middle ages, was a scroll of parchment or paper, containing a cross one fifteenth of the height of Jesus or a reproduction of the wound in his side. Scrolls, like girdles, could be laid across the belly during childbirth, and contained written promises that whoever viewed or wore them would have an easy delivery.[17] Certain mineral stones were believed to be helpful as well. These included iris (rock crystal), jasper, malachite, and best of all aetites or eaglestone. The last (a form of iron ore) was believed to be taken by eagles to their nests to assist them in breeding.[18] It was found in lumps with hard shells and soft cores, part of which sometimes broke loose and rattled inside, sug-gesting the marvel of a hollow stone and an analogy with the baby within the womb. Poor women, lacking scrolls or eaglestones, had to make do with humbler precautions. Reginald Scot tells how, at the end of the sixteenth century, they would tie their girdles or their shoe latchets to a bell, and strike on the bell three times. This too was believed to smoothe the process of birth.[19]

Spiritual preparation was also encouraged. John Mirk, canon of Lilleshall (Shropshire), who wrote a simple set of *Instructions for Parish Priests* in about 1400, urged them to tell pregnant women to come to confession and receive communion, 'for dread of peril that may befall', in other words death.[20] A prayer used in York diocese in the later middle ages invited listeners to pray for all women with child in the parish or other parishes,

> that God comfort them and deliver them with joy, and send their children christendom [*baptism*] and the mothers purifying of Holy Church, and release of pain in their travailing.[21]

There is more in this than meets the eye. We are praying not only for successful deliveries and healthy children. We are asking that babies may survive long enough to be baptised, in other words for just a few minutes, and their mothers long enough to be purified in church after forty days. The situation where a mother died in childbirth with the baby still inside her was common enough for Church leaders to rule that a caesarian operation should be done in such cases. Ælfric of Eynsham, writing soon after 1000, recalled that Julius Caesar was born in such a way, and said he had known another such person who lived into old age.[22] Several later clergy repeated the call, and Mirk told the midwife not to spare herself in using a knife. If her courage failed her, she should call in a man to do the work instead – a last resort indeed.[23]

Bartholomew thought that young women with small limbs were particularly at risk in childbirth; he wrote at a time when aristocratic girls married and gave birth in their teens.[24] Some noble girls and young women did not survive the crisis, despite the utmost care that the age could provide. Mary Bohun, countess of Derby, the first wife of Henry IV, died at or soon after childbirth in 1394, despite having borne several children. So did Jane Seymour, queen of Henry VIII, twelve days after giving birth to her first child, Edward VI. A pathetic memorial survives to Anne a Wode, wife of Thomas Asteley, esquire, in the church of Blickling (Norfolk). A monumental brass, it depicts Anne holding two swaddled babes in her arms (Fig. 8). An inscription explains that 'on the day of St Agapetus the martyr [in 1512], she bore a boy and a girl when giving birth, and after the peril of giving birth she suddenly passed to the Lord'. So apparently did her children.[25] Lady Margaret Beaufort, although she gave birth successfully to Henry VII when she was thirteen, had a difficult labour because of her small size, and seems to have been left infertile.[26]

It followed that birth needed expertise, and this was anciently provided by a woman rather than a man, a midwife rather than a male doctor. 'Midwife' means somebody 'with the wife' at the birth or (less certainly) who is 'amid the wife' to deliver her.[27] The Latin equivalent, *obstetrix*, signifies 'a woman who stands by'. Bartholomew defines her, in Trevisa's translation, as 'a woman that hath craft to help a woman that travaileth of child, that she bear and bring forth her child with the less woe and sorrow'. He tells how the midwife anoints the mother's womb with soothing balm to ease the birth. She takes the child out of the womb, and ties the navel-string four inches long. She washes away the blood on the child with water, anoints him with salt and honey (or salt and roses, pounded together) to dry him and comfort his limbs and members, and wraps him in clothes. His mouth

Ɂɪɑtɇ p̃ ɑɪɑ Ⱥɪɪɑɇ ɑɪɪoɪɇ ʋɪ° ſɇɪɪ̃ Ⱦɦoɇ Ⱥſtɇlɇɪɪ ɪɇ ɱɇlton Ⱦonſtɑɓlɇ ꝯ Ꞩ
Ⱥɪɪɪɪɑɡ ꝗɪɪɇ̃ ɪɪɪ ɔɪɇ ſɑ̃ Ⱥɡɑp̃tɪ ɱ̃ɪɪɪɓ ɱɑſɪɪlɪɪ ɇtſɇɱɇllɑ ɑɔ pɑɪtɪɪ ꝛɇp̃ɪt ɇt
poſt pɑɪɪɇɪɪɔɪ pɪɪɪɑlɪɪ ſɪɪɓɪto ɱɪɪɡɪɑɪɪɪt ɑɔ ɔɪɪɪɪ̃ ɑ̃° ꝗɡ° ɓɇ̃ɱꝓɪɪſɪ̃ɪɪɪ ɪɪ̃ ꝛɪɪ ꞩp̃ɪ.

8   Even the wealthy did not escape the dangers of childbirth. This brass commemorates Anne Asteley (d. 1512), and her dead baby twins.

and gums should be rubbed with a finger dipped in honey to cleanse them, and to stimulate the child to suck.[28] The midwife would usually be assisted by other women: servants in a big household, family or neighbours in a small one. Even great people might help with their presence or in supplying comforts for the occasion; Anne countess of Warwick (d. 1492) was remembered for her willingness to be with women in labour, and her generosity in giving material aid.[29]

Bartholomew's description of the midwife's duties is a medical one, but other sources suggest that she sometimes resorted to religious or superstitious devices to soothe her patients and ease their deliveries. During the pains of labour, the midwife and her assistants would pray to saints and urge the mother to do so. Henry III's queen called for help on St Margaret, Edward I's on St Thomas Becket.[30] The scrolls already mentioned advised those who used them to invoke St Cyr, the child-saint martyred with his mother Julitta, presumably because, as a child, he would be sympathetic to problems of childbirth.[31] Writers of the mid sixteenth century talk of Our Lady and St Margaret as popular choices for prayer.[32] By that time, Church Reformers had come to disapprove of such practices. In 1535, they began to destroy the childbirth relics, beginning with the Virgin's girdle at Westminster Abbey.[33] Nicholas Shaxton, bishop of Salisbury, told his clergy in 1538 to warn midwives not to cause women in labour to make vows to go on pilgrimage, but only to pray to God. They should not use 'any girdles, purses, or measures of Our Lady' during the labour. In 1551–2, John Hooper, bishop of

Gloucester and Worcester, sought to prevent midwives employing prayers to saints, or 'salt, herbs, water, wax, cloths, girdles, or relics' in super-stitious ways. Edmund Bonner, bishop of London, a good Reformation Catholic who had no objection to saints, condemned midwives in 1554 for using witchcraft, charms, sorcery, invocations, and prayers not approved by the Church.[34]

The midwife probably learnt her skills by assisting an older, established practi-tioner. She was not of high social status, and a reference to one who visited the Lestranges, a gentry family of Hunstanton (Norfolk) in 1520, calls her merely 'Mother Midwife'.[35] Equally, her role gave her prestige and importance, both secular and religious. The term for her in medieval French was *sage-femme*, 'wise woman', and a midwife appearing in a Church court in 1523 talked of 'the authority of mine office'.[36] That office included the duty of giving emergency baptism. Midwives with good reputations were in demand. John of Gaunt ordered Ilote, the midwife of Leicester who had attended his first wife Blanche, to be brought to Hertford to deliver his second wife Constance in 1372.[37] Katherine Tiler, midwife of Bristol, was summoned twelve miles to Thornbury Castle (Gloucs.) in November 1520 to minister to the daughter-in-law of the duke of Buckingham.[38] The midwife, however, was a transitory figure unlike the nurse, and the rewards for her work were less great. When Gaunt's sister-in-law, the countess of Buckingham, had a baby daughter in 1382, he gave the midwife 20s., less than a third of his gift to the nurse, and Katherine Tiler received only 10s.[39] The best-paid midwives were those of the royal family. Alice Massy, who attended Henry VII's queen, Elizabeth of York, at her first birth, earned £10 for this, the successful delivery of Prince Arthur in 1486.[40] She may have been retained to assist with the queen's later births, for in 1504, when these were all over and Elizabeth herself was dead, Henry awarded Alice a modest annuity of £5 a year as 'midwife to our dearest wife, the queen'.[41]

Descriptions of royal and noble births and baptisms survive from the middle of the fifteenth century. By that period, when so much of aristocratic life was highly regulated, a noble lady was expected to give birth in a style and dignity appropri-ate to her rank. Ordinances for the lying in and delivery of a queen may have been issued in the reign of Edward IV, and others were certainly approved by Henry VII in 1493.[42] A further set, inspired by those of the royal family, was drawn up in about 1500 for the Percy countess of Northumberland and adds some details not found in the royal ordinances.[43] The procedures laid down in these documents are elaborate, and it is not certain how far they were copied by lesser nobility and gentry, but they may well have had an influence. The queen or countess (let us call her the lady) was allowed to choose the chamber where she would give birth, and this had to be carpeted. Rich cloth of arras was to be hung across the roof, walls, and windows, leaving one window available to give light if the lady so wished. A darkened room was therefore visualised. Lamps were to be made ready and furniture provided in the form of a cupboard and a bed, appro-priate in splendour to the lady's rank. The Percy family planned to have a portable altar, so that mass could be said. One or two chambers beyond the bedchamber were also to be richly furnished: an antechamber and a great chamber with a

9   A lady receiving communion, as she might have done before retiring into seclusion to give birth.

'chair of estate' or throne.

The lady entered these rooms a month or so before she expected to give birth, and remained inside them for about six weeks after the event until she was purified or 'churched'.[44] Her entry to her suite was marked by a rite of passage, carried out in the chapel of the house in which she was staying. The Percy regulations, which have most to say about the chapel, assume that it will contain a high altar, two lesser altars, and a fourth in the 'closet' or gallery above the chapel, in which the lady sat during worship. The household steward, clergy, and gentlemen conducted the lady to the closet, when the dean of the chapel had made all ready for the service. While she watched from her closet, high mass was celebrated at the chapel high altar in honour of the Holy Spirit, and low (simple) masses at each of the other three altars – four masses going on at once, to give her as much spiritual benefit as possible. During high mass, she descended to the chapel by a stair and, as a special favour, went through the screen and into the chancel. She knelt, made an offering, and kissed the pax (the small metal or ivory disk kissed by the priest after consecrating the bread and wine of the mass). Then she was given communion or, as it was expressed, 'received her rights' (Fig. 9).

Receiving communion was unusual for lay people before the Reformation. It normally happened only on Easter Day and on occasions of great peril, of which childbirth was one. Following usual practice, a towel was held beneath the lady's chin by two gentlemen. This was to catch any crumbs that might fall from the consecrated wafer of bread as it was put into her mouth by the dean of the chapel. Household yeomen then brought wine from the cellar, which was inspected for quality. It was poured into the lady's own cup, from that into a chalice, and presented to her to drink. This wine, in late-medieval usage, was not consecrated. The consecrated wine of the eucharist was too holy to be given (what if it were spilt?), so those who received communion were given ordinary wine to cleanse their mouths and wash the wafer down. After communion, the lady returned to her suite of chambers. In the Percy household, she was given a 'voidee' or cup of spiced wine to sustain her, because she would have fasted before she took communion. Then she was ceremonially taken to her chambers by lords and ladies.

At this point, the men left the suite, and the outer door was fastened. Women alone were left inside. Food and wine were delivered to them when required, and they undertook the normal male duties of serving the lady and attending to her needs. Arrangements were made to bring the news of the labour and birth to the lord and his household, and the chapel clergy were warned to pray throughout the period of labour. If the lady was successfully delivered, it was their role immediately to sing the *Te Deum*, the hymn of praise and thanks for the joyful outcome.

BAPTISM: THE INSTITUTION

BY BEING BORN, a baby enters human society. English society, from the seventh century onwards, was a Christian society which sought to be more than human, and this aspiration affected babies. The Christian attitude towards them is well expressed by Robert Mannyng of Bourne, canon of Sempringham (Lincs.), in his English verse treatise, *Handling Sin*, begun in 1303. Mannyng set out to expound the Church's doctrines and practices to a popular audience. Like all Christians, he started from the belief that humanity fell from grace through Adam's sin of disobedience. Once this had happened, men and women by themselves could do nothing to rid themselves from sin, and would pass when they died to hell, a place where God was not.

The only way to salvation, says Mannyng, is to be baptised, a process in which one renounces sin, affirms one's faith in God, and receives God's grace, through being ceremonially washed with water:

> Saved we are through christendom [*baptism*]
> Of the deadly sin of Adam,
> In which sin all mankind is born:
> Is, shall be, and was before.
> Adam's sin was so severe
> That there is none to God so dear
> Who will not to hell be gone
> Unless he is washed in the font of stone.

Baptism raises us from human abjectness, frees us from slavery to the Devil, and opens a gateway to eternal life.[45] Its saving power was illustrated to Mannyng's contemporaries in a story from the East, reported in 1299. The brother of the king of the Tartars (a pagan) had married the Christian daughter of the king of Armenia. She bore him a son who was covered with bristles and hair, and the father ordered it to be burnt, but the mother asked for the child to be given to her and had him baptised by priests. Immediately, he lost his shaggy appearance and became smooth and beautiful. When the father saw the miracle, he believed in Christ, and so did the whole of his household.[46]

In the early years of Christianity, people were baptised in adulthood as Jesus had been.[47] Then, as the Church established rules and procedures, it laid down that recruits should first be instructed and examined in their faith. Baptism accordingly developed as a ceremony of two stages. First, the candidate was catechised: examined to ensure that he or she renounced the world, the flesh, and the Devil, and believed in the Trinity. Then the baptism took place, normally at Easter or Pentecost, the two great feasts of the early Church. Once there were Christian adults, however, it was natural for them to wish to have their children baptised, so that their family became a wholly Christian one. Infant baptism was practised at Rome by the third century when the priest Hippolytus suggested that, at celebrations of baptism, children should be admitted first, then men, then women. He added that since children could not speak for themselves, their parents or others from their family should do so for them.

The extension of baptism to children did not at first gain universal support. Tertullian (*c*.200) disapproved of it, and said that sponsors of baptised infants, by promising what these infants would believe and do, were in danger of perjuring themselves. But by the fourth and fifth centuries, most of the Roman Empire was nominally Christian. Children were so widely baptised that theologians began to worry about the salvation of those who were not. Ambrose of Milan (d. 397) said that he did not know if an unchristened child was worthy of heaven, and Augustine of Hippo (d. 430) went further. All who were born, he thought, were condemned, and no one was free of this judgment without being reborn. He recommended baptism as early as possible, to avoid eternal banishment from God. From his time onwards, baptism came to be seen not simply as permissible for children but as necessary, and therefore to be done when they were infants.

This view was well established by the time that England was re-converted to Christianity in the seventh century. True, many of the people baptised by the first missionaries were necessarily adults, but as soon as the new religion took hold among parents, the practice spread to their infant children. One of the earliest records of an English baptism is that of Eanflæd, the baby daughter of Edwin, king of Northumbria. She was born at Easter in 626, on the same day that her father, still a pagan, escaped an attack from an assassin sent by the king of Wessex. Edwin was so pleased by the double event that he allowed Eanflæd to be baptised at the following Pentecost, and promised to follow her example if he was success-ful in punishing Wessex.[48] Next Easter when this had been done, Edwin himself submitted to the ceremony, and his subsequent children were christened too, probably soon after birth, since two of them died within a week of their baptisms.[49]

A consensus about exactly when to baptise an infant was slower to emerge. Until the late twelfth century, there were two different views of the subject in England. One wished to confine the ceremony to the traditional times of Easter and Whitsuntide, even for babies. The Church council of Chelsea (787) ordered the 'canonical observances' to be observed, meaning these seasons, unless there was danger of death, and the Council of Winchester made a similar ruling as late as 1170.[50] Orderic Vitalis, the historian, tells us that he was born on 16 February 1075 but not baptised until the next Easter Eve (4 April), although the ceremony, at Atcham (Shropshire), took place locally.[51] The other practice was to christen as soon after birth as possible. This is recorded as early as about 690, when King Ine of Wessex issued a law code enforcing immediate infant baptism. Every child was to be baptised within thirty days of birth. If its guardian failed to comply, he was to be fined 30 shillings and, if the child died unbaptised, all that he possessed.[52]

Ine's law was practical to the extent that, by his time, there were minster churches with communities of clergy in many districts. One could hope that parents and priests would make contact within a month of a baby's arrival. By the tenth and eleventh centuries, when there were larger numbers of local parish churches, it became feasible to enforce baptism still closer to birth. The so-called Canons of Edgar (1005–8), actually issued by Bishop Wulfstan of Worcester and York, ordered priests to tell their parishioners that all children should be baptised within seven days.[53] A text of the same period, the 'Northumbrian Priests' Law' (*c.*1008–1123), made the period nine days, on penalty of a fine of six *ores* (about 10 shillings). If a child died unbaptised within this period, those responsible should do penance. If it died after nine days, without being christened, they were liable both for penance and a fine of twelve *ores*.[54]

Pronouncements about the time of baptism disappear after 1170, suggesting that, by about 1200, baptism was usually carried out close to birth and often on the day of birth itself. This was probably common in earlier times. It is true that Peter of Cornwall, the Augustinian canon and miracle collector (d. 1221), whose family came from Launceston (Cornwall), tells us that he had an uncle named Pagan in the early twelfth century, who was so called because he was not baptised until he was twelve.[55] But this may be mistaken family history. Pagan was a perfectly acceptable Christian name, and there was no obstacle to being christened in Launceston, which had two or three churches close by. Occasionally, baptisms might be delayed by a day or two through the need to contact godparents and by their travelling arrangements, especially if the birth happened earlier than expected.[56] The fourteenth-century English version of the romance *Lay Le Freine* imagines such a situation. A knight's wife gives birth to twins. He summons a messenger hastily and orders him to ride quickly to his neighbour, another knight, to ask him to come to be his child's godparent.[57] Ordinary people, on the other hand, were more likely to have friends and neighbours at hand to fill the role, and had no excuse to wait. A Church court in London in 1480 considered that a man who had fathered an illegitimate child compounded his sin by waiting two days before bringing it to be christened.[58]

The other exception to the timetable of speed after 1200 was one made by the Church itself, in an attempt to harmonise the claims of Easter and Pentecost with those of immediate baptism. Church service books laid down that solemn baptism should be held in churches on the Saturdays before these festivals, and it seems that babies born in the preceding days were reserved for the purpose. The practice was unpopular with parents. In 1237, the Council of London tried to reassure them that the pope himself christened babies on these days and that the Church did the same in other countries.[59] Eventually, the Council of Reading in 1279 produced a compromise. Babies would be held back only during the week before Easter and Pentecost, and not then if they were in peril of death. In the meantime all could receive the first part of the baptismal rite, the 'catechism', and need wait only for the baptism itself.[60] Occasionally one encounters Christian names like Anastasia ('resurrection') for women, Pascoe or Pascal ('Easter') for men, and Pentecost for both sexes. These may refer to baptisms in these, by now unusual, circumstances.

Formalities grew up about baptism. It had to be done in one's parish church, or in a recognised chapel-of-ease, not at home (save in emergency) or in a private chapel. The acquisition of a font by chapels was jealously regulated so as not to damage the rights of parish churches. Some clergy demanded a fee for baptising a child – a practice condemned by Ælfric of Eynsham as early as the 990s.[61] William of Malmesbury, writing in the twelfth century, implies that it happened widely at the time of the Norman Conquest and tells how St Wulfstan, provost of

Worcester and later its bishop (1062–95), distinguished himself by baptising poor people's children without charge.[62] Church prohibitions of baptismal fees are regularly found from the twelfth to the late thirteenth centuries, but the fact that they were so often repeated suggests that the practice was slow to die out.[63] Most of all, baptism required the presence of sponsors – people to support the person to be baptised. This was necessary whether he or she was a child or an adult. King Wulfhere of Mercia, for example, acted as sponsor to King Æthelwealh of Sussex when the latter became a Christian, and King Alfred did the same to his former enemy Guthrum the Dane.[64]

By about 1000, a male sponsor was called in English 'godfather' and a female one 'godmother'. If you needed to talk of both, the medieval word was not 'godparent' but 'godsib', later 'gossip', meaning 'relative under God'.[65] The modern custom that a boy or man at baptism should have two godfathers and a godmother, and a girl or woman the reverse, was established by the twelfth century.[66] A parent could not act except in an emergency, and a husband and wife could not do so for the same child. There was no bar to siblings, however, even children, and shortly after the earl of Kent was executed in 1330, with his family in disarray, his small son and daughter acted as sponsors to their newly born brother John.[67] Clergy too were eligible, and the officiating priest at a baptism could himself be a godparent.[68] In 1282, we hear of a pregnant mother doing the duty, but by the sixteenth century, some people thought this improper.[69] When Ralph Sadler, a servant of Henry VIII, needed to find a godmother for his newborn son in the mid 1530s, he was not sure whether to ask a Mrs Richards who lived nearby, in case she was pregnant. 'There is', he wrote in a letter, 'a certain superstitious opinion and usage amongst women, which is that in case a woman go with child, she may christen [*be godmother to*] no other man's child as long as she is in that case'.[70] Was this a superstition or a precaution for the future? Children, as we shall see, could not marry their godparents' children.[71]

Normally, then, baptism took place after the twelfth century on the day of birth or a few days later at most. Royal baptisms may have been the slowest. After the middle of the fifteenth century, they usually happened between two and four days after birth, perhaps to give time to prepare for the elaborate public ceremonies involved.[72] But not all births were normal. What happened if the delivery was difficult or the baby weak, and its death seemed likely at birth or soon afterwards? In that case, it was baptised as soon as it was born, or during the process. So important was this to ensure salvation that the Church waived the rights of the clergy in such cases. Any lay person might baptise in an emergency, even a father or mother, though parents should do so only if no one else was available. Writers for both the clergy and laity in the later middle ages took pains to describe the procedures, and priests were urged to ensure that everyone knew them, although in practice such emergencies were most often handled by midwives. Emergency baptism had to include two elements. The child must be washed, at least on the head, with pure water, and the person baptising must say 'I christen thee in the name of the Father, and the Son, and the Holy Spirit'. A name was preferably to be given as well, but was not essential. The words of baptism could be said in

English, French, or Latin, but it was imperative that they invoked all three persons of the Trinity.[73]

An enquiry into an emergency baptism by a midwife in Kent in 1523 shows what was done when the rules were followed correctly. The midwife, Elizabeth Gaynsforde, testified on oath in the bishop of Rochester's court that

> I, the aforesaid Elizabeth, seeing the child of Thomas Everey, late born, in jeopardy of life, by the authority of mine office, then being midwife, did christen the same child under this manner. 'In the name of the Father, the Son, and the Holy Ghost, I christen thee Denys.'

She was asked,

> whether the child was born and delivered from the wife of the said Thomas, whereto she answereth and saith that the child was not born, for she saw nothing of the child but the head, and for peril [that] the child was in, and in that time of need, she christened as is aforesaid, and cast water with her hand on the child's head; after which the child was born and was had to the church, where the priest gave to it that christendom [*baptism*] that [it] lacked, and the child is yet alive.[74]

All this was orthodox and sensible, including the choice of Denys, a name in use for people of both sexes. As Elizabeth noted, a baby who survived an emergency baptism was eventually taken to church where the priest enquired what had been done already and carried out the rest of the baptismal ritual.[75]

Inevitably, there were times when lay baptisms were not done properly. Incorrect words might be used, and Mannyng includes a story that warns about this. A midwife christened a child with a phrase of her own:

God and Saint John,
Christen the child, both flesh and bone!

The child died. When it was brought to the churchyard for burial, the priest questioned the midwife on what she had done. He told her that the child's soul was lost, and forbade her from ever again assisting at a childbirth.[76] Some laity, it seems, were so anxious not to make a mistake that several of them said the words instead of the single person who was meant to do so. One late-medieval treatise censured 'some foolish women' who did so, four or five taking part together.[77] Such actions speak of fear. If a priest were not present, would the words be said accurately? If not, and the child died, would its soul be deprived of grace and heaven? We shall see in a later chapter that the after-life of babies was a matter of great concern.[78]

BAPTISM: THE CEREMONY

THE NORMAL PROCEDURES at baptism in the later middle ages are set out in the Latin service-book known as the *Manual*, the book that clergy carried about in their hands when they ministered to their parishioners at birth, marriage, and death.[79] It is assumed in the *Manual* that baptism will take place in the parish church soon after birth and, because births might happen in a parish at any time, water was normally kept in the font and changed as often as it ceased to be pure. The baptismal party, including the midwife, baby, and godparents, gathered in the porch of the church, having sent word to the priest to meet them. The priest asked the midwife the sex of the baby; if male, it was placed to his right, and if female to his left – a custom which, at the very beginning of life, associated men with strength and dominance. Although, by the later middle ages, everyone was baptised at birth, the baptismal rite still kept its ancient two-fold form and was so presented in the *Manual*.[80] A baby had to be instructed before it could be christened, and the instruction had to be done outside the church because at this stage the baby was not yet Christian and eligible to go further in. The building of elaborate church porches was partly intended to provide shelter and splendour for these occasions (Fig. 10).

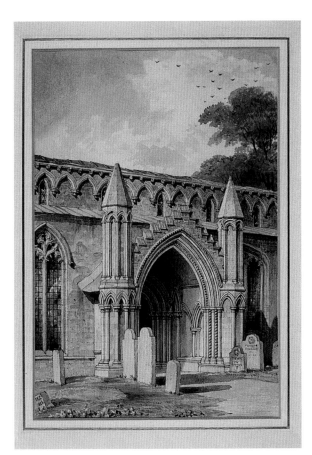

10   The church porch was the framework for the first part of the baby's baptism and for the mother's churching, six weeks later.

The making of a baby fit to enter the church could not be done by instruction in the traditional sense. Instead, it was exorcised from evil and infused with holiness in a series of ceremonies. The priest began by making the sign of the cross with his thumb on the baby's forehead. Then he placed his hand on the whole head and asked the child's name. The next ritual was the exorcism of some salt, which the christening party was expected to bring, and the putting of a little into the infant's mouth. This was accompanied by prayers, differing slightly for a boy or a girl, and two further signings of the cross on the forehead. After this, the priest spat into his left hand and used the thumb of his right hand to moisten the infant's ears and nostrils with saliva, recalling the way in which Jesus healed a deaf and dumb man. Then he made the sign of the cross in the infant's right hand, 'so that' (he said) 'you may sign yourself and repel yourself from the party of the Enemy. And may you remain in the Catholic faith and have eternal life and live for ever and ever. Amen.' Finally, he said to the baby, by name, 'Go into the temple of God'.

The christening party now went inside the church to the font which stood close to the entrance. If the font contained new water, this had to be made holy by the priest saying a litany of prayers and by further rituals. Water from the font was dashed out on all four sides. The priest breathed on the water three times, dripped in wax from a candle in the form of a cross to hallow the water, and made the sign of the cross in the water with the bottom of the candle. He added drops of oil and chrism (a mixture of oil and balm). Then, taking the baby (which had been removed from its christening robe), he placed his right hand upon it and again asked its name. He addressed questions in Latin to the baby, which were answered on its behalf by the godparents. They were expected to reply in Latin too, albeit of a very simple kind:

> *Abrenuncias sathane?* (Do you renounce Satan?)
> *Abrenuncio.* (I renounce him.)
> *Et omnibus operibus eius?* (And all his works?)
> *Abrenuncio.* (I renounce them.)
> *Et omnibus pompis eius?* (And all his pomp?)
> *Abrenuncio.* (I renounce it.)

The priest dipped his thumb into oil and made the sign of the cross on the baby's breast and back, between the shoulders. Then he said,

> *Quid petis?* (What do you seek?)
> *Baptismum.* (Baptism.)
> *Vis baptizari?* (Do you wish to be baptised?)
> *Volo.* (I do.)

The baby was now ready for baptism.

To do this, the priest held the baby in his hands with its head to the east and its face to the north, in other words on its right side. He said,

Et ego baptizo te in nomine patris (And I baptise you in the name of the Father),

plunging the whole of the baby beneath the water. He turned the baby's face to the south and did the same, continuing,

et filii (and of the Son).

Then he immersed the baby for a third time, with its face to the water, concluding,

et spiritus sancti (and of the Holy Spirit). *Amen.*

The laity, it seems, watched this process intently. 'We think', said a critic of the Church in 1546,

> that if our children be well plunged in the font, they shall be healthful in all their limbs ever after, but if they, by any misadventure, receive any hurt in any of their members, incontinent [*immediately*] we lay the fault in the priest, saying, 'That member was not well christened'.[81]

It was the priest's duty, therefore, to give the child complete and visible immersions.

When these were finished, the senior godparent took the baby from the priest's hands and literally 'raised it from the font' (Fig. 11). While the godparent held it, the priest dipped his thumb into chrism and make a cross on the top of the child's head. The baby was now put into its 'chrisom': a piece of cloth or a hooded robe which covered its head and body and kept the chrism and holy oil in place.[82] A lighted candle was put into the baby's hand with the words, in translation,

> Receive a burning and inextinguishable light. Guard your baptism. Observe the charge, so that when the Lord comes to the wedding, you may be able to meet him with the saints in the hall of heaven.

The rubrics for the service conclude with various directions which the priest had to pass on to those concerned. He must warn the parents of the baby that they should keep it from fire and water and all other perils until it was seven, and that if they did not do so, the godparents were responsible. The latter were told to teach the child, as it grew up, the three basic prayers that everyone was supposed to know: Paternoster (the Lord's Prayer), Ave Maria (the 'Hail Mary'), and the Apostles' Creed. There were two further instructions. One related to the chrisom cloth, which had to be kept on the baby's head for a time to protect the chrism there, and returned to the church in due course. It was usually brought back by the mother when she came to be purified. As a holy object (permeated by chrism), chrisom cloths could only be used again for religious purposes, such as towels or surplices, and clergy were forbidden to sell them for further baptisms.[83] The other

11   The baptism of a baby boy,
showing the priest, baby, two
godfathers, and a godmother.

instruction was that the baby should be brought to the bishop to be confirmed, as soon as he came within seven miles of the district.[84] Some clergy reminded the godparents to wash their hands before leaving church, presumably in case they had picked up traces of chrism.[85]

The *Manual* was not concerned with events away from church, but it is likely that hospitality was usually provided in the parental house to those who attended the christening. Godparents needed to be entertained, especially if they came from a distance. In return, their role included the duty of giving a present, and the higher the rank of giver or godchild, the greater the obligation. The richest gifts were given to royal babies. Prince Arthur, in 1486, received a gold cup and cover, a pair of gilt basins, a covered gold salt cellar, and a coffer of gold. Other royal children got similar kinds of gold or silver plate.[86] Early Tudor kings, Henry VII and Henry VIII, often presented 5 marks (£3 6s. 8d.) to their own godchildren, who were children of peers or, sometimes perhaps, of courtiers or household servants.[87] Queen Elizabeth of York gave £1 6s. 8d. to John Belle's child at Windsor in 1502, probably a child in the last category.[88] Knights were less generous: Sir Henry Willoughby of Wollaton (Notts.) in the 1520s dished out 10s. to gentle-

12 The birth of Alexander the Great, showing
the presents customarily given in medieval times.

men's children and sums of 3s. 4d., 1s. 8d., or merely 12d., to people of lower
rank.[89] Richard Hill, a London grocer of the same period, noted down the sums
that his children received, usually 3s. 4d.[90] Ordinary babies must have been lucky
to get a shilling, a groat, or merely a present in kind.

The sequel to the baptism was the mother's visit to church to be purified, or
'churched' as it was known by the fifteenth century.[91] Old Testament law laid
down that a woman who gave birth was unclean and should not touch a holy
object or enter a holy place for forty days after the birth of a son, or eighty following that of a daughter. She was then to make an offering to a priest and be
cleansed.[92] The Jewish custom was thought to have been followed by Mary after
the birth of Jesus, and (partly no doubt because of this) it passed into Christian
usage as a forty-day period in all cases. The practice was common in England by
the end of the twelfth century.[93] Christianity inherited the notion that birth
affected a woman's status, and by about 1400 a woman who died in childbirth was
supposed to be buried in the churchyard, rather than in the church itself.[94] But the
sense of impurity was less strong than in Judaism, and the exclusion of mothers
from church for forty days not insisted upon. Pope Gregory the Great, writing to
Augustine of Canterbury in about 600, advised that if women wished to enter
church to give thanks, straight after giving birth, they were not guilty of sin.[95] The
Manual too, although it refers to the 'purification of wives', goes on to

Note that wives may be purified after the issue of their offspring whenever they
wish to enter the church in thanks for the delivery . . . Nor is entry to churches

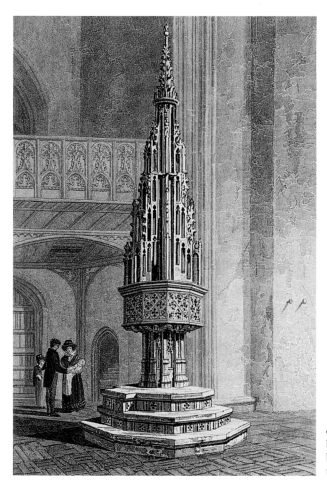

13   The font of Worstead church (Norfolk), dignified by being raised on steps and topped by an elaborate cover to protect the holy water.

to be denied to them, lest the penalty seem to be turned into blame for them. If, however, out of veneration they wish to abstain for some period of time, we do not believe that their devotion should be condemned.[96]

Officially, then, the Church did not insist on a particular span of time. Society may have been stricter in observing the forty days, either through clergy teaching or popular liking. Queen Eleanor of Provence went more than fifty days after the birth of Edward I in 1239, and almost exactly forty after that of his sister Katherine in 1253.[97]

Churching, as its name suggests, had to take place at church, and clergy were forbidden to do it at home.[98] A woman in London who failed to be churched in 1475, because her child was illegitimate, was made to do public penance in her parish church on three Sundays.[99] The mother to be churched was expected to bring women neighbours or friends to support her, and sometimes her midwife.[100] It was an occasion for a new dress and other finery. Queen Philippa was given a robe of cloth of gold faced with miniver fur when she was churched after the birth of the Black Prince in 1330, with a robe of silk and gold to wear in the evening.[101]

Even an ordinary woman might wish for 'a gown and other things against her churching, as she had the other time'.[102] The churching party met the parish priest and his clerk 'before the door of the church', which usually meant in the porch. The priest and clerk recited Psalm 121 ('I will look up to the hills'), some versicles and responses, and a prayer of thanks and hope for the mother's Christian vocation. Then she was sprinkled with holy water and the priest led her into church by the right hand, saying in Latin, as he had said to her baby six weeks earlier,

> Go into the temple of God, that you may have eternal life and live for ever and ever. Amen.

Inside, the mother offered her baby's chrisom cloth and a gift of money.[103] Sometimes, it seems, she stayed to hear mass.[104] Afterwards, there was often a feast at home. In 1246, the king, queen, and many nobility gathered at Wallingford (Berks.) to celebrate the churching of Sancha, wife of the king's brother Richard, earl of Cornwall.[105] That queen herself, Eleanor of Provence, had a similar banquet in 1253, attended by the archbishop of Canterbury, the bishop of Ely, and the earl of Gloucester.[106] Gentry invited their neighbours and entertained local worthies like abbots and priors, if they could get them, and ordinary people may have done the same within their circles.[107]

The wealthy elaborated the basic customs of baptism and churching as much as they did those of childbirth.[108] As the delivery of the child drew near, the church was made ready for the christening. In the case of the Tudors, the palace of Westminster seems to have been envisaged as a likely place of birth, and the nearby abbey as the appropriate church. The Percies, on the other hand, had to observe the rule of going to a parish church, like everyone else. The church-porch, where the baptismal service began, was hung and floored with cloth of gold, as was the area around the font and the whole of the chancel. A traverse (or curtained area) was set up beside the font with carpets, cushions, a brazier on which perfume could be cast, and basins of silver gilt containing water for washing. An ordinary church font seemed hardly grand enough for a prince or princess. The royal ordinances recommended that the silver font from Canterbury be brought for the occasion, or a similar new one made for the purpose, though it was conceded that a font of stone might be used 'as it hath been sometimes seen'. Whatever the case, the font was to be lined with soft linen and raised on a platform, so that the bystanders present might watch the ceremony.

Royal godparents were chosen before the birth and lodged nearby, ready for the event. A bishop too was secured to do the christening. When the baby was born, it was carried to church by the chief lady present – preferably a duchess in the case of the royal family, with another duchess to carry the chrisom upon her shoulder. The baby was dressed in a robe with a long train, held up (if a prince or princess) by an earl or a countess respectively. At Percy baptisms, the midwife went as well. The royal party was to be accompanied by an immense throng bearing 200 unlit torches (large candles), 24 of them borne by esquires surrounding the baby. A similar but smaller entourage attended the Percies. The sergeant of the pantry was sent to the church with the salt for the baptism, and the sergeant of the ewery with basins and water for hand-washing. The bishop received the child at the church-porch and carried out the first, catechising part of the service. Then the baby, with a canopy held over it, was brought into the church itself, taken out of its robe, and stripped for the christening. In royal practice, the abbot of Westminster was to consecrate the water in the font, and the christening was then done – presumably also by the bishop. When this was over and the lighted taper had been held in the baby's hand, the child was taken in procession up to the high altar of the church. A sum of money was offered on its behalf, the bishop con- firmed it, and prayers were said while the baby waited in another curtained tra- verse in the vicinity.

The completion of the spiritual formalities was followed by secular ones. Hands were washed, wine and spices served in church to the chief participants, and christening presents given. The procession formed to return to the palace, the presents going first, and the baby and its attendants next. A canopy was held over the baby and the attendants lit their torches. When the company reached home, the baby was taken to the nursery and the godparents' christening presents were handed over to the queen or lady (Fig. 12). Relatives or friends might also make gifts to the child. John of Gaunt in 1382 gave his niece Anne, daughter of his brother the earl of Buckingham, a pair of silver basins, a ewer, and other pieces of silver worth nearly £95. He tipped the baby's attendants and the messenger bringing the news.[109] Records of the gentry talk of presents such as a buckle of gold, gold rings set with precious stones, and sums of 2s. or 6s. 8d.[110] The fif- teenth-century pictorial life of Richard Beauchamp, earl of Warwick, shows, in the scene of his birth in 1382, one of his mother's attendants looking into a chest, apparently full of such gifts.[111]

These arrangements, of course, were ideal. Even those of royalty differed in detail and were overtaken by unplanned circumstances. Henry VII's first child, Prince Arthur, was born on a Wednesday, 20 September 1486, at Winchester not Westminster, and the christening was not carried out until the following Sunday.[112] It was a cold wet season, and the earl of Oxford, one of the intended god- parents, was delayed in arriving by floods. The earl was a long-standing supporter of the House of Lancaster, and Henry was unwilling to deprive him of the honour. So, in the meantime, the birth was celebrated by a procession of clergy in the cathedral, singing the *Te Deum*. Church bells were rung, bonfires lit in the streets, and messengers sent to spread the news throughout England. Inside the cathedral, a special font was erected on a stage, railed to keep off the crowds, and furnished with the appropriate hangings and traverse. On the Sunday, the baby was carried to the cathedral by the queen's sister Cecily, while another sister, Anne, carried the chrisom.

The christening party assembled when the earl of Oxford was reported to be a mile away, but this turned out to be a false alarm. Eventually, after waiting for three hours, it was decided to proceed without him. Cecily acted as godmother, and the earl of Derby and Lord Maltravers as godfathers. The prince was chris- tened by the bishop of Worcester, assisted by his brethren of Exeter and

Salisbury, and numerous other clergy. No sooner was the baby baptised than Oxford arrived, to be compensated by being asked to sponsor the prince at his confirmation, which was carried out by the bishop of Exeter. The prince returned home with burning torches and was piped into his nursery by trumpeters and minstrels. In the cathedral church-yard, two barrels of wine were broached so 'that every man might drink enough'.

How can one sum up baptism? Like the other services of the medieval Church it enshrined liturgical tradition and theological meaning. Being in Latin, it made its impact through its ceremonies, establishing Christian status in visible ways. It paid respect to the child as an individual. Once babies were baptised soon after birth, there were few group baptisms save at Easter, Pentecost, and in cases of twins or triplets. Most infants were christened individually. It was an emancipating process: the freeing of soul and body from sin and death to enjoy the possibility of salvation to everlasting life. At the same time, it was a process of binding, a rite of admission to a community, indeed at least four communities. In a public ceremony, it assigned you a gender and gave you a name – a name repeated some twenty-four times in the service. By acquiring a name, you became a member of society who could be identified, addressed, and commanded. By having your gender proclaimed, you were established as male or female in a world where the sexes had distinct identities, roles, and destinies. By receiving godparents, you gained a spiritual family alongside your natural one, and last (but not least) you became a member of the Church. This happened on the day you were born, without any consent on your part. For the rest of your life, always in theory and often in practice, you were subject to its rules on what you believed, how you behaved, and even when and what you ate and drank.

NAMES

'What is your name?'
'N. or M.'
'Who gave you this name?'
'My godfathers and godmothers in my baptism, wherein I was made a member of Christ, the child of God, and an inheritor of the kingdom of heaven.'[113]

THESE ARE THE famous opening words of Cranmer's Catechism of 1549: part of a lesson learnt by millions of children in England for the next four hundred years. They learnt it from clergy, teachers, and parents, and only when they could answer these and other questions were they allowed to be confirmed. Cranmer was a Protestant Reformer and his Catechism was a new way of teaching Christianity to children, but many of his assumptions were similar to those of medieval Catholics. From the Norman Conquest until the Reformation, christenings happened so soon after birth that the naming of the baby by the godparents in church was the first public announcement of the name. Often, as we shall see, the name was chosen by one of the godparents, and in these circumstances it was natural to say that they gave it.

Things had not always been so. The Anglo-Saxon child, especially in earlier centuries, may have been named by its parents days, weeks, or months before it had a chance of baptism. Baptism then endorsed the name rather than conferring it. After the Reformation, a gap began to reappear between birth and baptism. Cranmer himself forbade baptism on the day of birth (except in cases of necessity), and directed it to be held on a Sunday or festival day. His aim was to have it done in the presence of the whole church congregation and to use it as a teaching aid, so that 'every man present may be put in remembrance of his own profession made to God in his baptism'.[114] He did not stipulate which Sunday or festival, but for a long time baptism continued to take place soon after birth – often on the next such day available. In modern times, christenings have come to be delayed longer still, to give time for parents to recover and far-flung relations and friends to be invited. Nowadays, as with the Anglo-Saxons, the parental act of naming is the primary one. The baptism merely ratifies a choice already made, a fact already known.

Our names are our earliest possessions. As soon we can talk and understand, it is by them that we perceive our individuality and proclaim it to others. 'I am William', said the four-year-old prince to the herdsman's wife whose husband had found him alone in the forest, in the fourteenth-century romance *William of Palerne*.[115] Like any small child, he thought of his name as identifying him, not his rank as a king's son nor his splendid dress of cloth of gold. As we grow older, our names absorb our personalities and grow in resonance. John Smith, to those who know him, is not only a name but a person, and it is impossible to think of the name without imagining its owner as well. The paradox is that our names, for all their 'our-ness', are not of our own making. They are bestowed upon us by our elders, like our families, homes, and upbringings. Our names are chosen for reasons that matter to them, not to us. In order to understand the history of children's names, we have therefore to identify who chose them, and then try to discover why they chose as they did.[116]

In Anglo-Saxon times, names in the royal and aristocratic families whose members are best recorded seem to have been selected by parents, often with an eye on family tradition. Some families kept to recognisable patterns, so that most of the kings of Essex had names beginning with S (Saeberht, Seaxred, Saeward), while those of Wessex often began with C (Cerdic, Cynric, Cynegils). Others reused names, like the Alfreds, Edwards, and Edgars in the royal family from 900 to 1066, or (as we shall see) took parts of fathers' or mothers' names to make new ones. Yet other names were modelled on ancient heroes, who may have been regarded as family forebears. Eormenric, king of Kent, and Offa, king of Mercia, bore the names of famous kings of northern Europe. St Guthlac of Crowland was apparently called after the founding father of his tribe.[117] After about the time of the Norman Conquest, however, when infant baptism was universally established, a competing influence began to appear from a new quarter, that of the godparents. Each child, as we have seen, had three of these: two of its own gender and one of the other. The Church's service of baptism gave the godparents, not the parents, the role of announcing a baby's name in public. By the later middle ages, it was common practice for the senior of the two gender godparents to name the baby after himself or herself. This practice may have begun in the Anglo-Norman period, and was certainly widespread from the end of the thirteenth century onwards.

There has been some debate among historians as to the relative powers of parents and godparents in this matter. Philip Niles, in a study of the naming of feudal heirs from the thirteenth to the early sixteenth centuries, found that out of 302 documented children, 261 (86%) were given the name of one of their god-parents.[118] He drew attention to occasions when people at a baptism expressed surprise that a godparent's name was not given, implying that such an omission broke the accepted custom.[119] Names, he admitted, might sometimes be given in honour of a saint or a family member, but he concluded that the paramount right was that of the chief godparent to confer his or her own name. Louis Haas, on the other hand, has argued the need to look beyond the godparents. Using a smaller sample of feudal heirs in Yorkshire, he pointed out that parents may have chosen godparents who would give the name the parents wanted. Some godparents, he noticed, had the same name as the gender parent; others, he thought, were infe-rior in rank to the parents, implying that the latter selected them in order to dictate the choice of name.[120]

Both Niles and Haas are probably right in part. Some parents evidently decided what their children were called. Certain families, as we shall see, made a point of using distinctive, traditional names. In others, names were chosen to replicate those of parents, to glorify saints, or simply to distinguish each child from its siblings. Kings and queens normally gave each of their children a different name, though names might be reused if their owners failed to survive. Two sons of Edward III were christened William, the second after the first had died. Giving all one's children unique names is also found lower down in society. Robert Eyre, esquire, of Hathersage (Derbs.) (d. 1459) and his wife Joan had ten sons and three daughters, all but two of whom had dissimilar names, despite the likelihood that some died in infancy.[121] Other instances are those of the families of John Symondes, merchant of Cley (Norfolk) (d. 1512), and Humphrey Oker, esquire of Okeover (Staffs.) (d. 1538). Symondes had eight children (four of each sex) and Oker had thirteen (eight boys and five girls). No name was repeated in either family.[122] In such cases parents must either have chosen godparents with a wide selection of names or have told them the names they should give.

In other families, perhaps the majority, parents were more concerned to honour their godparents and give them the right to bestow their own names, than to interfere in the process. Such parents may have felt that the godparent would do more for the godchild if the two had a name in common. This policy, in a large family, might lead to the same name being given to more than one child. In Beddington church (Surrey), there is a memorial brass to Philippa Carew, daugh-ter of the lord of the manor, who died in 1414 (Fig. 14). She was one of fourteen children, seven of each sex, and the brass depicts their faces and lists their names. The boys were called Guy, John, John, John, John, William, and William. Their

14   The brothers and sisters of Philippa Carew of Beddington (Surrey) (d. 1414).

sisters were Eleanor, Lucy, Agnes, Agnes, Margaret, and Anne.[123] In the famous Norfolk gentry family, the Pastons, John Paston I (d. 1466) had five sons. The two eldest were both named John, one born in 1442, the other two years later, each of them living to adulthood and having important careers. It used to be supposed that names were reused because children died, and this might happen as it did in Edward III's family. But the explanation does not fit a case like the Pastons, where both children grew up. Here it is likely that the chief godparent's name was the primary factor, and that his or her right to give it (or the parents' wish to defer to this right) was more important than giving each child a separate name.

Having considered the people who gave the names, we can now turn to the names they gave. Anglo-Saxon names were of two main kinds: the monothematic (based on one element) and the dithematic (containing two).[124] Monothematic examples are names like Beorn ('man' or 'warrior'), Heafoc ('hawk'), or Wulf ('wolf'). The dithematic include Alfred ('elf counsel'), Edward ('rich or happy guardian'), or Æthelflæd ('noble beauty'). Both kinds of names were used throughout society, but kings and nobility especially favoured the dithematic type, while the monothematic was common among ordinary people. Important people might use elements of their own names to give to their children. King Edward the Elder of Wessex and his wife Ælflæd named their sons, born in the early 900s, Edwin, Edmund, and Eadred. These names duplicated the first element of the father's name, and Edmund likewise had sons called Eadwig and Edgar. The name of Edward's and Ælflæd's eldest son, Ælfweard, was made up of the first element of her name and the second of his. There were conventions about which names were male and which were female, but it is interesting to note that while some female names expressed gentle qualities, like Æthelflaed and Mildred ('mild strength'), others were similar in nature to those of men, such as Æthelthryth ('noble strength') and Edith ('happy war'). Such names might relate to the past or to the future. Edith might commemorate a father's successful campaign, Æthelflaed express a hope about how such a girl would develop.

The pool of Anglo-Saxon names was large. In Devon, some 562 certain or plausible personal names have been identified as embedded within place names alone.[125] Some of these may be variants of the same name, or pet names, because (like us) the Anglo-Saxons often shortened one another's names to be endearing or familiar. Ælfwine became Ælle, Nothelm Nunna, and Trumwine Tuma, and this usage was found at the highest level: the grown-up children of King Sæberht of Essex referred to him as 'Saba'.[126] It is likely that such pet names were used of children too, and represent their or their parents' mispronunciations, but this is difficult to prove because pet names can be given in adulthood. The conversion of the Anglo-Saxons to Christianity in the seventh century does not appear to have made a difference to naming customs for a long time. We might expect that Biblical or saints' names would have become popular, but although we encounter the occasional cleric with such a name, like John of Beverley or Boniface of Exeter, these were new names, taken after entering the Church. They were not given at birth, or even at baptism.

Children's names in England remained almost wholly Germanic up to the late eleventh century. The coming of Viking settlers to the Midlands and North introduced Scandinavian versions, but these were not vastly different in type or meaning from Anglo-Saxon ones. The same is true of the Normans in 1066, most of whose names were continental Germanic. Names that we regard as quintessentially Norman, such as Geoffrey, Henry, Hugh, Odo, Robert, Roger, and William, all fall into this category, as do those of some girls like Matilda, Millicent, and Rosamund. By the time of the Norman Conquest, however, a major change in naming practice was beginning to spread through western Europe. This was the use of Latin, saintly, and Biblical names, which was already taking root in northern France, though it was not yet common. We find a few such examples in late eleventh-century England (especially in Domesday Book), including Andrew, Laurence, Matthew, Maurice, Pagan (meaning 'countryman' rather than 'heathen'), and Stephen. Isaac and Moses appear as well, as Christian, not Jewish, names.

After 1066, these Biblical and saintly names spread steadily through the population of England, in a process which Robert Bartlett has aptly called one of 'transformation and convergence'.[127] 'Transformation' means that names changed from being largely Germanic to the mixture of Germanic, Hebrew, and Latin ones that is still with us today. 'Convergence' expresses the fact that particular names became widely adopted and that there were fewer of them in consequence. The process is observable throughout western Europe, reflecting a period of strong international links, notably in the Church and the crusades. In England, it was probably assisted by the Norman Conquest. This, by putting a French aristocracy in power, meant that English people who aspired to join them were tempted to give their children Norman names, especially William, Robert, and Henry which were used in the royal family. We can see this pressure at work in about 1120, in the case of Bartholomew, the hermit and unofficial saint of Farne Island (Nland.). He was born in Whitby (Yorks.) and named Tosti by his parents, but when he grew up his adolescent peers made fun of this name (a Viking one), and called him William. He then acquired Bartholomew as a religious name.[128]

The change is well illustrated in the family of Peter of Cornwall, prior of the monastery of Holy Trinity Aldgate (London), who died in 1221. Peter came from Launceston (Cornwall), and we can reconstruct his family tree from his writings and from a few surviving deeds of property. His great-grandfather was a certain Theodulf who lived at about the time of the Norman Conquest. Theodulf's sons had English names like himself, Ailsi and Brictric, but Ailsi's children (born about 1100) were given a mixture of Germanic, Latin, and Christian ones: Bernard, Nicholas, Jordan, and Pagan. In the next generation, in about the 1130s and 40s,

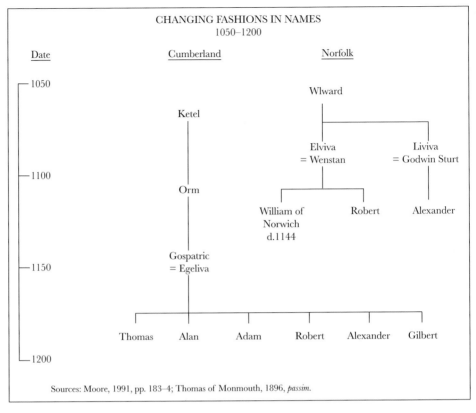

15   Name changes in the twelfth century. The families of William of Norwich and Gospatric of
Cumberland.

Bernard named his sons Luke, Peter, and John, while Jordan was the father of
Peter of Cornwall and possibly of a son named Richard.[129] This family radically
altered its naming habits during these four generations, and the same was true
elsewhere (Fig. 15). By the 1220s, Anglo-Saxon or Scandinavian names had
largely disappeared from the Lincolnshire countryside. A list of about 624 male
tenants from the Louth area shows only 6% of them having such names. The vast
majority bore 'modern' Norman or saintly ones, led by William (86 examples),
Robert (59), and John (40).[130]

Few pre-Conquest names, then, survived this process. A few endured for a
while in modified form as Ailmer (formerly Æthelmaer), Ailward (Æthelweard),
and Alured (Alfred) for boys, or Edith and Hilda for girls. Edward and Edmund
continued or returned as a result of the popularity of the saints who bore those
names. But generally, the pool of names grew more cosmopolitan. Norman ones
like those already mentioned became common, as did the names of saints and
Biblical characters. Adam, John, and Peter began their climb to popularity for
boys; Bartholomew, Christopher, Denis, Nicholas, and Philip became widely used
as well. Girls' names were slower to change, perhaps because Norman women
were less important role models than Norman men, but they too were trans-

formed by the early thirteenth century.[131] Two new kinds of girls' names became popular. One was that of a saint: Agnes, Isabel or Elizabeth, Katherine, Margaret, and Mary. The other was a name based on a Latin or French word with an attractive meaning, such as Clara and Clarice ('clear'), Christian (the modern Christine), Damsel ('lady'), and Pleasant. Many of the new names, both male and female, were made into pet names like the Anglo-Saxon ones. They were shortened (Bartholomew to Bat, Katherine to Kate, Mary to Mall), or had a diminutive ending added to them. Adam and Richard became Adcock and Hitchcock; John, Mary, and Peter turned into Jankin, Malkin, and Perkin. By about 1300, such names were certainly given to children as well as being used of adults.[132]

Names were also affected by the process of convergence. The total number in use remained a large one, but the individual names were not uniformly popular. List after list of people after 1200 – be it taxpayers, tenants, or guild members – contains vast numbers of a small group of names. John, Peter, Thomas, and William led the field for men; Adam, Henry, Stephen, and Walter were common as well. For women too, there was more conformity in choosing Elizabeth, Mary, and (a newcomer) Anne. Other names remained in use, but more rarely than before. Sometimes they survived as traditions within certain families. The de Vere earls of Oxford favoured Aubrey, and the Bohun earls of Essex and Hereford, Humphrey. Among the gentry, the Arundell family of Lanherne (Cornwall) used Remfrey, the Digby family of Stoke Dry (Rutland) Everard and Kenelm, and families in east Yorkshire (especially the Constables of Flamborough) Marmaduke – a name of Celtic origin. But in most families, the choice of names grew smaller, and it became necessary to find a way of distinguishing between so many Johns, Peters, and Williams. The result was a greater use of surnames during the twelfth and thirteenth centuries, giving people a further identification based on their address, occupation, characteristics, or the name of their father, mother, or husband. Some of the old Anglo-Saxon and Viking personal names lasted just long enough to become surnames, like Aylmer and Thurstan, Godwin and Orme.

Convergence seems to have happened for more than one reason. The giving of names by godparents may have helped here, since if people of relatively high status were often asked to do this duty, they would multiply their name in the next generation. The Norman Conquest has already been mentioned as a likely influence, and religion was undoubtedly a third. The Church's emphasis on figures such as the archangel Michael, the Virgin Mary, the apostles, and saints like Christopher and Nicholas, Katherine and Margaret, constantly brought their names to people's attention. Some clergy thought that name choice should be regulated. In 1281, a Church council at Lambeth warned priests not to allow the giving of names that were or sounded 'lascivious', especially to girls. If such names were given, the bishop might alter them at confirmation, a warning repeated in John de Burgh's popular late-medieval handbook for the clergy, *Pupilla Oculi*.[133] One wonders what were these immoral names. Did they include Amabel, Douce, or Iseult (a famous adulteress of fiction), all of which occur in gentry families in the fifteenth century?[134] If so, the ban was not altogether effective, at least among people of rank.

The royal family provides a good short history of naming practice in medieval England. In late Anglo-Saxon times, it used dithematic English names with a secular meaning, like Alfred or Edward. These often harked back to a famous king so called. When William conquered England in 1066, his family brought in continental versions of Germanic names: Henry, Robert, and William for boys, Adela and Matilda for girls. Names like these continued to be given after the Norman royal family died out in the male line in 1135, first in that of King Stephen and then in the Angevin branch of Henry II. Henry had sons called William and Henry, and a daughter named Matilda. But even in this period, changes of fashion are visible. Robert dropped out after 1100, William largely so after 1153, and Matilda after 1156. Henry was the only Germanic name to remain in constant use from the eleventh to the sixteenth centuries.

The Conqueror and his queen were not untouched by the growing popularity of non-German names. Two of their daughters were called Cecilia and Constance, both Roman names and the former that of a saint. In about the 1130s, King Stephen named one of his daughters Mary, the first royal response to the cult of the Virgin, a cult then vastly growing in importance. Henry II subscribed to another popular saint-cult by calling his youngest daughter, born in 1165, Joan, and his youngest son, born in 1167, John. John the Baptist too was a rising saint of the time. In the next generation, King John (like Henry II) mixed traditional family names (Henry and Richard) with new ones derived from saints (Isabel and Joan), but by the time that his son Henry III began to have children in 1239, saints' names were dominant. Two of Henry's daughters were named after popular women saints, Katherine and Margaret, the first because she was born on Katherine's day, the second because it was her grandmother's name and her mother invoked the saint's help during the birth.[135] Henry's sons received the Anglo-Saxon names of Edward and Edmund, both of which were now saintly rather than secular names in people's minds, since Edward recalled St Edward the Confessor and Edmund the martyred saint of Bury St Edmunds.

By the end of the thirteenth century, the royal penchant for saints' names embraced a third English figure, Thomas Becket. In one sense this was a curious choice. Becket was not a king like Edmund and Edward, but the child of a London merchant. Moreover, he had been the enemy and victim of Henry II in 1170. But in 1300, Edward I's wife Margaret prayed to him for help while giving birth to her first child, and the boy was named Thomas in gratitude. Evidently the popularity of Thomas's cult at Canterbury wiped out his earlier social and political significance, and his name was subsequently used for sons of Edward III and Henry IV. Other new saint-cults arose in the later middle ages, but these had less impact on the royal family, chiefly because fewer royal children were born after the 1350s than before. The family of Edward IV, the largest of the fifteenth century, also had the most adventurous names. They included George, by now the family's patron saint, and Bridget, whose name recalled two popular saints of the time: Bridget of Ireland and Bridget of Sweden. The latter Bridget was the patron saint of the monastery of Syon (Middx.), founded by Henry V and closely linked with the royal family.

From time to time, the family brought in new names of a secular kind as well. These were commoner for girls than boys, so that we find Berengaria, Blanche, and Philippa – usually as compliments to grandmothers. Edward I called his third son Alfonso, the name of the brother of his first wife, Eleanor of Castile, and had the young prince not died at the age of ten the name might have become established in England. Richard II, who was the second son of his father, the Black Prince, had a name not given in the family since 1209, but conceivably modelled on that of Richard I in the hope that the new Richard too would be a warrior and crusader. Henry VII, a king with a weak claim, tried to suggest his family's ancient lineage by calling his eldest son Arthur, and this too might have stuck had Arthur lived to adulthood. There is no sign that kings or queens took exception to the names of their unsuccessful predecessors. Those of John, Edward II, and Richard II were all reused in subsequent times. Edward I, Edward II, Edward III, and Henry IV each had a son called John, the most famous being John of Gaunt, and it was only the accidents of births and deaths that deprived us of a second such king.

Names, then, came to children carrying all kinds of significance. Some had clear meanings, pointing hopefully to future qualities or achievements. Most after 1200, however, recalled a person rather than conveying an idea. They were reminders of a saint, an ancestor, or a godparent, and (if you were lucky) might bring you such people's support. A few names marked out their holders as different because they were used only in certain families, but these were fairly unusual. The majority of names in the later middle ages were in common use, and formed a bond through society. You could reflect with satisfaction that you had the same name as your lord or lady, or your king or queen. A name might spur you to imitate those who had borne it. Edward the Black Prince came close to replicating Edward III. Or it might not do so at all. Edward II behaved quite differently to Edward I, and Henry VI was no Henry V.

BIRTHDAYS AND RECORDS

TODAY A BABY'S birth is a legal and civil event. It has to be reported to the state within so many days, by a formal process of registration. Registration establishes one's nationality and civil rights. The date of one's birth is recorded, and matters throughout one's life. From the date comes qualification for schooling, marriage, the electoral franchise, and a pension. Organisations ask for dates of birth on application forms, and use them as passwords to check one's identity. It is not surprising, therefore, that birthdays have social significance too. This is especially so in childhood when we have birthday parties and presents, and even in adulthood when we reach eighteen, twenty-one, or dates with round numbers.

Was this concern with birthdays shared by our medieval ancestors? The answer appears to be 'yes, but not so much'. Some people by the later middle ages were certainly aware of their own or their family members' birth dates. When Anne, the young daughter of William Boleyn, esquire, of Blickling died in 1479, her

16 The brass of Anne Boleyn (d. 1479), with its precise note of her age: three years, eleven months, and thirteen days.

father carefully noted on her tomb that she died at the age of three years, eleven months, and thirteen days (Fig. 16). It looks as though he knew that this was two and a half weeks short of her fourth birthday on or about St Luke's Day (18 October).[136] For people like the Boleyns, we have an obvious source of evidence in the so-called 'proofs of age', in which feudal heirs established that they had reached the age of majority: fourteen for a woman, twenty-one for a man. The evidence is not as impartial as one would wish because it comes from witnesses brought by the heirs, and was meant to support their claims rather than to record events with accuracy. Sometimes the witnesses do not specify the place of birth, and sometimes they are vague about the date. One in Kent in 1273 remembered only that his own son was born 'about' the time of the feast of the Nativity of the Virgin.[137] Roger of St Andrew, a Cambridgeshire heir in about 1280, was said to have been born both on about the feast of All Saints and on the second or third day afterwards.[138] The birthday of a Dorset heiress, Alice de Pidele, was placed in 1291 merely 'in March' and her age was given both as sixteen and eighteen.[139]

On other occasions, however, proofs of age assert definite, well-remembered facts about birth dates and ages. Heirs are often attributed with births on particular days, usually those of saints, in a particular year of a king's reign. They are said to have been baptised in particular churches, and sometimes the names of those present are stated. Thus Philip Paynel, a Wiltshire heir in 1291, is described as having been born on the day of the Assumption of our Lady, at about the first hour of the day. He was baptised in the local parish church of St Mary by the vicar in the early morning. Agnes de Writel took him to the baptism and was godmother, and two representatives acted for Philip Bassett who had been asked to be the chief godfather, to lift the baby from the font, and to give him his own name.[140] No records of this kind survive for the lower orders of society, but references sometimes show that there too some people remembered birth dates, accurately or approximately. William of Norwich, the young saint born in rural Norfolk of ordinary stock in 1132–3, was remembered or believed to have come into the world on Candlemas Day (2 February).[141] Margaret of Kilpeck, a Herefordshire widow in 1307, recalled bearing her son Adam on the feast of the Nativity of the Virgin Mary (8 September), and her son Roger 'a few days after Easter'.[142]

As these records show, the calendar was helpful in remembering dates of births. Religious festivals and saints' days enabled one to fix the day or at least the season. Thomas Becket must have known that he was born on the feast of St Thomas the Apostle, and named after the saint.[143] Richard II may have taken pride in his birthday on the Epiphany, the feast of the three kings, and on the fact that three real kings attended his baptism.[144] The day of the week or month might be remembered and given significance. The rhyme beginning 'Monday's child is fair of face' is not recorded before 1838, but similar folklore about birth days is very ancient indeed.[145] An Anglo-Saxon tract on the days of the month claims to reveal the different qualities possessed by children born on them. A boy who comes into the world on the first day, for example, will be 'illustrious, clever, wise, and book-learned', but he must beware of danger by water. A girl will be 'pure, chaste, mild, handsome, and acceptable to men', but will have a mark on her mouth or eyebrow.[146] Similar predictions survive from the fifteenth century, concerning the days of the week, days of the month, and signs of the zodiac (Fig. 18). A Sunday's child will be a great lord, a Wednesday's child strong and wise, but a Saturday's child and the mother who bears it will both experience peril.[147] A child born under one sign (no doubt Pisces) will become a fisherman, under a second (probably Libra) a handler of money, and under others a cleric or a soldier.[148]

Places of birth and baptism were remembered too. Gerald of Wales recalled how he was born in Manorbier Castle (Pemb.), Adam of Usk his origins in Usk (Gwent).[149] Biographers of saints – William of Norwich, Thomas of Hereford, and John of Bridlington – found out where their heroes first saw the light. For most people such evidence was never written down, but that does not mean that it was not once current knowledge. The proofs of age include many testimonies about the birth places of the aristocracy, and a series of records from the north of England does the same for some lesser people. In the city of York during the late fifteenth and early sixteenth centuries, men who came from the English side of the Scottish borders were sometimes alleged to be Scots and therefore ineligible for civil rights. To prove their English status, they produced witnesses to testify to their places of birth and baptism and, often, to the names of their parents and godparents. John Malson, girdler, for example, brought evidence in 1482 to show that he was the child of Richard Malson, born at Langwathby (Cumb.), and baptised in the church there. His godparents were John Mekyll of Penrith, John Walker of Langwathby, and the wife of William of Carleton.[150]

Birthdays not only remind us of the past; they are steps along the road of life to the future. Our age clicks on to a fresh number. Medieval people too must often have been aware of how old they were on their birthdays. This would have been especially so in childhood, as parents watched children grow up and children measured their progress towards adulthood. As we have seen, there was a well developed idea of the 'ages of man'.[151] The years three and seven were significant, three being the age of weaning while seven marked the transition from infancy to childhood. Adolescence was marked by a series of age thresholds regulating confession and communion in church, entrance into the system of law and order, the ability to marry, and the right to administer property.[152] Whether and how often children's birthdays were celebrated are uncertain. Readers of the Bible would have known that both Pharaoh and Herod Antipas commemorated theirs with feasts, and the word 'birthday' existed in English, but it was far less common than it is today.[153] More attention was given to the observance of people's death dates – 'obits' or anniversaries as they were called, when the dead were commemorated with masses or prayers for their souls. These events bulk larger in records than birthdays.

A further insight into this matter is provided by the records of Winchester College, the famous public school founded by William of Wykeham in 1382. The college gave scholarships to boys aged from eight to eighteen, and from 1472 it noted their ages at the time of their entry. The register of admissions states that the boy concerned was (for example) ten years old last Michaelmas (29 September). Up to the 1560s, the dates given were usually saints' days or other religious festivals. A few boys' ages were linked with the day of an unusual saint, like David (1 March) and Gregory (12 March), implying that they knew they were

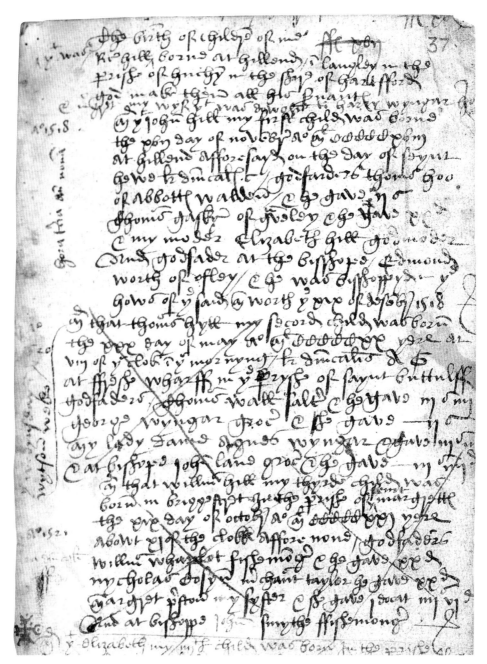

17   Richard Hill's notes of the births of his children, with careful details of times, godparents, and christening presents.

born on these days, but most boys were said to be of a particular age on a major festival, especially Christmas Day, Lady Day, St John the Baptist Day, and Michaelmas Day – the days that marked the quarters of the year. This suggests that they had only a rough, seasonal idea of their birth dates, and were unlikely to commemorate the day.[154] All the boys claimed to know how old they were, but even that was beyond the knowledge of the English schoolboy envisaged by Claude Desainliens in a treatise on French in the 1570s. The boy, when asked his age, says that he 'cannot tell', but knows that his father has written his birth date in the family Bible.[155]

Perhaps as this anecdote suggests, it was adults, rather than children, who noted such matters in their heads or in books. Certainly, remarkable numbers of medieval births were recorded by adults in writing, and the later one goes, the more survive. Chroniclers were beginning to note those of English royal children by the middle of the twelfth century, a fact that reflects the growing importance of primogeniture. The English crown and the lands of the aristocracy were coming to be passed down in a stricter order of succession, favouring eldest sons, and the sequence of births therefore mattered more than before. One of the earliest such chroniclers was Robert of Torigni, abbot of Mont St Michel, who wrote down those of Henry II's sons and daughters from 1155 to 1167, except for Matilda (born 1156). He also noted the death of William, the eldest, at about the age of three.[156] Matthew Paris, monk of St Albans, provided a similar coverage of five sons and daughters of Henry III and Eleanor of Provence, and the chronicle of Bury St Edmunds mentions several of the children of Edward I.[157] By the second half of the thirteenth century, some chroniclers were recording the births of lesser people. When George de Cantilupe was born at Abergavenny in about 1252, the date was allegedly written in the chronicles of the local priory and of Totnes Priory (Devon), where George's family were lords of the town.[158] In 1305, a Londoner who was probably Andrew Horn, fishmonger and subsequently chamberlain of the city, was moved to include in his chronicle the births of Elias and Julia, twin-children of his neighbour William the cooper on 3 April, and that of his own son 'J.' on 24 June, a baby who died twelve weeks later.[159]

More common than in chronicles was the insertion of information into Church service books. As early as the thirteenth and fourteenth centuries, some of the witnesses of feudal heirs claimed that they knew dates of birth or baptism because local clergy had recorded them in missals or psalters.[160] By the end of the middle ages, private prayer books survive into which their owners have entered family data of this kind. One late fifteenth-century 'book of hours' is particularly well supplied in this way. It belonged to William Roberts (d. 1508), a gentleman of Little Brackstead (Essex), and lists the birth of five of his children between 1478 and 1497. The entries give the name, weekday, hour, calendar date (or festival day), and year. Later, the book passed to William's daughter Margaret, who married first John Tymperley and then Edward Strangman. She or her husbands kept it in similar fashion, recording two of her children's births by the first husband and the unusually large total of seventeen by the second, including two sets of twins. The same information is given for each child down to the last of this generation, in 1537.[161]

One of the fullest records of family births is the one made by the London grocer, Richard Hill, during the 1510s and 20s, in the now famous anthology of

18 'Saturday's child works hard for a living.' Worse still, children born on Saturn's day might find themselves begging, in the stocks, or on the gallows

English prose and poetry which he compiled for his own or his family's use, known as Balliol College Oxford MS 354. In this book he noted his own place of birth at Hillend in Langley (Herts.), without date, and the births of his seven children.[162] The entry relating to the first child, John, is not as full as the rest, but the notes about Thomas, the second, are more typical:

> Anno 1520, the Wednesday in Whitsun week. Memorandum, that Thomas Hill my second child was born the 30 day of May, anno 1520 at 8 of the clock in the morning . . . at Fresh Wharf in the parish of Saint Botolf [London], godfathers Thomas Wall, salter, and he gave 3s. 4d.; George Wyngar, grocer, and he gave 2s.; my lady Dame Agnes Wyngar, and [she] gave 3s. 4d.; and at bishop [*confirmation*], John Lane, grocer, and he gave 3s. 4d.

There are a good many facts here, as we might expect from a successful trades- man. They include the place, parish, hour, weekday, day of the month, and year of birth, the names of the godparents, the sums of money that they gave, and the name of the sponsor at confirmation (Fig. 17). All these records were of potential value. Place and dates might be needed for legal reasons, and names of godpar- ents and sponsors might be relevant when marriages came to be planned. Money would have to be passed to children when they grew up, and the amounts of the sums testified to the family's social status. Three of Hill's children died in youth, and their dates and parishes of death are duly noted as well.

The parish clergy, as we have seen, might record the date of an important baby's christening as early as the thirteenth century. By the early sixteenth, a few may have been keeping fuller lists of baptisms, marriages, and sometimes funerals.[163] In 1538, the crown made such records compulsory. Royal injunctions to the clergy ordered them all to acquire a 'book or register' in which to write the day and year of every wedding, christening, and burial, and the names of those concerned (see Fig. 84). In the case of baptisms, the order was later expanded to include the names of the baby's father and mother.[164] The king claimed that this would enable legitimacy and illegitimacy to be recorded for legal purposes, but the wish to ensure that infants went on being baptised in parish churches was probably also important. At a time of growing religious divisions, Roman Catholics might be tempted to make separate arrangements for their babies, while radical Protestants like Anabaptists, who stressed voluntary adult baptism, might ignore the process completely. The English Reformers did not wish to dismantle the system by which the English all belonged to the same Church, like it or not.

It would be wrong, therefore, to deny our medieval ancestors an interest in places and dates of birth or in people's subsequent ages. Some of this interest may have had different motives from ours, such as the wish to predict a child's charac- ter or future from the calendar date or the disposition of the stars at the time. But practical reasons to record and remember births and ages already existed, even if they were not as pressing as they are today. The instinct to keep records of such things is an ancient one, and when Henry VIII's regime established parish regis- ters, it was building on tradition as well as introducing something new.

Chapter 2
———
Family Life

FAMILY SIZE AND SHAPE

WE DO NOT enter the world on an equal footing. We are shaped not only by the genes we inherit from our parents but by their health, the lives they lead, and the places they live. Wealth and poverty affect us in the womb, and increase their impact as soon as we leave it. Medieval children, like modern ones, grew up in a wide variety of homes in terms of family size and shape, housing, wealth, and standard of living. 'Family' comes from the Latin word *famulus*, meaning 'a slave' or 'a servant'. In Roman and medieval times, it applied both to what we now call a 'nuclear family' of parents and children, and to any servants who lived beneath the roof. The servants were under the authority of the head of the house like the children, and counted as family members. A richer child grew up in a larger household of this kind, interacting with servants as well as with parents. A poor one belonged to a nuclear family alone.

The best documented family of medieval England is the royal family, nearly every child of which is mentioned in chronicles or records from the mid twelfth century onwards.[1] About ninety-six children were born to English kings and queens between 1150 and 1540, ranging, within a single marriage, from none to about fifteen. Richard I and Richard II had no children, and Henry VI only one. At the other extreme, Edward IV had ten, Edward III twelve, and Edward I the largest total. He sired at least fifteen children by his first wife, Eleanor of Castile, and at least three more by his second, Margaret of France. A large family demonstrated the king's potency and the queen's good health. Kings needed male heirs, and both sons and daughters were valuable assets in governing the kingdom or forging alliances. The custom of employing wet nurses to suckle royal babies was another crucial matter. This quickened the mother's return to fertility, and led to briefer intervals between conceptions than if she fed her children by herself.

In practice, the royal family was smaller. Not all the children survived to grow up, despite the amount of nursing care and medical attention they received. In the next chapter, we shall see that about thirty-four of the royal offspring died at birth or soon afterwards, leaving a residue of only about sixty-two. If we divide this number by the number of married kings, fifteen, it produces an average number of only just over four children per monarch, rising to just over six if we include the infants who died. This average four was sometimes depleted by further deaths during childhood. Some royal children grew up together in groups, in a household of their own, and may have developed bonds of affection. In other cases, this did not occur. The family of Edward III was born over a twenty-five-year period. The youngest child, Thomas of Woodstock, born in 1355, was nine years behind his nearest sister, Margaret. Richard II, Henry VI, and Henry's son Edward each grew up without siblings for all or most of their childhoods.

Once we leave the royal family, records of births become less frequent, even among the highest ranks of society: the nobility, gentry, and the prosperous classes of the towns. Careful work by Dr J. S. Moore on barons and knights of the twelfth century, however, suggests that the average size of baronial families was between 4.15 and 4.83 members, and of knightly ones between 4.55 and 5.71. These figures include the parents, which leaves the average number of children at some-where between two and three. On either side of these averages, there might be a range in the number from one to ten, perhaps more.[2] The data on which such figures are based, however, are likely to ignore children who died in infancy, and some come from 'snapshots' of families at particular dates. Taking infant mortal-ity into account, the total number of children born to baronial and knightly parents is likely to have been higher, as it was in the royal family.

In the later middle ages, new sources survive for the family sizes of the nobility and gentry. One is that of prayer books or literary miscellanies, in which parents listed babies' names and dates of birth. These are not common and have not yet been studied in quantity.[3] The other source, less detailed but more plentiful, con-sists of monumental brasses, inlaid into flat 'ledger stones' on the floors of churches, marking the tombs of important people (usually adults). In the fifteenth century, it became fashionable for such brasses to depict not only the men and women they commemorated but also their children.[4] Exceptionally, the brasses name the children.[5] More commonly, they show them in a group of sons and a group of daughters. The numbers within these groups vary from brass to brass, and seem to indicate a convention of recording every child that was born, irrespective of its survival. Normally, however, all the children are shown as well grown, so that we do not learn how many died as infants or grew up to be adults.

The evidence of the brasses suggests that the offspring of nobility and gentry varied from one child upwards, but that six or eight were common and that totals occasionally rose above twelve. Thomas Stokes of Ashby St Legers (Nhants.) (d. 1414) and his wife Ellen had four sons and twelve daughters, while the Rochesters of Terling (Essex) in c.1500 had nine of each. John Lord Cobham and his wife Margaret achieved a total of eight sons and ten daughters up to 1506, and his suc-cessor Thomas thirteen: seven and six respectively. Still higher numbers were achieved by William and Agnes Aldriche of Burnham (Bucks.) c.1520, and Peter and Jane Coryton of St Mellion (Cornwall) up to 1551, each with twenty-four. The Aldriches had nine sons and fifteen daughters, the Corytons seventeen and seven respectively.[6] Brasses of yeomen are uncommon, but one of William Joye of Bramley (Hants.) shows him with twelve children, six of each sex.[7] Merchants and their wives seem rarely to have exceeded twelve, but one or two did so. John Gilbert, grocer and mayor of Norwich (d. 1467) had seventeen children by his wife Annore, and Nicholas Leveson, mercer and sheriff of London (d. 1539) had eighteen by his, Denys.[8] Margery Kempe, the famous burgess wife and mystic of King's Lynn in the early fifteenth century, accorded with this pattern: she claimed to have had fourteen.[9]

Such numbers must have been reduced by deaths (Fig. 19). Even the most pro-lific parents can rarely have had more than ten or twelve children alive at a time. Margery mentions only one of her children (a son) as having grown up and married. The average wealthy family of the later middle ages probably consisted of about two or three surviving children, as it had done in the twelfth century. This was true lower down in society too. Here, economic considerations might

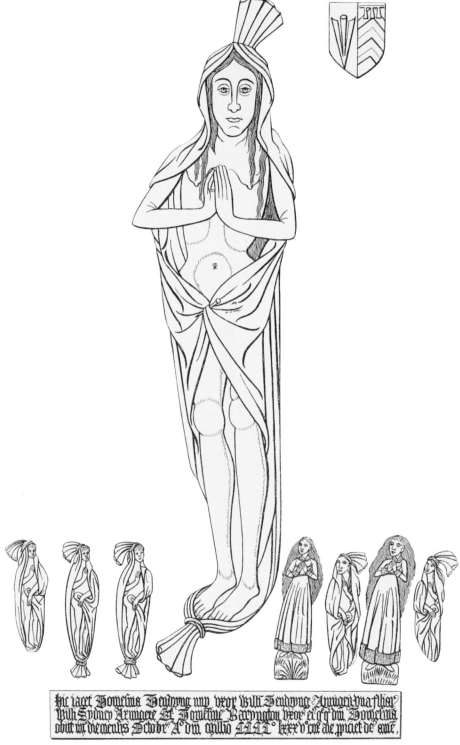

19   Birth and survival. The brass of Thomasine Tendryng (d. 1485), with three sons in shrouds and four daughters (two in shrouds, two in dresses with long hair). Apparently, only two survived infancy.

make parents cautious about begetting children, while poor housing, diet, and lack of medical care rendered children's survival more hazardous. Studies of rurual society between the twelfth and the mid fourteenth centuries suggest that, in poor labouring families, the average number of children who lived beyond infancy was slightly less than two. Among peasants who farmed their own holdings, the survival rate was better, rising to as many as five in the wealthiest families. After 1300, however, the population began to fall, in a process dramatically increased by the Black Death in 1348–9. By the late fourteenth century, these averages may have declined by as much as a quarter. [10]

Evidence about family size throughout society improves in the sixteenth century. In this period, the major new source is that of parish registers, which begin to survive in 1538. The registers aimed to record every baptism, a ceremony still compulsory for everyone soon after birth and therefore virtually a registration of the fact. They make it feasible to compile statistics of births, relating to the whole of the population. [11] By 1600, when this is fully possible, it appears that the mean age for men to marry was 28 and for women 26, so that most parents were fully adult by the time they had children. The nobility and gentry were exceptions because their members often married in their teens, but children born to such young parents would also have been brought up by older servants. By the 1540s, the average number of children born to an English marriage was 2.9, rising to 3.5 by the 1590s, numbers which now take account of all births, including those of infants who lived for short periods.

Taken together, these sources suggest that the typical English nuclear family was more or less constant in size across the medieval centuries with two or three live children, though this number tended to increase among the wealthy. [12] Most children did not have a large number of siblings, excluding those who died in infancy. Ordinary parents with large families must have been unusual, like the 'poor man that had thirteen children' to whom Henry VIII gave £3 6s. 8d. in 1530. [13] A child's parents were most likely to be married, living together, and aged between their late twenties and their early forties, again excluding some of the wealthy who might be ten or more years younger. The parents were normally the only adults in the household, unless there were servants. Grandparents or other relations may have lived nearby and contributed help, but rarely dwelt beneath the parental roof. We find a few rich grandmothers leaving bequests in their wills to their grandchildren: clothes, jewellery, money, or farm animals. [14] It is noticeable, however, that religious writers, when talking about the rearing of children, mention godparents, not grandparents, as the supporters of parents in this respect. In literature, grandmothers are sometimes baleful figures, resentful of their daughters-in-law and hostile to those daughters' children. It is a grandmother who sets the heroine and her baby adrift on the sea in Chaucer's 'Man of Law's Tale', and another who brings about the transformation of her grandchildren into birds, in the romance of the Knight of the Swan. [15]

Most children were brought up at home by their parents or their parents' servants. There was no general practice of fostering them elsewhere, at least in their early years. The word 'foster' was widely used in medieval times, but it meant simply 'to feed' or 'to bring up'.[16] Parents or nurses could be described as giving fosterage in the parental house. Fostering away from home was confined to certain specific groups. Kings and queens led mobile lives which did not easily permit them to have young children with them. By the late thirteenth century, such children lived in a special household of their own, looked after by a knight or lady of rank and some servants. Nobility and gentry sometimes made use of monasteries and nunneries, placing children there to be monks or nuns and later, after the twelfth century, to live as lay boarders.[17] At the other end of society, babies abandoned by their mothers would be taken into some kind of care, and brought up separately.[18] Most often, deaths of fathers led to children passing into hands of a guardian or relative. Even so, they were likely to stay with their mother (if possible) until at least the age of seven, and to move to the guardian's family after that.[19] All these kinds of children were exceptional, and they can only have formed a minority of the population. Not until ten or so was a child likely to leave home to be educated or to work as a servant.[20]

Another variation of family life arose from remarriage. A widowed father or mother might introduce a stepmother or stepfather, and sometimes stepchildren or (eventually) half-brothers and sisters. The word 'step' is an old Germanic one, meaning 'orphan', the step-parent being one's orphan parent and the stepchild one's orphan child. Some such parents may have been kind and loving, but the popular view of them was deeply hostile. Both, but especially mothers, were believed to lack the affections of natural parents and to wish harm to their partners' children. A meagre portion of bread was called a 'stepmother's slice'.[21] Stories down the ages told of their harsh or wicked ways. The twelfth century chronicle of Ramsey Abbey believed that, a hundred and fifty years earlier, a local magnate's wife had murdered her young stepson. When she was charged with the crime, her husband swore by his beard that she was innocent, but his beard came off in his hand and he gave the abbey an estate to atone for his unwitting perjury.[22] One famous medieval literary work, *The Seven Sages of Rome*, turns on a Roman prince facing death through the false accusation of his stepmother, and a story aimed at children, *The Friar and the Boy*, on how a farmer's son avenges himself on his father's mean and shrewish second wife.[23]

Others who lacked two full-time parents were the illegitimate, often brought up by a single mother. They, in contrast, experienced public disapproval and disabilities. By the twelfth century, both the Church and the English common law regarded a child as legitimate only if it was the offspring of a legitimate marriage. If its parents were not married, or were illegally united (cousins, for example, whose marriage had not been specially approved), its status was not legitimate. The Church was willing to accept a child born out of wedlock as legitimate if its parents subsequently married, but the common law did not make this concession. For religious purposes, the illegitimate were treated like the legitimate, in as far as rights and obligations were concerned, except that illegitimate men could not be ordained as clergy without a special dispensation, unless they also entered a religious order.[24] The common law was more discriminatory. It denied illegitimate children any right to succeed to their parents' property and status: matters affecting far more people. Only once did this make illegitimacy an advantage. From about the 1330s, lawyers held that the natural children of serfs were born free, because they could not even inherit their parents' serfdom.[25]

Children born outside marriage were probably unusual, at least by late Anglo-Saxon times when Christian ideas of morality took hold. In the sixteenth century, when the illegitimate birth-rate can first be measured, it was never more than about 4.5%.[26] Popular attitudes, feeding and feeding off those of the Church and the law, viewed such children with disfavour. They were described as 'bast', 'bastard', and later 'horcop', meaning 'whore head', or 'leir-child' ('child of the lair or lying').[27] 'Bastard' is first found in England soon after the Norman Conquest, when it was used to describe William the Conqueror – himself a man of doubtful birth.[28] It is itself a word of uncertain origin, which has been conjectured to mean 'bent', 'conceived on a pack saddle', or 'conceived in a grange' – all implying deviation from the marriage bed.[29] Later, it was extended to describe things of inferior quality, reflecting negative views of the illegitimate.[30] The poet Layamon, round about 1200, imagined how the young Merlin was abused by another boy about his supposed bastard status. 'I am a king's son, and you are a nobody . . . Your mother was a whore, for she never knew the man who fathered you . . . You are no man's son.'[31] Subsequent tellers of this story thought of other suitable taunts for the boy to use: 'foul shrew', 'black shrew', 'misbegotten wretch and fatherless', 'foul false foundling'.[32]

In practice, the treatment of the illegitimate was more varied and sometimes more tolerant. Mothers might bring them up, and fathers help with the process. By the fourteenth century, Church courts had the power to order fathers to support such children, and cases survive in which courts fixed payments for this at anything from 1d. to 6d. a week.[33] Some fathers acted more generously. The twelfth-century legal writer known as Glanvill conceded that a man might give land, even inherited land, to his natural child.[34] He wrote this in a century when Henry I is known to have had twenty illegitimate children and Henry II at least three.[35] Most of these children were provided by their royal fathers with only modest careers or marriages, but three were particularly favoured. Henry I's son Robert was made earl of Gloucester and his daughter Sybil was married to the king of Scots. Henry II's son Geoffrey became bishop of Lincoln and, after his father's death, archbishop of York. Such children lacked the full rights of their legitimate siblings, but (given paternal recognition) they could still enjoy a good deal of their family status.

The same was true in the later middle ages.[36] A close bond existed between Henry V's brother Thomas duke of Clarence and his bastard son John, perhaps because Thomas had no legitimate issue. Father and son fought at the battle of Beaugé in France in 1421, where Thomas was killed, but John boldly rescued his father's body as the French were preparing to take it away from the field. Later, he became a king's knight, constable of Dublin Castle, and the owner of lands in Ireland given to him by Henry VI.[37] During the early sixteenth century, there were several prominent men in English affairs whose mothers were unmarried. Charles Somerset, son of a duke of that name and a distant relation of the

Tudors, had a distinguished career at the courts of Henry VII and Henry VIII, and was created earl of Worcester in 1514. Arthur Plantagenet, son of Edward IV, enjoyed the friendship of Henry VIII, married a noblewoman in 1511, and duly became Viscount Lisle. In 1525, when Henry was beginning to worry about the succession to his throne, he promoted Henry Fitzroy, his son by Elizabeth Blount, to be duke of Richmond and Somerset. At this time and again in the early 1530s, it looked at though the duke might be chosen as Henry's royal heir, but the king never committed himself to this – wisely, since the young Henry died in 1536, aged only seventeen.[38]

BABY CARE

FROM THE DAY of its birth, a medieval baby fell into one of two unequal groups. Most were fed at the breasts of their mother – the usual practice unless she was sick or had died. In the upper reaches of society, however, it was common for mothers not to suckle their children but to employ a woman with a baby of her own to act as a wet nurse. This was the case in the families of the king, the nobility, the gentry, and some of the wealthy people of the towns who aspired to the same kind of lifestyle. Sometimes, no doubt, the mother's health and that of her baby were a consideration; she might be weak or sick. A quicker restoration of the mother's fertility may sometimes have been attractive to parents who wished to beget heirs – a son, say, after a daughter or two. Status and the desire to keep one's breasts small may have been other considerations. Equally, there may have been exceptions: wealthy women who nursed their own babies out of love for them or to delay another pregnancy. The Bible depicted such mothers in Sarah, Hannah, and above all the Virgin Mary (Fig. 20). So did one or two medieval romances.[39] In Malory's *Morte d'Arthur*, for example, Sir Ector's wife anticipates breast-feeding her own son Kay, but is asked to substitute Arthur and send her own son to another woman.[40] In real life, St Thomas Cantilupe, born into a baronial family in Lincolnshire in *c*.1218, is said to have been nursed 'by a very devout, noble, and holy matron' – a reference which may apply to breast-feeding.[41]

Those who employed wet nurses were urged to take care in choosing and supervising them. The high rate of mortality among babies seems to have been attributed, in part, to deficiencies in their milk, which made it essential to get a nurse who was right for the job. Giles of Rome, a thirteenth-century writer on royal and noble education, much read in later medieval England, recommended that a nurse should be chosen with similar physical characteristics to the real mother, because a mother's milk corresponds to the needs of its child.[42] Bartholomew, one of those who traced infants' illnesses to their feeding, advised that these should be treated by medicine fed to the nurse.[43] By 1493, the royal family was enforcing strict checks upon nurses' and babies' food. Whatever the nurse ate and drank herself was to be 'assayed' or tasted beforehand, for quality, by the household staff. A physician was also to be present at feeding times, to ensure that the baby was fed in appropriate ways.[44]

20   The Virgin Mary was the ideal of a mother
breast-feeding her child, here symbolically in W.
Bonde's *Directory of Conscience* (1527).

We know most about nurses in the royal family, where records capture their existence.[45] They appear to have been married women whose status was beneath the aristocracy but above the common sort. One was the wife of a tailor, another of a barber-surgeon. The nurses of the gentry may well have been of lower rank, the wives of peasant farmers, but hardly of the lowest, least well-nourished orders. Royal nurses benefited if their charges grew up to occupy the throne, and several kings are recorded giving them pensions of anything from £13 6s. 8d. to £40 a year. Their own children, the foster-brother or sister of the privileged child, might gain advancement too, as Kay did at the court of King Arthur. The best-known historical instance is Alexander Neckham, whose mother Hodierna, a woman of St Albans, nursed Richard I for his mother Eleanor of Aquitaine in 1157. Alexander subsequently had a distinguished career as a scholar, perhaps with royal support, and ended his life as abbot of Cirencester (Gloucs.).[46]

In a wealthy household, a nurse would have assistants. Walter of Bibbesworth, the English knight who wrote about everyday life in his late thirteenth-century treatise on how to learn French, recommended mothers to hire a *bercere* ('rocker' or 'rockster' in English).[47] This was a woman to rock the cradle and, no doubt, to give other help to the nurse. Royal and noble babies in the later middle ages had more attendants still, sometimes concerned not only with them but with the older toddlers often born in quick succession to non-nursing mothers. The Percy earls of Northumberland employed two rockers and a child servant in 1512, and the royal household ordinances of 1493 mention a nurse and four rockers. A slightly older prince, Henry VI, when aged three in 1424, had two nurses, a chamber-woman, a laundress, and two unidentified servants.[48] The lower down society, the less support there would be. A citizen's wife, or the wife of a yeoman farmer, could call on her female servants for assistance, but the vast majority of mothers had to bear the burden alone, unless they had a husband or other children willing and able to help.

Did husbands respond to such needs? Medieval writers and artists, when describing the roles of the sexes, assigned the chores of domestic life to women. Men were linked with more strenuous and outdoor pursuits. In literature, they are portrayed as inappropriate creatures to look after young children. Walter Map has a story of a knight, pursued by his enemies, who is sheltered by a woman in a cottage. She tells him to watch the baby while she misleads the pursuers, but he gives it his knife to play with, the baby falls on the knife, and it is killed.[49] The sheep-thief Mak, in the 'Second Shepherds' Play' performed at Wakefield in about 1500, uses his baby's cradle to hide his stolen sheep.[50] Robert Ferrar (d. 1555), the Protestant bishop of St David's, whistled to his baby son and said that the baby understood his whistle. He justified this as a way of bonding with his child and building a basis for teaching later on, but the habit formed one of the charges levelled against him by Catholics.[51] Similar disapproval hangs about Izaak Walton's story of the theologian Richard Hooker, when he was a married country parson in 1584. Two visiting friends were said to have found him immersed in domestic tasks at his wife's insistence, including the rocking of the cradle, a labour which they and Walton felt improper.[52] Much of men's energy must have been spent in directions other than child care, and there may have been prejudice against them doing otherwise. At the same time, wives may have wanted such help from their spouses, and some men have been glad or constrained to provide it.

Walter of Bibbesworth's treatise recommends that babies be swaddled in clothes and placed in a cradle (Fig. 21). He also talks of the bib, or 'slavering clout' as he calls it in English.[53] In fact, then as now, a wide variety of clothes and equipment might be procured for a wealthy baby or be replicated for a poor one in simpler ways. The range of items in a well-equipped baby's layette is outlined in Thomas Deloney's novel *The Gentle Craft* (*c*.1597). A young shoemaker tells his master's wife that he has got a maiden with child, and the wife exclaims at the expense that this will cost him:

> beds, shirts, biggins, waistcoats, headbands, swaddlebands, cross-clothes, bibs, tail-clouts, mantles, hose, shoes, coats, petticoats, cradle and crickets, and beside that a standing-stool and a posnet to make the child pap.[54]

As this list demonstrates, babies of those with means were given shaped clothes, both underclothes and top garments: shirts, petticoats, coats, hose, and shoes. Biggins were caps, and a cross-cloth a linen cloth worn across the forehead. Tail-clouts may be nappies (diapers) or rags for wiping the bottom. A cricket was a small stool for a mother or nurse to sit on while watching the cradle, or for the child to use when it became a toddler. The standing-stool was a frame to help the child to learn to walk, and the posnet a vessel with a handle and feet for cooking or warming soft food.[55]

deus salutis mee & exultabit lingua
mea iusticiam tua /
omine labia mea aperies et
os meum annunciabit laude tuam
uonia si voluisses sacrificiu
dedissem vtiqs holocaustis non de
lectaberis.
acrificium deo spiritus con
tribulatus cor contritum & humi
liatum deus non despicies
enigne fac domine in bona
voluntate tua syon vt edificentur
muri iherusalem
unc acceptabis sacrificium
iusticie oblationes et olocausta tuc
imponent super altare tuum vi
tulos.
equiem eternam. añ. Exulta
bunt domino ossa humiliata. añ.Ex
audi deus. Psalmus
E decet hymnus deus in sy

21   A baby in swaddling bands, lying in a cradle on rockers, enabling it to be moved with the foot.

One major difference in the medieval care of babies was the practice of tying them securely in their clothes: 'swaddling' as it came to be called. The Anglo-Saxons wrapped their babies in clothing, but it is not clear whether they bound them as well.[56] By about the thirteenth century, on the other hand, a baby's clothes were fastened into a compact bundle, the arms laid down the sides and the legs straight out. This was achieved with long strips of cloth, known as 'cradle-bands', 'swaddle-bands', or 'swaddling-bands', wound in a criss-cross fashion.[57] The custom reflected a belief that babies' bodies were flexible and that limbs, if not constrained, would grow crookedly. It may have had other advantages: promoting warmth in cold houses and even protection from animals. Children wrapped in this way could be held on a lap, or placed to lie in a cradle – an ancient invention, although the word is not recorded in English until about the year 1000.[58] Cradles varied in shape and elaboration, poor households perhaps affording only a box or a basket. Some, probably of basket form, hung from the roof, making them easy to rock. Others stood on the floor, sometimes painted in colours and resting on arc-shaped beams. This kind could be rocked with the foot, allowing the rocker to do other tasks with her hands.

Illustrations of the floor-based type of cradle survive from the fourteenth century onwards, especially in scenes depicting the nobility and the Holy Family, which was credited with a similar kind of rank (Figs. 21, 47). These cradles are portrayed as well-made pieces of furniture, often provided with buckles along the tops of the cradle sides, allowing the baby to be fastened inside for safety. The household ordinances of Henry VII describe the royal cradle of everyday use as being made of painted wood, 45 inches long and 22 wide. It had four knobs or pommels of silver and gilt at the corners, and a row of five silver buckles on each side. The frame was fitted with a canopy of linen cloth, sheets, and two counter-panes of scarlet trimmed with fur and bordered with cloth of gold. A larger 'cradle of estate' was used for public displays of the baby at court. It measured seven and a half feet in length and two and a half feet in width, and was made of wood covered with fine leather. There were eight buckles on each side and it was decorated with five posts, one at each corner and one in the middle of the head-board, engraved with the royal coat of arms. This cradle too was equipped with linen and costly coverings.[59]

Cradles needed careful management, since they and their occupants were prone to accidents. Clergy warned parents to ensure that cradles were kept upright so that they could not roll, and that children were carefully fastened in.[60] Two mishaps in this respect occur in the miracles of St Thomas of Cantilupe, recorded in 1307. In one case, a girl of sixteen weeks was found, apparently dead, dang-ling from her cradle by an arm; in another a baby was improperly secured and fell out, hanging from the object by its feet from dawn till prime (about 8.00 am).[61] In a third, a six-month-old boy of Brackley (Northants.) nearly strangled himself in the hanging cords of a cradle in 1491.[62] Some of these catastrophes, like the last, arose in cradles of the suspended variety, but the kind that stood on the ground was not without hazards. Such a cradle was vulnerable to the animals that so often ran about houses, overturning the article or attacking the child.[63]

22   Bathing the baby, here the Virgin Mary, with her mother St Anne in bed.

Bartholomew adds a little more about the care of babies in his encyclopaedia. Writing with the aristocracy in mind, he envisages them in the care of a nurse, but his remarks may reflect what mothers did as well. A baby should be washed when it dirties itself, be given frequent baths, and anointed with oil of myrtle or of roses, especially on the limbs. Boys need such anointing more than girls, because of their harder bodies. When babies cry, they should be offered the breast or moved about, now on the shoulders, now on the hands, now on the knees and lap. One should talk, whistle, and sing to them. They should be wrapped in sheets and cloths, making sure that their limbs are properly stretched out, and the cloths be bound with cradle-bonds to make the limbs grow straight, not crookedly. Babies should be put to sleep in the dark, because bright light injures their eyes and causes them to squint. For the same reason, they should not be left in such light while awake.[64] Guy de Chauliac, writing a century later, agreed that squints were often caused by babies being laid so that they looked aside to the light or to some prominent feature. This could be counteracted, he thought, by placing a shining or coloured object in the opposite direction.[65]

Other scraps of baby and toddler care occasionally surface in medieval writings. Aristotle, the major authority used by thirteenth-century writers on education, advised that babies be allowed to cry and scream, because this exercises the body and promotes growth.[66] Giles of Rome, however, understood Aristotle to say the opposite, and states that crying should be discouraged, because it dissipates breath and spirit. He also suggests accustoming children to cold, allowing them time to play, and refraining from giving them wine.[67] He does not mention daytime rests, but it is likely that babies and toddlers were put to bed for this purpose, if only to give some peace to their carers. Two miracle stories refer to midday sleeping by young children. In one case shortly before 1300, an eighteen-month-old boy met with an accident out of doors after rising from his sleep at about 12.20, apparently having been fed at about 11.00 and put down to rest about half an hour later.[68] In another, of the fifteenth century, a mother put her two-year-old child to sleep in his bed and went out to the fields. When she came back the house was on fire – perhaps through the child having woken and played with the hearth.[69]

It is not surprising, given the relatively high rate of mortality among medieval children, that parents worried about their well-being. Baby abductions by human hands were probably as rare as they are today, though Robert Mannyng, writing in 1303, envisaged the possibility that a woman might steal a child.[70] More commonly, infants died unexpectedly through cot-deaths or fatal infections, for which there seemed no medical explanation. William of Canterbury, writing in the 1170s, refers to the 'fabulous nonsense of the people' who, when a baby falls ill, think it has been changed or transformed.[71] His scepticism was not shared even by some of his clerical contemporaries. Gervase of Tilbury told how Humbert, arch-bishop of Arles, was taken as a baby at night from his cradle and placed in a foot-bath. Many infants, claimed Gervase, were found in the morning outside houses, and their cradles in the streets, despite closed doors.[72] Walter Map recounted a lurid story about a knight who lost three infant sons, all killed in their cradles by having their throats cut. The culprit was eventually discovered to be a demon in the likeness of a local woman, who flew out of the window on being arrested.[73]

Some parents took precautions to safeguard their children – precautions that were not essentially Christian. Eleventh-century writers refer disapprovingly to a practice by which adults drew children 'through the earth' at crossroads, apparently in a rite of dedication or protection.[74] Later on, it was common to place food by the beds of young children, to ward off or propitiate spirits that came to harm them. Robert Mannyng told parents that

> The food that you lay at the child's head,
> For such powers were better not left.
> If it for them there lie,
> Then is it a wicked heresy.
> Lay it for the love of the Holy Ghost,
> Father and Son, one God steadfast.[75]

He disliked the practice because it implied that there were supernatural powers in the universe other than God. But he did not feel equal to forbidding it; instead, he tried to make it orthodox by teaching people to leave the food in honour of the Trinity. The custom was still observed in the seventeenth century, when it was felt to guard against witches. Robert Herrick the poet describes two methods to keep them from sleeping children in the 1630s and 40s, one being the same as Mannyng's:

Bring the holy crust of bread,
Lay it underneath the head;
'Tis a certain charm to keep
Hags away, while children sleep.

Let the superstitious wife
Near the child's head lay a knife:
Point be up, and haft be down
(While she gossips in the town);
This, 'mongst other mystic charms
Keeps the sleeping child from harms.[76]

Bread may have been regarded as having virtue because it came from God ('Give us this day our daily bread'), or as a substitute for predators to take. Knives had power by reason of their iron, and might scare attackers away.

The changeling, swapped in the cradle by human or supernatural agency, was another figment of popular belief. Occasionally this had some basis, when a couple pretended to have a baby to secure a family inheritance. A sensational case in the 1290s came to the scandalised attention of the bishops of Lincoln and Worcester. Ella le Sor, the lady of a manor in Worcester diocese, feigned to be pregnant and sent her bailiff and other people in search of a suitable baby. Adam and Alice Coket of Banbury (Oxon.) sold them a boy-child two days old for 12d., a loaf of bread, and a dish of bacon. The boy was rebaptised and portrayed as Ella's heir, with some success because, when her husband died, the child was taken into wardship by the lord of the fief.[77] Rumours of similar origins sometimes surfaced about famous people. In a society that laid great stress on birthright, a good way to defame someone was to allege that he or she was not the true heir but a substitute. When John of Gaunt fell out with the citizens of London in 1377, libellous flyers were posted up in the city, claiming that he was the son of a Flemish butcher of Ghent, the town where Gaunt was born. The queen's real child, it was alleged, was overlain in bed by a nurse soon after birth, and for fear of the king, the queen and her household replaced him with the butcher's son.[78]

In 1318, the reverse situation arose in which an obscure person claimed to be royal. This was John de Powderham or John 'the writer', a scribe of Oxford in 1318, who announced that he, not Edward II, was rightfully king. John claimed that while in his royal cradle, he had received an injury which the nurse masked by exchanging him with the child of a carter. Edward, he said, displayed his ancestry by his love of rustic pursuits – an allusion to the king's known liking for workmen's skills. The story, one is told, was believed by many in Oxford, although the only evidence for John's claim was the trace of a wound. But when he tried to take possession of the royal palace of Beaumont outside Oxford, opposite what is now Worcester College, the local authorities put him in the city's Bocardo gaol. Eventually he was sent to Edward at Northampton where he continued to insist on his claim – the victim of his own delusions. Contemporary writers, on the other hand, asserted that he was a practitioner of black magic, and the crown extended him no mercy at all. He was handed over to the king's judges and, in short order, tried, condemned, and hanged as a traitor.[79]

WEANING

MEDIEVAL CHILDREN WERE fed at the breast for longer than usually happens today. We hear in the fifteenth century of a Somerset girl at the breast at the age of one, and a boy of Stoneleigh (Warks.) when he was two.[80] Weaning from breast-feeding seems to have been done at any time from one to three.[81] The Scottish poet Rait, who wrote in the early fifteenth century, defined the first age of human life as lasting from birth until three, perhaps with weaning in mind as the terminus.[82] One of the medieval lives of the Virgin Mary tells of her being weaned by St Anne at three, and the Nurse in Shakespeare's *Romeo and Juliet* recalls the same about Juliet.[83] The Nurse says that she weaned the child by painting her nipples with wormwood. This discouraged the child from seeking the breast and was an ancient practice, mentioned in Eadmer's twelfth-century Life of St Anselm.[84] By the age of two or three, of course, such children were already taking other foods than breast milk. Bartholomew observes that where a nurse was employed, she would masticate food in her own mouth for a toothless child and feed him with her fingers. This was still a common practice among nurses in Tudor and Stuart times, and doubtless also of mothers who brought up their children themselves.[85]

From ancient times, weaning was regarded as a significant point in a child's life. To adults, it was the first milestone after birth, marking a stage towards independence. In the Bible, the mother of the prophet Samuel put him to serve in the Temple when he was weaned, and the legend of the Virgin Mary represented her as going there at a similar time.[86] Weaning (or the period up to it) occurs as a landmark in medieval records as well. Edward the Confessor was said to have been sent to France to 'spend his infancy, the time of his weaning'.[87] Pope Adrian IV, born near St Albans, was believed to have been 'nourished there until the time of his weaning'.[88] The account of the pretended Edward II in 1313 talks about him being brought up by the queen's nurses 'until his weaning'.[89] In consequence, the time at which the child ceased to be breast-fed may have been significant: remembered by adults as Shakespeare implies in his picture of Juliet's Nurse. Sometimes there may have been a family celebration of the event. The Bible tells how Abraham held a feast to mark the weaning of his son Isaac, and the life of the child saint William of Norwich, born in 1132–3, claims that his father did the same – unless that is the author's invention, inspired by Abraham.[90]

Meanwhile, by about the age of six months, children are on the move: rolling, crawling, and finally standing and walking. This is both joyous and dangerous, for them and their elders. In a wealthy medieval household, there would be servants to keep watch. Walter of Bibbesworth recommends that, to avoid a child harming or dirtying itself, a boy or groom should be assigned to follow it about so that it does not stumble or fall.[91] Some manuscript illuminations show toddlers encased

23   Learning to walk. Mother and baby by the fire, and a toddler in a walking-frame.

from waist to feet in a frame or basket, which would support them if they fell over (Fig. 23). Thomas Deloney's standing-stool was a device of this kind. In most families, however, the supervision had to be done by parents or older siblings, especially the mother, and there were all kinds of potential dangers in houses where people coexisted with fire, water, tools, and animals.

The Church emphasised the duty of parents to keep their children safe. Bishop Bartholomew of Exeter (d. 1184) discussed who was to blame if a mother put her infant by the fire and a man put water into a cauldron which overflowed, scalding and killing the child. He concluded that the mother was guilty and should do penance for putting the child into a dangerous place.[92] Clergy at baptisms, as we have seen, warned godparents to ensure that parents guarded their child from fire, water, and other perils until it was seven.[93] Accidents occurred nonetheless, and these, as Barbara Hanawalt has shown, reflected gender differences.[94] Boys were more venturesome than girls and, by the ages of 4–6, most of their fatalities took place outside the home. In the case of girls, this happened a little later, in the period 7–12. Both boys and girls attached themselves to their gender parent from an early age, following and copying them. Accidents to small girls were more likely to take place in the home, and often related to the routine of their mothers in cooking or drawing water. Small boys tended to suffer more injuries through watching their fathers' work out of doors, especially with tools, animals, and vehicles.

Parents not only looked after their children, of course; they also sought to amuse and stimulate them. Mothers, as we shall see, sang lullabies or said nursery rhymes; parents played hand-games or provided toys. Artists liked to depict the Virgin Mary with the young Jesus on her lap in an attitude of play: he touching her chin, clasping a toy, or holding an apple. The early thirteenth-century treatise *Ancrene Wisse* imagined Jesus playing with his worshippers as a mother does with her child. 'She runs away from him and hides herself, and lets him sit alone and look anxiously around, and call "Dame! Dame!" and weep a while. Then she jumps out laughing, with outstretched arms, and embraces and kisses him and wipes his eyes.' The young child struggles to walk, bumps into something or stumbles against it, and knocks itself. When that happens, says the author, we smack the thing that it has run against, as if that had been naughty, and the child is amused and stops crying.[95]

Children bonded with animals too, as they do today, because of animals' more comparable size, their different activities, and the apparent friendliness of many of them. Adults encouraged the relationship by keeping domestic pets and telling fables with animal characters. One or two references to children playing with birds or animals occur in records of accidents. One small girl was knocked into water by a pig, while she was holding food, and another was drowned after taking a duck's head (presumably saved by her when the bird was killed) down to the river to wash it.[96] Household animals might be given names, and two or three are mentioned in fifteenth-century schoolbooks: 'Copple' (meaning 'crested') for a hen, 'Kob' for a fighting cock, and possibly 'Whitefoot' for a dog.[97] Noble children might own hawks or hounds, like the hawks of Edward I's small son Prince Henry in 1273–4, animals cared for by others but which the child could fancy to be its own.[98]

Infancy was considered to end at seven. When it ended, parents and god-parents lost some of their duties, since their charges could be reckoned stronger and more alert to protect themselves. By the later middle ages, theologians and lawyers thought that a child of seven might be tonsured as a clerk, be engaged to marry (but not fully married), be charged with a crime, and even (in the case of exceptional girls) be sexually active.[99] Aristotle suggested that boys should begin their formal education at seven, and there is some evidence that medieval princes were moved from women's rule to men's, or given schoolmasters, at about that age.[100] But seven should not be overemphasised as a watershed. Children could start their education as young as three or four, and childhood crimes and engage-ments were highly unusual. For most boys and girls, growing up was a gradual process marked by small changes and large continuities.

DAYTIME

TIME WAS COMMON to everyone, but its observance varied from family to family. Until the fourteenth century, it was largely governed by daylight. People of the lower orders rose at dawn and went to bed at dark, to save the cost of lighting. The wealthier got up a little later, when their servants had prepared the house for them, and used candles or lamps to linger into the evening. Daytime, especially for the poor, was longer in summer than winter, and workmen were paid more in

24 By the fifteenth century, life was increasingly regulated by clocks, private and public. The clock of Exeter Cathedral enabled bells to be rung, announcing time in the nearby city.

summer because they worked for more hours. This pattern, however, was gradually modified by a proliferation of clocks: domestic ones in large households and public ones in churches, marking time by bells and later by dials (Fig. 24). Clocks made it easier to measure the day in a constant way and to live it consistently, throughout the year. By about 1400, people were beginning, like us, to refer to times of the day by the clock, rather than by the older measures of morning, noon, and evening, or of times of worship like prime and vespers.

Even with clocks and candles, most medieval people made more use of daylight than we do, and therefore started and ended their days at an earlier hour. Rising at or soon after dawn, they took a drink or a small snack for breakfast, and often delayed doing so until as late as eight o'clock. Children lived according to this pattern. We hear most about their timetable from school records, which mention times when lessons began. These were early by our standards: six or seven in the morning, sometimes brought forward an hour in summer.[101] By the fifteenth century, courtesy literature, aimed at the sons of the gentry and wealthier townspeople, includes advice on getting up each day. One should make the sign of the cross on breast and forehead, and say the Paternoster and other prayers. Faces and hands should be washed, with attention to ears and nose, and hair should be combed.[102] Tudor moralists complained that boys in wealthy families were lazy, and inclined to lie in bed until broad daylight. Then they had breakfast, sometimes in bed, and were helped to dress by servants. One writer imagines a boy calling out for his clothes:

> Margerite, give me my hose. Dispatch, I pray you. Where is my doublet? Bring me my garters and my shoes. Give me that shoeing horn.

After dressing he demands to have water for washing and a towel.[103] But this is a rich man's son; the poor had no servants, though indulgent mothers may have filled the place for boys. And whether their children said prayers when they rose is unknown.

Breakfast seems to have been consumed individually. Sometimes it was eaten during work. Certain schools let boys bring breakfast to eat on the premises and stopped lessons for this, a custom forbidden by John Colet at St Paul's School (London) in 1518.[104] The other meals of the day were larger, more sociable, and more formal: dinner at eleven or twelve and supper at five or six. In large households, servants ate first and their employers later, lateness in eating (like rising) displaying one's status. Families seem to have joined one another at the two main meals, with the possible exception of young children. Schools suspended work in the late morning to allow boys to go home (or to their lodgings) for dinner. How families ate may have varied. The poor may have sat down together at one table, the rich have followed more elaborate customs. Bartholomew, describing meals in noble households, says that 'children are set in their places', leaving it open as to whether this was on the parents' table or another table.[105] The latter was certainly a practice followed in very great households. One Tudor source shows royal youths dining apart (Fig. 25), and another talks of a round table being set up for children at the end of the main board.[106]

25   Formal dining. A king sits at the high board, and two young men in lesser state at a separate table.

In pious and wealthy families, the formality of the main meals involved making children say grace before eating began. By the fifteenth century, in literate ones, it sometimes extended to having them read (or listen to) an improving text during the meal.[107] Older boys and youths might be expected to wait at table. Pages employed by other people did so, serving their master or mistress with food and drink, and taking their own meals separately.[108] This practice seems to have been copied in some homes, where sons were treated as if they were pages. Chaucer's Squire 'carved before his father at the table',[109] and Francis Seager's *School of Virtue* (1557) envisages boys, when large enough, attending their parents and guests. They offer the dishes, clear them away, serve the dessert, and bring water for washing the hands.[110] Meals conducted in these ways were educational as well as nutritious, teaching respect for God, parents, and guests. One learnt decorum, good manners, and the importance of social ranking expressed by the order in which people were seated and served.

Time ruled life in another way: the cycle of the year. This affected meals, dictating what kinds of food were available and what one could eat. Medieval Christianity emphasised diet: feasts at certain times and fasts at others, involving abstinence from particular foods or from food altogether. Meat was forbidden on Fridays and on the days before important festivals. A stricter fast was followed during Lent, in which not only meat but dairy products were prohibited and meals were sometimes delayed or omitted. On Mondays and Saturdays in Lent, known as 'scambling' or makeshift days, no supper was provided. Children were partly exempted from such fasts, continuing to have regular meals and sometimes foods forbidden to adults. The statutes of Winchester College, issued in 1400, allowed scholars aged less than fifteen to have breakfast as well as the dinner and supper served to older members of the college.[111] In the royal household of Edward IV, the aristocratic youths known as 'henchmen' were permitted to take supper on fasting days, while the Percy family in 1513 made similar concessions to the earl's children and the boys of his chapel.[112] The earl's children ate butter and eggs during Lent, food ruled out for their seniors.[113] Occasionally we are told of devout children who insisted on fasting like adults. William of Norwich was one, Edmund of Abingdon another.[114] William is said to have fasted on Mondays, Wednesdays, and Fridays from the age of seven, but his elder brothers did not do so.

Rank and wealth affected food, and here there was no uniformity. To do justice to all the food eaten by medieval children, we would have to chronicle the history of food itself. Certain foods, however, are mentioned specifically in relation to children. One is milk, which often appears in household accounts for their use. Katherine of Norwich, for example, an East Anglian widow of gentry rank, regularly purchased 'milk for children' as part of her household supplies in 1336–7.[115] Milk or water could be mixed with grain, flour, or bread to make porridge or gruel: 'pap' or 'papelotte' as it was known.[116] An early fifteenth-century medical recipe calls for cow's milk and fine white meal, boiled together in the manner of children's pap.[117] Once children were a few years old, they are likely to have drunk ale or beer like adults (probably brews of a weaker kind), ale being purer and more nourishing than water alone. In 1273–4, both milk and ale were regularly bought for Edward I's son, the six-year-old Prince Henry and for the two children who lived with him: his sister Eleanor aged nine and their cousin John of Brittany who was seven.[118]

Walter of Bibbesworth has some suggestions for feeding young children, just beyond the stage of weaning. If a child stretches out its hand in the morning towards the bread, give it a lump or merely a slice if you have no more. At midday dinner, take eggs (presumably boiled), remove the shells and the whites, and give the child the yolks. Apples are also good, as long as the stalk and peel are pared and the core cut out.[119] Early sixteenth-century writers mention bread and butter as a typical food of children, but this may apply to relatively wealthy people who could buy butter at market. A Venetian visitor to London in about 1500 noted that mothers gave their children bread spread with butter, 'in the Flemish fashion', and the Lestranges of Hunstanton bought 'butter for the children' in 1532–3.[120] Thomas More describes a mother giving her son bread and butter to take to school. The Venetian observed that the kites (scavenger birds) of London were so tame that they would take such bread from the children's hands.[121]

The reconstruction of children's diets is fully possible only in a few great households and colleges, where the framework of meals and the elements of diet have been recorded. Such places were typical only of the richer and better regulated parts of society. One such source is the household book of the Percy earls of Northumberland in 1513, which gives us insights into the food of two groups: the earl's own children and the boys who served in his chapel. The Percy household provided three meals a day for its members: breakfast, dinner, and supper. Breakfast for the earl's two oldest children (Henry, aged eleven, and his younger brother Thomas) consisted of a half loaf of basic 'household' bread, a manchet (a small loaf of fine wheat bread), two quarts of beer, and a chicken or three boiled mutton bones. Two other children, Margaret and Ingelram who were still in the nursery, were allowed a manchet, one quart of beer, and three boiled mutton bones.

The boys of the chapel had less grand food in keeping with their lower social status. Their breakfast included household bread, beer, and boiled beef, with salt fish on Fridays. If it was Lent, the meat was replaced by various kinds of fish: salt fish or herrings and, in the case of the earl's children, the butter or buttered eggs already mentioned. The Percy household book does not describe the menu for dinner, which would have varied from day to day and rank to rank, but it would certainly have included bread and meat or fish. Supper was varied too and is only specified for the scambling days, when it was remarkably like breakfast: a manchet loaf and butter for the earl's children, household bread for the chapel boys, and fish for all. The young Percies were favoured with fresh fish such as ling or turbot, while the chapel boys were given unspecified salt fish.[122]

In the 1570s, there is a good description of boys' food at a boarding school by Claude Hollyband, a French schoolmaster in London. Breakfast consists of a small piece of rough bread (containing bran) with butter, or fruit when in season. Dinner is usually a vegetable stew or, on fasting days, fresh fish, salt fish, or a bowl of bread and buttermilk. Supper includes a dressed salad and a meat dish – generally stewed mutton with vegetables, varied (once or twice a week) by roast meat such as veal or kid. On fasting days, the meat is replaced by two eggs apiece (roasted, fried, poached, or made into a pancake), or by fish and cheese. Bread is also available at dinner and supper, and is apparently unlimited in quantity. The crust may need to be chipped with a knife, if it has picked up ashes from the oven. Some pupils drink small (weak) beer, and in summertime there is fruit.[123]

Such diets were sustaining but might be monotonous, the latter even more so in poor households for whom bread and vegetables formed the staple of life. It is not surprising that children yearned for more exciting or seasonal food, and the subject turns up frequently in school exercises, where schoolmasters evidently hoped it would kindle their pupils' interest. One such set of exercises, from Exeter High School in about 1450, mentions capons, pheasants, and partridges before Lent; stuffed tripes, sausages, and haggises; cream, cream cheese, and flans at Rogationtide; and trout from the River Dart.[124] Such foods must have been rare or unattainable, save for the wealthy, and the same would apply to sweet treats such as crystallised sugar and fancy biscuits. Henry, the young son of Edward I, was given twisted sticks of sugar during an illness.[125] Most children must have slaked their craving for sweetness with fruit, and several writers refer to their fondness for this. The preacher Thomas Docking, in the late thirteenth century, talks of boys in autumn following the grape harvest, and the poet John Lydgate recalled in the fifteenth how he stole apples as a youth.[126] In an Oxford schoolbook of the 1490s, a schoolboy is imagined getting a present from home of 'wardens' (cooking pears) and looking forward to receiving pomegranates or oranges 'if there is any to be sold'.[127]

Clothes varied greatly like food, depending on wealth and status. Broadly speaking, medieval dress for both adults and children is likely to have included underwear of linen or flannel drawers, a shirt to cover the body, hose for the legs (especially in winter), and a top garment. Men and women of status, who were not involved in active work, wore this garment as a long robe going down to the lower legs or feet, belted or girdled at the middle. Men at work or play replaced the long robe by a short coat of hip or thigh length; working women by one that reached down to the calves. Hoods or hats were universal to protect from rain and cold, and gloves were widely worn, especially by the better off. Children were likely be similarly dressed, the girls with longer coats than the active boys, and the boys wearing full-length robes for special occasions or going to school (Fig. 26).

Such clothes could be made at home, commissioned from a neighbouring seamstress, purchased 'off the peg', or acquired second-hand. Certain articles seem to have been more commonly bought in finished form: hats, gloves, and shoes. One fifteenth-century dictionary has a special Latin word for a 'child's cap',[128] and glovers and shoemakers (working with more difficult materials) made up children's gloves and shoes in appropriate sizes (Fig. 27). Records of expenditure on children's clothes survive in the household accounts of wealthy families, but these tend to relate to cloth being bought for the purpose rather than ready-made clothes. The cloth, one presumes, was cut out and sewn up within the

hic iacet Iohes kent qudm scolaris novi collegii de wynchestr et fili simonis kent de Redyng cui aie piciet de

26 Children's dress included gowns for formal occasions, such as going to school. John Kent died in 1434 while attending Winchester College.

27 Clothes were often specially made for children, particularly leather goods like gloves, belts, and this fourteenth-century shoe, found at Baynard's Castle (London).

household. Nicholas, the schoolboy son of the Lestrange family in the 1520s, needed various pairs of shoes costing 6d. and 8d., three ells of linen to make two shirts (3s. 9d.), a cap (5s. 4d.), cloth for a coat and a pair of hose (10s.), and black fustian for a doublet (20s.). His younger sister Bess required a pair of shoes costing 4d., gloves 6d., and a yard of green satin decorated with birds at 2s. 2d., evidently for making into a dress. The kitchen-boy was given clothes of a cheaper kind, including 'clout leather', perhaps for an apron (5d.), a pair of shoes (6d.), blanket cloth to make him a pair of hose (7d.), two yards of canvas for a shirt (8d.), and four yards of frieze cloth for a coat (2s.). His set of clothes cost about 4s., but he needed two, the second to wear while the first was being washed.[129]

Dress, then, was significant; so was its opposite, undress. Nudity was a sign of innocence; Bartholomew noted how young children, before puberty, were happy to appear in public with nothing on.[130] Boys and youths might strip for games, as the earliest biographer of St Cuthbert describes them doing in the seventh century: taking off their clothes to stand on their heads and do other athletic feats.[131] The adolescent hero of the *Tale of Gamelyn*, current in Chaucer's day, wrestled 'barefoot and ungirt' apparently wearing nothing but his drawers.[132] Swimming (another sport of boys) would be done without any clothes. Older boys or girls (like their elders) might bare their arms and legs for work, like the 'bare-legged bold boy' on a barge who figures in the romance of *William of Palerne*.[133] In our own culture, stripping for work or leisure makes statements about youth, beauty, power, and sexuality. In the middle ages, such messages were mixed with ones that we have forgotten. Nakedness was linked with punishment. Boys bared their buttocks for beatings, criminals were whipped with their shirts off, and pilgrims or sinners went barefoot to gain merit or undergo penance. It also signified poverty. Writers and artists depicted the poor going unshod or in ragged clothing, exposing parts of their bodies. Havelok, the dispossessed prince in the thirteenth-century story of that name, sinks so low in fortune that he has to work as a fish-porter, barelegged and barefoot, with a cloak round his body made from sail-cloth. As soon as he finds a better job as a kitchen-servant, his employer buys him new clothes, including hose and shoes. Social status came from what you wore, not what you revealed.[134]

Once a child can dress and undress itself (and before that), it will be taught to keep itself clean and tidy: washing hands and combing hair. Customs in this respect may have varied by social rank, superior people being more fastidious and better able to keep themselves clean. Courtesy books aimed at boys of the wealthier classes emphasise hygiene and good table manners. Boys, as we have seen, were urged to wash their hands and faces when they got out of bed. Hands should also be washed before meals.[135] Body washing is a more obscure subject. Wealthy children might be bathed, and a miracle story of about 1200 tells how a nurse put a toddler of a year old into a leaden bath placed on a fire, went out to get more wood for the fire, and came back to find the child drowning.[136] The household accounts of Prince Henry and his siblings in 1273–4 mention baths on the eves of Christmas, Easter, and Whitsun, but these were evidently special events with a ritual or festal intention. The Christmas bath was a hot one, and the

Whitsun bath included a gallon of wine.[137] Two pounds of Spanish soap were bought for Henry's household, at 4d. a pound.[138] Ordinary people sometimes bathed out of doors in summer time. John le Wyte aged twelve of Wilden (Beds.) was drowned while bathing in a stream in 1269, and the sixteen-year-old John son of William de Redbourne in Houndsditch (London) in 1337 – an unpromising place to get clean.[139]

Toilet training and toilet procedures are another elusive topic. In well-provided households, chamber pots or close stools were widely used by adults and probably by children. Cheap pots were bought for the use of the young Prince Henry in 1273–4, costing a penny each.[140] Much of the population relieved itself in privies, indoors or out-of-doors, and it may be that girls and women were expected to do so in some privacy. Some men and boys, on the other hand, did so openly (see Fig. 1). John le Stolere, a pauper and beggar aged seven, was relieving nature in the street in 1339 when he was run over by a water cart drawn by two horses.[141] This openness was not confined to the poor. John Colet, who refounded St Paul's School London for the comparatively rich and privileged, provided only urinals in the building. 'For other causes', he said in 1518, the boys should go

down to 'the waterside'. This meant a longish journey to the River Thames to defecate on the shore or into the water.[142]

Civilised people cleaned themselves after defecating with something absorbent – an 'arsewisp' as it was known by the fifteenth century.[143] This, as the word 'wisp' suggests, was a handful of hay or straw, such as one used for cleaning shoes or rubbing down a horse.[144] The wealthy were more genteel in their habits. John Russell, in a fifteenth-century poem for household servants, tells the chamberlain (who looked after rooms) to see that the privy-house is kept clean, the sitting boards covered with green cloth, and the hole concealed by a cushion when not in use. Pieces of blanket, cotton, or linen should be kept available for wiping pur-

28   Home life: a mother prepares the oven, watched by her child.

poses. When the user has finished, the chamberlain should be at hand with a basin, ewer, and towel for washing.[145]

NIGHT-TIME

NIGHT FALLS AND lights are lit. Children see their shadows on the wall, and chase the shadows but never succeed in catching them.[146] We hear less about evenings than mornings, but families would have had to go to bed at around 9.00 pm to achieve eight hours of sleep, and younger children probably went earlier. No doubt they often tried to delay the process, as they do today. Some might wish to stay up to play, others be troubled by night-time terrors. Reginald Scot, writing in 1584, blamed adults for planting fears of the dark:

> But in our childhood our mothers' maids have so terrified us with an ugly devil having horns on his head, fire in his mouth and a tail in his breech . . . whereby we start and are afraid when we hear one cry 'Bough', and we have so affrayed us with bull beggers [*bogies*], spirits, witches, urchins, elves, hags, furies, satyrs, Pans, fauns, silens [*wood gods*], Kit with the candlestick [*Will o' the wisp*] . . . that we are afraid of our own shadows.[147]

Two notebooks of the kind kept by schoolboys talk of the witch's daughter, or nightmare, and the 'bloodless and boneless behind the door'.[148]

Some children encountered ghosts, or thought they did. In about the 1340s, a boy in Tynemouth Priory (Nland.) was helping a monk-priest to say early morning mass in what was called 'the chapel of the dead', when he saw something enter, dressed like a monk. It prostrated itself on its knees and elbows, with its face to the ground, giving the boy such a fright that he hid between the priest and the altar. When the priest finished celebrating mass, he too saw the figure and said to it, 'Arise, brother! Go to your rest!' It went out and disappeared.[149] In 1462, a boy of about eleven walking at dusk in Cambridge in the lane between King's College and Clare Hall, saw an old man with a long beard and poor clothing from whom he wished to flee but could not. He was ordered to return the next night to receive a message, and on doing so was told to come back on the third. Finally, the old man deigned to reveal his communication: a prophesy of pestilence, famine and death, more than anyone living had known. Questioned by a doctor of theology and others, the boy said that he did not see the old man walking on the ground, and the conclusion was that he had met a spirit.[150]

Prayers before going to sleep might calm these terrors. The famous English children's prayer at bedtime,

> Matthew, Mark, Luke, and John,
> Bless the bed that I lie on,

is not recorded until 1656, but it was then believed to date back to at least the middle of the sixteenth century, and support for this view comes from late-medieval literature.[151] Chaucer's 'Miller's Tale' refers to a 'night-spell' said by a householder on all four sides of his house and on the threshold of the front door to protect it from evil:

> Jesu Christ and Saint Benedight,
> Bless this house from every wicked wight [*creature*].[152]

A poem aimed at fifteenth-century schoolboys implies that they too knew such prayers. When they go to school, it reminds them, they will learn from their master to bless themselves in the name of the Trinity,

> *In nomine patris* teach he will thee,
> Then with Mark, Matthew, Luke, and John,
> With the *per crucis* and the high name.[153]

In nomine patris was the blessing 'In the name of the Father, the Son, and the Holy Spirit', said as one crossed onself, and 'Mark, Matthew' looks like a similar prayer to 'Matthew, Mark, Luke, and John'. Both would have been suitable for saying at bedtime.

Sleeping arrangements were often crowded by modern standards. Most people lived closely together, by night as well as by day, sharing beds and bedrooms to save space and keep warm. Parents and nurses frequently slept with young children, a practice opposed by Church leaders because of the risk of injuries and deaths. Bartholomew of Exeter suggested that those who 'oppressed' children fatally in bed should do penance of three years, each 'year' consisting of three periods of forty days, one of them spent fasting on bread and water. If a cleric was responsible, an extra year should be added.[154] In later centuries, the Church continued to take this problem seriously, and a series of bishops and councils urged the clergy to warn against doing so.[155] Parish clergy were told to send mothers who overlay their children to the bishop for judgment, and their husbands with them.[156] By the late fifteenth century, Church courts called up women accused of such deaths, though it is not clear whether punishments were given, or merely warnings.[157] Yet, notwithstanding this, adults continued to let young children into their beds. The list of miracles by Thomas Cantilupe, collected in 1307, features two children found apparently dead in their mothers' arms at midnight and two others overlain by their nurses; fortunately all recovered.[158]

Ideally, then, a very young child was supposed to sleep by itself in a cradle or cot. Once it was old enough, even clergy allowed that it could sleep with an adult. One bishop, Stavensby of Lichfield (d. 1238), laid down three 'or thereabouts' as the threshold at which a mother might put a child into her bed.[159] John Mirk, in Chaucer's time, said (less precisely) when a child could well look after itself.[160] A third cleric hit on, or recorded, an ingenious solution to the problem in about the fifteenth century. In his charge to parents and godparents at baptism, he told them to make sure that the child did not sleep by the father or mother until it could say '*Ligge outter!*', in other words 'Lie further over!'.[161] Children not in their parents' beds were likely to be laid with their siblings, but clergy cautioned against placing boys and girls together, at least after the age of seven, for fear of sexual consequences.[162] Children of the same gender often shared beds when older. At Winchester College, a well-endowed school, the scholars slept in pairs until they were fourteen; then, being adult, they had a bed each.[163] The choristers of Wells Cathedral slept three to a bed after 1460: two smaller boys at the bed-head and an older boy at the foot, with his feet between them.[164]

Parents, settling children in bed, may have had recourse to soothing phrases like the rhyme, first recorded in the nineteenth century, which gives each place in the bed a special value:

> He that lies at the stock [*outer side*] shall have a gold rock;
> He that lies at the wall shall have a gold ball;
> He that lies in the middle shall have a gold fiddle.[165]

Children without siblings may have slept alone, but a room to oneself was unusual. The six henchmen of the royal household, youths in their teens or early twenties, had their own chambers by the 1470s, though each had a personal servant who probably slept there too.[166] An Oxford schoolbook of the 1490s imagined the spoilt child of rich parents, aged between three and ten, in his own chamber decorated with hanging cloths. These, however, were rather special cases.[167] The king himself had servants who slept in his bedroom. Boys at least seem often to have gone to bed wearing nothing. In 1303, a small child named Roger, aged just over two, was lying naked in bed in a house near Conway Castle (north Wales) when he walked in his sleep, crossed a bridge, and fell into the castle ditch – fortunately without dying.[168] The Oxford schoolbook envisages lying in bed in a similar state. A schoolboy recounts how, 'in the morning early, as I waked out of my sleep, I heard a mischievous clap [*noise*], and for fear I leapt out of my bed as naked as ever I was born'.[169]

The crowded beds and bedrooms of the past may seem to have afforded little privacy. Yet people get used to sleeping in groups, and one can be as lonely in a dormitory as in a private room. Closing the eyes curtains off one's surroundings and creates a mental space of one's own. When sleep comes, dreams ensue, unique to every sleeper. Aristotle believed that children began to dream only after they were infants; Bartholomew fixed the age for this at five.[170] A boy in the Oxford schoolbook is pictured remembering that he had been 'troubled with marvellous visions in my sleep' but when he awoke 'I had forgot [them] altogether'.[171] All such dreams might be assumed to have vanished long ago but, oddly enough, some were recorded. This happened when they had a religious dimension which was thought by adults to be instructive. The dreams of medieval children, like ours, reflected personal experiences, problems, fears, and matters of current interest. They differed in reflecting the highly religious culture of the day: its art, ideas, and personalities.

Saints might appear in the dreams. The young Thomas Becket, ill of a fever, saw a lady, tall of stature, calm of expression, and beautiful of appearance, standing by his bed. Into his hand she put two keys, saying, 'Thomas, these are the keys of Paradise, of which you will be the keeper'; then she vanished.[172] Adam of Kilpeck glimpsed St Thomas Cantilupe, the former bishop of Hereford, while keeping vigil at his tomb in Hereford Cathedral. Not knowing what a bishop looked like, he described the man he saw as wearing priest's clothes. The figure cleaned the boy's blind eyes with his robe, and passed out of a great glass window to the east of the tomb. Opening his eyes, the boy said, 'Where has he gone?'[173] Lady Margaret Beaufort, when she was not more than twelve, was asked to make a choice between two suitors for her marriage. On the advice of an older woman she prayed to St Nicholas, patron saint of girls, and during the following night, at about 4.00 am, while waking or sleeping, a man appeared to her dressed like a bishop and told her to choose Edmund Tudor and marry him. The figure was, it seemed, the saint himself.[174]

Children might also dream of other worlds, of which they had heard from their elders. An adolescent girl of Mulbarton (Norf.) in the mid twelfth century saw a dove come down from heaven and tell her to follow it. She was changed into a dove herself and they flew together, first to the left (the sinister direction) seeing the places of punishment, with their stench, darkness, heat, and cold, and then to heaven where she beheld God, the Virgin, and the saints – including the new and local child saint, William of Norwich.[175] The young might suffer nightmares in which spirits or demons seemed to appear and threaten them. Such was the fate of Nicholas, a fifteen-year-old novice of Pontefract Priory (Yorks.) in the early 1170s, who thought that he was being suffocated by evil spirits. He jumped out of his bed in the convent dormitory and ran about crying, 'Save me! Save me! See, they crowd around me, holding me by the throat'. The nightmares happened again and again; he was given confession, without effect; but at last he was cured by praying to Thomas Becket and having his neck touched with a relic of the saint.[176]

One thirteenth-century miracle collection, that of St Richard of Chichester (d. 1253) includes a dream of the kind that is nowadays known as a 'near-death experience'. It tells how Nicholas, son of Walter de Dolinge of Romsey (Hants.), aged eight, fell ill with a tumour in the thirteenth century and appeared to die. Then he revived and said that he had come to a beautiful place where he met God and many glorious men attending him, including St Richard. He wished that he could live there for ever, but St Richard begged his life of the Lord. This was granted. The saint signed the boy's breast with his hand and strengthened it, driving all the pain and infirmity from his body. He emerged from his dream restored to life and health.[177]

PARENTS AND CHILDREN

MOST OF US still view the family as an ideal institution, with the potential to generate love, education, and sociability, however far it fails to do so in practice. People in medieval and Tudor England also conceived of ideal families and expressed the ideal in art and literature. Tombstones offer good visual clues to this subject. In the late fourteenth century, funeral monuments began to portray not only husbands and wives but children. One of the earliest to do so is the tomb of Edward III in Westminster Abbey, which still displays six of his children on one side and once had six on the other.[178] This custom spread after about 1400 to monumental brasses and, after the Reformation, to large wall monuments with sculptured effigies. As we have noticed, the inclusion of children on these memorials appears to extend to all who were born alive. A few are shown in swaddling clothes to signify that they died as infants, but normally the images ignore deaths and portray all the children as if they had reached mid childhood or adolescence. Occasionally, they are depicted as adults – priest, nun, or gentleman in armour – indicating that they grew up and followed these paths.[179]

Some of this iconography is religious. On the earliest monuments, like that of Edward III, the children are envisaged as 'weepers', accompanying their parents to the grave with tears and prayers. Later on, they are invariably kneeling and praying, as if interceding for their parents at and after their deaths. But the art of tombs carries other social and sexual messages. Father and mother are shown as

29   An ideal family: Thomas Heveningham (d. 1500), his wife Anne, and their eleven children. The children are all well grown, well dressed, and kneel to pray to and for their parents.

mature figures in the second of the three ages of life, at the top of the wheel of human vitality. The children demonstrate his potency and her fertility, and their depiction as well-grown figures confirms the point; to have shown some of them as dead infants would have weakened it. Equally, their physical immaturity ensures that they do not challenge their elders' power and sexuality. Their kneeling posture, though appropriate for prayer to God, is also submissive to their parents. A similar attitude was adopted when asking for parental blessings. The children's smart appearances proclaim that their father has transmitted to them his rank as well as his seed. He has been careful to provide for them, according to their status, and he has brought them with him to church. In short, these tombstone families are as ideal in their way as those in modern advertisements. Their children are numerous, devout, obedient, orderly, well maintained, and living in the estate to which God has called them (Fig. 29).

This is not to deny that tombstone children also have individuality. There is an image for each child, however idealised, and some of the images are named, like those of the Carew children, clearly intending them to be people in their own right.[180] Memorial art recognised the individual, and the individual child, long before portraiture became realistic. But when the fashion for realistic portraits developed in western Europe, during the fourteenth and fifteenth centuries, this eventually spread to children as well. One of the earliest paintings to include an English child is the famous Donne Triptych in the National Gallery (London) by

Hans Memling, dating from about 1479–80. It features kneeling figures of the donors, Sir John and Lady Elizabeth Donne of Kidwelly, accompanied by their daughter Anne. She was aged about eight at the time, and Memling may have painted her from life (Fig. 30).[181] By the end of the century, the rulers of Europe were commissioning portraits solely of their children. One, of the Dauphin Charles of France, aged two, survives from 1494, and three others, of children of the duke of Burgundy, from 1502.[182] The English royal family followed suit. Henry VII's sons Arthur and Henry VIII were painted when they were in their teens or younger, and we possess a number of likenesses of the infant Edward VI, produced from about 1539 onwards.[183]

The images of parents and children presented in art are repeated in literature. Christianity inherited the concern of Judaism with the duty of children to love and obey their parents; indeed the Ten Commandments expound the duty in the 'first table'

30   A realistic portrait of a child: Anne Donne of Kidwelly, painted by Hans Memling in about 1479–80.

31 A feckless family. Parents who wish their child to the Devil cause the fiend to appear and seize him.

(the obligations to God) rather than in the second (those to one's neighbour). Nor is the commandment merely an order, like the directions not to steal or kill. It is followed by the warning that the child's life and fortune depend on obeying the order, 'that you may live long, and that it may be well with you, in the land which the Lord your God is giving you'.[184] Medieval writers repeated the commandment and amplified it. Mannyng, for example, insists that it is a deadly sin to refuse to do your parents' will, and a lesser sin even to do so grudgingly. This is so too if you curse them or merely oppose them in speech. If you strike either parent, the sin is so great that a bishop himself may not absolve you, but only the pope.[185]

Duties applied in the other direction too. Mannyng observed that parents should love and cherish their children, and not curse them.[186] Geoffrey de la Tour Landry, whose *Book of the Knight of the Tower* was written in France in the 1370s and later translated into English, believed that fathers and mothers should pray for their children each day. He told a cautionary tale of two quarrelsome parents who verbally consigned their son to the Devil. The fiend appeared, seized the child by the arm, and left him maimed for life (Fig. 31).[187] Protestant writers of the sixteenth century took the same view. William Tyndale, quoting St Paul in 1528, urged fathers not to be churlish to their children, or to discourage them with continual chiding. Nor should they spoil and indulge them, but bring them up in a godly manner.[188] Nonetheless, Tyndale assigned the dynamic role in family life to the father or mother. He and his contemporaries regarded the relationship of parents to children as mirroring that of king to subject and God to humanity. The universe was framed on principles of rule and obedience. Children might deserve care, but they were bound to serve, to listen, and to obey.

Their manners were required to be submissive. Tyndale talks of children bowing the knee and doffing the cap to their parents, the customary etiquette.[189] Parents could bless their children, like priests, and children were expected to kneel for the purpose as they would do in church.[190] Words in writing had to be just as respectful. In the Paston family, the brothers John II and John III opened their letters to their father John I with variations on 'most reverend and worshipful father' and signed off as 'son and servant'. John II sometimes wrote to his mother Margaret shortly as 'mother', but this may have been a privilege of being the eldest son or her favourite child. At other times, he addressed her in the same way as he did his father, as 'right worshipful and right tender mother', and this latter mode was adopted by John II's younger brothers.[191]

Inevitably, there were strains. Gabriel Harvey (born about 1550) recalled a confrontation with an irritated father. 'My father began to chide and square with me at the table. I presently, and doing my duty, rise from the board, saying only "I pray you, good father, pray for me and I will pray for you"'.[192] Parents, faced with children they regarded as idle or disobedient, counter-attacked. Medieval England had a verb for exerting discipline: to 'chaste', 'chasten', or 'chastise', meaning to 'make chaste or pure'.[193] There was a noun for it, 'chastising'. These words could mean 'to correct' in the sense of giving advice or verbal warning, but they came to imply corporal punishment, as chastising does today. In this matter, medieval society differed markedly from our own, imposing such punishment widely, not only on children and young people but on adults. In the case of the young, it was acceptable for parents, employers, and teachers to punish them physically, and most educationists and moralists approved the practice when it was done for good reasons and not to excess (Fig. 55).

The great fourteenth-century poet William Langland, in his poem *Piers Plowman*, recommends beating as a means for the reform of society through the mouth of a character who is Reason itself. Reason directs a man with a shrewish wife to take two staves and bring her home, evidently to rule her by the threat of using them. Another, whose wife is idle, is told to cut a sapling or two and beat her until she goes to her work. Then Reason turns to children. He charges 'chapmen' or tradesmen to chasten their offspring and not to pamper them unreasonably through fear of the plague. Reason makes it clear that he uses 'chasten' in a physical sense. First, he quotes proverbial learning, what 'my father and mother taught me', that the dearer the child, the more it needs teaching. Then he cites the biblical Book of Proverbs,

> *Qui parcit virgo, odit filium.*
> The English of this Latin is, who-so will it know,
> 'Who-so spareth the spring [*rod*] spoileth his children'.[194]

Reason does not mention the beating or whipping of criminals, another well-established practice, but Langland does so elsewhere, with evident approval.[195]

Parental endorsement of corporal punishment, even in more 'civilised' households of gentry rank, is well attested. Agnes Paston, widow of William the judge, grew angry at the refusal of her twenty-year-old daughter Elizabeth to marry an elderly suitor in 1449. She forbade the girl social intercourse with anyone outside the house and, for at least a three-month period, so a shocked female cousin reported, beat her once a week 'or twice, and sometime twice in one day, and her head broken in two or three places'.[196] Nine years later, in 1458, Agnes wrote concerning her son Clement, then sixteen and studying in London,

> if he hath not done well, nor will not amend, pray him [i.e. his master] that he will truly belash him till he will amend. And so did the last master, and the best that ever he had, at Cambridge.[197]

An alternative to 'belashing' was public disgrace. During the 1520s, Sir William Carew of Mohun's Ottery in east Devon sent his son Peter to Exeter to board with an alderman and study grammar in the city high school. Peter played truant from class and climbed on the city walls; when his guardian arrived to apprehend him, the boy mounted a turret and threatened to jump, forcing the alderman to leave him to come down of his own accord. On Sir William's next visit to Exeter, he called his son before him, tied him to a line, and gave him to a servant to lead round the city 'like a dog'. Afterwards the boy was taken home to Mohun's Ottery in the same fashion and coupled, for a time, to one of his father's hounds.[198]

The corporal punishment of children was repeatedly urged by medieval and Tudor writers. This might cause us to suppose that the practice was well entrenched, until we ask why the writers stressed the point so much. Clearly, they felt society too lenient, not too harsh, in matters of discipline. This was especially thought to be so in towns, and just as Langland had singled out chapmen in this respect, early-Tudor critics picked on merchants and craftsmen. An Oxford schoolmaster of the 1490s grumbled that 'the most part' of rich men's children were ruined by parental indulgence, particularly from their mothers, so that they grew up wickedly; 'some be hanged, some be headed'.[199] Edmund Dudley, awaiting execution in the Tower of London in 1509–10, gloomily assessed the situation in almost identical terms. Speaking to merchants, he urges them not to let the pity of their wives destroy their children:

> pomp not them at home in furred coats, and their shirts to be warmed against their uprising, and suffer not them to lie in their beds till ten of the clock and then a warm breakfast ere their hands be washed.

He goes on to complain that a merchant's son is brought up so tenderly that he neither learns nor labours. 'Master John he must be called, and his father, Sir Merchant.' Earnestly he calls for discipline. Set young people to work straight-away. Remember how you won your wealth, and beware lest they squander what you gained with so much hardship and pain.[200]

THE POOR

DESCRIBING THE NORMAL procedures of birth and growing up can be misleading. This is especially true in the middle ages, when the surviving evidence is so
biased towards the wealthy. Many children were born into poor homes; some
scarcely into a family. Single women might fall pregnant as servants away from
home, as poor travellers, or as prostitutes. Wives who had followed their husbands
to a new town or village in search of work might find themselves widowed there,
with the prospect of giving birth or bringing up children almost alone. All such
people and their offspring faced extra problems from lack of support and sometimes from positive disapproval, because they were unmarried, poor, or migrants
from elsewhere.

Pregnant women in need, or needy women with small children, were chiefly
thrown on the mercy of their family, if they had one, or on private charity. The
only public help was provided by hospitals, which first appeared in England at the
end of the eleventh century and existed in most towns by the middle of the thirteenth. Medieval hospitals differed much from our own. Most of their care was
given through lodging and food rather than medical services, to poor visitors on a
temporary basis or to the infirm and elderly on a permanent one. In 1414, when
a parliamentary statute listed the kinds of people whom hospitals ought to
support, pregnant women were mentioned as one such group.[201] Robert
Copland's poem *The Highway to the Spitalhouse* (c.1530) features a well-conducted
hospital where admission is given to 'poor women in childbed'.[202] Occasionally,
we have more specific evidence about particular institutions. In 1240, Henry III
contributed £16 13s. 4d. to St John Oxford to make a chamber for women
labouring in childbirth.[203] The statutes of St Paul Norwich (c.1200–50) provided
for poor child-bearing women to be housed until they were fit to leave.[204] In 1446,
the small hospital of Blyth (Notts.) was refounded partly to receive and lodge such
women. This hospital, though in a rural situation, stood near the main roads
between the Midlands and the North, and may have ministered to poor women
passing along them.[205]

Not all hospitals were as helpful. Some of the larger and more dignified ones
preferred to restrict themselves to the easier tasks of catering for those who
needed only bed and board, avoiding the complications caused by pregnancy,
birth, and motherhood. The ordinances of St John Bridgwater (Som.) in 1219
forbade the admittance of pregnant women and sucking infants along with lepers,
lunatics, and persons with epilepsy or contagious diseases, irrespective of whether
they were poor or infirm.[206] Similar ordinances for St John Cambridge, made
between 1229 and 1254, likewise ruled out pregnant women, lepers, wounded
people, cripples and the insane.[207] Even St John Oxford in 1246 excluded 'lascivious' pregnant women, grouping them with lepers, people suffering from paralysis or dropsy, the insane, epileptics, and those with fistulas or incurable diseases.[208]
This suggests disapproval of prostitutes in a city of many single men.

The best-developed hospital facilities for pregnant women, mothers, and children were probably those of London. These reflected the city's greater problems

32 Some help for poor mothers, babies, and orphans was provided by hospitals. These usually lay in less prominent areas outside towns, as did St Bartholomew's (London).

in terms of migration from the countryside, a large servant population, poverty, and prostitution, leading to pregnancies which families could not or would not support. At least three major hospitals gave help. In 1341 and 1344, St Mary without Bishopsgate gained exemption from royal taxation because of its charitable work, including the reception of women during their confinement.[209] A similar concession was given to St Bartholomew in 1352, and both hospitals went on receiving such women during the fifteenth century.[210] The work of St Bartholomew was singled out for praise in that century by a London citizen, possibly William Gregory. It was, the writer states, a place of great comfort for the poor,

> and in specialty unto young women that have misdone, that are with child. There they are delivered, and unto the time of purification they have meat and drink of the place's cost and [are] full honestly guided and kept. And in [as] much as the place may, they keep their counsel and their worship.

His last remark meant that the hospital observed confidentiality with regard to the mothers and their babies (Fig. 32).[211]

The third London hospital doing such work was St Thomas in Southwark. There, says the author of the list,

> the noble merchant Richard Whittington made a new chamber with eight beds for young women that had done amiss, in trust of a good amendment. And he commanded that all the things that be done in that chamber should be kept secret outside, on pain of losing of their living, for he would not shame no

young women in no wise, for it might be [the] cause of letting [*hindering*] their marriage.[212]

Evidently, Whittington (who died in 1423) was an exponent of helping 'fallen' women, supporting them in giving birth, and perhaps arranging fostering so that they could resume normal life and be married. It is wise to remember, nevertheless, how hard the lot of most single mothers must have been. Their reception by hospitals might, in practice, be unsympathetic. In 1536, local people asserted that a poor woman, great with child, was denied a lodging at St Thomas and died at the church door. Rich men's women servants and mistresses, they claimed, were readily taken in.[213]

Two of these hospitals, St Bartholomew and St Mary without Bishopsgate, alleged that their work went beyond supporting pregnant women to maintaining the orphan children of those who died giving birth in the hospital, until such children were seven.[214] In York, the hospital of St Leonard played a similar role. It was granted two churches in 1155–65 for the support of the infirm and infants, and in 1255 it claimed to minister to the latter in particular.[215] By 1287, the hospital orphanage catered for eighteen children: boys and girls.[216] There was a housewife in charge, two cows provided milk, and forty-seven loaves of bread were dispensed each week.[217] In 1364, the building beneath the infirmary called 'Barnhous', meaning 'the children's house', was ordered to be prepared for nursing exposed infants, orphans, and other poor children. A sister was to look after the house, one or two cows were still to be kept for milk, and a good chimney was to be built in case smoke from the fire should trouble the children.[218] Lincoln too had hospital orphans as early as 1283. By 1504, there was a permanent group of them in the hospital of St Katherine's Priory, variously called the orphans, poor children, and fatherless or motherless children, who were regularly remembered with alms in the wills of local people.[219]

Even when children were born into a family with a home, poverty could make their upbringing hard for their parents. One of those who observed the privations of poor people and their offspring was Langland, whose poem *Piers Plowman*, first written in about the 1360s, centres on a hero who is sometimes presented as a small peasant farmer, sometimes as an agricultural labourer. The poem contains an episode in which the rural community is visited by a famine, personified by Hunger in human form (Fig. 33). Langland approved of hunger in one sense, because it disciplined people to work hard and avoid idleness and sin. Yet he conceded that it hurt the virtuous too. When Hunger demands food of Piers, the ploughman reminds him of the poor diet endured by a peasant or labourer in the early summer:

> 'I have no penny', quoth Piers, 'pullets to buy,
> Neither geese nor pigs, but two green [*unripe*] cheeses,
> And a few curds and cream and an unleavened cake,
> And a loaf of beans and bran baked for my children.
> And I say by my soul, I have no salt bacon,

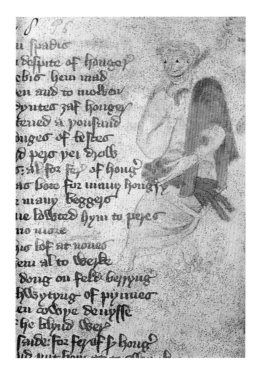

33 Hunger stalked poor families, not sparing children. Here, it is imagined in human form in Langland's *Piers Plowman*.

> Nor no cooking eggs, by Christ, collops [*bacon and eggs*] to make,
> But I have leeks and parsley and many cabbage plants. . .
> By this livelihood I must live till Lammas time [*1 August*];
> By then I hope to have harvest in my croft.'[220]

Piers's family are living largely on vegetables, with a little dairy produce. They have no grain left for bread. Until harvest in early August, the children must eat loaves formed of beans and bran – the ground-up husks of the grain – or, as Langland later rewrote the line, loaves of beans and peas. Such loaves were poor indeed, food which Langland elsewhere regarded as suitable for giving to idle beggars and not dissimilar to the fodder one fed to horses.

In the final version of his poem, written in about the 1380s, Langland returned to the theme of the poor and their children. He pointed out how the needy are to be found close at hand, among our neighbours,

> poor folk in cottages,
> Charged with children and chief lords' rent.
> What they with spinning may spare, [they] spend it in house-hire,
> Both in milk and in meal to make papelote [*porridge*]
> To satisfy their children that cry for their food.
> Also they themselves suffer much hunger,
> And woe in winter-time with waking at nights,
> To rise to the ruelle [*bedside*] to rock the cradle.

Children, runs the message, are a heavy burden. Babies need constant attention and break into adults' sleep, weakening them further. In this passage, the poet seems particularly concerned with mothers struggling to earn a living from spinning, carding, or combing wool, or by making clothes, washing, or peeling rushes. Though poor, they are ashamed to beg from their neighbours. Their food is cold meat and cold fish; on Friday or a fast-day, a farthing's worth of cockles or mussels is a feast to them.[221]

The subject surfaces a third time in an anonymous poem inspired by Langland called *Piers the Plowman's Creed*, composed in the 1390s. Here Piers is portrayed in a field, raggedly dressed, following the plough drawn by animals. His wife goes with him to drive them with a goad. Her coat is cut high to allow her to work, on this she has wrapped a winnowing sheet against the cold, and she goes barefoot despite the ice on the ground. Her tiny children have been brought, because they cannot be left at home. One, the baby, lies wrapped in cloth in a wooden bowl at the side of the field. Two others, two years old, stand or sit crying nearby, and the distracted ploughman sighs and tells them to be quiet.[222] Even in the fifteenth and early sixteenth centuries, when the population was smaller and more prosperous, there continued to be plenty of poor children. An Oxford schoolmaster, teaching his relatively well-off class in the 1490s, could note how

> Many children wear no shoes till they be thirteen or twelve years old at least, whose feet by long continuance of time be so hard that though they go over thorns, briars, and sharp stones, yet they feel no pain.[223]

Twenty years later, the poet Alexander Barclay observed boys in winter 'all rent and ragged'.[224]

Some poor children wandered begging, on their own or with their parents. We hear of a few by name in miracle records, because they were disabled and found healing. In Norwich, a boy named Robert, deformed from infancy, begged at houses while getting about on his knees with a pair of small crutches. He was cured at the shrine of St William in 1156.[225] A mad girl of Lincoln lived from the charity of the wives of the city, presumably going from house to house, before she was cured at the tomb of St Hugh in Lincoln Cathedral, soon after 1200.[226] At Orpington (Kent), a crippled boy took up his station at the church door, waiting for alms, and happened to meet St Richard of Chichester before 1253, while the saint was still alive; he was taken into care by Richard and healed.[227] John of Burton, aged about sixteen, begged in Ludlow (Salop) and Hereford at the end of the thirteenth century, able to speak only with a lowing sound. After going to the shrine of St Thomas Cantilupe at Hereford Cathedral, he could mutter Welsh and English, and a second visit improved his speech further.[228] These records show kindly attitudes to the poor and disabled. Local people, who probably knew them, gave them help, and the saints were portrayed as their patrons, poor as they were.

Not all were so lucky. Medieval observers did not always respond warmly to beggar children or their parents, especially in strange places. John of Burton was beaten before his cure, on the orders of a Hereford official, to see if his speech defect was a piece of fraud.[229] Langland, so sympathetic to the deserving poor, regarded beggars and their children with dislike. Such men and women, he claimed, produced children without benefit of matrimony, who suffered the status of bastards. Worse still, parents deliberately broke their children's backs or bones and went begging with them, the better to exploit people's kindness.[230] Barclay made similar charges in the early sixteenth century:

> Some other beggars falsely for the nonce [*occasion*]
> Disfigure their children – God knows, unhappily,
> Mangling their faces and breaking their bones,
> To stir the people to pity that pass by.[231]

A horrible story to this effect circulated in 1417, though it did not involve parents. Three children of King's Lynn (Norfolk) were allegedly kidnapped by thieving beggars. One had its eyes removed, another its back broken, and both had their tongues severed to silence them. The third was spared disfigurement and taken to London, where it was able to call for help when, accidentally, it saw its father. He had the beggars arrested, and they were hanged.[232]

Up to the Reformation, poor children were largely dependent on private charity. In the 1530s, however, the problem of the poor began to be addressed by legislation.[233] In 1536, an act 'for the punishment of sturdy vagabonds and beggars' made local authorities, in towns and parishes, responsible for gathering alms to finance the relief and support of the poor. They were empowered to take control of children aged between five and fourteen who were living 'in begging or idleness', as long as they were not suffering from some major disease or sickness. The children were to be handed over to substantial farmers or master craftsmen to learn to work, 'by the which they may get their livings when they shall come to age'. A set of clothes was to be given them when they entered service. Any young person aged between twelve and sixteen who refused such work, or left it, might be arrested, whipped with rods in public, and sent back to service, as often as was needed.[234] In 1563, the raising of money for this purpose became compulsory, and nine years later special overseers of the poor were appointed to see to their welfare, including that of young people. At Ashburton (Devon) in 1577–8, for example, there were three such children: a boy named Barrett, a girl called Yollond, and a boy referred to merely as 'the bastard'. Their board cost 6d. to 8d. a week, and they were provided with shoes and clothes: shirts and coats for the boys, smock, apron, and headkerchiefs for the girl. Altogether the three cost the parish £3 17s. 9d. in that year.[235]

Beggars' children, or children who begged, were sometimes at risk of their lives. It is illuminating that when Joan la Schirreve, aged nearly five, fell into a pond at Wisteston (Herefs.) in 1288 and apparently drowned, those who passed and saw her there did nothing. That was because they mistook her for the daughter of another local woman who begged with her child, and thought that her mother had thrown her in, out of desperation.[236] No one wanted the bother of raising the hue and cry. Three poor children came to grief in Bedfordshire in the 1270s alone. Roger, son of Agnes of Maulden, presumably the child of an unmarried mother or widow, sat in a road at twilight on 19 February 1272, weeping for lack of shelter. A neighbour came out to investigate, but met some passing thieves who murdered him and the child too, apparently as a witness.[237] In 1273, Joan Fine of Milton Bryant came into Houghton Regis (Beds.) and went from door to door seeking hospitality, carrying her son Henry, aged two, in her arms. Someone allowed them to stay in a barn, but Henry wandered off and fell into a ditch, with fatal results.[238] In the following year at about prime (early in the morning), a poor child named Joan, aged five, went through Riseley to beg for bread; she fell while crossing a bridge and was drowned.[239]

The 'green children' may have been poor children of a similar kind, brought up half-wild upon some East Anglian moorland or woodland in the twelfth century. Their story was told in about 1200 by two chroniclers, who were vague about the date when they appeared but agreed in describing what happened.[240] The children, a boy and a girl, were found by reapers on the edge of a pit at Woolpit near Bury St Edmunds (Suffolk), human in form, wearing clothes, and with a green tinge to their skins. No one could understand what they said. Crying inconsolably, they were taken to the house of a nearby knight, where many people came to see them. They refused all food till bean pods were produced; these they wanted to eat, but had to be shown how to open. The boy, apparently the younger of the two, languished and soon died, but the girl survived. She grew accustomed to a normal diet and lost her original colour. Duly baptised, she entered the service of the knight and eventually got married at King's Lynn.

Our own instinct may be to rationalise the children as orphans from the backwoods, anaemic through lack of a proper diet, but the chroniclers did not take this view. To them, the children radiated mystery and romance. The girl was said to have claimed that she and her brother came from the land of St Martin, whose people were Christians but green. It had no sun save for a glow in the sky, like that which comes after sunset. The land was not far from ours, but divided from it by a great river. When asked how she got into Suffolk, the girl explained that while she and the boy were looking after a flock of animals, they entered a cavern where they heard a delightful sound of bells. They went through the cavern and found themselves in our world, but could not discover the way back home. Starved and deprived though they were, there must have been something special about them to spark such a marvellous tale.

Chapter 3

Danger and Death

34   King Herod watches the slaughter of the Innocents, the classic medieval story of child abuse.

INFANTICIDE AND ABANDONMENT

INFANCY AND CHILDHOOD are times of frailty and danger. Birth needs expert help to make it safe. Our early years are fraught with potential hazards; plumbing, heating, cupboards, and their contents can all cause harm. As we venture away from home, we may meet other misfortunes at play or in the street. This is the case even in caring families, and not all families are caring. Parents and guardians may be neglectful or hostile, not loving and protective. Children may suffer from physical defects which make life difficult and affect the attitudes of other people towards them. They may fall ill and their illnesses may be fatal. The next stage of our journey is to explore these problems and perils as they affected medieval children.

Some babies survived for only an hour or two, not through their own frailty but that of their parents. Killed when born, they were the victims of terror, shame, indifference, or mental illness. Such was the baby girl, half a day old, found in the River Thames at Oxford near the Franciscan friary in 1343, its navel-string not tied – evidently a birth to a single girl or woman, without benefit of midwife.[1] Medieval people, like us, regarded such deeds with horror. From Ælfric in the 990s to Chaucer in the 1390s, religious leaders and writers categorised the killing of infants as murder, as serious as that of adults. Not only did it rob its victims of life in this world but of salvation in the next, for babies who died unchristened would go to hell and, added Ælfric, the murderers too unless they repented.[2] The Church required that infanticides, when found, should be sent to their bishops for penance, and that such penance should be set at a heavy rate.[3] Up to about the twelfth century, such sinners were excommunicated for life; later, the tariff was reduced, more humanely, to ten years.[4] Robert of Flamborough, writing soon after 1200, suggested fifteen years of penance. If the slayer was a mother so poor that she committed the act from inability to nourish a child, this might be reduced to seven years.[5] In the mid thirteenth century, the *Decretals* of Pope Gregory IX recommended that a mother who killed her son willingly should enter a religious house, although some lesser penance might be imposed if that were not feasible.[6]

The crown in England shared the Church's concern. The laws of Henry I, issued in about 1118, also refer to the old rule that women responsible for abortions should be excommunicated for life. Now, it laid down, they should do penance for three years if the embryo was less than forty days old and seven years if it was older and therefore endowed with a soul. The latter tariff was the same as for killing a live person.[7] By the thirteenth century, the killing of live children was treated as homicide and might incur capital punishment. Sabina de Coetingle, tried for making away with her newborn infant, claimed that it was still-born and pleaded insanity, but the jury found that the child was born alive and that she was sane. She was sentenced to be executed by burning.[8] Hers, however, was an unusual case; more commonly, royal courts accepted pleas of mental derangement where parents were concerned. When Matilda Levying of Bourton (Oxon.), 'suffering from ague and frenzy', murdered her two children with an axe in about 1275, the crown ordered her release from prison into the hands of her relatives, if they would undertake to look after her, and she was eventually pardoned.[9] We have no means of reckoning how many infants were deliberately destroyed in medieval England, but it is likely that (as today) the events were abnormal not normal. The disapproval of such killings by the Church and the crown is likely to have harmonised with the feelings of most people.

A less dreadful alternative to killing a baby was to abandon it. This practice is mentioned as early as the late seventh century, when King Ine of Wessex sought to provide support for those concerned. He ordered sums of money to be paid for the maintenance of a foundling child: 6 shillings in its first year, 12 in its second, 30 in its third, and afterwards 'according to its appearance', presumably its physique.[10] By the late twelfth century, the Church was also taking an interest in foundlings, because of the need to baptise them. Church councils at York (1195) and Westminster (1200) ruled that when children were abandoned, 'with or without salt', they should be christened unless this was known to have been done already.[11] The mention of salt refers to the practice by which the christening party took some of it to church for the priest to use in the service.[12] Those who abandoned infants with salt showed, by this little ritual, that they wished them to be preserved and baptised. One early-Tudor writer associates abandonment with prostitutes, but it was probably done by other single women, though we cannot say how widely.[13] Nor is it clear who took in such children to rear them. Some private people may have done so out of charity, some hospitals (as we have seen) did so from duty, and religious houses occasionally played such a role. In the late twelfth-century romance *Le Fresne*, by Marie de France, a lady-in-waiting abandons a baby outside an abbey of nuns, blessing her as she does so; the girl is then reared by the nuns.[14] This story had a real parallel: Queen Eleanor of Aquitaine found a small boy in the road, destitute of a mother, and arranged for him to be brought up in Abingdon Abbey (Berks.).[15]

DISABLEMENT

CHILDREN MAY BE born with disfigurements, with missing limbs, or as twins joined together. Successful births of these kinds were rare enough in the middle ages to be recorded as wonders by chronicle writers. Matthew Paris described two such cases in 1249. One was a miniature youth, aged eighteen, discovered in the Isle of Wight: only three feet in height, but proportionate in all his members. The other was a boy born in Herefordshire, allegedly the child of a female demon or *incuba*. Within half a year he was fully toothed and had the stature of a lad of about seventeen.[16] In 1399, Adam of Usk reported the birth of a boy at Llanbadoc (Mon.) with a single eye, placed in the middle of his forehead.[17]

Such wonders prompted a range of explanations. One came close to our notions of science and said that parents might physically generate too much or too little material to form a perfect child.[18] More often, disablement was traced to parents' thoughts or actions during love-making or pregnancy, which were then transferred to their offspring. Walter Map, for example, tells how a cruel French marquess had his right ear cut off by the king of France as punishment for his crimes. Within four days, the man's wife gave birth to a son without a right ear.[19] Intercourse between demons and humans was sometimes suspected, as it was by Paris,[20] or the influence of the heavens was seen as a factor. The stars might produce a monstrous child, and such a child, like a comet or an earthquake. be a sign of unusual events to come. The birth noted by Adam of Usk was one of a number of strange happenings which, he thought, reflected the turmoil of 1399–1400, when Henry IV dethroned Richard II and then met with rebellions in his turn. Many people, however, probably saw such children simply as freakish: objects for wonder or laughter. Paris described the youth of the Isle of Wight as a 'monster of nature'. He told how the young man was shown to the queen, who had him led around with her for the admiration of beholders. Some of the fools employed in noble households in the later middle ages are likely to have been children or young people, disabled in understanding or small in size. Making them fools is distasteful by modern standards, but contemporaries may have thought that they were giving them roles in which they could earn a living.

Badly disabled children also invited questions about their identity. Were they human, and if so, one human or more? In 1552, the wife of John Kenner of Middleton Stoney (Oxon.). gave birth to 'Siamese' twins. At least, we would say twins, but a London chronicler who recorded the event was not sure. He first wrote 'two children', corrected the words to one 'child', and then described them as two.[21] Three centuries earlier, Henry Bracton considered whether deformity affected a person's legal status. His judgment was a tolerant one. The law took no account of useless members, twisted limbs, hunch-back conditions, or fingers numbering six, four, or one. It would only reject a 'monster' or 'prodigy', which roared not cried and did not possess a human likeness.[22] John de Burgh, writing in the 1380s as an ecclesiastic, took a similar, charitable view. Asking whether those born in 'monstrous' form should be christened, he decided that they should if they were mainly human. This included joined twins or triplets. Burgh merely paused to observe that some people thought that the soul resided in the heart and some in the head, so that more than one baptism might be necessary in such cases.[23]

Deformity aroused compassion too. Some such children were loved and nurtured as dearly as the fully formed. Anglo-Saxon cemeteries produce occasional evidence of children and adults with cleft palates, who would have needed special care at birth because of their inability to suckle. Two graves have been found of disabled adults, one with a congenitally absent left arm and the second with an imperfectly grown right leg, due to a childhood disease. Both imply survival, thanks to care and support by others.[24] Someone looked after the young man of the Isle of Wight, and in the early fourteenth century a set of Siamese twins lived to the verge of adulthood. The pair, described in the chronicle of Meaux Abbey (Yorks.) as a 'human monster', were joined in their lower parts but separate above the navel. Their sexes were said to be male and female, though such twins are usually identical. They were born, probably in the East Riding of Yorkshire, in about 1330, and were cared for enough to grow up. Not surprisingly, they attracted attention and may have been visited by the public. One would eat, drink, sleep, or talk, while the other did something else. They were also accustomed to sing sweetly together. The pair died at Kingston-upon-Hull at about the age of eighteen, just before the onset of the Black Death in 1348, one outliving the other by three days.[25] The Kenner twins of 1552 lived for only fifteen days, but they too seem to have been regarded with sympathy. The London chronicler does not describe them as 'monstrous', but says that they were christened at home by the midwife with the Church's permission. He noted that they could sleep and wake separately, and responded to attention with a 'merry cheer' or expression.[26]

Nevertheless, when disabled children grew up, they were likely to find their physical handicaps increased by social and legal barriers. Marriage for women would be more difficult, and likewise employment for men – at least in the most prestigious posts and callings. A cleric with a deformity who wished to be a priest had to seek the sanction of the pope.[27] At least one expert on knighthood considered that lameness in any member ruled one out from receiving the accolade and, by the fifteenth century, 'disparagement', the attempt to marry a feudal heir to an unsuitable person, was held to include the deformed or the chronically ill.[28] Even servants were chosen or rejected for their physique. Havelok, in the thirteenth-century story, gets employment in an earl's kitchen because he carries up large loads of fish from the port, and the cook thinks him 'stalwart'. Two hundred years later, a writer who described the household of Edward IV thought that its boy-servants should be of 'clean birth' (legitimate) and 'clean-limbed' (well proportioned) – requirements endorsed by the mercers and cutlers of London for those who became their apprentices.[29]

ACCIDENTS

CHILDREN'S ACCIDENTS ARE one of the best known aspects of their lives in the middle ages, thanks to two kinds of sources, each of which points to the interest of adults in children. First, there are miracle stories. England, like other parts of Europe, generated saint-cults; these in turn led to miracles and writings about them. Those who recorded miracles wished to demonstrate the power of the saint and his or her willingness to help people out of their troubles. Good collections survive for saints such as Frideswide of Oxford, Godric of Finchale, Thomas Becket, Thomas Cantilupe (bishop of Hereford), and King Henry VI.[30] Many of the miracles involve children and their accidents, and show how desperate parents invoked the saint or took the child to the shrine, with beneficial results. Their stories are therefore ones with happy endings. They feature more boys than girls, perhaps because boys took greater risks, perhaps because parents were more concerned for their survival. But the records are remarkably open as far as rank is concerned, including poor and rich. The saint is presented as someone who cares for us all.

The other kind of evidence is that of coroners' rolls, and since coroners were concerned
with children only when they were dead, their
stories end unhappily. They resemble miracle
records, on the other hand, in having a concern
with children as well as with adults. Any unnatural death, at whatever age, was supposed to be
publicised and examined in a formal way. The
finder of the body had to raise the hue and cry
– drawing people's attention to the fact by shouting or blowing a horn. The four nearest neighbours had to be informed. They in turn were to
tell the local authorities, and the latter the
coroner. Fines could be levied on those who
avoided their duty. The coroner duly came to
view the body, and the first finder and the four
neighbours had to attend as witnesses. A jury of
local people was asked for its verdict on the
cause of death, and all these proceedings were
enrolled as a record.[31] Sometimes this procedure
may have been ignored, as it was in the case of
Joan la Shirreve in Herefordshire in 1288.[32] But
every system has its exceptions. Coroners'
records contain large numbers of cases involving dead children, including victims of simple
domestic accidents and, as we have seen, they
do not exclude the poor and marginalised. The
crown took seriously all unnatural deaths, from
the youngest babies upwards.[33]

Miracle stories and coroners' rolls reveal the
same kinds of accidents in medieval homes as
happen today and for the same reasons – childish curiosity and the existence of hazards, harm-
less to adults yet potentially lethal to children.
The baby in the cradle might be caught in straps
or cords, crushed by the fall of stones from the
wall, burnt in a fire, choked by smoke, or
attacked by an animal. Coroners' and miracle
records suggest that pigs were a particular
source of danger, wandering into houses
through open doors, biting babies, or overturning their cradles. The sow devouring the baby is
one of the images of death in Chaucer's

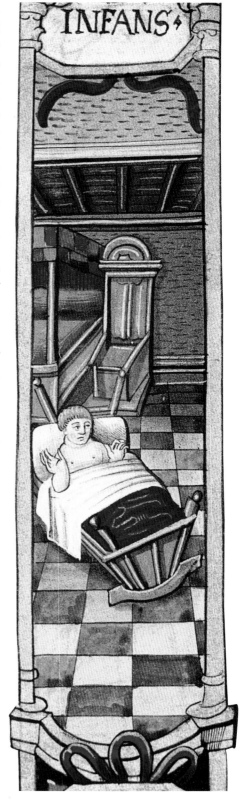

35 An unswaddled baby in its cot. Such babies might fall
out, or be attacked by domestic animals.

'Knight's Tale'.[34] As soon as infants could crawl or walk, these threats were increased by other potential dangers. The hearth was the chief of these, on which one might be burnt or scalded by overturning dishes placed upon it. Children fell into vessels of liquid: a pan of milk, a cask of water, a wooden vat. One was crushed by an opening door, another's head got entangled in the straps that fastened a door, a third fell from an upstairs window.

Infants able to touch loose objects are liable to put them in their mouths. Medieval children swallowed all manner of things they encountered: a ring, a silver groat, a badge, a brass pin, an ear of wheat. One put a plumstone up her nose, others a small stone or a bean in their ears. The boy with the bean in his ear did not lose it until thirty-seven years later. They injured themselves or were injured with tools: cut by a knife, struck by an axe-blade while watching Father chop wood, and pierced by his pitchfork while hiding in a pile of straw. Outside the house there were further dangers, especially from water. Children fell into the house well or into neighbouring ditches, pits, ponds, and rivers. Sometimes they did so while wandering about, at other times when washing, playing, trying to retrieve something, or fetching water. Once, a child drowned while allegedly watching its own reflection, and on another occasion after sleepwalking. In the yard or street, horse traffic posed a further threat. A child could be struck by a horse's hooves, or run over by a cart.

When accidents happened, the question arose what the parents were doing. Some claimed that they were momentarily distracted: eating a meal, heating the oven, hanging out the clothes. Others had gone on longer errands: to fetch ale, to attend church, or to work in the fields. Absent parents might provide a suitable baby-sitter; one hears of a girl watching a child in its cradle while the mother met with a fatal accident outside. At other times the guardian was too young, like John Cok, a boy of five who was left to look after his one-year-old brother William at Hilperton (Wilts.) in 1369. While he was in charge, the cradle caught fire and the baby died.[35] Coroners' inquests did not usually criticise parents, perhaps because once the cause of death was established as accidental, the crown had no interest in making further comment. Even miracle writers rarely lay blame upon parents, with a notable exception in the case of a mother and father who went to church, leaving their fifteen-month-old boy to crawl upon the hearth.[36] Instead, such writers seek to evoke the trauma of accidents: the apparent death, the anguish of parents and neighbours, and the desperate vow or prayer. All this built up the saints' reputations as successful helpers, however distressing the case.

ABUSE

WE ARE WELL aware of child abuse of one kind or another – physical, mental, and sexual. Our ancestors were mindful of it too; indeed, the Church had an annual festival of which it formed the subject. Holy Innocents' Day, 28 December, recalled the slaughter of the young boys of Bethlehem and its neighbourhood by the soldiers of King Herod. The slaughter was visualised as a holocaust, involving 144,000 children, a number suggested by the martyrs mentioned in the Book of Revelation. Book illustrations depicted the horror of the event in lurid detail (Fig. 34). But most medieval people probably saw the massacre as something exotic: the kind of cruelty typical of Jews. If it carried a lesson for their own society, it may have suggested that abuse of children had its origins outside families rather than inside, still a common assumption today.

Certainly, people appear to have found it easier to imagine abuse by strangers or guardians than by mothers or fathers. Physical abuse in the home, in particular, attracted little attention. Commentators, as we have seen, thought that parents punished their children too lightly, not too much. Courts, whether secular or religious, had small concern with the matter. Godparents, neighbours, clergy, or local authorities may have intervened from time to time to mediate and protect, but it is difficult to know how often this happened. Abuse was easier to spot away from home, when children were in other people's care. Then, their families were more likely to step in, or neighbours to report the matter. Schoolmasters were sometimes accused of exceeding the mark. Henry Machyn, the London chronicler of the mid sixteenth century, reports how in 1563, a man named Penred, who had a child to teach, beat him so severely with a buckled belt that the affair came to public notice. The master was set on the pillory, whipped till his blood ran down, and the boy's injuries were exhibited, 'the pitiest [sight to] see at any time'.[37] Occasionally, an employer was exposed as an abuser. The 'Greyfriars' chronicler of London records how, in 1552, a woman of Aldersgate Street, a maker of alcoholic spirits, 'carded' her maid with an iron-toothed comb of the kind used to raise the nap on cloth; the woman was paraded in a cart and sent to prison.[38]

Children could also suffer violence from one another: in school, at work, or in the street. Little is known about this, since it rarely came within the notice of the law, but it sometimes surfaces in relation to schools. An Oxford schoolbook of the early sixteenth century features a fictional bully named Anthony, who beats another boy about the head and face with his fists, leaving his victim black and blue in the cheeks, unable to sleep at night. The same book points to problems outside school. A schoolboy is imagined going into town one evening, on an errand. Returning home at about 8.00 pm, he is intercepted by three youths dressed like scholars 'but they were thieves in very deed'. While one keeps watch, a second claps his hand on the boy's mouth and beats him on the head to confuse him. The third steals his purse and money. Encounters of this kind would not be surprising. Many schoolboys were boarding away from home in a strange town, with ready money. Local youths were likely to see them both as strangers to attack and lucrative targets to rob.[39]

Abuse and exploitation might take mental or spiritual forms. Children sometimes appeared to have powers or perceptions beyond those of adults, which adults might then exploit. Some were thought to be able to open locks and bars, like St William of Norwich who, when a tiny child, was said to have met a man who wore iron fetters as a penance, and to have broken the metal in pieces by his touch.[40] In 1252, Matthew Paris reported a wonder-working infant at Stone

Pray for the sowle of Elyn bray dowghtur
of Sr Edmond bray knyght & Jane hys wyfe
Whiche elyn dyed y' xij day of may A° m° dxvj

36   Ellen Bray (d. 1516), a victim of infant
mortality. She wears her chrisom cloth to show
that she died baptized but before her mother's
churching.

near Dartford (Kent). The child, William son of William and Eustachia Coul,
aged two, had been born on Holy Cross Day (14 September) and could heal the
infirm, with his parents' assistance, by making the sign of the cross upon them
and speaking their names. Many of the sick flocked to him and were cured, and
his mother claimed that she had divine premonition of his powers after his birth.
But the miracles did not last and the wonder diminished.[41] This affair was not,
apparently, obnoxious to authority, but in 1555 (a less tolerant time) two women
were made to do penance at St Paul's Cross (London) for manipulating a child
to prophesy that the kingdom of God was at hand.[42]

A common practice was the use of children for crystal gazing. John of Salisbury tells us how, when he was a boy in about the 1120s, he was sent to learn
the psalms from a priest who engaged in this art. The priest made John and
another pupil peer at a fingernail smeared with oil and at the polished surface of
a basin.

> After pronouncing names which, by the horror they inspired, seemed to me,
> child though I was, to belong to demons, and after administering oaths of
> which, at God's instance, I knew nothing, my companion asserted that he saw
> certain misty figures, but dimly, while I was so blind to all this that nothing
> appeared to me except the nails or basin and the other objects I had seen there
> before. In consequence, I was adjudged useless for such purposes.[43]

Robert Mannyng, writing in 1303, was also aware of this practice, and warned
his readers and listeners against it:

> If thou in sword or in basin
> Any child madest look therein,
> Or in thumb or in crystal,
> Witchcraft men clepe [*call*] it all.[44]

It was, he insisted, an offence against the First Commandment, which forbids
Christians from worshipping others than God.

The activity went on, nonetheless. A story of about 1400, preserved in a manuscript of Byland Abbey (Yorks.) describes how a householder, troubled by thefts
of meat from his house, employed a wizard to solve the problem. The wizard
procured a boy, oiled his nail, and told him to study it and report what he
saw.[45] When Peter Idley of Drayton (Oxon.) wrote a poem of *Instructions* for his
son in the 1450s, he felt it worthwhile copying Mannyng's warning, word for
word, and added, 'Beware of this, it will have a fall.'[46] Meanwhile, in 1365, a
case of magic involving a child had surfaced in a London court. Richard Cook
claimed that Nicholas the clerk of Southwark had imprisoned him for half a day
and half a night, until he lost his mind through seeing evil spirits, stirred up by
the clerk's diabolical incantations. He sued for damages of £100. That Richard
was a child emerges from Nicholas's defence, in which he claimed that he was
teaching Richard and other boys to read and sing, and that he had detained him
for that purpose. The jury did not believe the clerk, and found in favour of
Richard.[47]

A third kind of child abuse is sexual, and this too was perceived in the middle
ages.[48] Church writers spent a good deal of time discussing sexual sins, and they
mention incest, rape, and the violation of virgin girls with strong disapproval.[49]
Priests at confession were advised to probe their parishioners about such
matters.[50] Today, we understand that children may be sexually abused at any age,
and that their parents may be responsible, but these possibilities seem to have
been less realised by our ancestors. The poet John Gower portrays the typical
lecher seducing a young virgin in her teens, because her previous childishness had
made this impossible.[51] Mannyng and Mirk saw incest arising from siblings rather
than adults, and both expressed concern about brothers and sisters sleeping
together.[52] Mannyng added a warning to godfathers. He tells a story from St
Gregory's *Dialogues* about such a man who, being drunk, slept with his goddaughter on the night before Easter Day. When day dawned, he recognised his
sin but decided to go to church in case people noticed his absence. Nothing happened to him there, but seven days later he died, and when he was buried a stink-
ing hot fire came out of the grave and burnt his corpse.[53] That showed his
destination only too clearly.

London is occasionally mentioned as a place of child abuse through prostitution, male and female. In 1179, a Jew was accused of killing a French boy in
Winchester. The boy's friend, also French, who levelled the charge, claimed that
a Jew in France had encouraged them to come to England but to hasten through
London because of its vices. 'Every quarter of it abounds in sad obscenities,
including pretty boys, effeminates, and pederasts.'[54] From time to time, sexual

activities involving young people caught the attention of the city authorities and were punished. Henry Machyn noted three such cases. In 1556, a woman was put into the pillory for procuring a child (apparently her own) for sex, and in 1560 two women were driven through the city in carts for similar offences. One of these, from Southwark (a notable brothel district), had procured a girl of eleven for a foreigner. The other was a woman of status, Mistress Warner, widow of a sergeant of the admiralty, who had done the same with regard to her daughter and maid, both of whom were pregnant in consequence.[55]

Religious communities, where men and boys lived in proximity, were other potential places of sexual abuse. Some of those in charge of such places seem to have envisaged this and to have sought to prevent it. Archbishop Lanfranc's rules for the monks of Canterbury Cathedral, issued in the late eleventh century, do not mention such abuse but imply a concern about it by the arrangements they make. The boy recruits in the monastery are to be governed by a monk of mature age and known discretion. He is to supervise them going to bed and be present if any other monk needs to talk to them. Monks are not to visit the boys' room.[56] Similar precautions are recorded in later times: thus at Durham Priory in 1446, the monks were told not to introduce unauthorised boys to their rooms.[57] In 1535, Henry VIII's commissioners, visiting all the English monasteries, asked 'whether the master, or any brother of this house, useth to have any boys or young men laying with him?'[58]

Nonetheless, monks had a reputation for pederasty as early as the twelfth century. Walter Map recounts a joke that he made on the subject. A Cistercian abbot was telling how St Bernard tried to revive the son of the marquess of Burgundy, who had died. The saint laid his body on that of the boy, in the manner of the Prophet Elisha, prayed, and got up, but no miracle occurred. Walter said 'He was the most unlucky of monks. I have never heard of any monk lying on a boy without the boy immediately getting up afterwards.' The abbot blushed, and some of the listeners went outside and laughed.[59] There was an outbreak of allegations of sexual abuse in monasteries on the eve of the Reformation. One concerned John Slythurst, canon of Missenden Abbey (Bucks.), who was seen through a hole in a wall embracing and kissing the bailiff's son in bed in 1530; it was his second such crime. The bishop's officer ordered him to be confined to the monastery and forbade boys to be alone with canons or to enter their dormitory or cells.[60] Henry's commissioners found (or were told of) a monk of Garendon Abbey (Leics.) who had been involved with ten boys, a canon of Thurgarton Priory (Notts.) with four, and another of the same house with several.[61] In the same year, 1535, a schoolmaster of Gloucester accused the prior and cellarer of Lanthony Priory, just outside the city, of sexually abusing schoolboys. He claimed to have discovered the evidence while stripping the boys to beat them![62]

Fear about child abuse reflects the preoccupations of society. Our own world is highly aware of sexual issues; in the middle ages, with its more religious culture, child abuse was easily linked with religion. Accusations against monks are a sign of this, because they often arose from those outside the cloister who had little sympathy with the monastic life-style. In the twelfth and thirteenth centuries, child

37 Christian perceptions of Jews (right) as the abusers of Christ, made it possible to see them also as abusers of children.

abuse was attributed to another unpopular religious group: the Jewish community.[63] Here, the charges centred on the alleged abduction of children for purposes of ritual. The earliest and one of the most famous cases was that of William of Norwich, the twelve-year-old boy found murdered near that city in 1144 and subsequently venerated as a saint. William had been boarding with a skinner in Norwich and learning his craft, work which brought him into contact with Jews. When the murder was discovered, it was blamed on them, and claims were made that a Jew had lured William away from his master's service. William, it was asserted, was taken to a Jewish house in Norwich on the eve of the Passover, and there on the day of the feast itself he was tortured and crucified like Jesus. His body was taken to Thorpe Wood near the city, where it was found by a woodcutter.[64]

A series of such allegations arose during the rest of the twelfth and most of the thirteenth centuries, the last of them in 1279, not long before the Jews were expelled from England in 1290. The children were always boys, who were variously said to have been circumcised, murdered, or crucified. Evidence of the facts was circumstantial at best. The body of little St Hugh of Lincoln, who died in

1255, was found in a cesspit in the city near the house of a Jew. In this case, torture of a Jew elicited a confession; he was drawn and hanged, and other Jews were tried in London and hanged for refusing to plead. Sometimes, as at Winchester in 1291, there was merely a report of a boy's disappearance, and no body was found. At other times, although there was a body, it could have been the victim of an accident or of a Christian murderer. William of Norwich, it was admitted, was enticed away from the skinner's service by a man who was or claimed to be the archdeacon's cook, a fact circumvented by claiming that the enticer was a Jew. Yet no Jew was tried for William's murder, though one was later killed by a knight's retainers. Apparently, people in England found it impossible to conceive that they themselves might murder children for the pleasure of homicide or sex. Instead, they interpreted such acts as religious ones, and laid them at the door of the most unpopular religious group of the time.

ILLNESS

ACCIDENTS WERE AVOIDABLE in principle; illnesses less so. Throughout society, disease posed threats to children's health and often to their lives. Infants at the breast might grow sick, the result (in Bartholomew's view) of impurities in the milk of their nurses, leading to

> full evil sores and wicked griefs [*sicknesses*], as whelks, blains, and pimples in the mouth, spewing, fevers, cramps, squirt [*diarrhoea*], the flux, and other such.[65]

Older children might suffer the epidemic diseases of childhood, or those that struck society regardless of age. From early times, medical writers (though mostly concerned with general or adult conditions) gave some attention to children's ailments. Anglo-Saxon texts, for example, prescribe hare's brain for sore gums during teething, and poultices of bull's gall or the herb lupine to lay on the navel for children's intestinal worms. Ashes of garlic blended with oil were recommended for children's scabby skin, probably especially for the scalp condition known as ringworm, and a mixture of four herbs as a cure for urinary troubles.[66]

Some of these disorders were perennial. Bartholomew also refers to ringworm in children, which he describes as 'scale' or 'moth . . . for it fretteth and gnaweth the over-part of the head as a moth fretteth cloth'. He mentions pox, apparently a mild disorder like chicken-pox, since he thought it boded well for health in later life: in particular it protected against leprosy. Children might nevertheless get leprosy, by transmission from a parent or a wet nurse, and he believed that small children might suffer from stones in their bladders – a problem that required an operation.[67] Guy de Chauliac's fourteenth-century treatise on surgery, which was translated into English, refers to mouth ulcers, scabs on the head (again, doubtless ringworm), and stones which he thought quite likely to occur up to puberty.[68] Records of saint-cults are another source for ailments. Benedict of Peterborough's

anmour dr. s'. midolas amiene
mias da midolaus pona
fica li dro:atus mfula om
ubus fe ama bilan achibunc. w.c.

38   Saints gave help to victims
of crimes, accidents, and
illnesses. Here, St Nicholas
restores three boys killed and
pickled by a butcher.

collection of the miracles of Thomas Becket, begun in the 1170s, lists some 56
cases involving children. They include both congenital and acquired conditions:
blindness and crippledness, impairments to speech and hearing, paralysis of a
limb, fits, mental illnesses, and infections described as 'fevers'. Other young people
are mentioned with swellings, hernias, pustules, lumps, sores, nose-bleeding, and
leprosy.[69]

Children suffered too in epidemics. Many may have died in the first onslaught
of the plague upon England in 1348–9. They certainly did so in its second major
outbreak in 1360–2, whose impact on the young was noticed throughout Europe.
In Yorkshire, the chronicle of Meaux Abbey described it as 'the second pestilence
in England, which was called the "pestilence of the children"'.[70] A writer at
the nearby abbey of St Mary in York called it 'the mortality of children, in which
many good people and a great number of children were taken away and entrusted
to God'.[71] It may be that more children than usual had been born after the
plague of 1348–9, causing a larger proportion of young people to suffer next
time. Many other epidemics of the later middle ages were recorded as having
severe effects upon young people. Take the late fourteenth century. In 1381, one

broke out at Oxford, spreading to London in the following year where it raged 'especially among boys and girls'. In 1383, an outbreak of plague in Norfolk affected men and women between the ages of seven and twenty-two. A year later, a plague ravaged Kent and elsewhere 'sparing neither age nor sex', and in September 1387 fatalities were recorded 'especially among the young of either sex'. The late summer of 1390 saw further epidemics in different parts of England, attacking 'the young rather than the old', 'particularly young people and children'.[72]

In wealthy households, medical advice would be sought for sick children, medicines purchased, and special foods brought in. Bartholomew recommended that, when babies fell ill, medicine should be given to them via their wet nurse.[73] Older children would be treated personally. Prince Henry, whose domestic arrangements have already been mentioned, was a delicate child who died at the age of seven in 1274. In his household accounts, we learn of Master Hugh of Evesham, a physician, 'visiting the lord in his sickness', a groom being sent to London to get sugar and oil of almonds for him and his sister, and a man 'bringing herbs from the country for the use of the lord, while ill'. Other items bought for his benefit included electuary, spices, syrup, borage, sandalwood, rose and violet sugar, and twisted sugar sticks. Pomegranates and 100 caleway pears are listed as well, perhaps to tempt an ailing appetite.[74] Another sickly boy was 'little Francis', a boy maintained by the duke of Buckingham, over two centuries later, in the priory of the Knights of St John at Clerkenwell (London). Francis too had a succession of illnesses. In November 1519, he was suffering from a skin complaint (perhaps the endemic ringworm). His head was shaved, 12d. was paid for healing his head and neck, and 5d. for a white cap for him to sleep in. In the following spring, he was afflicted by ague, a throat condition (including catarrh), and yellow jaundice. Each illness involved expenses for doctors' visits and medicines.[75]

Much about disease and its treatment must have been common to adults and children, but writers sometimes identified differences, especially the need to handle children more cautiously. Chauliac warned against subjecting them to blood-letting, purgatives, or an operation for the stone until they were fourteen. He thought, however, that a child's head might be cauterised to drain off water from within, and a fifteenth-century poem on blood-letting suggested opening the veins behind the ears to cure dizziness.[76] John Arderne, Chaucer's contemporary, mentions a plaster of white of egg, oil, wax, turpentine, and woody nightshade as good for pustules in children's mouths, and John Palsgrave, writing in 1530, recommended a little draught of malmsey for those with worms.[77] Some doctors may have specialised in children's ailments; certainly Copland, in *The Highway to the Spitalhouse* (c.1530), refers to the frauds of quacks in this respect. A man pretending to be a doctor from Europe, with an accomplice as interpreter, would call at a house and use a sham foreign language to convince the mother that her child was dangerously ill:

'Dis infant rompre un grand postum;
By Got, he a la mort tuk under thum'.

'What saith he?' saith the good wife.
'Hostess, he sweareth by his soul and life
That this child is vexed with a bag
In his stomach, as great as he may wag.'

The mother, impressed by the quack's expertise, would offer anything up to 20s. for a cure. A prescription was duly provided in a paper, consisting of a powder worth a mere couple of pence.[78]

Hospitals in medieval England, as has been noticed, did not concentrate on providing short-term treatment for illnesses, either of adults or children. Rather, they provided support for those with long-term disabilities. One such condition was leprosy (or Hansen's disease, as it is now called); others included blindness and crippledness. Children with these afflictions sometimes entered hospitals, like the young crippled youth brought up in one in the north of England before he was cured at St Godric's shrine at Finchale (Durham).[79] Hospitals, however, were usually limited in the number of their inmates, and their places were sought after, needing patronage to gain entry. When a girl of Halton (Nland.) appeared to contract leprosy in the twelfth century, her local priest procured her a place in the leper hospital at Bathel near Darlington (Durham). She stayed there for three years before recovering, also with Godric's assistance.[80] But we should not assume that such institutions took in all who needed their care.

Medieval medicine extended beyond its conventional modern boundaries into what we would call alternative medicine, and this applied to the treatment of children. One disease, scrofula or 'king's evil', was believed by the twelfth century to be curable from the king's touch, and people flocked to the monarch for this purpose from at least the reign of Henry II down to that of Queen Anne.[81] Records of the custom in England say little about the ages of those concerned, but the presence of sick children in miracle stories suggests that many boys and girls were taken to be touched, and there are occasional records of this. One of the earliest known candidates for healing, in Henry II's reign, was the fourteen-year-old daughter of a knight named Roger who took her to the king for her scrofula, with the result that the swellings subsided.[82] In 1531, Henry VIII gave 7s. 6d. 'to a poor child, the which the king's grace healed at Windsor'.[83] Even if the touch was not effective, it must have been something to remember as it was for the three-year-old Dr Johnson, taken to Queen Anne for the purpose in about 1712. Years later he told Boswell that he had 'a confused, but somehow a sort of solemn, recollection of a lady in diamonds and a long black hood'.[84]

Spells were another device of healing, involving the recitation of words invoking Christ or the saints against the malady concerned. In 1529, a London Church court prosecuted Elizabeth Fotman, a woman who claimed to cure diseases with charms and herbs, including toothache 'and the worms in children's bellies'.[85] Such women were familiar enough to be satirised in the Tudor play *Thersites*, written in 1537. In this, Ulysses sends his young son Telemachus to a middle-aged woman to be charmed from worms. She tells him to lie down with his belly upwards, and proceeds to recite a comic 'blessing' over it:

> The cowherd of Comerton with his crooked spade,
> Cause from thee the worms soon to vade [*depart*];
> And jolly Jack Tumbler that juggleth with a horn,
> Grant that thy worms soon be all to [*asunder*] torn.

She conjures the worms away by Isaac's cow, the bottom of Noah's ark, the stones that David slung at Goliath, the eyetooth of Tobias's dog, and the jawbone of the ox that was present when Christ was born. Then she concludes,

> Now stand up, little Telemachus, anon;
> I warrant thee by tomorrow thy worms will be gone.[86]

Scrolls containing prayers or charms were sometimes given to people to wear, including children, a practice acceptable even to the orthodox as long as the prayers were Christian.[87] Coral was another form of protection against epilepsy and devils as early as the thirteenth century, and in 1584 it still had a reputation for preserving 'such as bear it from fascination [*enchantment*] or bewitching'. Reginald Scot, who reports this belief, notes that it was common to hang a piece around a child's neck.[88]

When epidemics raged, children – at least those of the better off – might be dispatched elsewhere. This practice was particularly popular in colleges and religious communities in the late fifteenth and early sixteenth centuries. At times of sickness in Oxford, the fellows and scholars of Magdalen College decamped en masse to one or more of the college's rural manors: Brailes and Witney in 1500, Witney and Wallingford in 1502, and Highworth in 1507. The college school went with them, as did such of its teenage scholars as wished to go, camping out in farms or cottages.[89] A passage in a college schoolbook of the period observes that

> When we last [went] forth from the university for sickness, we had a foul slutty kitchen for our school, but now we be provided of a place a little more honest, how be it is but a stable.[90]

Sickness, for such people, could enlarge their world as well as contract it, and this could be true for children living at home. In 1480, William Worcester, the pioneer English antiquarian and traveller, noted down a piece of family history involving his aunt. She was the daughter of Adam Botoner of Coventry, who died there in a visitation of the plague in 1386. Just before he did so, he sent his small daughter Agnes out of harm's way to his brother Thomas in Bristol. The little girl was entrusted to a carrier and brought by him on the journey of 120 miles. She was four years old and lived to tell the tale.[91]

The other great remedy for children's sicknesses was spiritual: prayers, offerings, and pilgrimages. Sometimes prayer alone produced the cure; sometimes ailments responded only to pious actions. In the case of a sick child, its body might be measured and a wax candle of the appropriate length be sent as an offering to a shrine. This was a well-established practice by the twelfth century when it is mentioned in relation to miracles carried out by Thomas Becket and William of Norwich.[92] Benedict of Peterborough tells, for example, how Matilda of London, an unmarried mother with a sick baby, repented of her sin and made a candle of the measure of the baby to offer to St Thomas. Her baby revived and was able to feed at her breast.[93] When Prince Henry fell gravely ill in 1274, measured candles, each two pounds in weight, were sent to the shrines of St Thomas of Canterbury, St Fremund of Dunstable, St Momartre outside Guildford, St James of Reading, St Edward the Confessor and King Henry III at Westminster Abbey, and to one of the parish churches named Stapleford. Once, thirteen poor widows were paid a penny each to spend the night in prayers for the prince. He died, nonetheless, towards the end of October.[94]

In other cases, a personal pilgrimage was needed before a cure was received. Benedict mentions many in his account of miracles performed by Thomas Becket. A boy named Durand, who had a small stone lodged in his ear, could not be healed until he vowed to go to the saint's shrine; as soon as he did so, the stone came out.[95] Guibert of Thanet brought his crippled daughter to Canterbury; she needed a staff to support her on the way. A man of Folkestone came on horseback along with his daughter aged seven; she could not feed herself, having crippled fingers. Both girls were cured at the saint's tomb.[96] The countess of Clare made a pilgrimage barefoot after the recovery of her baby from a hernia; she had prayed to the saint and had, perhaps, promised the journey in recompense.[97] Francis, for his ague, was sent personally with an attendant to St Albans and to the shrine of Sir John Schorne, the unofficial saint of Windsor Chapel.[98]

Some pilgrimage centres did a further service by providing holy water, in which relics of the saint had been washed. Benedict describes how a baker of Canterbury borrowed a garment with the saint's blood on it, washed it in water, and gave the water to his sick boy who recovered in a few days.[99] Eventually, Canterbury water was marketed to pilgrims in small lead bottles. It cured Segiva, a three-year-old girl in Essex, who had got an ear of wheat stuck in her throat, a girl of Shropshire who suffered from insanity, and a knight's son who had been struck down by plague.[100] Its most dramatic effects were experienced by Henry, the ten-year-old son of a knight of Essex, who had long lost his appetite and looked sickly. His first drink brought no results, but his second caused him to vomit up a worm half a cubit in length with other putrid matter. He recovered his strength and the worm was hung up as a sign in his parish church.[101]

But not all gained the cures they sought at shrines. Benedict refers to a crippled boy who slept on Becket's tomb in the hope of a cure, yet the saint appeared to him and told him to go, because he, Thomas, would do nothing for him. A blind boy used the tomb in the same way with a similar lack of result; he died shortly afterwards. Benedict quoted these cases to demonstrate the power of the saint to give or withhold his favours; for the unlucky, the disappointment must have been great.[102]

DEATH

FOR CHILDREN LIKE these, treatment of every kind was a failure; at worst they died at any time from infancy onwards. This was not, of course, the fate of children alone. Death stood close to people of all ages and throughout society, as the greater hazards of life and less effective medicine and surgery led to shorter life expectancy. 'How many infants, daily how many children, how many flowering youths, how many robust young men', cried the preacher John Longland in the 1520s, 'are borne with weeping and great grief to the tomb.'[103] Moralists used such deaths to remind humanity of its frailty and of the need for submission to God's will in matters of life and death. When Caxton translated *The Book of the Knight of the Tower* by Geoffrey de la Tour Landry, he warned his readers that

> Men ought not to rejoice them too much when God sendeth to them children, for oft-time it displeaseth God, which soon taketh therefore his gift again from them.

The *Book* endorsed this statement with a story about a queen of Cyprus who gave birth to a son after a long period of infertility. Her court rejoiced and hailed the event with feasts and jousting, but God regarded these celebrations with disfavour, and the child died.[104]

In the fifteenth century, it became popular to imagine Death as a human corpse or skeleton, drawing people by the hand away from this life. A series of paintings on the subject was displayed in the church of the Holy Innocents, Paris, and widely imitated, notably in England at St Paul's Cathedral. Death was shown summoning everyone in society, from pope, emperor, cardinal, and king, down to minstrels and labourers. Inevitably, one was a child. John Lydgate, who composed verses to go with the pictures at St Paul's, imagined Death calling to it,

> Little infant, that were but late born,
> Shaped in this world to have no pleasance,
> Thou must with other that go here before,
> Be led in haste, by fatal ordinance.
> Learn of new to go on my dance;
> There may none age escape in sooth therefrom.

The child answers,

> A, a, a – a word I can not speak;
> I am so young I was born yesterday.
> Death is so hasty on me to be wreak [*avenged*],
> And list [*will*] no longer to make no delay.
> I came but now, and now I go my way;
> Of me no more no tale shall be told;

The will of God no man withstand may;
As soon dieth a young man as an old.[105]

A century after Lydgate, Hans Holbein made a memorable series of engravings of Death leading off all sorts and conditions of people. He too included the child, this time an older one, dragged from the very hearthside of his home as his horrified mother looks on (Fig. 39).

How many children died? We have already noted the estimated number of births per marriage, between 1540 and 1599, as ranging from 2.9 to 3.5. In the same period, a detailed study of twelve English parishes, based on informative parish registers, has suggested a large degree of infant and child mortality by modern standards, though less so than in the late seventeenth and early eighteenth centuries. Of every thousand children born in this late-Tudor period, 270 (27%, just over a quarter), died during the first year of life. Another 124 (12.4%, half as many) died aged between one and four, and a further 59 (about 6%) between five and nine. Altogether, therefore, 425 children died before they were ten (42.5%). Boys were more vulnerable than girls. In the first year of life, 148 boys might die compared with 127 girls. From the age of one to four, the balance was 65 boys to 59 girls; thereafter it was equal. The longer one survived, the better one's chances of reaching adulthood. Altogether, the expectation of life at birth in this period ranged between 27 and 41 years.[106]

These figures do not apply to the middle ages, of course, in which conditions changed from year to year and place to place. Medieval child mortality, however, was probably of at least a similar order, and this presumption is supported by studying the the royal family. About 96 children were born to the kings and queens of England between 1150 and 1500, counting Henry IV and Richard III who fathered their children before they came to the throne.[107] This is an approximate total, because records of royal births do not mention all the stillbirths and infants who died at birth, although some of these can be conjectured from gaps in the sequence of those who survived. About 34 of the 96 died in their first year. Eleven did so between the ages of one and ten, and a further eleven between that age and twenty. Three of the latter group were victims of violence during the Wars of the Roses, including the two princes in the Tower. Forty, less than half, reached their twenties, despite the better standards of living and medical care available to children of such status.

Although death came most often in the early years of life, it lurked throughout childhood and adolescence, still taking many by modern standards, in privileged households as well as in poor and deprived ones. Winchester College was the first modern public school in the sense of an endowed boarding establishment. It was founded by William of Wykeham in 1382 for seventy boy-scholars, aged between eight and eighteen (Fig. 40). Nominally, they were poor enough to need assistance with their education; in fact, they came mostly from families of gentry, rural yeomanry, and prosperous townspeople. Their accommodation and food were fairly good by contemporary standards and so, for most of the time, was their health. Normally, all could expect to survive their schooldays, but peri-

39   Death carries off a young child from a poor cottage, in Holbein's haunting engraving, as its mother cooks a meal.

odically the community was ravaged by epidemics with devastating effects. In 1401, there were at least twelve deaths of scholars, chiefly in April and May, and worse came a generation later. In 1430, nine boys died between April and December, and the toll continued with a further twenty in 1431, six in March alone. The boys suffered again during 1434, when eleven of them died, chiefly in August and September, and four more perished in August 1436. Altogether, at least 111

40   Winchester College, its founder, clergy, and scholars in the fifteenth century. Well provided
though they appear, a substantial number died while staying there.

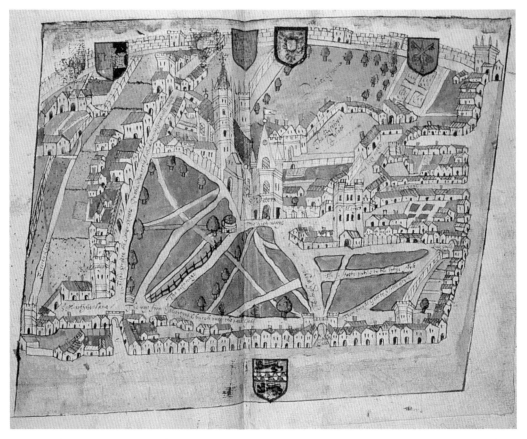

41   A landscape of death. Exeter Cathedral cemetery (criss-crossed by paths) in the sixteenth century, played in by children and traversed each day by the choristers.

scholars died in Winchester College between 1393 and 1471, when records of deaths were kept, including John Kent whose brass has already been pictured (Fig. 26). A number of others left the place, we are told, 'on account of their infirmity'.[108]

Death came visually into children's lives as well as pathologically. Some lived by cemeteries, or used them as open spaces for meeting and play, especially in towns. A few, who served as choristers or parish clerks, were professionally involved with death. The choristers of Exeter Cathedral in Devon lived in a house at the west end of the nave. This, however, was only their dormitory. During the day, they walked about the cathedral close, visiting the church for services, the song school for teaching, and the canons' houses for meals, each boy being fed in the house of the canon to whom he belonged. One of the functions of the cathedral and its close was to be a necropolis, an abode of the dead. The open ground that is now the cathedral green was then the cemetery of the city, where most local people were buried (Fig. 41). New graves were constantly dug within it, and the bones of previous burials, disturbed in this process, were gathered into a charnel house which stood near the choristers' dwelling.

The boys lived in this landscape. They passed the charnel and traversed the graveyard on most of their journeys each day. When they entered the cathedral, they trod a floor that was paved with the gravestones of canons. They walked by effigies of bishops and knights on altar-tombs. By 1500, two of these grander effigies were 'cadavers': stone representations of corpses, expressing the humility of their owners and warning the living to prepare for their own deaths. Sometimes the choristers attended funerals, when these were of wealthy people able to pay for a large number of clergy and singers; at other times they were present at 'obit' masses, commemorating the dead on their anniversaries. In the early sixteenth century, they ended the day by going to the west doors of the cathedral and singing an anthem facing the grave of Laurence Dobell, a cleric who left money for this to be done.[109]

How did such children cope with the closeness of illness and death? They have left no diaries or letters that deal with the subject, but a source exists in the early sixteenth century which casts some light on the matter. This is a set of passages for translation from English to Latin, written at Magdalen College School (Oxford), a grammar school intended (like Winchester) for boys in their teens from relatively prosperous families. The passages may have been written by a schoolmaster or a pupil, but whichever is the case, they reflect topics of interest to schoolboys. Four of them deal with epidemics and their consequences. In one, a pupil says that he has met a countryman skilled at foretelling the weather. His friend replies,

> I would God thou had asked that fellow that made himself so wise of things to come, what he perceived of this year: whether he thought it should be a year of health or of sickness.[110]

In another passage, a pupil complains that he missed a good deal of school last year,

> by the reason of sickness that continued here in the town. God give grace that it begin not again this [year].[111]

In a third, the falling ill of two pupils immediately raises fears of an epidemic:

> There be two scholars in our house that be very sick in their stomachs, of the which one wits [attributes] all his disease to the eating of a herring, the other knows not the cause of his disease. God grant they both escape their sickness and recover, for if it fortune them to die, their death will make not only us but many others to flee from the university.[112]

The alarm turns out to be a false one:

> Our scholars that we took such great heaviness for the last day be recovered, thanked be God, and therefore see that, when thou comest again, thou bring

thy school fellows, as many as be left at home with [thee] to school, for here is
no jeopardy to be afraid of.[113]

Clearly, rumour of illness were likely to trigger absences, at first from the school
and eventually from Oxford itself.

Epidemics and death, then, were factors of life, but we should not overestimate
their impact. Like theft or violence today, they had to be taken into account in
managing one's life, but they were not so powerful as to blot out everything else.
Medieval children experienced death more often than most of their modern successors: among neighbours, friends, and family. But life contained much else by
way of companionship, religion, education, work, and play. The choristers of
Exeter crossed a cemetery that doubled as the main recreational area of the surrounding city, a function shared by many other graveyards. People met, talked,
fought, and played games above the dead. A funeral had its wake and, for the
rich, its splendours of dress, hospitality, and almsgiving. In 1266, John son of
Hugh de Lodey and Henry son of Thomas of Duloe, both young people, went
to 'play' at the vigil of a dead man at Duloe in the parish of Eaton Socon (Beds.).
After a time, they left the house and played outside, falling into a pit where Henry
was stabbed by John's knife.[114]

Christianity also preached a message of hope: salvation, resurrection, and
eternal life with God. Far more tombs of wealthy people showed them in the
splendour of life than in the decay of death. Each day, the Exeter choristers
passed an outdoor statue of the Saviour Jesus, close to their house, and if they
had looked carefully at the cadaver of Canon William Sylke in the cathedral, they
would have seen behind it a painting of Christ's resurrection. Death was a pre-
occupation of the middle ages, as it was of the Renaissance, but only one of
many: a single strand of the rope of human concerns.

FUNERALS AND MONUMENTS

THE CHURCH RECEIVED all Christians for burial: everyone that is, except for
unbaptised infants, suicides, and those excommunicated.[115] Baptised children
were therefore treated like adults. When Prince Henry died at Guildford in 1274,
aged seven and a quarter, his heart was removed (in the manner often done to
important people) and buried in the local Dominican friary. The rest of his body
was wrapped in waxed cloth, put into a feretory or coffin, and taken to Westminster for burial. The citizens of London met his funeral procession to escort it
to the abbey. Masses were said for his soul in Guildford church and at Merton
Priory nearby.[116] Other royal children were buried with similar care, usually at
Westminster and with public ceremonies. Two infant children of Henry's sister
Elizabeth, Mary and Humphrey Bohun, had funerals and burials there in
1304–5.[117] In 1496, Henry VII's daughter Elizabeth, aged four, was brought from
Eltham and buried on the north side of the shrine of Edward the Confessor. Four
years later, her brother Edmund, aged just over a year, died at Hatfield and was

given a funeral like that of Prince Henry. His body was conveyed on a carriage, honourably attended. The duke of Buckingham acted as chief mourner, and the lord mayor and the guildsmen of London stood in their liveries as the cortège passed. Edmund too was laid by Edward's shrine.[118]

Royal children were exceptional in their status, but there is no reason to suppose that that they were unusual in being carefully buried. Some of the earliest references to children's funerals occur in the 'obit accounts' of Exeter Cathedral, between 1305 and 1327.[119] Every lay person in Exeter had to be taken to the cathedral for his or her funeral, and most were buried in its cemetery. The accounts inform us, for example, that the son of Robert de Neweton had a funeral in 1307, the son of Sir Henry de Bodrugan and the child of Walter Tauntifer in 1308, Thomas son of Thomas Baker in 1309, the son of Cheyne in 1316, and the son of O. de Haccombe in 1317.[120] A later and fuller record, the churchwardens' accounts of Lambeth (Surrey) which survive from 1504, lists the profits of the wax left from candles offered at funerals in the church or burnt around the corpse. In one typical period from March 1504 to March 1505, wax-money was received in respect of seventeen children's funerals and of the anniversary of the 'Barbon children'. The sums were usually small ones of 2d., but rose to 8d. in two cases and 9d. for 'Grene's child' – the higher amounts matching those recorded for adults.[121]

An Oxford source enables us to glimpse the whole cost of the funeral of a child of middling rank. In 1508, the boy-servant of the rector of Lincoln College fell ill in an epidemic and died, despite the purchase of 'treacle' (medicine) to cure him and the hiring of a nurse to look after him for two nights and two days. The college then spent 1s. 2½d. on laying him to rest. This included money for 'watching candles' to burn around his corpse overnight, ringing the bells of the parish church of All Saints, making an offering at his requiem mass, providing a shroud, and paying for the making of his grave.[122] His was evidently a modest funeral, but even this sum would have strained the resources of poor families, for whom a burial sheet, a grave, and minimal prayers may have been all that was feasible. The rich, on the other hand, could add whatever they wanted in the form of candles, offerings, masses of intercession, charity to the poor, and food and drink for guests. Funeral expenses of children in the seventeenth century mention the consumption of beer or wine, bread, cakes, and other victuals, depending on status, and such hospitality is likely to have been a traditional practice.[123]

The burials of infants gave rise to one or two special customs. A baby that died before its mother's churching was often buried in its chrisom cloth and was known as a 'chrisom child', a term that continued after the Reformation when babies were no longer anointed with chrism.[124] In some parishes, it was apparently also the practice for the clergyman to claim, as a fee, the 'bearing sheet' in which an older infant or child was wrapped for its funeral. This was an extension of the custom by which, when an adult died, his or her best robe was given to the clergyman as a 'mortuary' fee. In 1514, Richard Hunne, a London merchant taylor, refused the demand of the rector of St Mary's Whitechapel for the bearing sheet of his baby son Stephen. The baby had lived for only five weeks, and Hunne, who held radical religious views, argued that as an infant it had no property and could therefore owe no mortuary. A legal battle followed in the Church courts which ended in Hunne's arrest for heresy and his death in the bishop of London's prison, a death widely reckoned as murder.[125] The scandal helped to bring about a change in the law, and in 1529 an act of parliament forbade any clergyman to demand a mortuary fee for a child.[126]

Children in medieval England, like their elders, were normally buried in churchyards beneath shallow mounds. The mounds had no permanence or lasting memorials, because the ground was constantly re-used for burials, especially in towns. Children's graves might be scattered among those of the adults, or clustered in one spot. The Anglo-Saxons sometimes placed them beneath the eaves of the church; some later cemeteries reveal groups of graves at the east or west ends of the building.[127] Burial inside churches was restricted to adults and children of rank: clergy, nobility, gentry, merchants. These indoor graves were more permanent, and were often identified by monuments. Richard, son of the duke of Clarence, who died aged three months in the 1470s, was laid to rest in front of the high altar of Reading Abbey.[128] The Greyfriars' church in London, a list of whose tombs was made in the early-Tudor period, housed several that appear to be of children, buried either with parents or by themselves.[129] Most such monuments to children were probably flat ledger stones, sometimes inlaid with a monumental brass.[130] The earliest brass of a child consists of a simple cross and inscription in Westminster Abbey to Margaret, daughter of William of Valence, who died in 1276. The first to display an image of children is to be found in the church of Sherborne St John (Hants.), and may date from about 1360. It was erected in memory of Raulin and Margaret Brocas, possibly the son and daughter of Sir Bernard Brocas (d. 1395).[131]

A few more brasses of individual children survive from the late fourteenth, fifteenth, and early sixteenth centuries, but they are not common. Some represent babies in chrisom robes, such as Elyn Bray of Stoke d'Abernon (Surrey) in 1516, signifying that they died before their mothers were churched (Fig. 35).[132] Others show them in swaddling clothes, demonstrating that they lived little longer, like Thomas Greville of Stanford Rivers (Essex), who died 'in his tender age' in 1492.[133] There are brasses of older children too. One, of Anne Boleyn who did not quite reach her fourth birthday in 1479, has already been mentioned.[134] Three exist of boys in their teens: John Kent, scholar of Winchester College (d. 1434), John Stonor (d. 1512), and Thomas Heron (d. 1517) (Figs. 26, 42).[135] More elaborate tombs, in the form of altars with or without effigies upon them, are rarer still, but they were occasionally built for royal children. Four offspring of Henry III and two of Edward I were buried in a single marble altar-tomb, decorated with precious stones, in the south choir-aisle of Westminster Abbey. Edward III's daughter Blanche (d. c.1341) and his son William of Windsor (d. 1348) shared a second tomb-chest in the abbey, and this is exceptional in displaying their effigies. The tomb of their brother William of Hatfield (d. 1344), with a small alabaster figure on it, may still be seen in York Minster.[136]

Were such monuments a sign of affection by parents? They may have been,

42 Remembering a son. The memorial brass of John Stonor (d. 1512), in Wraysbury church (Bucks.).

because even the great and famous grieved for dead children. Katherine, daughter of Henry III and Eleanor of Provence, died in 1257 at the age of three and a half. She was a disabled child who could not speak, but Matthew Paris called her 'fair of face' and told how her mother grieved so much at her death that she became ill and could find no comfort in medicine nor human consolation.[137] In 1286–7, Eleanor of Castile gave a gold cloth to the Dominican friars of Bordeaux to keep the anniversary of her daughter, a child otherwise unknown to history who had died close to birth over twenty years before.[138] But monuments also expressed other notions. Sons and daughters, as we have seen, were proof of their fathers' virility, mothers' fertility, and family strength. The tomb or brass of a child was a sign that it came from a rich and important family. Elyn Bray's proclaims that she was the daughter of Sir Edmund Bray, knight; Anne Boleyn's displays her family coat of arms. Indeed, the very rarity of such monuments conveyed the special status of those they commemorated.

It followed that their absence too was no indication of a lack of affection for a child or of failure to recognise its individuality. A child beneath an unmarked churchyard mound might be as deeply mourned and as fondly remembered. Peter of Cornwall wrote with tenderness about the death of his niece in infancy, still wearing her chrisom, on virtually the same day as her grandfather. They were buried together, the girl between his legs.[139] The London chronicler, probably Andrew Horn, who recorded the birth of Horn's son 'J.' in 1305, noted with equal care his lifespan of twelve weeks and his burial in Colmanchurch near Aldgate.[140] In an Oxford schoolbook of the 1490s, a schoolboy tells how,

43   A burial, with child servers assisting at the last rites.

'A great while after my brother died, my mother was wont to sit weeping every day. I trow [*am sure*] that there is nobody which would not be sorry if he had seen her weeping.'[141]

The fact that so many children died did not necessarily lighten the pain of their loss for their parents.

THE AFTERLIFE

MEDIEVAL PEOPLE BROODED on life after death and had vivid mental maps of its geography: hell, purgatory, and heaven. Sorrow at losing children in this life might be deepened by fears of their fate in the next. Baptism was meant to give reassurance here. As Gregory the Great remarked in his *Dialogues*, 'we ought not to doubt but believe that all infants that are baptised and die in their infancy go to heaven'.[142] Their souls were free of their original sin and had not yet been sullied by new ones. But the question then arose how long the effects of baptism lasted. Gregory thought not long: once we can speak, we can sin. He told the tale of a boy of five, badly brought up by his parents and accustomed to utter God's name blasphemously. Plague broke out, the boy fell sick, and he saw dark men like Moors approach to take him away. In vain, he called to his father, 'Keep them off!', and died cursing God. Plainly, a child so young might go to hell.[143]

Some people in the early middle ages had similar concerns about children's sins. Early penitential treatises lay down penances for boys, probably meaning boys dedicated to the monastic life, indicating a belief that their sins needed to be paid for. In the late eleventh century, St Anselm imagined a young monk who had died being charged by the Devil with the sins he had committed after his baptism, before he entered the monastery as a boy or a youth.[144] Mannyng retold Gregory's story of the blaspheming boy as late as 1303, but by this time the Church had changed its view of sin.[145] During the twelfth century, children before puberty came to be seen as lacking the mental and physical capacity of adults. This meant that their sins were regarded as less serious, and their baptisms sufficient to atone for any they committed. In 1215, the Church obliged people to confess their sins to a priest, but only when they reached the age of discretion, effectively the early teens.[146] Only after that age was there a balance sheet, as it were, by which sins had to be paid for by penances or works of merit in this world and, if not in this world, by pain in the next. St Thomas Aquinas believed that, in consequence, those who died as children would not be called to account at the Last Judgment. They would attend merely as spectators, to behold the glory of Christ.[147]

This did not prevent people worrying about the fate of dead children, baptised or not. A story told how Bishop Bartholomew of Exeter (1161–84), was awakened at night while staying in a house near a country church, by the voices of innumerable infants in the churchyard. They were wailing 'Woe to us! Woe to us! Who will now pray for us, and give alms or celebrate masses for our souls?'

It turned out that a worthy local man had just died, who was accustomed to care for orphans and maintained a priest to pray for the dead.[148] These were apparently baptised souls; they should have needed no prayers, yet someone felt that they did. A need for reassurance about the fate of dead children emerges from Chaucer's 'Summoner's Tale', about a hypocritical friar who visits the home of a wealthy peasant and his wife. On learning that the couple's child has died within the last two weeks, the humbug hastens to soothe them about its salvation. 'I saw a vision of the child', he asserts, 'being carried to heaven within half an hour of its death. Two other friars saw it too. I went weeping to church, and we all sang *Te Deum* in thanks.'[149]

The fate of the unbaptised provoked still greater fears. St Augustine believed that the souls of all such infants were condemned to hell, by virtue of their original sin, and this became the orthodox view in medieval times. Ælfric, as we have seen, grieved that a baby killed at birth would go to hell, 'a loathsome heathen'.[150] Scholars came to identify the destination of unchristened children as *limbus inferni*, meaning a place on 'the edge of hell' yet still a part of that region (Fig. 44). Here their souls were spared the physical pains endured by wilful sinners, but they enjoyed no hope of salvation and might feel anguish from losing it.[151] This fate applied to stillborn children too. Although a foetus was believed to acquire a soul at about the age of forty days, or eighty for a girl, the Church did not regard a foetus as a complete body until it was born. It was therefore not capable of being reborn by baptism, and the christening of an unborn child was forbidden. Even during the dangers of delivery, a child could not be baptised until at least its head had emerged from the womb, so that those dying before this point were necessarily unbaptised.[152] Burial practices paralleled these beliefs. By 1400, stillborn children and unbaptised infants were not allowed a grave in consecrated ground, since they were not Christian, and they had to be buried outside.[153] All this gave cold comfort to parents coming to terms with the loss of such a child, anxious to give it decent burial, and yearning that its soul might be united with those of its family in heaven.

Some writers tried to mitigate such bleakness. William Lyndwood, the fifteenth-century English canon lawyer, suggested that a child in the womb might be sanctified by a special privilege from God, though it should always be baptised if born.[154] He was probably alluding to baptism by the Holy Spirit, a possibility widely discussed in the later middle ages.[155] The notion was suggested by the words ascribed in the gospels to John the Baptist: that he baptised with water but that someone after him (meaning Jesus) would baptise with the Holy Spirit.[156] Such a concept helped to explain how God would deal with good pagans, as well as with innocent children. A variant of the theory, that baptism could be done by an angel on God's instruction, is found in the writings of John de Burgh and of Lyndwood, who quoted Thomas Aquinas in its favour.[157] When people like these wished to soften the hard edges of Church doctrine, it is not surprising that the unorthodox did so too. The first great English challenger of orthodoxy, John Wycliffe, questioned whether an unbaptised child was incapable of salvation in his *Trialogus* (c.1382) – a proposition immediately attacked by his opponents but

44 The afterlife: a fifteenth-century English map of the underworld. Hell is at the bottom, and above it the abodes of uncircumcised Jewish children, unbaptised Christian children, and the patriarchs of the Old Testament.

influential among his supporters.[158] From then until the Reformation, we find
some of Wycliffe's Lollard followers declaring that it was not necessary to baptise
a child to save it. A child of Christian parents would be saved by grace in the
womb.[159]

Other people sought to get round the problem of the unbaptised by actions
rather than by reasoning. Sometimes, it seems, infants were christened when born
dead, in the hope of ensuring their salvation. Henry Bracton, writing in the thirteenth century, made a baby's legal birth dependent on its uttering a cry. Baptism
and burial as a Christian, he observed, were not a reliable guide because midwives were accustomed to say that children were born alive when this was not
so.[160] Those in charge of the birth of John, the son of Robert de Bokland of
Elmore (Gloucs.), towards the end of the same century, thought he had died at
birth but they baptised him nonetheless; only later did it become apparent that
he was alive.[161] When Emma de Hereford was crushed in a crowd at Oxford in
1300, giving birth to a stillborn child, an inquest into his death found that he died
in his mother's womb, but the fact that he had a name – Roger – suggests that
he too had been christened.[162] The rule excluding stillborn children from consecrated ground was not always followed, either. Most churchyards were easily
accessible, enabling babies to be buried under cover of darkness. That this happened is shown by a royal licence of 1389, allowing Hereford Cathedral to sur-
round its precinct and cemetery with walls and gates, locked at night. One of the
reasons given was to stop secret burials of unbaptised children.[163] A glimpse of
such a burial occurs in a Church-court case in London in 1493. Alice Wanten,
of the parish of St Nicholas in the Shambles, had been beaten while pregnant
by John Russell, causing her to give birth to a dead child. Then, the court was
told, the midwife ordered Agnes Coge to bury the child illegally in Pardon
Churchyard.[164]

Sometimes parents may have thought that prayers could save an unbaptised
child, although theologically this was not possible. A Latin folk tale of about 1400,
preserved in a manuscript of Byland Abbey (Yorks.), centres on the ability of a
human being to reverse a failure of baptism after the child had died. It tells
how a man from Cleveland in Yorkshire named Richard Rountre left his
pregnant wife at home, and went on a pilgrimage to Compostella in Spain. One
night, he and his fellow-travellers camped in a wood near a highway and took
turns to keep watch. While Richard was doing so, he heard a great noise of travellers going along the road: some on horses, others on sheep and cattle. These
were ghosts, riding to the next world on the animals which they had given the
Church as their mortuary fees. After these came a baby, tumbling along in a shoe.
He addressed it, and asked why it travelled in such a way. The baby answered,
'I am your son, abortive and buried without baptism or name.' Hearing this, the
father took off his shirt. He wrapped the baby in it, invoked the Trinity, and gave
it a name.

The baby, exulted, stood up on its feet, and sped away behind the other ghosts.
This, presumably, was because it was now free of its obligations to the Church.
Not only was it baptised but, by receiving the father's shirt, it was provided with

45 The afterlife: another view.
The *Pearl* poet sees his daughter
beyond the river of death, transformed into a mature woman
living in heaven.

the Church's burial fee. The shoe was left behind and the father retrieved it. When
he reached home, the midwives confessed that the baby had died unbaptised and
that they had buried it in the shoe. The story is such an attractive parable of the
triumph of lay devotion over law and doctrine that one is loath to admit that it
may not be wholly serious. It ends with the narrator pointing out that the father,
by baptising his son, had become its godfather. You could not marry your child's
godparent, and the husband and wife were obliged to get divorced! This was not
true in practice – emergency baptism by a parent was allowable when no one
else was at hand – so we may be dealing with a story that deliberately aimed to
tease and upset normal usages.[165]

We dream of those the dead we have known, and so did our ancestors. Peter
of Cornwall recounts at length a family tradition about a dream of his grandfather Ailsi in the early twelfth century. Ailsi's son Pagan died when twelve or so,
causing his father to ponder the nature of the next world with some fear for his
own and his son's prospects in it. One night, he dreamed that he was going on a
pilgrimage to Jerusalem with a group of travellers. Descending from a mountain,
they entered a valley thick with cloud where Ailsi lost his companions and wan-

dered alone. Reaching a river, he was amazed to be greeted by his dead son. Pagan explained that God had sent him to give consolation, and (despite their disproportionate sizes) took his father upon his back and flew with him over the river. They passed a place where souls were suffering, apparently in purgatory, and then crossed the valley of hell where demons threw firebrands at them. Finally, they reached a beautiful plain that was paradise. Pagan told his father that he himself now lived there, and that Ailsi would come there one day. Ailsi replied that he wished to stay there immediately, but the dream ended and his son disappeared. It was a disturbing dream, with its visions of horrors, and not altogether a reassuring one. Ailsi would reach paradise and be reunited with his son, but he must first endure pain in purgatory for the sins of his life.[166]

Two hundred years afterwards, in the late fourteenth century, a poet wrote an account of what he claimed to be a similar dream.[167] He described how he went to a garden where he lost a precious pearl, which rolled from a grassy mound into the earth. Only later are we made aware that the pearl was his infant daughter and the mound her grave. Distressed by the loss of the pearl, he laid his head on the mound and fell asleep. He dreamed that he wandered through a beautiful countryside to the banks of a stream. On the opposite side sat a child whom he knew: a maiden of courteous and gentle bearing. It was his daughter, dressed in white and wearing a crown of pearls (Fig. 45). She told him that Jesus had taken her to be his bride and crowned her as a queen. How could this be, asked the poet, when she lived for less than two years, and never learnt even her Paternoster and Creed? She reminded him of Christ's parable of the labourers in the vineyard. God rewards all equally at the end of the day, no matter how long they have worked.[168]

The poet wished to cross the stream to his child, but she warned him that this was impossible until he died. She had secured permission, however, for him to glimpse the place where she now lived. They walked up the stream to a vantage point from whence a city could be seen in the distance. It was built of gold and gems, and lit by the light of God. In it stood the Lamb of God, praised by the host of heaven, including his 'little queen'. The poet was so ravished by the sight that he tried to enter the water, but he awoke as he did so. Left once more in this world, 'the dungeon of sorrow', he expressed his thanks to the pearl for his vision and the reassurance that it gave him. Resigning himself to God's will, he acknowledged that God was his friend and committed his child to Him. Here, sorrow led to comfort. The poem, that we now call *Pearl*, dwells on none of the horrors of the afterlife, only on the assurance of God's greatness and mercy. Grace and faith heal grief, and the offer of heaven is made to us all.

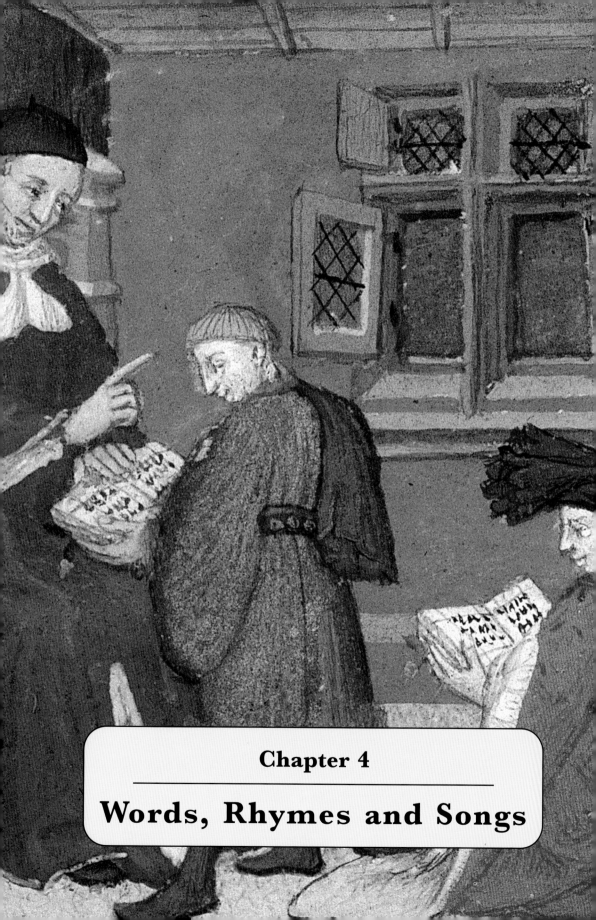

Chapter 4
Words, Rhymes and Songs

BABY TALK

WE CRY AS we enter the world, filling our lungs with air and announcing our coming as beings with selves and needs. For the first few months of life, we communicate largely with cries – cries for different reasons, often of different kinds. Hunger, cold, wind, boredom, or need for contact, all are expressed by cries. Yet, from the moment we are born, we are spoken to. We listen, and after about two months we start to copy what we hear. We still cry, but we experiment with sociable babbling and cooing. We do this all over the world, and there is little to distinguish the sounds we make from one country or language to another. Our first attempts to talk are made with vowels, 'aah', and 'ooh'. Next we add consonants, beginning with the lip sounds 'b', 'p', and 'm', and make single syllables, 'ba' and 'ma'. Later still we double the syllables and vary them; at last, usually after some ten or eleven months, we produce our first real words in the language of those around us. We now speak English, French, or Japanese.

All this is natural, and must have happened in medieval England in a manner and time-frame similar to those of today. There is no need to look for evidence to establish the fact, which is just as well since there are few contemporary references to infants' sounds and words. Moralists, hearing babies cry, sometimes reflected that they were expressing the sorrows of the human race. The fate of women after the fall of Eve was to bear children in sorrow, and 'the child at its birth', observed a twelfth-century writer, 'suffereth also bitter throes, and cometh at a doleful time into a grim habitation, and that it showeth by its weeping.'[1] Babies appear to make the sound of 'wa', which is not very distant from 'woe', and two or three fifteenth-century songs about the murder of the Innocents in Bethlehem imagined how 'The children of Israel cried "wa, wa"', as they met their fate at the hands of King Herod's soldiers.[2]

Another early infant noise is 'ba'. Song writers depicted the infant Jesus saying 'ba-bay' to his mother and her saying 'by, by' to him in return.[3] This syllable had more pleasant associations, since 'ba' was a word for kissing and its use expressed the loving relationship of Mary and her son. A third sound, 'da', is the same as the word for 'give!' in Latin. An Oxford schoolmaster of about 1380 built a joke on this in a model letter which taught a pupil how to write to his father for more money. Ever since he was an infant, says the son, he has had to speak with the same voice, like the cuckoo, 'Da! da! da!', and that is the song that he is obliged to sing now.[4]

Adults who speak to babies use baby-talk, mixing words with sounds like babies make. The practice may be as old as *Homo sapiens*, and it was noticed in the mid thirteenth century by Bartholomew in his encyclopaedia. Describing the duties of a nurse, he observes that she 'stammers and, as it were, breaks her speech as if to teach [the child] to speak more easily'.[5] As John Trevisa puts it in his translation of 1398, she 'whilispeth and semisouneth the words, to teach the more easily the child that cannot speak'.[6] 'Semisoun' means 'to talk quietly' and 'whilisp' is the old form of 'lisp'; both writers therefore imply that nurses spoke baby-language. Bartholomew was a broad-minded friar who not only noticed the habit but

46   Sir Thomas Elyot, the leading educationist of Henry VIII's reign. Though friendly to children in some respects, he deplored the use of baby-talk by nurses.

approved it as helpful to a child's development. That feeling was not shared by everyone. Sir Thomas Elyot (Fig. 46), the author of *The Governor*, a famous book on education published in 1531, described those using baby-talk as 'foolish women'. He criticised the custom as 'a wantonness, whereby divers noblemen's and gentlemen's children (as I do at this day know) have attained corrupt and foul pronunciation'. Nurses and other servants in charge of the young, he urged, should take care to speak proper English: 'clean, polite, perfectly and articulately pronounced, omitting no letter or syllable'.[7]

There can be little doubt that Bartholomew's views came closer to those of mothers and nurses than did Elyot's. Baby-talk continued; indeed, a few words in the English language come from sounds that infants make or adults copy. One is 'baby' itself, first recorded in English as *baban* in the early thirteenth century, and now also current in France (*bébé*), the French having borrowed it from the English in Georgian times.[8] Another may be 'pap', meaning the nipple of the breast and the infant's porridge.[9] Two more are found in the familiar names for our parents: 'dad' or 'daddy' and 'mam' or 'mamma'.[10] 'Mamma' is first recorded in a miracle story of the late fifteenth century. A woman of Stoneleigh (Warks.) came back to her house to find it on fire and her two-year-old son shouting 'Mamme, mamme' inside.[11] 'Mame', 'dadd', and 'daddye' all occur in a 1592 manuscript of the Chester play of 'Cain and Abel', in the mouth of the grown-up but churlish and rustic Cain.[12] Both words may be much older than these instances, escaping record because they were so colloquial.

Children are fascinated by their bodies, and adults often base their talk with them on body parts: pointing to them, naming them, and playing with them. There were medieval names for the fingers – thumb, toucher or lick-pot, longman or middlemast, leche or leche-man, and little-man – which must have been learnt by children, perhaps in a list or rhyme.[13] A further fragment of medieval baby-talk, real or imitated by adults, is the phrase 'handy-dandy', which arose from hand-play between adults and little children. An adult held out two hands to a child with an object in one of them. The hands were closed, the object was passed from one hand to the other, and the child had to guess which hand it was in. In due course, the words passed from the game to mean a secret payment slipped, as it were, in closed hands, and in this sense it turns up in Langland's *Piers Plowman*, in the late fourteenth century.[14] We possess this piece of talk only because it became a saying of adults.

Bartholomew noticed that babies are soothed with songs as well as aroused with talk. Adults, he says, sing to them in a soft voice or, in Trevisa's translation, 'sing lullings and other cradle songs' to comfort their babies; they 'please the child with whistling and songs when he shall sleep'.[15] This too is an ancient practice. The Romans had a name *lalla* for a song to send a child to sleep, and a verb *lallare* meaning 'to sing such a song'. There were similar words in English by the four-teenth century, 'lulla' for the song and 'to lull' for the verb, 'lulla' becoming 'lullaby' in the Tudor period through the addition of the syllable 'by' with its kissing associations.[16] No real lullabies survive from medieval England, but there are lyrics that copy their form. Poets, by the fourteenth century, liked to imagine the Virgin Mary singing to the infant Jesus, and to create a sense of pathos by making Mary or Jesus contemplate the suffering that awaited them. Some twenty-two such lyrics are currently known, in which lullaby words appear as a refrain or chorus.[17]

In one example, the Virgin sings simply 'by, by, lulley'.[18] In another, she repeats the syllables over and over:

> Lullay, lullow, lully, lullay,
> Dewy, bewy, lully, lully,
> Bewy, lully, lullow, lully,
> Lullay, baw, baw, my bairn,
>   Sleep softly now.[19]

In a third song, she mixes the sounds with words:

> Lullay, mine liking, my dear son, mine sweeting,
> Lullay, my dear heart, mine own dear darling,[20]

while in a fourth, she introduces statements and commands:

> Lullay, lullay, my little child,
>> Sleep and be now still;
> If thou be a little child,
>> Yet may thou have thy will.[21]

The business of these lyrics was to put forward ideas about Mary and Jesus, not to be realistic lullabies. There is no reason to think that medieval mothers and nurses sang to their babies only sadly; why should they not have done so teasingly, flatteringly, or ingratiatingly? The Marian lyrics are probably realistic, however, in showing the use of regular phrases – sometimes merely sonorous, sometimes including speech. Such phrases had a recognised format and constitute a little genre of oral literature – one of the earliest that children encountered.

Nor need all the songs sung over infants have been sleepy. One can imagine a mother or a nurse singing about the father, the house, the animals, or what the child might grow up to be or do. No lyric of this kind survives from medieval England, but there is one from Wales which helps to suggest what such songs might have contained. The Welsh song comes from a thirteenth-century manuscript, but its subject and language are far older. It is part of the *Gododdin*, a cycle of poems that appears to originate from the English and Scottish border regions and is traditionally said to have been written by the poet Aneirin in the sixth century. The poems are mostly elegies about a defeat of British warriors by the English at Catterick in Yorkshire, but one of them adopts the manner of a lullaby or cradle song. Its latest editor believes, on linguistic grounds, that it could well date from Aneirin's century or from the first half of the seventh:

> Dinogad's coat is speckled, speckled,
> I made it from martens' pelts –
> Whistle, whistle, a whistling;
> I used to sing to him, the eight slaves used to sing to him.
> When your father would go hunting,
> With the staff on his shoulder and club in his hand,
> He would call his [aggressive?] hounds,
> 'Giff, Gaff, catch! catch! fetch! fetch!'
> He would kill a fish in his coracle,
> As when the [brilliant?] lion slays.
> When your father would go to the mountain,
> He would bring back a roebuck, a wild sow, a stag,
> A speckled grouse from the Falls of Derwennyd.
> Of all that would come against your father and his flesh dart
> – Of wild sows and foxes from the Wood of Llwyfain –
> None would escape if it were not on wings.[22]

Like the Mary and Jesus songs, this is not a realistic copy of what mothers sang to children. It is longer and more elaborate than later English nursery rhymes, and the fact that it was anthologised within the *Gododdin* shows that it had literary status. Its past tense – what the father did rather than does – may be intended poignantly, to remind us that the British warriors left behind widows and orphans. Still, it implies the existence of similar songs, as do the Marian lullabies, and of songs that were optimistic. Like the modern nursery rhyme 'Baby bunting', it describes a father who goes out winning gains or spoils for his family. It is informative about things outside the home – terrain, animals, and hunting – and might, if the child was old enough, fire its imagination. It suggests that far more words and ideas passed between medieval adults and young children than have been recorded.

Lullabies, too, were not the only songs that babies heard. Mothers and nurses of any era may be moved to sing their own favourite lyrics to communicate with their infants or to entertain themselves. One fourteenth-century sermon writer states that they did so then. He tells us how, when mothers place their children in the cradle, 'they lull the child with their foot and sing an old song, saying thus:

> Watch well, Annot,
> Thy maiden bower,
> And get thee from Walterot,
> For he is lecher.'[23]

Annot ('little Agnes') and the lecherous Walterot ('little Walter') can hardly be characters in a lullaby. Rather, the words must be part of an adult song in which Agnes is seduced by Walter or is told that he has bad intentions towards her. Children would have overheard the songs of their elders from their earliest years; we shall presently see that they learnt and adopted them too.

CHILDREN'S RHYMES AND SONGS

WHEN WE GROW out of infancy, in our second or third years, our involvement with adult speech becomes more complex. This is the age of the nursery rhyme involving a story, a dialogue between adult and child, or a form of play between the two. 'Nursery rhymes' first occurs as a phrase in the early nineteenth century, perhaps in Ann and Jane Taylor's *Rhymes for the Nursery* (1806), which contained their famous composition 'Twinkle, twinkle, little star'. The title of the book appeared on the spine as *Nursery Rhymes*, and this has become the usual term for songs and rhymes associated with children. In America, they are also known as 'Mother Goose rhymes', probably due to the influence of another seminal work, *Mother Goose's Melody*, 'or Sonnets for the Cradle', first published in London in 1781.[24]

'Nursery rhymes' is useful as a phrase. Not all families have ever had nurses or nurseries, but the term implies younger children up to about the age of seven, and that is the audience which most of the rhymes address. Most (though not all) of

47   Children's literature began in the cradle, with the songs sung by their mothers, nurses, and rockers.

the pieces are indeed in rhyme. But the phrase can be misleading too. It suggests that nursery rhymes are solely childish – meant for children. As the Opies, the greatest modern students of the subject, have observed, they are rhymes 'preserved by the nursery' rather than 'coming from the nursery'.[25] Some, like lullabies, were indeed produced by adults for children of nursery age. Many others, however, are pieces by adults for adults. They are proverbs, verses, or scraps of songs that circulated first among grown-up people, and passed to children only later on.

'Nursery rhymes' also conveys, in our own times, a sense of quality and respectability. The term arose in a period when people were beginning to collect and publish rhymes for adults to use with children, or for children to read for themselves. The first such anthology was *Tommy Thumb's Pretty Song Book*, published at London in about 1744 and now extant only in a single incomplete copy in the British Library.[26] It printed children's rhymes already in use and was soon followed by other books, some similar like *Mother Goose's Melody* and others (like Ann and Jane Taylor's) containing specially-written poems. Since 1744, collections of new or traditional rhymes have become very common, and they have had two effects on the subject. First of all, they have caused the texts of nursery rhymes to become frozen. Before there were anthologies, the rhymes tended to vary a good deal because they passed about largely by word of mouth and were frequently altered. Once they were put into print, particular versions tended to be regarded as standard and orthodox. It would be hard nowadays to alter the accepted words of 'Hey diddle diddle', 'Jack and Jill', or 'Little Miss Muffet'.

Secondly, a gap has opened up between the rhymes that have got into the books and those that have not. Rhymes like the ones just mentioned have become classics of English literature, honoured by critics, illustrated by artists, and scrutinised for meaning by folklorists. Our concept of rhymes for young children is coloured by them. But children have never restricted themselves to such rhymes. They overhear and adopt many songs and sayings of their elders, most of which do not gain status as nursery rhymes or attract the attention of anthologists. As soon as children come into contact with siblings and other boys and girls, they meet other kinds of material: chants, rhymes, sayings, and parodies that are silly, satirical, or rude; ancient, modern, or original. This 'playground' or 'street' material was largely ignored by collectors and scholars until the Opies examined its manifestations in their book *The Lore and Language of School Children* (1959). Its pieces are still not generally thought of as nursery rhymes.

The middle ages differed in this respect. There were no published volumes of children's rhymes or songs, and those that circulated among the young cannot always be classified as 'adult' or 'child' in origin, or as 'nursery' or 'street' in character. It is therefore better to forget the concept 'nursery rhymes', with its modern connotations, before the eighteenth century. All we can do, further back in the past, is to trace the rhymes that were used with children or by children. This leads us through a wide range of material. It takes in songs and verses composed by adults for adults, which children copied and kept. It includes not only 'nursery rhymes' as nowadays understood, but 'the lore and language of children', often of an ephemeral and vulgar kind.

That medieval children learnt rhymes and songs, either from adults or from one another, as they have done in recent centuries, is predictable, given the constancy of human nature. John Trevisa, in his translation of Bartholomew, noted that children are 'witty to learn carols', meaning 'clever at learning songs for dancing'.[27] When the Opies first published *The Oxford Dictionary of Nursery Rhymes* in 1951, the standard modern collection, they identified at least seven rhymes which seemed to have medieval records or analogies, including 'Matthew, Mark, Luke, and John', 'Thirty days hath September' and 'I have four sisters beyond the sea'. As many as a quarter of the 550 texts in their dictionary, they thought, were likely to originate before 1599.[28] In 1978, Helen Cooper, a scholar of medieval English literature, pointed to another large body of potential nursery rhymes, which she collected and modernised in an anthology called *Great Grandmother Goose*.[29] Her material came from manuscripts and documentary records, from the thirteenth to the sixteenth centuries. Such sources sometimes contain short poems, single verses, and couplets, jotted down in margins or empty spaces, and often similar in format to the classic nursery rhymes.

The rhymes in Cooper's collection, given below in modernised versions, cover a variety of topics. Some are about animals:

> Clim, clam, the cat leapt over the dam.[30]

> My dame hath in a hutch at home
> A little dog with a clog;
> Hey, dogs, hey.[31]

> The hare went [to] the market, scarlet for to sell;
> The greyhound stood him before, money for to tell.[32]

Others refer to famous people and political events:

> Henry Hotspurs hath a halt,
>   And he is falling lame.
> Francis Physician for that fault
>   Swears he was not to blame.[33]

A third kind consists of practical advice:

> A white horse up the hill,
> A black horse down the hill,
> A gray horse in a gravel way,
> And a brown bay is best at all assay [*whatever the test*].[34]

A fourth looks like a rhyme to say while playing a game, like Grandmother's Steps, in which one person feigns to sleep while others come closer:

> When puckett [is] away, where shall we go play?
> When the puckett is asleep, then may we go sow our wheat.[35]

A fifth category is that of pure nonsense:

> Our dame milked the mare's tail;
>   The cat was licking the pot;
> Our maid came out with a flail,
>   And laid her under foot.

> A cow had stolen a calf away

> And put her in a sack;
> Forsooth, I sell no puddings today,
>   'Masters, what do you lack?'

punctuated, in this song, with the refrain:

> News, news, news, news!
> You never heard so many news![36]

Rhymes like these could all have been used with children. Their relative shortness, range of subjects, and popular rather than literary nature bring them close in character to the classic nursery rhymes of the eighteenth and nineteenth centuries.

Such material, however, raises several problems. We rarely know why it was noted down. Was a particular rhyme a popular piece of the day, or an original composition which did not necessarily become current? Are the rhymes complete or are they odd verses from something which, if we had it all, would turn out to be too big or unsuitable for children? To what literary categories do the rhymes belong? Is 'Clim clam', for example, a proverb (meaning, 'what a catastrophe!'), or a complete short piece to use with infants (perhaps with hand movements), or part of a longer rhyme or song? Most bafflingly, these jotted-down rhymes rarely possess a social context, except that they are written and were therefore current among adults or older children. The only ones to be labelled as 'Children's Songs' are 'When puckett [is] away' and 'My dame', both noted down (and then crossed out) by the Elizabethan scholar Gabriel Harvey in one of his printed books.[37] The rest could just as well belong to adults. Adults might have told a comic rhyme about Henry 'Hotspur' Percy; they would certainly have had maxims about the best kind of horse, and nonsense has amused them as well as children throughout history (Fig. 48).

To describe something as a children's rhyme or song in the middle ages, then, we need to establish its connection with children. This is not easy to do. Few rhymes contain internal evidence of such usage, and few medieval writers bothered to note what rhymes or songs were current among the young. The sermon reference to 'Watch well, Annot' is an outstanding exception, but a rare one. There is a valuable list of songs, including partial texts, sung by a child or youth in a Tudor play by the mysterious writer W. Wager: *The Longer Thou Livest the More Fool Thou Art*, published in 1569. The author makes the child say that he learnt them from a foolish woman servant of his mother, sitting upon her lap, and they could well date from at least the early sixteenth century. Eight songs are quoted and the child says that he knows twenty more; indeed, he sings one or two others later on.[38] But very little material is labelled 'for children' in this way. Much more is unlabelled but relevant because of its context and associations. When rhymes turn up in books that were used with children or by children, there is a likelihood that they were ones that children knew, even if the fact is not directly stated.

48 Medieval children (and their elders) loved nonsense and topsy-turvydom, a motif found in rhymes and pictures: here hares hunt boys.

One such kind of book is the miscellany or commonplace book, compiled by an adult for purposes of instruction and entertainment. A particularly good example, for our purposes, is the one put together by Richard Hill, the London grocer of the early sixteenth century, whom we have encountered recording his children's births.[39] Hill collected stories, songs, and other material, partly for his own amusement and interest, and partly, it seems, for use with or by his family. Two of its items in particular seem to be aimed at children. One is the song 'Twelve Oxen':

> I have twelve oxen that be fair and brown,
> And they go a-grazing down by the town.
> With hay, with how, with hay!
> Sawest thou not mine oxen, thou little pretty boy?[40]

In the three verses that follow, the oxen change to white, black, and red, and go grazing by the dyke, lake (or stream), and mead (or meadow). Although Hill gathered material relevant to both adults and children, the repetitive form of the verses and the address to the 'little pretty boy' make a child the likelier audience in this case. The song is soothing – it could be a lullaby. It is also imaginative. It is about somewhere else, it evokes a feeling of prosperity (twelve oxen), it teaches about colours. In these respects it reminds us of the lullaby in the *Gododdin*.

Hill's other song is a piece of nonsense.[41] It appears among adult material, but its humour is not strongly adult; rather, its depiction of animals doing human

tasks is close to that of many nursery rhymes. There are seven verses altogether,
the first two running as follows:

> I saw a dog seething [*cooking*] sauce,
> And an ape thatching an house
> And a pudding eating a mouse:
>   I will have the whetstone, and I may.

> I saw an urchin [*hedgehog*] shape and sew,
> And another bake and brew,
> Scour the pots as they were new,
>   I will have the whetstone, and I may.

Each verse is followed by the refrain:

> Hey, hey, hey, hey,
> I will have the whetstone, and I may,

because the rhyme is a carol: a lyric of verses and a chorus, originally sung in a
dance. False traders were sometimes sentenced to stand in the pillory with a whetstone hung around their necks, and the object became a symbol of dexterity in
telling untruths.[42]

   A third song in Richard Hill's book is a famous one, not normally linked with
children. This is the 'Corpus Christi' carol, which also contains a refrain,

> Lulley, lulley; lully, lulley,
> The falcon hath borne my make [*mate*] away.

The story tells how 'he' (presumably the falcon) carried 'him' (the mate) into a
brown orchard, in which lay a hall, in which was a bed, on which lay a wounded

49   Some children's words and rhymes related to games, and were chanted as part of play or ritual.

knight, by whom knelt a weeping maiden. The last verse is about a stone beside them, 'Corpus Christi written thereon'.[43] Is this a children's song? Two features might suggest so: the lullaby of the refrain and the unfolding sequence of places and people (as in the modern nursery rhyme, 'This is the house that Jack built'). It also occurs in the manuscript among pieces aimed at children. Equally, the imagery of the verses bears a sophisticated interpretation, relating to Christ, and the elements of the carol are so varied that it is difficult to be sure that the poem was primarily meant for the young. It remains a mysterious piece, eliciting little agreement among scholars.[44]

The best medieval record of a children's rhyme is that of 'How many miles to Beverleyham?', or 'to Babylon' as it became in later times, a rhyme which was used in a game.[45] This is another fragment of childhood culture recorded in a Latin sermon, one written at the end of the thirteenth century. The preacher was referring to people who wish to be good Christians at one moment and fall away at another. He compared them to

> children who play 'How many leagues [or miles] do I have to Beverleyham?' Another says 'eight'. The first says, 'Can I come by daylight?' The other says, with an oath 'Yes, you can', and the former begins a good run, as fast as he wishes to go, and then dances back and is in his original position and says, 'Ha, ha, petty pace, yet I am where I was'.[46]

The reference is to a game between two children. They both speak the first four lines, after which one runs across a space and back, while the other acts as catcher. If the runner returns successfully, he (or she) taunts the catcher with the final couplet.[47]

This game and rhyme were evidently long-lived. They were still remembered three hundred years later, when the Oxford scholar Gerald Langbaine (1609–58) wrote about his schooldays in Cumberland. He recalled that

> the Questions and responses were these. Q. Pe, pe, postola. How many miles to Beverlay? R. Eight, eight, and other eight. Q. Think you I shall get thither tonight? R. Yes if your horse be good and light.[48]

It looks from Langbaine's evidence as if the exchanges of the game have been abbreviated by the thirteenth-century writer, and that the version of his day was also in rhyme of a rough kind. It may have been chanted like this:

> How many miles to Beverleyham?
> – Eight, eight, and other eight.
> May I come there by daylight?
> – Yes, by God, if your horse be light.

A medieval rider on a light horse could travel much further than twenty-four miles a day: anything up to forty miles or so. As there is a suggestion of haste about the

50   Schoolmasters, like Robert Londe of Bristol (d. 1462), encouraged children to write about their own talk and play, as a way of interesting them in Latin.

journey (feeding into the game), perhaps the players should be envisaged meeting at midday or in the early afternoon. Twenty-four miles before dark would then be possible, but pushing it.[49]

Wager's play *The Longer Thou Livest* is a little late to be described as medieval, but it fills a number of gaps in our subject. Its eight poems, said to have been learnt on an adult's lap, cover several different categories.[50] One is a little story, of the kind so common in later nursery rhymes, like 'Humpty Dumpty' or 'Doctor Foster', with which it shares a focus on misadventure:

> Tom-a-lin and his wife and his wife's mother,
> They went over a bridge all three together;
> The bridge was broken and they fell in.

'The Devil go with all', quoth Tom-a-lin.

Another is imaginative – whether descriptive or riddling, it is hard to say:

> The white dove sat on the castle wall,
> I bend my bow and shoot her I shall,
> I put her in my glove, both feathers and all.

A third is a bit of a political song, about Martin Swart or Schwarz, the German mercenary who helped lead the forces of the pretender Lambert Simnel against Henry VII in 1487. The rebels were routed in the battle of Stoke near Newark, where Swart was killed:

> Martin Swart and his man, sodledum, sodledum,
> Martin Swart and his man, sodledum bell.

This must be part of a song or ballad composed and sung by adults after the battle, and picked up from them by their children.

The remaining items in Wager's list are also adult pieces: lyrics or love songs. Four of them are known from other sources. 'Robin, lend to me thy bow', a song still popular in Shakespeare's day, tells how Wilkin asks Robin for equipment to go hunting with his 'sweet lady'.[51] 'By a bank as I lay' opens with the singer in a melancholy mood, 'hey, how', until the nightingale sings that winter is past and calls on lovers to wake.[52] 'The gentle broom on Hive Hill' is a quotation from a ballad preserved in later, mainly Scottish, texts. A knight lays a bet with a lady that she cannot meet him on a broom-covered hill without losing her maidenhead. He arrives first at the hill, but she (or a witch) casts a spell that sends him to sleep. She then throws broom-flowers over his body and places her ring on his finger, to his shame when he wakes.[53] The oddest of the four is 'Come o'er the burn, Bessy', first recorded in the late fifteenth century. It begins like a love song,

> Come o'er the burn, Bessy, thou little pretty Bessy,
> Come o'er the burn, Bessy, to me,

then turns to allegory:

> The burn is the world blind, and Bessy is mankind,
> So proper I can none find as she.
> She dances and leaps, and Christ stands and clepes [*calls*]
> Come o'er the burn, Bessy, to me.[54]

It looks like something popular and secular has been adapted for religious purposes.

Songs and rhymes like these are tiny fragments from a huge lost repertory of popular music and verse. They show us, if we were doubtful, that young children came into contact with such material, and indicate something of its variety. Children sang songs, or had songs sung to them, concerning fantasy, nonsense, games, animals, people, politics, and love (including sex). Some of the songs or rhymes were largely used by children among themselves, like 'Beverleyham'. Others were appropriate for adults to say or sing to them, such as 'Twelve oxen'. A third kind, including 'Watch well Annot' and most of Wager's songs, were adult in origin, reaching the young at second hand. In rhymes and songs, as in other respects, children placed one foot in their elders' culture and kept one in their own.

OLDER CHILDREN

THE RHYMES AND songs of younger children are by no means the whole of the story. There is also a good deal of evidence about the oral culture of their older siblings, or rather older brothers, thanks to a more helpful source than any we have yet considered. This consists of school notebooks, put together by masters or pupils of grammar schools, and first surviving in the early fifteenth century (Fig. 51).[55] Notebooks reflect the wide availability of paper, a cheaper material than parchment and a more permanent one than wax tablets, the means of record used in earlier schools. A notebook grew out of individual quires of paper, on which the writer copied the shorter Latin texts and poems that were used in lessons, along with his own working notes and exercises. The notebook was there-fore a personal anthology, and could be used for non-academic jottings: names of ownership, pen trials, private memoranda, and scraps of songs or poems. Once there were thousands of such books, but only three or four dozen are now extant from before the Reformation.

They are mostly books of a fairly high standard of scholarship. Their tran-scripts of Latin texts were useful enough to be worth keeping during the writer's life and by others after he died. One or two books have survived by accident as wastepaper used to bind other volumes, but even these are of good quality. We do not have material from really bad or feckless writers. Frequently, the notebooks contain the names of the owners who made them or acquired them, but these people are usually hard to identify. It is not always clear whether a book belonged to a schoolmaster or a pupil, though the miscellaneous nature of the contents usually points to the latter. Still, whichever the case, there is a relationship with children. Either the material was being used by a master with schoolboys, or it was being written by schoolboys under a master. Grammar schools catered for boys between the ages of about seven and eighteen. It follows that the material in school notebooks was of interest to members of this age group, and need not have reached those who were younger.

Not every such notebook contains rhymes or songs in English, but several do. Sometimes the pieces appear as free-standing items in the book. When this happens they are usually short, like those that are found in adult manuscripts and documents, and seem to have been jotted down for personal reasons unconnected

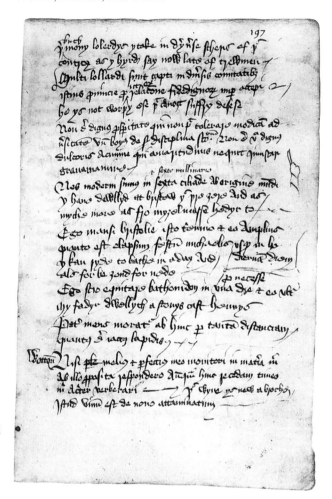

51 A page from the school notebook of Thomas Short (*c*.1430), who apparently studied in Robert Londe's school. It contains sentences about everyday life, in English and Latin.

with the work of the school. At other times, they are written in English and again in Latin, as if the schoolmaster has set them as a translation exercise or the pupil has been inspired to translate them for his own interest. Occasionally the two versions are part of a set of exercises, and when this happens their link with school work is indisputable. It may seem puzzling. The business of grammar schools was to teach Latin. Why should their masters have allowed the recording of English songs and rhymes, and the basing of Latin compositions upon them?

The answer lies in the nature of grammar-school teaching. Latin was a difficult language for pupils who spoke English (or Irish, or Welsh).[56] Its grammar and constructions were more alien than they were to speakers of French or Italian. Teachers of Latin in the British Isles after the fall of the Roman Empire had both to teach their pupils carefully and to maintain their interest in the subject. Grammars had to be written that taught Latin as a foreign language, unlike Roman grammars which assumed an understanding of basic Latin and aimed to improve one's skills. School work needed to be made attractive to pupils. We can see both strategies in the work of Ælfric of Eynsham, in about the year 1000. He produced the ancestor of all modern English grammars of foreign languages today. It was in English and taught Latin in an easy simple way, using Æthelstan and Dunstan as examples of nouns and including illustrative sentences about everyday life in England. Ælfric also wrote a Latin 'colloquy' depicting typical occupations of his time – the serf boy, the hunter, the scholar – which would amuse his pupils as well as instruct them.[57]

Schoolmasters of the fifteenth century pursued a similar strategy. They too used English as the teaching medium in schools, after a long period from the Norman era up to the Black Death when it was done in French, and made their pupils translate English into Latin. They too set topics for this purpose from ordinary life, familiar and interesting to the pupils. The writing of Latin in the lower parts of the school took the form of translating short passages of English prose or inventing Latin ones out of the head, the passages being known as 'latins' (*latinitates*) or 'vulgars' (*vulgaria*). Sometimes the master set the subject, and sometimes the pupil may have been allowed some freedom in choosing it. In either case, the exercise was likely to feature such topics as the schoolroom, the boy's family, the local town, news of the day, wise proverbs, and (occasionally) rhymes and songs. There was another reason for linking the study of Latin with daily life. It was not learnt only for reading but for speaking as a colloquial language. The best schools insisted on their older pupils talking Latin on the premises, because they were being prepared for life in the Church or a university where teaching and conversation might go on in Latin.

At least seven fifteenth-century school notebooks contain rhymes or songs in English: one each from Bristol, the Hampshire area, the Lincoln area, north-west Wales, and Winchester, and two from Exeter.[58] In six of them, the material looks as if it comes from popular culture – adult or child, either because of its format or because it is preserved in other manuscripts, showing its circulation beyond one writer or school. The topics of the rhymes fall roughly into five categories, of which the first is concerned with wordplay, oral or mental. One in the Lincoln notebook is a tongue-twister:

> Three gray greedy geese
> Flying [over] three green greasy furs [*furrows*];
> The geese was gray and greedy;
> The furs was green and greasy.[59]

Similar versions turn up centuries later. A Victorian antiquary noted one as:

> Three grey geese crossed through a green river;
> Grey was the geese and green was the river,

and a schoolgirl in Scotland quoted another to the Opies in 1952 as:

52   Riddles were popular with adults and children. This one illustrates the question 'Who comes neither driving, walking, nor riding; neither clad nor unclad; neither in the road nor out of it?'

> Twelve grey geese in a green field grazing;
> Grey were the geese and green was the grazing.[60]

The commonest wordplay items, however, are riddles (Fig. 52). Some of these, in the notebooks, are in Latin. A set turns up from time to time which asks 'Who died and was never born?' 'Adam.' 'Who was born and never died?' 'Elijah', and so on.[61] Riddles in English also occur. One of the Exeter notebooks contains two lines of English and four lines of Latin, which look like one, unless it should be viewed as a piece of nonsense:

> Three headless men played at ball,
> One headless man served them all.[62]

This appears in a longer form in an adult collection of songs, also of the fifteenth century:

> I saw three headless play at a ball,
> A handless man served them all;
> While three mouthless men lay and laughed,
> Three legless [men] away them drew.[63]

The same Exeter notebook includes a whole song or poem in English centred on riddles, which occurs in later ballad versions. A maiden is accosted by the Devil, who tells her that she must become his lover unless she answers a series of questions. The questions include,

> What is higher than is the tree?
> What is deeper than is the sea?
>
> What is sharper than is the thorn?
> What is louder than is the horn?
>
> What is swifter than is the wind?
> What is richer than is the king?

There are fourteen in all. The maiden prays to Jesus for support, and gives the right answers: 'heaven', 'hell', 'hunger', 'thunder', 'thought', and 'Jesus'. At the end, she rebukes the Devil and names him – a procedure which people believed would cause him to vanish immediately.[64]

A second group of rhymes is about birds and animals, treated like human beings as in fables. The Bristol notebook contains a verse reminiscent of 'Who killed Cock Robin':

> I saw a sparrow
> Shoot an arrow
> By an harrow
> Into a barrow.[65]

This, perhaps, is an original composition, inspired by the rhymes, rather than a current piece of verse. One of the Exeter books, on the other hand, contains a couplet already mentioned, which might be a proverb or come from a song or fable:

> The hare went [to] the market scarlet for to sell;
> The greyhound stood him before, money for to tell.[66]

The same notebook includes a four-line verse which is a piece of nonsense or part of another fable. It should be read with a Devonian accent; 'voxes' are 'foxes':

> Hares and voxes, mice and rats,
> Prayed reremice [bats], flies, and gnats
> That they should arm them with old mats
> To feeze [drive] out of town hounds and cats.[67]

The Welsh notebook echoes this topic. It has three four-line verses, possibly linked, possibly independent.[68] The first is about another battle between animals, here the cricket and the grasshopper:

> The cricket and the grass-hopper went here to fight

> With helmet and haburgeon [*mail coat*], all ready dight [*dressed*];
> The flea bore the banner as a doughty knight,
> The cherubud [*scarab*] trumpeted with all his might.

The next verse or poem turns to a hare on a hill:

> The hare sat upon the hill and fastened her shoon,
> And swore by the buttons which were thereupon,
> That she would not rise nor [be] gone
> Till she see twenty hounds and a one.

The last is about a miller sitting on the hill, and the village hens flocking around him:

> The miller sat upon the hill
> And all the hens of the town to him drew.
> The miller said, 'Shoo, hens, shoo!
> I may not shake my bag for you.'

Millers were notoriously covetous and allegedly stealers of other folk's grain. The implication is that this one will not even shake out his sack for the birds.

The mention of the miller leads us to a third kind of rhyme, which deals with unpopular people, reflecting the way in which schoolboys pick up the prejudices of their elders. A rhyme in the Winchester notebook collects friars, haywards (impounders of stray animals), and tapsters, and dumps them in the company of foxes and polecats:

> A fox and a foumart [*polecat*], a friar and a hayward,
> Standing in a row,
> A tapster [*ale-seller*] standing thereby,
> The best of the company is an old shrew.[68]

Another, in the same book, ridicules shoemakers, calling them by the word 'souter', which was coming to have an opprobrious meaning somewhat like 'cobbler' in recent times:

> Souters have a nice pride
> For they will ever on paniers [*panier baskets*] ride,
>   As poulterers on pokes [*bags*].
> Where in land we may them find
> We shall turn their arse against the wind,
>   For [they] stink like dogs.[70]

A further unpopular group were the Scots, the target of a rhyme in the Lincoln notebook. This is a fragmentary piece, which can be reconstructed with the help

53   Medieval children, like modern ones, were intrigued with the supernatural; here a youth apparently finds himself playing trap and ball with a ghost.

of the Latin that accompanies it. The rhyme was apparently triggered by an English victory, probably the battle of Verneuil in France in 1424, at which a Scottish contingent fought with the French and shared their defeat:

> [Rough-footed Scot with a raveling [*large boot*],
> Wast] thou at [Verneuil?] at the wrestling?
> In the crook on the moon went thou thitherward,
> And in the wild waning came thou homeward;
> There wast thou cast in midst of the place,
> That thy neck broke thee with evil grace.[71]

The verse tells how the (representative) Scot set out in the new moon and came home in the waning moon (unlucky times). He was thrown as in a wrestling match, metaphorically breaking his neck.

This last rhyme is evidently not an original piece. Chronicles written in London during the fifteenth century contain descriptions of the battle of Verneuil, and quote the middle two lines of the rhyme. The writer of one of the chronicles, exulting about the victory, states that 'the most vengeance fell upon the proud Scots, for they went to dog-wash [*died like drowned dogs*] the same day . . . so that they well may say,

> In the crook of the moon went they thitherward,
> And in the wild waning came they homeward.'[72]

We can also classify the piece as a political rhyme, in which case it reminds us of the song about Martin Swart and the verse concerning Harry Hotspur. Children evidently picked up popular songs or rhymes about current affairs. It is easy to imagine them taking an interest in events like wars, battles, and rebellions, and gloating over the downfall of the villains of the day.

A fourth kind of notebook verse explores another world: the supernatural. This is close to schoolboys' interests today and, as we have seen, was not far away before 1500.[73] The Bristol book has a sentence which might be the kind of saying that boys use to frighten one another about ghosts:

Bloodless and boneless standeth behind the door.[74]

The Winchester notebook contains a verse about being ridden by the 'witch's daughter' or nightmare; perhaps it is meant to be said as a charm against her:

If it so betide
The witch daughter over thee ride,
Both shall have God's curse:
The witch daughter and hers.[75]

Children are likely to have known their elders' safeguards against evil and their ways of transmitting it. One English poem, aimed at boys in the fifteenth century, specifically warns them against casting spells on other children or on animals – spells that apparently involved one turning round, sunwise or widdershins:

By street or way if thou shalt go,
From these two things thou keep thee fro:
Neither to harm child nor beast
With casting, turning west nor east.[76]

Another charm, not in verse, occurs in a Norfolk school notebook:

If thou wilt know who has stolen thy goods, write these letters in virgin wax and put under thine head, and he shall appear in thy sleep that hath thy goods.

The author goes on to supply the letters to be written, evidently on a lump of wax to be placed beneath the pillow.[77]

Finally, as in *The Longer Thou Livest*, notebooks incorporate lyrical rhymes or songs. A single line in the Bristol notebook looks like a scrap of one:

Light leaf of the linden [*lime-tree*] lay the dew a-down,[78]

while the Winchester book includes three longer fragments:

Wed me, Robin, and bring me home;

Have I aught, have I naught, then I am a dame.[79]

Flowers in mine arbour,
They grow green;
But if [unless] my lady love me well,
My dog will die for tene [grief].[80]

Underneath a louvre
Plucked I a plover;
Go to Joan Glover
And say that I love her;
By the light of the moon,
See that it be so done.[81]

The timbre of the first suggests a love song; the second is both lyrical and comic, because it is the lover's dog (not the lover) who is likely to die for grief. The third may be a song of love as well, unless the repeated rhymes are a sign that it is a school composition.

That some school rhymes were original works is suggested by the only notebook not yet considered: the one from Hampshire.[82] This contains five passages of English followed by Latin translations, the last of which is merely a proverb while the fourth may be a proverb or sentence, although it contains some rhymes:

When the clod clingeth and the cuckoo singeth and the broom springeth, then it is time for a youngling to go a wooing.

The remaining three passages are longer pieces of verse:

Today in the dawning
I heard the fowls sing,
The names of them it liketh me to ming [mingle]:
The partridge, the pheasant, and the starling,
The quail and the goldfinch and the lapwing,
The thrush, the mavis, and the woodwall [woodpecker],
The jay, the popinjay [parrot], and the nightingale,
The nuthatch, the swallow, and the seamew [gull],
The chough, the cuckoo, the rook, the raven, and the crow.
Among all the fowls that made glee [song]
The rearmouse and the owl could I not see.[83]

At my house I have a jay;
He can make many diverse lay [song]:
He can barking as a fox,
He can low as an ox,
He can hiss as a goose,

54 Education encouraged the collecting instinct. Boys learnt words for body parts, hunting terms, and (as here) types of birds.

He can bray as an ass in his cratch [*manger*],
He can croak as a frog,
He can bark as a dog,
He can chatter as a wren,
He can chatter as a hen,
He can neigh as a steed;
Such a bird it were mad to feed.[84]

It is [the case] in harvest [for] carts to clatter,
Paddocks [*frogs or toads*] for to crowd that sit by the water.
Whoso falls in the fen, he defileth his hat,
Whoso may not see he stumbleth the rather,
And he [that] hath an evil wife he thriveth the later.[85]

These look more like poems written in school, although the last one incorporates some proverbs. The first two in particular seem designed to test or show knowledge of Latin vocabulary – nouns for birds and animals, or verbs of making sounds (Fig. 54). But even if they were not in popular use, they are still interesting. Either they were pieces of original verse by a schoolboy, or produced by a schoolmaster to stimulate his pupils. They show a school tolerant of rhymes in English, and inspiring someone to imitate such rhymes.

They also remind us that schooling is not unfriendly to wit and fantasy. Learning a language makes one more conscious of grammar and syntax than might otherwise happen, and children may turn this awareness to humorous effect. It is well known that modern pupils learning (say) French will invent parodies of French or hybrid words, part French and part English. This kind of amusement can be traced in the middle ages, among both adults and children. They made up comic Latin, like the mock epistle in the fifteenth-century play of *Mary Magdalene*, discussed in a later chapter.[86] They devised Latin cryptograms, such as the one in the school notebook of Walter Pollard of Plymouth in the same century: a Latin sentence with the syllables reversed, *O Nebo tergisma dic bisno lambafa cranpuli*, which, rearranged, means 'Good master, tell us a lovely story'.[87] A few may even have invented languages of their own. The twelve-year-old Welsh schoolboy Eliodor, who claimed to have visited the underworld in the early twelfth century, alleged that he learnt its speech and used to repeat it to his listeners. Years later, Gerald of Wales recorded two of his phrases, *Ydor ydorum* ('Bring water') and *Halgein ydorum* ('Bring salt').[88]

SCHOOLBOY SONGS

THERE IS ANOTHER group of songs, not all preserved in children's notebooks, which are about children or rather schoolboys. At least four are recorded in manuscripts of the fifteenth or early sixteenth centuries, and apparently date from that period. All adopt the mode of being spoken by a schoolboy, or a group of such boys, and centre on the pains of attending school. They display resignation, impudence, or anger about this predicament, and ponder strategies to escape. The one recorded in Richard Hill's anthology is the best known.[89] It has the refrain,

> Hay, hay, by this day,
> What availeth it me though I say nay?

and begins:

> I would fain be a clerk,
> But yet it is a strange work;
> The birchen twigs be so sharp
> It maketh me have a faint heart.

The boy bemoans the torment of starting school at six o'clock on a Monday morning. When he arrives late, the master looks as if he were mad:

> 'Where hast thou been, thou sorry lad?'
> 'Milked ducks, my mother bade',

for which piece of sauce the master 'peppers his arse' till it bleeds. The boy then plans his revenge:

Lac pueror. M. holti Mylke for chyldren.

55 Beating children was widely recommended, especially in schools, whose masters are commonly shown holding rods or birches.

I would my master were a hare,
And all his books hounds were,
And I myself a jolly hunter;
To blow my horn I would not spare,
For if he were dead I would not care.

A second song is angrier. Its target is the usher – the schoolmaster's assistant, a man destined to be unpopular because he sat by the school door ('usher' means 'doorkeeper'), dealing with late-comers and those requesting to go out (Fig. 56):

Weenest [*thinkest*] thou, usher, with thy cleverness,
Each day [to] beat us on this wise,
    As [if] thou were lord of town?
We had liefer [*rather*] school forsake,

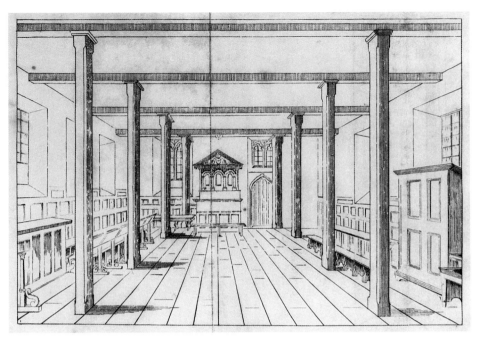

56   The usher's seat by the door of Magdalen College School (Oxford). Its occupant supervised entry and exit, an unpopular task.

> And each of us another craft take,
>   Than long to be in thy bandon [*power*].

'Would to God', says the next verse, 'that we might catch you by the millstones or the crab tree!' A millstone workshop would have had heaps of gravel and off-cuts lying about, and a crab tree have been full of little hard apples. If Sir Robert in his cloak (presumably the schoolmaster) turns up to defend the usher, he too will be warmed with blows. The boys have suffered from both men, and the singer wants a straight revenge.[90]

The Winchester school notebook contains a song that is 'macaronic', in both Latin and English. It seems to be a confession by a schoolboy who is preparing for a life in trade, since it refers to 'merchants', and its refrain (which is in Latin) introduces a more moral note than the two previous songs:

> *Frangens scola discipulus est mercator pessimus*
> [A pupil breaking off (or, out of) school is a bad merchant].[91]

In the first verse the boy complains how,

> O' mornings, when I am called to school,
>   *De matre vel matertera* [By mother or by aunt],

Then my heart beginneth to cool,
    Languescunt mentis viscera [The vitals of my courage grow faint].

He goes on to say how he comes late to school, plays in class, and takes no heed of how little he knows. If every merchant behaved like this, commerce would come to nothing. But, for all the tolling sound of the refrain, the song ends nonchalantly, indeed defiantly:

Fellows, be merry and make good cheer,
    Saltatis cum tripudio [dancing with jubilation]
For we shall not all thrive this year
    Qui exhibemur studio [who are maintained at study].

No thought here of revenge; rather, let's be merry, for we are not all going to do well anyway.

These three songs have no clear authorship or context. They could have been written by adults or by schoolboys, though they look like pieces for schoolboys to sing – perhaps on festal occasions at school or at concerts in households when boy singers took their turns. A fourth song has a more obvious purpose, because it mentions the end of the Christmas term of the school year. It is also in Latin and English, and was evidently meant to be sung at school by a group of boys to the master, as part of the end-of-term ceremonies. First there are four lines of 'goliardic' verse, with a fine surging rhythm, as if the boys were marching through the classroom up to the master's desk:

Ante finem termini baculum portamus;
Caput hustiarii frangere debemus!
Si preceptor nos petit, quo debemus ire,
Breviter respondemus, 'non est tibi scire!'

[Now that term is finishing, we've a stick to carry,
And the usher's head with it, we shall hit and harry!
If the master questions us, whither we are going,
Briefly we'll reply to him, 'that's not for your knowing!']92

The song then changes its mood. It turns into lines in both languages, and abandons defiance in favour of supplication:

O pro nobilis doctor [O noble teacher], now we you pray,
Ut velitis concedere [that you will grant] to give us leave to play.

The boys ask the master for permission to go away and to break up the school. After Christmas, they promise, they will come back and tremble again when they have to make their 'latins'.

CHILDREN'S TALK

THE RHYMES AND songs we have considered are precious, because their words were probably said or sung by medieval children. They are rare survivors of the great lost body of oral material that circulated among all children, literate and illit-erate. Little else remains of children's talk. What adults said, or were alleged to have said, appears in legal cases of slander, heresy, or treason, but children very rarely occur in such records. We have heard how the youths of Whitby teased Tosti because of his name, and how boys might have taunted someone who was illegitimate like Merlin.[93] But most of children's talk, what they said or shouted to one another, died as it passed from their mouths.

The few adults who noticed such talk usually did so with disapproval. Writers of sermons complained that parents not only allowed their children to use bad language but taught them to do so. 'Some', said a writer of about 1400, 'teach their children to swear and stare and fight, and to beshrew [abuse] all men about'.[94] 'Many fathers and mothers', agreed another some fifty years later, 'teach their children through their cursed oaths to despise God . . . , to blaspheme God'.[95] The practice which the preachers had in mind was that of swearing 'by God' (often meaning Christ specifically). God's commandment not to take His name in vain was broken – claimed one writer – throughout society, 'from a little young child that can scarcely speak, to an old bearded man'.[96] People swore by God's blood, body, bones, death, feet, flesh, guts, nails, sides, and wounds, not omitting his eyelids. 'Boys and mothers', wrote Thomas Becon in 1543, 'tear the most blessed body of Christ with their blasphemous oaths, even from the top unto the toe'.[97] When they were not abusing Christ, the foul-mouthed were obsessed by sex, as they are today. Modern parents, lamented an Oxford schoolmaster in the 1490s, indulged their children in every way, including bad language. 'If they happen to call the dame [mother] "whore" or the father "cuckold" (as it looketh sometimes), they [the parents] laugh thereat and take it for a sport, saying it is kind [natural] for children to be wanton in their youth'.[98]

It may then seem as odd to find abuse in school textbooks as it is to encounter rhymes and songs, but the same considerations apply. Schoolmasters might disapprove of speaking scurrilous words to one's parents, elders, and betters, but they were not averse to using scurrility to advance the cause of Latin. One who did so was John Stanbridge, the famous schoolmaster of Banbury, who published a book of *Vulgaria* in 1509 for translation from English to Latin. This includes such lines as 'Thou stinkest', 'Thou art a false knave', 'Thou art worthy to be hanged', 'Thou art a blab', and 'Turd in thy teeth'. His pupils also practised rude remarks to say about third parties: 'His nose is like a shoeing horn', 'He is a cuckold', 'He is the veriest coward that ever pissed'.[99]

Once or twice, the records furnish traces of short rhymes of the kind that pupils may have chanted at each other, with the formula 'I have something nice, and you have something nasty'. One, to be encountered again, occurs in the fifteenth-century morality play *Mankind*, as if it was meant to be said by one schoolboy to another:

> I have eaten a dishful of curds
> And I have shitten your mouth full of turds.[100]

Another occurs in a school notebook from Barlinch Priory in west Somerset, compiled in about 1500. This is in Latin, but it is followed by one English phrase which suggests that the Latin is a translation of a verse in English:

> *Ego habebo scuticam, tu habebis petuitam; ego habebo rosam et tu habebis catarrum.*

> I will have the whip [and you will have the pip.[101]
> I will have a rose and you will have a snotty nose].[102]

Far from restraining such insults, schools might develop pupils' skills in devising them.

The inclusion of sexual taunts in the juvenile repertory is an interesting matter in itself. Inklings of sex may have percolated down to young children. John Skelton, in his poem 'Why Come Ye Not to Court?' (1522), includes a couplet that looks like a quotation from a popular song:

> And Mocke hath lost her shoe;
> What may she do thereto?[103]

This bears a marked resemblance to a rhyme said to have been chanted by a girl of seven or so, in about 1606:

> Cocka doodle dooe,
> Peggy hath lost her shoe.[104]

Peggy, like Mocke, is a pet-form of Margaret. This second couplet is, in turn, an earlier version of the well-known modern nursery rhyme, first recorded in the eighteenth century,

> Cock a doodle doo!
> My dame has lost her shoe,
> My master's lost his fiddlestick,
> And knows not what to do.[105]

Now, Skelton's rhyme almost certainly contains a sexual double entendre. It turns up again in his poem 'A Garland or Chaplet of Laurel', as part of a discussion of Rosamond Clifford, the mistress of Henry II, in which the phrase 'losing one's shoe' seems to mean one's virtue or virginity.[106] It would be interesting if his couplet was taken from an early form of the later nursery rhyme and if the rhyme were said or sung by young children. Would they have realised the meaning it held for adults?

Older boys at school could certainly learn about sex as easily they did about terms of abuse. A sentence in the Barlinch Priory notebook warns:

Si sis vir fortis non des tua robora scortis
(If you are a strong man, do not give your powers to whores),[107]

and Stanbridge made boys translate,

He lay with a harlot all night.[108]

The most adventurous in this respect was William Horman, headmaster of Eton and Winchester. His published collection of *Vulgaria* (1519) includes a whole section on vices and improper manners. Here a pupil might learn that 'a common woman liveth by her body', and render into elegant Latin 'an exceeding strong whore'. He would learn of men who 'deflowered many women', 'keepeth other men's wives', 'gropeth uncleanly children and maidens', and consort with a 'sister openly as she had been his true wedded wife'.[109] There is a similar candour about the lavatory. Stanbridge's *Vulgaria* includes such sentences as 'I go to siege' (to defecate) and 'I am almost beshitten'.[110] Horman's goes further: 'he hath all be-smeared the seat that another cannot come at it'.[111] True, this is the material of lessons, not pupils' private talk. But it suggests less brakes upon such talk, more openness, than was the case in later centuries.

Songs and school sentences do not tell us all we would like to know about medieval children, but they are better than nothing. Reading them confirms, if we doubted it, our ancestors' similarity to ourselves. Medieval children shared many of the thoughts and interests of children today. They responded to wordplay, both in speech and in writing. They liked animals, and imagined them as people. They heard about political events like wars and rebellions. They had an interest in magic and the supernatural. They mocked one another, and derided unpopular occupations and races. They savoured scatalogical and sexual matters. As well as these broad similarities, there is a specific linkage in at least a few of the songs and rhymes in use. The tongue-twisting geese, 'How many miles to Beverleyham?', and probably 'Matthew, Mark, Luke, and John' have passed down the centuries, despite having largely done so in speech not in writing.

Much of this culture, like that of toys and games, was shared with adults. Parents and nurses sang children their first songs and probably taught them others. Adults had prejudices against certain social groups and races, which children picked up and repeated. Children copied their parents' oaths and abuse. Many of the songs and rhymes of childhood were those of adulthood too. The same applies today, and does not prove that there was no medieval childhood or children's culture as we understand the terms. There were special songs for children, and possibly some made by them. Children sang songs away from adults, sometimes, no doubt, with a different understanding. They also had contrasting experiences from most children today. They lived in a more violent world: cruel to animals and harsh to people, with corporal and capital punishments (see Figs. 18 and 119). It was also a world where lack of privacy may have made adult sexuality more obvious, and where some aspects of sex may have been more openly shared with children than is usually so today.

A TAILPIECE

THE ELEMENTS OF children's culture – humour, fantasy, nonsense, satire, sex, and scatology – make a grand coda in a poem written down in a printed book at the end of the late fifteenth century or early in the sixteenth.[112] The book is the *Dialogue against the Bohemians*, meaning the Bohemian Hussites, by Aeneas Sylvius Piccolomini, the secret agent who became Pope Pius II. It was printed at Cologne not later than 1472, and the poem is inscribed at the end of it. First comes an invocation, 'Christ's cross be my speed and Saint Nicholas', which announces that the speaker is a schoolboy, for these were words that pupils said before they recited the alphabet.[113] Next is a sentence which might be in prose or rough verse, 'Christ's curse be with you all, for I have fared the worse both for Saint Gregory and Saint Nicholas for beating of mine arse'. We are evidently at the beginning of a comic speech by a schoolboy: not an original or unique speech, because it has two verses missing, showing that it was copied from somewhere else. It is addressed to 'you', an audience, and must have been recited on some festal occasion, not unlike the schoolboy songs, although it is a good deal more ribald. A speech by a low-life character in a morality play would be a good comparison.

The poem is an alphabetical one, that is to say it consists of twenty-three rhyming couplets each beginning with a letter of the alphabet in sequence, but lacking the verses for 'e' and 'z'. Each couplet is an anecdote about an imaginary person:

> A is for Alyn Mallson that was armed in a mat,
> And rode to Rychmar [*Richmond?*] for to fight with a gnat,

rhyming words that we have already encountered.

> B is for Bartem the baker, that burst must he be;
> He claimed his heritage upon the pillory,

a baker who is evidently dishonest because he (or his father) has been put into the pillory for using false weights or selling bad bread. All the characters are men except for

> M for Margaret the mumbler that was a bold stot [*bullock*];
> She broke her husband's head with a foul pisspot.

There are fantasy and nonsense, as in nursery rhymes, and one or two mentions of animals:

57   Snowballing. Children, then as now, made their own culture, with games, words, and customs that differed from those of their elders.

> H for Harry Hangman, that gelded well an hog;
> For eating of a pudding he hung up his dog.

Insults are hurled at a cobbler, an oatmeal-maker, a pear-monger, a questmonger (a professional and, by implication, corrupt juror), a shoemaker, a thief, a tinker, a wire-drawer, and perhaps a lawyer, as well as the baker and hangman.

Finally, there are rude and sexual terms – 'stink' and 'fart' as well as 'pisspot', a joke about a cuckold with double horns, and another about the shrewish wife. The last two couplets begin with 'and' and *con*, two signs that followed the alphabet in the form that people then learnt it:[114] The second of these,

> Con- for all maids that will have no blame,
> God give you all ill marriage for ye are past shame,

is probably addressed to the audience. 'Con-', in the alphabet, was a Latin abbreviation, but it was also a French word for the most intimate part of the female anatomy, and was well known in England in that sense, at least by Shakespeare's time.[115] It is hard to believe that it was not meant as a double entendre, producing yet more sniggers or guffaws.

Chapter 5
Play

PLAY

IF OUR MOUTHS are the earliest organs on which we rely, our hands and feet soon strive to catch them up. Long before we can talk, we stretch them out and feel our cots and prams. Unable to hold a conversation or play a game, we are given simple toys to handle and keep us amused. Some are hard, bright, and noisy to stimulate our interest and teach us things. By using them we learn about colours, sounds, and substances, and practice physical skills. Others are soft and reassuring, to calm us down and give us comfort. Toys are the first things we possess and command, that we understand to be ours. We give them affection, and cry when they are lost or taken away. Then, as we grow older, our activities take new directions. They become more physical, so that we run and jump; more dexterous, so that we make and build; and more sociable, so that we join with others in games. In short, we play from our infancy and throughout our childhood, with a wide range of objects and outcomes. So it was in the middle ages, and for long before that.[1]

Play, as we now understand, is essential to children's development. It tests and develops their mental and physical skills. Like adults, they may play intently and seriously, with much labour. Yet the historic words for this process in English are condescending ones. 'Play', 'game', 'sport', and 'toy' convey the sense that such activities are primarily recreational, amusing, and (in the last case) childish. This attitude towards the play of children is closely related to a wish by adults to control it, a wish that goes back to the ancient Greeks, if not further. For centuries, adults have tried to use play to develop children's minds and bodies, and to move them on from infant forms of play to those of childhood, adolescence, and finally adulthood. Sometimes they have tried even to abolish play in favour of other activities. This has made play a more controversial subject than children's speech, and consequently a better recorded one. By having views about play, adults have been led to write about it, giving us a clearer picture of its nature in the middle ages than we possess for most other aspects of children's lives.

The observers of play in medieval England can be classified into several groups. One consisted of the ruling authorities, crown and parliament, who issued laws and orders about games which will come to our notice presently. Another was that of literary writers interested in human life and its various stages, the 'ages of man' with which this book began.[2] Those who wrote on the topic used play as a basic image or symbol of childhood and youth.[3] Not only were young people believed to love play, but it was seen as one of the defining features of the first stages of life that made them different from adulthood. A good example of such a writer is the poet John Lydgate. In 1426, he began to translate into English the famous French poem *The Pilgrimage of the Life of Man* by Guillaume de Deguileville, written in 1355. The poem is about the journey of life, and foreshadows such works as *Piers Plowman* and *The Pilgrim's Progress*. It imagines mankind as a pilgrim on a road, meeting characters who represent virtues and vices. One of them is a girl, running up and down while she bounces a ball at a wall. She has wings, and her legs are covered with feathers like those of a dove.

The pilgrim asks her name. 'I am Youth', she says, 'wild, fearless, and never constant'. She tells him that she spends all her time in play: running, leaping, singing, dancing, wrestling, stone-casting, and climbing trees to steal fruit. She mentions other games: 'closh' (a kind of croquet), 'camping' (football or hockey), hunting, fishing, catching birds, shooting at butts, playing nine men's morris, two games of dice, chess, 'tables' (backgammon), 'kayles' (skittles), and 'quek' (a game played on a chequer board). Deguileville was distrustful of Youth. She sends the pilgrim in the wrong direction, so that he strays from the road and falls into bad company. To a moralist, her passion for play was at best immature, at worst idle and sinful. Lydgate would have agreed, but she fired his imagination and he increased Deguileville's list of games, a mere seven, to about twenty-five. As a result he gives us a good idea of the range of activities popular in his day.[4]

A third group of writers about play were schoolmasters. As we have seen, they were used to empathising with their pupils to promote the work of their schools, and this led them to notice toys and games as they did rhymes and riddles. The pioneer in this respect was the mysterious recluse called Geoffrey, who lived in the Dominican friary of King's Lynn (Norfolk) in the mid fifteenth century. Geoffrey, one suspects, was either an ex-schoolmaster or a would-be one, because in 1440 he compiled a dictionary for schools entitled *Promptorium Parvulorum* ('a prompter for little ones'). It is a work of great distinction: the first significant English-to-Latin dictionary, the first English dictionary too, since it arranges large numbers of English words in alphabetical order, and the first dictionary to take an interest in children. Geoffrey included not only words common throughout society, but a number of names of toys and games, several of which he defined as 'children's play'. These were evidently playground words, because they are seldom or never recorded in other sources, and entitle him to be called the first collector of 'the lore and language of schoolchildren'.[5]

Other schoolbooks identified play as a topic, particularly those containing *vulgaria* for translation from English to Latin. Two such books from Magdalen College Oxford are particular useful here, the earlier composed in the 1490s and the later between about 1500 and 1520. They mention a number of games, especially those played or liked by the adolescent boys at whom the sentences were aimed.[6] The outstanding work of this kind, however, is the *Vulgaria* of William Horman, published in 1519. This is an encyclopaedia of English and Latin sentences, containing a section devoted to 'Exercises and Games' which mentions several toys, a number of games, and children's involvement in some of them. Dice, cards, hunting, fishing, and swimming are all described, because Horman thought that their vocabulary was relevant to pupils and would be likely to interest them.[7]

The list of observers of play is completed by the artists, especially those who illuminated manuscripts and later on made engravings for books. High-quality prayer-books and romances often included scenes of everyday life to illustrate their stories, to accompany the calendar of the year, or to provide decorations in the margins. Many of the best such manuscripts were produced in the Netherlands, and their artists, searching widely for subjects to paint, often turned

58   Pieter Bruegel's great celebration of play, 'Children's Games', painted in 1559. It depicts over 200 children and some 75 toys and games.

to children for the purpose. One strategy was to depict them alongside adults, to provide variety and authenticity in calendar pictures or narrative scenes. This is especially characteristic of finely painted Flemish manuscripts of the late fifteenth and early sixteenth centuries, like the Grimaldi Breviary in the Biblioteca Marciana, Venice (Figs. 1, 28).[8] Another approach was to portray children at play, in what was considered to be their most characteristic pursuit. Play had the advantage of taking manifold forms, enabling the artist to use it in a long series of scenes, a strategy followed (for example) in the famous *Romance of Alexander* in the Bodleian Library, illustrated by Jehan de Grise, probably in Flanders between 1338 and 1344 (Figs. 4, 53, 61, 67–9).[9]

These two approaches reached their climax in the work of the Flemish painter Pieter Bruegel the Elder in the mid sixteenth century. Not only do several of his major works feature children alongside adults, like the 'Battle between Carnival and Lent' (1559), but his 'Children's Games' (1560), now in the Kunsthistorisches Museum (Vienna), is devoted to them entirely (Fig. 58).[10] This painting depicts more than two hundred children and adolescents, playing with toys or taking part in games, differing from earlier art not so much in the range of activities it shows but by bringing them all together into one scene. The young people – boys and girls – are represented in a townscape during summer, playing singly, in pairs, and in groups. About 75–8 activities are included, chiefly outdoor ones for ease of representation. Some of the games are imitative (such as a wedding procession); others are skilful and involve toys or equipment. Objects depicted include dolls, dice, hoops, tops, windmills, a mask, and a hobby-horse. Physical activities are also depicted, which make use of the human body or the man-made environment. There is riding on rails and on barrels, piggy-back riding, acrobatics, wrestling, swimming, and climbing a tree. The scene is not realistic because the town contains virtually no adults; it has been taken over by children. Rather, it is an encyclopaedia of games and, because of their number and variety, a celebration of childhood and its ingenuity – one of the greatest in European art.

All these sources are immensely useful, but they involve some problems. So many toys and games were common to children, adolescents, and adults that it is often hard to know who played them when they are mentioned. Illuminations and paintings, particularly in their earlier history, do not always make it clear whether a little figure in a gown is a child or an adult drawn on a small scale. The same is true of archaeological finds, a further source that is beginning to add to our knowledge.[11] Discovering an object in an excavation does not necessarily reveal who used it. A ball, die, or draughtsman may have belonged to an adult, a child, or both; a small pot may have been intended as a child's toy or have had a separate, adult use. Archaeological finds are also limited by circumstances. Most come from towns, rather than from the countryside, and consist of objects capable of survival. Metal or pottery objects are more likely to be preserved in the ground than wooden or fabric ones. Altogether, our knowledge is strongest about toys and games as names and objects. How they were played, the skills they developed, and what they meant to their players are often beyond our grasp.

TOYS

OUR FIRST TOYS are the ones we are given as babies. They have to be of suitable sizes, shapes, and materials for children so young, and the practice of giving such toys is an ancient one. John Trevisa, writing in 1398, talks of noble children playing with 'a child's brooch' in their earliest lives, and we occasionally hear of babies and toddlers being given a brooch or a buckle as a present.[12] Sometimes, no doubt, these were intended as gifts for later in life, but some may have been used as toys for handling, being hard, smooth, decorative, and large enough to be fingered or bitten without being swallowed. Rattles existed in the time of Aristotle, who praised them as a means of allowing children to expend their energy without doing damage.[13] There is a word *thunung*, meaning something that creaks, in a late Saxon glossary, and the *Promptorium* mentions a 'child's bell' which may have been a similar kind of noise-maker.[14] The word 'rattle', however, is not recorded in English until Horman's *Vulgaria*: 'I will buy a rattle to still my baby for crying.'[15] Buying a rattle implies mass production, and manufactured rattles occur as archaeological finds in London in about the sixteenth century. They are made of lead-tin alloy and consist of a handle, about 9 cm long, ending in an open-work ball containing a bead to make the noise. This reduced the number of dangerous edges, and kept the rattling agent out of reach.

When children grew older, they could be given more complicated toys to shake or spin. One was the child's windmill, admirably described by John Florio in 1598 as 'a piece of card or paper cut like a cross, and with a pin put in at the end of a stick, which running against the wind doth twirl about. Our English children call it a windmill'.[16] This was often mounted at the end of the stick like a wheel on an axle (Fig. 3), rather than at a right angle to the stick as is usual today. A more elaborate twirling toy is shown in fifteenth- and sixteenth-century continental pictures, and may well have been known in England.[17] It consisted of a ball, small enough to be held in the hand and drilled to contain a spindle which projected from the top, holding a windmill in a horizontal plane. A second hole from the side of the ball to the middle allowed a string to be fixed to the spindle at one end and a handle at the other; the string could be wound up and then pulled to make the windmill revolve. Such toys took skill to make and were probably sold commercially.

Harder to manipulate, and therefore for older children, was the top, a word first mentioned in English in the story of *Apollonius of Tyre* (c.1060).[18] An example from the same century, made of maplewood, has been found in excavations at Winchester. The Winchester top is a small one, 6.9 cm high, with pointed ends at top and bottom, and a groove for whipping.[19] Other tops found on the continent have only a bottom point, and a third kind of top had no groove because it was designed for spinning with the fingers. Tops are not only personal toys but public and social ones. Walter of Bibbesworth talks about playing tops in the street, and there were common words among children for such objects.[20] The *Promptorium* lists four of them, all of which (it says) were used in children's play: 'top' itself, 'prill' (from a verb 'to twist'), 'spilcock' (meaning 'a little plaything'), and 'whirligig'.[21] Three other words for spinning objects appear in other fifteenth-century schooltexts: 'scopperil' (from a root meaning 'to jump about'), 'spilquern' (a variant of 'spilcock', from its quern-like shape), and 'whirlbone' (apparently relating to an animal bone – knee-bone or vertebra – that could be spun).[22] These words are precious because they are so seldom recorded. Four are unique to these sources, suggesting that they were only in use among children. In this respect they are like the unwritten words used in modern playground games, such as marbles.[23]

Dolls represent a different kind of toy, geared to the imagination, role playing, and the imitation of adult life. 'Doll' itself is a late word, a pet-form of Dorothy, which first meant a mistress or favourite and came to be applied to dolls only in the seventeenth century.[24] The earlier term was 'poppet', with variant forms such as 'popyn' and 'puppet' – the latter becoming the usual form in the sixteenth century.[25] 'Poppet' comes from the Latin word *pupa* or *puppa*, originally meaning a girl but also used of small images, such as one might offer at a shrine. The word passed into French, German, and Italian, and Chaucer's use of it to describe himself in *The Canterbury Tales*, 'a poppet in an arm t'embrace', suggests that it was already current in England as a term for something dainty like a doll. It is first recorded in that sense in the fifteenth century.[26] Then as now, dolls were chiefly toys for girl. The early-Tudor Latin dictionary, *Hortus Vocabulorum*, actually defines

59 A late-medieval votive doll, offered at the shrine of Bishop Edmund Lacy in Exeter Cathedral; a possible model for wax dolls for children.

them as 'small images which maidens are wont to make in the form of girls and to wrap in clothes'.[27]

Dolls came in several varieties and more than one kind of material. Earthenware figures, consisting of cones or tubes with faces and sometimes vestigial limbs, have been found in eastern France and Switzerland, and may have had functions with children though some could equally well be skittles. Wooden objects of a similar kind, truncheon-shaped with a head and simple body, are well attested in Tudor and Stuart England.[28] They were painted and suitable for dressing with costumes. Wax dolls may have existed too, because small images of the same material were made for people to offer at shrines when they needed help, or wished to give thanks for help received. At Exeter Cathedral, a cache of such images was discovered in 1943, including a model of a woman with hands joined in prayer, made in a mould and presumably sold commercially (Fig. 59).[29] Those who produced such objects could easily have made them for children.

A fourth kind of doll was made of cloth, and most of the earliest literary references are to these. In France, a fight between two women of Paris over a linen doll in 1396 allegedly caused one of them, who was pregnant, to miscarry.[30] In England, a religious text of 1413 compares idle knights and squires to 'legs of clouts [cloths], as children make poppets for to play with while they are young', and

60   By the Tudor period, dolls were extensively manufactured, imported, and exported. Here, a native American girl of about 1590 holds an English rattle or windmill and a fashion doll.

not long afterwards a Scottish text alludes to children making 'a comely lady of a clout'.[31] The *Promptorium* defines 'popyn' as 'child of clouts', and the Puritan writer Philip Stubbes derided women's fashions in 1583 as 'mawmets' (another word for doll) 'of rags and clouts compact together'.[32] Different doll materials were matched by variety of production and type. Children might make their own, as the Scottish source reminds us, or parents may have done so, a father using his carpentry skills or a mother hers at sewing. Poorer families may have been limited to home-made dolls, but by the sixteenth century dolls were manufactured for those who could afford them. Wax dolls were capable of being mass-produced from moulds, and wooden dolls were strong enough to be transported in quantities. William Turner's *Herbal* (1562) likens certain roots to 'little puppets and mammets which come to be sold in England in boxes'.[33] In 1582, the crown set a duty of 6s. 8d. on each gross of imported 'puppets or babies for children'.[34] The duty, amounting to just over a halfpenny per doll, implies that they were sold for about sixpence each.

What the doll depicted also varied. Some were probably babies or children, as the *Promptorium* implies with 'child of clouts'. Others were adults, generally female (it seems), reflecting the linkage of dolls with girls. Once a doll was to be clothed, a decision had to be taken about its social rank. Some were dressed relatively simply and cheaply, perhaps to give them an appeal to humbler children. Bruegel's 'Children's Games' shows two girls playing with dolls attired in workaday clothes: a white wimple and white apron over a black dress. For wealthy people, the doll's dress and status could be elaborated. A painting of 1502, now in Vienna, depicts the fifteen-month old Isabel, daughter of the duke of Burgundy, holding a doll that is itself a noblewoman wearing a headdress, collar, and a long robe, with hands together at the waist.[35] A contemporary account of Sir Richard Grenville's expedition to Virginia in 1585, describes how native American girls were 'greatly delighted with puppets and babes which were brought out of England'. An engraving in the book shows a girl of seven or eight, holding a toy like a rattle or windmill in one hand and a doll in the other. As imagined by the illustrator, this doll too was an adult woman in noble dress, with hat, ruff, and a full skirt, her hands clasped at the front (Fig. 60).[36]

The doll today is an object in common between children and adults. Grown-up people may keep their childhood teddies, or collect soft toys to display in their houses. In the middle ages too, the doll was not confined to the young. As a marionette, it might be operated by a man to make money. Horman tells how 'The tregetours [*jugglers*] behind a cloth show forth poppets that chatter, chide, joust, and fight together' (Fig. 61).[37] Adults might buy votive objects to offer at shrines, and statuettes of Christ or the saints to keep in their houses. Margery Kempe, the mystic of King's Lynn, when visiting Italy in 1414, met a woman who travelled about with an image of Christ as a baby. Other women dressed this image with clothes as an act of reverence, and Margery, seeing this happen, fell into tears for love of the infant Jesus.[38] Similar dolls of Christ and Mary are said to have been carried about by women during Advent in the north of England.[39] Dolls were used in magic too, and one of the earliest records of the word 'puppet' in English occurs in a fourteenth-century source about such a figure.[40]

61   Puppet dolls were used for entertainment by the fourteenth century, and are also mentioned in early-Tudor times.

62   Part of a sixteenth-century
toy, stamped on a sheet of metal
and capable of being folded into
a three-dimensional cupboard.

The narrowness of the line between child dolls and adult ones is revealed by the cleric Roger Edgeworth, preaching at Bristol in 1539–40. Edgeworth, a religious conservative, remarked with disapproval that

> Now, at the dissolution of monasteries and of friars' houses, many images have been carried abroad and given to children to play withal. And when the children have them in their hands, dancing them after their childish manner, cometh the father or the mother and saith: What Nasse [*Agnes*], what hast thou there? The child answereth (as she is taught) I have here mine idol; the father laugheth and maketh a gay game at it. So saith the mother to an other, Jugge [*Joan*] or Thommye, where haddest thou that pretty idol? John our parish clerk gave it me, saith the child, and for that the clerk must have thanks and shall lack no good cheer.[41]

These can hardly have been large wooden images; more likely they were small wax votive offerings like those from Exeter, left in churches until 1538 when royal injunctions forbade the paying of honours to saints or shrines. Such figures were thoroughly suitable in shape and size to serve as children's toys.

Playing with dolls helps children satisfy their instinct to copy adults. Other toys existed to feed the same desire, especially miniature utensils mimicking those of the home. These are found both in England and on the continent. A small ceramic pot, perhaps such a toy, survives from Strasbourg in the thirteenth century, and by the late fourteenth a little brass cauldron was being purchased for a French boy-prince and tiny bowls and plates of silver for a two-year-old princess.[42] Similar toys have been found in excavations in London.[43] They are

63 Boys' toys were often mass-produced, like this knight on horseback, found in London and made from a mould in about 1300.

made of lead-tin alloy using moulds and were evidently mass-produced, probably in England. As they are comparable in form to brooches and pilgrim badges, they may well have been manufactured by the same craftsmen and sold in shops, at fairs, or by pedlars.

Most common are tiny jugs and ewers, 2.5–3.5 cm high, furnished with handles and sometimes with lids and spouts (see Fig. 2). They may be linked with other small objects consisting of cups on stems (like chalices) and plates, all about 2.5 cm in size and suitable for make-believe meals or playing at housekeeping. Little tripod cauldrons and skillets of copper alloy appear in about the sixteenth century, and were robust enough to be filled with water and heated on a hearth. Miniature bowls, cutlery, fire-irons, and candlesticks survive as well. One of the most interesting toys to have been discovered from this time, the Tudor period, is part of an ornate cupboard, stamped out of a flat sheet of alloy. The stamped-out profile could be bent so as to recreate the cupboard in three dimensions, the ancestor of a modern self-assembly kit (Fig. 62).

Models of other kinds were also available. Archaeological finds from London include two metal soldiers, manufactured in about the reign of Edward I, to judge from the armour. One is complete, about 5 cm high, and the other a fragment of a similar shape, both knights in armour on horses, holding a sword (Fig. 63). They were made in a mould and must have been mass produced; very likely they were painted. A more complex toy of about the same date is a hollow bird, 2.5 cm high, originally mounted on a stand. When the bird was pivoted, a separately mounted tongue moved in and out of its beak (Fig. 64). By Tudor times, flat human figures were being produced, about 5.0–7.5 cm high. They are decorated to look like gentlemen and gentlewomen of the period, in datable costume, with arms like

64   A late-medieval toy bird, also from London,
with a moveable tongue.

handles capable of having a string or ribbon threaded through, them. The doll could then be danced like a puppet. Toys like these suggest that wealthier children in towns, where most of the alloy models have been found, had access to commercially made playthings which did not differ in essence from modern ones. The lead-tin models in particular went on being produced in fairly similar forms down to the Industrial Revolution.

Military and mechanical toys of a more elaborate kind are recorded in relation to royal children, and may have circulated in other important families. A toy cart was bought for Henry, the six-year-old son of Edward I, in 1273–4, at a price of 7d., and 2d. was paid to mend it.[44] A few years after, in 1279, money was spent on timber to make a 'little castle' for Henry's brother Alfonso (aged five) and to take it to Windsor Castle.[45] Alfonso had a siege engine too, and a painted boat – either a model or one big enough to contain him.[46] Later still, in 1290, an intricate castle was constructed for Edward's youngest son, Edward II, aged six, by the boy's master-cook, John Brodeye. It was painted, 'other things' were bought for it (possibly furniture or soldiers), and was so spectacular that it was shown to the queen (and doubtless many others) in Westminster Hall at the marriage feast of Edward's sister Margaret.[47] The two 'little cannons' delivered to Richard II, aged ten, in 1377 may have been models or miniatures to use in play or under supervision.[48]

Animal toys are popular today, and the question arises whether medieval children had such toys, made of fabric or of wood. Skilful fathers and mothers could easily have provided them. The only toys of which we hear, however, are imitation horses whose popularity is predictable in such an equestrian society. King Alfred noted how 'children ride their sticks and play many games in which they imitate their elders', and a Scottish writer of the fifteenth century talks of children who 'make a white horse of a wand'.[49] Jean Froissart, the Flemish historian born in the mid fourteenth century, recalled that he called his stick-horse 'Grisel' – a common name for a steed.[50] There is an English reference to a child's horse in a miracle story of about the 1470s or 80s, involving the five-year-old son of a man named

65   Imitation horses, like these hobby horses, were popular in a horse-dependent society.

Robert North who lived near the Thames. The boy, who suffered from a growth on his lip, saw a vision of the dead King Henry VI and was told by him to make a pilgrimage to his shrine. Reporting this message to his mother, the boy said to her that the king wished him to travel 'riding with you, and not on my wooden horse'. That meant, remarked the writer of the story, the stick that small children use in their games.[51] Some such 'horses' were no more than sticks; a child is shown astride one in a woodcut of 1495 (Fig. 3).[52] Others were probably more elaborate. A graffito in Wallington church (Herts.) shows the basic stick embellished with a head, ears, chest, and mane, which could have been made by parents or sold by craftsmen.[53] Sticks with carved heads also appear in continental illustrations of the period (Fig. 65).[54]

Children, of course, have never confined themselves to toys made specially for them. Poor or rich, they have fashioned their own from anything lying at hand. Gerald of Wales, describing his childhood at Manorbier Castle (Pembrokeshire) in the 1150s, recalls how he and his brothers played with sand and dust (perhaps on the nearby beach). They built towns and palaces, and he made churches and monasteries.[55] But the best account of children's own toy-making comes from the fifteenth-century Scottish poem *Ratis Raving*. Rait, the author, was a gentleman who wrote to advise his son about the seven ages of life. He was unusually observant about childhood, which he considered as covering the first three ages. Children in the earliest of these, until they were three years old, were concerned only with food, drink, and sleep. In the second, from three till seven, they began to make things: gathering flowers, building houses with sticks, and using bread, stalks, sedges, and rags to construct a horse, ship, spear, sword, or doll:

> So long has child [a] will always
> With flowers for to jape and play;
> With sticks and with spales [*splinters*] small
> To build up chamber, spence [*buttery*], and hall;
> To make a white horse of a stick,
> Of broken bread a sailing ship;
> A bunweed [*ragwort*] to a burly spear,
> And of a sedge a sword of war;
> A comely lady of a clout
> And be right busy thereabout
> To dight [*dress*] it featously [*handsomely*] with flowers,
> And love the puppet paramours.[56]

This must have gone on universally, but it was rare for anyone to record it in writing. Geoffrey's dictionary gives us another clue. It includes a word 'powpe', explained as meaning 'hollow stick'.[57] This could well be a tube of a balsam stem or a hollowed out branch of elder, used as a pea-shooter or a pop-gun.

GAMES

TOYS ARE ESPECIALLY things to be used by yourself; games are generally played with other people. There are games appropriate to all stages of childhood, and this was so in the past. 'Handy-dandy', a simple guessing exercise about which hand holds an object, has already been mentioned.[58] Cherry-stones, a cheap and easily available commodity, were used for rolling, throwing, or flicking. They are first mentioned by the blind poet John Audelay in the 1420s, when he reflected on children's lack of covetousness, content as they are with such stones.[59] One of the games for which they were employed was known as 'cherry-pit' from the practice of aiming the stones at a hole.[60] The bad child Wanton in the morality play *Mundus et Infans* (printed 1522) liked cherry-pit, and Horman mentions the general activity with approval: 'Playing at cherry-stone is good for children'.[61]

Cherry-stones remind us that children enjoy collecting or playing with insignificant things. Cobnuts, large cultivated hazelnuts, were used in the same way: one of the shepherds in the York cycle of mystery plays gave two to the infant Jesus.[62] They could be used in games as balls or as prizes; Randall Cotgrave, in his French dictionary of 1611, describes 'the childish game cobnut' as 'the throwing of a ball at a heap of nuts, which done, the thrower takes as many as he hath hit or scattered'.[63] In 1532, Sir Thomas More imagined a bad schoolboy playing games instead of going to school: 'cherry-stone, marrow bone, buckle-pit, spurn point, cobnut, or quoiting'.[64] It is not clear what all these games consisted of, but at least four of them centred on waste items of food or clothing, easily found. A later,

Elizabethan, source talks of children playing with small items such as points [*laces*], pins, cherry-stones, and counters.[65] Like cobnuts, these could be used both as the tools of a game and as the currency for measuring gains and losses.

The value placed by the young on such trifles is revealed by the chief archaeo-logical study yet made of a site dominated by children. At Coventry, the Carmelite friary after its dissolution in 1538 became for a time the free grammar school of the town. The friary church was turned into the classroom, and the choir stalls (which still survive at a different site) were used as desks for the pupils. During this period, numerous small objects fell into the foundations beneath the stalls and were recovered by excavation in the 1970s. Many were of iron or copper, such as arrowheads, buckles, buttons, pins, fragments of knives, and small trinkets including a cross, bells, and a Jew's harp. A large number of little copper tags from the ends of laces, about 400 of them, probably represent currency for games, like the ones mentioned above. There were beads of glass, paste, and bone, two children's teeth, discs and counters made from tile and shale, and small balls like marbles of green and red sandstone, brick, and clay.[66] The modern words for these balls – ally, marble, and taw – came into use only at the end of the seventeenth century, when higher-quality materials like alabaster, marble, and glass superseded older and cheaper ones. An earlier word may have been simply 'stones'; an engraving of 1659, showing a boy at play with balls like marbles, labels them 'bowling-stones' (Fig. 66).[67]

66   This seventeenth-century engraving shows a range of traditional children's games, including tops, 'marbles', bowling at ninepins, and swinging.

Marbles and cherry-stones develop manual dexterity; other games with things, such as dice, tables (or backgammon), draughts, chess, and cards, teach strategy and memory. All were played by children. When Edward the Black Prince was ten in 1340, money was paid for him to play not only *ad bill'* – a physical game with a stick – but *ad talos* (dice or knucklebones) with his mother the queen, Sir John Chandos, and the boys of his household.[68] Another board game, 'merels' or 'nine men's morris', is mentioned in Lydgate's translation of Deguileville, and is shown being played by a boy and a girl in an illustration in the *Romance of Alexander*.[69] Rait, who associated such games with the stage of life from seven to fifteen, names three of them,

> Now at the tables, now at the chess . . . ,
> And much with playing at the dice.[70]

Horman too refers to dice and chess. One of his sentences tells how 'men play with three dice and children with four dalies', a daly being a dialect word for a die or some similar cube. He refers to the French words used for the numbers on dice: 'a single ace is a losing cast; sice-ace winneth all; trey is cast good enough; cater is a very good cast'.[71] He imagines the purchase of a playing table 'with twelve points on the one side and chequers on the other side', suitable for playing backgammon and draughts or chess. He names the chess pieces – kings, queens, 'alfins' or judges (the modern bishops), knights, rooks, and pawns, in the correct numbers, and describes one of the colours as red.[72] Prince Arthur, son of Henry VII, played dice for money in 1496 when he was ten, and seems to have lost 40s. His younger brother Henry (VIII) did better two years later when he was seven; playing a game with his father (chess, dice, or cards), he won 6s. 8d.[73]

Chess had a higher status than other board games, because it was regarded as educational. Its pieces were seen as emblematic of society: king, queen, knights, judges, rooks (executive officers), and common folk, each having its own function and all being effective when working together. There were books explaining the method of play and expounding its relevance to the understanding of human affairs. The most popular of these was written in Latin in about 1300 at Genoa in Italy, by Jacques de Cessoles, a French Dominican friar, and soon translated into French. It was later turned into English by Caxton, who published it at Bruges in 1474 as *The Game and Play of the Chess*, and reissued it at Westminster with wood-cuts in 1483. In its English form, the work was praised by educational writers in the early sixteenth century, and it probably helped to create an encouraging context for the playing of chess by children, especially in wealthier families.[74]

Then there were physical games. The simplest of these were running and chasing games, requiring no equipment. William FitzStephen describes the youths of London running and jumping in summer in the late twelfth century, and Horman includes the sentence, 'I have wrestled and run, and I have had the worse at both the games', which envisages competition.[75] Running as part of a game has already been noticed in the thirteenth-century dialogue 'How Many Miles to Beverleyham?'.[76] Geoffrey mentions three activities of a similar kind in the *Promptorium*: 'running' (identified as a 'game'), playing 'buck hide', and 'base play' (described as a 'game of children').[77] 'Buck hide' was a form of hide-and-seek, perhaps because the hiders were the bucks and the seeker the hunter, and 'base play' was substantially the same as 'Beverleyham'. Children occupied a base and offered themselves to be caught by running out of it.[78] Rait mentions children of seven to fifteen running 'at bars', which may well be a similar game, since Geoffrey gives *barrus* as the Latin for 'base'.[79]

Throwing games of numerous kinds were played. Stone-casting is mentioned as popular with young men in the thirteenth century,[80] and Lydgate put it into Deguileville's list. Horman has a sentence, 'I have thrown a stone over the house'.[81] Rait refers to playing 'at the catch', while Horman praises one who 'casteth a quoit well'.[82] Thomas More wrote in about 1500 how boys love playing with the quoit and the cock-stele.[83] The cock-stele was a stick to throw at a cockerel in the cruel sport of burying the bird in the ground and aiming sticks or arrows at its head. One of the Magdalen College schoolbooks describes how,

> 'as I walked yesterday in the fields, I saw a hen set up to shoot at nine strides, so that the head only should appear out, all the remnant of the body hid under the ground'.[84]

In John Heywood's drama *The Play of the Weather* (printed 1533), various characters pester Jupiter for the kind of weather they want, ending with a boy who demands snow for snowballing.[85] There were also ways of throwing oneself: jumping, swinging, and balancing. Bruegel shows children swinging on railings, and Geoffrey mentions specially-made devices. He has two names for them, 'totter or merry totter, children's game'.[86] The words may have referred to any moving contraption – swing, see-saw, or spring-board – on which one 'waved', 'wavered', or 'tottered'.[87]

Ball games were always popular, both for small numbers of people in confined spaces and for crowds on open land. Lydgate's list includes 'closh' or croquet and 'kayles' or skittles, while Geoffrey refers to 'shuttle' (meaning shuttlecock) and 'tennis'. He defines shuttle as a 'child's game'.[88] Tennis emerges as a name in the fifteenth century and was first played simply against a wall. One of the shepherds in the Wakefield cycle of miracle plays gives baby Jesus a ball to 'go to the tennis'.[89] Ball games of the open kind were well developed by the late twelfth century, when FitzStephen's famous description of London includes an account of them taking place on Shrove Tuesday. He tells us how

> after dinner all the youth of the city goes out into the fields to a much-frequented game of ball. The scholars of each school have their own ball, and almost all the workers of each trade have theirs also in their hands. Elder men and fathers and rich citizens come on horseback to watch the contests of their juniors, and after their fashion are young again with the young.[90]

Geoffrey mentions a 'player at the ball,' and he has four entries about a game called 'camping', a participant at which he calls a 'camper, or player at football'.[91] Camping took its name from the Old English verb *campian*, 'to fight', and Geoffrey identifies it, both in English and Latin, as a game for the foot. Lydgate, on the other hand, associates it with crooked sticks, suggesting that it bore more relation to hockey. The name may have been used of more than one kind of game. It was popular in Norfolk, where the agricultural writer Thomas Tusser paid it a compliment in his popular book on husbandry in 1580:

> In meadow or pasture (to grow the more fine)
> Let campers be camping in any of thine;
> Which if ye do suffer when low is the spring,
> You gain to yourself a commodious thing.[92]

It is unusual to find a sport recommended as good for the grass!

Water was another enticing medium for swimming or fishing. Little is known about swimming in medieval England. It had some status up to the twelfth century (two literary heroes, Beowulf and Tristan, are described as doing it), but fell out of fashion among the nobility and gentry between 1200 and 1500.[93] The skill was practised unobtrusively during this period, however, and it improved its status in the early sixteenth century, due to more interest in classical Latin writings in which it was praised. Horman has two sentences on the subject, observing that 'Children do learn to swim leaning upon the rind of a tree or cork', and urging 'Learn to swim without a cork'.[94] By 1531, Sir Thomas Elyot was recommending it seriously as part of a noble education.[95] But there were limitations to swimming. It seems to been restricted to boys and men who did it naked, while girls and women merely bathed in clothes. Moreover it could only be done out of doors and in natural water, which confined it to the summer months.

Fishing, on the other hand, had the advantage of being possible all the year round. This too was apparently dominated by males, as it is today, and one of the Magdalen College schoolbooks contains two passages expressing the delight of boys in the sport and their anxiousness to get to the waterside.[96] Horman refers to the subject several times. He mentions anglers, those who set fish-traps, 'gins, grins [*snares*], pots, and other', and the use of nets. He names barbels, eels, lampreys, pikes, sturgeon, and tadpoles, and notes one or two of their characteristics. Fish breathe through their gills, swim either in schools or alone, and (in the case of eels) prefer clean running water.[97] Some of these details may have been taken from adult knowledge – there were already treatises on fishing by Horman's time – but the number of the references in his schoolbook suggests that he thought that the topic would interest his pupils as well.

Less formal than games, but no less formative, were explorations and experiments. Many children left home to play, sometimes with the disastrous results of which we hear in coroners' records and miracle stories.[98] Robert son of John of St Botulph of London, aged seven, was wounded climbing with other boys on pieces of timber in Kiron Lane in 1322, and the three-year-old Beatrice Shirley of Wiston (Sussex) while playing with other small children under a stack of

firewood in the fifteenth century.[99] Boys especially wandered afield, hunting for
birds and their nests. In the same century, Thomas Scott of Burnham (Bucks.)
climbed a tree one Sunday morning, for a prank or to take young birds from a
nest, and fell thirty feet; he survived through being nursed back to health in the
nearby nunnery and having prayers said for him to King Henry VI.[100] The boy in
Heywood's *Play of the Weather* (1533) confesses,

> All my pleasure is in catching of birds . . .
> And to hear the birds how they flicker their wings
> In the pitfall, I say, it passeth all things.[101]

Wanton in *Mundus et Infans* spies out 'a sparrow's nest' and torments animals,

> Yea, sirs, I can well geld a snail,
> And catch a cow by the tail –
> This is a fair cunning![102]

He was not alone in these tastes. The schoolbooks from Magdalen College
describe shooting at cocks and bear-baiting, and we shall shortly encounter the
popularity of children's cock-fighting.[103] Two fifteenth-century poems urge boys
not to throw sticks or stones at birds, dogs, pigs, or horses.[104] In an age when food
was hard to come by, violence widespread, and mutilation a legal punishment, the
teasing and chasing of birds and animals must have been only too common.

PLAYING AT WAR

SOCIETY IN MEDIEVAL England was a military society. Its leaders – kings, noblemen, and gentlemen – envisaged themselves as knights. They possessed military
equipment, used shields as badges of identity, and lay in their armour on tombs.
The Statute of Winchester of 1285, a major piece of legislation to promote law
and order, required every male over the age of fifteen to possess weapons in
accordance with his rank. Even the poorest were to have at least bows and
arrows.[105] Wars took place between the English and their neighbours, and there
was civil unrest from time to time. Boys became aware of fighting at an early age
and, as Rait observed, it entered into their play: spears being fashioned from stalks
and swords from sedges. The life of the famous warrior William Marshal, later
earl of Pembroke, tells how in 1152, when he was five, he played a game called
chevalers or 'knights' with King Stephen of England at Newbury. The game
involved taking two plantains or similar stalks with a knob at the top, and hitting
one against the other to knock off the head, in the manner of conkers.[106]

Adults were anxious to develop the interest in playing at war. In noble families,
it was encouraged from an early age. Henry son of Edward I had two arrows
bought for his use in 1274 when he was still only five, and his relative John of
Brabant had a wooden crossbow and swords for fencing fifteen years later.[107]

Henry V owned a sword in 1397 when he was nine, and his son Henry VI was provided with eight in the 1420s, 'some greater and some smaller, for to learn the king to play in his tender age'. When Henry VI went to France in 1430, at the age of seven, a little 'harness' or suit of armour was made for his use.[108] Children's bows were a distinct commodity by 1475 when the wood for them was imported from Spain.[109] One was bought for the five-year-old Prince Arthur, son of Henry VII in 1492, and his sister Margaret shot a buck at Alnwick (Nland.) in 1503 when she was fourteen, presumably with a similar light bow.[110] It was not only children of the nobility who played in this way. Maud Boylun of Tillbrook (Beds.), aged five, was hit by the ten-year-old John Phuch as he aimed his bow at a target in 1271, and children shooting arrows caused a similar accident to the four-year-old Thomas Fowle of Marden (Kent) in the fifteenth century.[111]

Hunting was often regarded as a kind of military training.[112] Horman called it 'a plain recording of war' and Elyot 'the very imitation of battle'.[113] John Hardyng, writing in 1457, urged that noble boys should be taught to hunt at fourteen, the beginning of adulthood. This would harden their bodies, accustom them to blood, and develop their cunning.[114] By the fifteenth century, there were texts to teach young men the terminology of hunting and the procedures to be followed.[115] Smaller boys of high birth took part too, with help from their elders. Henry III's son Edmund of Lancaster was allowed to hunt in Windsor Forest in 1254, when he was nine, and Henry VIII's son Henry Fitzroy was only six or seven in 1525 when his schoolmaster complained that his lessons were being disturbed by forays after hares and deer.[116] Even at gentry level, John Hopton, son of a Suffolk esquire, hunted as a schoolboy with a local vicar, and Thomas Cranmer's father encouraged him to do so in Nottinghamshire.[117] One of the schoolbooks from Magdalen College presumes an interest in hunting among boy pupils. It visualises a hare being chased with greyhounds when the ground is covered with snow, and men taking curs and mastiffs to kill a wild boar in the woods.[118] Ordinary children were unlikely to take part in hunting itself, but it is hard to believe that some did not follow to hold open gates or simply to watch what went on.

Boys also organised military games of their own, as they have always done (Fig. 67). A famous story of the discovery of the young Cyrus of Persia playing as king of the boys was told by Herodotus and known in late medieval England.[119] The second Magdalen College schoolbook, which repeats the story, imagines one of the school's own pupils acting the lord with his companions: appointing a carver, a butler, and a porter, and causing a boy to be beaten.[120] Kings were chosen by the children of London in Lent 1400, six months after Richard II had been overthrown by Henry IV. The chronicler Adam of Usk, who tells us this, believed that they gathered together 'in thousands', 'made war upon each other and fought to their utmost strength, whereby many died, stricken with blows or trampled underfoot or crouched in narrow ways – much to the wonder of the people what this might foreshow'. In the end, the new king had to order their parents and masters to restrain them.[121]

The wars of 1400 were not unique. Richard Carew, the Cornish topographer,

67   War influenced play; here boys imitate their elders by practising with a quintain.

records how a year before the Prayer Book Rebellion of 1549, at a time of religious unrest, the boys of Bodmin School (Cornwall) divided into two factions, 'the
one whereof they called the old religion, the other the new'. Each had a captain,
and the division affected all activities with 'eagerness and roughness'. 'At last, one
of the boys converted the spill [*stem*] of an old candlestick to a gun, charged it with
powder and a stone, and (through mischance or ungraciousness) therewith killed
a calf, whereupon the owner complained, the master whipped, and the division
ended.'[122] Five years later, after the failure of Wyatt's rebellion in January 1554,
boys gathered in Finsbury Fields outside London in March 'to play a new game:
some took Wyatt's part and some the queen's and made a combat in the fields'.
Renard the Spanish ambassador reckoned the number at three hundred and
heard that several were wounded; 'most of them', he wrote, 'have been arrested
and shut up in the Guildhall'.[123]

From at least the fourteenth century, the crown itself tried to affect the play of
young people. Although the Statute of Winchester had required all men to own at
least bows and arrows, the national skill at archery seemed deficient in the very
heyday of the Hundred Years War. In 1365, King Edward III complained that
people followed 'dishonest and useless' games like stone-casting, ball games, and
cock-fighting, and ordered his sheriffs to make the male population practise on
feast days with bows and arrows or bolts.[124] The Statute of Cambridge (1388)
ordered all 'servants' (a term implying young men) to give up quoits, dice, stone-
casting, and kayles, and to use bows and arrows on Sundays and festivals.[125] In
1410, the statute was reissued with penalties, and further re-enactments
(prompted by complaints of evasion) followed under Edward IV, Richard III, and
Henry VII.[126] All these injunctions were probably aimed at males over twelve or
fourteen, but in 1512 a statute of Henry VIII extended the legislation to younger
children. It laid down that all men with boys in their houses, aged between seven
and seventeen, should provide them with a bow and two arrows, and bring them
up to shoot. Justices of the peace were to enforce the statute, and butts were to be
set up in every town for practice on holidays.[127]

THE CHILDREN'S CALENDAR

CHILDREN'S GAMES TODAY vary during the year and go in and out of practice. Sometimes this is linked with the seasons, as with cricket in summer, but in other cases the changes are ones of fashion (like playing with marbles or skipping-ropes) and follow a cycle that is neither predictable nor related to the calendar.[128] Medieval children may have followed this second pattern in some of their games – nobody noticed their customs enough to say so – but they certainly observed the seasons of the year in other respects. They lived, after all, in a society that was strongly influenced both by the natural year and the Church's times and seasons. Adults had special customs all year round, involving indoor games at Christmas, eggs at Easter, and outdoor games and processions in May and June. Children shared in these, at least as spectators, but there are also signs that they had a calendar of their own: not wholly independent of the adult one, but semi-detached from it.

That children responded to the cycle of the year was noticed as early as the late thirteenth century by the Franciscan friar and preacher, Thomas Docking. A small boy, he comments, 'has his own particular favourite times of the year. In spring, he follows the ploughers and sowers; in summer and autumn, he accompanies those gathering the grapes'.[129] The early-Tudor poet Alexander Barclay went further than this, by drawing attention to a calendar of children's activities distinct from that of adults. In about 1518, Barclay published a translation of the sixth *Eclogue* of the Italian humanist Mantuan (Battista Mantovano Spagnuoli). Mantuan had observed that each time of life has its joys: children, for example, like playing at ball with a bladder. Barclay developed this to show how the joys of children alter with the seasons. He lengthened the account of ball playing and added two other activities, one in summer and one in early spring:

> Look in the streets; behold the little boys
> How in fruit season for joy they sing and hop;
> In Lent is each one full busy with his top,
> And now in winter for all the grievous cold,
> All rent and ragged a man may them behold.
> They have great pleasure, supposing well to dine,
> When men be busied in killing of fat swine.
> They get the bladder and blow it great and thin
> With many beans or peasen put within;
> It rattleth, soundeth, and shineth clean and fair
> When it is thrown and cast up in the air.
> Each one contendeth and hath a great delight
> With foot and with hand the bladder for to smite.[130]

Accidentally or instinctively, Barclay seems to have identified three of the main peaks of children's activity. The periods he mentions – Lent, the fruit season, and the time when pigs were killed (usually in November) – all feature in other sources.

68   Cock-fighting: the universal pursuit of boys on Shrove Tuesday.

Lent, the first of these seasons, was preceded by Shrove Tuesday in February or early March, depending on the date of Easter, to which it was tied. Shrove Tuesday was particularly important in the children's calendar. The last day before the six-week Lenten fast, it was a public holiday and one when children had their own activity: cock-fighting (Fig. 68). Mentions of this refer entirely to schoolboys, but it is not clear whether this reflects the better survival of records relating to schools or whether other boys and girls took part. According to the earliest major witness, William FitzStephen, describing London at the end of the twelfth century,

> Every year, on the day called *Carnilevaria* [Shrove Tuesday], boys from the schools bring fighting cocks to their master, and the whole forenoon is given up to boyish sport; for they have a holiday in the schools that they may watch their cocks do battle.[131]

The custom continued throughout the later middle ages. It seems to have taken place in the morning, as FitzStephen asserts, and the birds (dead or alive) to have been appropriated by the boys' schoolmasters. At Gloucester School in 1400, it was agreed that fifteen cocks were to be sent to the priory of St Oswald which had a claim over the school – suggesting that the birds were a recognised perquisite.[132] Even a boy in a noble household might have 7d. spent on his behalf 'for a hen at Shrovetide, for Francis to sport him with the children'.[133] The first signs of disfavour towards the sport emerge in the reign of Henry VIII. John Colet (Fig. 72) forbade it in his statutes for St Paul's School London (1518), and his ban was repeated at Hugh Oldham's foundation, Manchester Grammar School, seven years later.[134] But these, at first, were lone voices. Boys' cock-fighting and the throwing of cock-steles at birds were common down to the eighteenth century.[135]

One such fight has been recorded in a Latin poem written in about the 1430s, perhaps by a pupil of St Albans School (Herts.). The poem is in three parts, the second of which uses the metre of hymns like the *Stabat Mater* to praise the winning bird in terms not vastly different to those of Chaucer on Chanticleer in 'The Nun's Priest's Tale':[136]

> Cockerel denominated
> 'Kob', with feathers decorated,
>   Coloured yellow overall,
> At his beak the birds defenceless
> Quake in terror like the senseless,
>   With a clamour horrible . . .
>
> Wings outstretched at every comer
> Like a peacock in the summer,
>   All the feathers gleaming bright,
> Legs like posts ensure survival,
> Pressing hard on every rival;
>   He is victor in the fight.
>
> With a body as unyielding
> As a stone set in a building,
>   Never will he choose to flee,
> And the boys declare directly
> That, by custom and correctly,
>   Chelyng gets the victory.[137]

This gives us both the name of the cock and its owner. 'Kob' or 'Cob' means a male swan and suggests a large aggressive bird. Chelyng or Keeling is the boy who brought it to school, and the victory of his cock gives him glory among his schoolfellows.

As we have seen from FitzStephen, Shrove Tuesday was a day for ball games involving not only scholars but youths in general, including those at work. It is tempting to see such games as part of a renewal of physical activity by the young in the Lenten season. Lent, after all, is usually in March or April, when the weather is improving, yet still bracing enough for active outdoor pursuits. The battles of 1400 happened in Lent and those of 1554 were in March, nearly all of which fell within Lent that year. Barclay associated tops (another outdoor activity) with this season, a linkage confirmed by other observers.[138] One wonders if the whipping of tops in Lent was an echo of the scourging of Jesus or of penitent sinners, and was encouraged as such by adults (Fig. 69). In 1520, the city council of York ordered measures to be taken against boys who disturbed the peace by sounding clappers (rattles) on Maundy Thursday, Good Friday, and Easter Eve. On these days, it was customary not to ring the church bells but to summon people to services with clappers – a practice which the junior population in York apparently took to extremes![139]

ental sire fait il qui tant maunes chier
us toute riens aues ame bon cheualier

69   Tops were especially popular in Lent, perhaps alluding to the Passion of Jesus.

A second burst of activity took place in summer. Early summer – May and June – was the time of general holidays, especially in Rogation Week, Pentecost or Whitsuntide ten days later, and Midsummer Day (24 June). Late summer, from June to September, was the season of harvest and fruit-picking, in which children were likely to be involved, licitly or illicitly. The English 'Luttrell Psalter' of 1335–40 has a marginal scene with a boy up a tree, apparently picking cherries, with an angry man beneath.[140] Lydgate's Youth stole fruit, and Lydgate himself filched apples when he was young.[141] When summer ended, nutting was popular. Joan Barton of Leicestershire, aged nine, was accidentally wounded while looking for filberts in a garden with other boys and girls of her age in the fifteenth century.[142] By 1560–1, the boys of Eton College went nutting on a fixed day in September, possibly the 14th, Holy Cross Day.[143] The Eton nutting day was a recognised holiday, and the boys presented some of their spoils to the head-master and fellows.[144] A further custom, roasting beans, occurs in a unique reference among the miracles of Henry VI, relating to the late fifteenth century. A house at Berkhamsted (Herts.) was nearly burnt by a nearby bonfire on the Sunday before St Matthew's Day (21 September), before being saved by the dead king's intervention. This fire, says the miracle collector, was the result of 'a chil-dren's game', 'for children are accustomed in the autumn to burn beans or peas in their stalks, so that they may eat them half burnt'.[145]

The third time of excitement unfolded as winter approached. All Saints Day, 1 November, marked the commencement of winter for many people, and the killing of animals for winter food (and to spare scarce fodder) began on this day.[146] The slaughter of pigs in particular, by providing bladders for ball games, may have inaugurated the football season. Now that households were well-stocked with autumn fruit and ale, and with the stimulation of dark nights, young people (espe-cially boys) began to go about dressed up, singing songs, and asking for money or food. Horman hints at such doings in a sentence, 'He smeared his face with soot to affray [*frighten*] children'.[147] The earliest general account of these practices is a royal proclamation of 1541 which sought to abolish them as part of the Reformation attack on superstitions, ceremonies, and the worship of saints. It complains that on St Nicholas Day (6 December), Childermas or Holy Innocents Day (28 December), and the festivals of St Clement and St Katharine (23 and 25 November), 'children be strangely decked and apparelled to counterfeit priests, bishops, and women, and so led with songs and dances from house to house, blessing the people and gathering of money'.[148] The sixteenth-century Reformers were successful in suppressing ceremonies within churches, but their writ was less effective outside. Boys continued to go about on St Clement's Day begging for apples, pears, money, or drink, down to at least Victorian times, and boys (and sometimes girls) on St Katherine's Day. A Buckinghamshire record of the nineteenth century talks even of girls in men's clothing.[149]

The best recorded of these winter observances in the middle ages are the festivals of St Nicholas and Childermas. From at least the early thirteenth century, boys attached to churches as choristers or servers honoured St Nicholas, patron saint of boys and scholars, and boys from schools sometimes attended church on his feast-day.[150] The day was marked by licensed 'role reversal'. Each body of choristers or scholars chose one of their number to be bishop, and the rest acted as his clergy or servants. They put on clerical garments, travelled around the neighbourhood, administered blessings, and asked for gifts. These activities were chiefly extramural, but on 28 December the boy-bishop reappeared in church and took a leading part in the liturgy. At Salisbury, he was formally installed in the choir at vespers on the afternoon of the 27th. He led the services and administered blessings to the people until the vespers of the following afternoon.[151] At St Paul's Cathedral London by the fourteenth century, he preached a sermon, and two specimens of these survive from St Paul's and Gloucester in the Tudor era, written by adults for boys to deliver.[152]

Innocents Day had further customs outside church. At Exeter, the cathedral choristers had a special breakfast, and the boy-bishop and six companions a special dinner. They spent part of the day touring the city and suburbs, calling first at the local monastery of St Nicholas, and distributed gloves to local worthies, apparently in return for money. The fact that 'St Nicholas's clerks' became a common national expression for robbers suggests that, here and elsewhere, the boys begged with some forcefulness! Their takings, when totalled, went to the boy-bishop himself.[153] Exeter was a small city and the authorities firmly limited the boys' activities to the twenty-four hours of the feast. At St Paul's (London) the festivities were more expansive. Not only did the boys choose a bishop but a dean, archdeacons, and additional figures. Other boys formed a retinue of two chaplains, two taper-bearers, and five clerks to go in procession with the bishop, preceded by two servants of the cathedral carrying staves. The boys were entertained in the households of the dean and canons and, after midday dinner on the festival day itself, they gathered in the cathedral porch and mounted horses supplied by the adult clergy. Then they accompanied the bishop around the city, blessing the people.[154]

The customs of Innocents Day flowered most luxuriantly at York Minster. There, so much money was involved that financial accounts were produced to record it, one of which survives for the winter of 1396–7. This shows that £8 15s. 5d. was collected. Each of the senior clergy of the cathedral made a present in cash. Feasting took place on a lavish scale; the menu included ducks, chickens, woodcocks, fieldfares, and a plover. Wine, honey, and pears were also consumed. The boys of York did not restrict their travels to the city. On 4 January they went to call on a local knight at Kexby, six miles away, and returned the same day. On Sunday the 7th they left on horseback for a long journey which lasted until the following Saturday week. Returning on the 20th, they set off again on Monday the 22nd and finally came home on Saturday the 27th. During this period they toured the East and parts of the North and West Ridings, going as far as Northallerton to the north and Monk Bretton near Doncaster to the south. They visited fifteen abbeys and priories, seven lay lords and ladies (including the countess of Northumberland), and one parish rector. At each of these places they received a payment, apparently a customary one. Altogether, their expenses cost £6 14s. 10½d. and the boy-bishop took the balance of £2 0s. 6½d.[155]

The schools had a calendar of their own, affecting a smaller number of children – chiefly boys. Schools, then as now, seem to have operated a system of three terms starting with Michaelmas, followed by Christmas and Easter, and there are references in schoolbooks to the beginning and ending of these. This rhythm may have had its own calendar customs. Keith Thomas has drawn attention to the practice of schoolboys, after the Reformation, marking special holidays like Shrove Tuesday by a real or mock exclusion of the master, known as 'barring out'.[156] This custom is not recorded before the Reformation, the nearest approach to it being one of the songs discussed in the previous chapter: *Ante finem termini baculum portamus*. But this, as we saw, is a rather muted affair. Although it starts by threatening to cause mayhem, the song soon turns into a prayer for permission 'to break up the school', with a promise to return when Christmas was over.[157]

It would be unwise to assert that barring out did not exist in the middle ages, since we know so little of the details of school life. But if the lack of references to it reflects the real situation, it may be that barring out was less called for because pre-Reformation schools were more varied in their timetables. The year was often punctuated by festivals; most masters were self-employed and may have been indulgent about granting holidays. After the Reformation, festivals were fewer. More schools became endowed foundations, regulated by statutes, and the school year grew more uniform. Barring out may have been a response to this change.

MUSIC AND DRAMA

THERE ARE TWO other kinds of play left to consider: music and drama. Both are natural to childhood. Children, once they leave their infancy, begin to mimic the songs or music that they hear, and to copy the actions of their elders. So it was in

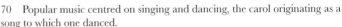

the past. True, the music of medieval children is an obscure subject, little noted by observers, but some of its likely forms can be conjectured. They certainly sang, spontaneously and artlessly, the nursery rhymes and songs of the previous chapter. They must have whistled, hooted through their fingers, or made simple pipes and percussion to beat or blow. Even at a popular level of society, there were parents who played musical instruments, for amusement or reward, and had motives for teaching such skills to their children. Barnwell near Cambridge is described in 1295–6 as a place where children and adolescents met on Midsummer Eve to entertain one another with songs and instruments.[158] John Stow tells how, in Elizabethan London, an adolescent girl might beat the timbrell (or tambourine) in the street while her friends danced, and a famous fifteenth-century story centres on a herd-boy who played the pipe with dramatic effects on his listeners (Figs 70, 107).[159]

Music was part of formal education too. Boys in school, it seems, often learnt plainsong to prepare themselves for work as parish clerks and adult clergy. Large churches, by the twelfth century, maintained choristers who were trained in singing plainsong and descant, and (by the mid fifteenth century) in the performance of elaborate polyphony.[160] Boys and girls of wealthy families were taught to play instrumental music as part of their education. Small boys might have drums, like Thomas and Edmund, the youngest sons of Edward I in 1306, when they were aged about four and five.[161] Older ones learnt to finger stringed instruments such as harps and lutes. Harp-strings were bought for Henry V in 1397, when he was ten, and all the surviving children of Henry VII, boys and girls, appear to have learnt the lute.[162]

70   Popular music centred on singing and dancing, the carol originating as a song to which one danced.

Chaucer describes his Squire as able to play the flute, and Henry IV possessed a recorder. Music entered into noble education because the ability to sing and play was a social accomplishment among adult men and women of the rank, and a few of them have left identifiable compositions, including a 'Roy Henry' who was either Henry IV or Henry V, and, of course, Henry VIII.[163]

Acting differed from music in being seen as a predominantly male activity. It is not mentioned in schemes of education, but boys were often encouraged to act by adults who valued their help in staging performances. Schoolmasters, who had the best access to groups of intelligent boys, seem to have used them as actors from early times. One of the oldest references to a play in England relates to a schoolmaster, Geoffrey of Maine, who arranged one on the life of St Katharine while teaching at Dunstable (Beds.) in about 1100. He borrowed vestments from St Albans Abbey to embellish it, and his pupils may well have performed it. The play was remembered because the vestments got burnt by accident, and Geoffrey made amends by joining the abbey as a monk.[164] In 1316, William Wheatley, schoolmaster of Lincoln, wrote two Latin hymns for 'playing' on Christmas Day, possibly in a dramatic presentation.[165] By the fifteenth century, references to plays single out the involvement of children. In 1430, boys from Maxstoke Priory (Warks.) acted in Maxstoke Castle on Candlemas Day, and in 1487, Henry VII watched similar boys from Hyde Abbey and Winchester Cathedral play 'Christ's Descent into Hell' in Winchester Castle.[166]

By this period references to plays proliferate, and they were clearly taking place all over England. Some were performed in the households of the aristocracy, gentry, higher clergy, and religious orders. Others were staged in public places in villages and towns. Their actors were sometimes members of a household or local community, performing for the occasion, and sometimes people who, if not professionals, were specialists presenting their work in several places. The plays fell into several categories. There were secular stories like those of Robin Hood. There were morality plays in which allegorical characters – good and bad – interacted to deliver a moral or educational message. There were religious plays depicting episodes from the Bible, a saint's life, or a miracle story. And there were whole cycles of plays, giving an outline of God's dealings with the world from the Creation to the Day of Judgment. These cycles, requiring large resources of staging and performers, were based in the larger towns, and four of them survive in written form: the Chester plays, 'N-Town' plays from East Anglia (possibly Norwich), 'Towneley' plays from Wakefield (Yorks.), and York plays.[167]

The chief evidence about children and the drama relates to the town cycles and the great households. Cycles, and indeed individual religious plays staged in smaller towns and villages, offered a good deal of scope for involving boys and youths. One reason for this was the existence of women's parts, which seem to have been normally played in England by males rather than females.[168] The early fifteenth-century 'Shrewsbury Fragments', from a cycle of town plays somewhere in the north of England, show that the same actor played a shepherd in the Nativity story and one of the three Maries in that of the Resurrection.[169] In Coventry, payments occur to boys or men playing St Anne and Pilate's Wife.[170]

Older women like Anne, or comic ones like Noah's Wife, were capable of being acted by grown-up men, but there was a need for pre-pubescent boys with soft complexions and no facial hair to play roles like those of Eve or the young Virgin Mary. The same may have been true of angels. Far from minimising female characters, the town cycles provided for them beyond the strict requirements of Biblical history. Virtues, cast as women, appear in one of the heavenly scenes in the N-Town series. A prophetess, Sibilla, joins the Old Testament prophets, and in two of the cycles the birth of Jesus requires the presence of midwives.

Boys and youths were also recruited to play themselves. The Bible stories of the town plays called for them on three occasions: the sacrifice of Isaac, the young Jesus with the doctors of the law, and the greeting of Jesus on his entry into Jerusalem by singing children. Other parts, however, like those for women, were often added to what the stories demanded. The Chester cycle had four shepherd boys in the Nativity scene, a boy to serve King Herod, a boy leading a blind man healed by Jesus, and a 'little God' speaking at Pentecost – presumably a small boy placed in a loft.[171] N-Town provided for an adolescent to lead the blind Lamech, and virgins to accompany Mary when she served as a girl in the Temple.[172] Towneley and York directed Abraham to take two boy attendants as he went to sacrifice Isaac, and York provided for children on other occasions. There, the 'children of Israel' in the play of Moses were presented literally as children, the young Virgin Mary was given girl companions, Herod and Pilate each had a voluble son, and King Herod Antipas possessed three.[173] All the cycles included messengers and grooms, who seem to have been adolescents or young men and were given humorous, bantering roles. Altogether, children and youths must have discharged a wide range of parts, large and small, stately, tragic, and comic.

The other important centres of drama about which records survive were the great households. These included the establishments of the king, nobility, bishops, and gentry, and religious communities such as cathedrals, monasteries, and colleges. Schools, too, can be classified with this group, especially the larger ones linked with cathedrals or colleges like Eton College, Magdalen College, St Paul's (London), and Winchester College. Life in such places lent itself to drama. The lord and lady, bishop or abbot, and their visitors had to be entertained, and feasts took place at which plays could be staged. There were numerous literate people able to write and act, and plenty of suitable players. Adult servants or clergy could be conscripted for men's parts, and choristers, schoolboys, wards, and pages for child or female ones. In schools, boys might do all the acting themselves, and in households, if they were not doing so, they might be spectators.

What kinds of performing roles did boys carry out in these places? At the simplest level, they may have delivered comic speeches or songs. Some of the earliest pieces of dramatic material to survive in English occur in a grammatical miscellany, probably connected with Bristol in about the 1420s. Along with the Latin texts which make up most of the contents, the manuscript contains three fragments of speeches and proclamations in English. One is a bidding prayer in verse, which begins 'We shall bid [*pray*] for the pope of Rome' and mentions 'the lord all of this hall' and his lady and children. It starts reverently enough, but becomes satirical when it turns to summoners, usurers, prostitutes, cuckolds, and false jurors, and ends by wishing them 'Christ's curse and mine'. The second item is a prologue, asking its hearers to listen 'to our play', and the third is another prologue, addressed to those 'in this hall'. It is followed by two three-line speeches, containing an exchange between Robyn Hoggys and Hawkyn Wynnegrett, picaresque characters. The material seems aimed at a secular household and, although the actors are not identified, the grammatical context suggests that a schoolmaster or scholar may well have been involved.[174]

Morality plays are particularly worth examining for traces of young actors. These were more sophisticated dramas, especially performed in households or by their members. Almost any character in a morality play was capable of being presented by a boy or a youth, and the existence of young female parts is a strong clue to their involvement. Stage directions sometimes mention children too. The three 'Macro' plays, written in East Anglia or nearby in the early and mid fifteenth century, are good examples. All are about humanity's progress through the temptations of life to final salvation. *The Castle of Perseverance* contains eleven female characters: seven Virtues and four 'daughters of God'.[175] *Wisdom* features Anima (the soul) as a maid, and five virgins who sing an anthem – very likely choristers.[176] It provides that, when Lucifer the Devil leaves the stage, 'Here he taketh a shrewd [*naughty*] boy with him and goeth his way crying'.[177] Later on, it presents Anima like a fiend and orders that 'Here runneth out, from under the horrible mantle of the Soul, seven small boys in the likeness of devils, and so return again'.[178]

The third Macro play, *Mankind*, is one where the presence of children is suggested by the text rather than the stage directions or characters. This play has a small cast of seven, all of them male, and it not clear how old they are meant to be. The dialogue, however, contains a good deal of Latin, suggesting an audience that included clergy, scholars, or competently literate people, and one of its comic characters – Nowadays – not only quotes Latin but refers in one of his speeches to a school Latin textbook:

> I pray you heartily, worshipful clerk,
> To have this English made in Latin:
> 'I have eaten a dishful of curds,
> And I have shitten your mouth full of turds.'
> Now open your satchel with Latin words
> And say me this in clerical manner![179]

The second line echoes one of the best-known basic schoolbooks of the day, *Informacio*, by the fifteenth-century Oxford schoolmaster John Leland. 'What shalt thou do when thou hast an English [sentence] to make in Latin?'[180] Line five may refer to another well known school text, the Latin verse vocabulary known as *Bursa Latini* ('the purse (or satchel) of Latin'),[181] and lines three and four are a parody of a school exercise. They constitute an English sentence for turning into Latin, and follow a comic formula, combining nice and nasty things, that we noticed in the

ᒿ🙰A new Enterlued for

Chyldren to playe named Jacke Jugeler, both
wytte, very playſent and merye, Neuer
before Imprented.

The Players names.
Mayſters. Boungrace.   A galant
Dame cope.   A Gentelwoman
Jacke Jugler.   the vyce.
Jenkin careaway   A Lackey.
Ales trype and go   A mayd.

71   Boys took part in plays, taking
roles not only as boys but as girls
and adults, as here in *Jacke Jugeler*
(*c*.1562).

previous chapter.[182] It is hard to resist the conclusion that Nowadays is a schoolboy or a character aimed at such boys.

A number of similar plays from the later fifteenth and early sixteenth centuries
contain signs of child participation. One important centre of drama in the 1490s
was the household of Cardinal Morton, archbishop of Canterbury, at Lambeth
Palace. It was here that the fourteen-year-old Thomas More, according to a later
account by his son-in-law William Roper,

> though he was young of years, yet would he at Christmastide suddenly some-
> times step in among the players, and never studying for the matter, make a part
> of his own there presently among them, which made the lookers on more sport
> than all the players beside.[183]

Two plays survive by Henry Medwall, one of Morton's notaries, which were
probably performed in the household during this decade. One, *Fulgens and Lucres*,
contains important female roles for Lucres and her maid, as well as parts for servants A and B, which were suitable for youths or young adults. The other, *Nature*,
has at least one female character, Innocency.[184] Signs of the presence of children

in plays continue as we move into the early sixteenth century. *Mundus et Infans*, as has been noted, features Infans, representing the first seven years of life, and Wanton, who embodies the next seven.[185] Heywood's *Play of the Weather* calls for a boy who is 'the least [*smallest*] that can play', and by about 1562 the play *Jack Juggler* was published with the assertion that it was suitable 'for children to play' (Fig. 71).[186]

Morality plays, then, indicate a significant input from the young in roles as varied as those of the town cycles. Moreover, the plays were not performed only in the households where they originated. As we have seen, the boys of Maxstoke Priory and the monasteries at Winchester staged their productions for important lay people elsewhere. In the 1520s, John Ritwise, high master of St Paul's School (London), led his pupils in performing a tragedy of *Dido* before Cardinal Wolsey, and a Latin play against Luther at Greenwich in front of Henry VIII.[187] Later in the sixteenth century, the choristers of the Chapel Royal and of St Paul's regularly put on plays in London that rivalled those of the professional theatres and furnished Shakespeare with a topic for discussion in *Hamlet*.[188] But the tradition on which this was based stretched back to the later middle ages.

PLAYERS AND SPECTATORS

THE PLAY OF children and adolescents flowed through society like a great river. There were large numbers of toys and games, sedentary and active, indoor and outdoor, solitary and social. Their players varied in age, wealth, and gender. Younger children might imitate older ones in their play, but lacked the strength, skill, and usually the equipment to make the same impact. Poorer children must have had fewer well-made toys and specialised equipment for games, yet they could make their own versions and, in purely physical feats, equal those who were better off. Some games, such as chess and hunting, were particularly associated with the wealthy and noble, but other youths might imitate them, like the ones who sparked off a riot in London in 1253 by trying to stage a tournament practice.[189] The more sedentary behaviour expected of girls acted as something of a brake on them joining in games, and childish convention may often have excluded them, but modern analogies suggest that they took part in a great many, at least up to puberty. They also had their own toys and activities including dolls, singing, and dancing.

Was the play of young people part of adult culture, or separate from it? As with rhymes and songs, the answer is doubtless 'both'. Although the moralists regarded play as typifying childhood and youth, most of the games played by the young were shared by adults too. The word 'play' was widely used of adult relaxations and recreations. Adults provided toys for children, in the sense of manufacturing and purchasing them. They helped to organise the boy-bishop ceremonies, and recruited and directed children in dramas. They tried to influence how children played, and to direct their play to adult purposes. Equally, play was special to children and adolescents, and took place separately from adult life. John Trevisa,

John Colet Dean of S.t Paul's

72   John Colet (d. 1519),
refounder of St Paul's School
(London), took a more critical
view of play than previous
schoolmasters. He forbade
cockfighting and 'riding about
of victory' at his school.

translating Bartholomew's encyclopaedia in 1398, observed how the young 'love talkings and counsels of such children as they are, and forsake and avoid [the] company of old men [*adult people*]'.[190] Children spent much time at play in streets and fields, with their peers rather than with their parents. They made their own toys as well as those that were given them, and used special names for the objects with which they played.

The great river had its spectators, as we saw at the start of this chapter. Some of the adults standing on its bank watched its progress with misgivings, often with discontent. They wished to divert its energies to useful purposes or to dam it completely. Play could be antisocial, or seem so. The child Wanton in *Mundus et Infans* uses his whip not only to spin his top but to hit his playmate.[191] At Exeter Cathedral, the dean and chapter complained bitterly about the invasion of their cloisters in about 1448 by 'young persons' who played at 'the top, quek, penny prick, and most at tennis, by the which the walls of the said cloister have been defouled and the glass windows all burst asunder'.[192] 'Quek', a board game, was sedate if inappropriate, but tennis and penny-prick were dangerous to property and people, the latter apparently involving the shooting of arrows at a penny piece.

Play seemed morally dangerous too. Guillaume de Deguileville and his English translators thought that it tempted young people to play truant, thieve, be wilful, and ignore parents. Youth literally set the camping crook against the cross.[193] Rait was indulgent about some aspects of children's play, particular the gentler and creative games, but he was critical of others and warned his son against them. Chess and backgammon drew children away from church attendance; dice playing was unwise.[194] *Mundus et Infans* took a similar view. Its badly brought-up infant becomes a wanton child, spends the next seven years playing games and shirking school work, and gives himself to self-indulgence when he grows up. He is rescued to virtue only at the end of the story. The play's implicit lesson is that, given more discipline and less play in childhood, he would have lived a better life.[195] One of the Magdalen College schoolbooks contains passages in which the natural tendency of children to enjoy ease and pleasure is framed with the necessity for them to accept discipline and education.[196] Laws against games and in favour of archery bear witness to similar views.

Even when it was neither immoral nor antisocial, children's play seemed an inferior activity to other human endeavours. Religious writers and moralists liked to use it not only as an image of children's immaturity but of the follies of adults. It was, after all, an attack on people's religious inconstancy that led the thirteenth-century preacher to refer to 'How Many Miles to Beverleyham?'. The Elizabethan *Book of Homilies* (1562), wishing to ridicule image-worship, quoted the saying of the early Christian writer Lactantius that 'as little girls play with little puppets, so be these decked images great puppets for old fools to play with'.[197] One of the Magdalen College schoolbooks satirises modern mothers as wishing to treat their children as dolls rather than to bring them up properly,[198] and Philip Stubbes's derisive comparison of dolls and women's clothes has already been mentioned. Such views left their mark on the treatment of play in literature, and presumably on individual parents and children, but their effects should not be overestimated. Play had too many supporters among clerics, schoolmasters, craftsmen, and parents. Most of all, children went on playing, despite all their elders' attempts to control what they did. Boys, after all, will be boys, and girls be girls.

Chapter 6
—
Church

THE CHURCH AND THE CHILD

LANGLAND'S GREAT POEM *Piers Plowman* begins by telling how its author falls asleep on the Malvern Hills and sees a vision of heaven, hell, and the world between them. Entering the world, the first person he meets is a lady with a beautiful face, clothed in pure linen. He does not recognise her, and she gently chides him. 'I am Holy Church. You ought to know me. I received you at the beginning, and taught you faith. You brought me pledges to do my bidding and to love me loyally while your life lasts.'[1] These words set out the relationship, in its ideal form, between the Church and children in medieval England. The Church admitted all to its membership on the first day of their lives, through baptism. As they grew up, it gave them teaching, provided by its clergy and (though Langland does not say so) by godparents and parents. In return, every child promised, through its godparents at baptism, to do the Church's bidding for the rest of its life. This promise affected how children behaved and what they believed.

The clergy's involvement with children formed part of their ministry to the whole of society through church services, pastoral work, and teaching. People needed to know how to pray, and the clergy were meant to see that they knew by heart the basic prayers of the Church. There were two of these by the late Anglo-Saxon period: the Paternoster (Lord's Prayer) and the Apostles' Creed, to which a third, the Ave Maria, was added by the thirteenth century.[2] People were also expected to have an elementary understanding of God, his rules about how to behave, and the evils of the world that they should avoid. An influential decree of the council of Lambeth in 1281, best known by its opening words *Ignorantia sacerdotum*, 'the ignorance of priests', laid down that the clergy should teach the people about the fourteen points of the Creed, the ten commandments, the seven sacraments, the seven works of mercy, the seven virtues, and the seven deadly sins.[3]

Most of the directions to medieval clergy about teaching relate to people as a whole, rather than children in particular. Church leaders seem usually to have expected instruction to reach the young from their parents and godparents, not directly from priests. In the thirteenth century, however, some diocesan synods made a point of encouraging parish clergy to teach children face to face. One held in Salisbury diocese, between 1217 and 1219, ordered them to call together children and instruct one or two, or cause them to be instructed, in the three basic prayers.[4] Another in Lincoln diocese, in about 1239, also told clergy to teach children these prayers, and several synods in other dioceses repeated the Salisbury or Lincoln decrees to their own parish priests.[5] Whether the clergy carried out these orders by holding regular classes is not clear. Some may have done so on their personal initiative, but there is no evidence that this happened on a normal or frequent basis. Much was written about the duties (and failings) of priests between 1250 and 1530, but it did not extend to discussing their work with children.

The Reformation marked a change in this respect. In 1537–8, we find certain English bishops – Latimer of Worcester, Lee of Coventry and Lichfield, Shaxton of Salisbury, and Veysey of Exeter – ordering their parish clergy and chantry

73   Baptism made everyone Christian at birth or soon after. Godparents had the duty to see that children were brought up safely and spiritually.

priests to teach the Paternoster, Ave Maria, Creed, and Ten Commandments in English to children and 'young people' specifically.[6] This seems to be a new initiative, reflecting the concern of Tudor Reformers with evangelism in general and the education of the young in particular.[7] When Cranmer's first Book of Common Prayer appeared in 1549, it contained the Catechism to teach children the form and meaning of the Creed, the Lord's Prayer, and the Ten Commandments in place of the Ave Maria.[8] The Book required the clergyman of each parish to spend half an hour in church for this purpose before the afternoon service on Sundays, at least once every six weeks – a duty increased to all Sundays and holy days in 1552. Here the clergyman was to instruct and examine them in the Catechism, so that each child knew the text by heart prior to being confirmed by the bishop.[9] The baptismal service continued to direct the godparents to ensure that children learned the three basic texts, but the clergy were now involved in the process to a greater extent than before.

Godparents, as we have seen, played an important part in the child's admission to the Church by baptism, but the Church did not regard their role as terminating with the christening ceremony.[10] They were envisaged as providing practical help in the child's upbringing, both spiritual and physical, in the ensuing years. Langland includes a warning of this in *Piers Plowman*:

> Godfathers and godmothers that see their children
> At misease [*trouble*] and at mischief, and may them amend,

Shall have penance in purgatory unless they them help,
For more belongs to the little bairn, ere he the law know,
Than naming of a name, and he never the wiser.[11]

By the end of the middle ages, the Salisbury or 'Sarum' service-books used in southern England included a charge for the priest to deliver to the godparents after a baby's baptism. This was in English, not in Latin like the service itself, so that it would be clearly understood:

> Godfathers and godmothers of this child, we charge you that you charge the father and the mother to keep it from fire and water and other perils to the age of seven years and that you learn [*teach*] or see it be learned the Paternoster, Ave Maria and Credo after the law of all Holy Church, and in all goodly haste to be confirmed of my lord of the diocese or of his deputy.[12]

A further rubric adds that they should teach it how to make the sign of the cross.[13] Godparents, then, should oversee the child's physical care, ensure that it learnt the basic prayers, and check that it proceeded to confirmation.[14] Even when it reached adulthood, they should continue to warn it to be chaste, love justice, and observe charity.[15]

How far were these tasks carried out? Anyone who has been a godparent knows that it is far easier to do one's duty at the christening than to make the role meaningful afterwards. Unless the parents are committed to the child's spiritual education, godparents have little opportunity to exercise an influence, and often become mere honorary uncles or aunts, sending greetings and presents on birthdays and at Christmas. The medieval godparent was potentially a stronger figure than this. First, there was the custom, already mentioned, by which the chief of the three often gave his or her own name to the child.[16] This set up a bond between them, easy to remember. Next, the Church's marriage laws regarded godparenting as establishing a spiritual family relationship. Your godparents and their children were your spiritual siblings, and you could not marry them.[17] This may have helped to perpetuate the link, not only between the parties concerned but among their clergy and neighbours. Finally, there was the higher mortality of the past, and the greater chance that godparents would need to take the place of absent fathers or mothers.

It is unlikely, however, that medieval parents chose godparents only or mainly on spiritual grounds. Secular motives mattered too, such as friendship and closeness at hand. The practice of selecting friends and neighbours as 'godsibs' or 'gossips' seems to be the reason why the word 'gossip' came to mean a crony and what cronies talk about.[18] Ralph Sadler's arrangements after the birth of his son in the mid 1530s were probably representative. The christening was to be held next day at Hackney, just outside London, where his wife had given birth, and godparents had to be found quickly. Sadler therefore wrote to Thomas Cromwell, the king's secretary, to ask him to be chief godfather and to give the child his name, envisaging that Cromwell could ride over from the king's court in

Dñs Galfridus louterell me fieri fecit

74   Sir Geoffrey Luttrell, of the famous Luttrell Psalter, was godparent to several children of his friends and servants.

Westminster or wherever else he was staying. The letter mentions that Sadler proposes to ask Mrs Richards or Lady Weston to be godmother, because they too were lodging near Hackney. Cromwell had already been godfather to another of Sadler's sons, but he had died; this one, the father hoped, would bring more joy.[19]

The choice of godparents was not a straightforward one. Many parents seem to have used the opportunity to gain the patronage of an important person, as Sadler did with Cromwell. Men and women of status and influence appear to have been often sought for their services. Sir Geoffrey Luttrell of Irnham (Lincs.) (d. 1345), the sponsor of the famous Luttrell Psalter (Fig. 74), mentions five godsons in his will, all named Geoffrey. One was the son of a knight but the remainder were the children of lowly people – two of them Sir Geoffrey's kitchen staff.[20] Simon Grendon, mayor of Exeter (d. 1411), made bequests at his death to nine godsons, each with his own forename.[21] Sir Henry Willoughby of Wollaton (Notts.), a knight and courtier of the early Tudor period, acted in similar ways. His household accounts show that he was called on three times to be a godfather in 1522, twice in 1524, and once in 1526. His daughter Mary acted twice in 1524, and her sister Alice two years later.[22] Their christening presents, graduated in scale, suggest that they too were approached both by neighbouring gentry and by lesser folk like tenants or former servants. The favour that the Luttrells and Willoughbys might provide in future, and the loyalty and good feeling produced in return, may have been valued as much or more as spiritual oversight.[23]

But not all godparents were superior socially. Others were equal or inferior in

rank to the child and its family. An analysis of christenings among the feudal aristocracy of Yorkshire in the later middle ages has suggested that out of fifty godfathers whose status is known, only four may have been superiors, while a greater
number were equals (15) and inferiors (31).[24] We certainly hear in the late thirteenth century of a steward, a steward's son, and an esquire doing duty at the baptisms of the sons of their employers, and not only in an auxiliary role but as chief
godparent, giving their names to the child.[25] Sometimes a recourse to inferiors
may have been forced by circumstances. Births were unpredictable, and the
arrival of a sickly child dictated immediate baptism. On other occasions, a preferred godparent failed to arrive in time.[26] A substitute had then to be found, such
as the presiding priest or a household servant. It is possible too that an inferior
person was used if he or she had the name which the parents wished to give to
their child. Superior persons might be offended if they were not allowed to confer
their own name.

Superior or inferior, it is difficult to summarise the effectiveness of medieval
godparenting. Logically, it must have varied from person to person. In pre-
Reformation times, claimed some Norfolk petitioners in 1556,

> 'Many good men of forty years, that had been godfathers to thirty children,
> knew no more of the godfather's office but to wash their hands ere they
> departed the church'.[27]

Others kept at least an avuncular relationship with their godchildren, expressed in
terms of gifts. One of the earliest such examples is Wulfric Spot, a Saxon
magnate, whose will of 1002–4 made a bequest of land and jewellery to his goddaughter.[28] Smaller gifts of money or goods occur in later medieval wills, similar
in scale to christening presents.[29] Giles Benet, for example, apparently a yeoman
farmer of Yeovil (Somerset) in 1521, gave 20s. each to Giles Benet, Giles Horsey,
and Giles Wynter, all godchildren whom he had named.[30] Occasionally, such
bequests are more obviously spiritual. William Revetour, a chaplain of York in
1446, bequeathed his goddaughter 'a large primer with images written inside it, in
the Flemish manner'.[31] A similar prayer book, the 'hours' of the Virgin, still exists
which Elizabeth Hull, abbess of Malling (Kent) presented to her goddaughter
Margaret Neville, daughter of a Kentish knight, between Margaret's baptism in
1520 and Elizabeth's death in 1524. Margaret kept the book all her life, and she
or someone else inserted a note of the gift inside it.[32] These last two instances, at
least, show that not all godparents forgot their religious functions.

RELIGION AT HOME

MOST CHILDREN LIVED at home in their early years. This left their parents as the
third, most dominant, influence on their religious upbringing. Since at least the
early eleventh century, Church leaders emphasised the duty of fathers and
mothers, as well as clergy, to teach their children the basic Christian prayers.[33] By

the later middle ages, they urged that this should extend to other basic knowledge and behaviour. John Thoresby, archbishop of York (d. 1372), told parents in his 'Lay Folk's Catechism' to pass on to their children the knowledge they gained from the clergy.[34] Reginald Pecock, bishop of Chichester, wrote in *The Donet* (*c*.1443–9) that they should inform their children about 'our belief and God's law'.[35] Critics of society, on the other hand, felt that too many parents failed in this respect. They laid the blame for social problems on the fact that children had not been brought up to respect God and to keep the laws that he and his Church had laid down for living.[36]

How far did parents exert themselves to bring up their children in a religious framework? A sign that some did so, in literate households, is the existence of primers – lay prayer books, first mentioned at the end of the thirteenth century.[37] These not only contain the basic prayers and other short religious pieces, usually in Latin, but sometimes start with an alphabet, suggesting that the primer was a book for parents or teachers to use with children. There is evidence that children learning to read were made to decipher the Paternoster as their first piece of prose after learning the basic letters.[38] Most homes, however, lacked books, and the practice of parents teaching prayers by word of mouth is poorly recorded. One person who remembered learning at home in this way was Hugh Buck of Barking (Essex), who asked his parish priest, John Adrian in about 1538, 'how shall a man

75 Parents too were expected to teach religion to children. Here, a father passes on the Word of God, enshrined in Henry VIII's English Bible of 1539, while all cry 'Long live the king'.

have knowledge for the spiritual life?' Adrian replied, 'Thy father and mother taught thee.' Buck admitted that 'my father and mother taught me my Paternoster, Ave, and Credo in Latin', but being touched by Reformation ideas he added 'and partly idolatry'.[39] There were different views in the later middle ages as to whether the basic prayers should be learnt in Latin or English. Both languages had their supporters, but Latin seems to have been widely used, even among ordinary and illiterate people.[40]

Hugh Buck's remark that he learnt 'partly idolatry' doubtless reflects the fact that home instruction, as well as spanning prayers, beliefs, and behaviour, included the outward observances that played so great a part in medieval religion. St Edmund of Abingdon (born *c*.1175) was 'nourished religiously' by his pious mother, to the extent that he prayed and fasted while he still was a child. When he was a student in Paris, she sent him a hair shirt.[41] In Chaucer's 'Prioress's Tale', a widowed mother teaches her seven-year-old son not only one of the basic prayers (the Ave Maria) but one basic observance: to kneel and repeat it in front of every image of the Virgin that he passes.[42] From at least the 1230s, Church leaders urged that children should not only be able to pray but to make the sign of the cross correctly – a ritual used before prayer or to ward off danger.[43] The right way of making the sign emerged in a case of alleged heresy in 1431, when Nicholas Canon of Eye (Suffolk) was accused of failing to do so. His mother had told him to cross himself against the devil with his right hand, and when he refused, she took his hand and crossed him saying, '*In nomine Patris, Filii, et Spiritus Sancti. Amen.*' Here we see maternal instruction at work, though in this case it was not effective since the son (by then an adult) refused to comply.[44]

By the fifteenth century, popular handbooks existed to give advice about children's upbringing. One meant for boys, *How the Wise Man Taught his Son*, exhorts them to begin each day with prayer, though its other contents are about wise behaviour rather than religious practices.[45] Another, Caxton's *Book of Courtesy*, says a good deal about both prayer and behaviour in church, and will be mentioned presently. There were similar works for girls. In *The Good Wife Would a Pilgrimage*, a mother leaving on a journey tells her daughter to pray with good devotion.[46] *How The Good Wife Taught Her Daughter* includes instructions to love God, go to church when possible, bid your beads when sitting there, observe holy days, and (in adulthood) pay tithes and give to the poor.[47] 'Bidding beads' may simply have meant praying, but beads were a synonym for the rosary commonly used to say multiples of the Paternoster, Ave Maria, and Creed. The memorial brass of Thomas Pownder, merchant of Ipswich (d. 1525), shows not only his wife but his eldest daughter with rosaries on their belts.[48]

Homes must have varied in their power to educate, from those of poor and indifferent families at one end to pious and wealthy ones at the other. Where religion was taken seriously, the home might turn into a house of God not dissimilar to a church in furnishings and observances. The house and well might be blessed by a priest to give them holy status.[49] Rooms might contain religious pictures and images: wall paintings and statues or figurines of saints. When printing developed, cheap woodcuts became available for display and veneration, showing

Christ on the cross or Our Lady of Pity sorrowing over his body. The existence of domestic images in England is mentioned by the government of Edward VI in 1547.[50] Families might own written indulgences, and literate people religious books. Lollard families were likely to engage in Bible reading and criticism of the contemporary Church, and prosecutions of Lollards sometimes mention their children.[51] Parents might undertake clergy functions, such as leading family prayers. They certainly gave solemn blessings to their kneeling children, as the biblical patriarchs had done.[52] Medieval writers told how Henry I and Edmund of Abingdon were blessed in this way, and the mother in the romance of *Freine* did the same to the baby that she left outside the nunnery.[53]

In civilised households, meals were a focus of family religion. The saying of grace before and after food was originally a monastic observance, copied by the lay nobility from at least the fourteenth century.[54] By the fifteenth, it had spread further down society, and the custom seems to have developed by which children (at any rate, boys) said or rather led the grace. Graces, like the basic prayers, were often in Latin, taking the form of short versicles and responses as well as pieces of prose. The texts sometimes appeared in primers, and might be taught by clergy or schoolmasters as part of the process of learning to read. In 1423, the abbot of Saffron Walden (Essex) forbade two local chaplains to teach the alphabet and graces to small children, but granted the request of the townspeople that any priest might do so to a single child.[55] At Hull in 1454, schoolchildren at the elementary stage of learning were taught graces after the alphabet.[56] It is possible that non-Latinate households said such prayers in English, but this practice lacked official encouragement until the Reformation. *The ABC both in Latin and English* (London, 1538) contained nine pages of graces in English for use before dinner or supper, with variations for fish-eating days and the season of Easter.[57]

Meals could be educational in other respects. The Church had dietary laws, the observance of which formed a large part of a Christian's duty. Adults were not supposed to eat meat on Fridays or on the days before major feasts, and had to abstain from meat and dairy products throughout Lent. Children would have become familiar with such rules, although they were not fully subject to them.[58] They would have joined in the feasting of Christmas and Easter, and the Rogationtide celebrations in May or June with their flans and dainty fish dishes.[59] Noble or pious households might follow another custom of religious houses: reading edifying literature at meals. An early fifteenth-century set of Latin instructions, apparently drawn up for a wealthy married layman, advised the improvement of family meals by reading aloud, lest people's tongues spoke vain or hurtful things. Reading should be done 'now by one, now by another, and by your children (*filiis*) as soon as they can read'.[60] When Edward IV planned the education of his son Edward V in 1473, a boy who was not quite three, he too included provision for the reading of 'noble stories' at his table.[61]

The most ambitious households followed daily patterns of prayer and worship, mirroring those of the clergy. King Alfred (d. 899) tried to devote half of his time to God by day and night, presumably in prayer and study.[62] In later centuries, it became common for royalty and the aristocracy to spend part of their day in prayer. Sometimes lay people said prayers by themselves in their bedrooms before rising and going to bed. At other times they did so in a chapel which became, by the later middle ages, an essential feature of a noble or gentle house, with a chaplain to serve it if resources allowed. By the fifteenth century, personal plans of religious observance begin to survive. The Latin instructions just mentioned recommended their recipient to begin the day by rising quickly from bed and making the sign of the cross. He should then go to church and say the short devotional service of mattins of the Virgin, probably from the prayer book in her honour known as the 'book of hours'. This was to be followed by hearing mass and repeating five decades of Our Lady's psalter (one third of the rosary). Vespers should be attended in the afternoon, while both main meals of the day – dinner and supper – should be preceded and followed by grace.[63] Later in the century, as clocks became common, pious people organised their days by clock time. Edward IV's mother, Cecily duchess of York (d. 1495), and Henry VII's, Lady Margaret Beaufort (d. 1509), both had daily timetables drawn up for them: arranging prayer, business, and meals in units as short as a quarter of an hour.[64]

Children and adolescents in wealthy families were brought up in a similar pattern. Geoffrey de la Tour Landry, writing in the 1370s told his daughters to begin saying 'mattins' (that is, of the Virgin) as soon as they rose from bed, before they had breakfast. They must read the service devoutly, and not think of anything else while doing so. Before going to sleep, they should pray to the Virgin Mary and the saints, and on behalf of the dead.[65] In about 1435, a plan of living for John Mowbray, duke of Norfolk, aged about twenty, recommended him to pray both morning and evening. He was to rise between 6.00 and 7.00 am, say mattins, prime, and the lesser hours with his chaplain, using the book of hours, and go to mass. In the afternoon, he should say the evensong of the Virgin.[66] The arrangements for Edward V contained similar provisions. After rising, he was to hear his chaplains say mattins in his chamber (presumably mattins of the Virgin), and then go to mass in his chapel or private closet. Like the duke, he was to attend evensong later in the day.[67]

Relatively few people lived in households with chapels and chaplains, but saying the hours of the Virgin from the book of hours seems to have been a common practice among the gentry and merchant class in the later middle ages. This is suggested by the large number of primers and hours belonging to such people, which are mentioned in documents or survive from the mid thirteenth century up to the Reformation. Occasionally, such books can be linked with children. Henry VI was nine when he was given the beautifully illuminated 'Bedford Hours' by his uncle and aunt in 1430.[68] Bridget Plantagenet, daughter of Viscount Lisle, was a year older when two mattins books were purchased for her in 1535, when she was boarding in the nunnery of St Mary at Winchester.[69] The saying of such prayers is mentioned in the *Book of Courtesy* published by Caxton in 1477, a work by an earlier unknown writer. This was constructed in verse to give advice to a 'little child' or 'little John'. It seems to be aimed at boys of relatively high status who were being educated in a noble household or attending a town grammar school. When the child gets out of bed, he is told to cross himself three times and repeat the Paternoster, Ave Maria, and Creed. He should then dress, while saying the hours of the Virgin with the pupil who shared his room.[70] Nothing is said here about evening prayers, but they were probably common: either from prayer books or in the form of traditional verses, like 'Matthew, Mark, Luke, and John', which we encountered in an earlier chapter.[71]

GOING TO CHURCH

BEING A CHRISTIAN also meant going to church and observing the customs in use there. In Caxton's *Book of Courtesy*, the boy reader is told to cast holy water on himself as he enters, from the bowl provided, and to kneel before the cross on the screen between the nave and chancel. There he was to say another Paternoster, Ave, and Creed.[72] Aristocratic children, who travelled with parents or guardians from one estate to another, or from court to country, were likely to experience a variety of churches, including household chapels and monasteries. As aristocracy, they were expected to be generous with their money. A roll of the expenses of Isabel and Joan, the daughters of Edward III, shows them travelling with their servants round the outskirts of London in 1341–2 and giving donations at the churches they visited. On 30 December 1341, they attended mass in the Tower of London, made an offering worth 6s., and gave 3s. 4d. to four friars singing at the service. On the following 17 February, they called on the nuns of Kilburn Priory (Middx.). On 1 April, they heard a friar preach a sermon, probably in the Cistercian abbey of Stratford Langthorn (Essex), and tipped him 3s. 4d. Later that week, while still at Stratford, they gave Maundy money to twenty-four poor people, and offered 6d. each to the cross on Good Friday.[73]

Most children were not aristocratic, and church for them was their parish church. Once baptised, there was no formal bar to their entry, even as infants, and in some respects medieval worship in parish churches was not ill-suited to the very young. Services took place in the chancel behind the rood-screen, while the laity followed their individual devotions in the nave, sometimes praying or read-ing aloud. These arrangements were less easily disturbed by babies than post-Reformation worship, in which clergy and people operated together in the nave. In practice, however, people's tolerance of baby noise in church varied, as happens today. St Cyprian considered it to be a kind of prayer, and some later moralists thought it a lament for the human condition.[74] Langland uses the simile 'as chaste as a child that in church weepeth', which affirms the chasteness rather than blaming the weeping.[75] Others, in contrast, found the presence of babies dis-tracting. A visitation of Lincoln diocese in the early sixteenth century was told that in the church of Kimpton (Herts.), 'infants for the most part laugh, cry, and call out during divine service'. At Gosberton (Lincs.) a certain Thomas Leyk was accused of impeding the service with an infant, apparently in a regular way.[76]

Because of their unpredictable behaviour or because some parents used church to escape from their families, very young children were not always taken there. In 1268, the Muchard family of Bedfordshire – father, mother, and household – all

76   Children who went to church would have watched the service through the chancel screen (omitted here), with other lay people.

went to church leaving behind a two-year-old boy, apparently in the care of an older sister; he wandered out of the house and fell down a well.[77] In 1377, Edith le Taylour of Lacock (Wilts.) put her infant daughter in a cradle by the fire at prime (about eight o'clock in the morning) while she attended mass – not reckoning that chickens would enter the house and scatter fire on the cradle with fatal results.[78] In the late fifteenth century, John Hargrave of Ketton (Rutland), a toddler of fifteen months, was left at home while his parents went to church for the service of vespers. The child crawled into the fire and burnt himself, and although he was later healed through prayers to the dead King Henry VI, the recorder of the miracle felt bound to say that the reason for this piece of negligence did not excuse it.[79]

Older children too made the journey to church. Some did so by themselves, out of curiosity or in search of play. In the late twelfth century, a little girl called Emeloth entered Durham cathedral illicitly while playing with others of her age. Unfortunately for her, the church was forbidden to women and she lost her senses, which she recovered only through a pilgrimage to St Godric of Finchale.[80] Other children were taken to church by adults, sometimes when they were sick, as we hear in miracle stories, but sometimes for other reasons.[81] Abbot Samson of Bury St Edmunds remembered his mother bringing him to the abbey church of the town to pray in about 1144, when he was nine.[82] A child could be a useful companion to a woman when going to church, because women were expected to be chaperoned when they travelled outside their homes. The Knight of the Tower urged his daughters never to be alone with a man other than their father, husband, or son, and a fifteenth-century poem from the north or from Scotland, *The Thews of Good Women*, advised women not to go on errands without a child or maiden to escort them.[83] Church attendance probably fell into this category. When Margery Kempe the burgess-wife of King's Lynn (Norfolk) visited the nearby church of Mintling in the company of two priests, they 'took with them a child or two and went to the said place all together'.[84] A woman courted scandal by going out with unrelated men, even to church, even with clergy; indeed, the Knight tells a cautionary tale of a woman who made love in church with the sexton.[85]

There were some pious children, or so hagiographers claimed, who attended church as part of a precocious interest in prayer and self-discipline. St William of Norwich is said to have enjoyed doing so in the mid twelfth century, and Edmund of Abingdon is credited with fasting and praying while he was still a boy.[86] Matthew Paris's Life of Edmund tells how, at the age of twelve, he often went to confession and made a vow of chastity to an image of the Virgin, giving her a ring as a token. During his adolescence, he left some fellow scholars who were playing in a field, and prayed in front of a flowering briar where he had a vision of the infant Christ.[87] St John of Bridlington (born in the early fourteenth century at Thweng in Yorkshire) was another godly child. On coming out of school, where he was sent in his fifth year, he refused to join in childish games but went to the church and gave himself to prayer and devotion. He too made a promise to be chaste in his twelfth year.[88]

77   Children were also taken to shrines. Here, the boy king Henry VI kneels at the tomb of St Edmund
at Bury (Suffolk).

The adult population was expected to come to church on Sundays and major
festivals, and this practice may have extended to children in noble families Prince
Henry's household accounts of 1273–4 show him and his siblings doing so on
thirty-seven occasions between 24 September and 31 December 1273 alone.
Dutifully and uniformly, they (or their guardian) offered 4d. on Sundays, 3d. on
saints' days, and larger sums on the great festivals.[89] The church-going habits of
the majority of young people, in contrast, are still little known. Some children
may have been brought by conscientious parents or sent by those who wished for
quiet at home. Others may have played truant or, in tolerant or indifferent families, may not have been made to go. In church, they had to fit into their elders'
arrangements for worship. Where one stood or sat reflected status and gender.
The chancel housed the clergy and probably any nobility and gentry who chose
to attend. Other leading parishioners are likely to have occupied the front parts of
the nave. Men and women were sometimes segregated on opposite sides of the
church. Children of high rank, one presumes, joined their gender parents in a
subordinate position, as they are shown on tomb monuments. Young men and

maidens, who formed groups in certain parishes as we shall see, may have done so in church as well. Ordinary children may have been put at the back of the building (an inferior location), as appears to have been the practice at Great Marlow (Bucks.) by the 1540s.[90] Placing of this kind must have become more rigid as churches instituted rows of benches, which was happening by the fifteenth century.

What did children and young people do inside the building? Much the same, one suspects, as their parents. The wealthy and literate might read devotional books: primers and hours, or more sophisticated psalters, breviaries, and missals. The less important might repeat the three basic prayers, with rosaries if they possessed them. Not all church-going, however, was linked with services. Lay people might enter church to pray alone or to light a candle to an image; children might go with them to do so. In 1531, Sir Thomas Elyot observed how they reproduced in their play both the formal and informal sides of church-going. 'We behold [how] some children, kneeling in their game before images and holding up their little white hands, do move their pretty mouths as [if] they were praying, other [or] going and singing as it were in procession.'[91] Processions of clergy and laity round the church or through the parish took place in the spring and early summer, and there is no reason why children should not have joined them too.

The young could also imitate their elders by bad behaviour in church. A Bristol guild in 1218–36 warned its adult members not to walk about church during services, but to stand or kneel as an example to other laity, and the author of *Sir Gawain and the Green Knight* felt it worth saying that his hero 'sat soberly' through the vespers of Christmas Eve.[92] At least two fifteenth-century courtesy poems for boys remind them that a church is a house of prayer in which one should avoid being noisy or playing about.[93] Tensions sometimes arose between younger and older people in these matters, as happens today. In Leicestershire in the early sixteenth century, the rector of Wymondham complained that children and older people made so much din that no one could hear the worship. A similar report at Kirby Bellars alleged that 'children there make noise indecently'.[94] Sometimes, they may have done damage. The protests of the dean and chapter of Exeter, about the 'young persons' who damaged the walls of their cloisters and broke the windows, are unlikely to have been unique.[95]

RITES OF PASSAGE

CHRISTIANITY SOUGHT, FROM the first, to embrace the young as well as the old. When people brought children to Jesus for blessings, he told his disciples not to forbid them, and talked of adults becoming like children in order to enter the kingdom of heaven.[96] Once the Church took an organised form, however, it had to learn to deal with children and adults in appropriate ways. Children did not need the same kind of teaching or discipline as their elders, and they could not be expected to support the Church economically. In due course, a tendency arose to consider some of the Church's services as appropriate either for children or for adults, rather than for both. Two of the sacraments (baptism and confirmation) became associated with children, while the other five (the eucharist, confession, marriage, ordination, and the anointing of the sick) were perceived as adult in nature. This distinction is more apparent in and after the twelfth century, when Church leaders began to lay more emphasis upon what people thought. Only an adult, it seemed, could understand the eucharist enough to receive it, or the obligations of marriage enough to be married. Only an adult could sin sufficiently badly to require confession and anointing. Children knew less, and needed different treatment.

The eucharist was the chief of the sacraments, along with baptism, because it was considered essential for salvation. From about the tenth century, when churches and clergy were common throughout England, it was the one most often celebrated. In the form of the Latin mass, it took place in all churches on Sundays and festivals. In major ones, it came to be carried out daily, sometimes several times a day. Its celebration involved at least one priest and one clerk, and often more. The officiating priest consecrated a wafer of bread and wine and consumed them himself; his assistants and any lay spectators did not participate. On Sundays in parish churches, substitutes were offered to the people. One was the 'pax' or 'paxbred', a small disk of ivory or metal, kissed by the priest after the consecration and taken around the church to be kissed by everyone else. The other was a loaf of holy bread (not to be confused with the consecrated wafer), divided among the laity when mass was over. Adults were given communion once a year as the special devotion of Easter Day, and at times of danger to life: childbirth, pilgrimage, and the sickbed. They received it, after the twelfth century, in the form of a consecrated wafer followed by a drink of unconsecrated wine.

In the late Anglo-Saxon and Norman periods, communion was given to children. Eleventh- and twelfth-century liturgical texts provide for bishops or priests to administer it to newly baptised infants, saying in Latin 'the body of our Lord Jesus Christ keep you in eternal life'.[97] By the end of the twelfth century, this practice was dying out. There was now a belief in the Real Presence: the view that the consecrated bread and wine were not merely memorials or symbols of Jesus, but changed their nature to become his body and blood. This dictated greater reverence. One had to guard against the elements being spilt or regurgitated, and a conviction grew among Church leaders that you needed to believe in the Presence to receive communion rightly. Children came to seem too young to understand what they were getting. The theologian Robert Pulleyn (d. 1146) still recommended the communication of a baptised infant by the priest dipping his finger in the chalice and putting it into the child's mouth. He censured a new practice by which children were given unconsecrated wine at communion – a procedure later extended to adults as well.[98] But his view did not prevail. In 1215, the Fourth Lateran Council of the Catholic Church, meeting at Rome, laid down that everyone should go to confession at least once a year and receive communion at Easter, provided that they had 'reached the age of discernment'.[99] This did not explicitly rule out children, but it implied as much (Fig. 78).

Evidence from England after 1200 confirms their exclusion. Robert of

Flamborough, writing at Paris in 1208–15, asserts that the eucharist could not be given to those with defective understanding, with whom he classed children.[100] William of Pagula, the author of the influential fourteenth-century handbook for priests, *Oculus Sacerdotis*, says that 'no one should be admitted to the sacrament of the body and blood of Christ outside the point of death unless he has been confirmed' – an event which William thought should take place at the ages of twelve (for girls) and fourteen (for boys).[101] His successor, John de Burgh, takes a similar view in his larger and more successful handbook, *Pupilla Oculi*. 'Out of reverence for what is contained under the forms [of bread and wine], defect of judgment and reason is excluded, as with children and the insane'. John pushes down a little the age at which the young might become eligible. 'Children when they are near to adulthood, that is to say when they are ten or eleven and when signs of discretion and reverence towards the sacrament appear in them, may receive communion.' Even this was permissible only if they had been confirmed, though John like William made an exception for those at the point of death.[102] Such influential books are probably guides to what happened in practice, with possible exceptions for children of high status.

Two other sacraments shared a similar history. In the early centuries, children were admitted to confession with a priest, and penitential guides of the Anglo-Saxon period envisage that a confessor might have to deal with children's sexual behaviour.[103] But by 1215, when the Fourth Lateran Council linked confession with years of discretion, it looks as though children were no longer required to confess – a view later shared by William of Pagula and John de Burgh.[104] The sacrament of extreme unction came also to be barred to the young. This was the rite in which the priest attended those who were gravely ill, heard their confessions, and anointed them with holy oil on parts of the face and body. In principle it was suitable for anyone, but by about 1200 Church leaders saw it too as requiring an adult level of understanding. In 1217–19, Bishop Poore of Salisbury restricted extreme unction to those of fourteen years and above, and his ruling was gradually adopted elsewhere in England during the thirteenth century.[105]

By the fourteenth, the withholding of unction from children was probably universal. Legislation attributed to Archbishop Reynolds of Canterbury in about 1322 made fourteen the minimum age, and this duly reappears in William Lyndwood's important commentary on Church law, the *Provinciale*, in the fifteenth century.[106] William of Shoreham, writing about the subject in Kent in about the 1320s, explained the restriction by the fact that 'he must have devotion who shall take [the sacrament] rightly. Therefore, children are not anointed, nor the insane, for they can have no understanding of its holy goodness'.[107] John de Burgh accorded with Shoreham. 'This sacrament is not conferred except on the adult sick who are in peril of death. . . . It is not given to children because they have no spiritual infirmity contracted through actual sin, nor can they have the disposition of devotion to this sacrament.'[108] Lyndwood agreed with the first of John's explanations. Holy unction was instituted to deal with the sins of adulthood, and was therefore irrelevant to children (Fig. 79).[109]

The twelfth-century emphasis on personal understanding can be seen in other

religious matters. Children were regarded as capable of swearing a formal oath only when they reached years of discretion: twelve, fourteen, or fifteen.[110] They were prohibited from taking monastic vows until an age variously reckoned at fourteen to eighteen.[111] If they wished to become parish clergy, they could be tonsured at seven and ordained to the minor orders of doorkeeper, reader, and exorcist, enabling them to become clerks or choristers, but such ordinations did not bind them to clerical life as adults. The next grade of ordination, that of acolyte, could only be given at thirteen or fourteen, and the next highest, that of subdeacon which involved a binding commitment to celibacy, only at seventeen.[112] Marriage, another process involving lifelong vows, was similarly modified. Lay society, particularly the nobility and gentry, tolerated the practice of child marriage, and some espousals of children took place in the middle ages. The Church, however, increasingly took the view that these marriages were not binding until the partners could understand their vows and consummate them, at the age of puberty.[113] In short, there seems to have been a large shift of opinion about children among the clergy during the twelfth century. After 1200, childhood was more likely to be regarded as a distinct sub-adult condition, requiring separate treatment.

78   Children became adults, in the eyes of the
Church, in their early teens. Only then were
they required, as here, to confess, and allowed
to receive communion.

79   By the thirteenth century, children were
not regarded as capable of committing mortal
sins, or
eligible for the sacrament of unction when sick.

80   Children could be confirmed at any age,
even when infants, as in this example.

If the Church came to stress more strongly the difference between childhood
and adulthood, did it mark the transition between the two stages with a rite of
passage? In the post-Reformation Church of England, the service of confirmation has come to play such a role, while the Catholic Church has preferred to
accentuate a child's first communion. Neither ceremony seems to have fulfilled
this role to any great extent in the middle ages. Confirmation began as a part of
baptism, its basic elements being the placing of hands on the baptised person's
head and the anointing of the forehead with chrism (oil and balsam). By about
the fourth century, a separation took place. Baptism was made the responsibility
of priests, and the other ceremonies became the sacrament of confirmation,
carried out by a bishop after the baptism was completed. Theologically, confirmation reinforces the gift of the Holy Spirit. Legally, it is the Church's official vali-
dation of one's Christian status. Historically, the placing of the hands forms a link
stretching back to the apostles of Jesus. Socially, the ceremony involves Church
leaders meeting their flock individually. This is usually the only time that such an
encounter takes place.

    In Anglo-Saxon England, when bishops were often missionaries and parish
clergy were few, baptism and confirmation continued to happen together in many

cases. St Cuthbert, bishop of Lindisfarne, laid hands on the recently baptised.[114] English 'pontificals' (the service-books of bishops) in the late Anglo-Saxon period assume that both rites will often or normally happen in tandem. They provide for the immediate imposition of chrism on a baptised infant if a bishop is present.[115] One (the pontifical of Sidney Sussex College Cambridge, probably a Winchester book of the early eleventh century) identifies the recipients of confirmation as 'infants'.[116] In the next century, the pontifical of Magdalen College states that, when baptism is complete, 'if a bishop is present, [the child] should be confirmed with chrism at once'.[117]

The confirmation of the newly baptised continued to be lawful throughout the rest of the middle ages. Pictures of the sacrament show bishops with infants, often indistinguishable in size from those who are being baptised (Fig. 80).[118] In noble and royal households, where bishops were easily available, confirmation might follow baptism right up to the Reformation. The practice is mentioned in the early-Tudor chapel book of the Percy earls of Northumberland, and was observed at the births of Henry VIII's children: Elizabeth I in 1533 and Edward VI four years later.[119] But children like these were exceptions after the Anglo-Saxon period. As the number of Christians grew and bishops acquired non-pastoral duties, it was rare for them to be at hand when most infants were christened. After the Norman Conquest, bishops often lived in London, engaging in royal or ecclesiastical business. Even those who came to their dioceses tended to journey chiefly between their estates, thought some made amends by appointing a suffragan bishop to travel and confirm on their behalf.

Not surprisingly, the absence of bishops to administer confirmation was matched by the failure of people to receive it. Neglect to be confirmed was a recognised problem by the thirteenth century, and bishops were obliged to set down periods of time for the rite to happen. In the dioceses of Chichester and Worcester, confirmation was ordered to be done within a year of baptism; in Exeter, Wells, and Winchester, three years; in Durham and Salisbury, five. Church leaders ordered negligent parents to be punished by fasting or exclusion from church but, as dioceses were often large and bishops away, such orders were not easy to enforce.[120] In 1213–14, the bishop of Salisbury envisaged children unconfirmed at puberty, while in 1281, the Council of Lambeth complained that many people neglected the sacrament and that 'innumerable' grew old in evil ways without receiving it.[121] The council tried to remedy this by insisting that no unconfirmed persons should be admitted to communion unless they were at the point of death, but whether the parish clergy enforced this policy is unclear. Archbishop Reynolds, in about 1322, anticipated 'adults' (those over fourteen) attending confirmation, and told them to come fasting and having confessed to their priests.[122]

One writer, William of Pagula, approved the delay of confirmation until children had reached years of discretion. Although he began with the neutral proposition that all faithful people should receive confirmation after baptism, he qualified it by adding that

they ought by right to be admitted to confirmation by the bishop who are fasting and of perfect age, i.e. twelve or fourteen years old, and they should be warned to make their confession first, so that, being clean, they may be worthy to receive this gift of special grace. This is the case, except for the sick and those in danger of death. It is better for their safety that they be confirmed before the age of adulthood.[123]

William's view anticipated that of Protestants at the Reformation, but it does not seem to have found much support in its day. His more influential successor John de Burgh kept to tradition. He recommended that children should be confirmed before adulthood, because they would have more glory in heaven if they died young.[124] He followed William in saying that all candidates should fast, but indicated confession beforehand only for those who were twelve or fourteen by the time they received confirmation.[125] Other writers concurred with an early age. John Mirk, in his *Instructions for Parish Priests*, said that children should be confirmed within five years of baptism.[126] Lyndwood gathered together the earlier legislation to recommend the confirmation of 'small children' as soon as a bishop comes 'nearby', explaining 'nearby' as 'within seven miles, as the common usage is'.[127] Large parts of England, however, did not see a bishop within seven miles for long periods; many people are likely to have been confirmed in adulthood, and some not even then.

The Reformation, with its emphasis on education, tried to change these customs.[128] In the 1530s, John Hilsey, bishop of Rochester, made one of the first proposals since Pagula that confirmation should be delayed to adolescence ('the years of discretion') and be preceded by an examination.[129] In 1549, Cranmer adopted a similar policy in the First Prayer Book of Edward VI, stating that children should come to years of discretion and learn the catechism before they received it. The Church 'in times past', he said, had ordained 'that confirmation should be ministered to them that were of perfect age', and though Cranmer understood people's fears that children who died unconfirmed might be in spiritual danger, he strove to reassure them on this point.[130] By 1562, the convocation of Canterbury proposed to levy a fine of 10s. on anyone with a child aged more than eight or an apprentice aged more than fourteen who did not know the catechism (unless incapacitated), implying a drive to ensure confirmation in about that span of life.[131] But the Reformers were always more successful at proposing reforms than achieving them. The perambulations of bishops and the attendance of candidates remained unpredictable. In 1577, the bishop of Durham tried to enforce confirmation on everyone who received communion under the age of thirty, only to concede that those unconfirmed over that age could communicate if they knew the Lord's Prayer, Creed, and Commandments.[132] As late as the seventeenth and eighteenth centuries, confirmations continued to involve a wide range of candidates, ranging from children as young as five to adults in their fifties.[133] It was only the coming of the railways that enabled bishops regularly to meet their flocks as lambs, rather than sheep.

For the child to be confirmed and for its family, the sacrament involved some preparation. First, they had to track down the bishop's movements or respond to him coming into their neighbourhood. Although some bishops made special tours to confirm, they often did so while they travelled on other business. The author of the Life of St Hugh of Lincoln (d. 1200) recalled a bishop he had seen who confirmed on horseback, with mounted retainers milling around him and the children at risk from the horses' hooves. Hugh, by contrast, always dismounted for the purpose, even when he was elderly.[134] Next, the child's family had to provide an adult sponsor to present the candidate or, in Robert Mannyng's word, to 'hold' it – an action appropriate in the case of a small child.[135] The sponsor had to be of the same sex as the child, someone other than a parent or godparent, and sponsorship set up a spiritual relationship like that of godparents. Finally, each person to be confirmed had to bring a linen bandage.

The rite, once it began, was a short one.[136] The bishop confronted each candidate separately and asked his or her name. It was possible to change your baptismal name at this point, though it is not clear whether or how often this was done.[137] The bishop anointed his thumb with chrism and used it to make the sign of the cross on the candidate's forehead. As he did so, he said in Latin,

> I sign you with the sign of the cross and confirm you with the chrism of salvation. In the name of the Father, and the Son, and the Holy Spirit. Amen.[138]

When the candidates had all been anointed, the bandages they had brought were wound round their foreheads to keep the chrism in place. The bandages had to be worn, at least around the neck, until the confirmees reached home and met their priest in the parish church within an interval variously fixed at three or eight days later. The priest then washed the confirmees' foreheads into the font to remove any chrism, and the bandages were taken off and burnt.[139]

These ceremonies had a visual impact, if only because new confirmees went about for a day or two wearing bandages. But confirmation did not act as a rite of passage for society in general. It was administered at too wide a range of ages and made no change to one's status in practical terms. A confirmed infant or child remained unqualified, after 1200, to receive communion or unction. Instead, the evidence for the spiritual transition from childhood to adulthood points to it being a process that was relatively unobtrusive and linked to age. The Church's view of growing up was that adulthood began, physically and intellectually, at twelve for girls and fourteen for boys.[140] At about these ages, in line with the decree of the Fourth Lateran Council, a parish priest was likely to tell his young parishioners to come to church to confession. This first confession would take place in church during Lent, as part of a process in which every adult was expected to come for the purpose. On the following Easter Sunday, the young person would receive her or his first communion, again alongside the rest of the community.

The young Christian would then be regarded as adult. He or she could make an oath, take monastic vows, marry permanently, and receive extreme unction. One became liable to pay church dues. In 1315, the archbishop of York laid down that all children in the parish of Maltby (Yorks), who lived in their parents' homes and received communion at Easter, should make an offering in church of a half-penny.[141] Henry VIII laid similar obligations on the children of London in 1536; if they were communicants, they had to make four offerings a year of 2d. each.[142] Transition to adult status at twelve or fourteen may well have been significant for a child and for its family. But the change was not marked in very special ways. Rather, it happened inconspicuously as part of the cycle of the Church year. Growing up in the Church resembled growing up in the world. In secular life, a child went through a number of transitions before adulthood, including school-ing, apprenticeship, enrolment in the system of law and order, and coming of age (if an heir).[143] All mattered to the person concerned, but none gave rise to a widely observed rite of passage.

GUILDS

GUILDS WERE A popular form of lay involvement in Church life, from at least the tenth century until the Reformation. Their purpose was to support a saint or a church and to provide social and religious benefits for their members, who were chiefly adults but not exclusively so. Records of some abbeys in the twelfth century, known as *libri vitae*, list benefactors who constituted a kind of guild of sup-porters, and these sometimes name their children as well.[144] The register of the Guild of Kalendars at Exeter, dating from the twelfth to the fifteenth centuries, and that of the Trinity Guild at Coventry, extant between about 1340 and 1450, include various people described as sons and daughters, though their ages are not given.[145] Young people might also form guilds of their own, imitating their elders while excluding them. An instinct to do this is found as early as 1264, when a guild of young men (*gilda iuvenum*) was formed at Bury St Edmunds, though in this case the members are also described as young adults (*bachelarii*) and formed a political group opposed to the local abbey and its privileges.[146]

The first young people's organisation mentioned as having a religious purpose occurs in the survey of religious guilds carried out by the government of Richard II in 1389. This was the guild of St William at King's Lynn, founded in 1383 and made up 'of young scholars' bound 'to maintain and keep an image of St William standing in a tabernacle in the church of St Margaret of Lynn' and to provide six tapers of wax to burn in the church on festival days. Appropriately, the patron was the child saint William of Norwich, killed at the age of twelve. In form and objec-tives, the guild was indistinguishable from an adult body. It met three times a year, held an annual festival on the Feast of Relics, provided funeral masses for broth-ers who died, and helped its members in need. By recruiting scholars, it probably relied on the local school or schools to give it an identity, and since scholars could be as old as eighteen, the leadership may have come from youths on the verge of adulthood. Or perhaps not, for the guild's return to the king's survey stresses its members' 'young age', its reliance on the help and counsel of wise men, and its dependence for revenues on other people's gifts.[147] There may have have been guilds elsewhere, or at any rate devotional cults, made up of chil-

81 The 'sisters' or young
women of St Neot (Cornwall)
in the early sixteenth century.
Church guilds and associations
were very popular, and some
included children and young
people.

dren. A boys' light is mentioned in the parish church of St John York in 1489, and
a children's light in St Michael Spurriergate nearby in 1519.[148]

The most frequent references to groups of young people, however, are to
maidens and young men – references which do not use the word 'guild' or
mention dedication to a saint. Such groups existed by the mid fifteenth century.
The church of St Margaret Southwark received 3s. 9d. in 1445–55 'in dancing
money of the maidens', and that of St Mary at Hill London 6s. 8d. 'of the gathering of the maidens of St Barnabas day' in 1512–13.[149] In Kent, we hear of
lights in churches between 1463 and 1533, maintained by the bachelors or young
men and the maidens or young women, implying the banding together of such
people to provide them.[150] In Cornwall during the same period, groups of young

men appear at Bodmin, Camborne, St Columb Major, St Neot, and North Petherwin, maidens at Antony, West Looe, and Bodmin, and sisters at St Neot (Fig. 81). Bodmin had associations of girls based on each of its two main streets.[151] In Devon, there were young men and maidens at Chagford and Morebath, young men (called grooms) at Modbury, and two groups of young men at Ashburton. One of the Ashburton groups is described as the young men 'on the land', meaning the rural part of the parish, while the other, whose membership is not specified, may have been drawn from the town itself.[152] Somerset had similar bodies: maidens at Croscombe and young men (otherwise known as 'younglings') there and at Pilton.[153]

Although no records survive of membership and ages within these associations, it looks as though they catered for those in their teens and early twenties, as the words 'groom' and 'bachelor' imply. Adult status at about the age of fourteen may have been the threshold for entry, and marriage in the mid twenties have triggered one's exit. The groups' activities, in as far as they are recorded, relate to parish churches, the records surviving among the accounts of parish churchwardens. It appears that both maidens and young men collected money, kept lights in the church, and sometimes contributed to parish finances. They may have held social events, too, such as an annual feast or ale, and have joined in other activities. Fifteenth-century songs, as we shall see, mention men seducing girls during communal dances at New Year and Midsummer, and while holding a vigil at a holy well.[154] At Morebath on Exmoor, where we know most about these groups, each one chose a pair of officers each year to handle its affairs, and the names of the officers survive after 1526. The maidens had two men as wardens in 1527, but this was exceptional; later, the wardens were always female until 1541 when the organisation was apparently disbanded. Their counterparts, the young men, had two male wardens until 1548 when they too disappeared – victims of the Reformation.[155]

CHILDREN AS CLERGY

AS WELL AS ministering to children, the Church recruited them to do duties in church and to become clergy. That is, primarily boys. Girls could be utilised only in nunneries, of which there were never more than 146 throughout England and Wales, whereas boys were suitable to work in cathedrals, colleges, monasteries, friaries, or parish churches. Children cost less to employ than adults and were more biddable. Asser noted that King Alfred, when trying to revive monasticism in England in the late ninth century, found it impossible to get recruits to be monks except for boys who had no choice in the matter.[156] Equally, service in a church had its rewards. It taught one to read, sing, and perform the liturgy as a chorister or clerk. It did not necessarily involve a commitment to life as a cleric, and many such boys went on to lay employment, sometimes with the help of their clerical employers. If a career in the Church was desired, on the other hand, there were plenty of openings. In about 1300, when the national population peaked at five or

82   Church tradition provided examples of children being placed by their parents to serve in churches; here the Virgin Mary is offered in the Temple.

six million, there were some 14,000 'regular' clergy living communally as monks and friars, and perhaps as many as 30,000 'secular' clergy living individually in parishes, colleges, and cathedrals.

To become a secular priest, one needed to be ordained, a process involving a number of stages. There were various 'minor orders', the chief of which was the grade of acolyte, all of which could be held in tandem with a secular life of work and marriage. The three 'major orders', on the other hand, bound one fully to life as a cleric, including a vow of celibacy, and they could not be conferred until adulthood. One had to be seventeen to be ordained as a subdeacon, nineteen as a deacon, and twenty-four as a priest.[157] In fact, many would-be priests seem to have waited until they were twenty-four and to have taken all the major orders at once. This was a prudent proceeding because, until you were assured of employment within the Church (and had no better prospects as a layman), it was unwise to bind yourself to celibacy. Some men were sustained through this long waiting period by family resources, going to school and sometimes to university to master the Latin texts required for life as a cleric. For others, service as a boy or young man in a church provided a means of support until they were twenty-four, became priests, and gained paid adult posts.

The other kind of clerical vocation, in a religious order, did not originally require ordination but was based on taking religious vows. In early times, this could be done at any age. Christian history provided models for binding children to careers in a church. The prophet Samuel was an infant when his parents committed him to serve in the Temple, and so, in legend, was the Virgin Mary (Fig. 82).[158] When St Benedict drew up his famous monastic rule in the middle of the sixth century, he permitted noble parents to offer their sons as monks before they had reached the age of majority. The parents had to make a written promise on their son's behalf that he would change his way of life and become obedient to the rule of the monastery. They had also to undertake never to give him any possessions or property, in case he was tempted to renounce the monastic life. In practice, the boy may have been consulted about his future and have consented to it, but the ceremony for admitting him did not stress that point. Rather, it represented him as a gift to the monastery by his parents. It took place in church at the point when the offertory of bread and wine for the mass was offered at the altar. The child brought up the offertory, and when he had done so his parents wrapped his hands in the altar cloth as a sign that he too was offered for the service of the church. By the eleventh century, he made a personal profession as a monk on reaching adulthood, but it was not envisaged that he would fail to do so.[159]

Child oblation of this kind, involving boys and girls, was practised in England up to the twelfth century, especially by the aristocracy.[160] It reflected a world in which there were relatively few churches or schools other than monasteries, and where monks or nuns usually had to be trained from youth within the cloister walls. The disadvantage of oblation was that the child might lack the will or the ability to follow monastic life, causing trouble in the future. During the twelfth century, opinion began to turn against the practice. One reason for this change was the emergence of reformed orders of monks like the Cistercians, who expected high standards of their recruits. Another was the proliferation of public schools, making it easier for youths to be educated in the world and enter the monastery at a mature age with a mature vocation. In 1134, the Cistercians prohibited the reception of boys as probationer monks until the age of fifteen, and raised this age to eighteen by 1175.[161] In 1186, the Benedictine monks of St Augustine at Canterbury followed suit by procuring a papal decree that their novices should be aged at least eighteen.[162] In 1234, the canon law of the Church ratified earlier papal pronouncements that no one should normally be professed as a permanent member of a religious order until the age of fourteen.[163] Youths in the later middle ages might be clad in the monastic habit while as young as fifteen, but formal profession as a monk was usually delayed until nineteen.[164]

Child recruitment lingered later in certain places. Some girls of aristocratic rank continued to be placed as nuns by their families after the thirteenth century.[165] Mary, daughter of Edward I, was veiled as a nun at Amesbury Abbey (Wilts.) in 1285, when she was only seven, and stayed there for the rest of her life.[166] Katherine, daughter of Sir Guy de Beauchamp, entered Shouldham Priory (Norfolk) by about the same age in 1359,[167] and Isabel daughter of Thomas duke of Gloucester was said to have been placed with the Minoresses of Aldgate (London) in her infancy. In Isabel's case, her entry seems to have been a conditional one. By 1401, she had taken no vows and retained the option of leaving, but she chose to stay and rose to be abbess.[168] The other kind of clergy to admit young entrants were the friars, who developed in the thirteenth century. At first, their two largest orders, the Dominicans and Franciscans, followed monks in fixing the normal age of entry as a novice at eighteen, but in later times both they and other friars took in boys who were in their early teens.[169] Normally, parents agreed to this, and the boys were only clothed in the friars' habit, which was conditional, rather than making a full profession of obedience, which was not. The practice, however, exposed the friars to criticism that they were recruiting children too immature to know better.[170]

They were also accused of ignoring parental consent. In 1357, Richard FitzRalph, archbishop of Armagh, told the pope at Avignon about an English father whom he had met only that morning, seeking the release of his son from the hands of friars. The father claimed that the boy, not yet thirteen, had been abducted at Easter while studying at Oxford, and that when he went to visit his son, he could not talk with him except in the presence of a friar.[171] Worse allegations still were made against the Crutched Friars of London in 1392. In their case, it was maintained that they enticed a ten-year-old schoolboy to translate into Latin the phrase 'I oblige me to be a friar of the Cross'. One of the friars then kissed him and said that all the bishops of England could not absolve him from their order, and they took him away and dressed him in their habit. Next day, the boy's schoolmaster complained to the city authorities, who ordered the boy to be restored at once to his guardian, the master of a local hospital.[172]

In 1402, protests about the recruitment of young friars were made in Parliament, and the House of Commons petitioned the king to forbid anyone to be received into the four largest orders of friars until he was twenty-one. The king, no doubt on advice from his senior clergy, refused to go so far, but he agreed to a statute prohibiting the four orders from receiving boys before the age of fourteen without the assent of their parents or guardians. This proviso still allowed for younger entrants when their families consented. No boy was to be moved from the friary he entered for one year, enabling him to be released if the parent or guardian so desired, and criminal charges could be brought against the friars concerned if the law was breached.[173] Despite this, charges of child abduction continued to circulate. 'Friar', taunted a Lollard writer of the fifteenth century, 'why steal ye men's children to make them of your sects?' Men, he contended, were hanged on gallows for thefts of less value. A friar replied that it was virtuous to bring people to God, but another Lollard rejoined that such thefts were worse than that of the ox, forbidden in the Ten Commandments. Children taken into the friars' orders, he claimed, became more worldly than secular men, and were made into beggars and sodomites.[174]

The decline of child oblation in the twelfth century may have been influenced from another direction: that of the minster. Minsters existed in late Anglo-Saxon times as communities of clergy living closer than monks to the life of the everyday world.[175] Their churches were often parish churches, and their clergy might have individual houses, incomes, and property. The most important of these foundations were the 'secular' cathedrals, so called because they were staffed by 'secular' canons living partly in the world in the minster manner. There were nine of these after the Norman Conquest: Chichester, Exeter, Hereford, Lichfield, Lincoln, St Paul's (London), Salisbury, Wells, and York. All nine supported bodies of young people by the twelfth century, and so did some other large minsters. Choristers, aged roughly between seven and fourteen or fifteen, filled the 'first form', the lowest of the three levels of the choir. 'Secondaries', 'clerks', or 'altarists' occupied the middle level or 'second form', and were usually in their late teens and early twenties. Some choristers graduated to the second form, after their voices broke, and rose in due course to the third (top) form as vicars choral or chantry priests of the cathedral. But there was no requirement to proceed in this way, as there was for monastic oblates. Boys might equally well leave the choir at puberty or later, and take up careers as parish clergy or laymen.[176]

Cathedral choristers were fully recognised members of their foundations from early on, and statutes were issued to regulate their lives. They lived in a special house although, as we have seen at Exeter, they sometimes had meals individually with the canons.[177] They went to a song school and mastered the plainsong used in the daily services. They attended some (but not all) of these services in the cathedral choir, and thereby learnt its work in a practical way. They did menial duties of fetching, carrying, and serving at mass. Sometimes, they sang special pieces of plainsong in the choir, or descants improvised to plainsong. Their voices, however, were not needed to a great extent, and they were learners rather than regular skilled practitioners. Their present-day role, which gives them a leading part in the choir, developed in the middle of the fifteenth century, as a result of developments in polyphonic music.[178] Polyphony was particularly associated with the worship of the Virgin Mary and with the Lady chapels named after her, which began to appear in large churches from the thirteenth century onwards. Clergy of the cathedral were deputed to hold services in her honour in these chapels, and by the middle of the fourteenth century these services were embellished with polyphony: music in several contrasting parts.

At first, this church polyphony was usually sung by a group of four men, taking three or four parts. During the 1450s, however, the number of parts was increased. Adult basses and boy trebles were added, and later on, boy altos. The number of singers rose from a small group to a large chorus of as many as two dozen. Boys became essential to the performance of polyphony, and acquired the central role in English cathedral choirs which endures in the present day. Cathedrals diverted their choristers to do more of this work, and sometimes increased the number of boys for the purpose. A special officer began to be employed to organise the music, a person usually called the 'clerk of the chapel', meaning the Lady chapel. He took over the instruction of the boys in music, including polyphony, and led the production of the music in church. The fashion spread to other large churches during the second half of the fifteenth century: minsters, collegiate churches, the household chapels of the king and the nobility, and (as we shall see) many of the greater houses of monks.

This topic brings us back to the monasteries, and their involvement with boys after the twelfth century. That involvement did not cease with the decline of oblation, but it turned towards the model of the secular cathedral. Boys were admitted not as oblates but as tonsured clerks, different in status from monks and not bound to the monastic life. The earliest references to them come from Bermondsey (Surrey), Bury St Edmunds, and Durham, round about 1200.[179] Similar bodies occur at many other large houses down to the dissolution of the monasteries in the 1530s. The boys lived in the monastic almonry – a building located outside the cloister area, where alms and hospitality could be given to travellers and to the poor. They were linked in some way with the abbey or priory concerned: relatives of monks, nominees of important local people, or sons of tenants. They may have entered the almonry at any age from seven upwards, but were probably most numerous and useful in their early and late teens. They were given board, lodging, and schooling – the latter sometimes from a special master in the almonry, sometimes at the local grammar school. In return, like choristers, they did helpful tasks in the church, notably by assisting the monks who were priests and said masses at altars in the building.

There were a good many almonry boys in late-medieval England. One of the biggest groups was at Westminster Abbey, which increased its roll of between twenty-two and twenty-eight in the 1380s to around forty in about 1405.

Glastonbury, another large house, may have reached forty in the 1370s.[180] Durham, a third, maintained thirty in the century or so before the Reformation. Smaller houses had smaller numbers, anything from four to twenty-four, but the national complement must have reached two or three thousand. The institution changed as time went on. During the thirteenth and most of the fourteenth century, almonry boys differed from choristers in having no significant musical duties. Music in a monastic choir was sung by monks alone, and the boys' roles were largely connected with serving and saying responses at masses. This began to alter in about the 1370s, when some of the bigger monasteries started to imitate the secular cathedrals by using boys to help sing the daily mass of the Virgin Mary in the Lady chapel, hitherto done by monks. A group of four, six, or eight almonry boys was collected for this purpose, and a professional musician from outside was sometimes employed to train them. Westminster Abbey used its boys in this way by 1373, Norwich by 1378, and Ely by 1383.

Musically, the skills required of these boys were not, at first, very great. The Lady mass was simple in form and based on plainsong, sometimes with improvised descant. It took a small part of the day, even when one adds the votive antiphon to the Virgin sung in the Lady chapel every evening. In the late fifteenth century, however, monks, like clergy elsewhere, further enhanced the Lady mass with polyphony, using the boys to sing in parts and therefore in a more ambitious way. Westminster was another leader in this respect in 1480, and other large houses like monastic cathedrals at Canterbury, Winchester, and Worcester soon followed. Once boys were involved in polyphony, a gap began to open up between those who performed it and the rest of the almonry boys. Monasteries began to use some of their almonry places for specialist boy singers, and these boys spent a larger part of their day in musical training. They usually continued to live with the almonry boys, however, and although their musical duties were now greater, these were still less than those of cathedral choristers. Indeed, the word 'chorister' was not in normal use in monasteries; the young singers were merely described as 'the boys'.

Some of the almonry boys, singers or not, went on to be monks. They may indeed have been viewed as potential recruits, whose capacity for cloister life could be observed and evaluated. At Canterbury Cathedral, four almonry boys were admitted as monks in 1486, and a similar practice is recorded at Furness Abbey (Lancs.).[181] There, after the house was dissolved in 1537, its former tenants claimed that it had received their children, given them schooling, and promoted them to be monks or abbey servants.[182] This second kind of career, as a monastic servant or a layman outside the monastery, must have been commoner still. In 1538, three witnesses in a lawsuit about property in Somerset recalled the days when they were boys in Glastonbury Abbey, some twenty years before. One was now a husbandman (small farmer), one a yeoman, and one a gentleman. The lawsuit centred on a fourth boy, Richard Beere, the abbot's nephew, who was brought up in the abbey as a layman and sent to Oxford and the Inns of Court. Richard, however, became a Carthusian monk. Some of these Glastonbury boys may have lived in the almonry, while others had a more genteel upbringing in the

83   The ubiquitous parish clerk, assisting his parish priest
to celebrate mass.

abbot's household, but the lawsuit testifies to
their varied later careers.[183] Monasteries
played an important role in educating boys
after 1200, both benefiting themselves and,
promoting literacy outside their walls.

Parish churches too had boyish or youthful
assistants. Every priest required a helper,
because church services were dialogues for at
least two people, and by the eleventh century
the English Church encouraged priests to
teach boys to help them in church.[184] There was a large requirement for such help,
greater even than that of cathedrals, religious houses, and household chapels.
Some 8,500 or more parish churches existed in late-medieval England, plus
chapels-of-ease – supporting three or four times that many priests, all engaged in
public worship at least once a week and often on a daily basis.[185] By the thirteenth
century, assistants in parish churches and chapels were known as holy-water clerks
(*aquebaiuli*), and by the fourteenth as parish clerks.[186] One murdered in
Bedfordshire in 1271 is said to have been eighteen.[187] Their duties, according to
Lyndwood, were threefold: to serve the priest at the altar, sing the service with
him, and read the epistle at mass (Fig. 83).[188] In return, they received a small
income from bell-ringing and supplying holy water for services or blessings. After
the Reformation, when such fees ceased, parishes went over to providing their
clerks with a regular income: at Ashburton (Devon), for example, it became £3.[189]

By the thirteenth century, there was an expectation that clerks would become
parish clergy. Bishops ordered that scholars should be given the posts in churches
near cathedral cities and castle towns, the assumption being that there were
schools in such places.[190] The practice probably lasted until the end of the middle
ages. In Devon, Latin exercises of about 1450 from Exeter High School contain a
reference to 'we three parish clerks of this city', suggesting that such clerks
attended the school.[191] Nearby at Witheridge, in the Devon countryside, a legal
dispute enables us to trace the careers of three of its parish clerks in the early fifteenth century. The first of them, James Edward, was born in about 1405 and
appears to have been appointed to his post when he was sixteen. He held it until
he was ordained as a priest eight years later. He and the two clerks who followed
him all became incumbents of parishes in the vicinity.[192] Such a career progres-
sion was so common up to the Reformation that it gave rise to a proverb: 'the
parish priest forgets that he was clerk'.[193]

Unlike choristers who made little impact on public opinion, clerks were
familiar enough to project an image in people's minds, like that of priests, monks,
and friars. It can be seen in Chaucer's description of Absolon, the parish clerk of
Oxford, a merry 'child' who can sing, dance, write, and flirt with women of the

parish.[194] True, Absolon's manliness is equivocal and he is humiliated by kissing the wrong end of the wife whom he tries to seduce, but this may be Chaucer's artful reversal of the stereotype. The usual image of the clerk appears in fifteenth-century songs, like the one with the refrain '*Kyrieleyson*'. It tells how he sings the service, reads the epistle, and tackles the intricate notes of the Sanctus. During the singing of the *Agnus Dei*, he takes round the paxbred, seducing a girl on the way:

> Jankin at the Agnus bore the paxbred;
> He twinkled but said nowt, and on my foot he trod,

with the result that,

> *Benedicamus domino*! Christ from shame me shield!
> *Deo gracias* thereto! Alas! I go with child![195]

Another song relates a similar story. The girl leads the parish dancing on Midsummer Day, and is kissed by Jack the 'stripling' clerk. He lures her to his chamber with a promise of gloves, she stays the night, and soon she is pregnant. Each verse ends with the plaintive line, 'Thought I on no guile' ('I thought of no trickery').[196]

The 'Digby' play *Mary Magdalene*, preserved in a manuscript of the early sixteenth century, draws on the same tradition. It has a scene in which a heathen priest leads a service with the assistance of Hawkyn, who is called both his 'clerk' and his 'boy'. The priest orders the clerk to make all ready, as if for mass:

> Now, my clerk Hawkyn, for love of me,
> Look fast [that] my altar were arrayed!
> Go ring a bell, two, or three!
> Lithely [*quickly*], child, it be not delayed,
> For here shall be a great solemnity.

Hawkyn asks if the priest would not prefer to have his mistress at his bedside, and teases him for his corpulence. He says that it is he, the clerk, who hooks the women when they come to sermons, both Kyrchon and Maryon. After further exchanges, the priest calls for his book, goes to the altar, and puts on his vestments. The boy reads the epistle, in mock Latin, from the 'Book of Mahomet':

> *Leccyo Mahowndys, viri fortissimi Sarasenorum,*
> *Glabriosum ad glumandum glumandinorum . . .*

Later, the priest and boy begin to sing the 'office' of the mass, but the boy distorts his voice and throws the priest out of order. The scene is a parody, but its attempt to convey a clerk's three major duties – altar-serving, reading the epistle, and singing responses – is perfectly accurate.[197]

Parish clerks were not the only young people employed in parish churches by the end of the middle ages. Sometimes there were boy servers, assisting the clergyman or other priests. Caxton's *Book of Courtesy* envisages its boy readers serving at mass. They should kneel or stand devoutly, not too near the priest nor too far away, and speak the responses in a moderate voice.[198] *The ABC both in Latin and English* of 1538 included the Latin invitation to confession (*Confitemini*) and the confession (*Confiteor*), under the heading 'To help a priest to sing'.[199] In the reign of James I, an elderly man of Wotton-under-Edge (Gloucs.) remembered how, in about the 1540s, he was one of two such boys who wore surplices and knelt on cushions in the parish church while mass was said by a chantry priest.[200] Some larger parish churches tried to compete with monasteries by establishing choirs of clerks and boys and performing more elaborate music. In the west of England, Ashburton (Devon) maintained four men and four boys by 1481. Cirencester (Gloucs.) was given an endowment for four boys to learn plainsong and polyphony in 1518, while Lyme Regis (Dorset) supported a clerk and children in 1548.[201]

Youthful clerks and choristers did not survive the sixteenth century in significant numbers. Long before that time, Lyndwood had conceded that married clerks might be appointed if unmarried ones were not available, and the clerk of Nutfield (Surrey) had a wife and son by about 1465.[202] At Ashburton, the clerks apparently continued to serve for short periods in the early sixteenth century, implying younger men, but then stayed longer. One man held the post from 1519 to 1537 and another from 1537 until at least 1576.[203] The Reformation removed boy servers and choristers from most churches, and the career route for parish clerks to become parish clergy diminished as the latter fell in numbers and rose in academic qualifications. In 1604, the Church laid down that parish clerks should be at least twenty years old, and the typical parish clerk of Stuart, Georgian, and Victorian England was older and less learned than his medieval predecessors.[204]

CHILDREN IN THE LITURGY

BY THE LATER middle ages, there were certain days in the year when boys not only supported the liturgy but helped to lead it. Like the times of dressing up and begging for money, these days were especially located in November and December: before and around Christmas. November began with All Saints Day, a major feast of the Church. On this day, the 'Sarum' or Salisbury Cathedral service, which came to be followed throughout southern England, provided for the cathedral choristers to sing and act a text after the eighth lesson at mattins (the service said at midnight). The presentation recalled Christ's parable of the Wise Virgins. Five boys, dressed in surplices, covered their heads with white amices or hoods 'in the manner of virgin women', and held burning candles in their hands. They went to the high altar of the church and stood before it singing a text beginning *Audivi vocem*: 'I heard a voice from heaven, "Come all wise virgins. Put away the oil into your vessels until the Bridegroom arrives." '[205] This piece of drama is interesting because of its use of boys to represent women; it comes close to the cross-dressing customs which also took place in this season.[206]

Eight weeks after All Saints Day, boys in large churches took part in another night service. This was the mattins held late on Christmas Eve, preceding the first mass of Christmas at midnight. The Sarum service provided that, after the first lesson, two clerks of the second form should sing a text in front of the high altar, *Hodie nobis celorum rex* ('Today the king of heaven is born for us'). Five boys wearing surplices, with amices covering their heads and candles in their hands, then sang a response from behind the altar: *Gloria in excelsis Deo* ('Glory to God in the highest').[207] The dramatic effect of this custom was improved at Exeter Cathedral, which developed its own version. Here, instead of the older clerks, a bareheaded boy, chosen for his good clear voice and dressed in an alb with an amice about his neck, appeared from behind the high altar towards the end of the first lesson.[208] He stood on the highest altar step, facing eastwards, with a lighted torch in his left hand. When the lesson was over, he turned to the choir and began to sing *Hodie nobis celorum rex de virgine nasci dignatus est*: 'The king of heaven consented on this day to be born for us of a virgin'.[209] His singing was accompanied by dramatic gestures. At *celorum rex* he raised his right hand to heaven, at *de virgine* he extended it to the image of the Virgin Mary on the north side of the altar, and at *dignatus est* he genuflected. The choir replied *Ut hominem perditum ad celestia regna revocaret* ('That he should call home outcast humanity to the kingdom of heaven'). Meanwhile, three other boys from the south side of the choir and three from the north, wearing the same dress as the first, came to the lowest step of the altar. The first boy descended to them, and all seven sang the *Gloria in excelsis Deo* together, facing the choir.

The other two days when boys carried out important functions in church were those of St Nicholas (6 December) and the Holy Innocents, or Childermas (28 December), the days of the boy-bishop already mentioned.[210] Salisbury custom gave him his main role on the later date, and this was probably widely followed elsewhere. In the Sarum rite, the boy-bishop ceremonies started after vespers in the mid afternoon of 27 December, St John the Evangelist's Day. The boys and their bishop, the latter in mitre and with a pastoral staff, went to the altar of the Holy Innocents wearing silk copes and holding lighted candles. There they sang a Latin text from the Book of Revelation, which was thought to refer to the children whom Herod had killed:

> The one hundred and forty-four thousand who were redeemed from earth, they are those who were not defiled with women, they remained virgins. Therefore they reign with God, and the Lamb of God with them.

After further singing by the boys, the boy-bishop entered his stall in the choir – presumably the real bishop's throne – and presided over the services of the next twenty-four hours. His main duties were to lead parts of the singing, to give blessings, and sometimes to preach a sermon.[211] The bishop's cross-bearer, who seems to have been his deputy, took the bishop's staff, and sang before him an antiphon, in translation:

> Prince of the church, shepherd of the fold, may you deign to bless all your people. With gentleness and charity, humble yourself to give your blessing.

He returned the staff, and the boy-bishop gave the blessing, addressing in turn the choir, the lay people watching, and the altar:

> I sign you with the sign of the cross. May your defence be he who bought you and redeemed you with the price of his flesh!

On Holy Innocents Day itself, the boys came into the choir for mattins, and possibly other services, although their feasting and money collecting must have taken up much of their time. Finally, they returned for vespers, at which the boy-bishop delivered his blessing once more. Then – say the service-books, firmly – 'let the office of the boys for this day be completed'![212]

A CHILD-FRIENDLY CHURCH?

ACTIVE MODERN CHURCHES acknowledge children as a group within their congregations. They seek to minister to them in appropriate ways, and their ministry makes an impact on their buildings. Medieval parish churches were not without signs of a concern with children. Entering such a church, the first thing that one normally saw (and still sees) was the font by the west door: a child-friendly object in form and in function, adopting a size and height appropriate for immersing a baby in water. The font possessed a greater status before the Reformation than it has today. It was a more sacred object, permanently full of holy water, sometimes emphasised by being raised on steps, and often topped by an elaborate cover, locked to keep the holy water safe (Fig. 13).

Many churches contained images of children. Statues of the Virgin Mary carrying the child Christ would have been common; so too paintings of St Christopher with Christ on his shoulders. There were a few child saints, not the most famous figures of the Church but remembered in its calendars and sometimes portrayed in its art.[213] Two early Roman martyrs, Cyr and Pancras, were believed to have been boys, and both had a few churches dedicated to them in England. So had the Anglo-Saxon saints Kenelm and Rumwold, popular in the Midlands and celebrated in extravagant legends. Kenelm, who actually died in his twenties, was said to have been killed when seven, the news being brought to the pope in a letter conveyed by a dove. Rumwold, who lived for only three days, was alleged to have repeatedly exclaimed 'I am a Christian', to have demanded baptism and communion, and even to have preached a sermon. Some of the so-called victims of the Jews, notably Little St Hugh of Lincoln and William of

84   An Elizabethan transcript of the original parish register of Colyton (Devon), beginning in 1538. The Reformation, far from relaxing compulsory Church membership, tried to enforce it by recording infant baptisms.

Norwich, were venerated in their neighbourhoods. And if all these were boys, there were plenty of young virgin saints with whom girls might identify: Mary or Margaret, Katherine or Barbara, and others.

Nor should we think of churches, as we usually do, solely in terms of adults. Shrines and images in churches were not only centres of worship for grown-up people but places where children were brought for healing, candles offered in their measure, and votive objects left in hope or appreciation of their recovery. Tombs of children were not frequent in churches, but wealthy parents were often depicted with their offspring as kneeling groups in windows, on pulpits, or on monumental brasses.[214] Some churches served a further purpose for the young by accommodating schools, especially schools of an elementary nature, held in a corner, in the tower, or in a room over the porch. Such a school is mentioned at Norham (Nland.) as early as the twelfth century, and by the end of the sixteenth they were common enough for Shakespeare to base a joke on the 'pedant that keeps a school i' th' church'.[215]

The services of the medieval parish church can hardly be called child-friendly in the way that modern worship aims to be. Their language was Latin, and they set out to worship God in the language and concepts of adults. Sermons were in English but addressed themselves in a similar way. Only the boy-bishop cere-monies gave children a central role in church, and that excluded girls. Yet worship was less wholly orientated towards adults in practice than it was in theory. By the fifteenth century there might be boy choristers in larger churches, helping with masses or anthems of the Virgin, requiring small forms to sit on and a place to be taught. Other children, though not necessarily required to be in church, might be present as part of the congregation. Occasionally there were enough of them to have a disturbing effect, and in the case of Great Marlow they seem to have occu-pied a distinct part of the building. Nor was medieval worship much more friendly to its adult congregations than to its children. Carried out in Latin by the clergy, it favoured the old no more than the young. The devotions recommended during the service – the saying over of the three basic prayers – could be done as easily by children as by their elders.

A good many of the rites in parish churches were also for children or triggered by them. An infant's birth required not only a baptism but its mother's purifica-tion.[216] Confirmations sometimes took place in churches and always required church attendance for the washing of foreheads and burning of bandages. Ordinations might include children, since boys were often marked with the first tonsure, and this rite might be carried out in a church by a passing bishop.[217] A few children of gentle or noble rank were married in church, and many more had funerals there. Sometimes children assisted with the funerals of adults, their prayers being valued because of their innocence. In 1471, for example, a Bristol merchant named John Gaywood asked for scholars to attend his funeral and say a Paternoster, Ave, and Creed.[218] In 1524, Maud Gowsell of London willed money for fifteen tapers of wax to be carried by children at hers.[219] True, children were not admitted to communion in church nor, it seems, required to attend confession. But these exclusions should not be overvalued. Even adults were not bound to go to confession except in Lent, and most received communion only at Easter.

Church, then, must have had significance for children, and particular churches have lodged in their memories as they grew up. There they were baptised, learnt the forms of services, sang or served as boys, and helped to bury their siblings or their parents. There they made the first confession and communion that signalled their status as adults. There, later on, they congregated with other young men or maidens, taking their share in fund-raising and (if sermons and songs may be trusted) carrying on courtships. Langland's view of church as a place where children learnt the faith was correct, but it touched their lives in many other ways.

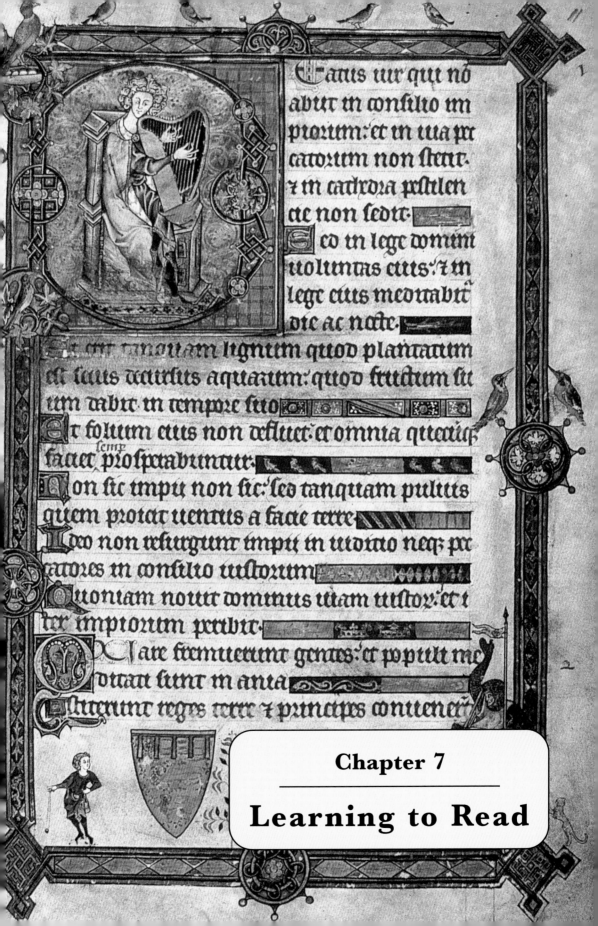

Chapter 7

Learning to Read

LITERACY AND SCHOOLS

EVERY CHILD TODAY, at about the age of five, must start to learn to read and write. 'Must' is a recent verb in this respect. School attendance did not become compulsory in England until 1880, or in most of the United States until about the same period. Before then, people lived in a conditional era when children 'might' begin to master these skills, also at five or so. The popular assumption of today is that the further back one goes into the past, the fewer the number of children who learnt to read. Certainly, the practice was never universal. Some who could read in pre-Victorian times mastered the art in later life, rather than in childhood. Nonetheless, there were always some children in medieval England, and after about 1200 several thousands of them, learning to read in schools or at home. The experience was part of growing up for many people.

Literacy in England dates back to at least the arrival of the first Christian missionaries in the year 597. They came from Italy and were speakers and readers of Latin. The Bible they brought and the services they held were in Latin, and when they recruited English boys and men to become clergy, these had to learn to read and speak Latin too. Within a short space of time after 597, however, this clerical Latin culture broadened out. First, because Latin was a difficult language to learn, writing (and therefore reading) began to be done in English. This happened surprisingly early; King Æthelberht of Kent, the king who received the first missionaries, issued a written code of laws in his native language by the time of his death in 616.[1] Secondly, reading spread beyond the clergy. Bede tells us in his *Ecclesiastical History* that Aldfrith, who became king of the Northumbrians in 685, had previously been in contact with clergy and was able to read Latin.[2] Aldfrith is the first clear case of a literate layman in England. Within a hundred years of the coming of St Augustine to Canterbury in 597, the English had entered modern times as far as education and learning were concerned. Those who could read were both clergy and laity, and reading and writing went on in English as well as in Latin.

The proportion of literate people, of course, was for a long time far smaller than it is today – not that we have any means of measuring it. Information about who could read or write in medieval England is fragmentary.[3] The clergy were meant to be able to read and understand Latin, but there were plenty of accusations about individuals who allegedly fell short in this respect. Evidence about lay people is scattered and hard to collect. By the end of the ninth century, the historian Asser was praising Alfred the Great as a literate king who encouraged literacy within his family and among his nobility.[4] By the twelfth century, when large numbers of texts and documents survive, there are references to the reading abilities of various kings, queens, noblemen, and noblewomen. By the early thirteenth, it is manifest that towns too were centres of literacy. Town councils were keeping records and individual townsmen could read or write. By the middle of that century, if not before, there were stewards and bailiffs in the countryside, with similar skills.

By 1250, at the latest, the whole of the population was in contact with writings

85   The ascent of knowledge. Lady Grammar gives a child the alphabet, with which to climb through the castle of learning to Theology on its topmost tower.

and literate people, whether or not they were personally literate. Even a serf attended a church where a cleric used books and a lord's court which kept written records, including ones relating to the serf's tenancy and duties. Even such serfs might have charters of their property to which they could refer with the help of educated people, and might acquire or convey property by means of further char-

86   Aristotle teaching Alexander the Great, as a master might do in a noble household. Each well-
dressed boy has his own book.

ters, authenticated with their own seals.[5] We think of literacy as a personal skill,
because we live in a society that places an emphasis on people as individuals. In
the middle ages, communities were equally important: families, households,
towns, manors, and villages, all of which included literate people. English society
was collectively literate by the thirteenth century, and perhaps much earlier.
Everyone knew someone who could read, and everyone's life depended to some
extent on reading and writing.

How did people learn to read, and children in particular? In the case of the
Latin needed by clergy, scholars, and administrators, the process was a difficult
one. It required formal teaching by a Latinist with access to books: grammars,
vocabularies, and reading texts. From the moment of its reintroduction to
England, Latin was normally learnt in a special environment, a school.[6] In Anglo-
Saxon times, schools were chiefly attached to religious houses where recruits
needed to be trained and literate clergy were available to be teachers. Many religious houses – cathedrals, monasteries, and collegiate churches – continued to
have schools up to the Reformation, though these mostly catered for small
numbers of boys or young men attached to the houses, such as altar-boys, choristers, or novices, rather than for the general public. Great households were other
centres of education. King Alfred is said to have maintained children and to have

had them trained in letters and good manners, as early as the late ninth century.
By the end of the middle ages, the royal household and those of the great
nobility and clergy often included one or more schoolmasters to teach the lord's
children, wards, and the boys who sang in the chapel (Fig. 86).

Schools such as we have today – free-standing public institutions taught by professional schoolmasters – first appear in records soon after the Norman Conquest
and were common in later centuries. They were especially to be found in towns.
Some were officially recognised bodies, controlled by a local bishop, cathedral,
monastery, or lay patron, with their own buildings and a monopoly of local teaching. Others were private ventures, run by a master from his own house for a
handful of pupils. Nearly all charged fees until the late fourteenth century, when
a movement began to provide free schools. One such school was Winchester
College, founded in 1382: a large boarding establishment offering free instruction
and accommodation to seventy pupils chosen from the founder's family and the
places where the college held land. Another was the grammar school of Wotton-
under-Edge (Gloucs.), endowed by Lady Katherine Berkeley in 1384, offering free
instruction to any boy wishing to study there. Though Winchester is the more
famous, Wotton was the more typical, and many similar day-schools, small and
free, were founded in England during the fifteenth and sixteenth centuries
(Fig. 87).

87 Modern free-standing
schools appeared in the late
eleventh century. By the fifteenth, some like Magdalen
College School (Oxford),
founded by William Waynflete
in 1481, provided free education.

*Elevation of the South front of Saint Mary Magdalene Hall, Oxford
as it appeared in 1820.* *from Dublin 1830.*

Most schools were limited to boys and youths. Boys needed Latin for careers as clergy, merchants, and administrators, or for lives as gentlemen and noblemen. Girls did not become clergy or administrators, but those of the wealthy classes learnt to read enough Latin to look at a prayer book and French or English to read romances or works of instruction. We know less about the education of girls, but they may have gone to elementary schools, sometimes with small boys, sometimes without.[7] The thirteenth-century treatise *Ancrene Wisse* forbids a woman enclosed as an anchoress to teach children, but allows her maid to do so to little girls who cannot be taught with boys.[8] Nunneries often boarded small numbers of girls of gentry or merchant status, and these too were probably taught to read elementary Latin, French, or English. A priest of early-Tudor Norwich paid tribute in his will to a nun who 'was the first creature that taught me to know the letters in my book'; if she taught him, she may well have taught girls as well.[9] In 1404, a woman named Matilda Maresflete occurs as a schoolmistress (*magistra scolarum*) in Boston (Lincs.),[10] and at least two women in London had this word as a surname, presumably from pursuing a similar kind of work. One, E. Scolemaysteresse, is mentioned in a will of 1408; another, Elizabeth Scolemaystres, paid a tax levied on foreigners in 1441.[11] These mistresses are likely to have taught small girls, and some male teachers may have done the same. An elderly priest in London named William Barbour was said to have thirty young children in his care between 1505 and 1515, when he was accused of abusing one of them, a girl of eight years old.[12]

TEACHING AT HOME

SCHOOLS PROVIDE SO much of our schooling today that there is a tendency to assume that they must have done so in the past. This is not necessarily true of the middle ages. Learning Latin was best done at school, and schools (at least by the end of the middle ages) often had an elementary class in which small boys learnt the alphabet and how to read simple Latin or English prayers (Fig. 92). Elementary learning, however, did not need to be done in a school. It required only an ABC and a prayer book, and any literate adult could teach a child to do it. Once a child had learnt to read letters and words, he or she could abandon Latin as a subject and concentrate on the easier task of reading English. This involved no complicated grammar and little strange vocabulary. The process could take place in a child's own home, in that of an employer such as a tradesman, or in the households of the king and the aristocracy where noble children were brought up as wards or pages.[13] It is reasonable to envisage gentlemen- and gentlewomen-in-waiting, clergy (friars, chaplains, or nuns), and merchants or their clerks, all teaching reading to children or young people, though evidence of the fact is hard to find. Some parish clergy certainly taught in this way. The recommendation of about the year 1000 that they should teach boys to help them in church never developed into an obligatory system, but instances of the practice are found from time to time.[14] Orderic Vitalis tells us of his studies with Siward, priest of Montgomery (Wales) in the 1080s,[15] and the vicar of Bridgwater (Somerset) had a boy in his house in about 1500, being taught by the curate to 'learn [to] read and sing'.[16]

Parents too were potential teachers. 'The wise man taught his child gladly to read books and well understand them.' So runs the opening sentence of the register of Godstow Abbey (Oxon.), compiled in about 1450 to teach the abbey's nuns to read their charters in English.[17] The sentence may have been proverbial. There was an ancient tradition of fathers instructing their sons, sometimes by writing texts for them to read.[18] The books of Proverbs, Ecclesiastes, and Ecclesiasticus in the Bible profess to be aimed at sons, and Roman authors such as Marcus Portius Cato, Cicero, and Livy wrote with similar intentions. The Emperor Augustus himself was said to have taught his grandsons to read and write.[19] A number of works by fathers for their sons were written in medieval England, and may owe something to these Biblical and classical models. They include Walter of Henley's treatise on *Husbandry* in the thirteenth century, Chaucer's *Astrolabe* at the end of the fourteenth, and Peter Idley's *Instructions* in the fifteenth. In France, Geoffrey de la Tour Landry began to compose *The Book of the Knight of the Tower* for his daughters in 1371, a book which later made its way to England, and he wrote another for his sons.[20] By the early sixteenth century, Sir Thomas Elyot used *The Governor* (1530), his influential book about the education of noblemen and gentlemen, to argue that it was 'no reproach to a nobleman to instruct his own children, or at least to examine them, by the way of dalliance or solace'. He cited Augustus as a precedent.[21]

Some of the writings by fathers for children are ambitious. *The Book of the Knight of the Tower* is indeed accessible to older children, and Chaucer's *Astrolabe* may have been used to teach reading to younger ones.[22] Walter of Henley's *Husbandry*, on the other hand, is a technical handbook, as is Sir Thomas Littleton's great fifteenth-century legal work on *Tenures* in law French, also addressed to his son. Such works were suitable only for an adolescent boy or a young adult. In the earlier stages of life, children who were learning to read may have been closer to their mothers than to their fathers. One of the earliest stories in English history about a boy and his reading, in Asser's Life of King Alfred, tells how Alfred's mother showed him and his brothers a book of English poetry and promised it as a gift to the first one who learnt it. Alfred took the book, went to his 'master', learnt it, and recited it to his mother.[23] The account does not say that his mother taught him, nor that he learnt the book except by memory, but it features her as a benign and positive influence. In less important families, without specialist teachers, a mother's role in this respect may have been still greater.

There are certainly signs, later on, of mothers taking an interest in their children's education. A good example is that of Denise de Montchensey, an Essex lady of the thirteenth century. She wished to teach her children French, a language already difficult to acquire in England, and Walter of Bibbesworth obliged by composing his *Tretiz de Langage* for her in about 1250.[24] By about 1300, the linkage of women with children's reading was familiar enough for a poem comparing men and women to include the statement 'woman teacheth child on book'.[25] The mother in London who taught her daughter to say mass in 1391, evidently from a missal, was highly unusual in the nature of her teaching, but mothers who helped children simply to read a prayer book must have been common.[26] When the Yorkshire knight Sir Robert Plumpton was away from home in about 1506, it was his wife Isabel who wrote to remind him, 'Sir, remember your children's books'.[27] Literary works by mothers for their children are rarer than those by fathers, but there is one from the fifteenth century: the treatise on hunting in English verse known as *Tristram*, which claims to be composed by a woman for her son.[28] The claim could hardly have been made if mothers had not been regarded as possible teachers.

Another indication of their role in this respect is the rise of interest in St Anne as the teacher of her daughter, the Virgin Mary. In the second century AD, a work was written, called the 'Book of James', to supply the gaps in the Gospels about Mary, Joseph, and the birth of Jesus. It claimed that Mary was the only child of long-infertile parents, Joachim and Anne. In gratitude, her father and mother dedicated her to God, and sent her at the age of three to live and serve in the Temple at Jerusalem. She stayed there until she was twelve and reached puberty, when the priests arranged for her to be married. The widowers of the district were summoned, and Joseph was chosen after the appearance of a dove which settled upon his head.[29] Nothing is said about reading or teaching in this story, or in medieval writings based upon it. The best-known of these, the famous collection of saints' lives known as *The Golden Legend*, written by Jacopo da Varazze in about 1260, gives a similar account to the 'Book of James'. Mary is offered in the Temple at the age of three, stays there until she is fourteen, and spends her days in prayer and at weaving.[30]

Artists, in contrast, developed a different tradition. By the early fourteenth century, they were portraying Anne and Mary in an educational relationship for which there is no room in the the older account of Mary's childhood. Mary is pictured as a well-developed child or adolescent, reading a book under her mother's instruction (Fig. 88).[31] The scene occurs in continental sources, but it was especially popular in England where it is found in manuscripts, wall paintings, and stained-glass windows.[32] In one example, Mary's reading appears to consist of a tablet or primer used to teach children the alphabet.[33] In another, now destroyed, it was a roll containing the letters ABC.[34] Most often, she holds a book containing a text of scripture. One of the earliest portrayals of the scene in England, a window image in the church of Stanford-on-Avon (Northants.), represents the words of the book as being *Domine, labia mea aperies, et os* . . . ('O Lord, open my lips, and my mouth will proclaim your praise').

There are two ways of interpreting such scenes. One is that they were symbolic. Mary's reading may be meant to emphasise her role in conceiving and giving birth to the Word of God, hence the liking of artists to place texts on her book which speak of praise to God.[35] 'O Lord, open my lips' was the opening sentence of the medieval 'hours' or liturgy in honour of the Virgin, said by thousands of worshippers each day. Equally, her act of reading may have been meant to be real. The scene of Mary and Anne appears in art just as we hear in literature that

88   Parents too might teach their children to read. Here St Anne instructs her daughter the Virgin Mary.

'woman teacheth child on book', at a time when artists were portraying Mary and Jesus in lifelike houses and landscapes. These portrayals tended to imagine the Holy Family living in the style of wealthy people of the later middle ages, and it would have been natural to attribute Mary with the kind of education current among such people. In turn, the scene may have affirmed such education, encouraging mothers to teach their children to read.

Whoever did such teaching – fathers, mothers, or tutors – it seems to have started at an early age, at least in wealthy and enlightened households. Margaret Plumpton, daughter of a Yorkshire esquire and granddaughter of a knight, had nearly learnt to read from a psalter in 1463 when she was only four.[36] A few years later, the ill-fated Edward V, eldest son of Edward IV, had ordinances drawn up for his education in 1473, including his 'learning', when he was two months short of his third birthday.[37] Henry VII's sons Arthur and Henry VIII had schoolmasters by the ages of four or five.[38] Sir Thomas Elyot thought that noble boys should learn to read well before seven, despite contrary views by certain ancient authors, and an early start continued to find support in later times.[39] Charles Hoole observed in his book *The Petty Schoole* (1659) that four or five was the usual age of beginning school in towns, and six or seven in the countryside where journeys to school were more lengthy. He thought the earlier the better, and considered that a child of three or four was already capable of looking at a book.[40] Lower down in society, of course, it was less easy to get educated: to find a school, pay school fees, or (most of all) conceive that schooling was useful. Poorer children, even if they or their parents were favourable to reading, might have to postpone the undertaking until adolescence or adulthood, and might not begin it at all.

THE ALPHABET

LEARNING TO READ involves learning the alphabet: its characters, their names, and their sounds.[41] You can do this by memorising the twenty-six letters in order, and then use your knowledge to spell words. Alternatively you can begin with words, learn the letters out of order, and get to know the order last of all. It has been suggested that children in Anglo-Saxon England may have learnt by the word method,[42] and the same may have been true of some who learnt informally in homes in the later middle ages. By Chaucer's time at the latest, however, it was common practice to learn the alphabet first, especially in schools and probably in many homes. This is the better documented of the two procedures, and the easier to reconstruct and imagine. Learning the alphabet for the first time is a fresh experience for a child, interesting and stimulating or hard and baffling. This must have been as true in the middle ages as it is today, but in another respect the medieval experience was very different from ours. Our ancestors' alphabet contained more than the twenty-six letters. It gave some letters in alternative forms, it contained additional signs, and it was set in a religious framework. It was like an historic building which had grown organically and acquired an aura of mystery. Its teachers, let alone its learners, may not have known exactly why it was like it was.

The alphabet used in medieval England came, like writing in general, from Latin. It was based on that of the Romans, and was similar to the alphabets in use in the other countries of western Europe. The Roman letters numbered twenty-two – excluding 'j', 'v', 'w', and 'y' – and this became a twenty-three-letter alphabet during the middle ages through the addition of 'y', originally a Greek letter and still known in France as 'i-grec' and in Germany and Italy as 'ypsilon'. The twenty-three letters, however, were not wholly adequate for use in medieval England. One shortcoming was that they did not cater for all the sounds of English, especially 'th' and 'w'. The Anglo-Saxons therefore borrowed two signs for this purpose from the independent runic alphabet, consisting of 'thorn' [þ] for 'th' and 'wyn' [ƿ] for 'w'. They also developed two additional signs: [ð], a form of 'd' that modern scholars call 'eth', which was also used for 'th', and 'yogh' [ȝ], a form of 'g', for 'gh' and 'y'. 'Wyn' and 'eth' disappeared by about 1300, 'wyn' having been replaced by 'w', but 'thorn' and 'yogh' survived until the late fifteenth century. Indeed 'thorn', by then indistinguishable in shape from 'y', persisted later still in one or two abbreviations such as 'ye' and 'yt' for 'the' and 'that', the basis of the modern humorous misunderstanding, 'ye olde inne'.

The other problem about the Roman alphabet was that people did not write it uniformly. In an age of writing everything by hand, different forms of letters were in use, notably the famous long 's' like an 'f', which went on being used in England down to the eighteenth century. The modern 's' was used only at ends (and sometimes beginnings) of words. Abbreviations were employed to save time – lines and twirls for 'n', 'per', 'pre', 'pro', 'que', and so on – and whole signs for one or two common works like *et* ('and') and *est* ('is') in Latin, as well as for 'and' in English. Learning to read was therefore a complex task, though not necessarily more so than today. You needed to know the classic letters, variant forms, and abbreviations, just as modern children learn printed letters in one form, encounter them in others, and practice writing them in yet more.

Teachers of reading were already grappling with these difficulties by the late Anglo-Saxon period. Although we have no ABC books from this period, we possess copies of alphabets which people scribbled in books during the tenth and eleventh centuries. A particularly good one occurs in the margin of a manuscript now in the British Library (Harley MS 208), a copy of the *Letters* of Alcuin.[43] This gives the alphabet from 'a' to 'z', the signs for Latin *et* and English 'and', and four Anglo-Saxon letters:

a d [*sic*] c d e f g h i k l m n o p q r ∫ t u x y z & 7 ᵽ þ æ ð

It is followed by

pater noster qui es in celis sanctificetur nomen tuum adveniat reg

– in other words by the opening phrases of the Lord's Prayer in Latin.[44] Some other Anglo-Saxon alphabets contain the extra signs and letters, with slight variations, so that 'æ' may come after 'eth' and 'eth' appear in its capital and minuscule (lower-case) versions. The ABC is beginning to ripen into its characteristic late medieval forms. Its regular troop of letters has acquired a group of camp followers – runes and abbreviations, a more disorderly throng which does not always keep to the same sequence. The layout of the letters and signs is already designed to prepare one for reading both Latin and English. And, once the letters are mastered, the first text to be learnt is the Paternoster, the Lord's Prayer.

These developments continued during the twelfth century. Here valuable information is forthcoming from another British Library manuscript (Stowe MS 57), a miscellany including a Latin poem in which a father undertakes to instruct his son.[45] The poem is followed by five alphabets including one in Latin. Its letters appear in capitals, and in some cases also in minuscule forms, and they are given their pronouncing names, similar to our own. Then, as before, come the camp followers:

A B C D E F G H I K L M N O P Q R S T V X Y Z & ÷ Amen

Finally the writer lists 'letters in English' (*Anglice littere*), consisting of 'wyn', 'eth' (which this text uniquely, but perhaps correctly, calls 'thet'), 'thorn', and the sign for 'and' in English. Two important changes are visible here, also significant for the future. First, the sign '÷' for *est* in Latin has crept in after *et*. The alphabet gives it a name, 'titel', from *titulus* in Latin, meaning 'a sign'. Secondly, the word 'amen' has arrived at the end. 'Amen' is the word for concluding a prayer. The ABC is no longer a mere list of letters; it has become something that you offer to God, just as you do when you pray.

Alphabets become more common at the end of the fourteenth century, when they start to appear on the first pages of some lay prayer books of the kind known as 'primers', or 'primmers' as the word was pronounced.[46] Primer alphabets are broadly similar from the late fourteenth to the mid sixteenth centuries and from England to the continent, although there are slight variations of detail.[47] One of the oldest primers to contain an ABC, a manuscript in Glasgow University Library (MS Hunter 472), dating from Chaucer's time, sets out the letters as follows (Fig. 89):

+ a.a.b.c.d.e.f.g.h.i.k.l.
m.n.o.p.q.r. ꝛ. ſ.s.t.u.v.
x.y.z.&. est ⁚ amen:[48]

At the other end of the timescale, *The ABC both in Latin and English*, a primer printed in 1538, gives them as follows:

+ A a b c d e f g h j k l m n o p
q r ꝛ ſ s t v u x y z & ꝗ ÷ est Amen.[49]

The primer alphabets, therefore, begin with a cross and present the letters, usually in minuscule form, sometimes divided by stops and sometimes not. 'A' now appears twice, and three other letters are given in alternative forms: 'r', 's', and 'u/v'. The traditional '&' after 'z' is followed by the Latin abbreviation for *con-* and by an arrangement of dots. '*Est* has been inserted in front of 'amen'. Continental alphabets were set out similarly, except for differences in the abbreviations and the absence of the words *est* and 'amen'.

Some features of this pattern need explaining. Excluding the cross for the moment, the first problem is the double 'a' at the beginning. Some alphabets, like that in the Hunter manuscript, present each 'a' in minuscule. Others put the first 'a' in capitals – a practice found in Italy by about 1400, and in England by the late fifteenth century.[50] This second usage became very common in Tudor times, and eventually, as we shall see, the three strokes of the capital A came to be interpreted as a symbol of the Trinity. That, however, is unlikely to have been the original function of the first 'a', in view of its minuscule form in some of the late-medieval alphabets. The Hunter primer and one other from the fifteenth century give each minuscule 'a' in a slightly different shape.[51] A better explanation might therefore be that the two were put in because pupils might meet different forms of 'a', as they would in the case of 'r' and 's'.

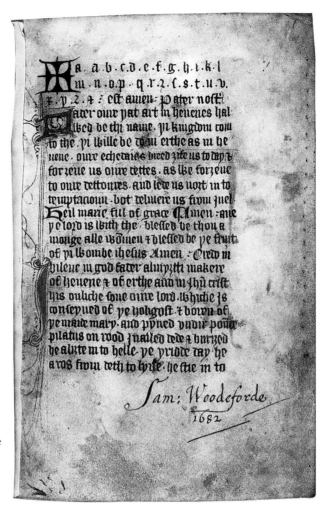

89   The opening page of a late fourteenth-century 'Hunter' primer, containing the Latin alphabet and basic prayers in English.

There is also a third possibility that the first 'a' stands for something other than the second. The double 'a' is common in alphabets throughout Europe, making it likely that the doubling stems from one tradition of teaching. All the teaching of Latin in medieval Europe went back ultimately to the grammarians of the Roman Empire, and if we consult the most famous of these, Priscian and Donatus, we find that, in trying to identify the most basic elements of language, they begin with *vox*, the voice or vocal sound, and then go on to discuss the written letters.[52] Schoolmasters, trying to follow this scheme, may have spent their first lesson with pupils by getting them to articulate sounds. Support for this view comes from a fifteenth-century *Ballade de ABC* from France, which tells us how a pupil went to school and learnt, in his first lesson, 'a' 'a' 'a', and then 'a' 'b' 'c' in his second.[53] 'A' was supposedly the basic sound, the first one to be articulated by a new-born baby.[54] Making children start by pronouncing a sound would have had the value of getting the young, shy, and tongue-tied to speak clearly enough for the master to be able to check that they were indeed all speaking. This was an essential step

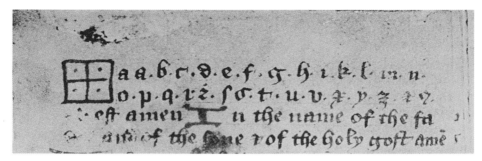

90   The cross and alphabet from another primer of about 1400.

to ensuring that they learnt the ABC, because that process involved them pronouncing the letters aloud.

The rest of the primer letters down to 'z' were straightforward except for the alternative forms of 'r', 's', and 'u/v', included because pupils would encounter them in manuscripts. One might expect that a separate 'i' and 'j' would also have appeared in the table, since they were originally variant forms of the same letter, and this was so on the continent but not in England, where only one of the two appears, usually 'i'. By putting in these double forms, the primer alphabets followed the Anglo-Saxon practice of making the ABC a guide to palaeography, the art of reading manuscripts. For the same reason they included, after 'z', at least a couple of the common abbreviations used in handwriting: '&' and *con-*. The dots after *con-* are evidently the descendants of the sign for *est* in the twelfth-century alphabet. They too were known as 'tittle' or 'tittles', as the *est* sign had been. Their form varies: two dots like a colon, three such dots, a line between two dots (like a division sign), four dots placed in a diamond shape, and three lines. The reason for this seems to be that the *est* sign fell out of use in the thirteenth century. While this was happening, the word *est* was added after the tittles, as an explanation. The meaning of the tittles was eventually forgotten and they became mere decorations, but *est* kept its place. Other European countries put the '&' and *con-* signs after the alphabet, but the tittles and the *est* seem to have been unique to England.[55]

One or two further observations can be made about the primer alphabets. There was no accepted way of setting them out, other than the sequence of letters. Writers of books did not assign so many letters to each line; they simply wrote them out in the space available. Most alphabets are Latin ones, but versions with English letters are occasionally found, as in earlier times. One example from York in the late fifteenth century has a 'thorn' at the very end, and a second, from Winchester at about the same period, has a 'w' before the 'x', a 'thorn' after 'y', and perhaps the letter 'yogh' (for 'gh' and 'z'), unless it is an alternative form of 'z'.[56] 'Yogh' was dropping out of use by this time and 'thorn' was becoming indistinguishable from 'y', so one would not expect to find them in alphabets after 1500, but it was long before 'w' gained general recognition. Indeed this was still not always the case by the Reformation.

The alphabet, then, as normally presented to children in late-medieval and

Tudor primers, had evolved a good deal from its classical form. It had been Christianised with a cross at the beginning and 'amen' at the end. It had been adjusted to medieval writing practices. It had become a rigmarole relating to the past as well as to the present, since the original function of the tittles no longer existed. Did Tudor teachers and pupils understand the meaning of the tittles and of the word *est*? It is possible that they did not, and that when they said the word *est*, they felt that they were making an affirmation. They had recited the alphabet, and 'it is so!'

THE CHRIST-CROSS ROW

THE OTHER DISTINCTIVE feature of the late-medieval alphabet was the cross. It led the letters like a cross-bearer and the letters marched behind it like a force of crusaders or a parish procession. In due course, the cross also gave its name to the letters that followed. The word 'alphabet' was not common in English speech or writing until the late sixteenth century. Medieval people were more likely to talk of the ABC or 'abece', which means much the same as 'alphabet',[57] but by the 1520s a third name was becoming popular: 'Christ-cross row', or 'cross row' for short, and this name was widely used in Tudor and Stuart times.[58] The alphabet cross was more than a symbol too. It was a rubric: an instruction to readers to say a short prayer before they pronounced the letters that followed. The recitation of the letters also became a prayer, and the word 'amen' was said at the end of the process, just as it was at the end of a prayer.

That the alphabet should be presented as a Christian text or icon, with 'amen' for good measure, is not surprising in a society and culture as Christian as that of medieval England. Indeed, the linkage of letters and religion is far older than the middle ages. Christians do not have a story about the invention of the alphabet, but the Bible comes close to giving it a divine origin. Writing is first mentioned in the Old Testament in the accounts of God's delivery of the Ten Commandments to Moses, in the books of 'Exodus' and 'Deuteronomy'. 'The Lord said to Moses, "Come up to me on the mountain. Stay there and let me give you the tablets of stone, the law and the commandments, which I have written down so that you may teach them".' He then gave the prophet two tablets 'written with the finger of God'. These first tablets were broken by Moses in anger at the worship of the golden calf by the people of Israel, and replaced by new ones written, according to 'Deuteronomy', by God himself, but in 'Exodus' by Moses at God's dictation.[59]

It is not explained how Moses learnt to write, and the gift of writing is not clearly ascribed to God. But God could certainly write, and his new relationship with his people was expressed through this means. Not only were the Commandments preserved on tablets; they were copied by people and kept on their bodies in amulets. God's later communications with his prophets were also recorded in writing. The religion of Israel became 'a religion of the book', which depended on written texts for its understanding and practice. So did Christianity. 'I am the alpha and omega', says Christ in the 'Book of Revelation', 'the beginning and the end' – an image which links him with the first and last letters of the Greek alphabet.[60] Christianity too was based on books: the Bible, Roman and canon law texts, and prayer books for worship. The leaders of the Church and its worship – the clergy – had to be able to read these and other relevant spiritual works.

Most Christians, of course, did not use the alphabet and language of Israel; they wrote in Greek in the East and Latin in the West, using the appropriate letters. The Greeks had a legendary hero named Cadmus who was said to have introduced their alphabet, and the Latins had a female one, Carmentis. When Isidore of Seville (d. 636) wrote his famous dictionary called the *Etymologies*, he took a broad view of the origin of writing. He thought that the Syriac and Chaldaean alphabets stemmed from Abraham, the Hebrew from Moses, and the Greek and Latin from Cadmus and Carmentis – a view that did not see alphabets as particularly holy in themselves.[61] Later in the middle ages, however, Latin and its writings so dominated the culture of western Europe that there was less awareness of other alphabets and their scripts. The Latin ABC of twenty-two letters came to be seen as part of God's scheme of things, just as the Hebrew alphabet did to the writers of 'Exodus' and 'Deuteronomy', although in reality the Latin version was a comparatively late development.

There is a good example of this view in a ninth-century tract on the alphabet, surviving in a manuscript from Berne in Switzerland. The author of the tract attempts to show that the Latin letters have Christian characteristics. He asks 'why is the first letter "a"?' He explains that this is because it is the first letter of angel, *anima* ('life'), and Adam – all early creations of God. The three strokes of the capital 'A' signify the Trinity, and the whole letter stands for God as a unity. He tries to give similar values to other letters: 'c' is the Church, 'e' the Trinity, 's' the Old and New Testaments, and 'x', of course, the Cross.[62] A similar kind of approach can be seen in Bartholomew's thirteenth-century encyclopaedia, *De Proprietatibus Rerum*. God, says Bartholomew, did twenty-two works in the first week of his creation. The generations from Adam to Jacob were twenty-two in number, the Old Testament was written in twenty-two books, and there are 'two and twenty letters of ABC, by the which all the lore of God's law is written'.[63] In the same way, a medieval French book illustrator could imagine Moses coming down from Mount Sinai with ABCD written on his tablets.[64]

By the tenth century, the fact that the Church was grounded on writings was visibly demonstrated every time a new church building was consecrated. During the consecration ceremony, the presiding cleric – the bishop – wrote letters across the floor of the church. The directions about this state that 'the bishop shall begin at the left-hand [corner] of the east end to write the alphabet on the pavement with his staff up to the right-hand corner of the west end, and he shall write the alphabet similarly from the left-hand corner of the west end up to the right-hand corner of the east end'.[65] A great St Andrew's cross of letters was thereby scratched across the floor of the building: one alphabet in Latin and one in Greek. In *The Golden Legend*, Jacopo da Varazze tried to attach meanings to this cross of letters. It represented the joining together of the Gentiles with the Jews under

Christ, and the two Testaments of the Bible (which interlink with one another). Thirdly, it stood for Christian belief. 'The pavement of the church is like the foundation of our faith, and the characters written on it are the articles of the faith.'[66] Learned extrapolation, perhaps, but the consecration alphabets were an appropriate symbol of the ways that Christianity rested on the written word and that letters, in consequence, acquired religious significance.

It fitted with all this that medieval children learnt the alphabet in a Christian form and as a Christian task. It was not only to be looked at, but pronounced aloud and pronounced like a prayer. The cross at the beginning was not simply a visual reminder of Christianity; it was a trigger for a phrase that you spoke before you started saying the letters. John Trevisa, in his translation of Bartholomew's encyclopaedia, begun in 1398, included a prologue recalling how, in his school-days,

> [A] cross was made, all of red
> In the beginning of my book,
> That is cleped [*called*] 'God me speed',
> In the first lesson that I took.
> Then I learned 'a' and 'b',
> And other letters by their names.[67]

The first thing that a child learnt in school, according to John Alcock, bishop of Ely, in the 1490s, was ' "Christ's cross be my speed", and so beginneth the ABC'.[68] You pronounced the phrase, crossed yourself, and were ready to say the alphabet. In fact, although these were the commonest words, the phrase existed in several versions. We find it in texts associated with, or alluding to children, as:

God me speed [also, God speed me].[69]
Du gveras ['God help', in Cornish].[70]
Cross Christ [me] speed.[71]
Cross of Jesus Christ be ever our speed.[72]
Christ cross me speed.[73]
Cross and courteous Christ this beginning speed.[74]
Christ cross me speed, and St Nicholas.[75]
Christ cross be our speed, with grace, mercy in all our need.[76]
Christ's cross be my speed, in all virtue to proceed.[77]

The phrase was not unique to children, and was said by adults too when making the sign of the cross. Thus the hero of the poem *Sir Gawain and the Green Knight* exclaims 'Cross Christ me speed' while he is riding on an adventure and prays to God for somewhere to stay during Christmas.[78] Schools probably took the phrase from general use, but it became especially identified with them. By the early fifteenth century, a character in a story could ask another how long ago he said 'Christ cross me speed', knowing that readers would associate the words with being a schoolboy.[79]

Saying the text before you recited the alphabet meant that you commended yourself to God and entered into a spiritual mode. When you had finished the recitation, you said 'amen' as in a prayer. Indeed, on the first page of a primer, the alphabet with its 'amen', placed above other short prayers with theirs, looked remarkably like a prayer itself.[80] The process that we have seen beginning in the twelfth century had become fully developed. Once the alphabet was seen as religious text or icon, it was tempting to go on spinning religious meanings from it. Bartholomew's twenty-two letters are one instance of this, and we shall encounter others in which even the alphabet book and its rubrics could be compared to the cross and wounds of Christ.

LEARNING THE ALPHABET

HAVING ESTABLISHED THE shape of the alphabet, we need to know how it was put into children's hands and heads. Modern schools have blackboards, whiteboards, or projectors to show material to a class. Medieval schools may have displayed large alphabets, and three Tudor ABCs survive on the vestry wall of the church of North Cadbury (Somerset), apparently from its use as a schoolroom. But pupils then, like pupils today, needed their own copies of the alphabet, and this was especially true in homes where reading might be taught to one child at a time. It was already common by the thirteenth century to use small wooden tablets for this purpose with a parchment cover attached to one or both sides. The sermon writer Odo of Cheriton, writing early in that century, uses such a tablet as an illustration of the crucifixion of Jesus. 'Just as the sheet (*carta*) on which the ABC taught to children is fixed with four nails to a board, so the flesh or skin of Christ was stretched out on the cross'. Christ on the cross was an image of the ABC, 'rubricated with the vermilion of his own blood'.[81] The alphabet tablet is mentioned again by Friar Robert Holcote, writing between 1326 and 1349. 'You know', he says, 'that children, when they are first instructed, are not put to learn anything complicated but only what is plain. Therefore, they are first taught from a book with letters written large, affixed to a piece of wood, and afterwards, by progress, in letters from a more sophisticated book'.[82]

The fullest account of the tablet appears in an English poem about the passion of Christ, written in the late fourteenth or early fifteenth century. This poem survives in two versions, one in a Harley manuscript in the British Museum, the other in a Bodleian manuscript, which differ slightly in details.[83] The Harley text, which is perhaps the earlier, begins as follows:

> In [every] place as man may see,
> When a child to school shall set be,
>   A book [for] him is brought,
> Nailed on a board of tree [*wood*],
> That men calleth an ABC,
>   Prettily wrought.

Wrought is on the book without [*outside*],
Five paraphs [*paragraph marks*] great and stout,
    Boled [*embellished*] in rose red;
That is set without doubt
[Full of letters about]
    In tokening of Christ's death.

Red letter in parchment
Maketh a child good and fine
    Letters to look and see.
By this book men may divine
That Christ's body was full of pain
    That died on rood tree [*on the cross*].

On tree he was done full blithe
With great paraphs, that be wounds five,
    As you may understand.
Look in his body, maid and wife,
When they began [to] nails drive
    In foot and in hand.

The poem then goes on to discuss the crucifixion, in terms of the alphabet tablet. Christ's body was marked with red wounds, like paragraph marks, and with blue bruises from the blows delivered to him. His marks, says the poet, can be read like an ABC, and he or she proceeds to discuss a number of aspects of Christ's passion alphabetically, such as his bonds, faintness, love, mercy, and suffering. The Harley alphabet ends with the abbreviation '&', but the Bodleian version contains two further stanzas incorporating the three tittles, *est*, and amen.

These literary sources teach us at least three things about the medieval alphabet tablet. First, people called it both an 'abece' and a 'book', although it was not a book in the usual sense. Secondly, the tablet was covered with a piece of parchment (doubtless for durability), attached by nails, and containing writing. The Harley text talks about red letters on the tablet; the Bodleian version refers to letters of red and black. Most tablets probably displayed the alphabet letters in black, for cheapness and durability, though there may have been rubrics or embellishments in red. The mention of five paragraph marks may mean that the writing was divided into five sections or contained five items (alphabet, Paternoster, and other basic prayers). Finally, there is the emphasis on the tablet's religious significance. Not content with the alphabet cross as a reminder of Christ, Odo and the alphabet poet seek to use the whole tablet and its red ink as images of the cross, Christ's wounds, and his sacrifice for us. In their view, not only was the alphabet a religious text, but the tablet itself an icon which you could venerate just as you did an image of the crucified Christ in a church. 'The word made flesh' becomes 'the flesh made word' (Fig. 91).

The writers mentioned so far do not tell us, unfortunately, what was written on

91   Christ on the cross was seen as a kind of book, and the marks of his Passion as letters that teach us lessons.

the tablet. For this, we have to go to sources from the continent and from later in English history, because alphabet tablets were widely used in western Europe during the late medieval and early modern periods. Illustrations of them on the continent suggest that they were oblong, at first often lateral in shape but later more usually vertical, especially by the sixteenth century. They had one or more handles or a carrying cord, which might be at the top, sides, or bottom, the latter being especially associated with the later, vertical form. Pictures of alphabets on lateral tablets appear in fifteenth-century Italian paintings, one of them depicting the young Jesus and two illustrating the school days of St Augustine of Hippo. The Jesus alphabet begins with a capital 'A', followed by 'a' and the rest of the letters in minuscule.[84] The others start with a cross and then give 'a' and so on in minuscule.[85] A fourth example comes from a woodcut in Gregor Reisch's *Margarita Philosophica Nova*, printed at Strasbourg in 1508, which depicts Lady

92   An elementary class, about 1450. One boy reads the
letters A B C D, with physical encouragement from the
master; others recite the Paternoster in Latin.

Grammar giving one to a schoolboy. This is a
vertical tablet, and contains an alphabet of
twenty-three letters in minuscule (Fig. 93).
None of these alphabets appears to contain
alternative forms of the letters or abbreviations.

Real tablet-books survive from England after
the Reformation, chiefly from the seventeenth
and eighteenth centuries. By the 1580s, these
were known as 'horn-books', because by then they were often covered for protection with a thin transparent sheet of horn, but it is not clear if this material was
used in earlier times.[86] The typical horn-book was a vertical oblong tablet, about
three inches wide and six high, with a handle at the bottom (Fig. 94).[87] A printed
sheet was pasted on the tablet containing two alphabets, one in minuscule and one
in capitals. This was followed by a list of vowels and a table of two-letter syllables,
the invocation 'In the name of the Father, the Son, and the Holy Ghost', and the
Lord's Prayer in English.

Medieval tablets in England certainly contained the alphabet. But was it a
simple ABC, as in the continental pictures, or the more complicated one of the
primers with the alternative letters, abbreviations, *est*, and 'amen'? It is difficult to
be sure about the alternative letters. The refer-
ences we possess to children reciting the alphabet suggest that they simply named the basic
twenty-three letters and did not say, when they
got to 's', 'long s' and 'short s'. If the alterna-
tives were in their copies,   children may have
been told to ignore them for reciting purposes.
There are several pieces of evidence, however,
that the abbreviations, *est*, and 'amen' were
said, and these may well have appeared in the
tablet alphabet. But, before discussing that
point, we need to establish how children pronounced the ABC when they said it. Naming
the letters aloud, after all, is fundamental to
understanding them. When we are accom-
plished readers, we read at sight and usually
silently, with little attention to sound. For children who are learning to read, a different

93   An alphabet board, 1508 (detail from Fig. 85).

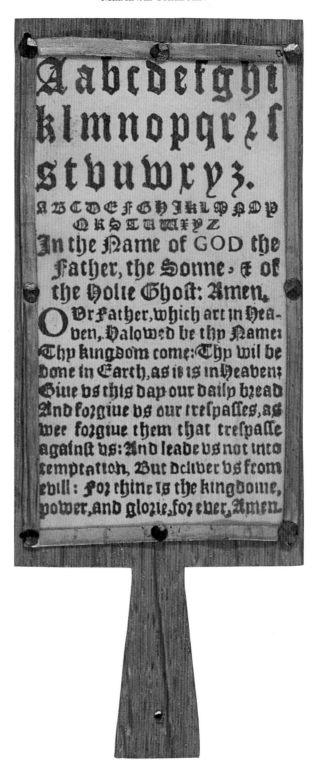

94   A horn-book of a type used in Tudor and Stuart England, containing the alphabet and Lord's Prayer.

approach is needed. They have not only to look at letters and recognise their shapes and values, but to pronounce their names and understand their sounds. Only by naming the letters can they learn their qualities and relate them to words that they have hitherto known only as sounds. Only by children reading aloud can adults ascertain that they are doing so correctly.

The Greek alphabet possesses letters with names which once had meanings. 'Alpha' itself came from the Semitic word *aleph*, 'an ox', and a capital letter 'A' is an ox's head that has been turned upside down. The names of our own letters, 'a', 'be', 'ce', are merely pronouncing names which tell you the sound of the letter, apart from 'zed' which comes from the Greek word *zeta*. These names, like the alphabet, go back to the Romans. Medieval teachers adopted them from Roman grammarians and they appear in such texts as the Stowe manuscript, already mentioned. There are plenty of references to show that they were used in late-medieval England, in popular speech as well as in school, as they have been down to the present day.[88] Their names in France – a, bé, cé, dé, e, ef, gé, ah, i, ka, el, em, en, o, pe, qu, er, es, té, u, iquece, i-grec, zed – were almost exactly the same.[89] People in England differed mainly from their continental neighbours in having their own name for 'y'. This appears as 'fix' in the twelfth-century alphabet, and as 'wy' by about 1200.[90]

One of the earliest references to a pupil saying the alphabet in England occurs not in the English language but in the fifteenth-century Cornish text *Beunans Meriasek*.[91] This is a play about the life of the Breton saint Meriadec, written for performance at Camborne whose parish church was dedicated to him. It tells how Meriadec was sent to school, and describes the scene when he got there. One of the schoolboys begins to recite the alphabet:

> *Du gveras! A, b, c,*
> *An pen can henna yv d,*
> *Ny won na moy yn lyver.*

> [God help! A, b, c;
> The end of the song is 'd'.
> I do not know any more in the book.]

He is presumably a beginner, who is learning the first four letters. Another boy says,

> *E, s, t, henna yv 'est'.*
> *Pandryv nessa ny won fest;*
> *   Mur na reugh ov cronkye;*
> *Rag my ny ve3af the well . . . .*

> [E, s, t, that is 'est'.
> I do not quite know what is next.
> Do not beat me greatly, because I shall be no better.]

This scholar has reached the end of the alphabet, but the play makes the joke that having reached *est*, he does not realise that he has only to say the word 'amen' in order to finish.

We learn something else from this scene: that reciting the alphabet continued after 'z' with the additional material. Writers in Tudor England record that this material was pronounced 'and per se, con per se, tittle est amen'; indeed, 'tittle est amen' became a figure of speech for an end or conclusion.[92] *Per se* is Latin for 'by itself', and meant that the signs for 'and' and *con-* were complete in themselves. Further light on reciting the alphabet comes from Thomas Morley's musical setting of 1597, a setting not necessarily meant for children but aiming to use a familiar (and perhaps amusing) text for instruction in music. His version goes:

> Christ's cross be my speed, in all virtue to proceed, A.b.c.d.e.f.g.h.
> i.k.l.m.n.o.p.q.r.s and t. double-u.v.x. with y. ezod, and per se, con per se.
> tittle tittle est amen. When you have done begin again, begin again.[93]

There may have been a method of chanting the alphabet similar to this musical arrangement, in which the letters were arranged in roughly stressed or metrical lines. And unless his final sentence is his own addition, it may represent an instruction used in schools to make children go on chanting indefinitely. Hoole says that in his day children were usually 'made to run over all the letters in the alphabet, forwards and backwards', until they could tell any one.[94] This was still done in the nineteenth century. Flora Thompson recalled the beginners in an Oxfordshire village school in the 1880s chanting the ABC forwards, then backwards in a metrical form, over and over again. 'Once started, they were like a watch wound up, and went on alone for hours.'[95]

Was there a scheme by which children built up their knowledge of the alphabet? Did they learn one letter per lesson, or more than one? The words in use for the alphabet may throw some light on this. 'Alphabet' itself, of course, comes from Greek and relates to the first two Greek letters, but two other words were common in medieval Europe. One is *abecede*, found in Latin as far back as Roman times, and the other 'abece', especially popular in English. They suggest that there may have been two schemes in operation, one teaching the letters in threes, beginning with 'a', 'b', and 'c', and one in fours including 'd' as well. The French *Ballade de ABC* says that after the first lesson, when the master taught 'a' 'a' 'a', the pupil learnt three letters at each lesson, beginning with 'a' 'b' 'c', down to the ninth, containing 'y' and 'z'.[96] A French treatise called *Civilité honeste pour les Enfans*, published at Paris in 1560, proposes that the four letters 'a' to 'd' be learnt on the first day and four more on each of the next four days, leaving the last three to be mastered on the sixth.[97] Another French writer, Jacques Cossard in 1633, joins in recommending the method of three letters per lesson.[98] A third alternative is suggested by the alphabet tablet in Gregor Reisch's book. This tablet, which divides the letters into two lines of four followed by three lines of five, may reflect a five-day scheme (Fig. 93).

In England, the Cornish play provides the best evidence found so far for a system of learning four letters each day. The mention of five paragraph marks in the poem about the alphabet tablet might indicate something similar to the Reisch book, but it is not clear if the marks refer to divisions of the alphabet, or to the alphabet and other prayers. One can well imagine medieval teachers liking a scheme of four letters, because it would enable the alphabet to be taught from Monday to Saturday, leaving Sunday as a holy day. This would have been an elegant imitation of God's creation of the world in one week, and would have chimed with Bartholomew's comparison between God's twenty-two acts in that week and the letters of the alphabet. But we need to be cautious in this matter. The system of three letters, implied by 'abece', may have been in use as well, and the abbreviations had also to be learnt. Teachers may not all have taught in the same way, a situation suggested by the lack of a standard layout of the alphabet in the primers. Moreover, schemes of learning letters are more suited to a school environment, where pupils do the same task in a classroom. They need not have been followed in a domestic relationship between a parent and child.

If pupils followed one of the schemes mentioned above, they might have learnt to say the ABC in as little as a week. Understanding what the letters meant, and linking them with their symbols, normally took longer. A comic story about Edward IV's jester Scoggin, recorded in 1626, tells how Scoggin taught a rustic boy, the son of a husbandman (or farmer), the first nine letters of the ABC. The boy took nine days to learn them, and he then asked in dialect 'Am I past the worst now?'.[99] Hoole, a careful observer, noted a wide variation in his day. He knew of one child who learnt the alphabet, both names and signs, in eleven days, thanks to a toy box and wheel showing one letter at a time. Slow witted children, on the other hand, could take a whole year, even when beaten to make them.[100]

LEARNING SYLLABLES

'A CHILD', OBSERVED John Wycliffe in about 1378, 'first learns the alphabet, secondly how to form syllables, thirdly how to read, and fourthly how to understand.'[101] Having mastered the ABC, the next stage was to recognise and pronounce the letters in syllables. In medieval times, the first groups of letters which children encountered were prayers, perhaps on the tablet and certainly in the primer: the Paternoster, Ave Maria, and Creed. As we shall see presently, these were often in Latin up to the 1530s, so the learning of syllables (and later of words) was frequently done in a language which children did not understand. It is not easy to find how this stage of learning worked in the middle ages, but some light is thrown on it in the sixteenth century by playwrights who show dull or rustic people trying, or being taught, to read. In John Rastell's play *The Four Elements*, written in about 1520, a comic character mocks another for his learning, and offers to teach him:

> Lo, he hath forgotten, you may see,
> The first word of his ABC.
> Hark, fool, hark! I will teach thee:
> P, a, pa; t, e, r, ter.[102]

In *Doctor Faustus* by Christopher Marlowe (*c*.1593–4), the clown Robin steals one of the doctor's conjuring books and tries to read out a spell:

> A per se, a; t, h, e, the; o per se, o; deny orgon, gorgon.[103]

These examples suggest that children were made to read out the letters of each syllable individually, and then pronounce it, finally putting the syllables together to make the whole word. 'P, a, pa; t, e, r, ter; pater'. If the word contained only one letter, as in 'a', they were taught to say, in Latin, *a per se a*, meaning 'a by itself is a'. There were four words which required you to say *per se* when you spelt them out, the others being 'I', 'O', and '&'. The modern word 'ampersand' for the '&' sign comes from the practice of making children say 'and per se and' when they encountered it.[104] Rastell's evidence indicates that 'Pater' was the first whole word that most children learnt to spell and pronounce; it was, after all, the opening word of the prayer that usually came first after the alphabet in primers.[105] The custom may go back to Anglo-Saxon times, as the Harley manuscript of Alcuin implies, and would have been appropriate in a Christian society. Just as one of the first whole words that children learnt to say was the name of their earthly father, so the first whole word that they learnt to read would be that of their heavenly one.

By the fifteenth century, educationists (at least in Italy) were giving children practice at saying syllables before they attempted whole words. A painting of about 1400 at Lucca shows the child Jesus holding an ABC tablet containing the alphabet in two lines, followed by two rows of syllables:

> Ba. be. bi. bo. bu.
> Ca. ce. ci. co. cu.[106]

Gerardus de Lisa published an *Alphabet and Syllabary* in Italian in about 1478–80, which printed the alphabet, then the vowels, and lastly lists of syllables, some beginning with a vowel ('ab eb ib ob ub') and others with a consonant ('ba be bi bo bu').[107] It is possible that medieval English children were trained in pronouncing syllables in this way, but the method is not recorded until it is found in printed Latin primers of the mid and late 1530s (Fig. 96).[108] These books resemble the Italian sources in giving the alphabet, vowels, and a shortened list of syllables, down to the letter 'g':

> + A a b c d e f g h i k l m n o p
> q r ⁊ ſ s t v u x y z & ⁊ est Amen.
> a e i o u   a e i o u

ab eb ib ob ub	ba be bi bo bu
ac ec ic oc uc	ca ce ci co cu
ad ed id od ud	da de di do du
af ef if of uf	fa fe fi fo fu
ag eg ig og ug	ga ge gi go gu

It may be, although this is not specified in the English texts, that children worked through the whole of the alphabet in this way. The method was a slow one, but it would have grounded pupils more securely. Pupils would take longer to get to *Pater* but be more likely to say it correctly when they did so.

LEARNING WORDS AND TEXTS

HAVING LEARNT SYLLABLES, pupils could practice reading whole words and sentences. Which words and sentences? Teachers of reading were not necessarily clergy, especially if they were parents, and the Church did not formally specify how they should teach. Nevertheless, Christianity was a powerful influence on the process. We have seen that Church leaders, from Anglo-Saxon times, emphasised the need for all children and adults to learn the Paternoster, the Creed, and (by about 1200) the Ave Maria.[109] People should know these basic prayers 'at least in the mother tongue', meaning in English or French, but 'at least' implies a concession for less intelligent people. In church, the clergy said these prayers in Latin, and schools and schoolbooks were more likely to teach them in that language. The Anglo-Saxon alphabet in the Harley manuscript, followed by the opening words of the Paternoster in Latin, suggests as much.

Alphabet tablets may have included basic prayers like the Paternoster, as hornbooks did in later centuries. But a tablet had only limited space for texts, and sooner or later readers were likely to go on to a book with pages. Up to the thirteenth century, Latin church service-books were probably used for this purpose, notably psalters and antiphonals. The psalter included the 150 psalms, which were said or sung by clergy in their daily prayers, the whole sequence being read through every week. The antiphonal contained antiphons, short biblical texts which were said or sung before and after the psalms. Such material was especially suitable for boys or girls training as clergy or nuns, and, from Anglo-Saxon times, the most junior members of the clergy were known as 'psalmists', implying that one learnt the psalms before going on to higher studies and duties.[110] But learning them was not confined to religious trainees. King Alfred's children, Edward and Ælfthryth, both did so in their youth, and both grew up as lay people.[111] Later, in the twelfth and thirteenth centuries, many major churches and towns had a 'song' school, whose business apparently centred on learning to read and sing the psalter. These schools too probably catered not only for future clerics but for children who would stay in the secular world.[112]

In the thirteenth century, new kinds of prayer books developed alongside the older church service-books.[113] One was a book of basic prayers, sometimes in Latin, sometimes in English. It included the Paternoster, Ave Maria, Creed, confessions, graces, and other texts, and sometimes began with an alphabet, as we have seen. Another was the 'book of hours', 'hours of the Virgin', 'hours of Our Lady', or simply 'hours'.[114] This contained shorter, simpler versions of the daily church services said by the clergy, with special devotions to the Virgin Mary. Books of basic prayers and hours were usually in Latin, although there were a few in English by the late fourteenth century. The hours were sometimes read in church by clergy in addition to the normal daily services, but they and the basic prayer books were specially suitable for use by literate lay people. They could be read at home as a private devotion, or in church while attending a service. The well-known Venetian account of England in about 1500 mentions how people took the hours of Our Lady to church, and read it verse by verse, with a companion.[115] Books of hours became common possessions of wealthy people, sometimes in beautiful and expensive copies, and they are frequently mentioned in wills and inventories of books.

A special word developed to describe lay prayer books, 'primer' – a term apparently special to England. It is found in Latin by 1297, and in English by Chaucer's time.[116] Rather confusingly, it seems to have been applied both to books of basic prayers and to books of hours. The word is an interesting one, because it means 'first [book]', and may have come into use, as John Hilsey believed in 1539, because a prayer book or book of hours was 'the first book that the tender youth was instructed in'.[117] There are a number of references to children reading basic prayer books and hours during the later middle ages. The Carthusian priory of Hinton (Som.) owned two books called 'primers of children' in 1343.[118] Bishop Grandisson of Exeter wrote in 1357 of pupils learning to read and write the basic prayers and the hours of the Virgin before they went on to study Latin grammar.[119] In the 1490s, Bishop Alcock of Ely mentioned children in school learning graces and the hours.[120] We have already noticed the encouragement of wealthier and nobler boys and girls to say the hours when rising in the morning.[121] But prayer books and hours do not seem to have quite driven out the use of the psalter and antiphonal for teaching the young. Song schools would have continued to use such books, and some children in noble households did so. A beautiful illuminated psalter was begun for the use of Prince Alfonso, son of Edward I, when he was eleven in 1284, and after his death in that year it apparently passed to his younger sister Elizabeth (Fig. 95).[122] Walter of Dinedor, a young noble ward of the bishop of Hereford, had a psalter bought for his use in 1290–1, and Margaret Plumpton, as we have seen, was learning one as late as 1463.[123]

Because most books of hours were in Latin, as were psalters and antiphonals, there was a strong Latin framework to learning to read, even for those who did so privately at home. Primer alphabets were normally Latin ones, though some (as we have seen) had extra English letters. They contained a Latin word, *est*, and the phrase *per se* used in spelling was Latin too, implying that you were engaged in a Latin process. Most readers therefore began as Latin scholars, and seem to have read their earliest texts in that language. When your master teaches you, observed

95   The Psalter of Prince Alfonso, a beautiful manuscript produced for a boy prince who died in 1284 before it was finished.

the writer of a fifteenth-century courtesy book for boys, he will teach you the Paternoster, Ave Maria, *Credo, In nomine Patris, Confiteor,* and *Misereatur* – in other words the basic prayers in Latin.[124] This made learning to read a different process from today for many children, because it was in an unfamiliar language. Pupils would learn to recognise words and pronounce them, but they could not understand the meaning without being told.

Chaucer's picture of a school in the 'Prioress's Tale' depicts two pupils at this stage of learning. The boy hero of the story, aged seven, sits in the school at his primer, whatever that means: alphabet tablet, basic prayer book, or book of hours. A second older boy is part of a group learning the antiphonal. Its members are singing the text in praise of the Virgin, *Alma Redemptoris Mater.* The younger boy, through listening, learns the first verse by heart. He asks the older pupil what it means, but this boy is not sure. He has merely heard that it is a hymn to the Virgin, saluting her, and asking for her help. He explains the defect in his knowledge thus,

I learn song; I know but little grammar.[125]

At the moment, he is mastering reading at sight and pronunciation. He will not understand the meaning of the words and sentences until he learns Latin grammar.

This makes it hard to say how long it took to read, from beginning the ABC to understanding whole sentences. A Tudor estimate of 1561, shortly to be discussed, makes the optimistic prediction that someone could do so in six weeks, probably imagining a keen adult or a well-motivated child. But such a person, of course, could only have understood a text in English after such a short time. He or she would have got no further in reading Latin than word recognition and pronunciation. Some children must have struggled to decipher Latin words and pronounce them properly, and probably took months to do so. A sentence in John Palsgrave's French grammar of 1530 says, of a dull pupil, 'He hath been at school this half year, and yet he cannot spell his Paternoster'.[126] Even intelligent boys had to spend months, perhaps years, in a grammar school to master the grammar and vocabulary of Latin sufficiently to understand what it meant.

Some readers (chiefly boys) went on to learn such things. Many others probably did not, but all children, whatever their next stage of learning, would sooner or later meet with material in their own spoken language: French or English. Children, especially girls in homes, may have deviated from Latin to reading English soon after learning the ABC. Alfred's children are said to have learnt not only psalms, implying Latin ones, but 'English books, especially English poetry'.[127] An Anglo-Saxon alphabet, as we have seen, might include the letters peculiar to English. Some early fourteenth-century primers may have contained the basic prayers in French, and primers in English like the Hunter manuscript certainly existed by the end of the century.[128] We saw in a previous chapter how English rhymes and songs might creep into notebooks in grammar schools, showing that pupils were evidently used to writing (and therefore reading) English. In our next chapter, we shall explore the wide range of literature in English, available for children to read after about 1400. Some of it was practical, some recreational; some was produced for children, some for adults, but all shows signs of usage by young people.

In one area of reading, however, Latin clung on tenaciously. This was the reading and reciting of prayers from prayer books, including the basic prayers. One might expect this practice to have changed from Latin to English in Chaucer's time, when English was coming into use for so many official and literary purposes. But this happened only to a limited extent. Some basic prayer books and hours were written and used in English during the late fourteenth and fifteenth centuries, and some orthodox devotional works for the laity included the basic prayers in English. The late fourteenth-century treatise called *The Chastising of God's Children* observes that some folk 'say in English their psalter and mattins of Our Lady, and the seven psalms, and the litany'.[129] The Lollards, who emerged in the same period, emphasised the value of prayers said in a language that people understood. John Mirk, an orthodox writer, supported such practices too. His *Instructions for Parish Priests*, written in the late fourteenth century, provided rhymed versions of the basic prayers in English, and his book of model sermons, *Festial*, urged the use of English too. 'It is much more speedful and meritable to you', he told his lay readers, 'to say your Paternoster in English than in such Latin as you do. For when you speak in English, then you know and understand well what you say, and so, by your understanding, you have liking and devotion to say it.'[130]

But Mirk's words reveal that he was trying to alter ingrained habits of prayer. No doubt people made use of English to pray personally and extemporally, but where the basic prayers and other formal prayers were concerned, the majority view, both in and after Chaucer's day and among both clergy and laity, seems to have been that Latin should be used. This applied both to the literate who read such prayers from books and those (literate or illiterate) who said them from memory. When Langland compiled the 'B' version of *Piers Plowman* in the 1370s, and the 'C' version a few years later, he wrote in English with a deep feeling for the language. Yet he criticised slothful parishioners for not having a perfect knowledge of the Paternoster 'as the priest it singeth', in other words in Latin.[131] Prayer books and hours in English were a minority of their kind, up to the Reformation. Most manuscript primers and hours, and the printed versions which began to take their place in the late fifteenth century, were wholly or largely in Latin. Even those with alphabets, implying use with the young, were just as likely to contain the basic prayers and other devotions in Latin as in English.[132] Most people who read the hours up to the Reformation therefore did so in Latin, as the Virgin Mary was shown doing in pictures. Indeed, some devout lay people in the later middle ages owned copies of the same breviaries and missals that were used by the clergy; these too were in Latin.

There was more than one reason why Latin remained so popular as the medium of prayer. It was the language of the clergy and of Church services. English, by contrast, may have seemed an inferior substitute. The author of *The Chastising of God's Children* noted that some authorities disapproved of translating religious texts into English, because this could not be done with sufficient accuracy. He himself was willing to allow such translations to help people understand their Latin prayers, but not as replacements for them.[133] When John Wycliffe's radical followers, the Lollards, appeared in the 1380s, the use of English for religious texts became more controversial. The Lollards translated the Bible into English and produced sermons and tracts in the language, but they were accused of holding heretical views about the Church, which tended to discredit the use of English for religious purposes. The Lollard translation of the Bible was prohibited in 1409, and some people in the fifteenth century came under suspicion of Lollardy in part because they possessed English primers – though not necessarily wholly for that reason.[134] Praying in Latin, by contrast, was approved officially, and demonstrated one's orthodoxy. It helped accustom children to the language they would have to learn if they wished to attend a grammar school. And it conferred on adults, whatever their rank in society, a sense of superiority, of being like the clergy.

Nor was the appeal of Latin confined to the higher ends of society. It reached far down. There is a late but telling instance of this in Thomas Ingelend's play *The Disobedient Child*, written by 1553.[135] A cook-maid says that although she now works in the kitchen, she once went to school and learnt her primer in Latin. Challenged to say how the text began, she replies, *Domine, labia aperies*, the opening phrase of the hours of the Virgin, with one word missing. Even people who could scarcely read – or not at all – still clung to using Latin by memory. Nicholas Canon's mother knew how to cross herself and invoke the Trinity in Latin, and tried to teach him to do the same.[136] In about 1510, the printer Wynkyn de Worde published a humorous story called *A Little Jest how the Ploughman Learned his Pater Noster*.[137] It tells how a parish priest tricked a rich but ignorant farmer into learning the prayer by heart, and this too was done in Latin not in English.

The primacy of Latin in people's formal prayers does not appear to have changed, in fact, until the Reformation. It was only in the 1530s that English began to to oust Latin widely from popular prayers and devotions, and not until 1549 that its dominance became absolute with the introduction of the Book of Common Prayer. The first *Primer in English*, 'very necessary for all people that understand not the Latin tongue', was printed in London in 1534.[138] In 1536, royal injunctions of Henry VIII ordered clergy, parents and masters to teach their children and servants the Paternoster, Creed, and Ten Commandments in English – the Commandments now taking the place of the Ave Maria.[139] John Moreman, vicar of Menheniot (Cornwall) at that time, was said to have been 'the first in those days that taught his parishioners and people to say the Lord's Prayer, the Belief, and the Commandments in the English tongue'.[140] The earliest known ABC with prayers in English as well as in Latin appeared in 1538, and by 1545 there was a similar work entirely in English, 'set forth at the king's commandment'.[141]

For a while, in the middle of the sixteenth century, there continued to be ABCs in print with the basic prayers in Latin and English. During the reign of Mary Tudor (1553–8), there may indeed have been a revival of Latin. *An A.B.C. for*

96 A sixteenth-century printed primer, still recognisably similar to its medieval ancestors.

Children, published in about 1561 and perhaps a reprint of a 1550s edition, still provided the Paternoster, Ave Maria, and Creed in Latin and English, albeit with the Latin in smaller type, and apparently aimed itself at adults as well as children. It asserts that 'by this book a man that hath good capacity and can [*knows*] no letter on the book may learn to read in the space of six weeks, both Latin and English'. That meant reading Latin in Chaucer's sense of recognising and pronouncing the words correctly, not understanding the meaning.[142] Even after the last known bilingual ABC came out in about 1570, when copies contained only English material, their contents and layout remained broadly traditional.[143] Protestant horn-books in English during the seventeenth century continued to head the alphabet with a cross and to follow it with the invocation to the Trinity and the Lord's Prayer.[144] As late as 1630, an English book of anecdotes by Thomas Johnson explained the alphabet, as learnt by children, in a thoroughly medieval manner:

A is thought to be the first letter of the row because by it we may understand
Trinity and Unity: the Trinity in that there be three lines, and the Unity in that
it is but one letter. And for that cause, in old time, they used three pricks at the
latter end of the cross row . . . which they caused children to call tittle, tittle,
tittle: signifying that as there were three pricks, and those three made but one
stop, even so there were three Persons and yet but one God.[145]

Eight hundred years after the ninth-century commentator, the alphabet could still
be viewed as a religious text.

SWEETENING THE PILL

MEDIEVAL SCHOOL EDUCATION may seem primitive in its resources, dour and
dogged in its nature. That is because we know little about it, especially about its
less formal aspects. After 1500, when more writings survive on the subject of education, they show greater signs of inventiveness and humanity than are visible
earlier. Sir Thomas Elyot, for example, suggested that children's first letters should
be 'painted or limned in a pleasant manner', in other words in a decorative
book.[146] Hoole in the mid seventeenth century mentions toys for teaching the
young to read. These included ivory dice with letters on their faces, playing cards
with letters on their backs, and boxes containing a wheel or a scroll which showed
a letter when turned.[147] Evidence like this may tempt us to think that the phi-
losophy of education changed markedly after 1500; the deduction, however,
would be an unsafe one.

Although medieval methods of teaching young children to read are elusive,
enough is known to suggest that some teachers devoted both time and ingenuity
to making the process attractive.[148] We hear in fifteenth-century Italy of alphabet
letters 'in fruit, cake, sugar, and other children's foods'. Pottery bowls occur in
France, Spain, and the Netherlands in the same period which carry the text of the
Ave Maria and may well have had a function with children. Some books of hours
were decorated and illustrated, and although these were usually meant for adults,
they may have been shown to children or commissioned for those of high status,
like Alfonso's psalter. A list of jewellery – rings, brooches, and crowns – belonging
to Henry III in 1255 included an *abece*, which may have been an alphabet tablet
of precious metal, or an object decorated with the ABC.[149] In 1415, an alphabet
with letters of gold was purchased for the five-year-old Jeanne, daughter of
Charles duke of Orleans in France.[150] In Yorkshire, an esquire named John
Morton bequeathed 'a silver bowl with ABC written on the cover' to one of his
male relatives in about 1431.[151]

A real bowl, similar to Morton's, still exists in the Victoria and Albert Museum,
London. The 'Studley Bowl', as it is known, consists of a bowl on a foot with a
matching cover. It is of silver gilt, 14.5 cm high with a diameter of 14.3 cm, and
was made in England in about the late fourteenth century (Fig. 97).[152] Its original
owners are not known and nothing is recorded about it until it appears in the pos-

session of a Yorkshire gentry family in the late nineteenth century; it could have been Morton's or another example of the same type. The cover of the bowl has a knob on the top, decorated with a minuscule 'a', and the cover and bowl are each engraved with an alphabet, embellished with foliage. Counting the knob produces the double 'a'. Each alphabet is laid out in an identical way, with some differences from those in the primers:

+ a b c d e f g h i k l m n o p q r s t u x y z & est : ꝛ

The cross is present, but there are no alternative letters; the *est* is placed before the tittles and *con-*, and there is no 'amen'. It is tempting to interpret the bowl as a utensil for a child who was learning to read, and such a function is plausible but

97   The Studley bowl. Was it meant to be used by a child, who would learn the alphabet while doing so?

not certain. The alphabet may be a decorative motif, or reflect the view that the ABC harmonises with God's creation and underlies all knowledge. Such a bowl could well have been produced with both adults and children in mind, or intended for one group and also used by the other.

Did the ingenuity in making visual alphabets extend to presenting them in other written or graphic forms? There are a number of late-medieval poems whose lines each start with letters in alphabetical order. They deal with such topics as the Passion of Christ, the Virgin Mary, flowers, morals and manners, satire on the clergy, and the ribald poem 'A for Alyn Mallson'.[153] None of these, however, seems aimed at young children. The earliest poem to survive with such a purpose appears to be one by Richard Whitford, brother of Syon Abbey (Middx.), in his religious treatise for lay people, *The Work for Householders*, published in about 1531.[154] This poem addresses itself to a 'child', and someone has scribbled an alphabet beside it in the British Library copy. The verses begin,

> Always love poverty, with vile [*humble*] things be content.
> Be also in good works busy and diligent.

The rest of the letters give advice on behaviour (don't speak too much, be charitable, forgive your enemies) and religious observances (keep fast days, receive the sacraments frequently, and remember your Lord's passion). At the end come the abbreviations, and the poem manages to pack *con-*, the tittles, and the other final elements into the last two lines:

> Conceive here two tittles more, two precepts for ten:
> Love God and your neighbour both, so conclude *est*, amen.

Was Whitford a pioneer of alphabet teaching to children, whose seriousness others would lighten in years to come? Or was he trying to make serious a method of teaching that already existed in more playful forms? By the seventeenth century, children were learning the famous sequence 'A was an apple-pie, B bit it, C cut it', and so on, and by the Georgian period there were rhyming alphabets in print.[155] It would be risky to rule out the existence of similar devices in medieval England, given the variety of teachers and pupils, and the frivolity even of lessons in grammar schools.

Noeur
Eus in adiuto
rium meü ltëde.
Domine ad ad
uuandum me

Chapter 8

Reading for Pleasure

LITERATURE FOR CHILDREN

CHILDREN WHO LEARN to read today may enter (if they wish) a whole world of literature. Not only can they read what adults read, but a vast array of material is produced and published especially for them. There are works of fiction from comics to novels, some for throwing away and others for keeping as classics. There are works of non-fiction – books about hobbies, animals, history, geography, and technology, ranging from introductions to encyclopaedias. Some of this literature is read in school or at home with parental encouragement; some is read unofficially, by children's own preference. Medieval England was far less well provided with such reading, yet we can glimpse the same tastes and tendencies among its children as among their modern successors. Literate children tackled more than prayer books and schoolbooks. By 1400, they had access to a growing body of writing in English, both works directly aimed at them and works primarily intended for adults. Children's literature in England, in terms of both content and readership, begins in the middle ages.

How much young people read today depends a good deal on their family circumstances. Is there a culture of reading at home, or not? This must have been equally true in the past. A child from an unbookish family who was sent to school, perhaps as part of the family's attempt to better itself, might not encounter books other than school texts. A boy brought up in a priest's household might meet only with prayer books, unless the priest had others for recreation. The medieval families that came closest to modern ones in providing support for children's reading were those of wealthier and literate people. They included the nobility, gentry, and merchants, and possibly yeomen farmers in the countryside and better-off craftsmen and shopkeepers in the towns. Such families, of course, varied greatly in the amount of books they owned or could borrow. Those of high status might have access to dozens, others no more than one or two. We, as historians, have problems in finding out what was the case. Family books are not well recorded. Inventories of volumes are confined to those of a few important people; usually we hear only of individual titles, listed in wills or mentioned in letters. Such casual references do not reveal a family's whole resources, and the naming of a book rarely tells us who read it or whether it was read at all.

There are indications, however, that literate parents shared books with their children. Social reading, aloud in a group, was popular in medieval times among people who could read by themselves. Since at least the eighth century when *Beowulf* was written – the first great story to survive in English, the wealthy had enjoyed owning such books and hearing someone read them (as *Beowulf* is certainly meant to be read). Throughout the middle ages, indeed as late as the time of Jane Austen and even of *Brideshead Revisited*, the wealthy read stories to one another for pleasure. In the remote past, this arose in part from scarcity of books and variable degrees of literacy, but it was popular for its own sake too. The nobility, gentry, merchants, and other wealthy folk lived in larger households than we do, accompanied by kinsfolk, servants, or visitors. Reading aloud was a means of entertainment.[1] Most such households included children or adolescents: sons,

98   Family instruction. The Knight of the Tower presents his daughters with the book he has written for them.

daughters, pages, wards, or servants. Life in such places must have often given young people the opportunity to hear or overhear what their elders read.

Writers also recommended that parents should encourage their children to read, or showed them doing so. Asser tells us how King Alfred arranged for his children to be educated, and how they came to be familiar with books in English, including poems.[2] In the story of *Yvain* by Chrétien de Troyes, composed in France in about the 1170s, a girl of sixteen is depicted reading a romance to her knightly father – a scene which gives her skills her father's approval.[3] Almost exactly two hundred years later another French writer, Geoffrey de la Tour Landry, compiled his *Book of the Knight of the Tower* for his daughters to read, in the form of stories teaching wisdom and good behaviour (Fig. 98). He based it on other books that he owned: the Bible, deeds of kings, and chronicles of France, Greece, England, and other lands, which acquainted them with a range of religious and historical literature.[4] Not long after this, in about 1400, an English author who was probably a follower of John Wycliffe mentions parents introducing their children to similar kinds of works. This author wished to stress the importance of teaching children the Paternoster, Creed, and Ten Commandments, but he added disapprovingly that 'some men set their children to learn gestes [*deeds*] of battles and of chronicles, and novelties of songs that stir them to jollity and to harlotry'.[5] Like some later Protestant writers, he was irked that adults should teach their offspring what was amusing rather than what was godly.

A good guide to the literary activities of wealthy families is to be found in miscellanies or commonplace books, compiled by members of the gentry and merchant classes, or by other people on their behalf. Examples of such books survive from the late thirteenth century onwards, one of the oldest being the so-called Digby manuscript in the Bodleian Library.[6] It was written by or for a small landowner in Worcestershire, possibly Richard of Grimhill, between about 1272 and 1282, and seems to have passed to Richard's daughter Amice. She married Simon of Underhill, and the book descended to their son William. Its pages contain a large number of short literary pieces in Latin, French, and English. They need not represent all that the owners read, of course, since there are no long romances or saints' lives, which may have been owned in separate volumes.

The contents of the Digby manuscript fall into three main categories. First, there is religious matter: a Church calendar, Latin prayers and psalms, and short accounts in French of the Seven Deadly Sins, Ten Commandments, Twelve Articles of Faith, Seven Sacraments, and a model confession. Next come various kinds of practical works, also in Latin or French: how to interpret dreams, foretelling the year from the day when Christmas falls, medical advice and prescriptions, chemical experiments, arabic numbers, and the care of hawks. There is the famous Letter of Prester John (the legendary Christian ruler in Asia) to the pope, and a poem called 'The Complaint of Jerusalem', both bringing vistas of foreign places to this corner of England. Finally, there are poems in French and English: religious, moral, and narrative. They include a short life of St Eustace, miracles of St Nicholas, a fable about the fox and the wolf in the well, and the fabliau or comic tale called *Dame Sirith*. This last is about a procuress who seduces a merchant's wife for a clerk, by making the wife believe that a woman who turned down a clerk's advances was changed into a dog.

One can imagine the owners of the book being interested in all these things, and turning to it (as to an encyclopaedia) for information or entertainment on many occasions. But they did not necessarily read it alone: *Dame Sirith* is marked with voice parts for performance aloud by one or more people (Fig. 99). And it is conceivable that some of the items in the book were meant (or used) for educating children or adolescents. The prayers and religious tracts are close in nature to the those of a primer. There is a French translation of Peter Alfonsi's twelfth-century *Disciplina Clericalis*, a book of wise and moral stories from Arab sources, aimed at educating clergy and superior lay people.[7] There is a French version of the *Elegies* of Maximian, a late classical work which was commonly read in grammar schools at the time, and a French text called *Le Doctrinal Sauvage*. This last is a work of wise counsel, not specifically aimed at children but close in form to the courtesy literature which was so important in the teaching of well-born English youths.[8]

Some other late-medieval miscellanies give a similar sense of concern with young people.[9] One such, compiled in the second half of the fifteenth century, is a manuscript in the National Library of Wales at Aberystwyth (MS Porkington 10): a book produced for a gentry family in the west Midlands, possibly Shropshire.[10] Here we find the poem 'The Good Wife Would a Pilgrimage' (a mother's instruction to her daughter), 'Arise Early' (a popular list of maxims for daily living), 'terms of association' (collective names for animals), and vocabularies of words proper to hunting and cookery. Although the technical terms about these subjects were of interest to adults, they were appropriate to be learnt by the young and appear (as we shall see) in works directed at them.[11] Particularly suggestive of young people is *The Friar and the Boy*, a comic tale about a farmer's son which will be told in due course.[12] If the relevance of the Porkington manuscript to children and young people is acceptable, other parts of its contents might be envisaged as coming within their sphere. These include the romance of *Sir Gawain and the Carl of Carlisle*, 'The Knight and his Wife' (a miracle story involving the Virgin Mary), a Life of St Katherine, and an account of the Siege of Jerusalem.

The miscellany with the strongest signs of being used with children is Balliol College Oxford MS 354, the volume already mentioned as having been put together by Richard Hill (fl. *c.*1490–1540), the London merchant and grocer.[13]

99 A family miscellany. The Digby manuscript, containing the opening of the racy story *Dame Sirith*. The letters t, c, v, and f mark the speaking parts for the narrator, clerk, wife, and procuress.

His book is a large anthology of songs, poems, and short practical works, mainly in English and current among adults. But Richard and his wife had seven children too, born between 1518 and 1526, of whom three boys and two girls lived beyond infancy. Several of the pieces he collected seem more appropriate for them, or for reading with them, than for him or his wife alone. They include the lyrics that were discussed in the context of nursery rhymes, 'I have twelve oxen' and 'I saw a dog seething sauce', as well as one of the songs of complaint by a schoolboy.[14] *The Friar and the Boy* is present and so are some short pieces from a pamphlet for children printed by Caxton, including John Lydgate's poem about good manners, *Stans Puer ad Mensam* ('O boy standing at the table').[15] There are two other poems about good behaviour, one on 'How the Wise Man Taught his Son', a set of fifty-five maxims and proverbs in English with Latin translations, and a further set of proverbs in Latin alone – kinds of material that appear in grammar-school note-books.[16] It looks unlikely that Hill gathered these pieces for his sole benefit; rather, his book seems designed for his family as well.

DIDACTIC LITERATURE

THE INSIGHTS THAT we gain from miscellanies are reinforced, after about 1390, by evidence from individual works of literature. The late fourteenth and fifteenth centuries are a period in which far more writings in English survive than before, both practical and recreational, including ones that state a concern with children. One of the earliest such works is Chaucer's prose treatise on the *Astrolabe*, which he began to write in 1391 but never finished. It is a technical study of an important astronomical and navigational instrument, but it starts with a prologue addressed to the poet's son Lewis, then aged about ten. Chaucer says that Lewis has asked him how to use the astrolabe and that he, his father, has written him an explanation in simple English, instead of the Latin in which such works have hitherto appeared.

Lewis may have been an unusually studious boy, and he certainly had an exceptionally literary father. It is possible, however, that the *Astrolabe* was read by other boys than Lewis. Four of the extant manuscripts of the work do not give it the title *Astrolabe*, but 'Bread and Milk for Children'.[17] Does this mean that it was regarded as suitable for teaching not only astronomy but reading itself? Three of the four manuscripts do not look promising in this respect, because they contain astronomical diagrams and survive in the company of other adult texts. The fourth, on the other hand, which dates from the second quarter of the fifteenth century, could well have been used with a child. Its leaves are small like a schoolbook, it contains no diagrams, and it is not bound up with any other work in its modern state.[18] Nowadays we would not use a technical treatise to teach children, but when there are few suitable works available, people will have recourse to anything available. One is reminded of Dr Johnson, travelling through the Highlands in 1773. Wishing to present a book to a girl he met, he gave her *Cocker's Arithmetick* and, when his friends later laughed, retorted 'I had no choice in the matter', nothing better to give.[19]

100   A marginal drawing from a fifteenth-century treatise on hunting. Such treatises taught young people the complicated rules and terms of the sport.

A number of other non-fictional works for children can be identified from the fifteenth century.[20] One category is made up of wise and moral writings which parents, clergy, and teachers wished young people to learn as a basis for ruling and transfiguring their lives. Boys in grammar schools had long read the famous late-Latin poem called the *Distichs of Cato* – sober observations about human life in the form of distichs or couplets. This text was translated into English verse in the mid fifteenth century by Benedict Burgh for a noble youth named William, son of Viscount Bourchier, who may not have been able to read the Latin with ease.[21] In the 1450s or 60s, George Ashby wrote a comparable work for Edward, Prince of Wales (1453–71), the ill-fated son of Henry VI and Margaret of Anjou. It consisted of Latin quotations, 'the sayings and opinions of various philosophers', with English verse translations.[22] The text survives in only a single manuscript, but a similar work in French, called the *Dicts and Sayings of the Philosophers*, achieved a wide circulation later in the century through being turned into English prose by Anthony Wydeville, Lord Rivers, in 1473–4. Rivers was guardian to another unfortunate prince of Wales, Edward (later Edward V) the son of Edward IV. The prince was then aged four, and Rivers says that the translation was intended for his education; it was eventually printed by William Caxton.[23]

Works were also produced for young people on two technical subjects: courtesy and hunting (Fig. 100). Literature about courtesy – the behaviour of courts and courtiers especially (but not only) at the table – was first written in medieval Europe in the twelfth century, in Latin and for adults.[24] But good behaviour is such a large objective in the upbringing of children in any society that, by the middle of the thirteenth century, there was a text about courtesy for boys. This was *Stans*

Puer ad Mensam by Robert Grosseteste (d. 1253), the bishop of Lincoln famous for his manners.[25] It became a standard text in grammar schools and was turned into English verse by John Lydgate during the early fifteenth century, a translation that became well known in manuscript copies and in Caxton's printed edition of 1476.[26] Lydgate set a fashion in this respect, or followed one, and at least six other poems for children about good manners and table etiquette made their appearance later in the century.[27]

The earliest writings about hunting in England were composed in Anglo-Norman French and English in the early fourteenth century, probably also for adults, though they are not specific about their readership.[28] Somewhere around 1400, however, a treatise was produced in English verse which came to be known as *Tristram*, after the knightly hero famed for his hunting skills. It professes to be written by a 'mother' for her 'son' or 'sons', and seems to be envisaged as an educational work for a boy or a youth.[29] The poem deals with some basic rules of hunting: close seasons, how to speak to hounds, and the way to butcher carcasses. Above all it teaches terminology, because hunting was a pedantic sport with exact words for animal body-parts, animals of different ages, and groups of animals. Two shorter works from the fifteenth century have similar links with young people. 'A Little Book of Doctrine for Young Gentle Men' lists the names for groups of animals and people, with the correct verbs to use for carving meat (brawn, for example, is 'leached').[30] A similar text, containing names of groups ('a herd of harts') and the right verbs to describe how animals sit or lie ('a hare in his form is shouldering or leaning'), was used by Caxton to fill up space in Lydgate's fable *The Horse, the Goose, and the Sheep* which he published in 1476.[31] The juxtaposition of the two suggests that he thought them both appropriate for children.

All the texts mentioned so far were written for boys, or addressed to them in the first instance. Much less was produced for girls. Three courtesy poems aimed at them survive in fifteenth-century manuscripts – *How the Good Wife Taught her Daughter* and similar works. They advise girls to be pious, modest, and circumspect, especially towards men, and seem to be aimed at wealthy mothers and daughters of the towns rather than of the gentry and nobility.[32] For the latter, there was one larger and more ambitious work in the form of Geoffrey's *Book of the Knight of the Tower*. This reached England in at least one copy in French, and was turned into English during the reign of Henry VI (1422–61), although that version too is confined to a single known text.[33] The work achieved a wider circulation when Caxton retranslated it and printed it in 1484 – at the request, so he claimed, of 'a noble lady' with 'many noble and fair daughters', who may have Elizabeth Wydeville, the widow of Edward IV.[34] Even his version was not a bestseller since it was never reprinted, but it was remembered in England as late as 1534.[35]

Girls, then, were less well provided with books about morals and manners, but it is conceivable that they (or their mothers) used the ones produced for boys. After all, noble and gentle girls needed to learn table manners like those of their brothers, and some of them took part in hunting of a less exacting kind. It is interesting that Lydgate, when he translated *Stans Puer*, rendered *puer* as 'child' and the child's lord (*dominus*) as 'sovereign' – gender-neutral words. Perhaps he was trying to extend the poem's appeal to both sexes.[36]

STORIES: THE MENU

THE HEART OF 'children's literature' today consists of stories, and there is no reason why children and adolescents should not have read stories too, as far back as they were written. Chrétien's *Yvain* features a teenage girl with a romance, but most of the evidence for children reading stories, or being encouraged to read them, survives only after the late fourteenth century, as it does in the case of non-fiction. We have already encountered the Knight of the Tower emphasising the value of the Bible and of chronicles for young people, and the Lollard reference to 'false chronicles', probably meaning stories about the deeds of fictional knights. The earliest English writer, as far as I know, who claims to have written a story especially for a young person is Thomas Hoccleve. He translated the 'Tale of Jonathas' in the early 1400s from the Latin story collection called the *Gesta Romanorum*, and says that he did so for a fifteen-year-old boy, the child of a friend who was worried about his son's lack of discipline.[37]

Some other people offered advice on story reading to young people in the second half of the fifteenth century. George Ashby advised Prince Edward to read the Bible (especially stories about righteous and ungodly people) and chronicles – similar sources to those of the Knight of the Tower.[38] At about the same time, an unknown author wrote a poem about courtesy in the manner of Lydgate, beginning, 'Little child', which can be dated after 1449–50 (because it mentions Lydgate's death) and before 1477 (when it was published by Caxton).[39] The poet tells the child, who was evidently a boy rather than a young man, that he should spend his time in reading, which combines learning with pleasure and stops one being idle. Four authors are recommended by name, as masters of style and wisdom: Chaucer, Gower, Hoccleve, and Lydgate. In Gower's case the child is particularly directed to the *Confessio Amantis* and in Hoccleve's to the *Regement of Princes*; in those of Chaucer and Lydgate he is encouraged to read anything.

What children actually read, compared with what they were recommended, is a more difficult matter. In the case of boys, it may sometimes be guessed from the contents of manuscript miscellanies, like the Gawain romance in the Porkington collection, and *The Seven Sages of Rome* and the stories from the *Confessio Amantis* in Richard Hill's book. More clearly, there are instances of boys receiving books from adults or being advised what to read. In 1472, Sir John Paston II sent *The Seven Sages* to his younger brother Walter, who was then about fifteen years old.[40] Five years later, Geoffrey Spurleng, citizen of Norwich, made a copy of the *Canterbury Tales* with the assistance of his son Thomas, a youth of about sixteen.[41] In the same year, 1477, Caxton translated Raoul Le Fèvre's French prose version of the story of *Jason*, and dedicated it to Prince Edward, son of Edward IV, then aged seven. He did this, he said, 'to the intent he may begin to learn read English', a phrase which asserts that the work was fit for a boy.[42] Another of Caxton's translations, *Eneydos* – the story of Aeneas, published in 1490, was similarly inscribed to Prince Arthur, son of Henry VII, and then aged four. In this case, it is not suggested that the prince should read it, but *Eneydos* is a knightly story like *Jason*, and Caxton may well have wished to place it on the menu for noble boys, at least when they grew older.[43]

There are also a few clues to reading by girls. One is an early fourteenth-century collection of Arthurian romances in French, containing the signatures of Elizabeth Wydeville, later queen of Edward IV, and her daughters Elizabeth (wife of Henry VII) and Cecily. The fact that each signature gives the woman's maiden name suggests that they all read the book in their teens, before they were married.[44] In 1472, Anne Paston, Sir John's younger sister, lent a book 'of the Siege of Thebes' (probably Lydgate's translation) to the Scottish earl of Arran, who was then living in London. She was probably then in her late adolescence, since she is thought to have been born not long before 1455.[45] Caxton provides us with two further insights, relating to books from his press that he wished to appeal to young women. One was his own translation of *The Book of the Knight of the Tower* (1484), which he advertised as suitable for all readers 'but in especial for ladies and gentlewomen, daughters to lords and gentlemen', exhorting 'every gentleman or woman' having children to acquire a copy.[46] The other was the romance of *Blanchardyn and Eglantine* (1489), which he claimed to be relevant to 'gentle young ladies and damsels for to learn to be steadfast and constant'.[47] This is true in the sense that much of the story is about the exploits of the knightly hero; the heroine's role is a more passive one.

The fullest account of girls' reading may be the list of books mentioned by John Skelton in his poem *Philip Sparrow* as being known to Joan Scrope, a knight's orphan daughter who went to live as a boarder in Carrow Priory outside Norwich in 1502.[48] The poem cannot be dated more precisely than between that year and 1509, and Joan's age at the time is not certain, but she was born not later than 1485 and seems to have been about twenty when Skelton wrote.[49] He credits her with reading widely in English, largely from romances. In verse, these included Chaucer's *Canterbury Tales* (those of the Knight, Wife of Bath, and Nun's Priest being specified), a romance of Sir Gawain, Gower (presumably *Confessio Amantis*), *Guy of Warwick*, and *Lybeaus Desconus*. In prose, Skelton mentions *The Four Sons of Aymon*, *Jason*, a book about Troy (which may have been Caxton's translation of Le Fèvre's *Recueil of the Histories of Troy*), stories of Arthur and Tristram (possibly Malory's *Le Morte d'Arthur*), and *Paris and Vienne*. Joan is further attributed with knowledge of the poet Lydgate and of characters from biblical and classical history, whom she could have encountered in Lydgate's translation of Boccaccio's *Falls of Princes* or in Ranulf Higden's history of the world, *Polychronicon*.

Joan's reading list is an impressive one, but is it true? Did Skelton aim to flatter her or to display his own literary erudition?[50] Perhaps; yet the titles are feasible for a wealthy lay person to have read in early-Tudor England. All were available in English and most had been published by Caxton except for *Guy of Warwick*, which is not recorded in print until about 1500, and the Gawain work and *Lybeaus Desconus* which may have been accessible only in manuscripts.[51] Quantitatively the list is a long one, even for women with literary tastes unless they were rich or lived in a major city. Qualitatively, on the other hand, the volumes look plausible as ones that would interest adolescent girls. They are the same as, or similar to, the writings mentioned in other sources as suitable for reading by young people.

STORIES: THE INGREDIENTS

COMPILING THE MENU of stories for children enables us to gauge the kinds of food it offered. Its dishes belonged to several genres of literature. There were pure stories, divisible into chansons de geste like *Guy of Warwick* which centre on the deeds of knights, and romances such as Chaucer's *Troilus and Criseyde* which turn on love affairs between knights and ladies (Fig. 101). There were also stories (often in a collected format) with a moral or message. Some of Chaucer's *Canterbury Tales*

101   Sir Ector meets a lady in the forest, in the famous French 'Prose *Lancelot*'. Romances introduced young people to love, violence, social structure, and geography – not always accurately.

come into this category, and so does Lydgate's most ambitious work, *The Falls of Princes*. One could add *The Book of the Knight of the Tower* which, though educational, makes its points through a series of tales. Chronicles may be thought of as embodying stories, and so may the Bible. Along with its prophetic and instructive books, it contains many that are narratives: the chronicles of the Old Testament, the gospels, and the books of 'Esther', 'Judith', 'Ruth', and 'Tobit', which are especially story-like in their form.

Two other popular kinds of story literature do not appear among the books already mentioned, but may have reached children as well. One is the saint's life, which was widely read by literate people in French or English versions. The other is the fable: a short story usually featuring animals, with a distinct message or moral (Fig. 102). Fables in Latin prose and verse ascribed to Aesop (*Isopet* in medieval French), or to Avianus or Romulus, circulated in western Europe from early times.[52] Vernacular ones in French appeared in the twelfth century, and three well-known collections were written in English during the later middle ages, all claiming to be based on those of Aesop. They include seven fables in verse by John Lydgate early in the fifteenth century, a large prose anthology translated from French by Caxton and published in 1484, and thirteen in verse by Robert Henryson, produced in Scotland late in the century or early in the next.[53] Lydgate wrote two longer works like fables, called *The Churl and the Bird* and *The Horse, the Goose, and the Sheep*. These have animal characters but are discussions rather than stories: the first about wisdom and happiness, the second about who is best, with a warning not to despise other people.[54]

The relationship of fables to children, however, is not straightforward. Schoolboys certainly read them in Latin. The verse fables of Avianus were often studied in schools up to about 1300, and linger in one or two later school notebooks.[55] Another Latin collection, the *Novus Esopus*, was used in some late-medieval schools, more commonly on the continent than in England.[56] Fable collections in English, on the other hand, seem to have been meant for adults as much as for children. Lydgate believed that Aesop originally wrote 'in Rome to

102 Fables, like Aesop's Cock and the Fox, were apparently read widely, by adults as well as children.

please the senate', and Henryson addressed his fables to 'my masters', 'worthy folk', 'lords of prudence', and men 'of every estate'. He ends by saying that he has left the rest of his material to the friars.[57] Caxton's edition of Aesop contains woodcuts, which would have appealed to children, but his text is a large one of 142 leaves, unlikely to have been bought as a children's book in the first instance. It includes not only animal fables but human stories about sexual morality and capital punishment. The fables most likely to have been read by children in English were Lydgate's *Churl* and *Horse*, if we should call them fables. These were both published by Caxton in 1476 in a modest format, suggesting that he had young people in mind.[58] But there is no reason to suppose that fables in England were primarily or solely a genre of stories for children.

Counting in saints' lives and fables does not alter the character of our menu of stories. It is a menu in English. If we could gather similar evidence from the thirteenth and early fourteenth centuries, it would probably include material in French which was spoken in England up to about 1400. Many boys learnt Latin as well, but, apart from those who were especially scholarly or intending to become clergy, they seem to have preferred to read or hear stories in a language they could easily understand. Girls, who learnt Latin less often, were even more dependent on literature in the vernacular. As we saw in the previous chapter, literature had spread from Latin into English during the Anglo-Saxon period for these very reasons. Romances and chansons de geste had been written in French since the twelfth century and in English since the thirteenth; chronicles, although still sometimes written in Latin, were also available in both the other languages. There was a Bible in French by the thirteenth, copies of which are mentioned in aristocratic wills in England up to about Chaucer's time. In the 1380s and 90s, the Bible was translated into English by the Lollards, but their translation aroused hostility because of their other unorthodox views, and the Church authorities did not allow it to be read without permission after 1409. This restricted it to those relatively few people who read it surreptitiously or who were allowed to do so openly. We know, for example, of English Bibles belonging to Henry IV, his son Thomas and his uncle Thomas duke of Gloucester.[59]

Socially, it is clear that most story literature was common to adults and children. All the works recommended to the young before 1500, like Chaucer and Gower, are ones which we normally think of as adult. It is a moot point, of course, if there can be such a thing as adult literature until there is a separate children's literature; authors may have assumed an 'all-age' readership. Still, matters are different today, when children have their own stories rather than being expected to cope with adult ones. We will examine presently the question whether fiction for children existed, but such a thing is lacking from the recommended reading lists. The evidence indicates too that girls and women read works similar to their brothers and husbands, and vice versa; Joan Scrope's reading was just as appropriate for a young man. In an age of fewer books, many were probably common to both sexes. Thus Caxton, who aimed *The Book of the Knight of the Tower* primarily at women, claimed that anyone might learn from it, and although he recommended *Blanchardyn* to young female readers, it was equally suitable for male ones.

This was true of many other romances, chronicles, and Bible stories, and meant that girls and women had often to put up with stories which portrayed men as active and women as more passive. Fortunately, there was some literature that offered girls more dynamic models: Guinevere in the Arthurian stories, Chaucer's Wife of Bath, and some of the lives of saints.

Let us now explore some of these works in more detail, to see why they might have attracted child readers. Medieval story literature might be primarily meant for adults, but it contained much that would appeal to children or adolescents. Some books (like *The Book of the Knight of the Tower*) were collections of short prose stories, appropriate for the briefer attention spans of young people. Romances and chansons de geste were usually longer works, some very long, but they centred on adventures with fast-moving plots, suspense, exotic locations, and (usually) happy or victorious endings. The text was frequently in verse, usually couplets of eight syllables, which had advantages for child readers. Such verse was laid out in columns of short lines, and the rhymes may have helped decipher the reading and pronunciation. Many medieval stories featured characters who were children or adolescents. This is true of saints' lives, notably those of St Katherine and St Margaret, and of some miracle stories like Chaucer's 'Prioress's Tale'. It also applies to many romances and chansons de geste from the twelfth century onwards, such as *Bevis of Hampton*, *Guy of Warwick*, *Havelok*, and *Tristan*.

Works like these often start with their hero's or heroine's birth and upbringing. Details of their teachers may be given, and of the skills or studies that they learnt.[60] Sometimes this information forms an unrelated prologue to the adult life-story, but in other cases the events of childhood determine what happens later. A child may be abducted or abandoned, brought up away from home, revealed in adulthood through virtue or deeds of arms, and finally restored to its rights or reconciled with its parents.[61] Thus the twelfth-century *Lay Le Freine* by Marie de France, translated into English in the fourteenth century, is about a baby girl placed by her mother outside a nunnery, who recovers her identity and finally marries her lover.[62] The thirteenth-century English romance *Floris and Blauncheflur* tells how a boy and girl go to school together, fall in love, and (when older) have adventures which end in their marriage.[63] *William of Palerne*, translated from French into English verse in the mid fourteenth century, is a story of a boy carried off by a werewolf, brought up by a cowherd, and (after many adventures) reunited with his mother and crowned Roman emperor. In the single surviving copy of the English version, someone in the late fifteenth century wrote a prayer of thanks for the translation, because it is a 'goodly story', and one 'to keep youth from idleness'. Clearly, he thought it suitable for the young.[64]

Another romance about young people, with a strongly didactic theme, is *The Seven Sages* (or *Seven Wise Masters*) *of Rome*: correctly a cycle of short stories originating in the Orient, translated into French in the mid twelfth century, and subsequently turned into most major European languages, including English and Welsh.[65] The story centres on Florentyne, the fictional son of the Roman Emperor Diocletian, who is put to school at the age of seven with the sages of Rome – the wisest men on earth. The first part of the romance describes the

103   The famous story of the *Seven Sages of Rome*. Diocletian on his throne, the wicked empress, and the innocent prince in prison.

sages, including the famous Cato, and says a little about the prince's studies. In one version, he is housed in a hall painted to represent the three parts of Donatus's Latin grammar and the seven liberal arts.[66] When Diocletian remarries, his new wife accuses Florentyne, now a teenager, of rape. The emperor condemns him to death, but the sages tell a story each day to postpone the execution (Fig. 103). The empress counters these with tales of her own to keep the sentence in force, and the final story is told by Florentyne, after which the empress confesses her deceit and is burnt, while the prince is restored to favour. Three of the tales feature children, including those of the knight who kills the greyhound that guarded his son, and of the boy (aged seven or fifteen in the English versions) who prophesies that he will be greater than his parents and is thrown in the sea by his father. *The Seven Sages* therefore has both an educational setting and children or adolescents as characters. It is not surprising that it featured in the reading of the Hill and Paston families.

Another important category of popular literature was that of ballads, which exist in written form from the fifteenth century onwards. The earliest are outlaw stories about Robin Hood and his counterparts in Cumberland who feature in the tale of *Adam Bell*.[67] Like the verse romances, the ballads have swift and simple plots, and are composed in short lines of verse, easy to read or remember. They were frequently printed after 1500, usually in cheap versions, and their popularity was strong among the reading and listening public.[68] Robin Hood and the outlaws of *Adam Bell* were yeomen between the ranks of the aristocracy and those of ordinary people, and attractive to both groups. They attacked corrupt members of the social elites, like avaricious monks and the sheriff of Nottingham, and spared or helped the poor. At the same time, they deferred to honest knights and to the king, and did not challenge the framework of society. They could even be viewed as models for the young, since they embodied the traditional skill of archery which the authorities wanted to keep alive (Fig. 104). In 1512, as we have seen, a parliamentary statute ordered that boys as well as men be taught to shoot.[69]

One would expect the ballads, with their simple form and exciting stories, to have appealed to children and adolescents, and by the 1520s Protestant writers were certain this was so. It was something they deeply regretted. William Tyndale, attacking restrictions on Bible reading in 1528, complained that the clergy allowed the reading of 'Robin Hood and Bevis of Hampton, Hercules, Hector, and Troylus, with a thousand histories and fables of love and wantons and of ribaldry, as filthy as heart can think, to corrupt the minds of youth withal'.[70] Miles Coverdale agreed a few years later: 'As for the common sort of ballads, which now are used in this world . . . what wicked fruits they bring. Corrupt they not the manners of young persons?'[71] In 1550, Walter Lynne, a London publisher, tried to counteract the attraction of ballads with a religious work called *The True Belief in*

104   Boys shooting arrows at a target. The Robin Hood ballads reflected the emphasis that boys should learn archery skills.

Christ, which he recommended to men, women, and children instead of 'the feigned stories of Robin Hood, Clym of the Clough [one of the heroes of *Adam Bell*], with such like' that 'they have been heretofore accustomed to read'.[72] But the publishing and reading of ballads went on, nevertheless, and it is safe to say that the liking for them was far stronger than the strictures of their critics.

Historians of early ballads have not normally considered them in terms of their appeal to the young. The tales of Robin Hood and Adam Bell are chiefly studied today for what they are thought to reveal about adult tastes and preoccupations: hostility to royal officials, anticlericalism, predilection for violence against one's enemies, and nostalgia for the greenwood and the archer.[73] Yet they may also throw light on children's tastes and on the way that children grew up to share the values of their elders. Like the romances, the ballads sometimes feature youthful characters. Those about Robin Hood are indeed largely restricted to adult men, but *Adam Bell* contains two children with whom young male readers might identify. One is the 'little boy', a swineherd, who carries the news of William Cloudesly's arrest to his fellow-outlaws in the forest. The other is William's seven-year-old son who stands with the apple on his head to be shot at by his father, as in the legend of William Tell, and is rewarded by being made a boy-servant of the queen's wine-cellar.[74]

One fifteenth-century outlaw ballad or song, the mysterious *Robyn and Gandelyn*, goes further in featuring boys or youths as its characters. The story, which exists in a single manuscript, tells how two 'children' go to shoot deer in a forest. There, Robyn is shot dead by a rival, Wrennok of Donne, after which Gandelyn avenges his friend by killing Wrennok, and the ballad ends with his exultation. A 'child' could mean a young man as well as a child, but Wrennok is described as 'a little boy' and, although this may be meant derisively, the poem looks more like a story about adolescents than one about older men.[75]

TALES ABOUT CHILDREN

WERE THERE, THEN, stories especially for young people? Nowadays we possess a great body of such fiction, whose central characters are children or teenagers. The plots may educate or transform their participants, but the young remain young at the end of the story, unlike most medieval child heroes such as Guy of Warwick who grow up shortly after the story begins. Fiction of this modern kind is harder to identify before 1500. Even if we allow (as we must) for literature having been lost, few stories aimed primarily at children have survived compared with the large number aimed at their elders. It is probably rooted in human nature, however, for adults to tell children stories about children, or for boys and girls to tell them to one another. Such stories may be invented, based on events of family history, or adapted from literature. One can imagine a medieval child being told the story of David and Goliath (Fig. 105), or that of Arthur and the sword in the stone.

There is a small group of such stories in late-medieval English literature. The

105   The Bible contained many stirring stories, some involving young people, most famously David and Goliath.
The latter is shown as a knight in chain mail.

best example is the romance of the *Chevelere Assigne*, 'the knight of the swan', a
version of the legend of Lohengrin. This story was taken from a longer medieval
French romance about the family of Godfrey de Bouillon, and made into a self-
contained short tale in English alliterative verse at the end of the fourteenth
century.[76] It tells how Beatrice, the wife of King Oryens, had seven children at a
birth, six boys and a girl, each born with a silver chain around the neck. The king's
wicked mother, Matabryne, took the babies away and replaced them with
puppies, causing the angry king to consign his wife to prison. A hermit rescued the
babies and brought them up, but Matabryne heard of their existence and sent a
forester named Malkedras to take away their chains and to kill them. When he cut
off their chains with his sword, they turned into swans, except for the eldest boy
who was not present. Malkedras went back with the chains, and Matabryne
ordered them to be made into a cup. The goldsmith she employed found that half
of a chain sufficed for this, and purloined the rest; the other half chain was given
to Malkedras.

Twelve years passed, and the wicked mother-in-law persuaded the king to burn
his imprisoned wife. An angel carried news of this to the surviving twelve-
year-old son, and told him to go and fight in his mother's defence. The boy
had been brought up in seclusion; he had not been baptised or ever encountered
a horse, but he went to the court, where he was christened Eneas. The king
gave him a steed and armour, including a shield marked with a cross, and in due
course he was put to challenge Malkedras. When the latter struck the cross on the
shield, an adder sprang from it and attacked him, and flames gushed out and

blinded him. Eneas then killed him. Beatrice was rescued, Matabryne burnt, and the goldsmith restored the five chains that he had taken. The chains were returned to five of the swans, enabling them to change back into children, but there was no chain left for the last boy-swan which had to remain as it was. In the longer story, this provides the basis for further adventures of Eneas with his swan-brother (Fig. 106).

It is possible that this story was told to children by itself, and that the English *Chevalere Assigne* was abridged for that purpose. The sole surviving text is in a collection of romances and courtesy poems, three of which were commonly used with young people.[77] Children were also likely to learn the story in the two noble English families that claimed descent from the knight of the swan. One was that of the Bohun earls of Hereford and Essex, who named a son Eneas in about 1310–15. Their claim passed to their descendant Edward Stafford, duke of Buckingham, and in 1512 he commissioned Robert Copland to retranslate the story into prose, to make it better known. This version was printed at least three times in the course of the sixteenth century.[78] The other family was that of the earls of Warwick. When their historian, John Rous, drew his well-known pictorial roll of the earls and their history in 1483–4, he included Eneas as one of their ancestors, placing him roughly in the Anglo-Saxon period. He also told the story in its English, abbreviated, and child-centred form with one or two differences, describing the chains as gold and Eneas as seven, not twelve. Rous added that Matabryne's cup was still preserved at Warwick Castle, and said that the countess had allowed him to drink from it.[79]

Two similar stories about marvellous boys occur in the famous Percy miscellany of songs and ballads, put together in the mid seventeenth century. Both are in ballad form and could be a couple of hundred years older, since one of them, 'The Boy and the Mantle', refers to the Catholic practice of confessing one's sins, while the other, 'Sir Aldingar', contains features like those of the *Chevelere Assigne*. 'The Boy and the Mantle' is about a mysterious child who comes to Arthur's court with

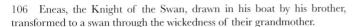

106   Eneas, the Knight of the Swan, drawn in his boat by his brother, transformed to a swan through the wickedness of their grandmother.

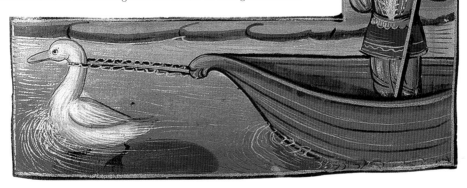

magic gifts. He produces a mantle, small enough to fit in a nutshell and able to change its appearance according to the virtue of the woman who wears it. Guinevere tries it on and it turns yellow, green, and black; other ladies do so and look naked. When Sir Craddocke's wife attempts the test, the gown fits her well, save for a crinkle at the bottom. She confesses that she kissed her husband before they were married, and as soon as she says so the mantle gleams like gold. Guinevere spitefully rejoins that the lady has lain by fifteen men, 'priests, clerks, wedded men', but the 'little boy' tells Arthur to control his wife. 'She is a bitch and a witch, and a whore bold.' Craddocke's lady receives the mantle as a present, and her husband gets a boar's head and a golden drinking horn for passing two tests about cuckoldry. Is this a story for children or for adults? Its sequence of tests is like those of other folk-stories which have, in later times, become children's literature. True, it is about chastity and immorality but (as we have seen) such topics were not unknown to late-medieval children or thought improper for them.[80]

The ballad of 'Sir Aldingar' is another tale about adultery, and one that occurs in the folklore of many countries. Sir Aldingar is a wicked knight who tries to seduce the queen. Rebuffed by her, he arranges for a leper to be put into her bed and reveals the fact to King Harry, who orders the leper to be hanged and the queen burnt. The queen begs a respite of forty days, and sends out messengers to search for a champion to defend her. One of them,

> As he rode then by one river side,
>   There he met with a little child;
> He seemed no more in a man's likeness
>   Then a child of four years old.
>
> He asked the queen's messenger how far he rode;
>   Loth he was him to tell;
> The little one was offended at him,
>   Bade him adieu, farewell.
>
> Said, Turn thou again, thou messenger,
>   Greet our queen well from me;
> When bale [*evil*] is at highest, boot [*good*] is at next;
>   Help enough there may be.

The forty days pass, and the queen is taken to execution:

> Our queen was put in a tun to burn,
>   She thought no thing but death;
> They were ware of the little one
>   Came riding forth of the east . . .
>
> Said, Draw away these brands of fire
>   Lie burning before our queen,

>And fetch me hither Sir Aldingar,
>   That is a knight so keen.

The child pulls out 'a well good sword' and, with his first stroke, severs his opponent's legs at the knees. Aldingar confesses all and dies. The child tells the king to take his wife and love her, but his own identity is not revealed.[81] This is a simple and powerful story, with dramatic tension, and although there is no proof that it was meant for children, it would have made a good tale for parents to read or tell them, or for children to tell or read themselves.

The best example of a story for children before 1500, however, is not a romance but a fabliau or comic tale, which came to be known as *The Friar and the Boy*, a poem in six-line stanzas, which first appears in manuscripts of the fifteenth century.[82] There was once a 'husband' or farmer who had three wives, and a son Jack by the first of them. His second wife dislikes the boy and tells her husband to send him away into service, but the farmer says he is too young and puts him in charge of the herd in the field. On taking the animals there, Jack opens the dinner which his stepmother has provided, finds it paltry, and presents it to a poor old man who asks him for charity. In return, Jack is given three magic gifts: a bow that always hits its target, a pipe that makes everyone dance, and a charm to make the stepmother fart when she is angry. Jack plays the pipe and leads home his animals dancing. When he goes indoors, his parents are having their supper. He asks for food and his father throws him a capon's wing. The stepmother scowls and immediately explodes like a gun going off. All those present roar with laughter. She makes another noise as loud as a bomb, and turns red with shame.

A friar now arrives to spend the night, a friend of the stepmother. She tells him to give Jack a good beating, but when the boy meets the friar next day, Jack diverts his attention by shooting a bird in a thorn-bush. The friar goes into the bush to retrieve it and Jack starts piping. The friar dances among the thorns until his body is bleeding and his clothes are in tatters. When Jack goes home that night, his father asks him what he has done to the friar and demands to hear the pipe. The friar, in terror, begs to be tied up. Jack plays and everyone dances. The stepmother explodes again, the friar twitches even in his bonds, and Jack leads the dancers down the street, drawing the neighbours naked out of bed. Finally, the friar summons Jack before the local Church court. The court official asks for the pipe to be played, universal dancing ensues, and Jack stops only when he is allowed to go free. This story is virtually a tale and nothing more. It has a whiff of anticlericalism and a moral to the extent that disagreeable people get punished, but there is nothing improving about it; the plot is simply a series of funny incidents with a boy as the hero and victor.

The Friar and the Boy was published by Wynkyn de Worde, 'imprinted at London in Fleet Street at the sign of the sun' between 1510 and 1513.[83] It came out in a cheap and cheerful format, making a small folded pamphlet of eight leaves. The work has no title page and the text is simply headed 'Here beginneth a merry jest of the friar and the boy', followed by an attractive woodcut and the beginning of

107   *The Friar and the Boy*, the first children's story to be printed and illustrated. The boy Jack plays his magic pipe, while the friar dances in the thorn-bush.

the poem. The woodcut shows a rural scene with a village or town in the distance (Fig. 107). Jack sits with his herd beyond him, playing his pipe, while the friar dances in the brambles. A pamphlet like this cost only a couple of pence, and could be easily sold to parents and children by pedlars or at fairs. The demand for the story is shown by the number of editions – at least three in the sixteenth century, five in the seventeenth, six in the eighteenth, and four in the early nineteenth. There must have been more, because such humble books were read to pieces and very few have survived. It was last published as a popular work in 1820, before its uproariousness and farts were suppressed by Victorian prudishness. So long a literary life is remarkable. The late middle ages may have little to show in terms of stories primarily for children, but this one work did sterling duty in that role for over three hundred years.

PRINTING

The Friar and the Boy was written in the age of manuscripts, but it found its widest public through print. How then did printing, introduced to England by Caxton in 1476, affect young people and the literature they read? The early history of printing is a much misunderstood subject. Popular folklore imagines that books were scarce before Caxton, most of them written by monks, and that the mass production of books, and hence the spread of literacy and education, were largely the result of the new technology. This, of course, is nonsense. Printing, like many inventions, came when it did because the demand for its product was sufficiently high. Literacy and education were widespread. There was already a huge production of literature, written by readers themselves or manufactured for sale by scriveners and book scribes. By 1476, one could buy single or multiple handwritten copies of anything from a one-sheet charter or indulgence to a whole book. The early printers, like the professional copyists who preceded them, produced material to supply an existing demand.

Caxton realised the popularity of religious, educational, and recreational reading in English among the nobility, gentry, and rich of the towns. His second major printed book, produced at Bruges in 1474 before he set up his press in England, was *The Game of Chess*, a book part manual, part social analysis, which was in both respects a work of education.[84] When he moved to Westminster, he identified the education of children and adolescents as a promising field. They already constituted a large body of readers, either in schools or in households, and books were already produced especially for them: school grammars in Latin, and moral, courtesy, and hunting works in English. Caxton seems to have made a policy decision not to involve himself with school textbooks. As far as we know, he printed only one (probably at the request of a patron), in marked contrast with printers after his death who issued schoolbooks in large quantities.[85] But he was well aware of the demand for books for young people to read in English in their homes, and took an interest in it throughout his career in England.

108 The opening page of Caxton's first printed book for children, *Stans Puer ad Mensam*: Lydgate's treatise on table manners.

Accordingly, when Caxton got ready to print in Westminster, he planned his first list of titles to include four cheap works in English aimed at children or at adults on their behalf. All are now thought to belong to 1476, his opening year in England.[86] The shortest of the four was Lydgate's verse translation of Grosseteste's poem on table manners, *Stans Puer ad Mensam* (Fig. 108). This poem, as has been said, was widely read in grammar schools in its original Latin form, and Lydgate's translation had made it available for use in homes. Caxton issued it as a single sheet of print which could be folded into an eight-page pamphlet and, because *Stans Puer* was too short for this purpose, he supplemented it with *Salve Regina*. This is an ingenious poem which conveys the words of a famous Latin hymn to the Virgin Mary within an English explanation of their meaning. Odd corners of the pamphlet were filled up with proverbs and maxims in English.

The other three works were longer. Two were Lydgate's debates in the manner of fables: *The Churl and the Bird*, which made a booklet of ten leaves, and *The Horse, the Goose, and the Sheep*, totalling eighteen leaves including the lists of words about animals, already mentioned. The longest of the four was *Cato* in the original Latin with Benedict Burgh's translation, which occupied thirty-four leaves. *Cato* was read in all schools and probably in some households, so Caxton's version looks partly intended for children, but equally the poem was a famous repository of wisdom and, being a larger book, may have been partly directed at adults. All three of these longer works were reprinted by Caxton at least once, and *Cato* on two further occasions – once in a new translation by Caxton himself, so they certainly found a market. It may be that *Stans Puer* was reprinted too, since the first edition survives today in only two copies and a second could easily have disappeared altogether.

Caxton's educational interests did not stop with these relatively small productions. In his second year of activity, 1477, he issued his own version of the romance of *Jason* with the dedication to the young prince of Wales, and Rivers's translation of *The Dicts and Sayings of the Philosophers*, another work produced with the prince in mind. He also published in that year *The Book of Courtesy*, a verse treatise on good manners for boys, similar to *Stans Puer* but covering more aspects of behaviour. For the rest of his career in England (he died in 1491), Caxton regularly printed works in English suitable for teaching or entertaining children or adolescents. They include the short popular encyclopaedia called *The Mirror of the World* (1481), *Reynard the Fox* (1481), the *Fables of Aesop* and *The Book of the Knight of the Tower* (1484), the *Book of Good Manners* (1487), *Blanchardyn and Eglantine* (1489), and the *Eneydos* (1490) with its inscription to Prince Arthur. It is possible too that some of Caxton's other narrative works were read by young people, like Chaucer's *Canterbury Tales* (1476) and Malory's *Le Morte Darthur* (1485), although he does not mention this in his editions.

Caxton, then, deserves to be called a pioneer of publishing for young people. He was aware that they constituted a market for books, and aimed to supply them with both works of their own and adult works, both stories and works of education. Some of his titles were suitable for boys, others (at least in his view) for girls and women. By personally translating books from French to English, and printing works less readily accessible in manuscript, he increased the body of literature available to the young – at least the wealthier young. The printers who succeeded him in England, beginning with Wynkyn de Worde and Richard Pynson, took matters further. They went on printing large classic works, as he had done, but they broadened the scope of their activity. First, they opened up the school market, printing more school grammars and reading texts, and increasing their circulation and usage.[87] Secondly, they produced a wider variety of amusing and recreational works, some of which were especially suitable for younger readers.

During the 1490s, more English classics came into print through their efforts. *The Seven Sages of Rome* was printed by Pynson in 1493 and by de Worde in about 1506, and another anthology of stories, the *Gesta Romanorum*, by de Worde in about 1502.[88] The romance of *Guy of Warwick* came out from de Worde's press in about 1497 and from Pynson's in about 1500, followed by *Bevis of Hampton* from de Worde in 1500 and from Pynson about three years later.[89] *A Little Geste of Robin Hood*, the earliest-known printed ballad about the outlaw, was issued by Pynson in about 1500, by de Worde in about 1506, and at London, York, and possibly Antwerp during the next ten years – a sign of its huge popularity.[90] All these titles continued to be printed in one form or another during the sixteenth century, and were evidently well established in popular taste. The shorter ones, like *The Friar and the Boy* and *Robin Hood*, were particularly apt for children. They took only a few large sheets to print and cost very little: a *Robin Hood* could be bought for 2d. at Oxford in 1520, and short 'ballads' for as little as a halfpenny.[91] One can imagine such texts being widely available at fairs or from pedlars as well as from booksellers, and being bought by children with their own pocket money – a practice known to have happened by the seventeenth century.[92]

Literature for children, then, did not start with the early printers, but they promoted it. They made it more easily available and increased its profile by pointing out the utility of certain works for children and young people. In addition, they enhanced its visual appeal. There were illustrated manuscripts long before printing, but these were costly works confined to children of high status, like Prince Alfonso and Henry VI.[93] Hand-written texts for children, like schoolbooks and short moral or practical works, were plainer, and Caxton followed this pattern in works like *Stans Puer*. It had no title page or illustrations – simply a short title followed by the text, as in a manuscript (Fig.108) By the 1480s, however, Caxton was including woodcuts in a few of the larger works he printed, some copies of which may have come into children's hands. Notable in this respect are *The Mirror of the World* (1481), the second edition of *The Game of Chess* (1482), the second edition of the *Canterbury Tales* (1482), and Aesop's *Fables* (1484).[94]

Caxton's successors made more use of woodcuts to enhance their books. De Worde, for example, included over three dozen in his lost edition of *Reynard the Fox* (*c*.1500) and seven in his *Seven Sages* (*c*.1506), while Pynson put ten into his *Bevis of Hampton* (1503) – all books which may have found young readers. By the 1490s, both men were issuing their Latin grammars with pictorial title pages. Sometimes, the title page shows a schoolmaster occupying a large chair with his birch in his hand, while a group of pupils sit obediently in front of him. In other cases, it depicts a scholar in his study, implying that the grammar is scholarly or else that the pupil, if he is diligent, may become a great scholar himself. Other small books for children or basic readers began to be given similar illustrated title pages or first pages, like *The Horse* and *The Churl* printed by de Worde in the 1490s. The same cuts circulated widely in different books and among different printers, and some basic productions like *Robin Hood* merely had 'factotums' – moveable figures, such as Lady Fortune, a jester, and a swordsman, to decorate their opening pages. *The Friar and the Boy*, with its cut of the two main characters, is the earliest illustrated children's story, just as it is the first printed story centred on a child. By the time it came out in the 1510s, printers were well aware that a picture enhanced the appeal of even a cheap book, when laid on a counter or stall.

A READING EXPERIENCE

COMPILING MENUS OF children's reading is all very well, but reading (like feeding) is a personal experience. We can all remember books we encountered when young and, sometimes, how they struck us at the time: exciting or dull. What did medieval children think of what they read? This kind of information is hard to discover when so little survives in the way of personal records like letters, diaries, or autobiographies. One possible source, however, exists in copies of books which show signs of having been used by children. Little attention has yet been paid to such volumes, but an example survives in the Bodleian Library at Oxford which tells us a good deal. Stripping away the layers of its history, like peeling an onion, brings us closer to what children in our period might have felt about a story that they read.

If you order item 'Douce B subt. 234' in the Bodleian Library, it arrives in a neat grey box fastened with strings and buttons, representing modern times and conservation practice. Opening the box, you discover a book in a leather binding (now broken), with a title on the spine in gold on red: BEUYS OF SOUTHAMPT. The binding is later than its contents, and comes from a period when the book was considered a bibliographical rarity, meriting dignified dress. Inside the covers stands the bookplate of Francis Douce (1757–1834), the book collector who acquired the volume and bequeathed it to the Bodleian. Before it was cherished by bibliophiles, however, the book led a different life. Turning the pages reveals that some of them are disfigured by scribbles, drawings, and names: notably those of 'John Good' and 'John Bettes'. These were boys who used the book in the sixteenth and seventeenth centuries, and to them it was not an antique but a functional book. Indeed, they used it so well (or badly) that parts of it are missing.

The boys were not the book's first readers, however. It was manufactured and published by the London printer Richard Pynson in about the year 1503, and because it is a work of many pages with woodcut illustrations, costing more than a few pence, we can be pretty sure that it was originally bought and read by an adult. It was well treated at first, since none of the scribbles in it appear to go back to the early sixteenth century. But even 1503 does not bring us to the heart of the onion, because the work existed before Pynson printed it. His text (which is in English) dates from the fifteenth century, and is a reworking of an earlier English text of the late thirteenth or early fourteenth. That text in turn was a translation of something first written in England in Anglo-Norman French in about the early thirteenth. Nobody knows who wrote the original story, *Bevis of Hampton*, but it was one of the works most widely read in medieval England and for long after-wards.[95] After circulating for three hundred years in manuscript versions, it was published at least nine times in England in the sixteenth century, six times in the seventeenth, and five times in the eighteenth. The last edition came out in about 1780. Outside England, it was translated into Dutch, continental French, Icelandic, Italian, and Welsh. There is even a version in Russian.

A work like *Bevis of Hampton* is hard to classify as adult or as children's reading. It is about a boy who grows up to be a knight, so it could have appealed to boys or to men. It gives a major role to Bevis's sweetheart Josian, so it holds an interest for girls and for women. In genre it is a romance, a word suggestive of fantasy and adventure, and *Bevis* contains plenty of both. But its opening pages are also disturbing; they are about the break-up of a family and a child's expulsion from home. Bevis's parents are ill matched. His father Guy, the earl of Southampton, is a brave but elderly knight. His much younger mother, the daughter of the king of Scotland, would have preferred to marry the Emperor of Germany (or his brother, in Pynson's version of the story).

By the time that Bevis, their only child, is seven, the wife is tired of her husband's piety and sexual inadequacy. She sends a messenger to her former lover to come and kill her husband. The lover, aptly named Sir Murdour, arrives with his men, ambushes Guy, and kills him viciously. He brings Guy's head to the lady, who tells him to come to her chamber that night and prepares to marry him immediately. Bevis learns of his mother's betrayal and, young as he is, confronts her. When he calls her 'whore', she knocks him down and orders his tutor, Sir Sabere, to have him killed, but Sabere fakes the death and sends Bevis to keep his sheep on the hill (Fig. 109). Bevis looks down on his old home, where the wedding is in progress, and cannot resist going in. He kills the porter who bars his way (Fig. 110) and knocks down Sir Murdour, but he is overpowered and eventually sold to heathen merchants. They take him away by ship, and he duly finds himself (now aged fifteen) as a servant of the king of Armenia. There Bevis meets the king's daughter, Josian, who falls in love with him.

The story that follows is immensely complicated. It takes thirteen pages to summarise the plot, although the poem is only 4,332 lines long![96] Bevis has a series of adventures, first in Armenia and the neighbouring lands, and then in England, after which the story alternates between the two places. Supported by his magnificent horse Arondel, a gift from Josian, he fights with armies, knights, giants, snakes, a boar, and a dragon. Josian is not inactive, either. When Bevis is taken captive, she is given in marriage to somebody else, but maintains her vir-

109   The young Bevis of Hampton, driven from home, keeping sheep on the down near Southampton.

110   Bevis storms his home, killing the porter, while his mother and murderous stepfather feast inside

ginity by means of a magic girdle. When a third man tries to marry her by force, she strangles him with it and nearly gets burnt for the crime. Even when she is married to Bevis, she is attacked by lions, gives birth to twins alone in a forest, and gets carried off by a giant. Eventually the various plots are resolved. Bevis comes back to England, and avenges his father by plunging his stepfather into a cauldron of boiling lead. His mother throws herself to her death from a tower. One of his sons becomes king of Armenia and the other king of England. In the end Bevis, Josian, and Arondel all die in the East on the same day, and their elder son buries his parents in a chapel, founding a monastery to pray for their souls.

We can learn how this story struck the boys who read it from the scribbled entries in the Bodleian copy. The scribbles are of various kinds. There are notes of names and ownership: '*John Betts of Aylysb . . .*', '*thys boke longgyth to John Betts*', '*John Gowd* [written over a previous name, apparently *Thomas Bett] owth thys boke*', '*Thes Boke [belongs] to John Good of Aylysb . . .*', and '*Stephen Aldhouse 1696*'. The name 'Thomas' is written several times. There are a couple of scraps of Latin, of the sort that boys studied or wrote in grammar schools: *Iste sanus est pater meus* ('this wise man is my father') and *vesperi sunt prolyxitantes* ('the nights are drawing out'). Sketches have been done in the margins. One or two of these are copied from the woodcuts of the book, including a dog's head which is imitated twice. Others are free-style, mainly faces, one of a man in a typical Tudor hat.

The scribbles must be substantially later than the date when the book was published, probably from the late sixteenth and early seventeenth centuries. Their untidy nature suggests that they were made by children rather than adults, with the probable exception of Stephen Aldhouse whose name occurs on a flyleaf. It looks as if the book first belonged to men or women who treated it carefully, and then came into the hands of boys: John and Thomas Betts, very likely living or studying at Aylesbury in Buckinghamshire, followed by John Good or Gowd of the same place, and then Aldhouse.[97] By the time that the boys were reading it, the story was a rather old-fashioned one. It made references to Catholic religious practices, which may have lessened its interest to adults after the Reformation. It had come under attack from Protestant clergy for its extravagant fantasies, and was being ridiculed by writers like Nashe and Shakespeare for its rough verse and incredible happenings.[98] None of these issues need have bothered the boys, for whom the poetry would have been simple and accessible, while the religious framework may have seemed merely another romantic feature.

Eight passages in the book have been marked with lines or crosses. One cannot be sure who made them, because such marks cannot easily be linked with hand-writing, but the boys are plausible candidates. They were using the book in circumstances where they were able to disfigure it, and the marks refer to topics likely to have interested young people between about seven and eighteen. The earliest relates to the episode when Bevis kept the sheep on the downs above Southampton, and looked down at his father's house from which he had been ejected:

> As he beheld toward the tower,
> Trumpet he heard and tabor;
> There was harping and much bliss
> In the place that should be his.

This is one of the most pathetic parts of the story. A child would have been able to sympathise with the anguish of being driven out of one's home; a boy who had been sent away to school might well have had similar feelings.

Several of the other marked passages are to do with unusual events and marvels. One is about a wild boar who eats the men he slays ('The blood he drank, the flesh he gnew'). Another draws attention to Bevis's noble nature when he gives a fine robe to Josian's messenger – no 'churl's deed', as the messenger remarks. A third describes the wicked King Brademond's exotic palace, with its gold-painted walls and brass doors and pillars, and another the giant Ascopard whom Bevis fights and tames:

> This giant was both mighty and strong,
> And fully thirty foot long;
> He was bristled like a sow,
> A foot [*in length*] he had between each brow.

Marks have been made against two lines relating to the long period when Brademond kept Bevis in a dungeon:

> Rats and mice and such small deer
> Was his meat that seven year.

These very lines are quoted in *King Lear* by Edgar, while he is acting the role of Tom the madman. They may have been the most famous words of the poem or, by Shakespeare's time, the most ridiculous.

Finally, two marked passages show a budding interest in the opposite sex. Early on, when Josian comes into the story, there is a twelve-line description of her beauty, which has been scored:

> Her visage was white as lily flower,
> Therein ran the red colour . . . ,
> Her body was gentle without lack,
> Well shapen both body and back.

This is a typical romantic description of a heroine and keeps to conventional phraseology, but in a later love scene between Bevis and Josian, someone has noted one of the most sexually explicit parts of the book:

> Bevis says, No man in the world but would have
> You as queen if they once saw you.
> I am a knight of strange land;
> I have no more than I in stand.
> Mercy, Bevis, said Josian.
> I had thee liever [*rather*] to my lemman [*lover*],
> Thy body in thy shirt all naked
> Than all the good that Mahounde [*Mohammed*] maked.

This whole passage has been marked once, and the last three lines a second time. The readers did not fail to note its erotic suggestions!

Books like *Bevis*, then, presented young readers with an exciting tale and a good deal more as well. Romances fed the mind with all kinds of ideas, both true and false. Society was presented in a simplified way: made up knights and ladies, clergy (priests, monks, and friars), outlaws, farmers, and servants. England was shown as a country of castles and monasteries, its landscape partly of tamed fields and partly of forests, rivers, and seas. Much of the action of stories flitted between the wilds and the civilised world of towns and great households. It was not an isolated country. Heroes and heroines crossed to France, Germany, Italy, and Spain, all of which were depicted with similar landscapes and societies. England, like these lands, was a part of Christendom, a faith at war with Islam, and stories sometimes took their characters to the Middle East on crusade. It was also a part of the whole world, a world which scholars believed that they knew completely. Caxton's *Mirror of the World* describes the world's roundness, its three continents (excluding the Americas), and its natural history, including giants, pygmies, elephants, and salamanders. Romances too portrayed these wonders: the great

111 'Greedy hypocritical clergy'. The Friar in Chaucer's *Canterbury Tales*, introducing his tale maliciously aimed at one of his fellow-pilgrims.

extent of the globe, its large non-Christian areas, strange inhabitants, and fearsome monsters.

Reading gave children a sense of the past as well as one of the present. Saints' lives, romances, and chansons de geste were set in the Greek or Roman worlds, or in the reigns of King Arthur, Charlemagne, or King Athelstan. Heathen worship was often mentioned, revealing that ancient times were pagan and different. True, in other respects the characters and scenery of these stories – knights, ladies, and castles – were often typical of the twelfth and thirteenth centuries when the stories were written. But that period, by the later middle ages, was a little old-fashioned. The stories depicted a world where monasteries were still being founded and crusades fought – activities less frequent after 1300. Reading such stories thereafter was a backward-looking experience, just as the reading of so many modern children's classics evokes a vanished world of cooks and housemaids, steam trains and deserted roads.

Young readers would also have learnt a good deal about behaviour. Some of the literature put into their hands, like *Cato* and the courtesy books, was meant to instruct them in wisdom, virtue, and good manners. Romances too presented heroes and heroines who were models of bravery, chastity, generosity, piety, and fortitude. The reverse was shown as well. Love took place not only in an ideal sense, but coarsely in terms of desire, seduction, and adultery. There were tyrannical kings, cruel stepmothers, treacherous knights, and greedy hypocritical clergy (Fig. 111). Young listeners or readers would encounter violence, both in the formal sense of battles and combats, and in the anarchic one of quarrels and murders. They would be encouraged to condone the brutality done by a hero – like Bevis's murder of his own porter – and to disparage any actions by the villains. These darker sides of human life complemented, and to some extent undermined, the literature of wisdom and virtue. It is not therefore surprising that romances and ballads were seen as subversive by Wycliffite and Reformation writers, and some strict parents may have attempted to censor stories viewed as tainted in this way. More commonly, however, such works coexisted with 'good' literature, and both were imbibed by children. Through literature, as well as through life, they grew up to share the complex tastes and prejudices of their elders.

Through literature as well as through life – because children and adolescents formed a significant group of readers and listeners by 1500. Sometimes, they took the initiative in reading or listening to literature primarily meant for adults. At other times, they were the targets of literature – didactic works, stories, miscellanies, and the output of the printers – aimed at them by authors, publishers, and parents. They deserve to be regarded, more than they have been, both as generators of medieval literature and as its consumers.

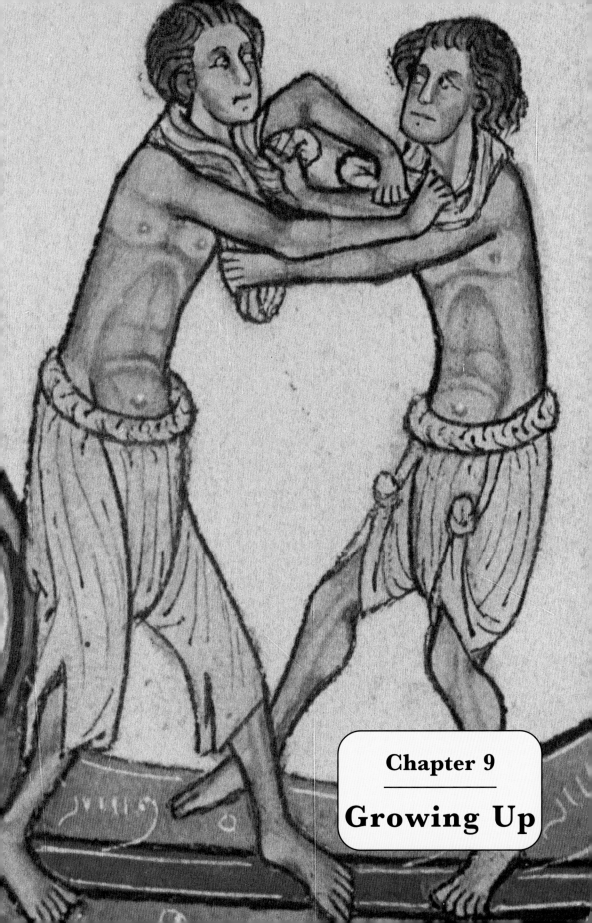

Chapter 9

Growing Up

LEARNING TO WORK

A BOY AT SCHOOL in Oxford in the 1490s is reviewing the course of his life:

> The world waxeth worse every day, and all is turned upside down, contrary to th' old guise. For all that was to me a pleasure when I was a child, from three years old to ten (for now I go upon the twelfth year), while I was under my father and mother's keeping, be turned now to torments and pain.

While he lived at home, he remembers, he used to lie in bed until broad daylight, looking at the rafters of his chamber and the hangings that lined the walls. He got up when he wished, and summoned a servant to lay out his clothes for the day. His breakfast was brought to his bedside as often as he called for it.

> But now the world runneth upon another wheel. For now at five of the clock by the moonlight I must go to my book and let sleep and sloth alone, and if our master happens to awake us, he bringeth a rod [in]stead of a candle. Now I leave pleasures that I had sometime; here is nought else preferred but admonishing and stripes. Breakfasts that were sometime brought at my bidding are driven out of country and never shall come again.

He would tell more of his troubles, but there is no pleasure in doing so. All his thought is now given to making his life easier, so that he may get up and go to bed when he pleases, out of the fear of beatings.[1]

This piece of prose is so evocative that the reader may be disappointed to learn that it is not real autobiography but passages in a Magdalen College schoolbook for turning into Latin prose: passages meant to criticise what the boy says as much as to sympathise with him. Educationists, as we saw in an earlier chapter, regarded childhood as an immature and irresponsible time when children (given their head) do nothing but idle and play.[2] Parents, particularly wealthy townspeople, were blamed for indulging their children and exerting too little control. Preachers and schoolmasters urged the need for correction. Children should be hardened with discipline, educated with skills, and infused with good manners and morals. Long before anyone had heard of Protestantism, medieval Christians preached that humanity should be led away from childishness to an adult life marked, spiritually and physically, by hard work and self-discipline.

The Magdalen College schoolbook was written or set to be written by a schoolmaster, and schooling was one of the established ways of teaching children the skills and behaviour of adults. An outline of the range of schools has already been sketched: free-standing public schools in towns, schools in religious houses and great households, private schools, and individual tuition by clergy.[3] How many people went to school is impossible to say, and the process was not a straightforward one. There had to be a reason to justify paying for a child to learn in a classroom rather than helping with household tasks or earning money from work. There had to be a suitable teacher at hand, or resources to send the child away

112   Learning to work: a child might be given an easy task like driving domestic birds to pond or pasture.

from home – then, as now, far more expensive than schooling alone. In the case of the children of serfs, the lord of the manor had to give permission for schooling, and parents might have to pay a fee for the privilege. Schooling implied a career elsewhere as a cleric or in a town, threatening the lord with the loss of an adult labourer. So although many went to school, some stayed for only short periods and others (the majority, it seems) did not go there at all.

Most medieval people therefore learnt through work rather than at school. Even literary skills such as keeping accounts and writing them up, which could be acquired from specialist teachers, must often have been mastered 'on the job' as an apprentice or a trainee clerk in a household.[4] The process of learning to work starts early in life, for even young children take pleasure in copying adults and helping them with tasks. This was so in the middle ages. We have seen how small girls followed their mothers in cooking or drawing water, while small boys were attracted to their fathers' work with tools and animals.[5] Coroners' inquests and cases of trespass and damage show how older children gradually became involved in doing such tasks themselves. Already before they were seven, when they were still infants in medieval parlance, they might be given simple household duties such as looking after younger siblings or fetching water from the well. Once they were seven or so, their liking to wander and explore could be utilised for the benefit of their families. Records show them gathering fruit and nuts, fishing in rivers, collecting shellfish on the shore, harvesting reeds in marshland, finding firewood, or digging peat from a turbary.

Both girls and boys might do these things in childhood. But as they grew older, physique and convention opened up a gap between the sexes. Girls would concentrate on household work and food collecting, adding cooking and washing to their experience. They learnt textile skills such as spinning, sewing, and weaving, and these were practised throughout society, from the king's daughters to the lowliest unmarried 'spinster'. Boys would take on harder physical tasks involving the care of animals or work in the fields. A lad as young as seven could be given a simple agricultural job such as bird-scaring or herding geese (Fig. 112). Working with larger and more valuable beasts – sheep, pigs, cows, oxen, or horses – needed greater strength or experience (Fig. 113). John Serle of Cheriton Bishop (Devon) was only eight when, in the late fifteenth century, he goaded the oxen as they pulled a plough or cart for his stepfather and was gored by one of them. The recorder of the event (a miracle collector) observed that 'he was really too small' for the task.[6] Sometimes a miracle story or coroners's record allows us to follow such work in some detail. One morning in late summer, shortly before 1300, Nicholas son of John the Fisher of How Capel (Herefs.) took his father's white cow to a field near the land of the lord of the manor, called Lord's Croft. The cow was wild and ran about, first into the lord's corn and then towards the River Wye. The youth decided to shackle its legs, and went to the river where his father kept a small boat, in which there were some osiers – pliable willow shoots. Trying to enter the boat, he tumbled into the river and was not found until the early afternoon. Fortunately, he did not drown but survived through the help of St Thomas of Hereford.[7]

Some girls might work at home until they married, some boys until they inherited the home from their parents. Equally, the sending of children away to work, either on a daily basis or to board permanently, was common among the working population. Even a relatively small child might be deputed to help a neighbour in return for some reward. A girl of seven, described as the 'little servant' of a woman of Staplehurst (Kent) in the late fifteenth century, was sent by her mistress to draw water from a well with a wooden bucket when she fell in – with luck, not fatally.[8] A girl called Helen Constune, who appears in a legal dispute of the early

113   Older children could be set to work with larger animals.

sixteenth century, was sent into service with a London tallow chandler at the age of nine, and stayed with him for a year before moving to work for a clerk of St Stephen's Chapel, Westminster.[9] It was probably more common for children to take up regular work between the ages of about twelve and fourteen. Till then they scarcely had the strength and understanding to give their employers value for money.

Of course, a master or mistress who wanted a servant did not necessarily look for a child or adolescent. 'Servant' is not itself an age-related term, and adults have always fulfilled the role. But there is no doubt that a great many medieval servants – perhaps most – were aged between about twelve and the mid twenties. This fact has left its mark in our language. The words in use for servants in the middle ages often carry a strong implication of youth: page, child, maid, and groom. Even 'yeoman', which was being used by the late fourteenth century to convey social superiority and sometimes seniority of age, is a compound of the words 'young man'.[10] Young people were attractive to employ because they lacked dependents and were cheap to hire. They could be trained for whatever purpose was required, and replaced when they grew older and needed more wages. In return, children and their parents saw early employment as a means of gaining maintenance, training, and patronage outside their own families. Homes lost mouths to feed and bodies to clothe.

All this attracted little comment from English writers; it was normal and taken for granted. Round about 1500, however, an Italian visitor to London wrote a description of England and the English for the benefit of the authorities in Venice, a work now known as the 'Italian Relation'. In it he drew attention to what he called the 'want of affection' of the English towards their children, in remarks that have become famous:

> After having kept them at home till they arrive at the age of 7 or 9 years at the utmost, they put them out, both males and females, to hard service in the houses of other people, binding them generally for another 7 or 9 years. And these are called apprentices, and during that time they perform all the most menial offices; and few are born who are exempted from this fate, for every one, however rich he may be, sends away his children into the houses of others, whilst he, in return, receives those of strangers into his own.

On asking the reason for this severity, said the author, the English answered that they did so in order that their children might learn 'better how to live'. He considered rather that 'they do it because they like to enjoy all their comforts themselves, and that they are better served by strangers than they would be by their own children'. Other people's children cost less to keep, and could be made to work harder.[11]

Ariès would have liked this passage, with its apparent endorsement of his views about the coldness of parents and the brevity of childhood. A modern reader will be wise to weigh it cautiously. The 'Italian Relation' embodies the view of a stranger, based chiefly in London and talking primarily about apprentices, who were more numerous there than anywhere else in England. What he says about them is not altogether accurate since, as we shall see, most apprentices started their training at twelve or fourteen. His analysis of parents' motives in sending their children away is also debatable. Why should such motives have been selfish rather than altruistic: the wish for children to better themselves through acquiring skills and patronage? As he himself conceded, his analysis was not shared by the English themselves. Writers from Langland and the fourteenth-century preachers, through Dudley and the Magdalen College schoolbook to the leaders of the Reformation, thought that the problem with parents was their indulgence, not their severity. The need was to make them less fond and more strict.[12]

OPPORTUNITIES FOR WORK

THERE WERE FOUR large areas of potential employment for young people in medieval England. They included the countryside, the towns, and the great households of the aristocracy, as well as the Church which has already been considered.[13] The opportunities for working in the countryside are illustrated by the admirable, if patchy, survey of the English population in the poll-tax records of 1377–81, which survive for much of England, albeit fragmentarily. Many of these records list the inhabitants of towns and villages by name, and some go further by mentioning people's status, including that of servants. The returns of 1379 from Leicestershire, for example, enumerate 162 people in the rural village of Lubenham, 21 of whom were servants: eleven men, six women, and four of unspecified sex.[14] Carleton Curlieu has eight servants out of 51 people; Frisby-on-the-Wreak, twelve out of 88; Hungarton, eight out of 50; Queniborough, nine out of 95; and Whetstone, seven out of 81.[15] There were usually more men servants than women in these lists. Unfortunately for us, the poll-taxes were an unfamiliar and unpopular form of taxation. They prompted much evasion, and servants in particular may have been concealed because their employers did not wish to pay for them. In Gloucestershire in 1381, a second enquiry revealed a dozen and sometimes two dozen or more new names of 'labourers and servants' in the average village, so the surviving totals of rural servants may often be defective.[16]

The poll-tax records suggest that most such people worked for the élites of society: the gentry, the parish clergy, and those who approached the gentry in rank and were known as franklins or yeomen, operating large farms. Young servants might live with their employers, or come into work each day on a full-time or part-time basis. For youths, the work might involve outdoor crop-growing and stock-raising tasks, and for girls, the indoor ones. One familiar room on a farm, the dairy, takes its name from 'dey', a medieval word for a female servant, indicating the use of women to make butter and cheese on the bigger farms which generated enough milk for the purpose.[17] Some rural craftsmen (of whom there were many) may also have kept young assistants, but peasant smallholders were less able to afford hired servants and more likely to use the labour of their own children.

114   By adolescence, children could be apprenticed to adult trades, here as assistants to a smith or cutler.

Many people in the medieval countryside were serfs, known as 'bondmen' or 'villeins', bound to the land. They were unfree in the physical sense that they could not leave their manor without permission, and their children were supposed to find work locally – a fact that suited lords of manors who required a ready supply of cheap labour. Neither this rule nor the work available in the country-side, however, could counteract the desire to move to the towns. Medieval towns were unhealthy places with high death-rates, but they had the attraction of offer-ing freedom to any villein who lived in them for a year and a day. More impor-tantly, they provided more jobs, of a wider variety, than existed in most rural communities. A small market town, Ashby-de-la-Zouch (Leics.) in 1379, recorded 36 servants out of 163 taxpayers, twenty male and sixteen female, a higher pro-portion than in the villages.[18] Two years earlier, the poll-tax lists for Dartmouth (Devon), a flourishing seaport, show that of 121 households, 66 (just over half) kept servants. Of these, 45 employed one such person, 13 two, 8 three, and 2 had four and six respectively – a total of 105 employees.[19] In the same year, 1377, the lists for Colchester (Essex), a still larger town, enumerate 478 servants, 16% of a taxpaying population of 2,978. Of these, 212 were men, 227 women, and the remaining 39 not identified.[20]

The tendency of workers, especially the young, to drift to the towns from the countryside is confirmed by the formulation of laws to control or prevent the practice. Manorial law forbade a bondman to put his child to be an apprentice without his lord's consent, on the assumption that apprenticeship involved a move to other work, often in a town. Fees were imposed on those who sought permis-sion, and fines on those who evaded it. At the end of the fourteenth century, when labour was in short supply after the Black Death, migration to the towns became an issue in Parliament (the mouthpiece of lords of manors), and laws were passed to restrict it. The Statute of Cambridge (1388) laid down that any person, male or female, who had been accustomed to work at the plough, cart, or other agricul-tural labour up to the age of twelve, should continue in the same work, and not be put to any trade or craft.[21] In 1406, there were complaints that the statute was not effective, and that children of humble parents had been apprenticed, sometimes at the age of twelve, sometimes younger. The statute was therefore re-enacted. This time, it was decreed that parents should not apprentice a child in a city or borough unless they possessed land or rent worth at least 20s. a year. Apprenticeships were not to be granted unless the parents brought a bill, signed by two justices of the peace, testifying to the value of their property.[22] Medieval statutes are evidence of Parliament's wishes rather than of its power to enforce them, but this one had effects for decades to come. In 1429, the citizens of London petitioned against its restrictions and gained exemption.[23] A similar immunity was given to Norwich in 1496 and, subsequently, to some other places.[24]

Notwithstanding all these laws and statutes, it is likely that many rural youths went to towns to take up menial work, and rural girls to serve as maids in households.[25] Some crafts and trades of a less exalted kind may have admitted apprentices from relatively poor families. Apprenticeship, however, tended to be an institution for young people of some status and money.[26] The word 'apprentice', which is first found in England in the late thirteenth century, signified a learner and implied that he or she had a good deal to learn.[27] Most trades were run by men and their apprentices were therefore boys, but girls were sometimes apprenticed, especially in crafts like silk making, embroidery, mercery (the cloth industry), and tailoring.[28] Apprentices had to be of suitable strength and intelligence to profit from their training, and fourteen was often laid down as a minimum age, although records of younger boys are sometimes encountered. The period of service involved was a long one, usually of seven years or more, and many employers demanded a payment before it began. In London, such premiums ranged from as little as £1 10s. to as much as £13 6s. 8d., depending on the status of the boy's family, that of the employer, and that of the trade to be learnt. Sometimes, the apprenticeship included provision for schooling. All this suggests that such places were not as easily obtainable by children of the poor as the statute of 1406 might suggest.

It became common to define the terms of an apprenticeship in a written indenture, a document of which each party kept an identical copy. In 1396, Thomas son of William Edward of Windsor contracted to serve John Hyndlee of Northampton, a brazier (worker in brass), as his apprentice for seven years. He promised to learn in a humble manner, keep confidence about his master's affairs, and not to do any damage to his master. He was not to absent himself unlawfully from his master's service, nor to use his master's goods without permission. He agreed not to patronise taverns or whores, engage in dice-playing or games at his master's expense, commit fornication or adultery with any woman of John's household, or marry without his master's agreement. He pledged himself to obey all the lawful and reasonable orders that his master gave him, and undertook, if he broke any of the terms of the indenture, to make appropriate amends or to double the term of his apprenticeship.

The arrangement placed John in place of a parent to Thomas, with powers over him like those of a father. On his side, he agreed to teach Thomas the craft of a brazier and pewterer in the best possible manner, concealing nothing from him, and to chastise him in an appropriate way and no other. He promised to find Thomas food, clothing both linen and woollen, bed, lodging, shoes, and other things every year, in accordance with Thomas's age. Very likely, though the document does not say so, Thomas would learn or improve arithmetical and literary skills as well as industrial ones, through helping to buy and sell and to record the transactions. Finally, the document was witnessed by the mayor of Northampton, the two bailiffs of the town, and other people.[29] Their presence and endorsement gave the arrangement public status. John became responsible for Thomas's behaviour in the town, and when Thomas had finished his term he would qualify to be made a burgess of Northampton with rights to work and trade there.

The other large area of employment for young people lay in great households, ranging from that of the king with several hundred members, through those of the nobility with up to two hundred, to those of knights, merchants, and clerical dignitaries with a dozen or two. These households differed from those of yeoman farmers and tradesmen, both in size and in other respects. Most of their members were male. A queen or lady might have a few female companions and servants, but even such women were otherwise served by men and boys, and the clergy entirely so. Great households also contained a wider span of ages, ranks, and skills than smaller ones. The lord's or lady's own attendants would be noble or gentle in status, the heads of the working departments yeomen, and the rest of the servants grooms of ordinary rank. There would often be priests and clerks of a secretarial kind, keeping records of the income and expenses of the household and its estates. Young people formed a significant presence, chiefly youths, who ranged in status like the adult men from noble children, wards, and pages through choristers to menial boy servants. Girls were largely restricted to adolescents of gentry rank, whose parents paid for them to board in a household with a wife or widow in charge, until they were married.

Detailed household records begin to survive in the thirteenth century and, from the first, reveal the presence of boys and youths. The household roll of Richard Swinfield, bishop of Hereford, in 1289–90, shows the bishop maintaining his nephew, a ward, and various 'pages' and 'boys' of servant rank in his bakery, kitchen, and stables, as well as Hardy, page of his huntsman.[30] During the fourteenth century, the numbers of boys in such households appears to have grown, perhaps because the fall in the population after the Black Death and the consequent rise in wages made adolescents cheaper to hire than adults.[31] Thomas Arundel, bishop of Ely, had eight or nine boys, described as 'pages', in his household in the 1380s, as well as nine to eleven choristers. The boys worked (usually singly) as assistants to the porter, launderer, poulterer, larderer, and in the stables.[32] In the fifteenth and early sixteenth centuries, these numbers grew still larger. The household book of Henry Algernon Percy, earl of Northumberland, in 1511 lists some twenty-seven boys or adolescents out of a household of 160 members, serving the earl, his wife, and his children.[33]

The young people in the Percy family belonged to a hierarchy of ranks, with the earl's four children at the top of the tree. Beneath them came attendants from knightly or gentry families: carvers, sewers, cupbearers, henchmen, and young gentlemen as they were variously called. Some of these were paid for by their families to enjoy the benefits of serving in the earl's household. They totalled eleven. Further down, there were boys from lower orders of society. The chapel employed

Seignoz fait aluximo
vous maues teffic
Depar uofttre amual
quel vous a gmande

115   Great households employed many youths, the kitchen needing a particularly large work-force.

six 'children', and the working departments of the household had a boy each (also called a 'child') in the nursery, the wardrobe, the kitchen, the scullery, the stable, the coach-house, the bake-house, the butchery, the catery, and the armoury. The chamberlain of the household, the steward, and the 'arrasmender' who looked after the tapestries had a further boy apiece: thirteen working boys altogether. In return for their work, the boys received board, lodging, and a wage reflecting their rank: £3 6s. 8d. a year for noble attendants, £1 5s. for chapel boys, and 13s. 4d. for working boys. The noble boys also enjoyed the services of a grammar master, and the boys of the chapel those of a 'master of the children' to instruct them in song.

The biggest household and the greatest employer of boys was that of the king. In 1445, ordinances for its staffing mention sixty-two children. Twelve of these were henchmen and pages in attendance on the king and queen, and therefore of noble rank. Seven were choristers of the Chapel Royal. One boy assisted in the counting-house (the financial department), and three in the great hall. The remainder, some thirty-nine, were scattered among the various departments of food and laundry, of which the kitchen employed eight, the cellar, larder, and scullery four each, and the rest two or one.[34] This number was pruned a little in 1454, but remained in the region of the upper forties and fifties.[35] The 'Black Book' of Edward IV, a description of the household made by one of its clerks in 1471–2, adds valuable material about the duties and perquisites of these young servants, and makes philosophical observations about them. Its author believed that the presence of children in the household went back to at least the time of

King Harthacnut (1040–2), who allegedly provided for their breakfasts – a meal denied to adult servants.[36] A proliferation of boy assistants, he thought, had taken place since the reign of Edward III. All departments had them. They ought to be of 'clean birth' (free and legitimate), clean-limbed, personable, and virtuously disposed. They were subject to discipline from the sergeants and yeomen who headed their departments.[37]

Some insight into how such a boy or youth might be trained comes from the French hunting treatise *La Chasse* by Gaston count of Foix, which was translated into English as *The Master of Game* by Edward duke of York early in the fifteenth century. A lord's huntsman is advised to choose a boy servant as young as seven or eight: one who was physically active and keen sighted. This boy should be beaten until he had a proper dread of failing to carry out his master's orders. He was to sleep in a loft above the one-storey building where the hounds were kept, to intervene in case they fought at night. He was to learn all their names and colours, so as to recognise them, and to carry out menial tasks. These included cleaning the hounds' kennel each day, replacing the straw on which they lay, and giving them a fresh supply of water. He was to lead them out to take exercise and relieve themselves every morning and evening, comb them, and wipe them down with wisps of straw. In addition, he was to learn to spin horse-hair to make couples or leads for the hounds, to speak carefully, and to use the technical terms of hunting, so loved by its devotees.[38] As time passed, such experience would turn a boy into a skilled practitioner.

Posts for boys in households must have been valued, and the requirements for entry mentioned above suggest that the biggest establishments could pick and choose from relatively well connected people. Household service offered board, lodging, clothing, wages, and education. Only the lord's children, wards, and choristers were likely to have formal lessons from teachers, but lesser boys would be trained in the skills of service and many would partake as onlookers of the etiquette and culture of household life. Status was another attraction. Household staff were visibly well-dressed in the livery of their lord and reflected his glory. Aspiring parents could advance their children socially by boarding them in a household, and Chaucer owed his rise to such an arrangement. The son of a London wine merchant, his father bought (or procured) him a place in the household of the countess of Ulster, from which he progressed to the royal household, the rank of an esquire, and a marriage that later linked him with John of Gaunt.[39]

Finally, household service gave one patronage. Lords with young servants had a degree of obligation to find them employment when they grew older. The author of the Black Book states that, if the king's boy-servants behaved well, they would be promoted to higher offices.[40] The children of the royal chapel were particularly favoured. In 1317, Edward II sent twelve of them to study at Cambridge, an arrangement which developed into the endowment of a permanent college to house them, King's Hall, in 1337.[41] The career prospects of the boys continued to be good in later times. The Black Book notes that, when their voices broke, they were offered either an adult post in the chapel, a different office in the household, or a place at Cambridge or Oxford where they would be supported to study until

116   From Anglo-Saxon times, young men at home or away bonded through games or unruliness.

the king could give them further advancement.[42]

Many lesser lords acted in similar ways. Bishop Arundel, for example, promoted two of his choristers to posts as yeomen in 1383–4, music then (and later) being as likely to lead to secular as to clerical work.[43] A lord's death dealt a serious blow to such prospects, but he could still do a little for his young dependents in his will. In 1451, Sir Thomas Cumberworth, a knight of Somerby (Lincs.), left bequests to four boys of his household: 'little Tom', child of his hall, 'little Will' of his stable, and unnamed children of the kitchen and the shippon or cow-shed. Tom was given his master's hose, Will his boots and spurs, and the kitchen boy a pair of gloves – thick ones, perhaps, for handling hot utensils. Each of them also received a small sum of money and a yearling calf.[44] Child labour in households was to die out, like households themselves, in the twentieth century, but one of its skills remains today, though now done by a small adult: the jockey. In 1530 Henry VIII gave a reward of 10s. to a boy who 'ran' a white nag, as well as smaller sums to individual members of his 'riding children'.[45]

Reviewing how institutions function gives the impression that they work well, and not all households may always have done so. There must have been cases where children were exploited, or discharged without acquiring major skills or patrons. Peter Carew, a reluctant schoolboy, was attending St Paul's School London in the early 1520s, when the schoolmaster advised his father to take him away. The discomposed father, Sir William, went for a walk in St Paul's Cathedral where he met a gentleman friend, who served at the French court and offered to bring up Peter there 'like a gentleman'. Sir William provided his son with apparel and other things appropriate for a gentleman's page, but the new employer, on taking the boy to France, demoted him from his chamber to his stable, and made him a lackey in charge of his mule. Fortunately, in Peter's case, his family kept an eye on the situation; a relative came on a visit and rescued him.[46] Others may have been less lucky.

LEAVING HOME

IT FOLLOWED THAT growing up, for many children, meant leaving home. Going to school was one reason, because schools were not plentiful in the countryside and pupils were often obliged to go to a town and attend one there. Becoming an apprentice, taking service in a household, or entering a monastery usually required you to live under the roof of the employer concerned. Young noble children might be left in a family house while parents travelled elsewhere. Leaving home could be triggered by accident too. Among the gentry and nobility, the death of a father before his children grew up caused them to fall into the wardship of the feudal superior, who might take them into his custody or sell them into that of somebody else.[47] Even lower down in society, losing parents might involve children going away to live with relatives. Equally, not all left their homes. Sometimes, their labour was required to help with the family business or the work of the household. Sometimes, parents may have ignored the advantages of sending their offspring elsewhere, or have lacked the resources to do so.

There was no special age for leaving home. In the case of a ward or an orphan, the change might happen early in life, as it did in the case of the four-year-old Agnes Botoner in 1386.[48] Normally, however, it was understood that children would remain at home until the age of seven, and for a few years after that they were likely to go, if at all, to relatives or friends. The aristocracy, with their pattern of frequent movement, were an exception here, and we encounter children in nunneries – small boys under the age of ten and girls under that of fourteen – whose parents (probably noble or gentle in rank) put them in effect into a boarding school.[49] Dispatching a boy to a town school, to serve as a chorister, or to be educated in a great household, was likely to be delayed until he was at least ten. Thomas Whythorne, the Tudor musician, went from Somerset at that age to live with his clergyman uncle near Oxford in 1538.[50] Occasionally, boys may have left home to work before puberty, like William of Norwich, who was only in his eighth year when he was sent to work with a skinner in Norwich, perhaps because he had relatives living near his new employer.[51] But the major exodus from home to be an apprentice or servant probably took place for both sexes in the early teens, when childhood formally ended. As early as the seventh century, we are told that St Wilfrid left at fourteen to enter the Church and St Guthlac at fifteen to train as a warrior.[52] A similar pattern is likely in later times.

Leaving home can be a wounding experience. Parents may seem uncaring at such times, and children feel hurt and resentful. The emotions aroused can be remembered for life. Orderic Vitalis was a ten-year-old boy in Shropshire in 1085 when his father sent him to become a monk in the abbey of Saint-Evroult in Normandy. This was no brutal rejection; his father had planned the move three years before and had paid the abbey for the privilege. But Orderic left home, 'a weeping child', in the charge of a monk named Reginald, and remembered years later how he crossed the sea to France not knowing its language, because he obeyed his father and had been told that life as a monk would ensure his salvation. He never saw his father again.[53] Orderic became learned enough to write about his feelings, but there is no reason why they should not have been shared by those less educated. In the fourteenth-century romance *William of Palerne*, the hero (a lost prince) is brought up in humble circumstances by a herdsman. When, after a time, the boy's real father rediscovers him and takes him back to court, the author imagines his regrets on leaving his adopted family and friends. William asks his foster father to pass on his best wishes to all the lads with whom he has played – Hugonet and Huet, Abelot, Martynet, and Akarin – using their familiar forms, as a modern teenager might do.[54]

Difficulties of travel meant that even short-term absences to board at a nearby school or monastery tended to be longer than they are today. Alexander de la Pole, son of the earl of Suffolk, went only twenty miles from Wingfield (Suffolk) to school at Ipswich in September 1416, but he did not come home again until the following July. His sister Philippa travelled less far, ten miles to Bungay Priory in July, but she too stayed there for ten months, with the exception of a two-week holiday at Christmas.[55] At such distances, a child or young person might feel as isolated as in a foreign country. Dorothy, daughter of Sir Robert Plumpton of Plompton (Yorks.), was sent (apparently in her teens) to be brought up in the household of Lady Darcy at Birkin nearby, in the first decade of the sixteenth century. The distance was only about twenty-five miles, but the girl felt lonely and unhappy. She sent her father 'diverse messages and writings', and asked a traveller who was passing Plompton to relay a plea to come home. No answer was returned. In due course, Lady Darcy noticed her low spirits and reacted sympathetically, becoming 'to me more better lady than ever she was before' and promising to find her another place if she could. But Dorothy continued to feel neglected. Her father's failure to answer her, she told him in a letter, 'is thought in these parts by those persons that list [*like*] better to say ill than good, that you have little favour unto me, the which error you may now quench, if it will like you to be so good and kind father unto me'. Trying to finger some responsive chord, she asked for a fine hat and some good cloth to make kerchiefs.[56]

Late-medieval schoolbooks, reflecting the presence of boys away from home, say a good deal about this kind of separation though (not surprisingly) they tend to tone it down. A boy at Magdalen College School grieves that he is kept at school when others go home on holiday:

> Well is [it for] my school fellows which have leave to go see their fathers and mothers to sport them. As for me, I cannot so much as a moment depart from my master's side.[57]

Another looks forward to a visit from his parents, who appear to live twenty or thirty miles away:

As it is said, the next fair shall be kept here within this fortnight, and then I
ween my father and my mother will be here, and if they come, I put no doubt
but that I shall lack nothing that I have need of.[58]

A third takes comfort from a letter:

My brother hath written to me from London that my father and mother and all
my friends fare well, the which letter hath made me right merry. For why? The
more I love them, the more I rejoice [at] their health and welfare.[59]

A fourth is soothed by presents:

My father sent my brother and me 200 wardens [*pears*]. While I was absent my
brother hath chosen the best and left me the worst, but I am sure my father will
send us pomegranates other [*or*] oranges if there be any to be sold; then I shall
serve him likewise.[60]

A fifth goes home at last, reporting that on meeting his father and mother 'we
wept for joy, each to other'.[61]

By the later middle ages, literacy provided a means of bridging this gap. Those
of wealthier status, boarding at school or in a household, could write to their
parents and receive a written reply. Some light is thrown on this practice by collections of model letters, composed by schoolmasters (especially at Oxford) as part
of the process of teaching their pupils to write.[62] Although not real, and often
deliberately ironic, the letters suggest a practice of correspondence among the
families of the gentry or rich burgesses. Sons write to fathers complaining of their
poverty and asking for subventions; sometimes they call on their mothers for extra
help. Parents reply to sons, deploring the extravagence and bad behaviour of
which they have heard, and warning of the consequences. Mention is made of
letters from parents to teachers, suggesting that fathers and mothers used an alternative route to keep in touch with what their sons were doing. Once, a boy grieves
that he has had no reply from his father for a request of 10s. to settle his boarding
fees; the debt has now grown to 15s. The father replies indignantly that he
received no earlier letter, and sends the money together with a further 20s. for the
coming term.[63]

The trauma of leaving home is often increased by new surroundings.
Newcomers from elsewhere in medieval England might experience homesickness,
difficulties of communication (due to linguistic differences), bullying, and tyranny
from employers. More positively, the change led to the phase of life between childhood and marriage, in which family ties give place to comradeship (Fig. 117). We
have heard John Stow's account of girls in Tudor London, dancing in the street to
music, under the watchful eyes of their employers (Fig. 118).[64] Some such girls
may have joined parish companies of maidens. Youths bonded with others of
their kind: schoolboys, apprentices, or household servants. They shared, as they
do today, in a male adolescent culture, fondly remembered by the old men of

117 'Assay thy friend ere thou hast need.' Teenage comradeship might end in betrayal, as in the fable of the youth attacked by a bear and deserted by his friend.

Shakespeare's *Henry IV Part Two* as the time when 'lusty lads roam here and there' and ' 'Tis merry in hall when beards wag all'.[65] Even in a monastery, boys might make mischief together, like the four noble youths of Ramsey Abbey (Hunts.) who got into the abbey belfry in the late tenth century, jangled the bells, and broke one.[66] In a lay household, half military in character, such rowdiness might be worse. Bishop Grosseteste of Lincoln (1235–53), advised the countess of Lincoln to allow her adolescent and young adult 'grooms' to come into hall for meals only when their seniors were seated. Two men should be assigned to keep order and stop noise. The grooms should leave together, and care be taken in case they pilfered the left-over food, intended as alms for the poor.[67]

Youthful energy easily turned to violence in public: mimic among the younger (as in the battles of kings) and real among the older. Country youths pitted themselves against town youths, household servants against apprentices, guildsmen

118 Girls also bonded in conversation, dancing, and games – here playing blind man's buff.

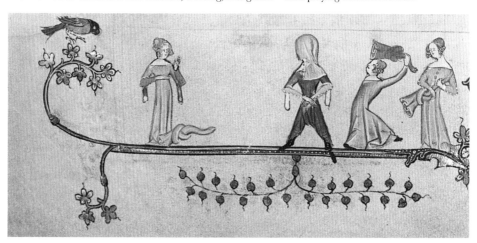

against guildsmen, all against foreigners. This was especially so in London, where each of these groups was larger than elsewhere.[68] Matthew Paris tells how, in 1253, young men of London played tournament games on horses with a quintain, arousing the jealousy of the junior staff of the royal household, who called them 'scurvy rustics' and 'soap-makers'. A fight began, in which the household men were put to flight, causing the angry king to fine the city.[69] Many London apprentices, it was said, joined in the Peasants' Revolt: a general uprising against authority, resulting in looting, paying off personal scores, and the murder of aliens such as Flemish immigrants.[70] Foreigners were targets again in 1455 when London apprentices assaulted the Lombards, provoking the intervention of the mayor and sheriffs and the trial and execution of two or three rioters.[71] Four years later, there were conflicts between the inhabitants of Fleet Street and those of the Inns of Court, mostly young men. Clifford's Inn was plundered, the Temple was invaded, and there were deaths on both sides.[72]

The worst of these conflicts was the famous Ill May Day of 1517, which was remembered for the rest of the century. It began with attacks on foreigners by young men on 28 April, and rumours circulated that the city would rise on May Day. Cardinal Wolsey replied by imposing a curfew on the night of the 30th, but when that evening Sir John Monday, one of the aldermen, tried to arrest two youths who were playing with swords and bucklers in Cheap, other young men came up and raised the cry of 'Prentices and clubs!', the traditional call to riot. The resulting disturbances lasted all night, involving men, youths, and children as young as thirteen. Prisons were broken open, shops looted, and houses sacked. When order was restored, a ringleader, John Lincoln, and thirteen others were hanged; lesser offenders were pardoned, after appearing before the king in Westminster Hall with halters round their necks.[73]

CHILDREN AND THE LAW

HOW OFTEN DID young people become involved with the law? Not at all, if both their parents were alive and if they were not accused of serious crime. A child with parents was not normally considered as having property of its own until it reached its teens and began to work and earn money.[74] If it was involved in damage or petty theft, its victims would seek redress from its father. The standard late-medieval treatise on manorial courts imagines a complaint about boys going into the the garden of the lord of the manor, and stealing fruit. Their fathers, not they, are called to answer the charge, and this occurred in practice.[75] The control of a child belonged to its parents, and if they administered punishment too severely or abused their children sexually, the child had no recourse to law. No one else was formally responsible for protecting its interests. A child could not be a witness against its parents, and its safety rested chiefly on the restraints imposed by public opinion.

The question then arose, as it does in every society, when childhood ended and adulthood began. When could a child undertake adult responsibilities, and incur adult punishments? In the Church, opinion varied about this, placing the water-shed at different times, for different purposes, between twelve and seventeen. Participation in confession and communion, as we have seen, probably began at puberty and liability to pay ecclesiastical dues at about the same age.[76] Men could take oaths, according to a Council of Rouen in 1096, from the age of twelve, but a century later Bishop Bartholomew of Exeter quoted another Church council to the effect that children should not be forced to do so until they were fourteen.[77] Later still, Winchester College required its scholars to swear oaths of allegiance only at fifteen, and Church courts did not normally allow children to give evidence until they were sixteen.[78] Wills of personal property (goods and chattels), which were administered in the Church courts, could be made by girls at twelve and boys at fourteen – a custom following that of Roman law. By the sixteenth century, however, an executor of a will was required to be at least seventeen.[79]

In the field of secular law, there were similar variations and a tendency also for age thresholds to rise as time went on. Laws from Kent and Wessex in the late seventh century regarded ten as the age at which a child no longer needed a guardian and could be tried as an accessory to a theft.[80] By the eleventh century, on the other hand, King Cnut (1016–35) provided that freemen should join the organisations of local government, the hundred and tithing, when they were twelve, and take an oath not to be a thief or the accomplice of one.[81] This requirement developed into the system of frankpledge. By the twelfth century, every boy who reached the age of twelve (other than members of the aristocracy, prosperous freeholders, and clergy) was obliged to swear to keep the peace, and was placed in a tithing of ten or twelve men. The group was responsible for its members' conduct and had to bring one another to court, if charged with a crime.[82] It followed that no youth could be outlawed until he was twelve, since he was not in the law.[83] Twelve, then, was the threshold of adulthood for keeping the peace, but this was not true for all legal purposes. Full criminal responsibility, as we shall see, came to be fixed at fourteen. The laws of Henry I (c.1118) made fifteen the age at which a child might bring a legal action, or sit on a jury.[84] In 1377–81, when Parliament sanctioned poll-taxes on the whole population, the age of liability was set first at fourteen, then sixteen, and finally fifteen.[85]

It is easy to prescribe the age at which an activity shall be lawful; more difficult to deal with unlawful actions. The age of criminal responsibility poses problems in all ages and societies.[86] While there is an instinct to moderate the law for children, children are capable of crimes so serious that they counteract the instinct. The Anglo-Saxons themselves were perplexed by these issues. Two of the laws of King Æthelstan (924–39) laid down that thieves seized in the act should be subject to the full rigour of the law if they were over twelve, which might involve the death penalty.[87] Later, Æthelstan thought this rule unsatisfactory when dealing with young offenders. He felt it cruel to execute

> such young people and for such slight offences as he has learnt is the practice everywhere. He has declared now that both he himself and those with whom he has discussed the matter, are of opinion that none should be slain who is

under fifteen years old, unless he is minded to defend himself or tries to escape
and refuses to give himself up.

Only youths who resisted or re-offended beneath that age were to be killed. Those
who submitted to the law were to be imprisoned and then liberated, or made to
find surety for their good behaviour.[88]

We know little more about the treatment of children for crimes until the thirteenth century, when evidence begins to survive about those accused of causing
the death of others – 'homicide' in legal terminology.[89] By that time, two contrasting views were held about such children, as is the case today. One was that
crimes and injuries are absolute and have to be paid for, whoever does them,
however accidentally. The other, promoted both by natural feelings and by the
Church, saw children as defective in understanding, limited in ability to sin, and
needing special treatment if they did.[90] The first view was responsible for the
imprisonment of even young children, involved in unintentional homicide, until
they could be tried at the next arrival of the king's justices. An extreme case was
that of Katherine Passeavant, aged four, in 1249. She had allegedly opened a
door, thereby pushing a younger child into a vessel of hot water, with fatal results.
She was confined in the abbot of St Albans's gaol to await trial. A few similar
cases are recorded involving children aged between six and eleven. In one
of them, a six-year-old boy actually died in prison before the justices could hear
his case.

Such actions show a substantial lack of consideration, by modern standards, for
tender minds and bodies. They reflect, of course, the belief that the operation of
the law and the rights of the victim should, in the first instance, have priority over
the age of the child. Homicide was a serious matter. Only when the justices heard
the case or the king was informed about it, could the child's status be taken into
account. At that point there was indeed consideration for children, even in the
thirteenth century. In Katherine Passeavant's case, her father appealed to the king
before her trial, the king pardoned her, and told the local sheriff to release her. In
other instances when children accidentally killed one another, the accused child
had to wait in prison until the justices arrived but was then freed or, at most,
remanded back to prison until the king issued a pardon. Such pardons were freely
given to children, though they usually had to be actively sought by the child's
family and sometimes required the child to stand trial on coming of age, if the
victim's family wished to pursue the matter.

Leniency was extended even to those who committed homicide with a degree
of violence and deliberation. A boy of six who hit another on the head with a
stone, causing his death, gained a pardon without any plea that the blow had been
an accident. By the 1270s, too, the justices were taking a more positive view of
children's status than merely recommending them for pardon. They were beginning to acquit those brought before them, on the grounds that the accused were
too young to have committed an offence. In 1302, Henry Spigurnel, a prominent
royal justice, spoke in court on behalf of the moderation of the law where children were concerned. Trying some young men in 1302 for the manslaughter of a

person whom (they claimed) they had found stealing wheat, he observed that a child who committed a crime before the age of seven should not suffer judgment at all. A child of seven to twelve should answer for a crime only if it affected life or limb, because until that age it was not sworn to keep the peace.[91]

Then as now, of course, the justices were occasionally confronted with children who had done a wicked crime while apparently fully aware of its wickedness. In 1299, a boy named Thomas of Hordlegh, from Great Chart (Kent) or nearby, was tried for murder at Maidstone by Spigurnel and a colleague. A jury of local people reported that Thomas, while passing through a certain unnamed village, entered the house of Thomas Gibelot and found it untenanted save for his daughter Joan, aged five. When Thomas tried to steal some bread, Joan protested, at which the boy grabbed a hatchet, hit her on the head to stop her cries, and killed her. The justices asked the age of the boy at the time of the offence, and were told that he was ten. They found the accusation proved, and Thomas was sentenced to hang.[92] Spigurnel recalled the case some fourteen years later, when he was judging another teenage crime. He remembered that the boy, when sentenced, was eleven, and he justified the decision on the ground that Thomas knew what he was doing: 'the fact that, after having killed the child, he also hid its body, was taken as evidence of his heinous malice, and he was condemned'.[93]

We hear of one or two other such executions. The hanging of a 'boy' of unspecified age at St Albans in 1243 led to protests by local people.[94] A fourteenth-century source refers to the burning of a girl of thirteen (the usual capital punishment for women), because she had killed the mistress to whom she was servant.[95] But punishments like these must have been unusual, even in a more violent society. By the sixteenth century, the law in general had adopted Spigurnel's view that a child below the age of seven could not be guilty of a felony – a serious crime. Between the ages of seven and twelve or fourteen, there was a strong presumption to the same effect, though it could be rebutted. Only over the age of puberty, at twelve or fourteen, was someone fully capable of committing a felony, an age fixed definitely at fourteen by the seventeenth century.[96] Once past that threshold, on the other hand, young people were treated as adults and, from our point of view, with little regard to their youth (Fig. 119). In January 1538, a 'boy' servant of Thomas Culpepper, gentleman of the king's privy chamber, was tried at Westminster and convicted of stealing his master's purse, containing £11 of money, and a jewel belonging to the king. He was condemned to death and ordered to be hanged in the tilt-yard of the Palace of Westminster next day.

The execution reached the point at which the hangman was taking away the ladder on which the youth stood, when the king's pardon arrived 'and so he was saved from death, to the great comfort of all the people there present'.[97] Richard Mekins was less fortunate; in 1540–1, he was burnt for heresy at Smithfield under the draconian 'Act of Six Articles'. The chronicler Edward Hall reported that the 'child', as he called him, was not more than fifteen when he spoke heretical opinions about the eucharist and criticised the execution, also for heresy, of Dr Robert Barnes. Mekins was tried before commissioners, including Edmund Bonner, bishop of London, and although two juries failed to convict

119 Teenage crime was blamed on bad parenting. A youth attacks his mother for her negligence as he goes to the gallows.

him, a third did so. He repented in prison and 'was taught', according to Hall, to speak good of the bishop and to curse the time that ever he knew Dr Barnes. He was burnt nevertheless.[98] As in the middle ages, such cases were rare and aroused people's pity. They do not point to a regular practice of treating the young like their elders.

If relatively few children were caught in the net of the criminal law, far more – and of a wider spread of ages – became involved with the law of property. This was an issue when a father or mother died, leaving an inheritance to which the child had a claim. Questions then arose about who should administer the property until the child reached a suitable age to do so.[99] Usually, there was a need to provide for the care of the child as well, a care often considered to include the arrangement of its marriage. The regulation of these matters varied, depending on the type of property and the gender of the child. Property might be moveable (goods or chattels) or immovable (lands and tenements). During the middle ages, the custom grew up that a father should leave a third of his moveable goods to his wife and a third to his children, if he had any, or half to the children if he had no wife.[100] Such goods would, in practice, have been guarded and administered by those who looked after the children concerned, but that was a separate issue and one that was chiefly determined by the other kind of property: lands and tenements or 'realty'.

At the top of society, the nobility and gentry held their lands by feudal tenure from a superior lord who might be the king, another member of the nobility, or an important ecclesiastic such as a bishop or abbot. In this form of tenure, property legally passed to the eldest son by the principle known as primogeniture, though most fathers made provision during their lives for their other children. If there was no son, the property was divided equally among the daughters. When a father died leaving a male heir under the age of twenty-one or a female heir under fourteen, however, the heir was not allowed to administer the property until reaching that age.[101] Instead, both he or she and the property passed into the wardship of the superior lord – a custom which may go back to the Norman Conquest, and was certainly common by the twelfth century. A small child and its brothers or sisters might be left in the care of the mother.[102] Older children were often taken into the household of the lord, and brought up there. But, whoever had the custody of the child-heir, the lord had ultimate control of the heir's affairs. He or she had the right to administer its property, and bestow its marriage. These rights could be given or sold to someone else, and often were: royal wardships, in particular, passed as favours to courtiers.

Wardship became a controversial matter during the reign of King John (1199–1216), because of his alleged abuses of the system. In 1215, his opponents inserted clauses 3–6 into Magna Carta to give wards more protection. These provided that lords or guardians should take only reasonable produce, customs, and services from their wards' properties, and avoid laying them waste. Those who failed to do so would be deprived of their wardships. They had the duty to maintain buildings and equipment, and to ensure that the property was stocked with ploughs and carts when the heir came of age. The king was to allow his wards to inherit without imposing charges upon them ('relief' and 'fine'), and guardians who arranged their wards' marriages were not to 'disparage' them by matching them with unsuitable partners.[103] In 1263, the Statute of Merton defined disparagement as marriage with a burgess or villein – a definition later extended to a bastard, a foreigner, or anyone defective in mind or body such as a lunatic, a disabled person, or a woman unable to bear a child.[104]

Beneath the nobility and gentry were those who held their lands by socage tenure in the countryside and burgage tenure in the towns. The property of these people – prosperous rural freeholders and urban merchants, shopkeepers, and craftsmen – descended differently from that of the aristocracy. In some places, it was shared by the sons in equal portions or, lacking sons, by the daughters.[105] In others, it was inherited by one son, who could be the eldest but was more often the youngest. The latter custom, named 'borough English' from the 'English' part of Nottingham where it applied, may reflect the assumption that a father would provide for his older children while he was alive.[106] At this level of society, it was rare for a superior lord to have rights of wardship. Socage or borough heirs and their property usually passed to the guardianship of the nearest relative who was not a potential inheritor, likely to harm the child or its interests. A child's mother was the obvious choice in such cases. In the absence of a mother, the guardian was picked from her family if the child's property came from the father, and from his family if it came from the mother.[107]

Up to the reign of Henry III, a guardian in socage appears to have had similar rights to those of a feudal lord over his ward's property and marriage. In 1267, however, the Statute of Marlborough introduced important qualifications. It laid down that the guardian could bestow the heir in marriage, or sell the marriage, only if this was to the heir's profit. And when the heir inherited, the guardian had to return the profits arising from the property during the heir's minority.[108] Young socage heirs usually took control of their property earlier than feudal heirs, in their mid teens. Henry Bracton, writing in the mid thirteenth century, states that a youth inherited a socage tenancy when he was fifteen and strong enough to work the land himself. A girl did so in her fourteenth or fifteenth year when she knew how to run a household and understood what belonged to *cove and keye* ('store-chamber and key').[109] A burgess's son could inherit when he knew how to count money, measure cloth, or do similar tasks – that is to say, when he could handle such matters like an adult.[110]

Lower still in social ranking came those who were not free, who lived in the countryside, and held their property – a smallholding or a cottage – by villein tenure. Technically villeins had no property of their own, either realty or chattels, since they and all they had belonged to their lords. When a villein father died leaving young children, the lord of the manor had the right to take decisions about the future of the father's possessions and the custody of the children. Normally, the family's expectation to keep its holding of land was respected, but the lord would ensure that a suitable guardian looked after it and after the children, until one of the latter was capable of doing the services or paying the rent due from the land. Such a guardian might be the widow, a relative, or another senior man who lived on the manor. If a villein had more than one child, there were different customs about inheritance, varying from manor to manor. As in higher society, these might favour the eldest son, the youngest son, or all the sons, and if there were no sons, daughters would succeed with a similar mixture of practice.[111]

The topic of children and the law, then, was a complicated one. It differed according to status, gender, and property. There was no single age of responsibility or majority. In the early seventeenth century, Sir Edward Coke discerned seven age-thresholds of noble girls alone.[112] Aspects of adult life seeped down to the early years of childhood in a manner astonishing today. Tiny girls and boys could be joined in marriage, or be put permanently into religious houses. Children nearly as young might suffer imprisonment, and be executed from about the age of ten in exceptional cases. The formal demarcations between childhood and adulthood were often placed lower than they are today, between the ages of twelve and fifteen. But these possibilities should not be exaggerated. Those who inherited, married, or were punished in their mid-teens were exceptions. Most people's adulthood, in the modern sense, was postponed until much later. Noble and gentle heirs did not inherit until twenty-one, allegedly because their military duties needed greater strength and understanding.[113] In the world of work, apprentices came out of service only in their twenties, and in that of the Church, clerks could be made priests only at twenty-four. Children who followed their parents' occupations stood in their parents' shadow until their twenties, sometimes longer. Most, partly for that reason, did not marry until then. On the whole, young people were not propelled suddenly from childhood into adulthood. There was (as there is today) a long intermediate period of youth or adolescence, with its own culture, as literary writers so often observed.[114]

SEXUALITY

EVERY MEDIEVAL CHILD was assigned a gender on the day of its birth, a gender proclaimed in public. Taken to church for baptism, it was placed (if a girl) on the priest's left side, and (if a boy) on his right. Its name was given, usually one distinctly male or female. Toddlers soon acquired a sense of their gender and of the opposite one, partly from how they were treated, partly from what they observed.[115] But gender boundaries are not always simple. There must have been unboyish boys and ungirlish girls in the middle ages, as in any society, and those who (for some reason or other) wished to cross the line. Ambiguity of this kind could be hazardous and unpopular. Words like 'effeminate', 'feminine', and 'womanish' were in derogatory use for men by at least the fifteenth century, and wild girls were known as 'tomboys' in Shakespeare's day.[116] Equally, males at least could safely take on attributes of the opposite sex in certain circumstances. One's surname could be that of one's mother, not one's father, perhaps through being brought up by a widow. Names like Annett, Marriot, and Parnell are examples. A boy might cross-dress as a chorister, a St Katherine's Day singer, or a character in a play. Even a knight like Perceval in Arthurian legend might be called, with approval, a 'maiden', not because he was woman-like but because he was chaste.

Sexuality, as distinct from gender, may be learnt from our peers, our elders, rhymes, or books. All were available for this purpose in the middle ages. A mother's song to a baby might tell of a lecher who seeks to seduce a girl.[117] In homes where privacy was often restricted, young people may have become aware of the sexual activity of adults sooner than happens today. Some, victims of child abuse, encountered it all too early.[118] Boys who went to grammar schools learnt to say *amo*, 'I love', as their first verb. They were taught the parts of the human body in Latin, including the male and female sexual organs, and composed or translated sentences in which sexual relations were mentioned.[119] Romances provided further oblique information.[120] Early-Tudor writers, as we have seen, lamented the use of sexual words by children, such as 'whore' and 'cuckold', and the complacency of parents when this occurred.[121] Many adults, it seems, were not concerned to keep their offspring innocent of such matters. Even the Church, by excusing children from its rules about confession, implied that childish sexual play and invective, imperfectly understood and incapable of fulfilment, were matters not worth its attention.

From about eleven or so, we experience changes in our physical shape and characteristics as we advance to puberty: the onset of our reproductive powers. Bartholomew noted some of these changes in his encyclopaedia. Boys grow in size and muscularity. Girls develop in a different way, their upper bodies staying narrow and their lower broadening between the navel and the knees. Puberty itself is signalled by the acquisition of pubic hair and changes in the voice. Young people become self-conscious when naked, which is not the case among children.[122] Medieval writers understood that girls reached puberty first, and conventionally reckoned this to happen at twelve, and at fourteen for boys. The difference of age required an explanation, one of which was that women's bodies were hotter than men's and therefore developed earlier. Another suggested that more time was needed to develop the power to generate children than to bear them, and a third said sourly that bad plants grow more quickly![123]

How accurate were the conventional dates of puberty? This is a complicated question, because the onset of reproductive powers differs from person to person. It ranges in the modern western world from about ten for girls and eleven for boys, until about sixteen, but most commonly happens to girls between about twelve and thirteen and to boys about a year later. There were also variations in the middle ages, and these were recognised by contemporaries. The English canon lawyer William Lyndwood believed correctly that exceptional children might experience puberty early in childhood. Less accurately, he located the threshold for this at seven in the case of a girl and nine in that of a boy, citing Gregory the Great about a nurse made pregnant by a boy of that age. In fact, rare cases are recorded even younger. In 1414, a Welsh girl and boy appeared with their baby, she allegedly seven and he nine. They were given to the earl of March as a marvel, and impressed him so much that he sent them to the king, Henry V.[124] Scholarly writers accepted too that a boy might not be sexually mature at fourteen. Not until he was eighteen did they feel it safe to assume that he was congenitally impotent.

Most medieval people probably reached puberty in the early to mid teens, just as they do today. Girls could be sexually fertile by the age of twelve, especially if they came from the better-fed upper orders of society. Mary Bohun, the first wife of the future Henry IV, conceived her first child in the summer of 1381 when she was about twelve and her husband just over fifteen.[125] Lady Margaret Beaufort was impregnated with her son Henry VII in late April 1456, about a month short of her thirteenth birthday. Thomas duke of Clarence, who died in the battle of Beaugé in 1421 at the age of about thirty-three, must have sired his illegitimate son John at about fifteen, since John was old enough to rescue his body.[126] The Virgin Mary herself was thought to have been only fifteen when Jesus was born – an assumption which tallied with the custom of portraying her in art like a noble girl of the day.[127] Puberty among poorer and less well-nourished children may have lagged by a year or two, but its normal onset does not seem to have been vastly later, as is sometimes suggested. Penitential treatises of the sixth century lay down penances for boys of twelve who masturbate (apparently boys in monasteries) and for 'boys' (as opposed to men) who fornicate.[128] The Church and the common law allowed girls to marry permanently at twelve and boys at fourteen, evidently assuming that they could consummate their marriages at those ages.[129] Evidence about boy choristers in the fifteenth century points to their voices breaking at fourteen or, at most, a year later.[130]

We know about the sexuality of Henry IV, Mary Bohun, and Lady Margaret because they married in their early or mid teens and soon produced children. This practice, as we shall see, was largely confined to the wealthy. Most people's marriages were delayed till their twenties, when they had mastered adult skills and, in the case of men, acquired a permanent job or an inheritance.[131] For the vast majority of young people, there was a long period of ten or twelve years in which their sexuality could not be expressed within marriage and had to be managed in other ways. In the view of the Church, this could be done only through chastity. It was sinful to have sex with a woman except for one's wife. It was worse still to engage in masturbation or homosexual sex. Both of these were seen as actions, not orientations, but both came to be regarded by theologians and Church lawyers as unnatural in principle and sinful in practice, especially after the eleventh and twelfth centuries. There was a sharp, severe condemnation of homosexual acts from a Church council at London in 1102, and they are mentioned disapprovingly in some later Church legislation.[132] Bartholomew attacked those who used their organs against the law of nature, not to beget children, and Thomas Aquinas placed such people in the worst class of sexual sinners. To the objection that masturbation did not involve anyone else, he replied that, on the contrary, it was an injury to God.[133]

These views, however, were not necessarily expounded by parish clergy or held by lay people. References to masturbation are rare outside scholarly writings. The Latin words to describe it, *masturbatio*, *mollicies*, and *pollutio*, seldom occur, and their English counterparts are elusive.[134] In the thirteenth century, some Church leaders advised clergy to enquire about 'unnatural' sex during confession, a heading which would have involved both masturbation and homosexual acts.[135] But two of the most influential writers for the parish clergy in the later middle ages seem little concerned with either subject. John Mirk recommended confessors to run through heterosexual activities, lustful thoughts, and nocturnal emissions.[136] John de Burgh suggested asking men about sex with others than their wives, apparently more concerned with husbands than adolescents.[137] In practice, young people, especially boys, must often have masturbated for experiment or pleasure, without reproof. Even homosexuality was not much of an issue outside monasteries, perhaps because it was not viewed as a permanent disposition. Mirk indeed counselled parish clergy not to preach about it; maybe he feared encouraging people to do it.[138] The prince of Wales, later Edward II, had a famous relationship with Piers Gaveston in the early 1300s, which may have had a sexual dimension, but contemporary writers do not say so. When Edward I sent Gaveston into exile, he seems to have done so not on sexual grounds but because the prince had asked for him to be given a major royal fiefdom.[139]

The vast majority of evidence about adolescent sex in medieval society relates to contacts between young men and women. This, to commentators, constituted the heart of sexual activity. Then as now, youths and girls flocked together in groups for recreation, to dance, play games, and make or listen to music.[140] Some such encounters were purely social; others had an emotional side (Fig. 120). One thirteenth-century song tells how the boys competed at feats of strength while a girl watched and selected one as her lover:

> At stone-casting my lemman [*lover*] I chose,
> And at wrestling I did him lose.
> Alas! that he so soon fell;
> Why stood he not better, vile gorrel [*low, fat fellow*]?[141]

Such emotions might lead further still. The early thirteenth-century poem, 'A Little True Sermon', portrays young men and women of the parish gathering together at church on holy days. One girl is more interested in her sweetheart Watkin than in the worship; her Lord's Prayer is left at home. Another, named Gilot, lets Robin take her to the ale-house. Then, in the evening, they go off by themselves and make love. Her parents scold her about her attachment, and threaten to beat her, but she refuses to give him up. In the end she falls pregnant.[142] Several songs survive from the fourteenth or fifteenth centuries, telling how dancing, dressing a holy well, and even church attendance lead to the seduction of girls by clerks, priests, or travelling chapmen.[143] Some of the songs approach the subject with humour and look as if they were meant to amuse young men. One or two concentrate on the girls' despair at their predicament, and may have been intended to warn young women.

Teenage sex and pregnancies could be as surprising and unwelcome to adults as they are today. 'Is it not a wonder to see a boy do such a deed?' wrote John Palsgrave in 1530. 'I weened he had not been able to beget a child.'[144] Clergy

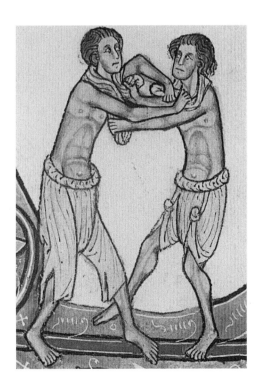

120 'At stone-casting my lover I chose, and at wrestling I did him lose.' Medieval sports, like modern ones, might have erotic undertones.

121 'Prostitutes and other dirty things'. A
young man meets a common woman.

denounced such things in sermons and writings, and enquired about them in confessions. Church courts had a jurisdiction over fornication and could, in principle, call up offenders. Whether this was done in the case of a casual pregnancy
is uncertain, though it is always possible that an angry family may have initiated
Church-court proceedings to make a father accept responsibility. From the
eleventh and twelfth centuries, lords of manors levied penalties called *leirwite*
('lying fine') when one of their villein women was found to have fornicated, and
childwite ('child fine') when one of them had a child outside marriage. On one
large manor, that of Wakefield (Yorks.), fines were imposed on seven girls or
women of the manor in 1316 alone for what was there called *lecherwytt*, or 'lechery
fine'.[145] On another, that of Broughton (Hunts.), twenty-six extra-marital births
were recorded and penalised between 1288 and 1340.[146] The motives for such
fines may have varied. Lords may have taken the opportunity to gain money from
a breach of social conventions, or they may have feared that women with illegitimate children would not get married. That would rob the lord of another
payment, *merchet*, paid by villeins when their daughters wed.[147]

There is no reason to think that medieval society was unduly permissive about
teenage pregnancy compared with our own.[148] Many parents seem to have taken
as strong a line against it as the clergy. One fifteenth-century song imagines a girl
coming home after spending the night out, to be met by an angry mother:

> The other day at prime [*early morning*] I came home, as I ween;
> Met I my dame [*mother*], bad-tempered and keen:
> 'Say, thou strong strumpet, where hast thou been?
> Thy tripping and thy dancing, well it will be seen!'

The tirade ends with a clout from the dame to the girl.[149] Parents with children
away from home did their best to provide advice and exert control. Two of the
model letters mentioned above express fears by fathers that teenage sons in
Oxford are spending their time and money on 'prostitutes, brothels, and other
dirty things' (Fig. 121).[150] An apprentice's indenture, as we have seen, might rule
out sexual contact both in his master's household and outside. Geoffrey de la Tour
Landry grew anxious even about his daughters. As noblewomen, they were
subject to supervision and would not have wandered the parish with boys, but he

122   Young women were constantly warned about vanity and lust. A girl preoccupied with her comb and mirror is ridiculed by a devil behind her.

was still concerned to warn them about bodily temptations (Fig. 122). He urged them to fast three or four days in the week to subdue the flesh, and recounted a number of cautionary tales in which men seduced women with tragic results.[151]

A trio of English poems in the fifteenth century gave similar advice to parents and daughters of burgess and yeoman families. *How the Good Wife Taught her Daughter* tells girls to walk demurely, and avoid taverns and popular sports. If any man courts and offers to marry them, they should answer him guardedly and discuss his offer with their families.[152] *The Good Wife Would a Pilgrimage* envisages more dangerous situations. It counsels girls against going from house to house, among young men, because they will say that you are 'nice' (a word originally meaning 'wanton') and encourage you to do wrong. Girls spending a holiday in company, dancing, singing, or playing, should not hang their girdles low, but take the knot away and wear no beads. Clothes that showed their legs should be avoided, lest men think them reckless of their bodies. Only by care will a girl avoid temptation and secure a good husband.[153] *The Thews of Good Women* is also concerned with potential loss of virtue. Girls should be careful to avoid getting drunk when good drink is available. They should not sit up late, drinking, calling 'wassail' and 'drink-hail', but go to bed early. Holidays should be spent at worship, and girls should shun male sports like wrestling and cock-steling, because women who attend these are strumpets or 'gigelots'.[154]

CHILD MARRIAGE

FOR A SMALL number of people, marriage took place before they reached their twenties. In families of noble, gentle, or merchant rank, there was a tradition that parents should arrange their children's matches, and that this could be done at any point after infancy (Fig. 123). Marriage, in such families, was linked with important issues of rank and property. Family pride and status required children to take partners equal (or superior) to their own degree. Parents saw marriage as a way of providing for sons by joining them to heiresses or girls with dowries, and of ensuring that daughters were maintained in their accustomed style of life. All this was more easily achieved when children were younger and more pliable. If they did not marry young, there was the danger that fathers might die and children fall into the wardship of a guardian. In that case, the guardian would arrange a marriage in his interests, not those of the family. Child marriage avoided such an outcome.

It was never universal, even among the rich. In the royal family, there were more projects to get children married than substantive marriages. Most royal brides and bridegrooms were in their teens and technically adults. The children of the Paston family in the fifteenth century married between nineteen and thirty-three, but mostly in their twenties, and Margery Kempe, although the daughter of the mayor of King's Lynn, did not do so until she was twenty 'or somewhat more'.[155] Nevertheless, there are examples of the practice in all the higher levels of society: royal, noble, and gentle.[156] Joan of the Tower, daughter of Edward II, married Prince David of Scotland in 1328 when he was four and she was seven.[157] Richard II wed Isabel of France in 1396, a week short of her seventh birthday, although she was given the right to change her mind at twelve.[158] Normally, no more is known of child weddings than that they occurred, but by the Tudor period picturesque accounts survive in Church-court records. One is that of the marriage of John Somerford and Joan Brereton, offspring of a gentleman and knight of Cheshire, who were joined in Brereton church in the county in 1552. He was three and she was two. John's uncle later testified that he carried the boy in his arms at the wedding and spoke some of the marriage vows 'that the said John, by reason of his young age, could not speak himself'. Another adult said the words for Joan.[159]

When children had no parents, the parental power over their marriages passed to their guardians or overlords. Guardians had a legal right to arrange the

123 Marriage involved not
only two partners but their
families, and often led to tensions
between personal and family
wishes.

matches of their wards, just as they had to administer their property. Bracton,
summarising the position in the mid thirteenth century, states that a male heir
without a father might marry whom he wished only if he was an adult out of
wardship. A female heir in the same situation must get her lord's permission, even
in adulthood. If an heir was under age and in feudal wardship or socage
guardianship, the guardian had control of the marriage and could arrange it personally or sell the right to do so to another person. These rights were becoming
modified a little by Bracton's time. Magna Carta provided that a feudal heir
should not be disparaged with a marriage to someone of lower rank; a lord who
broke that rule stood to forfeit the wardship.[160] Socage heirs, as we have seen,
acquired some protection from the Statute of Marlborough, which ordered that
the ward's marriage must be for his or her profit.

   The greatest support for the rights of children in marriage, however, came not
from the crown but the Church. To the clergy, a valid and permanent marriage
required the free consent of the partners, taken at an age when they fully understood what they were doing and could consummate their union sexually. These
requirements made marriage possible only after puberty. 'Where there is no
consent by both parties', states the *Decretum* of Gratian, the great handbook of
canon law, 'there is no marriage. Those who give boys to girls in their cradles
achieve nothing unless each of the children consents when it comes to the age of
discretion, even if the father and mother have arranged and willed the marriage'.[161] In 1175 an English Church council at Westminster repeated these words,
though it weakened them by conceding that younger marriages might be made in
exceptional cases to bring about peace.[162] Some Church leaders added their own
disapproval of young brides or bridegrooms. St Hugh of Lincoln frowned on a
marriage that took place in the late twelfth century between Adam de Neville and

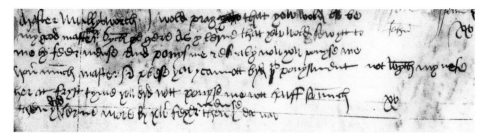

124   'You punish me overmuch and I cannot bide this punishment.' Robert Yall's pitiful complaint to his tutor.

his four-year-old ward, the heiress of the Hartshill family in Lincolnshire. The marriage went ahead, but Hugh told his clergy not to attend it.[163] At least four bishops of the thirteenth century forbade the marriage of pre-pubescent children, one adding the rider that his consent was necessary.[164]

The Church's view was a powerful one, since what the clergy said they were able to put into effect officially. The division of the law between the Church and the lay authorities gave the Church jurisdiction over marriages until the nineteenth century. Questions of what was a valid marriage and what was not were decided in the Church courts, normally within each diocese but occasionally at a higher level, and exceptionally (in a case like that of Henry VIII and Katherine of Aragon) in the court of the pope himself. Robert of Flamborough, in his penitential written between 1208 and 1215, confirmed that no child could marry or promise to do so before the age of seven. After that, a promise might be made to marry in the future, but it could not be finalised until the age of puberty when, by implication, it could be completed sexually. Robert likewise fixed this age at twelve for girls and fourteen for boys.[165] Lyndwood's attitude, in the fifteenth century, was similar. A betrothal or engagement could take place at seven, but a binding marriage was possible only at the ages laid down in the Council of Westminster, effectively the same as those set out by Robert.[166]

The clergy's refusal to regard a marriage as binding until puberty meant that, until then, it was provisional and could be undone. Those cases of child marriage that came into the Church courts represent failures of the arrangements. They arose because one or more of the parties or families repented of the fact before the marriage was consummated, and applied to have it annulled. Witnesses were then brought who were careful to stress the formal nature of the marriage, the youth of the participants, the lack of consent, and the absence of physical contact. This allowed the Church to implement its policies about consent and consummation, and to annul the marriage. John Somerford and Joan Brereton, it appears, lived together at Brereton or at least saw each other regularly for ten years after their marriage, but when they came to puberty (John being fifteen and Joan about a year younger) they refused to ratify the marriage. John's uncle attributed the fact to Joan's 'unkindness', but another witness claimed that both young people were loath to proceed.[167]

We know little about how marriages were offered to children and teenagers, and how far choice or compulsion entered into the process. No doubt circumstances varied. Very small children must have been cajoled into their matches without real understanding. Bishop Fisher stated in his funeral sermon for Lady Margaret Beaufort that she was offered a choice between marrying John de la Pole, son of the duke of Suffolk, and Edmund Tudor, earl of Richmond, when she was not yet nine.[168] In fact, she had already made a childhood marriage with John, and when she was consulted about leaving him for Edmund, she must have been at least nine and may have been twelve. By the teens, a young person's views must have mattered and might be unfavourable. Some youths and maidens were capable of resisting parental pressure, causing serious family disputes. We have seen how Agnes Paston beat her twenty-year-old daughter Elizabeth for spurning a proffered match, but Elizabeth remained stubborn and won her point.[169] A generation later, Agnes's grand-daughter Margery caused a still greater furore at about the same age by becoming engaged to her family's bailiff, Richard Calle – a man of lower rank. Her mother forbade her to enter the house and her elder brothers expressed their indignation. One predicted that she would end up selling candles and mustard in Framlingham. The bishop of Norwich was asked to investigate the engagement and to press Margery to break it off – to no avail. The obstinate lovers got married.[170]

Nor were free choice and consent altogether denied to children who were under the care of a guardian. Here the English common law was also involved, to the extent of sorting out the financial aspects of the matter. By the thirteenth century, a youth in feudal wardship could legally refuse the marriage proposed by his guardian, provided that he paid compensation on reaching his majority, so that the guardian did not lose by the arrangement. The amount was fixed at what anyone else would have paid to secure the heir's marriage. A ward could marry without his guardian's licence if he was over fourteen, but in that case the guardian could administer the inheritance beyond the age of majority to recoup the value of his loss. The Statute of Merton allowed the lord twice the value.[171] A female ward could refuse her marriage too, but if she did so her guardian could prolong her wardship until she was twenty-three 'as a mark of displeasure at contradiction and disobedience'.[172] In practice, guardians seem to have treated marriage simply as a financial perquisite. If heirs and heiresses wished to select their own spouses, they did so and paid the guardian for his loss – sometimes after the marriage.[173]

There were provisions, then, to protect the freedom of young people to choose their marriages. But we must remember that most such marriages never came before the law and have left no record of the partners' opinions. The likelihood is that parents had their way in some cases, and that some children entered marriage without a real consent. Such marriages could also be shortlived. Even Mary Bohun was no more than twenty-five when she died in 1394, having borne at least seven children.

STORIES AND MEMORIES

IT IS EASY to find evidence about medieval children as they were seen by others. But what have they told us themselves? We are not well supplied with personal records made by young people. The best are school notebooks, which contain not only school-work but scraps of songs and scribbles.[174] Chaucer's Squire 'could songs make' and his poem *Troilus and Criseyde* features a song composed by a Trojan 'maid' who seems to have been envisaged as a young adult like the Squire.[175] Real teenage boys or girls may have written or adapted verses or tunes, but any such work is lost in the anonymity of most extant medieval lyrics. Letters were probably more often composed than lyrics by those of wealth and literacy, as we see from the model collections, but few real children's letters survive. One of the earliest is a draft of a letter or a speech, scribbled in the margin of a book during the last years of Henry VII's reign (Fig. 124). The writer was apparently a schoolboy named Robert Yall who was under the tutelage of a fellow of Magdalen College Oxford and, very likely, a pupil at the college grammar school. His spelling is worth printing as he wrote it:

> *Master Mullysworth, I wold pray and beseytt yow that yow wold be my good master, for syche gere as y lerne that yow wold sew ytt to me by feer mense and ponys me resnably. Now yow ponyse me houer much, master, and plese yow, y cannot byd this ponysment. Her at fryst tyme yow dyd nott ponyse me nott hauff so much; then y dyd lerne more by yowr feyer mense then I doo now.*

Master Mullysworth, I would pray and beseech you that you would be my good master; for such gear [*matters*] as I learn that you would show it to me by fair means and punish me reasonably. Now you punish me overmuch, master, and, please you, I cannot abide this punishment. Here at first time you did not punish me not half so much; then I did learn more by your fair means than I do now.[176]

This contains pleasing traces of immaturity, although the writer may well have been in his early teens.

Such letters as exist in finished form are less obviously childlike. Edward IV and his brother Edmund 'wrote' two letters in English to their father, Richard duke of York, in about 1454. They were twelve and eleven respectively, but may have been helped to write by a schoolmaster or a secretary. Their letters are carefully formulated, addressing the duke in respectful terms, and one of them affirms that the boys are attending to their learning.[177] In the other, they acknowledge the gift of green gowns and ask for a prayer book and some fine bonnets. The boys' style differs little from that of an adult, and much the same is true of the Paston Letters, some fifteen of which originate from young men of the family between the ages of sixteen and twenty.[178] One, written by William Paston II at sixteen in 1452 conveys a youthful excitement in its gossip about a local cleric who has been slandering the family. Another, by the nineteen-year-old William Paston III in 1479, breathes a certain callowness in its confidences about an eligible girl he has met, mixed with his pride at a Latin couplet that he has written as a pupil of Eton College.[179] Generally, however, Paston youths wrote in a mature and business-like fashion by their late teens.

One further letter is worth mentioning here, though it was written to a young person rather than by one. In 1476, Thomas Betson, a merchant of Calais, was courting Katherine Ryche, the stepdaughter of his partner William Stonor of Stonor (Oxon.). She was almost a child in our terms, aged thirteen or so, but almost an adult in theirs. They corresponded. Katherine sent Thomas a 'token' and a letter written by her stepfather's squire, and his reply survives. In part, it is an adult piece containing expressions of love and looking forward to Katherine's growing up, presumably so that they might be married. But it contains additional touches of humour that Thomas felt appropriate for his young love. Katherine is urged to eat well 'that you might wax and grow fast to be a woman'. She is asked to greet Betson's horse 'and pray him to give you four of his years to help you', and to address the household clock at Stonor 'and pray him to amend his unthrifty manners, for he strikes ever in undue time'. And it ends with a private joke: 'At great Calais, on this side of the sea, the first day of June, when every man was gone to his dinner and the clock smote 'noon' and all our household cried after me and bade me "come down! come down to dinner at once!" and what answer I gave them, you know it of old.'[180]

Some children told stories about themselves, stories so strange that they caught the attention of adults. That of the 'green children' of Suffolk has already been mentioned, with its claim that they came from another land by an underground passage.[181] Others look as if they were shaped by mental illness, but achieved record because they seemed to signify the victory of Christianity over the forces of evil or disorder. The miracles of St Thomas of Hereford, collected in the early fourteenth century, recounts the experiences of Christian Nevenon of Inglethorp (Norfolk), a girl perhaps in her teens. She was vexed for five years by a devil who promised her gifts to sleep with him, but was kept at bay when she made the sign of the cross. One day, he took her to a lovely place and showed her wonders, including a table with delectable food, but again she escaped by crossing herself. Later still, she fell ill and became paralysed – a condition from which she was freed by visiting the saint's shrine at Hereford. This made her story worth adding to the materials being collected to support St Thomas's canonisation.[182]

The chronicle of Thomas Walsingham of St Albans describes the adventure of a youth or young man of the household of William Lord Greystoke, who was riding through a field of wheat in 1343. The wheat rippled like the sea and out of it peered the head of a small red man. As the rider watched him, the creature grew in stature. He seized the youth's bridle and led him through the wheat to a beautiful lady attended by many damsels. She ordered him to be put down from his horse, lacerated in his skin and flesh, and flayed. Then, cutting open his skull, she took out his brain, and closed up the head again. She had the youth put back upon his horse and sent him away. As a result he grew insane and had to be chained up, but his girlfriend stayed faithful to him and led him to many shrines in search of a cure. At last, after six years of misery, he had a dream at Beverley in which he saw the beautiful lady. Once more, she opened his head, but this time she put back the brain. Restored to sanity, he married the girl and they had fifteen children; after she died, he took holy orders and became a parochial rector. There was a sequel to the story. While the rector was celebrating mass and elevating the consecrated wafer, the red man came once more and surrendered his power. 'Your keeper now', he said, 'is He whom you hold in your hands.'[183]

Were medieval people more forthcoming in preserving childhood memories when they had grown up? Here too, the evidence is relatively scanty. Autobiography was not a well-established literary genre in the middle ages. St Augustine indeed describes his life, including his childhood and youth, in his *Confessions* of about 400. A few twelfth-century writers tell us stories about their early years. Orderic Vitalis, as we have seen, recalls his baptism and his departure from home, and John of Salisbury his boyhood involvement with magic.[184] Walter Map looked back on his early teens, when he was in his fifties, as the happiest time of his life.[185] Gerald of Wales wrote a good deal about himself in his writings, although only a little of it is concerned with his childhood. He identifies his family, mentions his birth-place Manorbier Castle (Pembs.), and includes the story of himself and his brothers playing in the sand.[186] He also records the childhood reminiscences of the old priest Eliodor, relating to the first half of the twelfth century. This man claimed that, when he was twelve, he met two tiny men who led him through a dark tunnel to a beautiful land whose sky was covered by clouds, without sun, moon, or stars. It was inhabited by little people with horses and dogs of proportionate size, who welcomed him and allowed him to come and go between their land and Wales. The story ended like a fairy tale. Eliodor's mother incited him to steal a golden ball; he did so, was pursued, and lost the ball. The way to the beautiful land disappeared, and he never found it again.[187]

Interest in recording one's childhood, however, failed to grow and blossom from these shoots. Little survives after Gerald by way of autobiography until the fifteenth century, and when the genre began again it did not place an emphasis on people's early years. Adam of Usk, who frequently mentions himself in his chronicle of events under Richard II and Henry IV, includes but a single incident from his childhood, and one that scarcely involved himself. Most of his reminiscences begin in 1387 when he was a student at Oxford.[188] Margery Kempe, whose mystical writings are even more highly self-centred, opens her career with the birth of her first child in the mid 1390s.[189] The fifteenth-century poet John Lydgate wrote briefly in verse about his youth, but not historically or affectionately. Rather he portrayed himself as a typical moralist's child: playful, irreverent, and unstable. He viewed his childhood and the adolescence which followed it as times of immaturity, compared with his later life.[190] Not until the mid sixteenth century did autobiography begin to focus on childhood in a significant way (Fig. 125).[191]

More exists by way of medieval biography than autobiography, but this too is limited in its concern with young people. Lives of saints are common, but tend to

125   Biography and autobiography became more popular in
the sixteenth century. The memorial brass of Robert Pursglove,
bishop of Hull (d. 1579) provides a resumé of his career.

be highly generic in their portrayal of childhood.
The saintly child is already the future saint: its
birth foreshadowed by miraculous events and its
life marked by wisdom and piety well in advance
of its age. Lives of kings and knights are scarcer
and usually begin with their heroes' adolescent
feats of war. That of William Marshal contains an
account of him being held hostage at about the
age of five, and playing 'knights' with King
Stephen, but Richard earl of Warwick's, a more
typical example, leaps from his birth and baptism
to his knighting at seventeen.[192] Such writings
reflect a lack of interest in childhood by the biographers rather than a lack of memories about it.
When authors bothered to do so, they were quite
capable of finding evidence about their heroes'
origins. Thomas of Monmouth discovered a good
deal about the childhood of William of Norwich,
presumably from members of his family.[193] The
biographers of St Edmund of Abingdon and St
Richard of Chichester in the thirteenth century, St Thomas of Hereford in the
fourteenth, and St John of Bridlington in the fifteenth all collected information
about their early lives from those who had known them.[194] Most of all, legal
records that involved reconstructing the past – proofs of age, marriage litigation,
and cases about ownership of property – show that witnesses could recall events
of their youths and other people's, when required.

It is unlikely, then, that medieval adults remembered less of their early lives, or
talked about them less, than we do today. One person who did so and valued his
origins was John Shillingford, canon of Exeter Cathedral in 1388. When he made
his will in that year, he had the opportunity to choose a grave in the cathedral that
had given him status in life, where he could lie close to the stately round of services. But he did not take it. Instead, his thoughts turned to the moorland church
of Widecombe on Dartmoor in which his mother lay buried, and he asked to be
laid beside her there, so that 'where I had my first greeting, there I may take my
last farewell'.[195] Few of us nowadays ask for such a burial, but like him, we never
quite lose our parents and never altogether leave our homes. People, possessions,
and happenings remind us of our childhood throughout our lives. Its scenes and
characters return in our dreams. We leave it fully only when we die.

LIST OF ABBREVIATIONS

BL	British Library, London
Bodleian	Bodleian Library, Oxford
CCR	*Calendar of Close Rolls*
CIPM	*Calendar of Inquisitions Post Mortem*
CPL	*Calendar of Papal Letters*
CPR	*Calendar of Patent Rolls*
EETS, es	Early English Text Society, extra series
EETS, os	Early English Text Society, original series
EETS, ss	Early English Text Society, supplementary series
HMC	*Historical Manuscripts Commission*
Index	Carleton Brown and R. H. Robbins, *The Index of Middle English Verse* (New York, 1943), and R. H. Robbins and J. L. Cutler, *Supplement to the Index of Middle English Verse* (Lexington, Kentucky, 1965)
LPFD	*Letters and Papers, Foreign and Domestic, Henry VIII*
MED	*Middle English Dictionary*, ed. Hans Kurath and Sherman M. Kuhn (Ann Arbor, Mich., and London, 1956–, in progress)
MLD	*Dictionary of Medieval Latin from British Sources*, ed. R. E. Latham and D. R. Howlett (London, 1975–, in progress)
OED	*Oxford English Dictionary*
PRO	Public Record Office, London
RS	Rolls Series, 99 titles (London, 1858–96)
STC	A. W. Pollard and G. R. Redgrave, *A Short-Title Catalogue of Books Printed in England . . . 1475–1640*, 2nd ed., 3 vols (London, 1976–91)
VCH	*Victoria History of the Counties of England*, ed. H. A. Doubleday, William Page, and others (London, 1900–, in progress)

NOTES

References follow the Harvard style, and relate to the bibliography. Authors are identified by surnames, with initials if there are two such surnames, dates if there are more than one relevant work, and a letter after the date if two works appeared in the same year. Sources not listed in the bibliography are described in full

INTRODUCTION

1. For a good survey of the historiography of this subject, see Crawford, pp. 1–8.
2. P. Ariès, *L'Enfant et la vie familiale sous l'Ancien régime* (Paris, 1960); *Centuries of Childhood* (London, 1962).
3. On what follows, see Ariès, 1962, especially pp. 31–47, 125–30, 353–99.
4. Ibid., p. 125.
5. See the bibliography, p. 372.
6. For the Opies' work, see ibid., p. 372.
7. On what follows, see *MED* and *OED* under the words cited.
8. Shakespeare, *The Winter's Tale*, III.iii.70; ed. J. H. P. Pafford (London and Cambridge, MA, 1965), p. 70.
9. On this subject, see Rowland, pp. 17–29, and with more detail, Burrow.
10. *Byrhtferth's Manual*, ed. S. J. Crawford, EETS, os, 177 (1929), pp. 10–11; Furnivall, 1868a, pp. 166–9.
11. Isidore of Seville, *Etymologiarum sive Originum Libri XX*, ed. W. M. Lindsay, 2 vols (Oxford, 1909), ii (book xi, chapter 2); *On the Properties of Things i, 300*; *As You Like It*, II.vii.139–66
12. See above, pp. 213–17.
13. See above, pp. 321–8.
14. See above, pp. 311, 322.
15. See above, pp. Chapters 4–7.

CHAPTER 1: ARRIVING

1. *The York Plays*, pp. 126–7.
2. *The Chester Mystery Cycle*, pp. 115–18; *The N-Town Play*, pp. 156–62; ultimately derived from James, 1953, pp. 46, 74.
3. *Beues of Hamtoun*, pp. 171–2.
4. For an outline of the subject, see Dunstan, pp. 39–57.
5. Aristotle, 'On the Soul', sections 402a–405b; idem, 'History of Animals', sections 583a–b; idem, *De Partibus Animalium I and De Generatione Animalium I*, ed. D. M. Balme (Oxford, 1972), sections 731a, 734b–736a.
6. John, ii.20.
7. Augustine, 'De Diversis Questionibus LXXXI-II', in *Opera Omnia*, vol. 4 (*Patrologia Latina*, ed. J.

P. Migne, vol. 40, Paris, 1887), col. 39.
8. Dunstan, pp. 39–57; M. Anthony Hewson, *Giles of Rome and the Medieval Theory of Conception* (London, 1975), pp. 166–78; Pamela M. Huby, 'Soul, Life, Sense, Intellect: Some Thirteenth-century Problems', in *The Human Embryo: Aristotle and the Arabic and European Traditions*, ed. G. R. Dunstan (Exeter, 1990), pp. 113–22.
9. Thomas of Chobham, pp. 463–4. Chobham was here citing the version of the Mosaic law in the Septuagint (Dunstan, p. 42).
10. Bracton, ii, 341.
11. There are early printed editions of the Latin text, e.g. Bartholomaeus Anglicus, *De Rerum Proprietatibus* (Dillingen, 1506). The English translation has been edited as *On the Properties of Things*, i–iii; for its early printed editions see STC 1536–8.
12. On what follows, see *On the Properties of Things*, i, 294–7. For other accounts of gestation and gynaecology, see *The Early South-English Legendary*, vol. i, ed. C. Horstmann, EETS, os, 87 (1887), pp. 319–22; Beryl Rowland, *Medieval Woman's Guide to Health: the first English gynecological handbook* (Kent, OH, and London, 1981); and Helen Rodnite Lemay, *Women's Secrets: a translation of Pseudo-Albertus De Secretis Mulierum, with commentaries* (Albany, NY, 1992).
13. *On the Properties of Things*, i, 234–5.
14. Eadmer, 1962, p. 165.
15. *Customary of the Benedictine Monasteries of . . . Canterbury, and . . . Westminster*, ed. E. M. Thompson, vol. ii, Henry Bradshaw Society, 28 (1904), pp. 49, 73; PRO, E 101/370/20; Charles Peers and L. E. Tanner, 'On Some Recent Discoveries in Westminster Abbey', *Archaeologia*, 93 (1949), p. 151; Nicolas, 1830, p. 78.
16. *Pierce the Ploughmans Crede*, p. 4, lines 78–9; *LPFD*, ix, 11, 49; *Three Chapters of Letters Relating to the Suppression of Monasteries*, ed. Thomas Wright, Camden Society, 26 (1843), pp. 59, 198; Strype, i part i, 396–7; J. W. Clay, *Yorkshire Monasteries: Suppression Papers*, Yorkshire Archaeological Society, record series, 48 (1912), pp. 16–18.
17. Bühler, pp. 274–7.
18. *On the Properties of Things*, ii, 845–6, 853–5, 862.
19. STC 21864; Scot, p. 205.
20. Mirk, 1974, lines 77–84.
21. *The Lay Folk's Mass Book*, ed. T. F. Simmons,

EETS, os, 71 (1879), p. 71.

22. *Councils and Synods I*, i, 248.

23. *Councils and Synods II*, i, 70, 183, 234, 441, 453, 635; Mirk, 1974, lines 97–106.

24. *On the Properties of Things*, i, 303.

25. Stephenson, p. 324.

26. M. K. Jones and M. G. Underwood, *The King's Mother: Lady Margaret Beaufort* (Cambridge, 1992), p. 40.

27. *MED, OED*, s.v. midwife.

28. *On the Properties of Things*, i, 298, 305.

29. Rous, section 56.

30. Above, p. 42.

31. Bühler, pp. 274–5.

32. *The Early Works of Thomas Becon*, ed. J. Ayre, (Cambridge, Parker Society, 1843), pp. 138–9; J. Calfhill, *An Answer to John Martiall's Treatise of the Cross*, ed. R. Gibbings (idem, 1846), p. 20; R. Hutchinson, *Works*, ed. J. Bruce (idem, 1842), pp. 171–2; T. Rogers, *The Catholic Doctrine of the Church of England*, ed. J. J. S. Perowne (idem, 1854), pp. 226–8.

33. Charles Wriothesley, *A Chronicle of England during the Reigns of the Tudors*, ed. W. D. Hamilton, vol i, Camden Society, new series, 11 (1875), p. 31.

34. *Visitation Articles*, ii, 58–9, 292, 356–7.

35. Gurney, p. 429.

36. Above, p. 26.

37. *John of Gaunt's Register*, ed. Sydney Armitage-Smith, 2 vols, Royal Historical Society Camden 3rd series, 20–1 (1911), ii, 55, 321.

38. *LPFD*, iii part i, p. 499.

39. *John of Gaunt's Register, 1377–1383*, ed. Eleanor C. Lodge and Robert Somerville, 2 vols, Camden 3rd series, 66–7 (1937), ii, 258–9.

40. *Materials for a History of the Reign of Henry VII*, ed. William Campbell, 2 vols (RS, 1873–7), ii, 65, 84.

41. *CPR 1494–1509*, p. 354.

42. The undated ordinances are in BL, Harley MS 6079, fols. 26r–29r, printed in Leland, iv, 179–80, with an unwarranted ascription to Lady Margaret Beaufort. BL, Cotton MS Julius B.XII, fol. 56, contains an account of a confinement of Queen Elizabeth of York (printed in Leland, iv, 249). The ordinances of 1493 are in BL, Harley MS 642, fols. 207r–24v, printed in *A Collection of Ordinances and Regulations for the Government of the Royal Household* (London, Society of Antiquaries, 1790), pp. 125–8, with a further text in BL, Harley MS 4712, at fol. 15r.

43. Bodleian, MS Eng.hist b.208, fols 1r–22r.

44. E.g. E. W. Ives, *Anne Boleyn* (Oxford, 1986), p. 230.

45. Mannyng, lines 9509–16, 9560–2.

46. William Rishanger, *Chronica et Annales*, ed. H. T. Riley (RS, 1865), pp. 189–90; Walsingham, 1863–4, i, 113.

47. On the history of baptism in the middle ages, see J. D. C. Fisher, 1965, and Cramer.

48. Bede, pp. 164–7 (book ii, chapter 9).

49. Ibid., pp. 186–9 (book ii, chapter 14).

50. *Councils and Ecclesiastical Documents*, iii, 448–9; *Councils and Synods I*, ii, 575.

51. Orderic Vitalis, vi, 552–5.

52. Attenborough, pp. 36–7.

53. *Councils and Synods I*, i, 319.

54. Ibid., i, 455.

55. Hull and Sharpe, pp. 26–7.

56. Above, p. 25, 34, 202–3.

57. *The Middle English Lai le Freine*, lines 35–58.

58. Hale, p. 2.

59. *Councils and Synods II*, i, 247; cf. pp. 297, 368, 590; ii, 988.

60. Ibid., ii, 836; Mirk, 1974, lines 142–50.

61. *Councils and Synods I*, i, 211.

62. *Three Lives of the Last Englishmen*, ed. Michael Swanton (New York and London, 1984), p. 100.

63. *Councils and Synods I*, ii, 774, 979, 986; *Councils and Synods II*, i, 68, 70, 117, 180, 246, 453; ii, 988.

64. Bede, pp. 372–3 (book iv, chapter 13); Asser, pp. 47, 140.

65. *MED*, s.v. 'godsib', 'godsibbe-rede'; *OED*, s.v. 'gossip', 'gossipred'.

66. *Councils and Synods I*, ii, 1048–9.

67. *CIPM*, ix, 455.

68. *CIPM*, vii, 381–2.

69. *CIPM*, iv, 109.

70. *Original Letters Illustrative of English History, Third Series*, ed. Henry Ellis, 4 vols (London, 1846), ii, 225–6.

71. Above, p. 202.

72. For examples of this, from 1480 to 1537, see BL, Add. MS 6113, fols. 31v–33r, 74r–78v, 79v–80r, 81r–86v, 115r–119v.

73. Mannyng, lines 9591–626; Bodleian, MS Bodley 828 (William of Pagula, *Oculus Sacerdotis*), fols 115r–117v, 120v; STC 4115: Burgo, fol. 4r–v; *Manuale*, pp. 38–42; Mirk, 1974, lines 85–96, 125–40.

74. W. Maskell, *Monumenta Ritualia Ecclesiae Anglicanae*, 2nd ed., 3 vols (Oxford, 1882), i, pp. ccxlviii–l.

75. *Manuale*, p. 39.

76. Mannyng, lines 9627–56.

77. STC 791: *The Art of Good Lyvyng and Good Deyng* (Paris, 1503), sig. I.iv recto.

78. Above, pp. 123–8.

79. *Manuale*, pp. 25–43.

80. Ibid., pp. 25–31, 35–43.

81. *Four Supplications*, ed. F. J. Furnivall and J. Meadows Cowper, EETS, es, 13 (1871), p. 90.

82. *MED* s.v. 'crisme'; *OED* s.v. 'chrisom'.

83. *Councils and Synods II*, i, 69–70, 141, 427, 512; ii, 1087.

84. Above, p. 219.

85. Littlehales, 1903, p. 5; Foxe, viii, 126.

86. BL, Cotton MS Julius B.XII, fols. 19v–27r, printed in Leland, iv, 206–7; cf. BL, Add. MS 6113, fols. 79v–80r, 81r–86v, 116v–117r, 117v–119v.

87. Samuel Bentley, *Excerpta Historica* (London, 1831), p. 110; Nicolas, 1827, pp. 106, 117, 136, 145.

88. Nicolas, 1830, p. 28.

89. *HMC, Report on the Manuscripts of Lord Middleton* (London, 1911), pp. 338, 343–4, 365, 367–8, 376, 381–2.

90. Dyboski, pp. xiii–xiv; above, p. 50.

91. *MED* s.v.'chirchen'; *OED*, s.v. 'church'.

92. Leviticus, xii.1–8.

93. M. R. James, 'Two Lives of St Ethelbert, King and Martyr', *English Historical Review*, 32 (1917), p. 235; *Councils and Synods II*, i, 35.

94. Mirk, 1905, p. 298.

95. Bede, pp. 90–1 (book i, chapter 27).

96. *Manuale*, p. 44; *Dives and Pauper*, i part ii, 116.

97. Paris, iii, 539, 566; v, 415, 421.

98. Hale, pp. 14, 111.

99. Ibid., p. 10.

100. Ibid., pp. 206, 225.

101. PRO, E 404/2/10; Rickert, pp. 94–5.

102. *Cely Letters*, p. 167.

103. *Manuale*, pp. 43–4. For the offerings, see Brightman, ii, 884, and Cox, pp. 59–63.

104. Hale, p. 119.

105. Paris, iv, 568–9.

106. Ibid., v, 632; T. Stapleton, 'A Brief Summary of the Wardrobe Accounts . . . of King Edward the Second', *Archaeologia*, 26 (1836), p. 337.

107. *CIPM*, iv, 224; v, 50; vi, 118, 204–5; vii, 381, 385.

108. BL, Cotton MS Julius B.XII, fols. 19v–27v; Harley MS 6113, fols. 31v–117r passim; Leland, iv, 180–4; Bodleian, MS Eng.hist b. 208, fols. 15r–18r.

109. *John of Gaunt's Register*, ed. Lodge and Somerville, ii, 258–9.

110. *CIPM*, v, 36; vi, 476; vii, 188, 385.

111. Dillon and Hope, pp. 1–2.

112. BL, Cotton MS Julius B.XII, fols. 19v–27v; Leland, iv, 204–7.

113. Brightman, ii, 778.

114. Ibid., ii, 724.

115. *William of Palerne*, p. 127, line 70.

116. On the history of English personal names, see Withycombe, and Reaney.

117. *Felix's Life of Saint Guthlac*, ed. Bertram Colgrave (Cambridge, 1956), pp. 76–7.

118. Niles, pp. 95–107, at p. 98; cf. Bennett, pp. 1–14.

119. E.g. *CIPM*, viii, 90; ix, 137–8.

120. Haas, pp. 1–21, at p. 18.

121. Stephenson, p. 83.

122. Ibid., pp. 328, 444.

123. Ibid., p. 478; idem, *A List of Monumental Brasses in Surrey*, ed. J. M. Blatchly (Bath, 1970), pp. 23–31.

124. On Anglo-Saxon names, see W. G. Searle, *Onomasticon Anglo-Saxonicum* (Cambridge, 1897; repr. Hildesheim, 1969), especially pp. xii–xxiv, and Clark, 1987, pp. 31–60.

125. *The Place-Names of Devon*, ed. J. E. B. Gover, A. Mawer, and F. M. Stenton, 2 vols, English Place-Name Society, 8–9 (1931–2), ii, 681–7.

126. Bede, 1991, pp. 132–3 (book ii, chapter 5).

127. Robert Bartlett, *The Making of Europe* (London, 1994), pp. 270–80 at 274.

128. *Symeonis Monachi Opera Omnia*, ed. T. Arnold, 2 vols (RS, 1882–5), i, 296.

129. Hull and Sharpe, pp. 36, 45–50. For similar cases, see Clark, 1987, p. 42, and Moore, pp. 183–4.

130. Gillian Fellows Jensen, 'The Names of the Lincolnshire Tenants of the Bishop of Lincoln, c.1225' in *Otium et Negotium: Studies in Onomatology and Library Science Presented to Olof von Feilitzen* (Stockholm, Acta Bibliothecae Regiae Stockholmiensis, 16, 1973), pp. 86–95 at 86–7.

131. Cecily Clark, *Words, Names and History*, ed. Peter Jackson (Cambridge, 1995), pp. 117–43 at 128–9.

132. E.g. 'Watekyn', noble boy in the bishop of Hereford's household in 1290–1 (Webb, i, 135). See also above, pp. 172, 319.

133. *Councils and Synods II*, ii, 897; Burgo, fol. 9v; Lyndwood, p. 246.

134. Clayton, pp. 82, 85, 87.

135. Paris, iv, 48; v, 415.

136. Stephenson, p. 324.

137. *CIPM*, ii, 31–2.

138. Ibid., p. 195.

139. Ibid., pp. 498–9.

140. Ibid., p. 500.

141. Thomas of Monmouth, p. 12.

142. *Acta Sanctorum*, October, i, 638–9.

143. Frank Barlow, *Thomas Becket*, 2nd ed. (London, 1997), p. 10.

144. Nigel Saul, *Richard II* (New Haven and London, 1997), p. 12.

145. Opie, 1997a, pp. 364–5.

146. Cockayne, iii, 184–97.

147. Robbins, pp. 63–67, 67–70; *The Works of John Metham*, ed. H. Craig, EETS, os, 132 (1916), pp. 148–56.

148. *Dives and Pauper*, i part i, 130–1.

149. *The Autobiography of Giraldus Cambrensis*, ed. H. E. Butler (London, 1937), p. 35; Adam of Usk, pp. 118–19; cf. pp. 98–9.

150. *A Volume of English Miscellanies*, ed. James Raine, Surtees Society, 85 (1890), pp. 40–1. See also *York Civic Records*, ed. Angelo Raine, Yorkshire Archaeological Society, Record Series, 98, 102, 106 (1938–42), i, 24, 169, 175; iii, 15–16, 130.

151. Above, pp. 6–7.

152. Above, pp. 213–21, 321–8.

153. Genesis, xl.20; Matthew, xiv.6; Mark, vi.21; *MED* s.v. 'birth'; *OED*, s.v. 'birthday'.

154. Winchester College Archives, 21490A (Registrum Primum), pp. 38 et seq. There are a few earlier entries for 1431 (ibid., p. 22).

155. Byrne, p. 5.

156. *Chronicles of the Reigns of Stephen, Henry II, and Richard I*, ed. R. Howlett, 4 vols (RS, 1884–9), iv, 176, 183–4, 189, 195, 197, 211, 226, 233.

157. Paris, iii, 539; iv, 48, 224, 406; v, 415; *The Chronicle of Bury St Edmunds 1212–1301*, ed. Antonia Gransden (London, 1964), pp. 47, 52, 56, 62, 67, 77.

158. *CIPM*, ii, 20–1.

159. Stubbs, i, 134, 137.

160. *CIPM*, ii, 505–6; v, 355; vii, 90, 341–2, 383, 481; viii, 41, 150, 233–4; ix, 247, 410–11, 413, 449.

161. *Sotheby's Catalogue*, no. 92: *Western Manuscripts and Miniatures* (London, 1992), section 92. For the family, see P. Morant, *History and Antiquities of Essex*, 2 vols (London, 1768), ii, 144. Similar volumes include BL, Harley MS 5793 (Danet family); BL, Royal MS 2 A.XVIII (family of Henry VII); Bodleian, MS Dugdale 47, fols 4r, 5r (Hales family); and Bodleian, MS Gough liturg. 3, fol. 94v (Coope family).

162. Dyboski, pp. xiii–xiv.

163. Cox, pp. 236–9; the Tipton register there mentioned, however, should be dated 1573 not 1513.

164. *Visitation Articles*, ii, 39–40.

CHAPTER 2: FAMILY LIFE

1. On what follows, see Fryde, pp. 38–42, and Parsons, pp. 245–65.

2. Moore, pp. 153–96.

3. Above, p. 48.

4. The standard list of monumental brasses, including references to children, is Stephenson. On children in particular, see Page-Phillips.

5. E.g. Stephenson, pp. 83, 329, 444.

6. Ibid., pp. 20, 34, 37, 39, 76, 83, 87, 135, 221, 273, 278, 283, 378, 401, 478, 502, 536, 549–50; Page-Phillips, Figs. 34 and 44.

7. Stephenson, p. 158.

8. Ibid., pp. 4, 148, 184, 234, 276, 308, 350.

9. Kempe, pp. 115, 221.

10. Moore, pp. 167, 188; Razi, pp. 75, 85–8, 93, 139–44; Howell, pp. 232, 235.

11. On what follows, see Wrigley and Schofield, especially pp. 189, 255, 260, 307, 423, 528.

12. Moore, p. 193.

13. Nicolas, 1827, p. 93.

14. E.g. *Somerset Medieval Wills (1383–1500)*, ed. F. W. Weaver, Somerset Record Society, 16 (1901), pp. 179, 375, 384; idem, *(1501–1530)*, ibid., 19 (1903), pp. 70, 140–1, 191.

15. Chaucer, 'Canterbury Tales', II (B^1) 694–896; above, p. 290–91.

16. *MED* s.v. 'fostren'; *OED*, s.v. 'foster'.

17. Above, p. 225; Power, pp. 568–81.

18. On abandonment, see above, pp. 88, 96.

19. Above, p. 326.

20. Above, pp. 308–9, 317.

21. *MED*, s.v. 'step-', 'step-child', 'step-dame', 'step-fader', 'step-moder'; *OED*, s.v. 'stepdame', 'stepfather', 'stepmother'.

22. Macray, pp. 129–34.

23. Above, pp. 287,293, ••.

24. Lyndwood, p. 26. The bishop could give a dispensation for minor orders, but the pope alone for major ones including the priesthood.

25. Pollock and Maitland, i, 422–3, for an earlier contrary view, see Bracton, ii, 30.

26. Peter Laslett, *Family Life and Illicit Love in Earlier Generations* (Cambridge, 1977), pp. 112–14.

27. *OED, MED*, s.v.

28. *The Anglo-Saxon Chronicle*, ed. Dorothy Whitelock *et al.*, 2nd impression (London, 1965), p. 141.

29. Paul Robert, *Dictionnaire alphabétique et analogique de la langue française*, 12th edn, 9 vols (Paris, 1985), s.v. 'bâtard'.

30. *OED*, s.v. 'bastard'.

31. Layamon, *Brut or Hystoria Brutonum*, ed. W. R. J. Barron and S. C. Weinberg (Harlow, 1995), lines 7765–79; the episode is derived from Wace's *Le Roman de Brut* and that in turn from Geoffrey of Monmouth's *Historia Regum Britanniae*.

32. *Of Arthour and of Merlin*, ed. O. D. Macrae-Gibson, vol. i, EETS, os, 268 (1973), pp. 92–3; *Merlin*, ed. H. B. Wheatley, vol. i, EETS, os, 10 (1865), p. 30; *Lovelich's Merlin*, ed. E. A. Koch, vol. i, EETS, es, 93 (1904), p. 57.

33. *Registrum Hamonis Hethe, Diocesis Roffensis*, ed. Charles Johnson, vol. ii, Canterbury and York Society, 49 (1948), p. 951; *Act Book of the Ecclesiastical Court of Whalley Abbey 1510–1538*, ed. Alice M. Cooke, Chetham Society, new series, 44 (1901), pp. 170–1; Ralph Houlbrooke, *Church Courts and the People during the English Reformation, 1520–1570* (Oxford, 1979), p. 77; cf. Robbins, p. 20.

34. Glanvill, pp. 70–1.

35. On what follows, see Given-Wilson and Curteis.

36. On support for the illegitimate in London, see Hanawalt, 1993, pp. 59–61.

37. Walsingham, 1863–4, ii, 339; *CPR 1422–9*, pp. 489–90, 543.

38. On Fitzroy, see Given-Wilson and Curteis, pp. 174–6.

39. Genesis, xxi.7; 1 Samuel, i.24; Luke, iii.16.

40. Sir Thomas Malory, *Works*, ed. Eugène Vinaver and P. J. C. Field, 3rd edn, 3 vols (Oxford, 1990), i, 10–11.

41. Unless 'nursed' (*nutritus*) meant merely 'brought up' (*Acta Sanctorum*, October, i, 600).

42. Giles of Rome, *De Regimine Principum*, part ii, book ii, chapter 15.

43. *On the Properties of Things*, i, 299.

44. Leland, iv, 183.

45. On what follows, see Orme, 1984, pp. 11–12.

46. London, College of Arms, MS Arundel 6, fol. 135v; *Rotuli Litterarum Clausarum*, ed. T. D. Hardy, vol i (London, Record Commission, 1833), p. 416.

47. Walter of Bibbesworth, p. 3.

48. Orme, 1984, p. 12.

49. Map, pp. 382–3.

50. *The Towneley Plays*, p. 145.

51. Foxe, vii, 9; Andrew J. Brown, *Robert Ferrar* (London, 1997), pp. 121–3.

52. Izaak Walton, *The Life of Mr. Richard Hooker* (London, 1665), pp. 43–4.

53. Walter of Bibbesworth, p. 3.

54. *The Works of Thomas Deloney*, ed. Francis Oscar Mann (Oxford, 1912), p. 103.

55. *OED* s.v. 'biggin', 'cricket', 'cross-cloth', 'posnet', 'standing'.

56. Crawford, p. 68.
57. *OED*, s.v. 'cradle' 17, 'swaddleband', 'swaddling-band'.
58. Ibid., s.v. 'cradle'.
59. Leland, iv, 183–4.
60. Thomas of Chobham, p. 215; *Councils and Synods II*, i, 214.
61. *Acta Sanctorum*, October, i, 643–4, 645.
62. Grosjean, pp. 260–3.
63. Above, pp. 99–100.
64. *On the Properties of Things*, i, 298–9, 304.
65. Chauliac, p. 443.
66. Aristotle, 'Politics', book 7, chapter 17, section 1336a.
67. Giles of Rome, *De Regimine Principum*, part ii, book ii, chapter 15.
68. *Acta Sanctorum*, October, i, 614–15.
69. Grosjean, pp. 92–4.
70. Mannyng, lines 2153–4.
71. J. C. Robertson, i, 203–4.
72. Gervase of Tilbury, *Otia Imperialia*, ed. F. Liebrecht (Hannover, 1856), p. 40.
73. Map, pp. 160–2.
74. Crawford, pp. 89–90.
75. Mannyng, lines 9671–80.
76. Robert Herrick, *Poetical Works*, ed. L. C. Martin (Oxford, 1956), p. 284.
77. *The Rolls and Register of Bishop Oliver Sutton*, ed. Rosalind M. T. Hill, vol. v, Lincoln Record Society, 60 (1965), pp. 126–8; *The Register of Bishop Godfrey Giffard*, ed. J. W. Willis-Bund, part iv, Worcestershire Historical Society (1902), p. 538.
78. Galbraith, pp. 104–5. A variant of the story, allegedly emanating from William of Wykeham, is told by Thomas Walsingham (*Chronicon Angliae*, ed. E. M. Thompson, (RS, 1874), p. 107).
79. On the episode, see *CPR 1317–21*, p. 273; *Le Livere de Reis de Brittanie e le Livere de Engleterre*, ed. J. Glover (RS, 1865), p. 335; Stubbs, i, 282–3; *Vita Edwardi Secundi: The Life of Edward the Second*, ed. N. Denholm-Young (London, 1957), pp. 86–7; and *Chronica Monasterii de Melsa*, ed. Edward A. Bond, 3 vols (RS, 1866–8), ii, 335–6.
80. Grosjean, pp. 21–3, 92–4.
81. Palsgrave, fol. 407r, implies over one.
82. *Ratis Raving*, lines 1112–25.
83. *The Middle English Stanzaic Versions of the Life of Saint Anne*, ed. R. E. Parker, EETS, os, 174 (1928), p. 8; *Romeo and Juliet*, I.iii.20–5.
84. Eadmer, p. 81; see also *Jacob's Well*, ed. A. Brandeis, part i, EETS, os, 115 (1909), p. 231.
85. *On the Properties of Things*, i, 304; Palsgrave, fol. 234r; *OED*, s.v. 'blabber'.
86. 1 Samuel, i.23–4; James, 1953, p. 41.
87. *The Life of King Edward*, ed. F. Barlow (London and New York, 1962), p. 8.
88. John Amundesham, *Annales Monastici S. Albani*, ed. H. T. Riley, 2 vols (RS, 1870–1), i, 349.
89. *Annales Monastici*, iv, 344–5.
90. Genesis, xxi.8; Thomas of Monmouth, pp. 12–13.
91. Walter of Bibbesworth, p. 3.
92. Morey, p. 224.
93. *Manuale*, p. 32.
94. Hanawalt, 1977, pp. 15–19. On accidents, see also above, pp.99–100.
95. *Ancrene Wisse*, pp. 97, 119.
96. PRO, JUST 2/106 m. 1d; 2/107 m. 7.
97. Orme, 1989, pp. 80, 83, 85; Thomson, 1979, p. 150.
98. Johnstone, p. 408.
99. Above, pp. 216,324, 327.
100. Aristotle, 'Politics', book 7, chapter 17, section 1336b; Orme, 1984, pp. 9, 17–18.
101. Orme, 1973, p. 124; above, p. 154.
102. Furnivall, 1868a/1931, pp. 265–6; idem, 1868b, pp. 4 7.
103. Byrne, p. 1. See also above, p. 75.
104. Orme, 1973, p. 124; Lupton, p. 278; Byrne, p. 8.
105. *On the Properties of Things*, i, 329.
106. Byrne, p. 23.
107. Above, p. 207.
108. Furnivall, 1868a/1931, pp. 186, 252, 275–6.
109. Chaucer, 'Canterbury Tales', I (A) 100.
110. Furnivall, 1868a/1931, pp. 229–31.
111. Kirby, pp. 487–8.
112. Myers, p. 126; Percy, pp. 80–1, 84.
113. Percy, pp. 73, 78.
114. Thomas of Monmouth, pp. 13–14; Lawrence, p. 203.
115. *Household Accounts from Medieval England*, ed. C. M. Woolgar, 2 parts, London, British Academy, Records of Social and Economic History, new series, 17–18 (1992–3), i, 182–3, etc.
116. *MED*, s.v. 'pap', 'papelote'; *OED*, s.v. 'pap', 'papelotte'.
117. John Arderne, *Treatises of Fistula in Ano*, ed. D'Arcy Power, EETS, os, 139 (1910), p. 72.
118. Johnstone, pp. 400, 402, etc.; cf. Byrne, p. 9.
119. Walter of Bibbesworth, p. 7.
120. Sneyd, p. 11; Gurney, p. 517.
121. More, xii, 45–6; Sneyd, p. 11.
122. Percy, pp. 73–6, 79–81.
123. Byrne, pp. 8–11.
124. Orme, 1995, pp. 287, 290–1.
125. Above, p. 108.
126. Lydgate, 1911, pp. 352–4.
127. Nelson, p. 16.
128. *Promptorium Parvulorum*, i, 75.
129. Gurney, pp. 433–62.
130. Above, p. 329.
131. Colgrave, pp. 64–5.
132. *The Tale of Gamelyn*, ed. W. W. Skeat, 2nd ed. (Oxford, 1893), lines 215, 259, 269.
133. *William of Palerne*, p. 202, line 2,767.
134. *The Lay of Havelok the Dane*, ed. W. W. Skeat, 2nd ed. (Oxford, 1956), lines 855–62, 962–74.
135. Furnivall, 1868a/1931, pp. 265–6.
136. *The Vita Wulfstani of William of Malmesbury*, ed. R. R. Darlington, Royal Historical Society, Camden 3rd series, 40 (1928), p. 120.
137. Johnstone, pp. 402–3, 405.

138. Ibid., p. 411.
139. Hunnisett, p. 11; Sharpe, p. 190.
140. Johnstone, pp. 401–2, 408.
141. Sharpe, pp. 219–20.
142. Lupton, p. 279.
143. *MED*, s.v. 'ars' (2); *OED*, s.v. 'arse' sb.
144. *OED*, s.v. 'wisp'.
145. Furnivall, 1868a/1931, pp. 63–4.
146. Brown, 1957, p. 146.
147. Scot, pp. 152–3.
148. Above, p. 151.
149. Walsingham, 1867–9, ii, 368–9.
150. *Three Fifteenth-Century Chronicles*, ed. J. Gairdner, Camden Society, new series, 28 (1880), p. 165.
151. Opie, 1997a, pp. 357–60.
152. Chaucer, 'Canterbury Tales', I (A) 3483–4.
153. Furnivall, 1868a/1931, p. 181.
154. Morey, p. 224; cf. Robert of Flamborough, p. 222.
155. *Councils and Synods II*, i, 32, 70, 183, 204, 214, 235, 274, 302, 351, 410, 432, 441, 444, 457, 520, 590, 618; Thomas of Chobham, p. 215.
156. Mirk, 1974, lines 1657–8.
157. Hale, pp. 21, 41.
158. *Acta Sanctorum*, October, i, 645, 669.
159. *Councils and Synods II*, i, 214.
160. Mirk, 1974, lines 155–6.
161. BL, Add. MS 30506, fol. 23v; Littlehales, 1903, p. 5.
162. Mannyng, lines 7659–62; Mirk, 1974, lines 216–21.
163. Kirby, pp. 509–10.
164. *Dean Cosyn and Wells Cathedral Miscellanea*, ed. Aelred Watkin, Somerset Record Society, 56 (1941), p. 107.
165. Opie, 1997a, pp. 475–6.
166. Myers, p. 126.
167. Nelson, pp. 1–2.
168. *Acta Sanctorum*, April, i, 626–8.
169. Nelson, p. 3.
170. Aristotle, 'On Dreams', section 461a; *On the Properties of Things*, i, 338.
171. Nelson, p. 2.
172. J. C. Robertson, iii, 162.
173. *Acta Sanctorum*, October, i, 638–9.
174. John Fisher, pp. 292–3.
175. Thomas of Monmouth, pp. 74–7.
176. J. C. Robertson, i, 380–1.
177. *Acta Sanctorum*, April, i, 213.
178. *An Inventory of the Historical Monuments in London*, vol. i: *Westminster Abbey* (London, Royal Commission on Historical Monuments (England), 1974), p. 30.
179. Above, p. 53; Page-Phillips, passim; Stephenson, passim.
180. Above, pp. 37–8.
181. K. B. McFarlane, *Hans Memling* (Oxford, 1971), pp. 8–9, 53, 56, plates 1, 4.
182. Riché and Alexandre-Bidon, p. 64; Vienna, Kunsthistorisches Museum, no. 4452; cf. nos. 4430, 5618.
183. Oliver Millar, *The Tudor, Stuart and Early Georgian*

184. Exodus, xx.12; Deuteronomy, v.16.
185. Mannyng, lines 1057–169.
186. Ibid.
187. Caxton, 1971, p. 114; compare Mannyng, lines 1243–74.
188. STC 24446; William Tyndale, *The Obedience of a Christian Man* (Antwerp, 1528), fols. 48v–49r.
189. Ibid., fol. 25r.
190. Above, p. 207.
191. *Paston Letters*, i, passim.
192. *Gabriel Harvey's Marginalia*, ed. G. C. Moore Smith (Stratford-upon-Avon, 1913), p. 143.
193. *MED*, *OED*, s.v. 'chaste', 'chasten', 'chastise'.
194. Langland, A.v.28–32; B.v.28–41; C.vi.131–40; Proverbs, xiii.24.
195. Ibid., C.ix.163.
196. *Paston Letters*, ii, 32.
197. Ibid., i, 41.
198. Hooker, p. 5.
199. Nelson, pp. 13–14.
200. Edmund Dudley, *The Tree of the Commonwealth*, ed. D. M. Brodie (Cambridge, 1948), p. 68. Compare also Palsgrave, fols. 186v, 312r.
201. *Rotuli Parliamentorum*, iv, 19–20; *Statutes of the Realm*, ii, 175.
202. Judges, p. 3.
203. *Calendar of Liberate Rolls*, i, *1226–40*, p. 455.
204. E. H. Carter, 'The Constitutions of St. Paul Norwich', *Norfolk Archaeology*, 25 (1935), pp. 350–1.
205. *VCH Nottinghamshire.*, ii, 165.
206. *Reg. Bekynton, Wells*, ed. H. C. Maxwell-Lyte & M. C. B. Dawes, 2 vols, Somerset Record Society, 49–50 (1934–5), i, 289.
207. Miri Rubin, *Charity and Community in Medieval Cambridge* (Cambridge, 1987), pp. 300–1.
208. *A Cartulary of the Hospital of St John the Baptist*, ed. H. E. Salter, 3 vols, Oxford Historical Society, 66, 68–9 (1914–20), iii, 3.
209. *CCR 1339–41*, p. 600; *CPR 1340–3*, p. 434; *CPR 1343–6*, p. 432.
210. *CCR 1349–54*, pp. 414–15; *CPR 1354–60*, p. 11; *CPR 1436–41*, p. 48; *CPL 1431–47*, pp. 489–90.
211. *The Historical Collections of a Citizen of London in the Fifteenth Century*, ed. J. Gairdner, Camden Society, new series, 17 (1876), p. viii.
212. Ibid., p. ix.
213. *LPFD*, xi, 73.
214. *CCR 1343–6*, p. 432; *CCR 1349–54*, pp. 414–15.
215. *Early Yorkshire Charters*, ed. W. Farrer, 3 vols, Yorkshire Archaeological Society Record Series, extra series (1914–16), i, 248–9; *CPL 1198–1304*, p. 319.
216. Patricia H. Cullum, 'Hospitals and Charitable Provision in Medieval Yorkshire', University of York, PhD thesis (1989), p. 191, quoting Lichfield, Joint Record Office, QQ7; idem,

Pictures in the Collection of Her Majesty the Queen, 2 vols (London, 1963), text p. 53, plate 7; *The Drawings of Hans Holbein . . . at Windsor Castle*, ed. K. T. Parker (Oxford and London, 1945), p. 49, plate 46.

Cremetts and Corrodies, University of York, Borthwick Papers, 79 (1991), pp. 28–9.

217. *Cal. Inquisitions Miscellaneous*, ii: *1307–49*, pp. 178–9.

218. PRO, C 270/20; *VCH Yorkshire*, iii, 340.

219. *Lincoln Wills*: vol i, *A.D. 1271 to A.D. 1526*, ed. C. W. Foster, Lincoln Record Soc., 5 (1914), references listed on p. 213.

220. Langland, A.vii. 267–77; B.vi. 282–92; C. ix. 304–14.

221. Ibid., C.x.71–97.

222. *Pierce the Ploughmans Crede*, pp. 16–17.

223. Nelson, p. 86.

224. Barclay, 1928, p. 184.

225. Thomas of Monmouth, p. 270.

226. Gerald of Wales, 1861–91, vii, 134–5.

227. *Acta Sanctorum*, April, i, 302.

228. *Acta Sanctorum*, October, i, 625–6.

229. Ibid., p. 629.

230. Langland, C.x. 166–70.; cf. A.viii. 73–8; B.vii. 90–4.

231. Barclay, 1874/1966, i, 304.

232. *The St. Albans Chronicle, 1406–1420*, ed. V. H. Galbraith (Oxford, 1937), p. 103.

233. For a summary of the legislation, see J. R. Tanner, *Tudor Constitutional Documents A.D. 1485–1603*, 2nd ed. (Cambridge, 1930), pp. 469–73.

234. *Statutes of the Realm*, iii, 559.

235. Hanham, p. 184.

236. *Acta Sanctorum*, October, i, 610–12.

237. Hunnisett, pp. 39–40.

238. Ibid., pp. 66–7.

239. Ibid., p. 82.

240. Ralph of Coggeshall, *Chronicon Anglicanum*, ed. J. Stevenson (RS, 1875), pp. 118–20; William of Newburgh in *Chronicles, Stephen, Henry II and Richard I*, ed. R. Howlett, vol. i (RS, 1884), pp. 82–4. See also the inverse story told by Gerald of Wales, above, p. 340.

CHAPTER 3: DANGER AND DEATH

1. *Records of Medieval Oxford*, ed. H. E. Salter (Oxford, 1912), p. 27.

2. Ælfric, *Lives of Saints*, ed. W. W. Skeat, vol. ii, EETS, os, 82 (1885), pp. 374–5; Chaucer, 'Canterbury Tales', X (I) 577.

3. Thomas of Chobham, p. 215.

4. Morey, p. 222.

5. Robert of Flamborough, p. 222.

6. Friedberg, ii, col. 792.

7. Downer, pp. 222–3. The laws also talk anomalously of a ten-year penance.

8. Hurnard, p. 169; PRO, JUST 1/818, m. 47.

9. Hurnard, p. 162; *CCR 1272–9*, p. 206; *CPR 1281–92*, p. 146.

10. Attenborough, pp. 44–5. It is not clear who was responsible for these payments or whether they continued in later times.

11. *Councils and Synods, I*, ii, 1048–9, 1061–2.

12. Above, p. 28.

13. Horman, fol. 68v.

14. Marie de France, *Lais*, ed. A. Ewert (Oxford, 1944), lines 156–224; cf. *The Middle English Lai le Freine*, lines 135–85.

15. Two different versions of the episode appear in J. C. Robertson, i, 213; ii, 245.

16. Paris, v, 82.

17. Adam of Usk, pp. 86–7.

18. For a range of explanations, see Helen Rodnite Lemay, *Women's Secrets: a Translation of Pseudo-Albertus Magnus's* De Secretis Mulierum *with commentaries* (Albany, NY, 1992), pp. 112–16.

19. Map, pp. 442–7; Gerald of Wales, 1861–91, vi, 131–2.

20. *Dives and Pauper*, i part ii, 118–19.

21. Brewer and Howlett, ii, 236–7.

22. Bracton, ii, 31; iv, 361.

23. Burgo, fol. 7v.

24. Crawford, pp. 94–6.

25. *Chronica Monasterii de Melsa*, ed. E. A. Bond, 3 vols (RS, 1866–8), iii, 69–70.

26. Brewer and Howlett, ii, 236–7.

27. Lyndwood, p. 29; *CPL*, xiii part i, pp. 20, 45, 224, 237–8, 403, 409.

28. Ramon Lull, *The Book of the Ordre of Chyvalry*, trans. W. Caxton, ed. A. T. P. Byles, EETS, os, 168 (1926), pp. 63–4; Thomas Littleton, *Treatise on Tenures* (London, 1841), II.iv, section 109.

29. *The Lay of Havelok the Dane*, ed. W. W. Skeat, 2nd ed. (Oxford, 1956), lines 880–908; Myers, p. 118; Hanawalt, 1993, pp. 139, 253.

30. The subject is studied by Gordon, and Finucane. For the miracle collections mentioned, see *Acta Sanctorum*, October, viii, 567–90; Reginald of Durham, *Libellus de Vita et Miraculis S. Godrici*, Surtees Society, 20 (1845); J. C. Robertson, i–ii; *Acta Sanctorum*, October, i, 610–705; and Grosjean.

31. R. F. Hunnisett, *The Medieval Coroner* (Cambridge, 1961), especially pp. 9–36; Pollock and Maitland, ii, 578.

32. Above, p. 91.

33. The topic of children's accidents in coroners' records is surveyed by Hanawalt, 1977, pp. 1–22, and idem, 1986, pp. 171–87. Examples of the records include *Select Cases from the Coroners' Rolls, A.D. 1265–1413*, ed. C. Gross, Selden Society, 9 (1896); *Records of Mediaeval Oxford*, ed. Salter; Sharpe; Hunnisett; and *Calendar of Nottinghamshire Coroners' Inquests 1485–1558*, ed. R. F. Hunnisett, Thoroton Society Record Series, 25 (1969).

34. Chaucer, 'Canterbury Tales', I (A) 2019.

35. PRO, JUST 2/200, m. 2.

36. Above, p. 211. Thomas of Chobham (p. 215) ordered parents of children killed by negligence to be sent to the bishop for penance.

37. Machyn, p. 311.

38. Brewer and Howlett, ii, 236.

39. Orme, 1989, pp. 139, 145; Orme, 1995, p. 275; see also above, pp. 320–1.

40. Lemay, *Women's Secrets*, pp. 117–19; Thomas of Monmouth, pp. 12–13.
41. Paris, v, 302–3.
42. Machyn, p. 88.
43. John of Salisbury, 1909, i, 164; idem, 1938, pp. 146–7.
44. Mannyng, lines 351–4.
45. James, 1922, pp. 420–1.
46. *Peter Idley's Instructions to his Son*, ed. Charlotte D'Evelyn, Modern Language Association of America, Monograph Series, 6 (Boston and London, 1935), p. 113.
47. *Select Cases of Trespass from the King's Courts, 1307–1399*, vol i, ed. M. S. Arnold, Selden Society, 100 (1984), pp. 17–18.
48. For some context on this, see Boswell, 1980.
49. See, e.g. Aquinas, vol. xiii, part ii (second part), question 154, articles 1–12; Chaucer, 'Canterbury Tales', X (II) 835–914.
50. Mirk, 1974, lines 1347–414.
51. John Gower, *Mirour de l'Omme*, trans. William Burton Wilson (East Lansing, 1992), p. 120.
52. Mannyng, lines 7659–62; Mirk, 1974, lines 216–21. But see above, p. 160 (Horman).
53. Mannyng, lines 9709–85; Gregory the Great, *Dialogues*, book iv, chapter 32, in J. P. Migne, *Patrologia Latina*, vol. 77 (Paris, 1896), cols. 372–3.
54. *The Chronicle of Richard of Devizes of the Time of King Richard the First*, ed. J. T. Appleby (London, 1963), p. 65.
55. Machyn, pp. 112, 228, 239.
56. Knowles, 1951, pp. 115–18.
57. R. B. Dobson, *Durham Priory 1400–1450* (Cambridge, 1973), pp. 75, 78.
58. Wilkins, iii, 787.
59. Map, pp. 80–1.
60. *Visitations in the Diocese of Lincoln, 1517–1531*, ed. A. Hamilton Thompson, vol. iii, Lincoln Record Society, 37 (1947), pp. 19–21.
61. Strype, i part i, 396–7.
62. PRO, SP 1/100, pp. 5–8; *LPFD*, ix, 373–4.
63. On the subject, see Cecil Roth, *A History of the Jews in England*, 3rd edn. (Oxford, 1964), pp. 9–56.
64. Thomas of Monmouth, pp. 15–34.
65. *On the Properties of Things*, i, 299.
66. Cockayne, i, 123, 227, 347, 351; ii, 241; iii, 87.
67. *On the Properties of Things*, i, 344, 409, 420, 426.
68. Chauliac, pp. 315, 393, 515.
69. J. C. Robertson, ii, passim.
70. *Chronica Monasterii de Melsa*, ed. Bond, ii, 159.
71. Galbraith, p. 50.
72. Hector and Harvey, pp. 20–1, 28–9, 44–5, 56–7, 204–5, 438–9; Walsingham, 1863–4, ii, 197.
73. *On the Properties of Things*, i, 299.
74. Johnstone, pp. 406–14.
75. *LPFD*, iii part i, pp. 499, 502–4.
76. Chauliac, pp. 131, 515, 537, 546, 556; Robbins, p. 78.
77. John Arderne, *Treatises of Fistula in Ano*, ed. D'Arcy Power, EETS, os, 139 (1910), p. 32; Palsgrave, fol. 172r.
78. Judges, pp. 11–12.
79. Reginald of Durham, *Libellus*, pp. 432–3.
80. Ibid., pp. 455–8.
81. On the royal touch, see Marc Bloch, *The Royal Touch: Sacred Monarchy and Scrofula in England and France*, trans. J. E. Anderson (London and Montreal, 1973), especially pp. 21–7.
82. *Acta Sanctorum*, October, viii, 575.
83. Nicolas, 1827, p. 150.
84. *Boswell's Life of Johnson*, ed. G. Birkbeck Hill and L. F. Powell, 6 vols (Oxford, 1934–50), i, 43.
85. Hale, p. 34.
86. STC 23949; *Three Tudor Classical Interludes*, ed. Marie Axton (Cambridge, 1982), pp. 57–9, lines 687–754.
87. *Dives and Pauper*, i part i, 158.
88. *On the Properties of Things*, ii, 843; Scot, p. 294.
89. Orme, 1989, pp. 132–3.
90. Ibid., p. 147.
91. William Worcester, *Itineraries*, ed. John H. Harvey (Oxford, 1969), pp. 310–11.
92. Thomas of Monmouth, p. 134.
93. J. C. Robertson, ii, 94; cf. pp. 153, 259, 263–6.
94. Johnstone, pp. 399, 409, 420.
95. J. C. Robertson, ii, 200.
96. Ibid., pp. 116–17, 125.
97. Ibid., pp. 255–7.
98. *LPFD*, iii part i, p. 503.
99. J. C. Robertson, ii, 58.
100. Ibid., pp. 208, 221–2, 229–34; cf. p. 259.
101. Ibid., p. 105.
102. Ibid., pp. 67–8.
103. J. W. Blench, *Preaching in England in the late Fifteenth and Sixteenth Centuries* (Oxford, 1964), p. 235.
104. Caxton, 1971, pp. 115–16.
105. *The Dance of Death*, pp. 68–71.
106. Wrigley and Schofield, pp. 248–9, 528.
107. A complete count has been made only for Edward I's first family (Parsons). In the meantime, there are only the incomplete lists in Fryde, pp. 37–42.
108. Winchester College Archives, 21490A (Registrum Primum), pp. 1–37, summarised with omissions of month dates and some inaccuracies in T. F. Kirby, *Winchester Scholars* (London and Winchester, 1888), pp. 18–81.
109. Orme, 1983b, pp. 85–100.
110. Orme, 1989, p. 140.
111. Ibid., p. 143.
112. Ibid., p. 137.
113. Ibid.
114. Hunnisett, pp. 3–4.
115. For Anglo-Saxon burial practice involving children, see Crawford, pp. 19–21, 27–8, 66, 169–70, and Lucy; for later medieval practice, Daniell, especially pp. 124–8; for post-Reformation practice, Gittings, pp. 80–1.
116. Johnstone, pp. 399, 414, 420.
117. Charles Peers and L. E. Tanner, 'On Some Recent Discoveries in Westminster Abbey', *Archaeologia*, 93 (1949), pp. 151–2.
118. A. H. Thomas and Thornley, pp. 260, 294,

374–5.

119. Orme, 1988, pp. 195–203.

120. Exeter Cathedral Archives, Obit Accounts, D&C 3673, fols 74, 84v, 85v, 90v; 3764, fols 19, 25.

121. *Lambeth Churchwardens' Accounts, 1504–1645*, ed. C. Drew, part i, Surrey Record Society, 40 (1940), pp. 1–5.

122. Andrew Clark, 1914, p. 27; cf. Gittings, pp. 80–1.

123. Gittings, pp. 80–1.

124. Cox, pp. 59–63.

125. Arthur Ogle, *The Tragedy of the Lollards' Tower* (Oxford, 1949), pp. 48–56, 196–7.

126. *Statutes of the Realm*, iii, 288–9.

127. Daniell, p. 128; Crawford, p. 87.

128. Rous, 1980, section 58.

129. C. L. Kingsford, *The Grey Friars of London* (Aberdeen, 1915), pp. 92, 96, 100, 104, 124.

130. On brasses of children, see Page-Phillips; Stephenson, passim; and Clayton, especially pp. 77–8, 120, 132–4, 138–9.

131. Page-Phillips, p. 9 and Fig. 1.

132. Stephenson, pp. 36, 304, 498.

133. Ibid., pp. 133, 222, 262, 324, 436, 558.

134. Above, pp. 43–4.

135. Page-Phillips, Figs. 16–18.

136. Joan P. Tanner, 1953, pp. 25–37; *An Inventory of the Historical Monuments in London*, vol. i: *Westminster Abbey* (London, Royal Commission on Historical Monuments (England), 1974), pp. 30–1, 34, 38.

137. Paris, v, 632.

138. Parsons, p. 257.

139. Hull and Sharpe, pp. 26–7. Daniell (pp. 101–2) notes a number of cases of medieval parents asking in wills to be buried with children.

140. Stubbs, i, 137.

141. Nelson, p. 17.

142. Gregory, *Dialogues*, book iv, chapter 18, in Migne, *Patrologia Latina*, vol. 77, col. 349.

143. Ibid.

144. Eadmer, p. 18.

145. Mannyng, lines 4865–904.

146. Norman P. Tanner, 1990, i, 245.

147. Aquinas, vol. xxi (supplement, question 89, article 5); see also above, pp. •• (John de Burgh), •• (unction).

148. Roger of Wendover, *The Flowers of History*, ed. H. G. Hewlett, vol i (RS, 1886), pp. 18–20.

149. Chaucer, 'Canterbury Tales', III (D) 1765–884.

150. Ælfric, *Lives of Saints*, ed. Skeat, ii, 374–5.

151. G. G. Coulton, *Infant Perdition in the Middle Ages* (London, 1922); *MED* and *OED*, s.v. 'limbo', 'limbus'; Aquinas, vol. xx (supplement, question 69, articles 5–7); Mannyng, lines 9565–76.

152. Mirk, 1974, lines 85–96; Lyndwood, p. 246.

153. Mirk, 1905, p. 298; Gittings, pp. 82–3.

154. Lyndwood, p. 246.

155. On baptism by the Holy Spirit, see Bernard Manning, *The People's Faith in the Time of Wyclif*, 2nd edn. (Hassocks, 1975), pp. 54–8.

156. Matthew, ii. 11; Mark, i. 8; Luke, iii. 16.

157. On baptism by angels, see Burgo, fol. 4r, and Lyndwood, p. 245.

158. Anne Hudson, *The Premature Reformation: Wycliffite Texts and Lollard History* (Oxford, 1988), p. 291.

159. Ibid., pp. 99, 114, 141–2, 469, 494, 510; J. A. F. Thomson, *The Later Lollards 1414–1520* (London, 1965), pp. 33, 45, 64–5, 67, 76, 104, 122, 127.

160. Bracton, iv, 361.

161. *Acta Sanctorum*, October, i, 643.

162. *Oxford City Documents, Financial and Judicial, 1268–1665*, ed. J. E. Thorold Rogers, Oxford Historical Society, 18 (1891), p. 155.

163. *CPR 1388–92*, p. 160; *Hereford Cathedral: a history*, ed. Gerald Aylmer and John Tiller (London, 2000), p. 304.

164. Hale, p. 34.

165. James, 1922, p. 421.

166. Hull and Sharpe, pp. 26–35.

167. *The Poems of the Pearl Manuscript*, ed. Malcolm Andrew and Ronald Waldron (London, 1978), pp. 53–110.

168. Matthew, xx. 1–16.

CHAPTER 4: WORDS, RHYMES, AND SONGS

1. *Old English Homilies of the Twelfth Century*, ed. R. Morris, EETS, os, 53 (1873), pp. 180–1; Owst, p. 37.

2. Brown, 1939, p. 294.

3. Ibid., pp. 4–7; Greene, pp. 89–90; *MED, OED*, s.v. 'ba'.

4. Richardson, 1942, p. 389.

5. Bartholomaeus, book vi, chapter 10.

6. *On the Properties of Things*, i, 304.

7. Elyot, fols. 19v–20r (book i, chapter 5).

8. *MED*, s.v. 'baba', 'babe'; *OED*, s.v. 'baban', 'babe', 'baby'.

9. *MED, OED*, s.v. 'pap'.

10. *OED*, s.v. 'dad', 'daddy', 'mam', 'mamma'.

11. Grosjean, pp. 92–4.

12. *The Chester Plays*, ed. Hermann Deimling, part i, EETS, es, 62 (1892), pp. 40, 46.

13. Thomas Wright, 1884, i, 752–3.

14. Langland, A.iv.61; *MED*, s.v. 'handi-dandi'; *OED*, s.v. 'handy-dandy'.

15. 'Sibilis et cantilenis demulcet puerum dormientem' (Bartholomaeus, book vi, chapters 5, 10); translated in *On the Properties of Things*, i, 299, 304.

16. *MED*, s.v. 'lullai', 'lullen', 'lulling', 'bissen'; *OED*, s.v. 'lulla', 'lullaby', 'byss'.

17. Greene, pp. 85–104; compare Brown, 1957, p. 70; Brown, 1939, pp. 3–8; Baker, p. 163.

18. *Index*, no. 3597; Greene, p. 95.

19. *Index*, no. 1352; Greene, p. 87.

20. *Index*, no. 1351; Greene, p. 87.

21. *Index*, no. 1264; Greene, p. 90.

22. J. T. Koch, *The Gododdin of Aneirin: Text and Context from Dark-Age North Britain* (Cardiff, 1997), section A.87, pp. lxxxi, lxxxix, 126–9, 233–4.

23. *Index*, no. 3859.5; BL, Cotton MS Faustina A.V, fol. 10r; Robbins, p. xxxix.

24. On this and on what follows, see Opie, 1997a, pp. 1–43.

25. Ibid., p. 3.

26. BL, C.59.a.20.

27. *On the Properties of Things*, i, 300.

28. Opie, 1997a, pp. 6–7.

29. London, 1978.

30. *Index*, no. 635.5.

31. Eleanor Relle, 'Some New Marginalia and poems by Gabriel Harvey', *Review of English Studies*, new series, 23 (1972), pp. 401–16.

32. *Index*, no. 3372.5; S. B. Meech, 'A collection of Proverbs in Rawlinson MS D 328', *Modern Philology*, 38 (1940–1), p. 124.

33. *Index*, no. 1185.

34. Rachel Hands, 'Horse-Dealing Lore, or a Fifteenth-Century 'Help to Discourse'?', *Medium Aevum*, 41 (1972), p. 237.

35. Relle, *Review of English Studies*, 23 (1972), pp. 401–16.

36. *Index*, no. 102.3; Greene, p. 290.

37. Magdalene College Cambridge, Old Library, Lect. 26; Relle, *Review of English Studies*, 23 (1972), pp. 401–16.

38. STC 24935; W. Wager, *The Longer Thou Livest the More Fool Thou Art* (London, *c.*1569), sig. A.iii recto, cf. D.ii recto; ed. R. Mark Benbow (London, 1968), pp. 6–8, cf. pp. 39–40.

39. Above, pp. 48–50.

40. *Index*, no. 1314; Dyboski, p. 104.

41. *Index*, no. 1350; Dyboski, p. 110.

42. *Index*, no. 1350; Greene, p. 504.

43. *Index*, no. 1132; Dyboski, p. 103; Greene, pp. 195–6.

44. Greene, pp. 423–7.

45. For the history of the rhyme, see Opie, 1997a, pp. 73–5.

46. Oxford, Balliol College, MS 230, fol. 153v; Mynors, p. 242.

47. Opie, 1969, pp. 124–6.

48. Oxford, Bodleian Library, MS Wood donat. 4, p. 384.

49. Nicholas Orme, 'From Exeter to London in 1562', *Friends of Exeter Cathedral, 58th Annual Report* (Exeter, 1988), pp. 16–17.

50. Wager, *The Longer Thou Livest*, sig. A.iii recto; ed. Benbow, pp. 7–8.

51. Printed in Joseph Ritson, *Ancient Songs and Ballads*, ed. W. Carew Hazlitt, 3rd edn. (London, 1877), pp. 207–8.

52. W. Chappell and H. Ellis Wooldridge, *Old English Popular Music*, 2 vols (London and New York, 1893), i, 46–7.

53. Child, 1882–8, i, 390–9.

54. *Early Tudor Songs and Carols*, ed. John Stevens, Musica Britannica, 26 (London, 1975), p. 17.

55. On this subject, Orme, 1973, pp. 98–100; Thomson, 1979, passim; and Orme, 1989, pp. 73–151.

56. On this subject, see Vivien Law, *The Insular Latin Grammarians* (Woodbridge, 1982), pp. 53–4, and idem, *Grammar and Grammarians in the Early Middle Ages* (London, 1997).

57. Law, *Grammar and Grammarians*, pp. 202–16.

58. The manuscripts are respectively: Bodleian Library, Lincoln College Oxford MS lat. 129 (E) (Orme, 1989, pp. 87–112); British Library, MS Harley 1002 (Thomson, 1979, pp. 239–53); Yale University, Beinecke Library, MS 3 (34) (Orme, 1989, pp. 74, 82–5); Aberystwyth, National Library of Wales, MS Peniarth 356B (Thomson, 1979, pp. 114–31); British Library, Add. MS 60577 (E. Wilson); Cambridge, Gonville and Caius College, MS 417/447 (Thomson, 1979, pp. 148–57); and Bodleian Library, MS Rawlinson D 328 (ibid., pp. 290–315; S. B. Meech, 'A Collection of Proverbs in Rawlinson MS D 328', *Modern Philology*, 38 (1940–1), pp. 112–32).

59. Orme, 1989, p. 84.

60. Ibid.

61. Thomson, 1979, pp. 107, 202, 293.

62. Meech, *Modern Philology*, 38 (1940–1), p. 125.

63. *Index*, no. 1354; Oxford, Bodleian Library, MS Eng. poet e. 1, fol. 26v.

64. *Index*, no. 4169; Thomson, 1979, p. 309; Child, 1882–8, v, 283–4.

64. Opie, 1959, pp. 22–6.

65. Orme, 1989, p. 102. This is not dissimilar to verse 4 of the comic song 'I saw a dog seething sauce', which has also the rhymes arrow-barrow-harrow (Greene, p. 289).

66. Above, note 32.

67. Thomson, 1979, p. 146.

68. *Index*, no. 3324; Robbins, p. 104.

69. *Index*, no. 35.5; E. Wilson, fol. 76v; compare R. H. Robbins, 'Middle English Lyrics: Handlist of New Texts', *Anglia*, 83 (1965), p. 44.

70. E. Wilson, fol. 76r.

71. Orme, 1989, pp. 80–2.

72. *The Brut or The Chronicles of England*, ed. F. W. D. Brie, part ii, EETS, es, 136 (1908), p. 441; cf. *Chronicles of London*, ed. C. L. Kingsford (Oxford, 1905), p. 284.

73. Above, p. 77.

74. Orme, 1989, p. 100. Or is this a riddle?

75. E. Wilson, fol. 76r.

76. Furnivall, 1868a/1931, p. 187.

77. Thomson, 1979, pp. 202, 204.

78. Orme, 1989, p. 100.

79. E. Wilson, fol. 76r.

80. Ibid., fol. 76v.

81. Ibid.

82. BL, Harley MS 1002, fols. 72v–75r; Thomson, 1979, pp. 239–53; C. E. Wright, 'Late Middle English Parerga in a School Collection', *Review of English Studies*, new series, 2 (1951), pp. 114–20.

83. *Index*, no. 3788.5.

84. *Index*, no. 430.8.

85. *Index*, no. 1632.5.

86. Above, p. 230.

87. Thomson, 1979, p. 292.

88. Gerald of Wales, 1861–91, vi, 75–7; see also above, p. 340.
89. *Index*, no. 1399; Oxford, Balliol College, MS 354, fol. 252r, with variant text in Bodleian Library, MS Laud misc. 601, fol. 115v, both printed in Greene, pp. 245–6.
90. *Index*, no. 3895; Lincoln Cathedral Library, MS 132, fol. 100v, printed in Robbins, p. 105.
91. *Index*, no. 2683; BL, Add. MS 60577, fol. 93r, printed in E. Wilson, fol. 93r. A variant text (London, BL, Add. MS 14997, fol. 44v) is printed in K. Hammerle, 'Verstreute me. und frühne. Lyrik', *Archiv für das Studium der neuren Sprachen*, 166 (1934), pp. 203–4.
92. *Index*, no. 320.5; BL, Sloane MS 1584, fol. 33r, printed in *Reliquiae Antiquae*, ed. T. Wright and J. O. Halliwell, 2 vols (London, 1841–3), i, 116–17.
93. Above, pp. 39, 57.
94. BL, Harley MS 2398, fol. 94v; Owst, p. 466.
95. Owst, pp. 466–7.
96. Ibid., p. 416.
97. STC 1732; Thomas Becon, *An Invective against Swearing* (London, 1543), fols. 17r, 24v.
98. Nelson, p. 13; Elyot, fol. 17r (book i, chapter 4).
99. Stanbridge, pp. 17–18, 20, 22.
100. Orme, 1989, p. 77.
101. I.e. 'pip' in the sense of a respiratory disease.
102. Orme, 1989, p. 119.
103. *The Poetical Works of John Skelton*, ed. Alexander Dyce, 2 vols (London, 1843, repr. New York, 1965) ii, 29; Skelton, *The Complete English Poems*, ed. John Scattergood (Harmondsworth, 1983), p. 281.
104. Opie, 1997a, p. 149.
105. Ibid.
106. Skelton, ed. Dyce, ii, 416; ed. Scattergood, p. 351.
107. Orme, 1989, p. 118.
108. Stanbridge, p. 23.
109. Horman, fols. 64v–78v.
110. Stanbridge, pp. 14, 17.
111. Horman, fol. 171r.
112. *Index*, no. 0.1; C. F. Bühler, 'A Tudor "Crosse Rewe"', *Journal of English and Germanic Philology*, 58 (1959), pp. 248–50.
113. Above, p. 253.
114. Above, p. 248.
115. Gordon Williams, *A Dictionary of Sexual Language and Imagery in Shakespearian and Stuart Literature*, 2 vols (London, 1994), i, 289–90. The same pun on the alphabetical 'con' is found in a fifteenth-century French poem: Pierre Champion, 'Pièces joyeuses du xve siècle', *Revue de Philologie française et de littérature*, 21 (1907), p. 192.

CHAPTER 5: PLAY

1. The pioneer work on toys and games in England, still worth consulting, is Strutt, especially pp. 485–513. More recently, see W. Endrei

and L. Zolnay, *Fun and Games in Old Europe* (Budapest, 1986); Riché and Alexandre-Bidon; and Alexandre-Bidon, 1997, pp. 141–50.
2. Above, pp. 6–7.
3. For examples, see *The Parlement of the Thre Ages*, ed. M. Y. Offord, EETS, os, 246 (1969), pp. 4, 6–9; More, i, 3–7; and STC 25982: *Mundus et Infans* (London, 1522), pp. 4–5, reprinted in Lester, p. 116.
4. John Lydgate, *The Pilgrimage of the Life of Man*, ed. F. J. Furnivall and Katherine B. Locock, 3 vols, EETS, es, 77, 83, 92 (1899–1904), ii, lines 11068–229.
5. *Promptorium Parvulorum*, p. 555. See also *Catholicon Anglicum*, a later fifteenth-century English-Latin dictionary, with similar, but fewer, entries on games, e.g. pp. 62, 192, 324, 390.
6. Nelson; Orme, 1989, pp. 134–49.
7. Horman, fols. 276v–283v.
8. Cod. Marc. Lat. I. 99 (2138); compare Bodleian, MS Douce 135 and Douce 276.
9. Bodleian, MS Bodley 264; James, 1933.
10. Pieter Bruegel, *Complete Edition of the Paintings*, ed. F. Grossmann, 3rd edn. (London, 1973), plate 51, p. 191; Jeannette Hills, *Das Kinderspielbild von Pieter Bruegel d.Ä (1560)* (Vienna, 1998).
11. See, for example, Egan.
12. *Polychronicon Ranulphi Higden*, ed. C. Babington, 9 vols (RS, 1865–86), ii, 159; *CIPM*, vi, 476; Johnstone, pp. 396–7.
13. Aristotle, 'Politics', book 8, chapter 6, section 1340b.
14. J. Bosworth and T. Northcote Toller, *An Anglo-Saxon Dictionary* (Oxford, 1898), p. 1076; *Promptorium Parvulorum*, p. 75.
15. Horman, fol. 147r.
16. STC 11098; John Florio, *A Worlde of Wordes* (London, 1598), p. 443.
17. Riché and Alexandre-Bidon, pp. 69, 72.
18. *The Anglo-Saxon Version of Apollonius of Tyre*, ed. Benjamin Thorpe (London, 1834), p. 13.
19. Martin Biddle, *Object and Economy in Medieval Winchester*, 2 vols, Winchester Studies, 7 (Oxford, 1990), ii, 706.
20. Walter of Bibbesworth, p. 4, line 36.
21. *Promptorium Parvulorum*, pp. 413, 469, 496, 525; *MED* s.v. 'prille', 'spilcock'.
22. *Catholicon Anglicum*, pp. 192, 324; *MED*, s.v. 'scopperil', 'spilcock'; *OED* s.v. 'whirlbone'. The latter does not recognise the word as applying to a children's toy, but the *Catholicon* reference quotes a Latin verse to that effect.
23. Opie, 1997b, passim.
24. *OED*, s.v. 'doll'.
25. *MED*, s.v. 'popet'; *OED*, s.v. 'poppet', 'puppet'; Nelson, p. 13.
26. *MED*, s.v. 'popet'.
27. STC 13830; *Hortus Vocabulorum* (London, 1509), s.v. 'pupa'.
28. There are examples in the Museum of Childhood at Bethnall Green, London.
29. Ursula M. Radford, 'The Wax Images Found in

Exeter Cathedral', *The Antiquaries Journal*, 29 (1949), pp. 164–8.

30. Claude Gauvard, *'De Grace Especial': Crime, Etat et Société en France à la fin du Moyen Age*, 2 vols (Paris, 1991), i, 309.

31. Guillaume de Deguileville, *The Booke of the Pylgrimage of the Sowle*, ed. K. I. Cust (London, 1859), pp. iv, xxxvi, 84; *Ratis Raving*, p. 58.

32. *Promptorium Parvulorum*, p. 409; Philip Stubbes, *Anatomy of the Abuses in England*, ed. F. J. Furnivall, 2 vols (London, 1877–82), i, 75.

33. STC 24366; William Turner, *Herball* (London, 1562), part 2, fol. 46r.

34. STC 7689; *The Rates of the Custome House* (London, 1582), sig. D.viii.

35. Vienna, Kunsthistorisches Museum, no. 4452.

36. STC 12786; Thomas Hariot, *A Briefe and True Report of the New Found Land of Virginia* (Frankfurt, 1590), plate VIII.

37. Horman, fol. 282v; cf. fol. 281r.

38. Kempe, pp. 77, 297.

39. A. R. Wright, iii, 192.

40. *MED*, s.v. 'popet'.

41. Roger Edgeworth, *Sermons Very Fruitfull, Godly and Learned: Preaching in the Reformation, c.1535–c.1553*, ed. Janet Wilson (Cambridge, 1993), pp. 143, 388.

42. Alexandre-Bidon, 1997b, p. 148.

43. On what follows, see Egan.

44. Johnstone, pp. 400, 403.

45. PRO, E 372/123, m. 21.

46. H. M. Colvin *et al.*, *The History of the King's Works*, vol. i: *The Middle Ages* (London, 1963), p. 202; PRO, E 101/467/7 (3), (7).

47. PRO, C 47/4/5, fol. 53r.

48. PRO, E 101/396/15; T. F. Tout, 'Firearms in England in the Fourteenth Century', *English Historical Review*, 26 (1911), p. 695.

49. *King Alfred's Old English Version of Boethius*, De Consolatione Philosophiae, ed. W. J. Sedgefield (Oxford, 1899, repr. Darmstadt, 1968), p. 108; *Ratis Raving*, p. 57. The word hobby-horse is not found in literature, however, until the mid sixteenth century (*OED*, s.v. 'hobby-horse').

50. *Oeuvres de Froissart: Poésies*, ed. A. Scheler, 3 vols (Brussels, 1870–2), i, 93, lines 213–14.

51. Grosjean, pp. 284–6.

52. STC 1536; Bartholomaeus Anglicus, *De Proprietatibus Rerum* (London, 1495), sig. M.ii recto.

53. N. J. G. Pounds, *A History of the English Parish Church* (Cambridge, 2000), p. 353.

54. Bodleian, MS Douce 12, fol. 16; MS Douce 276, fol. 124v.

55. Gerald of Wales, 1937, p. 35.

56. *Ratis Raving*, pp. 57–8.

57. *Promptorium Parvulorum*, p. 411; *MED*, s.v. 'poupe'.

58. Above, p. 132.

59. *The Poems of John Audelay*, ed. Ella K. Whiting, EETS, os, 184 (1931), p. 197.

60. *OED*, s.v. 'cherry-pit', 'cherry-stone'.

61. *Mundus et Infans*, p. 5; Lester, p. 116; Horman, fol.

281v.

62. *The York Plays*, p. 132.

63. STC 5830; Randle Cotgrave, *A Dictionarie of the French and English Tongues* (London, 1611), s.v. 'chastelet'.

64. More, viii part i, 492.

65. Byrne, p. 6.

66. Woodfield, pp. 81–159.

67. Comenius, pp. 276–7.

68. Bodleian, MS Bodley 264, fol. 112r.

69. PRO, E 101/386/6.

70. *Ratis Raving*, p. 61.

71. Horman, fol. 280v; cf. fol. 281v; *MED*, s.v. 'dali'.

72. Horman, fol. 282v.

73. Anglo, pp. 30, 33.

74. STC 4920–1; Jacques de Cessoles, *The Game of Chess*, trans. W. Caxton (Bruges, *c.*1475; Westminster, *c.*1483); facsimile, ed. Norman Blake (London, 1976); Grente, pp. 728–31.

75. J. C. Robertson, iii, 11, translated by H. E. Butler in F. M. Stenton, *Norman London* (London, 1934), p. 30; Horman, fol. 279v.

76. Above, p. 141.

77. *Promptorium Parvulorum*, pp. 20, 404, 430.

78. *MED*, s.v. 'bas'; *OED*, s.v. 'base'.

79. *Ratis Raving*, p. 61.

80. Above, p. 331.

81. Horman, fol. 282r.

82. *Ratis Raving*, p. 61; Horman, fol. 281v.

83. More, i, 3–7.

84. Orme, 1989, p. 136.

85. John Heywood, *The Play of the Weather* (Malone Society, Oxford, 1977), sig. D.iii, lines 1032–42.

86. *Promptorium Parvulorum*, pp. 498, 518.

87. *MED*, s.v. 'totir'; *OED*, s.v. 'totter', 'merry-totter'.

88. *Promptorium Parvulorum*, pp. 447, 488; *MED* s.v. 'shitel'.

89. *The Wakefield Pageants*, p. 62, line 736.

90. J. C. Robertson, iii, 9; Stenton, *Norman London*, p. 30.

91. *Promptorium Parvulorum*, pp. 60, 269, 404.

92. STC 24380; Thomas Tusser, *Five Hundred Pointes of Good Husbandrie* (London, 1580), fols 25v, 27v.

93. On what follows, see Orme, 1983a.

94. Horman, fol. 278r.

95. Orme, 1983a, pp. 52–4; Elyot, fols. 64v–68r (book i, chapter 17).

96. Nelson, pp. 23–4.

97. Horman, fols. 277v, 283r.

98. On children in coroners' records, see Hanawalt, 1986, especially pp. 171–87.

99. Sharpe, pp. 63–4; Grosjean, pp. 35–7.

100. Grosjean, pp. 101–3.

101. Heywood, *The Play of the Weather*, sig. D.iii, lines 1032–42.

102. *Mundus et Infans*, p. 5; Lester, p. 116.

103. Nelson, p. 27; above, p. 185–6.

104. Furnivall 1868a/1931, p. 382; Furnivall, 1868b, pp. 8–9.

105. *Statutes of the Realm*, i, 97–8.

106. *L'Histoire de Guillaume le Maréchal*, ed. P. Meyer, 3 vols, Société de l'Histoire de France (Paris,

1891–1901), i, lines 602–19.

107. Johnstone, p. 408; PRO, E 301/352/6; *Records of the Wardrobe and Household 1286–1289*, ed. Benjamin F. Byerly and Catherine R. Byerly (London, 1986), pp. 411–12.

108. Orme, 1984, pp. 183–4.

109. *Rotuli Parliamentorum*, vi, 156; *Statutes of the Realm*, ii, 432.

110. Orme, 1984, pp. 201, 204.

111. Hunnisett, pp. 33–4; Grosjean, pp. 37–8.

112. On what follows, see also Orme, 1984, pp. 191–8.

113. Horman, fol. 277r; Elyot, fol. 69v (book i, chapter 18).

114. *The Chronicle of John Hardyng*, ed. H. Ellis (London, 1812), pp. i–ii.

115. Above, p. 280.

116. *Close Rolls, 1253–4*, p. 41; *LPFD*, iv part iii, pp. 2593–4 (no. 5806).

117. Colin Richmond, *John Hopton: a Fifteenth Century Suffolk Gentleman* (Cambridge, 1981), p. 133; J. G. Nichols, *Narratives of the Days of the Reformation*, Camden Society, 77 (1859), pp. 238–40.

118. Nelson, pp. 23–5.

119. Herodotus, *Histories*, book 1, chapter 14, told in Ranulph Higden, *Polychronicon*, vol. iii, ed. J. R. Lumby (RS, 1871), pp. 140–3.

120. Orme, 1989, pp. 142–3, 150.

121. Adam of Usk, pp. 94–7.

122. R. Carew, *The Survey of Cornwall* (London, 1602), fol. 124v.

123. *The Chronicle of Queen Jane*, ed. J. G. Nichols, Camden Society, 48 (1850), p. 67; *Calendar of State Papers Spanish, 1554* (London, 1949), p. 146.

124. *CCR 1364–8*, pp. 101–2; T. Rymer, *Foedera, Conventiones, Literae*, 20 vols (London, 1704–35), vi, 468.

125. *Statutes of the Realm*, ii, 57.

126. Ibid., pp. 163, 432, 462–3, 472–3, 494, 569, 649–50.

127. Ibid., iii, 2–3.

128. On this subject, see Opie, 1997b, pp. 1–8.

129. Jenny Swanson, p. 327.

130. Barclay, 1928, p. 184.

131. J. C. Robertson, iii, 9; Stenton, *Norman London*, p. 30.

132. Orme, 1976, p. 62.

133. *LPFD*, iii part i, p. 503.

134. Lupton, p. 278; *VCH Lancashire*, ii, 584.

135. Hutton, 1996, pp. 153–8.

136. Chaucer, 'Canterbury Tales', VII 2859–64 (B^2 *4049–54).

137. Cambridge, St John's College, MS F.26, fols. 28v–29r; Thomson, 1979, p. 150. There is another less specific school cock-fighting poem in Bodleian, MS Rawlinson D 328, fol. 72r.

138. Opie, 1979b, pp. 7–8; Bruegel, 'The Battle between Carnival and Lent' (1559).

139. *York Civic Records*, ed. Angelo Raine, vol. iii, Yorkshire Archaeological Society, Record Series, 106 (1942), p. 70.

140. British Library, Add. MS 42130, fol. 196v;

141. Millar, fol. 196v.

141. Lydgate, 1911, pp. 352–4. See also *Mundus et Infans*, p. 5; Lester, p. 116.

142. Grosjean, pp. 61–2.

143. For nutting on 14 September, see *Grim the Collier of Croyden*, II.i, in Robert Dodsley, *A Select Collection of Old English Plays*, ed. W. Carew Hazlitt, 4th edn., 15 vols (London, 1874–6), viii, 418.

144. H. C. Maxwell-Lyte, *History of Eton College, 1440–1910*, 4th edn. (London, 1911), p. 152.

145. Grosjean, p. 54.

146. Tusser, *Five Hundred Points of Good Husbandrie*, fol. 23v.

147. Horman, fol. 280r.

148. Wilkins, iii, 859–60; Hughes and Larkin, i, 301–2. A further day, St Edmund's (probably 20 November), is mentioned in Chambers, i, 367.

149. A. R. Wright, iii, 167–86.

150. On what follows, see Chambers, i, 336–71, and Shahar, 1994, pp. 243–60.

151. Above, pp. 232–3.

152. Rickert, p. 121; Nichols and Rimbault.

153. G. Oliver, *Lives of the Bishops of Exeter and a History of the Cathedral* (Exeter, 1861), pp. 228–9.

154. *Registrum Statutorum et Consuetudinum Ecclesiae Cathedralis Sancti Pauli Londinensis*, ed. W. Sparrow Simpson (London, 1873), pp. 91–4.

155. Chambers, ii, 287–9.

156. Keith Thomas, 1976.

157. Above, p. 157.

158. *Liber Memorandorum Ecclesie de Bernewelle*, ed. J. W. Clark (Cambridge, 1907), pp. 41–2.

159. John Stow, *A Survey of London*, ed. C. L. Kingsford, 2 vols (Oxford, 1908), i, 95; above, p. 319.

160. Above, pp. 227–8.

161. PRO, E 101/368/12, fol. 3.

162. PRO, DL 28/1/6, fol. 36r; Anglo, pp. 29–40.

163. On this subject, see Orme, 1984, pp. 163–70.

164. Walsingham, 1867–9, i, 73.

165. Oxford, New College, MS 264, fols 262r–265v.

166. Thomas Warton, *History of English Poetry*, ed. W. Carew Hazlitt, 4 vols (London, 1871), iii, 310, 312.

167. *The Chester Mystery Cycle*; *The N-Town Play*; *The Towneley Plays*; *The York Plays*.

168. On this topic, see Rastall, pp. 308–27.

169. *Non-Cycle Plays and Fragments*, ed. Norman Davis, EETS, ss, 1 (1970), pp. xvi, 1–7.

170. *Records of Early English Drama: Coventry*, ed. R. W. Ingram (Toronto and Buffalo, NY, 1981), pp. 86, 168, 186.

171. *The Chester Mystery Cycle*, i, 132, 151, 173, 231–3, 259, 385.

172. *The N-Town Play*, i, 45, 90–1.

173. *The Towneley Plays*, i, 52–3; *The York Plays*, pp. 93, 105, 119, 135–40, 257, 278–80.

174. Bodleian, Lincoln College MS lat. 130, fols 1–2; Cynthia R. Bland, *The Teaching of Grammar in Late Medieval England* (East Lansing, Mich., 1991), p. 115.

175. *The Macro Plays*, p. 2.
176. Ibid., pp. 114, 119.
177. Ibid., p. 132.
178. Ibid., p. 144.
179. Ibid., p. 158.
180. Thomson, 1984, p. 111.
181. Thomson, 1979, p. 125.
182. Orme, 1989, pp. 77, 119; above, p. ••.
183. Roper, p. 5.
184. *The Plays of Henry Medwall*, ed. Alan H. Nelson (Cambridge, 1980), especially pp. 32, 42–3, 102.
185. *Mundus et Infans*, pp. 3–5; Lester, pp. 112–17.
186. Heywood, *Play of the Weather*, sig. D.ii verso; STC 14837, *Jacke Jugeler*, sig. A.i recto.
187. M. F. J. McDonnell, *A History of St Paul's School* (London, 1909), p. 94.
188. *Hamlet*, II.ii; Norman Sanders *et al.*, *The Revels History of Drama in English*, vol. ii: *1500–1576* (London and New York, 1980), pp. 117–29.
189. Above, p. 321.
190. *On the Properties of Things*, i, 301.
191. *Mundus et Infans*, p. 4; Lester, p. 115.
192. *Letters and Papers of John Shillingford, Mayor of Exeter 1447–50*, ed. Stuart A. Moore, Camden Society, new series, 2 (1871), p. 101.
193. *The Pilgrimage of the Life of Man*, ed. Furnivall, ii, 304–6.
194. *Ratis Raving*, p. 61.
195. *Mundus et Infans*, passim; Lester, pp. 111–56.
196. Above, p. 306.
197. *Certain Sermons or Homilies Appointed to be Read in Churches*, repr. (London, 1843), p. 275.
198. Nelson, p. 15.

CHAPTER 6: CHURCH

1. Langland, A i.73–6; B i.75–8; C i.72–5.
2. *Councils and Synods I*, i, 321; ii, 1070–1; *Councils and Synods II*, i, 61, and passim.
3. *Councils and Synods II*, ii, 900–5.
4. Ibid., i, 61.
5. Ibid., i, 228, 269, 346, 405, 439, 518, 648.
6. *Visitation Articles*, ii, 17, 21, 56, 63, 85, 105–6, 129.
7. Some chantry and guild priests statutorily acted as schoolmasters from the 1380s onwards, and others may have taught schools privately, but a requirement that all should teach is not found before the legislation of the 1530s (Orme, 1973, pp. 6–7, 196–7, 274–82.).
8. Brightman, ii, 778–90.
9. Ibid., pp. 796–8.
10. In addition to what follows, see Lynch, 1986, and Coster, pp. 301–11.
11. Langland, B.ix 74–8.
12. *Manuale*, p. 32; cf. Mirk, 1974, lines 151–8. On baptism and instruction, see also Duffy, pp. 53–87.
13. *Manuale*, p. 42.
14. Compare STC 4115; Burgo, fols 9v–10r.
15. *Manuale*, p. 42.

16. Above, p. 37.
17. *Councils and Synods I*, i, 465, 474; ii, 1067; *Councils and Synods II*, i, 88, 644.
18. *OED*, s.v. 'gossip'.
19. *Original Letters Illustrative of English History, Third Series*, ed. Henry Ellis, 4 vols (London, 1846), ii, 225–6; see also above, p. 24.
20. Millar, pp. 53, 55.
21. *The Register of Edmund Stafford, 1395–1419*, ed. F. C. Hingeston-Randolph (London and Exeter, 1886), pp. 397–8.
22. *HMC, Report on the Manuscripts of Lord Middleton* (London, 1911), pp. 338, 343–4, 365, 367–8, 376, 381–2.
23. See also above, p. 30–1.
24. Haas, p. 11.
25. *CIPM*, iii, 379; v, 37, vi, 78; cf. vii, 480.
26. E.g. *CIPM*, iii, 128–9; vii, 340; above, p. 34.
27. Foxe, viii, 126.
28. *Anglo-Saxon Wills*, ed. Dorothy Whitelock (Cambridge, 1930), pp. 50–1.
29. See, for example, *Notes or Abstracts of the Wills contained in . . . the Great Orphan Book* (Bristol), ed. T. P. Wadley (Bristol, 1886), pp. 19, 25, 27, 38–9, 43, 143; *Somerset Medieval Wills (1383–1500)*, ed. F. W. Weaver, Somerset Record Society, 16 (1901), pp. 107, 128, 161, 320, 355, 357, 405; idem, *1501–1530*, ibid., 19 (1903), pp. 213–14.
30. *Somerset Medieval Wills 1501–1530*, ed. Weaver, pp. 213–14.
31. *Testamenta Eboracensia*, vol. ii, ed. J. Raine, Surtees Society, 30 (1855), p. 117.
32. N. R. Ker, *Medieval Manuscripts in British Libraries*, 4 vols (Oxford, 1969–92), ii, 109–11; F. J. Furnivall, 'The Nevile and Southwell Families of Mereworth in Kent', *Notes and Queries*, 4th series, 2 (1868), pp. 577–8.
33. *Councils and Synods I*, i, 321; *Councils and Synods II*, i, 61, 228, 423–4.
34. *The Lay Folk's Catechism*, ed. T. F. Simmons and H. E. Nolloth, EETS, os, 118 (1901), pp. 21–3; *Religious Pieces in Prose and Verse*, ed. G. G. Perry, EETS, os, 26 (1867), p. 2.
35. Reginald Pecock, *The Donet*, ed. Elsie Vaughan Hitchcock, EETS, os, 156 (1921), p. 70.
36. Above, pp. 84–5.
37. Above, p. 264.
38. Above, p. 262.
39. *LPFD*, xiii part ii, p. 223.
40. Above, p. 267–8.
41. Lawrence, pp. 203, 223.
42. Chaucer, 'Canterbury Tales', B^2 1695–1705.
43. *Councils and Synods II*, i, 269, 346, 405, 518, 648.
44. Foxe, iii, 599.
45. *Index*, no. 1891; Furnivall, 1868a/1931, pp. 48–52.
46. Mustanoja, pp. 173–5.
47. Ibid., pp. 159–60.
48. Clayton, plate 44.
49. *Liber Pontificalis of Edmund Lacy, Bishop of Exeter*, ed. Ralph Barnes (Exeter, 1847), 212–13, 235–6.
50. *Visitation Articles*, ii, 126.

51. E.g. Foxe, iv, 123, 177, 182.

52. Keith Thomas, *Religion and the Decline of Magic* (London, 1971), pp. 505–6.

53. *The Metrical Chronicle of Robert of Gloucester*, ed. W. A. Wright, vol. ii (RS, 1887), p. 621, line 8704; *The Early South-English Legendary*, ed. C. Horstmann, vol. i, EETS, os, 87 (1887), p. 435, line 129; *The Middle English Lai le Freine*, lines 135–230.

54. *MLD*, p. 1099; Stone, 1977–92, p. 339; *MED*, *OED*, s.v. 'grace'.

55. *HMC, 8th Report*, Appendix (London, 1908), part i, section ii, no 281b.

56. Moran, p. 41, quoting Hull Corporation Archives, Bench Book, IIIa, fol. 58.

57. STC 19; *The ABC*, ed. Shuckburgh.

58. Above, p. 71.

59. On Rogationtide food, see Orme, 1995, pp. 273–4, 290.

60. Pantin, p. 399.

61. Orme, 1989, p. 185.

62. Asser, pp. 89–90; Keynes and Lapidge, pp. 107–8.

63. Pantin, pp. 398–422.

64. C. A. J. Armstrong, 'The Piety of Cecily, Duchess of York', *For Hilaire Belloc*, ed. D. Woodruff (London, 1942), pp. 79–80; John Fisher, pp. 294–5.

65. Caxton, 1971, pp. 14, 16–17.

66. Orme, 1989, p. 183.

67. Ibid., p. 185; see also Roper, p. 25.

68. BL, Add. MS 18850, fol. 256r; Janet Backhouse, *The Bedford Hours* (London, 1990), pp. 59–61.

69. *The Lisle Letters*, ed. Muriel St Clair Byrne, 6 vols (Chicago and London, 1981), iii, 93.

70. Furnivall, 1868b, pp. 4–5.

71. Above, p. 77–8.

72. Furnivall, 1868b, pp. 8–9.

73. PRO, E 101/389/11.

74. Cramer, p. 118; Owst, p. 37.

75. Langland, B.I.178.

76. *Visitations in the Diocese of Lincoln, 1517–1531*, ed. A. Hamilton Thompson, vol i, Lincoln Record Society, 33 (1940), pp. 69, 112.

77. Hunnisett, p. 9.

78. PRO, JUST 2/200, m. 6.

79. Grosjean, pp. 156–9.

80. Reginald of Durham, *Libellus de Vita et Miraculis S. Godrici*, Surtees Society, 20 (1845), p. 403.

81. Above, pp. 98, 110–11; Finucane, passim.

82. *The Chronicle of Jocelin of Brakelond*, ed. H. E. Butler (London, 1949), p. 37.

83. Caxton, 1971, p. 87; Mustanoja, p. 187.

84. Kempe, p. 200.

85. Caxton, 1971, p. 59.

86. Thomas of Monmouth, pp. 12–14.

87. Lawrence, pp. 203, 224–6.

88. *Acta Sanctorum*, October, v, 137–8.

89. Johnstone, pp. 417–20.

90. Foxe, v, 454.

91. Elyot, fol. 17r-v (book i, chapter 4).

92. Orme, 1978, p. 35; *Sir Gawain and the Green Knight*, line 940.

93. Furnivall, 1868a/1931, p. 382; idem, 1868b, pp. 10–11.

94. *Visitations in the Diocese of Lincoln*, ed. Hamilton Thompson, i, 23, 26. For post-Reformation examples of children's disturbances, see Hale, pp. 268, 276, 278.

95. Above, p. 196–7.

96. Matthew, xviii.5, xix.13–14; Mark, ix.36, x.13–14; Luke, ix.47, xviii.15–17.

97. *The Leofric Missal*, ed. F. E. Warren (Oxford, 1883), p. 238; *Manuale et Processionale ad Usum Insignis Ecclesie Eboracensis*, ed. W. G. Henderson, Surtees Society, 63 (1875), part ii, pp. 136, 147, 150; H. A. Wilson, p. 178.

98. Robert Pulleyn, 'De Officiis Ecclesiasticis', book i, chapter 20, in *Patrologia Latina*, ed. J. P. Migne, vol. 177 (Paris, 1879), cols 392–3.

99. Norman P. Tanner, 1990, i, 245.

100. Robert of Flamborough, p. 268.

101. Bodleian, MS Bodley 828, fols 121v–2r.

102. Burgo, fols 10v, 19v–20r; compare also Aquinas, vol. xvii (part iii, question 80, article 9); vol. xviii (supplement, question 32, article 4).

103. E.g. *Councils and Ecclesiastical Documents*, iii, 328–9. See also Meens, pp. 53–65.

104. Norman P. Tanner, i, 245; compare Aquinas, vol. xix (supplement, question 39, article 2).

105. *Councils and Synods II*, i, 90; cf. pp. 146, 444, 645; but no age seems implied in i, 305, 372–3, 457, 596, 706–7, and ii, 995–6.

106. Wilkins, ii, 512; Lyndwood, p. 36.

107. *The Poems of William of Shoreham*, ed. M. Konrath, vol i, EETS, es, 86 (1902), p. 41.

108. Burgo, fol. 70r.

109. Lyndwood, pp. 35–6; compare Aquinas, vol. xviii (supplement, question 32, article 4).

110. Morey, p. 244; Kirby, pp. 464–5; *Dives and Pauper*, i part i, 250.

111. Above, p. 225.

112. Friedberg, ii, cols 570–1, 1140; Aquinas, vol. xix (supplement, question 39, article 2); Bodleian, MS Bodley 828, fol. 178r; Burgo, fol. 81r.

113. Above, pp. 335–6.

114. Colgrave, pp. 252–3.

115. *Manuale . . . Eboracensis*, ed. Henderson, part ii, pp. 136, 147, 150.

116. Banting, pp. 168–9.

117. H. A. Wilson, p. 178.

118. Alfred C. Fryer, 'On Fonts with Representations of the Seven Sacraments', *The Archaeological Journal*, 59 (1902), pp. 46–7; G. McN. Rushforth, 'Seven Sacraments Compositions in English Medieval Art', *The Antiquaries Journal*, 9 (1929), pp. 83–100.

119. Bodleian, MS Eng. hist. b 208, fol. 20; Hall, pp. 806, 825.

120. *Councils and Synods II*, i, 32, 71, 298, 369, 441, 453, 591, 703; ii, 989.

121. Ibid., i, 32; ii, 897.

122. Wilkins, ii, 512.

123. Bodleian, MS Bodley 828, fols 121v–122r.

124. Compare Aquinas, vol. xvii (part iii, question 72, article 8).

125. Burgo, fol. 10r-v.

126. Lyndwood, p. 34; Mirk, 1974, lines 157–8.

127. Lyndwood, p. 34.

128. On what follows, see J. D. C. Fisher, 1970.

129. Strype, i part ii, 344–7.

130. Brightman, ii, 776–8.

131. E. Cardwell, *Synodalia*, 2 vols (Oxford, 1842), ii, 510.

132. *The Injunctions and Ecclesiastical Proceedings of Richard Barnes, Bishop of Durham* [ed. J. Raine,] Surtees Society, 22 (1850), pp. 14–15.

133. Susan J. Wright, pp. 203–28.

134. Douie and Farmer, i, 126–7.

135. Mannyng, lines 9870–88.

136. Texts of the rite in England go back to the tenth century: see Banting, pp. 14–15, 167–9. Later examples include H. A. Wilson, p. 221, and *Liber Pontificalis of Edmund Lacy*, ed. Barnes, pp. 9–10.

137. *Councils and Synods II*, i, 636; ii, 897.

138. The formula varies slightly in the pontificals. This example comes from *Liber Pontificalis of Edmund Lacy*, ed. Barnes, pp. 9–10.

139. Wilkins, ii, 512; Burgo, fol. 10v; Mirk, 1974, lines 661–70; Lyndwood, p. 34.

140. Lyndwood, p. 34.

141. *The Register of William Greenfield, Lord Archbishop of York, 1306–1315*, vol. ii, ed. W. Brown and A. Hamilton Thompson, Surtees Society, 149 (1934), pp. 220–1. Compare the rates for funerals at St Margaret Lothbury, London in 1571: 10d. for children up to fourteen, and 16d. above that age (Legg, p. 73).

142. Hughes and Larkin, i, 216, 225.

143. Pollock and Maitland, i, 568; ii, 438–9.

144. Moore, pp. 168–80.

145. Orme, 1977, pp. 161–9; *The Register of the Guild of the Holy Trinity, Coventry*, ed. Mary Dormer Harris, Dugdale Society, 13 (1935), passim.

146. H. W. C. Davis, 'The Commune of Bury St. Edmunds, 1264', *English Historical Review*, 24 (1909), pp. 313–17.

147. *English Gilds*, ed. Toulmin Smith, 2nd edn., EETS, os, 40 (1892), pp. 51–3.

148. Angelo Raine, *Mediaeval York* (London, 1955), pp. 160–1, 250.

149. J. C. Cox, *Churchwardens' Accounts from the Fourteenth Century to the Close of the Seventeenth Century* (London, 1913), p. 22; *The Medieval Records of a London City Church (St Mary at Hill)*, ed. Henry Littlehales, part i, EETS, os, 125 (1904), p. 283.

150. Arthur Hussey, *Testamenta Cantiana*, part ii (London, 1907), pp. 18–19, 136, 181, 255, 260, 380.

151. Joanna Mattingly, 'The Medieval Parish Guilds of Cornwall', *Journal of the Royal Institution of Cornwall*, new series, 10 part 5 (1989), pp. 311, 320–2.

152. Robert Whiting, *The Blind Devotion of the People: Popular Religion and the English Reformation* (Cambridge, 1989), pp. 105, 107, 110–12;

Exeter, Devon Record Office, 296A/PW4–5 (on Modbury); Hanham, entries indexed on p. 216.

153. *Church-wardens' Accounts of Croscombe, &c.*, ed. E. Hobhouse, Somerset Record Society, 4 (1890), pp. 9–40, 67–8.

154. Above, p. 331.

155. *The Accounts of the Wardens of the Parish of Morebath, Devon, 1520–73*, ed. J. Erskine Binney (Exeter, 1904), passim.

156. Asser, p. 93; Keynes and Lapidge, p. 103.

157. Canon law specified that the candidates must have reached their eighteenth, twentieth, and twenty-fifth years (Friedberg, ii, col. 1140; Bodleian, MS Bodley 828, fol. 178r; Burgo, fol. 81r).

158. 1 Samuel, i.24–ii.11; James, 1953, pp. 41–2.

159. *The Rule of St. Benedict*, ed. D. O. Hunter Blair, 5th edn. (Fort Augustus, 1948), pp. 150–1; Knowles, 1951, pp. 110–11.

160. On this subject, see Crawford, pp. 135–8.

161. *Statuta Capitulorum Generalium Ordinis Cisterciensis, ab anno 1116 ad annum 1786*, ed. Joseph Canivez, 8 vols (Louvain, 1933–41), i, 31, 84.

162. *Historiae Anglicanae Scriptores X* [ed. Roger Twysden,] (London, 1652), col. 1815.

163. Friedberg, ii, cols. 571–2.

164. *Chapters of the English Black Monks*, ed. W. A. Pantin, 3 vols, Royal Historical Society, Camden third series, 45, 47, 54 (1931–7), i, 10, 99; Knowles, 1948–59, ii, 230–1.

165. On this topic, see Power, especially pp. 4–14.

166. *VCH Wiltshire*, iii, 247, 249.

167. Power, p. 26.

168. *CPL, 1396–1404*, p. 385; *VCH London*, i, 518–19.

169. On boys in friaries, see Orme, 1973, pp. 227–8.

170. E.g. *The Major Latin Works of John Gower*, trans. E. W. Stockton (Seattle, 1962), p. 189.

171. J. R. H. Moorman, *The Grey Friars in Cambridge, 1225–1538* (Cambridge, 1952), pp. 107–8; Katherine Walsh, *A Fourteenth-Century Scholar and Primate: Richard FitzRalph* (Oxford, 1981), pp. 424–5.

172. *Calendar of Select Pleas and Memoranda of the City of London, 1381–1412*, ed. A. H. Thomas and P. E. Jones (Cambridge, 1932), p. 182.

173. *Rotuli Parliamentorum*, iii, 502; *Statutes of the Realm*, ii, 138.

174. *Jack Upland*, ed. P. L. Heyworth (Oxford, 1968), pp. 63, 89, 109.

175. *Minsters and Parish Churches: The Local Church in Transition, 950–1200*, ed. W. John Blair (Oxford, 1988).

176. On this subject, see Kathleen Edwards, *The English Secular Cathedrals in the Middle Ages*, 2nd edn. (Manchester, 1967), pp. 303–17, and Orme, 1983b, pp. 85–100.

177. Above, p. 116.

178. On what follows, see Roger Bowers, 'The Vocal Scoring, Choral Balance and Performing Pitch of Latin Church Polyphony in England, c.1500–1558', *Journal of the Royal Musical Association*, 112 (1987), pp. 38–76 at p. 48; idem,

1995, pp. 1–47 at 17–35; idem, 'The Musicians and the Music of St George's, *c.*1400–1500', in *Saint George's Chapel, Windsor, in the Fifteenth Century*, ed. Eileen Scarff (Stroud, forthcoming); A. F. Leach, *English Schools at the Reformation 1546–8* (Westminster, 1896), pp. 31, 219.

179. On what follows, see Bowers, 1999, pp. 177–222.

180. Orme, 1991, pp. 292–3.

181. W. G. Searle, *Christ Church, Canterbury*, Cambridge Antiquarian Society, 34 (1902), p. 106.

182. T. West, *The Antiquities of Furness*, 3rd edn. (Ulverston, 1822), p. 195.

183. Orme, 1991, pp. 291–5.

184. *Councils and Synods, I,* i, 331.

185. On clergy numbers, see J. R. H. Moorman, *Church Life in England in the Thirteenth Century* (Cambridge, 1955), pp. 53–6, and R. N. Swanson, pp. 30–1.

186. *MLD,* s.v. 'aquaebajulus'; *MED, OED,* s.v. 'parish clerk'. On the office of clerk, see Legg.

187. Hunnisett, pp. 37–8.

188. Lyndwood, p. 142.

189. Hanham, p. xvii.

190. On this subject, see Orme, 1973, pp. 180–1.

191. Orme, 1995, pp. 281–2.

192. *The Register of Edmund Lacy, Bishop of Exeter, 1420–1455:* Registrum Commune, ed. G. R. Dunstan, 5 vols, Devon and Cornwall Record Society, new series, 7, 10, 13, 16, 18 (1963–72), ii, 214.

193. *The Oxford Dictionary of English Proverbs*, ed. F. P. Wilson, 3rd edn. (Oxford, 1970), p. 609.

194. Chaucer, 'Canterbury Tales', A 3,310–38.

195. Robbins, pp. 21–2.

196. Ibid., pp. 23–4; cf. pp. 18–19, 24–5.

197. *The Late Medieval Religious Plays of Bodleian MS Digby 133*, ed. D. C. Baker *et al.*, EETS, os, 283 (1982), pp. 62–5.

198. Furnivall, 1868b, pp. 10–11.

199. *The ABC*, ed. Shuckburgh fol. 2v.

200. Orme, 1976, p. 198.

201. Ibid., pp. 111, 130, 150.

202. Lyndwood, p. 142; Stephenson, p. 493.

203. Hanham, p. xvii.

204. *Constitutions and Canons Ecclesiastical 1604*, ed. J. V. Bullard (London, 1934), p. 94. Material on the history of clerks is collected in Legg, pp. xvii–lxii, where the tendency of the clerk to become an adult also seems to emerge.

205. *Breviarium ad Usum Insignis Ecclesiae Sarum*, ed. F. Procter and C. Wordsworth, 3 vols (Cambridge, 1879–86), iii, col. 975; cf. *The Hereford Breviary*, ed. W. H. Frere and L. E. G. Brown, 3 vols, Henry Bradshaw Society, 26, 40, 46 (1904–15), ii, 389.

206. Above, p. 188.

207. *Breviarium ad Usum Sarum*, ed. Procter and Wordsworth, i, col. clxxiv.

208. *Ordinale Exon*, ed. J. N. Dalton, vol i, Henry Bradshaw Society, 37 (1909), p. 64.

209. *Breviarium Sarum*, ed. Procter and Wordsworth, i, col. clxxiv.

210. Above, pp. 188–9. On the feast of the Innocents, see also Dudley, pp. 233–42.

211. On the sermon, see above, p. 188.

212. *Breviarium ad Usum Sarum*, ed. Procter and Wordsworth, i, cols. ccxxix–ccxlv; cf. *The Hereford Breviary*, ed. Frere and Brown, i, 161–3. The account is fuller in *Ordinale Exon*, ed. Dalton, i, 74–6, but some details here may represent Exeter practice.

213. David Farmer, *The Oxford Dictionary of Saints*, 3rd edn. (Oxford, 1992), pp. 120–1, 151–2, 279–80, 377, 424–5, 496.

214. On this subject, see Page-Phillips.

215. Reginald of Durham, *Libellus*, p. 149; *Twelfth Night*, III.ii.72–3.

216. Wilkins, ii, 553.

217. See, for example, *The Register of Edmund Lacy, Bishop of Exeter*, ed. Dunstan, iv, 71, 79, 80, 82, 84, 92, etc.

217. *Notes or Abstracts of Wills*, ed. Wadley, p. 145.

219. Susan Brigden, *London and the Reformation* (Oxford, 1898), p. 33.

CHAPTER 7: LEARNING TO READ

1. Bede, pp. 150–1 (book ii, chapter 5).

2. Ibid., pp. 430–1 (book iv, chapter 26); Colgrave, p. 237.

3. On medieval literacy in England, see Clanchy, with bibliography, and Orme, 1996, pp. 35–56.

4. Asser, pp. 21, 58–60, 67, 73, 75; Keynes and Lapidge, pp. 75, 90–1, 96–7, 99–100.

5. *Carte Nativorum: a Peterborough Cartulary of the Fourteenth Century*, ed. C. N. L. Brooke and M. M. Postan, Northamptonshire Record Society, 20 (1960).

6. On medieval English schools, see Orme, 1973, 1976, and 1989.

7. See the romance of *Floris and Blancheflur*, above, p. 286.

8. *Ancrene Wisse*, pp. 216–17.

9. J. C. Dickinson, *An Ecclesiastical History of England: the Later Middle Ages* (London, 1979), p. 387.

10. *VCH Lincolnshire*, ii, 451.

11. Sylvia Thrupp, *The Merchant Class of Medieval London*, p. 171; idem, 'Aliens in and around London in the fifteenth century', *Studies in London History presented to P. E. Jones*, ed. A. E. Hollaender and W. Kellaway (London, 1969), p. 269.

12. PRO, C 1/290/78.

13. On what follows, see Orme, 1984, pp. 16–28, 55–60.

14. Above, p. 229.

15. Orderic Vitalis, v, 6–9.

16. Orme, 1976, p. 95.

17. Clark, 1905, p. 25.

18. On what follows, see Orme, 1984, pp. 103–6.

19. Suetonius, *The Twelve Caesars*, book ii, chapter 64.

20. Caxton, 1971, p. 192.

21. Elyot, fol. 19r (book i, chapter 5).

22. Above, p. 278.

23. Asser, p. 20; Keynes and Lapidge, p. 75.

24. Tony Hunt, *Teaching and Learning Latin in Thirteenth-Century England*, 3 vols (Cambridge, 1991), i, 11–12.

25. W. W. Skeat, 'Nominale sive Verbale', *Transactions of the Philological Society* (1903–6), p. 7.

26. Knighton, pp. 540–1.

27. *Plumpton Letters*, p. 181.

28. Above, p. 280.

29. James, 1953, pp. 38–49.

30. Jacobus de Voragine, *The Golden Legend*, trans. William Granger Ryan, 2 vols (Princeton, NJ, 1993), ii, 152–3; compare also *The Middle English Stanzaic Versions of the Life of Saint Anne*, ed. Roscoe E. Parker, EETS, os, 174 (1928), pp. 9–11.

31. On this topic, see Wendy Scase, 'St Anne and the Education of the Virgin', in *England in the Fourteenth Century*, ed. Nicholas Rogers (Stamford, 1993), pp. 81–96, and Pamela Sheingorn, '"The Wise Mother": the Image of St Anne Teaching the Virgin Mary', *Gesta*, 32 (1993), pp. 69–80.

32. For discussion and examples, see Christopher Norton, David Park, and Paul Binski, *Dominican Painting in East Anglia* (Woodbridge, 1987), pp. 51–3, and Richard Marks, *Stained Glass in England during the Middle Ages* (London, 1993), p. 75; Figs. 13, 43, 45, 56, 142.

33. Bodleian, MS Douce 231, fol. 3r.

34. Norton *et al.*, *Dominican Painting*, p. 53 note 110.

35. Dr Michael Clanchy, private communication.

36. *Plumpton Letters*, p. 30.

37. Orme, 1989, pp. 184–5.

38. Orme, 1973, p. 28.

39. Elyot, fol. 18r (book i, chapter 5).

40. Hoole, pp. 1–2.

41. On what follows, Alexandre-Bidon, 1989, pp. 953–92, is a valuable and relevant survey, especially of continental European material; see also B. L. Wolpe, 'Florilegium Alphabeticum: Alphabets in Medieval Manuscripts', in *Calligraphy and Palaeography: Essays Presented to Alfred Fairbank*, ed. A. S. Osley (London, 1965), pp. 69–74.

42. Parkes, 1997, p. 8.

43. On Anglo-Saxon alphabets, see Robinson, pp. 443–75.

44. BL, Harley MS 208, fols. 87v–88r.

45. BL, Stowe MS 57, fol. 3r; Robinson, p. 450.

46. On primers, see above, p. 264.

47. On continental alphabets, see Paul F. Grendler, *Schooling in Renaissance Italy: Literacy and Learning 1300–1600* (Baltimore and London, 1989), pp. 142–61.

48. Young and Aitken, pp. 392–3.

49. STC 19; *ABC*, ed. Shuckburgh, fol. 1r.

50. Schreiner, plate 19, no 32.

51. Bodleian, MS Rawlinson C 209.

52. *Grammatici Latini*, ed. H. Keil, 8 vols (Leipzig, 1855–80), ii, 5–6; iv, 367.

53. Pierre Champion, 'Pièces joyeuses du xve siècle', *Revue de Philologie française et de littérature*, 21 (1907),

pp. 191–2; Alexandre-Bidon, 1989, p. 968.

54. *The Dance of Death*, pp. 68–9.

55. See, for example, Alexandre-Bidon, 1989, p. 986.

56. Bodleian, MS Wood empt. 20, fol. 97v; E. Wilson, fol. 120r.

57. E.g. *Pierce the Ploughmans Crede*, p. 1.

58. *OED*, s.v. 'christ-cross-row', 'cross-row'.

59. Exodus, xxiv.12, xxxi.18, xxxii.16–19, xxxiv.1, 28; Deuteronomy, ix.9–17, x.4.

60. Revelation, i.8, xxi.6, xxii.13.

61. *Isidori Hispalensis Episcopi Etymologiarum sive Originum*, ed. W. M. Lindsay, 2 vols (Oxford, 1911), i, I.iii.4–5, I.iv.1, V.xxxix.10–11.

62. *Grammatici Latini*, ed. Keil, viii, 302–5.

63. *On the Properties of Things*, ii, 1373–4. Compare, however, Bartholomew's contemporary, Vincent of Beauvais, whose *Speculum Doctrinale* (Venice, 1591), book ii, chapters 6–8, gives a more just and historical account of the Hebrew, Greek, and Latin alphabets in the manner of Isidore.

64. Alexandre-Bidon, 1989, pp. 957–8.

65. Banting, p. 38; cf. *The Claudius Pontificals*, ed. D. A. Turner, Henry Bradshaw Society, 97 (1971), p. 44; *Pontificale Lanaletense*, ed. G. H. Doble, Henry Bradshaw Society, 74 (1937), p. 7; H. A. Wilson, p. 105.

66. Jacobus de Voragine, *The Golden Legend*, ed. Ryan, ii, 182.

67. *On the Properties of Things*, i, 40.

68. Nichols and Rimbault, p. 2.

69. *Index*, no. 33; *On the Properties of Things*, i, 40.

70. Orme, 1993, p. 9.

71. Furnivall, 1868a/1931, p. 181.

72. Clark, 1905, p. 4.

73. STC 14546.5; J. Ames, *Typographical Antiquities*, ed. T. F. Dibdin, 4 vols (London, 1810–19), ii, 367–9.

74. *Pierce the Ploughmans Crede*, p. 1.

75. *Index*, no. 604; Cambridge, Caius College, MS 174/95, p. 482; *Cambridge Middle English Lyrics*, ed. W. R. Person (Seattle, 1953). pp. 5–6.

76. E. Wilson, fol. 56v.

77. STC 18133; Thomas Morley, *A Plaine and Easie Introduction to Practicall Musicke* (London, 1597), p. 36.

78. *Sir Gawain and the Green Knight*, lines 761–2.

79. *A Selection from the Minor Poems of Dan John Lydgate*, ed. J. O. Halliwell, Percy Society, 2 (1840), p. 42. The text is not now attributed to Lydgate.

80. See, for example, Plimpton, p. 19.

81. H. Leith Spencer, *English Preaching in the Late Middle Ages* (Oxford, 1993), pp. 140, 417.

82. Beryl Smalley, *English Friars and Antiquity in the Early Fourteenth Century* (Oxford, 1960), p. 192.

83. *Index*, nos. 1523 (BL, Harley MS 3954, fol. 87r; also Edinburgh, National Library of Scotland, MS Advocates 18.7.21 fol. 122v) and 1483 (Bodleian, MS Bodley 789, fol. 152r). The first of these is printed in *Political, Religious and Love Poems*, ed. F. J. Furnivall, 2nd ed., EETS, os 15 (1903), pp. 271–8.

84. Reproduced in Schreiner, plate 19, no 32.

85. Reproduced in Grendler, *Schooling in Renaissance Italy*, pp. 145–6.

86. *OED*, s.v. 'horn-book'.

87. On horn-books, see the detailed but rhapsodical account of Tuer, with numerous illustrations.

88. See *OED*, under the letters of the alphabet.

89. Alexandre-Bidon, 1989, p. 968.

90. Robinson, p. 450; *OED*, s.v. 'Y'.

91. Orme, 1993, pp. 9–10.

92. *OED*, s.v. 'tittle'.

93. Morley, *A Plaine and Easie Introduction*, p. 36.

94. Hoole, p. 4.

95. Flora Thompson, *Lark Rise* (Oxford, 1939), chapter 11.

96. Alexandre-Bidon, 1989, p. 968.

97. Ibid., p. 967.

98. Ibid., p. 968.

99. STC 21850.7; *The First and Best Part of Scoggins Jests* (London, 1626), pp. 10–11.

100. Hoole, pp. 4, 8–9.

101. John Wycliffe, *De Veritate Sacrae Scripturae*, ed. Rudolf Buddensieg, 3 vols, Wyclif Society, 29–31 (1905–7), i, 44.

102. Rastell, p. 55.

103. Christopher Marlowe, *Doctor Faustus*, ed. John D. Jump (London, 1962), scene vii, lines 7–8.

104. *OED*, s.v. 'I', 'O', 'ampersand'.

105. Compare the Hunter primer, which places the Latin words *Pater noster* in red after the alphabet, and before the English text of the Paternoster (Young and Aitken, pp. 392–3).

106. Schreiner, plate 19, no 32.

107. Alexandre-Bidon, 1989, pp. 986–7.

108. STC 19, dated 1538: *ABC*, ed. Shuckburgh, fol. 1r; compare STC 17.7, dated *c*.1535: *ABC*, ed. Allnutt.

109. *Councils and Synods I*, i, 321, 483; *Councils and Synods II*, i, 61, 134, 465; ii, 1076.

110. Banting, pp. 17, 157; Lyndwood, p. 117.

111. Asser, p. 59; Keynes and Lapidge, pp. 90–1.

112. Orme, 1973, pp. 63–6.

113. Clanchy (p. 111) suggests that the book of hours originated *c*.1240.

114. On the nature and history of primers, see Littlehales, 1895–7; Clark, 1905, pp. 4–12; *ABC*, ed. Allnutt; E. Birchenough, 'The Prymer in English', *The Library*, 4th series, xviii (1937–8), pp. 177–94; Plimpton, pp. 18–34; Wolpe, 'Florilegium Alphabeticum', pp. 69–74.

115. Sneyd, p. 23.

116. *Visitations of Churches Belonging to St. Paul's Cathedral in 1297 and in 1458*, ed. W. Sparrow Simpson, Camden Society, new series 55 (1895), pp. 49–50.

117. STC 16010: *The Manuall of Prayers, or the Prymer in Englyshe* (London, 1539), sig. C.i verso.

118. E. Margaret Thompson, *The Carthusian Order in England* (London, 1930), p. 323.

119. *The Register of John de Grandisson, Bishop of Exeter*, ed. F. C. Hingeston-Randolph, 3 vols (London and Exeter, 1894–9), ii, 1192–3.

120. Nichols and Rimbault, p. 10.

121. Above, pp. 69–70, 208.

122. Alexander and Binski, p. 355.

123. Webb, i, 132, 135; *Plumpton Letters*, p. 30.

124. Furnivall, 1868a/1931, p. 181.

125. Chaucer, 'Canterbury Tales', VII 495–538 (B^2 *1685–1726).

126. Palsgrave, fol. 368v.

127. Asser, p. 59; Keynes and Lapidge, pp. 90–1.

128. Examples include the Hunter MS; the MS featured in Plimpton, pp. 19–33 (late 14th or early 15th century); Bodleian, MS Rawlinson C 209 (15th century); and primer material in BL, Add. MS 60577 (E. Wilson, fols. 120r–180r (late 15th century)).

129. Margaret Deanesly, *The Lollard Bible* (Cambridge, 1920, repr. 1966), p. 337.

130. Mirk, 1974, lines 410–53; Mirk, 1905, p. 282.

131. Langland, B.v.401; C.viii.10.

132. E.g. *ABC*, ed. Allnutt.

133. Deanesly, *The Lollard Bible*, p. 338.

134. Ibid., pp. 357, 368.

135. STC 14085; *The Dramatic Writings of Richard Wever and Thomas Ingelend*, ed. John S. Farmer (London, 1905), p. 59.

136. Above, p. 206.

137. STC 20034.

138. STC 15986.

139. *Visitation Articles*, ii, 6–7.

140. Frances Rose Troup, *The Western Rebellion of 1549* (London, 1915), p. 108.

141. STC 19, 19.6.

142. STC 19.4.

143. STC 17.7–19.5.

144. Tuer, passim.

145. STC 14708.5; Thomas Johnson, *A New Booke of New Conceits* (London, 1630), sig. A.v recto.

146. Elyot, fol. 18v (book i, chapter 5).

147. Hoole, pp. 6–9.

148. On what follows, see Alexandre-Bidon, 1989, pp. 971–9.

149. *CPR 1247–58*, p. 400.

150. Alexandre-Bidon, 1989, p. 973.

151. *Testamenta Eboracensia*, vol. ii, ed. J. Raine, Surtees Society, 30 (1855), p. 15.

152. For description and bibliography, see Alexander and Binski, pp. 525–6.

153. *Index*, nos 0.1, 160, 239, 312.5, 455.8, 604, 607, 1378.5, 1483, 1523, 2201, 4155.

154. STC 25412, sigs. K.viii recto – L.i. verso.

155. Opie, 1997a, pp. 53–4, 57.

CHAPTER 8: READING FOR PLEASURE

1. On this subject, see Coleman.

2. Asser, p. 59; Keynes and Lapidge, pp. 90–1.

3. Chrétien de Troyes, *Yvain*, ed. T. B. W. Reid (Manchester, 1948), lines 5360–79.

4. Montaiglon, p. 4; Caxton, 1971, p. 13.

5. BL, Harley MS 2398, fol. 94v; another version is printed in *Select English Works of John Wyclif*, ed.

Thomas Arnold, 3 vols (Oxford, 1871), iii, 195–7. I am grateful to Professor Anne Hudson for the Harley MS reference.

6. Tschann and Parkes, especially pp. xii–xxxviii, lvi–viii. The ownership of the volume is discussed by Brian D. H. Miller, 'The Early History of Bodleian MS Digby 86', *Annuale Mediaevale*, 4 (1963), pp. 23–56.

7. *The Disciplina Clericalis of Petrus Alfonsi*, trans. Eberhard Hermes (London, 1977).

8. *Doctrinal Sauvage*, ed. Aimo Sakari, Studia Philologica Jyväskyläensia, 3 (Jyväskyl, 1967).

9. For example, Cambridge University Library, MS Ff.2.38 (Parkes, 1973, pp. 568–9).

10. Kurvinen, pp. 33–67.

11. Above, p. 280.

12. Above, p. 293.

13. Above, pp. 48–50; Mynors, pp. 352–4; Dyboski.

14. Above, pp. 139–41.

15. Above, pp. 279–80, 296.

16. On English and Latin *vulgaria* and the use of proverbs in schools, see Orme, 1989, pp. 73–85.

17. Chaucer, pp. 661–83, 1195.

18. Bodleian, MS Bodley 619 (S.C. 2151). It belonged, however, to a monk of Great Malvern (Worcs.).

19. *Johnson's Journey to the Western Islands of Scotland and Boswell's Journal of a Tour to the Hebrides*, ed. R. W. Chapman (London, 1924), pp. 32, 247.

20. On what follows, see Orme, 1984, pp. 98–111 (general and political treatises), 136–9 (courtesy books), and 194–5 (hunting works).

21. *Index*, nos. 854, 3955. It was also translated into Welsh: D. Simon Evans, *A Grammar of Middle Welsh* (Dublin, 1964), p. xli; J. Lloyd-Jones, 'Lexicographical Notes: Cynghorau Catwn', *The Bulletin of the Board of Celtic Studies*, ii (1925), pp. 16–36.

22. *George Ashby's Poems*, ed. Mary Bateson, EETS, es, 76 (1899).

23. STC 6826–30; *The Dictes or Sayengis of the Philosophhres* (Westminster, 1477).

24. On courtesy literature, see Orme, 1984, pp. 134–40; J. W. Nicholls; and Severs and Hartung, ix, 3354–77.

25. Gieben, pp. 47–74.

26. Lydgate, 1989/1990.

27. J. W. Nicholls, pp. 191–5.

28. On hunting, see Orme, 1992, pp. 133–53.

29. *Index*, no. 4064; Hands, passim. Terms of association for animals had previously appeared in Walter of Bibbesworth, p. 8.

30. J. Hodgkin, 'Proper Terms', *Transactions of the London Philological Society* (1909); Hope Emily Allen, 'The Fifteenth-Century "Associations of Beasts, of Birds, and of Men": The Earliest Text with "Language for Carvers"', *Publications of the Modern Language Association of America*, 51 (1936), pp. 601–6.

31. Above, p. 296.

32. Index, nos. 671, 3362–3; Mustanoja.

33. BL, Royal MS 19 C.VII (George F. Warner and

Julius P. Gibson, *British Museum: Catalogue of Western Manuscripts in the Old Royal and King's Collections*, 4 vols (London, 1921), ii, 335–6); Thomas Wright, 1868.

34. STC 15296; Caxton, 1971, pp. 3, 194.

35. Ibid., p. xvi.

36. It is true that *puer* in Latin means 'child' not just 'boy', but Grosseteste's poem almost certainly envisages boys in a male household.

37. Orme, 1984, p. 104.

38. Ashby, *Poems*, ed. Bateson, pp. 17, 25.

39. *Index*, no. 1919; Furnivall, 1868b, especially pp. 32–40.

40. *Paston Letters*, i, 576. For calculations of Walter Paston's age, see ibid., i, p. lxiii; ii, 365.

41. Young and Aitken, pp. 138–41 (MS U.1.1.).

42. Raoul Le Fèvre, *The History of Jason*, ed. John Munro, EETS, es, 111 (1913), p. 2.

43. *Caxton's Eneydos*, ed. M. T. Culley and F. J. Furnivall, EETS, es, 57 (1890), p. 4.

44. BL, Royal MS 14 E.III, fly-leaves; Warner and Gibson, *Catalogue of the Old Royal and King's Collections*, ii, 140.

45. *Paston Letters*, i, pp. lxii–iii, 575.

46. Caxton, 1971, p. 3.

47. *Caxton's Blanchardyn and Eglantine*, ed. Leon Kellner, EETS, es, 58 (1890), p. 1.

48. Skelton, 1983, pp. 87–92.

49. Ibid., p. 405.

50. I am grateful to Professor Derek Pearsall for this comment.

51. STC 801, 1007, 5082, 12142, 12540, 13438, 15375, 15383, 19206. Two Gawain romances in English were, however, published in the early sixteenth century: STC 11691a.3–7, 11984. For *Lybeaus Desconus* see the edition by M. Mills, EETS, os, 261 (1969).

52. L. Hervieux, *Les Fabulistes latins depuis le siècle d'Auguste jusqu'à la fin du moyen âge*, 5 vols (Paris, 1894–9); Wells, pp. 180–2; Grente, pp. 716–18; Severs and Hartung, ix, 3477–86; *The Poems of Robert Henryson*, ed. Denton Fox (Oxford, 1981), pp. xli–l; Marie de France, *Fables*, ed. Harriet Spiegel (Toronto, 1994), pp. 5–7.

53. Lydgate, 1934, pp. 566–79; Caxton, 1976; Henryson, *Poems*, ed. Fox, pp. xli–l, 3–110. The Caxton translation was frequently reissued down to 1634: STC 175–84.

54. Lydgate, 1934, pp. 468–85, 539–66.

55. M. Boas, 'De librorum Catonianorum historia atque compositione', *Mnemosyne*, new series, 42 (1914), pp. 17–46; Thomson, 1979, pp. 137, 250.

56. Thomson, 1979, p. 273.

57. Henryson, *Poems*, ed. Fox, pp. 4, 26, 34, 63, 96, 110.

58. Above, p. 296.

59. A. I. Doyle, 'English Books in and out of Court from Edward III to Henry VII', in *English Court Culture in the Later Middle Ages*, ed. V. J. Scattergood and J. W. Sherborne (London, 1983), pp. 168–9; *The Cambridge History of the Book in Britain* vol. iii, ed. L. Hellinga and J. B. Trapp

(Cambridge, 1999), p. 261.

60. For examples, see Orme, 1984, pp. 82–5.

61. On this subject, see Ramsay, especially pp. 26–44, 157–88.

62. Marie de France, *Lais*, ed. A. Ewert (Oxford, 1944), pp. 35–48; *The Middle English Lai le Freine*, lines 135–230.

63. *Floris and Blancheflour*, 1927; *Floris and Blauncheflur*, 1986; Sands, pp. 279–309.

64. *The Romance of William of Palerne*, ed. W. W. Skeat, EETS, es, 1 (1867), p. xxiii.

65. Grente, pp. 1317–20. For English texts, see *The Seven Sages of Rome*, 1907 and 1933, and for Welsh, Jarman and Hughes, pp. 329–30.

66. *The Seven Sages of Rome*, 1933, p. 6.

67. Dobson and Taylor print all the earliest texts of the Robin Hood ballads, and that of *Adam Bell* (pp. 258–73).

68. For printed editions, see STC 13688–92.

69. Above, pp. 183–4.

70. STC 24446; William Tyndale, *The Obedience of a Christian Man* (Antwerp, 1528), fol. 20r.

71. STC 5892; Miles Coverdale, *Goostly Psalmes and Spirituall Songes* (London, *c*.1535), fol. 3v.

72. STC 24223.5; *The True Beliefe in Christ* (London, 1550), sig. C.ii verso.

73. Dobson and Taylor, passim.

74. Ibid., pp. 261, 263–4, 273.

75. *Index*, no. 1317, printed in Dobson and Taylor, pp. 255–7.

76. *The Romance of the Cheuelere Assigne*, ed. H. H. Gibbs, EETS, es, 6 (1868), pp. 1–19; W. R. J. Barron, '*Chevalere Assigne* and the *Naissance du Chevalere au Cygne*', *Medium Aevum*, 36 (1967), pp. 25–37; *The Old French Crusade Cycle*, vol. i, ed. Emanuel J. Mickel and Jan A. Nelson (Alabama, 1977).

77. BL, Cotton MS Caligula A.II.

78. G. E. Cockayne, *The Complete Peerage*, ed. Vicary Gibbs *et al.*, 13 vols (London, 1910–59), vi, 469–77; STC 7521–2: *The Knyght of the Swanne* (London, *c*.1560), sig. A.i verso.

79. Rous, p. 18.

80. *Bishop Percy's Folio Manuscript*, ii, 301–11; Child, 1882–8, i, 257–74.

81. Christopherson, pp. 168–73; Child, 1882–8, ii, 33–48.

82. *Index*, no. 977; Severs and Hartung, ix, 3497–8. For an edition of the MS versions, see Flügel, pp. 104–32.

83. For the sixteenth-century printed editions, see STC 14522–4.3.

84. Above, p. 178.

85. STC 7013.

86. Hellinga, pp. 68, 83.

87. On this subject, see Orme, 1999, pp. 459–64.

88. STC 21297–8, 21286.2.

89. STC 12540–1, 1987–8.

90. STC 13688–13690.

91. F. Madan, 'Day-Book of John Dorne', in *Collectanea, First Series*, ed. C. R. L. Fletcher, Oxford Historical Society, 5 (1885), pp. 79, 149.

92. Spufford, pp. 72–3.

93. Above, pp. 208, 264.

94. On what follows, see Hodnett.

95. Grente, pp. 173–4; *Der anglonormannische Boeve de Hantone*, ed. A. Stimming (Halle, 1899); *Beues of Hamtoun*, 1885–94. The latter edition includes the text printed by Richard Pynson.

96. For a summary, see *Beues of Hamtoun*, 1885–94, i, pp. xxi–xxxiii.

97. There were Betts and Good families in Long Crendon, Bucks., in the seventeenth century, a Gowd family in Aylesbury around 1700 (too late), and a Stephen Aldhouse was born in Norwich in 1672 (International Genealogical Index).

98. See, for example, Calfhill, Hooper, and Tyndale, in H. Gough, *A General Index to the Publications of the Parker Society* (Cambridge, Parker Society, 1855, p. 113); Thomas Nashe, *The Anatomie of Absurditie* (London, 1589), in *The Works of Thomas Nashe*, ed. R. B. McKerrow, 5 vols (London, 1910), i, 26; and Shakespeare, *Henry VIII*, I.i.38.

CHAPTER 9: GROWING UP

1. Nelson, pp. 1–2.

2. Above, pp. 84–5.

3. Above, pp. 240–2.

4. On this subject, see Orme, 1973, pp. 75–9.

5. Hanawalt, 1977, pp. 1–22, and idem, 1986, pp. 156–62, 273.

6. Grosjean, pp. 275–6.

7. *Acta Sanctorum*, October, i, 618–20.

8. Grosjean, pp. 293–4; cf. Hanawalt, 1993, p. 114.

9. PRO, C 1/424/58; Gardiner, p. 117.

10. *OED*, s.v. 'yeoman', 'young man'.

11. Sneyd, pp. 24–5.

12. Above, pp. 84–5.

13. Above, pp. 223–31.

14. Fenwick, p. 534.

15. Ibid., pp. 535–66.

16. Ibid., pp. 308–13.

17. *MED*, s.v. 'daie'; *OED*, s.v. 'dey'.

18. Fenwick, p. 544.

19. Ibid., pp. 143–4.

20. Ibid., pp. 194–205.

21. *Statutes of the Realm*, ii, 57.

22. Ibid., pp. 157–8.

23. *Rotuli Parliamentorum*, iv, 354; *Calendar of Letter-Books . . . of the City of London: Letter-Book K*, ed. R. R. Sharpe (London, 1911), pp. 104–5.

24. *Statutes of the Realm*, ii, 577, 636; iii, 211.

25. On London servants, see Hanawalt, 1993, pp. 173–98.

26. On the history of the institution, see Lipson, pp. 308–25, and on London in particular, Sylvia Thrupp, *The Merchant Class of Medieval London, 1300–1500* (Chicago, 1948), pp. 213–19, and Hanawalt, 1993, pp. 129–71.

27. On the term, see *MLD*, s.v. 'apprenticius'; *MED*, s.v. 'apprentis'; *OED*, s.v. 'apprentice'.

28. Thrupp, *Merchant Class*, pp. 171–2.
29. 'Indenture of Apprenticeship, Temp. Ric. II', *The Archaeological Journal*, 29 (1872), pp. 184–5.
30. Webb, i, 171–2, 196; ii, pp. xxxii–iii.
31. Woolgar, p. 39–41.
32. Margaret Aston, *Thomas Arundel: A Study of Church Life in the Reign of Richard II* (Oxford, 1967), pp. 413–14.
33. Percy, pp. 43–5.
34. Myers, pp. 70–4.
35. *Proceedings and Ordinances of the Privy Council of England*, ed. N. H. Nicolas, 7 vols (London, Record Commission, 1834–7), vii, 220–33.
36. Myers, p. 83.
37. Ibid., p. 118.
38. Edward duke of York, *The Master of Game*, ed. W. A. and F. Baillie-Grohman (New York, 1909, repr. 1974), pp. 123–7.
39. Crow and Olson, especially pp. 1–22.
40. Myers, p. 118.
41. Alan B. Cobban, *The King's Hall within the University of Cambridge in the Later Middle Ages* (Cambridge, 1969), especially pp. 9–28.
42. Myers, p. 137.
43. Aston, *Thomas Arundel*, pp. 411–14.
44. Andrew Clark, 1914, pp. 51, 55.
45. Nicolas, 1827, pp. 29, 39.
46. Hooker, pp. 6–10.
47. Above, pp. 325–7.
48. Above, p. 110.
49. Power, pp. 568–81.
50. Whythorne, p. 10.
51. Thomas of Monmouth, pp. 14, 16.
52. Eddius Stephanus, *The Life of Bishop Wilfrid*, ed. Bertram Colgrave (Cambridge, 1927), pp. 6–7; *Felix's Life of Saint Guthlac*, ed. Bertram Colgrave (Cambridge, 1956), pp. 80–1.
53. Orderic Vitalis, vi, 552–5.
54. *William of Palerne*, p. 135, lines 359–66.
55. BL, Egerton Roll 8776, m. 5.
56. *Plumpton Letters*, pp. 182–3.
57. Nelson, p. 14.
58. Ibid.
59. Ibid., p. 16.
60. Ibid.
61. Ibid., p. 15.
62. Richardson, ii, 331–430.
63. Ibid., pp. 401–3.
64. Above, p. 190.
65. *2 Henry IV*, V.iii.20, 33.
66. Macray, pp. 112–14.
67. Walter of Henley, pp. 400–3.
68. See further, Hanawalt, 1993, pp. 116, 124–8.
69. Paris, v, 367–8.
70. Knighton, p. 217.
71. Thomas and Thornley, 1938, p. 188.
72. R. Flenley, *Six Town Chronicles of England* (Oxford, 1911), p. 146.
73. Hall, pp. 588–91; Brewer and Howlett, ii, 187–8.
74. Above, p. 220–1.
75. *The Court Baron*, ed. F. W. Maitland and W. P. Baildon, Selden Society, 4 (1890), pp. 36–7, 53;

cf. *Halmota Prioratus Dunelmensis*, ed. W. H. D. Longstaffe and John Booth, Surtees Society, 82 (1889), pp. 144, 147.
76. Above, p. 220–1.
77. Orderic Vitalis, v, 20–1; Morey, p. 244.
78. Kirby, p. 465; R. H. Helmholz, *Marriage Litigation in Medieval England* (Cambridge, 1974), p. 155.
79. Holdsworth, ii, 510–11.
80. Attenborough, pp. 20–1, 38–9; Crawford, p. 52.
81. A. J. Robertson, pp. 184–5.
82. Bracton, ii, 351–3; Pollock and Maitland, i, 568–71, 580–2.
83. Bracton, ii, 353.
84. Downer, pp. 194–5.
85. Fenwick, pp. xiv–xvi.
86. For an outline of the topic, see Kean, pp. 364–70.
87. Attenborough, pp. 126–7, 156–7.
88. Ibid., pp. 168–9.
89. On what follows, see Hurnard, especially pp. viii, 152–6.
90. Above, p. 123, 214.
91. *Year Books of the Reign of King Edward the First, Years 30 and 31*, ed. A. J. Horwood (RS, 1863), pp. 510–13.
92. PRO, JUST 3/26/2, m. 4d. The boy's name is given both as Reginald and Thomas (but mainly as Thomas), and his surname as Hordtegh, of which Hordlegh seems a likelier form.
93. *Year Books of Edward II*, vol. v: *The Eyre of Kent 6 & 7 Edward II*, vol. i, ed. F. W. Maitland, L. W. V. Harcourt, and W. C. Bolland, Selden Society, 24 (1909), pp. 148–9; *Year Books of Edward the Third, Years XI and XII*, ed. A.J Horwood (RS, 1883), pp. 626–7; cf. a case of 1488 quoted by Kean, p. 367.
94. *Annales Monastici*, i, 134.
95. *Year Books of the Reign of King Edward the Third, Years XI and XII*, ed. Horwood, pp. 626–7.
96. Holdsworth, iii, 372; Kean, pp. 367–9.
97. Charles Wriothesley, *A Chronicle of England during the Reigns of the Tudors*, ed. W. D. Hamilton, vol i, Camden Society, new series, 11 (1875), p. 73.
98. Hall, p. 841; Foxe, v, 441–2.
99. On what follows, see Pollock and Maitland, i, 318–28; ii, 436–45.
100. Bracton, ii, 180; Holdsworth, iii, 350–4.
101. On what follows, see Glanvill, pp. 82–7; Bracton, ii, 250–1; Pollock and Maitland, i, 318–28; Walker, 1975–6, pp. 104–16; Walker, 1988, pp. 13–31; and Waugh, passim.
102. E.g. Attenborough, pp. 18–19; *CPR 1232–47*, pp. 229, 301.
103. W. S. McKechnie, *Magna Carta*, 2nd edn. (Glasgow, 1914), pp. 203–14.
104. Ibid., p. 214.
105. On what follows, see Glanvill, pp. 71, 75–6.
106. Holdsworth, iii, 271; *Borough Customs*, vol. 2, ed. Mary Bateson, Selden Society, 21 (1906), pp. xcv–c.
107. Glanvill, pp. 84–5; Bracton, ii, 254, 263.
108. Pollock and Maitland, i, 322–3.

109. Bracton, ii, 250–1; *MED*, s.v. 'cove'. *OED*, s.v. 'cove', suggests possible alternative meanings, 'bed-chamber' or 'store-chamber', but medieval Latin *cova* points to the latter (*MLD*, s.v.).

110. Glanvill, p. 82; Bracton, ii, 250.

111. Elaine Clark, 1985, pp. 333–48.

112. Edward Coke, *Institutes of the Laws of England*, ed. F. Hargrave and C. Butler (London, 1788), fol. 78b.

113. Bracton, ii, 251.

114. Above, p. 6–7, 230.

115. Above, p. 67.

116. *OED*, s.v. 'effeminate', 'feminine', 'tomboy', 'womanish'.

117. Above, p. 134.

118. Above, pp. 100–6.

119. Above, pp. 159–60.

120. Above, pp. 299,302.

121. Above, p. 158.

122. *On the Properties of Things*, i, 301–2, 306–7.

123. On this and on what follows, see Lyndwood, p. 272. Rastall, pp. 308–27, argues the case for later puberty among boys, but his evidence seems only to show the survival of some pre-pubescent characteristics among some boys for a few years after fourteen.

124. Adam of Usk, pp. 244–5.

125. *CIPM*, xiii, pp. 130–5; J. H. Wylie, *History of England under Henry the Fourth*, 4 vols (London, 1898, repr. New York, 1969), iii, 324–5; iv, 132.

126. Above, p. 57.

127. Nicholas Love, *The Mirrour of the Blessed Lyf of Jesu Christ*, ed. L. F. Powell (Oxford, 1908), pp. 46–7.

128. McNeil and Gamer, 1938, p. 170; Bieler, pp. 66–7, 74–5.

129. Lyndwood, p. 272; Bracton, ii, 251.

130. Above, p. 358, note 178.

131. By about 1600, the mean age of marriage for men in England was 28 and for women 26 (Wrigley and Schofield, pp. 255, 423). Lower ages have been argued for peasants at Halesowen (Worcs.) in the fourteenth century (Razi, pp. 63–4, 135–7), but the truth of this is still not clear.

132. *Councils and Synods I*, ii, 678–9.

133. *On the Properties of Things*, i, 263; Aquinas, vol. xiii (part ii, second part, question 154, articles 11–12); *Councils and Synods II*, i, 219; *Dives and Pauper*, i part ii, 58. See also, in general, James A. Brundage, *Law, Sex, and Christian Society in Medieval Europe* (Chicago and London, 1987), especially pp. 60–1, 109–10, 165–7, 212–14.

134. *Novum Glossarium Mediae Latinitatis*, ed. Franz Blatt, vol. M–N (Copenhagen, 1959–69), s.v. *mollities*; *MED* and *OED* s.v. 'pollution'; *Dives and Pauper*, i part ii, 58.

135. *Councils and Synods II*, i, 219; ii, 1064.

136. Mirk, 1974, lines 1347–1414; cf. *Yorkshire Writers: Richard Rolle of Hampole and his Followers*, ed. C. Horstman, 2 vols (London, 1895–6), ii, 341–3.

137. Burgo, fol. 40r.

138. Mirk, 1974, lines 223–5.

139. J. S. Hamilton, *Piers Gaveston, Earl of Cornwall 1307–1312* (Detroit and London, 1988), pp. 16–17; Pierre Chaplais, *Piers Gaveston: Edward II's Adoptive Brother* (Oxford, 1994), pp. 7–8, 21. For a similar view that homosexuality was not a great issue, see Pollock and Maitland, ii, 556–7.

140. Robbins, pp. xxxix, 7, 22.

141. *Index*, no. 445; Robbins, p. xxxix.

142. *Index*, no. 1091; *An Old English Miscellany*, ed. R. Morris, EETS, os, 49 (1872), pp. 190–1.

143. Above, p. 230; Robbins, pp. 6–7, 18–25.

144. Palsgrave, fol. 159r.

145. *Court Rolls of the Manor of Wakefield*, ed. John Lister, vol. iv, Yorkshire Archaeological Society, Record Series, 78 (1930), pp. 53–4, 155.

146. Britton, pp. 50–3.

147. *MLD*, s.v. 'childwita', 'legerwita'; *MED*, s.v. 'child-wite', 'leir', 'leir-wite'; *OED*, s.v. 'child-wite', 'lairwite'; *The Court Baron*, ed. Maitland and Baildon, p. 102.

148. Above, p. 57.

149. Ibid., p. 23.

150. Richardson, ii, 368, 409.

151. Caxton, 1971, pp. 19–20, 59, 79–92.

152. Mustanoja, pp. 158–63.

153. Ibid., pp. 173–5.

154. Ibid., pp. 162–9.

155. *Paston Letters*, i, pp. liv–lxiii; Kempe, p. 6.

156. See, for example, *CIPM*, xiii, pp. 91, 166, 168.

157. Fryde, pp. 39, 59.

158. Nigel Saul, *Richard II* (New Haven and London, 1997), pp. 226–30.

159. Furnivall, 1897, pp. 25–8.

160. Bracton, ii, 257, 263–4; *Statutes of the Realm*, i, part ii, 3.

161. Friedberg, i, 1100; M. M. Sheehan, 'Marriage Theory and Practice in the Conciliar Legislation and Diocesan Statutes of Medieval England', *Mediaeval Studies*, 40 (1978), pp. 408–60.

162. *Councils and Synods I*, ii, 991; cf. 981.

163. Douie and Farmer, ii, 20–7.

164. *Councils and Synods II*, i, 135, 351–2, 376, 412.

165. Robert of Flamborough, pp. 64, 85; Helmholz, *Marriage Litigation*, pp. 98–9.

166. Lyndwood, p. 272; Aquinas, vol. xix (supplement, question 43, article 2); Mannyng, lines 1663–76.

167. Furnivall, 1897, pp. 25–8.

168. John Fisher, pp. 292–3.

169. Above, pp. 84–5.

170. *Paston Letters*, i, 341–3, 409, 541.

171. Bracton, pp. 257, 264; *Statutes of the Realm*, i, part ii, 3.

172. *Fleta*, ed. H. G. Richardson and G. O. Sayles, vol. 2, Selden Society, 72 (1953), p. 27.

173. Walker, 1982, pp. 123–34.

174. Above, pp. 144.

175. Chaucer, 'Canterbury Tales', I (A), line 95; 'Troilus and Criseyde', book ii, lines 824–6, 876–82.

176. Orme, 1998, p. 76.

177. The letters are preserved in BL, Cotton MS Vespasian F.III, fol. 9 (printed in *Original Letters Illustrative of English History*, ed. Henry Ellis, 3 vols (London, 1824), i, 9–10), and Cotton MS Vespasian F.XIII, fol. 35 (printed in S. Bentley, *Excerpta Historica* (London, 1831), pp. 8–9).

178. *Paston Letters*, i, nos. 81, 83–4, 114–17, 231, 317–20, 406–7, 421.

179. Ibid., nos. 81, 407.

180. *Stonor Letters*, ii, 6–8.

181. Above, p. 92.

182. *Acta Sanctorum*, October, i, 677–8.

183. Walsingham, 1863–4, i, 261–2.

184. Orderic Vitalis, iii, 6–9, 146–7; vi, 552–5; above, p. 102.

185. Map, pp. 166–7.

186. Above, p. 175.

187. Gerald of Wales, 1861–91, vi, 75–7.

188. Adam of Usk, pp. 12–16, 86–7.

189. Kempe, p. 6.

190. Lydgate, 1911, pp. 352–4.

191. E.g. Whythorne, pp. 7–18.

192. Above, p. 181; Dillon and Hope, plates 1–3.

193. Thomas of Monmouth, pp. 12–53.

194. Lawrence, pp. 203, 223–6; *Acta Sanctorum*, April, i, 278–9; ibid., October, v, 137–8.

195. *The Register of Edmund Stafford, [Bishop of Exeter,]*, 1395–1419, ed. F. C. Hingeston-Randolph (London and Exeter, 1886), p. 387. For other requests to be buried by a parent, see Daniell, pp. 101–2.

BIBLIOGRAPHY

1. Unpublished Sources

Aberystwyth, National Library of Wales

  MS Peniarth 356B
  MS Porkington 10

Cambridge, Gonville and Caius College

  MS 174/95
  MS 417/447

Cambridge, St John's College

  MS F.26
  MS N.24

Cambridge, University Library

  MS Ff.2.38

Exeter, Cathedral Archives

  D&C 3673–4

Exeter, Devon Record Office

  296A/PW4–5 (Modbury)

Glasgow, University Library

  MS Hunter 472
  MS Hunter U.1.1.

Lincoln Cathedral Library

  MS 132

London, British Library

  Add. MS 4712
  Add. MS 6213
  Add. MS 14997
  Add. MS 18850
  Add. MS 30506
  Add. MS 42130
  Add. MS 60577
  Cotton MS Caligula A.II
  Cotton MS Julius B.XII
  Cotton MS Faustina A.V
  Cotton MS Vespasian F.III
  Cotton MS Vespasian F.XIII
  Egerton Roll 8776
  Harley MS 208
  Harley MS 642

  Harley MS 1002
  Harley MS 2398
  Harley MS 3954
  Harley MS 4712
  Harley MS 6079
  Royal MS 14 E.III
  Royal MS 19 C.VII
  Sloane MS 1584
  Stowe MS 57

London, College of Arms

  MS Arundel 6

London, Public Record Office

  C 1 Early Chancery Proceedings
  C 47 Chancery Miscellanea
  C 270 Chancery Ecclesiastical Miscellanea
  DL 28 Duchy of Lancaster, Accounts (Various)
  E 101 Exchequer, K. R., Accounts (Various)
  E 372 Exchequer, L. T. R., Pipe Rolls
  E 301 Exchequer, Augmentations, Certificates of
    Colleges and Chantries
  E 404 Exchequer of Receipt, Writs and Warrants
    for Issues
  JUST 1 Records of the Justices Itinerant, Assize
    Rolls
  JUST 2 Records of the Justices Itinerant, Coroners'
    Rolls
  JUST 3 Records of the Justices Itinerant, Gaol
    Delivery Rolls
  SP 1 State Paper Office, State Papers (Henry VIII)

Oxford, Balliol College

  MS 230
  MS 354

Oxford, Bodleian Library

  MS Ashmole 176
  MS Bodley 264
  MS Bodley 619
  MS Bodley 789
  MS Bodley 828
  MS Digby 86
  MS Douce 12
  MS Douce 135
  MS Douce 231
  MS Douce 276
  MS Dugdale 47
  MS Eng. hist b. 208
  MS Eng. poet e. 1
  MS Gough liturg. 3

MS Laud misc. 601
MS Lincoln College lat. 129 (E)
MS Lincoln College lat. 130
MS Rawlinson C 209
MS Rawlinson D 328
MS Wood donat. 4
MS Wood empt. 20

Oxford, New College

MS 264

Winchester, Winchester College

21490A (Registrum Primum)

Yale University, Beinecke Library

MS 3 (34)

2. Published Sources

The ABC both in Latyn & Englyshe, ed. E. S. Shuckburgh (London, 1889).

An Early Sixteenth-Century ABC in Latin after the Use of Sarum [ed. W. H. Allnutt (Lanhydrock, 1891)].

Acta Sanctorum, 69 vols (Antwerp and Brussels, 1643–, in progress).

Adam of Usk. *The Chronicle of Adam of Usk 1377–1421*, ed. C. Given-Wilson (Oxford, 1997).

Aesop – see Caxton.

Alexander, Jonathan, and Binski, Paul. (eds.) *Age of Chivalry: Art in Plantagenet England 1200–1400* (London, 1987).

Alexandre-Bidon, Danièle. 'La Lettre volée: apprendre à lire à l'enfant au moyen âge', *Annales*, 44 (1989), pp. 953–92.

Alexandre-Bidon, Danièle, and Lett, Didier. *Les Enfants au Moyen Age: Ve–XVe siècles* (Paris, 1997a); translated as *Children in the Middle Ages: Fifth–Fifteenth Centuries* (Notre Dame, Indiana, 2000).

Alexandre-Bidon, Danièle. 'La vie en miniature: dînettes et poupées à la fin du Moyen Age', *Ludica*, 3 (1997b), pp. 141–50.

Alexandre-Bidon, Danièle. 'Images du père de famille au Moyen Age', *Cahiers de Recherches Médiévales (XIIIe–XVe siècles)*, 4 (1997c), pp. 41–60.

Ancrene Wisse, ed. J. R. R. Tolkien, EETS, os, 249 (1962).

Anglo, Sydney. 'The Court Festivals of Henry VII', *Bulletin of the John Rylands Library*, 43 (1960–1), pp. 12–45.

Annales Monastici, ed. H. R. Luard, 5 vols (RS, 1864–9).

Aquinas, Thomas. *Summa Theologica*, 22 vols (London, 1920–4).

Ariès, Philippe. *L'Enfant et la vie familiale sous l'Ancien régime* (Paris, 1960); translated as *Centuries of Childhood* (London, 1962).

Aristotle. *The Complete Works of Aristotle: the revised Oxford translation*, ed. Jonathan Barnes, 2 vols (Princeton, 1984).

Asser. *Life of King Alfred*, ed. W. H. Stevenson, new ed. (Oxford, 1959).

Attenborough, F. L. (ed.) *The Laws of the Earliest English Kings* (Cambridge, 1922).

Baker, D. C., Murphy, J. L., and Hall, L. B. (eds.) *The Late Medieval Religious Plays of Bodleian MSS Digby 133 and e Museo 160*, EETS, os, 283 (1982).

Banting, H. M. J. (ed.) *Two Anglo-Saxon Pontificals*, Henry Bradshaw Society, 104 (1989).

Barclay, Alexander. *The Ship of Fools*, ed. T. H. Jamieson, 2 vols (Edinburgh and New York, 1874; reprinted New York, 1966).

Barclay, Alexander. *The Eclogues of Alexander Barclay*, ed. Beatrice White, EETS, os, 175 (1928).

Bartholomaeus Anglicus. *De Rerum Proprietatibus* (Dillingen, 1506). See also *On the Properties of Things*.

Bede. *Ecclesiastical History of the English People*, ed. B. Colgrave and R. A. B. Mynors (Oxford, 1991).

Bennett, Michael. 'Spiritual Kinship and the Baptismal Name in Traditional European Society', in *Principalities, Powers and Estates: Studies in Medieval and Early Modern Government and Society*, ed. L. O. Frappell (Adelaide, 1979), pp. 1–14.

The Romance of Sir Beues of Hamtoun, ed. Eugen Kölbing, 3 parts, EETS, es, 46, 48, 65 (1885–94).

Bieler, L. (ed.) *The Irish Penitentials* (Dublin, Scriptores Latini Hiberniae, vol. 5, 1963).

Bishop Percy's Folio Manuscript: Ballads and Romances, ed. J. W. Hales and F. J. Furnivall, 3 vols (London, 1867–8).

Blake, N. F. *William Caxton: a Bibliographical Guide* (New York and London, 1985).

Boswell, John. *Christianity, Social Tolerance, and Homosexuality* (Chicago and London, 1980).

Boswell, John. *The Kindness of Strangers: the Abandonment of Children in Western Europe from Late Antiquity to the Renaissance* (New York and London, 1988).

Bowers, Roger. 'To Chorus from Quartet: the Performing Resource for English Church Polyphony, c.1390–1559', in *English Choral Practice 1400–1650*, ed. John Morehen (Cambridge, 1995), pp. 1–47.

Bowers, Roger. 'The Almonry Schools of the English Monasteries, c.1265–1540', in *Monasteries and Society in Medieval Britain*, ed. Benjamin Thompson (Stamford, 1999), pp. 177–222.

Bracton, Henry. *On the Laws and Customs of England*, ed. G. E. Woodbine and S. E. Thorne, 4 vols (Cambridge, MA, 1968–77).

Brewer, J. S., and Howlett, R. (eds.) *Monumenta Franciscana*, 2 vols (RS, 1858–82).

Brightman, F. E. (ed.) *The English Rite*, 2 vols (London, 1921).

Britton, Edward. *The Community of the Vill* (Toronto, 1977).

Brown, Carleton. (ed.) *Religious Lyrics of the XVth Century* (Oxford, 1939).

Brown, Carleton. (ed.) *Religious Lyrics of the XIVth Century*, 2nd edn. (Oxford, 1957).

Brown, Carleton, and Robbins, R. H. *The Index of Middle English Verse* (New York, 1943), with *Supplement to the Index of Middle English Verse*, ed. R. H. Robbins and J. L. Cutler (Lexington, Kentucky, 1965).

Bruegel, Pieter. *Complete Edition of the Paintings*, ed. F. Grossmann, 3rd edn. (London, 1973).

Bühler, Curt F. 'Prayers and Charms in Certain Middle English Scrolls', *Speculum*, 39 (1964), pp. 270–8.

Burgo, John de. *Pupilla Oculi* (London, 1510).

Burrow, J. A. *The Ages of Man: A Study in Medieval Writing and Thought* (Oxford, 1986).

Byrne, Muriel St.Clare. (ed.) *The Elizabethan Home, Discovered in two Dialogues by Claudius Hollyband and Peter Erondell*, 3rd edn. (London, 1949).

Calendar of Close Rolls, 47 vols (London, Public Record Office, 1900–63).

Calendar of Inquisitions Miscellaneous (London, Public Record Office, 1916–, in progress).

Calendar of Inquisitions Post Mortem (London, Public Record Office, 1904–, in progress).

Calendar of Liberate Rolls, 6 vols (London, Public Record Office, 1917–64).

Calendar of Papal Letters (London, Public Record Office, 1894–1960; Dublin, 1978–, in progress).

Calendar of Patent Rolls (London, Public Record Office, 1901–, in progress).

Catholicon Anglicum, ed. Sidney J. H. Herrtage, EETS, os, 75 (1881).

Caxton, William. *Caxton's Blanchardyn and Eglantine*, ed. Leon Kellner, EETS, es, 58 (1890).

Caxton, William. *The Book of the Knight of the Tower*, ed. M. Y. Offord, Early English Text Society, supplementary series 2 (1971).

Caxton, William. *The History and Fables of Aesop*, ed. E. Hodnett (London, 1976).

The Cely Letters, ed. Alison Hanham, EETS, os, 273 (1975).

Chambers, E. K. *The Medieval Stage*, 2 vols (London, 1903).

Chaucer, Geoffrey. *The Riverside Chaucer*, ed. Larry D. Benson, 3rd edn. (Oxford, 1988).

Chauliac, Guy de. *The Cyrurgie of Guy de Chauliac*, ed. Margaret S. Ogden, vol. i, EETS, os, 265 (1971).

The Chester Mystery Cycle, ed. R. M. Lumiansky and David Mills, vol. i, EETS, ss, 3 (1974).

Child, Francis James. (ed.) *The English and Scottish Popular Ballads*, 5 vols (New York, 1882–8, reprinted 1965).

Christopherson, Paul. *The Ballad of Sir Aldingar: its origin and analogues* (Oxford, 1952).

Clanchy, Michael. *From Memory to Written Record: England 1066–1307*, 2nd edn. (Oxford, 1993).

Clark, Andrew. (ed.) *The English Register of Godstow Nunnery*, part i, EETS, os, 129 (1905).

Clark, Andrew. (ed.) *Lincoln Diocese Documents 1450–1544*, EETS, os, 149 (1914).

Clark, Cecily. 'English Personal Names ca.650–1300: some prosopographical bearings', *Medieval Prosopography*, 8 part 1 (1987), pp. 31–60.

Clark, Elaine. 'The Custody of Children in English Manorial Courts', *Law and History Review*, 3 (1985), pp. 333–48.

Clayton, Muriel. *Victoria and Albert Museum: Catalogue of Rubbings of Brasses and Incised Slabs* (London, 1968).

Close Rolls, Henry III, 14 vols (London, Public Record Office, 1902–38).

Cockayne, Oswald. (ed.) *Leechdoms, Wortcunning, and Starcraft of Early England*, 3 vols (RS, 1864–6).

Coleman, Joyce. *Public Reading and the Reading Public in Late Medieval England and France* (Cambridge, 1996).

Colgrave, B. (ed.) *Two Lives of St Cuthbert* (Cambridge, 1940).

Comenius, Jan Amos. *Orbis Sensualium Pictus*, trans. Charles Hoole (London, 1659; repr., Menston, 1970).

Cooper, Helen. *Great Grandmother Goose* (London, 1978).

Coster, William. '"From Fire and Water": the Responsibilities of Godparents in Early Modern England', in *The Church and Childhood*, ed. Diana Wood (Oxford, 1994), pp. 301–11.

Councils and Ecclesiastical Documents Relating to Great Britain and Ireland, ed. A. W. Haddan and W. Stubbs, 3 vols (Oxford, 1869–73).

Councils and Synods I: A.D. 871–1204, ed. Dorothy Whitelock, M. Brett, and C. N. L. Brooke, 2 vols (Oxford, 1981).

Councils and Synods II: A.D. 1205–1313, ed. F. M. Powicke and C. R. Cheney, 2 vols (Oxford, 1964).

Cox, J. Charles. *The Parish Registers of England* (London, 1910).

Cramer, Peter. *Baptism and Change in the Early Middle Ages, c.200–c.1150* (Cambridge, 1993).

Crawford, Sally. *Childhood in Anglo-Saxon England* (Stroud, 2000).

Crow, Martin M., and Olson, Clair C. (eds.) *Chaucer Life-Records* (Oxford, 1966).

The Dance of Death, ed. Florence Warren and Beatrice White, EETS, os, 181 (1931).

Daniell, Christopher. *Death and Burial in Medieval England, 1066–1550* (London and New York, 1997).

De Mause, Lloyd. (ed.) *The History of Childhood* (New York, 1974).

Dillon, Viscount, and Hope, W. H. St J. (eds.) *Pageant of the Birth, Life and Death of Richard Beauchamp, Earl of Warwick* (London, 1914).

Dives and Pauper, ed. Priscilla Heath Barnum, vol. i, parts i–ii, EETS, os, 275, 280 (1976–80).

Dobson, R. B., and J. Taylor. *Rymes of Robyn Hood: an introduction to the English outlaw* (London, 1976).

Douie, Decima L., and Farmer, D. H. (eds.) *Magna Vita Sancti Hugonis*, 2nd edn., 2 vols (Oxford, 1985).

Downer, L. J. (ed.) *Leges Henrici Primi* (Oxford, 1972).

Dudley, Martin R. '*Natalis Innocentium*: the Holy Innocents in Liturgy and Drama', in *The Church and Childhood*, ed. Diana Wood (Oxford, 1994), pp. 233–42.

Duffy, Eamon. *The Stripping of the Altars: Traditional Religion in England c.1400–c.1580* (New Haven and London, 1992).

Dunstan, G. R. 'The Human Embryo in the Western Moral Tradition', in *the Status of the Human Embryo*, ed. G. R. Dunstan and Mary J. Seller (London, 1988).

Dyboski, R. (ed.) *Songs, Carols and other Miscellaneous*

Pieces from the Balliol MS. 354, Richard Hill's Commonplace-Book, EETS, es, 101 (1908).

Eadmer. *The Life of St Anselm*, ed. R. W. Southern (London, 1962).

Egan, Geoff. *Base-Metal Toys* (Oxford, Finds Research Group, Datasheet 10, [1985]).

Elyot, Sir Thomas Elyot. *The Boke Named the Gouernour* (London, 1531; repr. Menston, Yorks., 1970).

Fenwick, Carolyn C. (ed.) *The Poll Taxes of 1377, 1379 and 1381*, part i (London, British Academy, Records of Social and Economic History, new series, 27, 1998).

Finucane, Ronald C. *The Rescue of the Innocents: Endangered Children in Medieval Miracles* (London, 1997).

Fisher, John. *The English Works of John Fisher*, ed. J. E. B. Mayor, vol. i, EETS, es, 27 (1876).

Fisher, J. D. C. *Christian Initiation: Baptism in the Medieval West*, Alcuin Club Collections, 47 (1965).

Fisher, J. D. C. *Christian Initiation: the Reformation Period*, Alcuin Club Collections, 51 (1970).

Floris and Blancheflour, ed. A. B. Taylor (Oxford, 1927).

Floris and Blauncheflur, ed. F. C. de Vries (Groningen, 1986).

Flügel, E. 'Liedersammlungen des XVI Jahrhunderts, besonders aus der Zeit Heinrichs VIII', *Anglia*, 26 (1903), pp. 104–32.

Fossier, Robert. (ed.) *La petite Enfance dans l'Europe médiévale et moderne* (Toulouse, 1997).

Foxe, John. *Acts and Monuments*, ed. J. Pratt, 4th edn., 8 vols (London, 1877).

The Middle English Lai le Freine, ed. Margaret Wattie, Smith College Studies in Modern Languages, 10 part 3 (Northampton, Mass., 1929).

Friedberg, E. (ed.) *Corpus Juris Canonici*, 2 vols (Leipzig, 1879–81).

Fryde, E. B., Greenway, D. E., Porter, S., and Roy, I. *Handbook of British Chronology*, 3rd edn. (London, Royal Historical Society, 1986).

Furnivall, F. J. (ed.) *Early English Meals and Manners*, EETS, os, 32 (1868a, repr. 1931).

Furnivall, F. J. (ed.) *Caxton's Book of Curtesye*, EETS, es, 3 (1868b).

Furnivall, F. J. (ed.) *Child-Marriages, Divorces, and Ratifications, &c. in the Diocese of Chester, A.D. 1561–6*, EETS, os, 108 (1897).

Galbraith, V. H. (ed.) *The Anonimalle Chronicle 1333 to 1381*, 2nd edn. (Manchester, 1970).

Gardiner, Dorothy. *English Girlhood at School* (London, 1929).

Gerald of Wales. *Opera*, ed. J. S. Brewer *et al.*, 8 vols (RS, 1861–91).

Gerald of Wales. *The Autobiography of Giraldus Cambrensis*, ed. H. E. Butler (London, 1937).

Gieben, Servus. 'Robert Grosseteste and Medieval Courtesy Books', *Vivarium*, 5 (1967), pp. 47–74.

Giles of Rome. *De Regimine Principum* (Rome, 1556).

Gittings, Clare. *Death, Burial and the Individual in Early Modern England* (London, 1984).

Given-Wilson, Chris, and Curteis, Alice. *The Royal Bastards of Medieval England* (London, 1984).

Glanvill. *The Treatise on the Laws and Customs of the Realm of England Commonly Called Glanvill*, ed. G. D. G. Hall (London, 1965).

Gordon, Eleanora C. 'Accidents among Medieval Children as Seen from the Miracles of Six English Saints and Martyrs', *Medical History*, 35 (1991), pp. 145–63.

Greene, R. L. (ed.) *The Early English Carols*, 2nd edn. (Oxford, 1977).

Grente, G. (ed.) *Dictionnaire des Lettres françaises: Le Moyen Age*, ed. R. Bossuat, L. Pichard, and G. Raynaud de Lage, 2nd edn. (Paris, 1994).

Grosjean, Paul. (ed.) *Henrici VI Angliae Regis Miracula Postuma* (Brussels, Société des Bollandistes, Subsidia Hagiographica, 22, 1935).

Gurney, Daniel. 'Extracts from the Household and Privy Purse Accounts of the Lestranges of Hunstanton', *Archaeologia*, 25 (1834), pp. 411–569.

Haas, Louis. 'Social Connections between Parents and Godparents in Late Medieval Yorkshire', *Medieval Prosopography*, 10 part i (1989), pp. 1–21.

Hale, W. H. *A Series of Precedents and Proceedings in Criminal Causes*, 2nd edn. (Edinburgh, 1973).

Hall, Edward. *Chronicle Containing the History of England* (London, 1809).

Hanawalt, Barbara. 'Childrearing among the Lower Classes of Late Medieval England', *Journal of Interdisciplinary History*, 8 (1977), pp. 1–22.

Hanawalt, Barbara. *The Ties that Bound: Peasant Families in Medieval England* (New York and Oxford, 1986).

Hanawalt, Barbara. *Growing up in Medieval London* (New York and Oxford, 1993).

Hands, Rachel. *English Hawking and Hunting in 'The Boke of St Albans'* (London, 1975).

Hanham, Alison. (ed.) *Churchwardens' Accounts of Ashburton*, Devon and Cornwall Record Society, new series 15 (1970).

Hector, L. C., and Harvey, Barbara. (eds.) *The Westminster Chronicle 1381–1394* (Oxford, 1982).

Hellinga, Lotte. *Caxton in Focus: the beginning of printing in England* (London, 1982).

Hodnett, Edward. *English Woodcuts 1480–1535*, 2nd edn. (Oxford, 1973).

Holdsworth, W. S. *A History of English Law*, 12 vols (London, 1922–38).

Homans, G. C. *English Villagers of the Thirteenth Century*, 2nd edn. (New York, 1960).

[Hooker, John.] *The Life and Times of Sir Peter Carew, Kt.*, ed. J. Maclean (London, 1857).

Hoole, Charles. *The Petty Schoole* (London, 1659).

Horman, William. *Vulgaria* (London, 1519, repr. Amsterdam, 1975).

Houlbrooke, Ralph A. *The English Family, 1450–1700* (London, 1984).

Howell, Cicely. *Land, Family and Inheritance in Transition: Kibworth Harcourt 1280–1700* (Cambridge, 1985).

Hughes, Paul L., and Larkin, James F. (eds.) *Tudor Royal Proclamations*, 3 vols (New Haven and London, 1964–9).

Hull, P. L., and Sharpe, Richard. 'Peter of Cornwall and Launceston', *Cornish Studies*, 13 (1985), pp. 5–53.

Hunnisett, R. F. *Bedfordshire Coroners' Rolls*, Bedfordshire

Historical Record Society, 41 (1961).

Hurnard, Naomi. *The King's Pardon for Homicide before A.D. 1307* (Oxford, 1969).

Hutton, Ronald. *The Stations of the Sun: a History of the Ritual Year in Britain* (Oxford and New York, 1996).

Hutton, Ronald. *The Rise and Fall of Merry England: the Ritual Year 1400–1700* (Oxford and New York, 1994).

James, M. R. 'Twelve Medieval Ghost-stories', *English Historical Review*, 37 (1922), pp. 413–22.

James, M. R. (ed.) *The Romance of Alexander* (Oxford, 1933).

James, M. R. (ed.) *The Apocryphal New Testament* (Oxford, 1953).

Jarman, A. O. H., and Hughes, Gwilym Rees. (eds.) *A Guide to Welsh Literature c.1182–c.1550*, vol. ii, 2nd edn., rev. Dafydd Johnston (Cardiff, 1997).

John of Salisbury. *Policraticus*, ed. C. C. J. Webb, 2 vols (Oxford, 1909).

John of Salisbury. *Frivolities of Courtiers and Footprints of Philosophers*, trans. J. B. Pike (Minneapolis, 1938).

Johnstone, Hilda. 'The Wardrobe and Household of Henry, Son of Edward I', *Bulletin of the John Rylands Library*, 7 (1922–3), pp. 384–420.

Judges, A. V. *The Elizabethan Underworld* (London, 1930).

Kean, A. W. G. 'The History of the Criminal Liability of Children', *Law Quarterly Review*, 53 (1937), pp. 364–70.

Kempe, Margery. *The Book of Margery Kempe*, ed. Sanford Brown Meech and Hope Emily Allen, EETS, os, 212 (1940).

Keynes, Simon, and Lapidge, Michael. (eds.) *Alfred the Great: Asser's Life of King Alfred and other Contemporary Sources* (London, 1983).

Kirby, T. F. *Annals of Winchester College* (London and Winchester, 1892).

Knighton, Henry. *Knighton's Chronicle*, ed. G. H. Martin (Oxford, 1995).

Knowles, David. *The Religious Orders in England*, 3 vols (Cambridge, 1948–59).

Knowles, David. (ed.) *The Monastic Constitutions of Lanfranc* (Edinburgh and London, 1951).

Knowles, David. *The Monastic Order in England*, 2nd edn. (Cambridge, 1963).

Kurvinen, Auvo. 'MS. Porkington 10', *Neuphilologische Mitteilungen*, 54 (1953), pp. 33–67.

Kussmaul, Ann. *Servants in Husbandry in Early Modern England* (Cambridge, 1981).

Langland, William. *The Vision of William concerning Piers Plowman*, ed. W. W. Skeat, 2 vols (Oxford, 1969).

Latham, R. E., and Howlett, D. R. (eds.) *Dictionary of Medieval Latin from British Sources* (London, 1975–, in progress).

La Tour Landry, Knight of – see Caxton; Montaiglon; Wright, T.

Lawrence, C. H. *St Edmund of Abingdon* (Oxford, 1960).

Legg, J. Wickham. (ed.) *The Clerk's Book of 1549*, Henry Bradshaw Society, 25 (1903).

Leland, John. *De Rebus Britannicis Collectanea*, ed. T. Hearne, 2nd edn., 6 vols (London, 1770).

Lester, G. A. (ed.) *Three Late Medieval Morality Plays* (London, 1981).

Letters and Papers, Foreign and Domestic, Henry VIII, 21 vols and addenda (London, Public Record Office, 1864–1932).

Lipson, E. *The Economic History of England*, 12th edn., vol. i (London, 1959).

Littlehales, Henry. (ed.) *The Prymer*, 2 vols, EETS, os, 105, 109 (1895–7).

Littlehales, Henry. 'A Few Notes on the Primer', reprinted from *The Tablet*, 22 August 1896, intended to be added to EETS, os, 109 (1897).

Littlehales, Henry. (ed.) *English Fragments*, EETS, es, 90 (1903).

Lucy, Samantha. *The Anglo-Saxon Way of Death* (Stroud, 2000).

Lupton, J. H. *A Life of John Colet*, 2nd edn. (London, 1909).

Lydgate, John. *Table Manners for Children: Stans Puer ad Mensam*, ed. Nicholas Orme (Salisbury, 1989; reprinted London, 1990).

Lydgate, John. *The Minor Poems of John Lydgate*, ed. H. N. MacCracken, vol. i, EETS, es, 107 (1911).

Lydgate, John. *The Minor Poems of John Lydgate*, ed. H. N. MacCracken, vol. ii, EETS, os, 192 (1934).

Lynch, Joseph H. *Godparents and Kinship in Early Medieval Europe* (Princeton, NJ, 1986).

Lyndwood, William. *Provinciale* (Oxford, 1679).

Machyn, Henry. *The Diary of Henry Machyn*, ed. J. G. Nichols, Camden Society, 42 (1848).

McNeill, John T., and Gamer, Helena M. *Medieval Handbooks of Penance* (New York, 1938, reprinted 1990).

Macray, W. D. (ed.) *Chronicon Abbatiae Rameseiensis* (RS, 1886).

The Macro Plays, ed. M. Eccles, EETS, os, 262 (1969).

Mannyng, Robert. *Handlyng Synne*, ed. Idelle Sullens, Medieval and Renaissance Studies, 14 (Binghampton, NY, 1983).

Manuale ad Vsum Percelebris Ecclesie Sarisburiensis, ed. A. Jefferies Collins, Henry Bradshaw Society, 91 (1960).

Map, Walter. *De Nugis Curialium: Courtiers' Trifles*, ed. M. R. James, C. N. L. Brooke, and R. A. B. Mynors, 2nd edn. (Oxford, 1983).

Meens, Rob. 'Children and Confession in the Early Middle Ages', in *The Church and Childhood*, ed. Diana Wood (Oxford, 1994), pp. 53–65.

Mehl, Jean-Michel. *Les Jeux au royaume de France du xiiie au début du xvie siècle* (Paris, 1990).

Millar, E. G. *The Luttrell Psalter* (London, 1932).

Mirk, John. *Mirk's Festial*, ed. T. Erbe, EETS, es, 96 (1905).

Mirk, John. *Instructions for Parish Priests*, ed. Gillis Kristensson, Lund Studies in English, 49 (Lund, 1974).

Montaiglon, A. de. (ed.) *Le Livre du Chevalier de la Tour Landry* (Paris, 1854).

Moore, John S. 'The Anglo-Norman Family: Size and Structure', *Anglo-Norman Studies: Proceedings of the Battle Conference*, 14 (1991), pp. 153–96.

Moran, Jo Ann Hoeppner. *The Growth of English Schooling 1340–1548* (Princeton, 1985).

More, Thomas. *The Complete Works of St. Thomas More*, ed. R. S. Sylvester *et al.*, 15 vols (New Haven and London, 1963–97).

Morey, Adrian. *Bartholomew of Exeter* (Cambridge, 1937).

Mustanoja, Tauno F. (ed.) *The Good Wife Taught her Daughter*, Annales Academiae Scientiarum Fennicae, series B, 61 part 2 (Helsinki, 1948).

Myers, A. R. *The Household of Edward IV* (Manchester, 1959).

Mynors, R. A. B. *Catalogue of the Manuscripts of Balliol College Oxford* (Oxford, 1963).

Nelson, William. (ed.) *A Fifteenth Century School Book* (Oxford, 1956).

Nicholls, J. W. *The Matter of Courtesy* (Woodbridge, 1985).

Nichols, J. G., and Rimbault, E. F. 'Two Sermons Preached by the Boy Bishop', *The Camden Miscellany, VII*, Camden Society, new series, 14 (1875).

Nicolas, N. H. (ed.) *The Privy Purse Expenses of King Henry the Eighth* (London, 1827).

Nicolas, N. H. (ed.) *Privy Purse Expenses of Elizabeth of York* (London, 1830).

Niles, Philip. 'Baptism and the Naming of Children in Late Medieval England', *Medieval Prosopography*, 3 part i (1982), pp. 95–107.

The N-Town Play: Cotton MS Vespasian D.8, ed. Stephen Spector, vol. i, EETS, ss, 11 (1991).

Opie, Iona and Peter. *The Lore and Language of Schoolchildren* (London, 1959).

Opie, Iona and Peter. *Children's Games in Street and Playground* (Oxford, 1969).

Opie, Iona and Peter. *The Singing Game* (Oxford, 1985).

Opie, Iona and Peter. (eds.) *The Oxford Dictionary of Nursery Rhymes*, 2nd edn. (Oxford and New York, 1997a).

Opie, Iona and Peter. *Children's Games with Things* (Oxford and New York, 1997b).

Orderic Vitalis. *The Ecclesiastical History of Orderic Vitalis*, ed. Marjorie Chibnall, 6 vols (Oxford, 1968–80).

Orme, Nicholas. *English Schools in the Middle Ages* (London and New York, 1973).

Orme, Nicholas. *Education in the West of England, 1066–1548* (Exeter, 1976).

Orme, Nicholas. 'The Kalendar Brethren of the City of Exeter', *Reports and Transactions of the Devonshire Association*, 109 (1977), pp. 153–69.

Orme, Nicholas. 'The Guild of Kalendars, Bristol', *Bristol and Gloucestershire Archaeological Soc. Transactions*, 96 (1978), pp. 33–52.

Orme, Nicholas. *Early British Swimming, 55 BC–AD 1719, with the first swimming treatise in English, 1595* (Exeter, 1983a).

Orme, Nicholas. 'The Medieval Clergy of Exeter Cathedral: II. The Secondaries and Choristers', *Reports and Transactions of the Devonshire Association*, 115 (1983b), pp. 85–100.

Orme, Nicholas. *From Childhood to Chivalry: the Education of the English Kings and Aristocracy 1066–1530* (London and New York, 1984).

Orme, Nicholas. 'Mortality in fourteenth-century Exeter', *Medical History*, 32 (1988), pp. 195–203.

Orme, Nicholas. *Education and Society in Medieval and Renaissance England* (London and Ronceverte, 1989).

Orme, Nicholas. 'Glastonbury Abbey and Education', in *The Early History and Archaeology of Glastonbury Abbey*, ed. Lesley Abrams and J. P. Carley (Woodbridge, 1991), pp. 285–99.

Orme, Nicholas. 'Medieval Hunting: Fact and Fancy', in *Chaucer's England: Literature in Historical Context*, ed. Barbara A. Hanawalt (Minneapolis, 1992), pp. 133–53.

Orme, Nicholas. 'Education in the Medieval Cornish Play *Beunans Meriasek*', *Cambridge Medieval Celtic Studies*, 25 (1993), pp. 1–13.

Orme, Nicholas. 'An English Grammar School ca.1450', *Traditio* 50 (1995), pp. 261–94.

Orme, Nicholas. 'Lay Literacy in England, 1100–1300', in *England and Germany in the High Middle Ages*, ed. Alfred Haverkamp and Hanna Vollrath (London and Oxford, 1996), pp. 35–56.

Orme, Nicholas. *Education in Early Tudor England: Magdalen College Oxford and its School* (Oxford, 1998).

Orme, Nicholas. 'Schools and Schoolbooks, 1400–1530', in *The Cambridge History of the Book in Britain*, vol. iii, *1400–1557*, ed. Lotte Hellinga and J. B. Trapp (Cambridge, 1999), pp. 449–69.

Owst, G. R. *Literature and Pulpit in Medieval England*, 2nd edn. (Oxford, 1961).

Page-Phillips, John. *Children on Brasses* (London, 1970).

Palsgrave, John. *Lesclarcissement de la Langue Francoyse* (London, 1530; repr. Menston, 1969).

Pantin, W. A. 'Instructions for a Devout and Literate Layman', *Medieval Learning and Literature: Essays Presented to Richard William Hunt*, ed. J. J. G. Alexander and Margaret T. Gibson (Oxford, 1976), pp. 398–422.

Paris, Matthew. *Chronica Majora*, ed. H. R. Luard, 7 vols (RS, 1872–84).

Parkes, M. B. 'The Literacy of the Laity', in *Literature and Western Civilization: the Medieval World*, ed. David Daiches and Anthony Thorlby (London, 1973), pp. 555–77.

Parkes, M. B. '*Raedan, areccan, smeagan*: how the Anglo-Saxons Read', *Anglo-Saxon England*, 26 (1997), pp. 1–22.

Parsons, J. C. 'The Year of Eleanor of Castile's Birth and her Children by Edward I', *Mediaeval Studies*, 46 (1984), pp. 245–65.

Paston Letters and Papers of the Fifteenth Century, ed. Norman Davis, 2 vols (Oxford, 1971–6).

[Percy, Thomas. (ed.)] *The Regulations and Establishment of the Household of Henry Algernon Percy* (London, 1827).

Pierce the Ploughmans Crede, ed. W. W. Skeat, EETS, os, 30 (1867).

Plimpton, G. A. *The Education of Chaucer* (Oxford, 1935).

The Plumpton Letters and Papers, ed. Joan Kirby, Royal Historical Society, Camden 5th series, 8 (1996).

Pollock, F., and Maitland, F. W. *The History of English*

Law before the Time of Edward I, 2nd edn., 2 vols (Cambridge, 1968).

Power, Eileen. *Medieval English Nunneries, c.1275 to 1535* (Cambridge, 1922).

Promptorium Parvulorum, ed. A. Way, 3 vols, Camden Society, 25, 54, 89 (1843–65).

On the Properties of Things: John Trevisa's Translation of Bartholomaeus Anglicus De Proprietatibus Rerum, ed. M. C. Seymour *et al.*, 3 vols (Oxford, 1975–88).

Ramsay, Lee. *Chivalric Romances: Popular Literature in Medieval England* (Bloomington, IN, 1983).

Rastall, Richard. *The Heaven Singing: Music in Early English Religious Drama*, vol. i (Woodbridge, 1996).

Rastell, John. *Three Rastell Plays*, ed. Richard Axton (Cambridge, 1979).

Ratis Raving, ed. J. R. Lumby, EETS, os, 43 (1870).

Razi, Zvi. *Life, Marriage and Death in a Medieval Parish* (Cambridge, 1980).

Reaney, P. H. *A Dictionary of British Surnames*, ed. R. M. Wilson (London, 1976).

Richardson, H. G. 'Letters of the Oxford Dictatores', in *Formularies which Bear on the History of Oxford*, ed. H. E. Salter *et al.*, 2 vols, Oxford Historical Society, new series, 4–5 (1942), ii, 329–450.

Riché, Pierre, and Alexandre-Bidon, Danièle, *L'Enfance au Moyen Âge* (Paris, 1994).

Rickert, Edith. *Chaucer's World* (New York and London, 1948).

Robbins, R. H. (ed.) *Secular Lyrics of the XIVth and XVth Centuries*, 2nd edn. (Oxford, 1955).

Robert of Flamborough. *Liber Poenitentialis*, ed. J. J. Francis Firth (Toronto, 1971).

Robertson, A. J. (ed.) *The Laws of the Kings of England from Edmund to Henry I* (Cambridge, 1925).

Robertson, J. C. (ed.) *Materials for the History of Thomas Becket*, 7 vols (RS, 1875–85).

Robinson, Fred C. 'Syntactical Glosses in Latin Manuscripts of Anglo-Saxon Provenance', *Speculum*, 48 (1973), pp. 443–75.

Roper, William. *The Lyfe of Sir Thomas More, Knyghte*, ed. Elsie Vaughan Hitchcock, EETS, os, 197 (1935).

Rotuli Parliamentorum, ed. J. Strachey, 6 vols (London, 1767–77).

Rous, John. *The Rous Roll*, 2nd edn. (Gloucester, 1980).

Rowland, Beryl. 'Classical and Medieval Ideas on the "Ages of Man" and the Middle English Poem "The Parlement of the Thre Ages"', *Poetica*, 3 (1975), pp. 17–29.

Sands, D. B. (ed.) *Middle English Verse Romances*, 2nd edn. (Exeter, 1986).

Schreiner, Klaus. 'Marienverehrung, Lesekultur, Schriftlichkeit', *Frühmittelalterliche Studien*, 24 (1990), pp. 314–68.

Scot, Reginald. *The Discoverie of Witchcraft* (London, 1584).

The Seven Sages of Rome, ed. Killis Campbell (Boston, 1907).

The Seven Sages of Rome (Southern Version), ed. K. Brunner, EETS, os, 191 (1933).

Severs, J. Burke, and Hartung, Albert E. (eds.) *A Manual of the Writings in Middle English 1050–1500*, 9 vols (New Haven, 1970–93).

Shahar, Shulamith. *Childhood in the Middle Ages* (London, 1990).

Shahar, Shulamith. 'The Boy Bishop's Feast' in *The Church and Childhood*, ed. Diana Wood (Oxford, 1994), pp. 243–60.

Sharpe, R. R. (ed.) *Calendar of Coroners Rolls of the City of London* (London, 1913).

Sir Gawain and the Green Knight, ed. J. R. R. Tolkien, E. V. Gordon, and Norman Davis, 3rd edn. (Oxford, 1967).

Skelton, John. *The Complete English Poems of John Skelton*, ed. J. Scattergood (Harmondsworth, 1983).

Skelton, John. *The Poetical Works of John Skelton*, ed. A. Dyce, 2 vols (London, 1843; repr. New York, 1965).

Sneyd, Charlotte Augusta. (ed.) *A Relation . . . of the Island of England*, Camden Society, 37 (1847).

Spufford, Margaret. *Small Books and Pleasant Histories* (London, 1981).

Stanbridge, John. *The Vulgaria of John Stanbridge and Robert Whittinton*, ed. Beatrice White, EETS, os, 187 (1932).

The Statutes of the Realm, from Magna Carta to the End of the Reign of Queen Anne, 10 vols (London, Record Commission, 1810–24).

Stephenson, Mill. *A List of Monumental Brasses in the British Isles* (London, 1926).

Stone, Lawrence. *The Family, Sex and Marriage in England, 1500–1800* (London, 1977).

Stone, Louise, Rothwell, W., and Reid, T. B. W. (eds.) *Anglo-Norman Dictionary* (London, 1977–92).

The Stonor Letters and Papers, 1290–1483, ed. C. L. Kingsford, 2 vols, Royal Historical Society, Camden 3rd series, 29–30 (1919).

Strutt, Joseph. *The Sports and Pastimes of the People of England*, ed. William Hone (London, 1876).

Strype, John. *Ecclesiastical Memorials Relating Chiefly to Religion*, 3 vols in 6 (Oxford, 1822).

Stubbs, William. (ed.) *Chronicles of the Reigns of Edward I. and Edward II.*, 2 vols (RS, 1882–3).

Swanson, Jenny. 'Childhood and Childrearing in *ad status* Sermons by Later Thirteenth Century Friars', *Journal of Medieval History*, 16 (1990), pp. 309–31.

Swanson, R. N. *Church and Society in Late Medieval England* (Oxford, 1989).

Tanner, Joan D., 'Tombs of Royal Babies in Westminster Abbey', *The Journal of the British Archaeological Association*, 3rd series, 16 (1953), pp. 25–40.

Tanner, Norman P. (ed.) *Decrees of the Ecumenical Councils*, 2 vols (London and Washington, 1990).

Thomas of Chobham. *Summa Confessorum*, ed. F. Broomfield (Louvain, 1968).

Thomas of Monmouth. *The Life and Miracles of St William of Norwich*, ed. A. Jessopp and M. R. James (Cambridge, 1896).

Thomas, A. H., and Thornley, I. D. (eds.) *The Great Chronicle of London* (London, 1938).

Thomas, Keith. *Rule and Misrule in the Schools of Early Modern England* (Reading, 1976).

Thomas, Keith. 'Children in Early Modern England', in *Children and their Books: a Celebration of the Work of*

Iona and Peter Opie, ed. Gillian Avery and Julia Briggs (Oxford, 1989), pp. 45–77.

Thomson, David. *A Descriptive Catalogue of Middle English Grammatical Texts* (New York and London, 1979).

Thomson, David. (ed.) *An Edition of the Middle English Grammatical Texts* (New York and London, 1984).

The Towneley Plays, ed. M. Stevens and A. C. Cawley, vol. i, EETS, ss, 13 (1994).

Tschann, Judith, and M. B. Parkes. (eds.). *Facsimile of Oxford, Bodleian Library, MS Digby 86*, EETS, ss, 16 (1996).

Tuer, A. W. *History of the Horn-Book*, 2 vols (London, 1896).

Victoria History of the Counties of England, ed. H. A. Doubleday, William Page, *et al.* (London, 1900–, in progress).

Visitation Articles and Injunctions of the Period of the Reformation, ed. W. H. Frere and W. McC. Kennedy, 3 vols, Alcuin Club Collections, 14–16 (1910).

The Wakefield Pageants in the Towneley Cycle, ed. A. C. Cawley (Manchester, 1958).

Walker, Sue Sheridan. 'Widow and Ward: the Feudal Law of Child Custody in Medieval England', *Feminist Studies*, 3 (1975–6), pp. 104–16.

Walker, Sue Sheridan. 'Free Consent and Marriage of Feudal Wards in Medieval England', *Journal of Medieval History*, 8 (1982), pp. 123–34.

Walker, Sue Sheridan. 'The Feudal Family and the Common Law Courts: the pleas protecting rights of wardship and marriage, *c.*1225–1375', *Journal of Medieval History*, 14 (1988), pp. 13–31.

Walsingham, Thomas. *Historia Anglicana*, ed. H. T. Riley, 2 vols (RS, 1863–4).

Walsingham, Thomas. *Gesta Abbatum Monasterii S. Albani*, ed. H. T. Riley, 3 vols (RS, 1867–9).

Walter of Bibbesworth. *Le Tretiz*, ed. William Rothwell, Anglo-Norman Text Society, Plain Texts Series, 6 (1990).

Walter of Henley. *Walter of Henley and other Treatises on Estate Management and Accounting*, ed. Dorothea Oschinsky (Oxford, 1971).

Waugh, Scott. *The lordship of England: Royal Warships and Marriage in English Society and Politics, 1217–1327* (Princeton, NJ, 1989).

Webb, J. (ed.) *A Roll of the Household Expenses of Richard de Swinfield, Bishop of Hereford*, 2 vols, Camden Society, 59, 62 (1854–5).

Wells, J. E. *A Manual of the Writings in Middle English, 1050–1400* (New Haven and London, 1916). See also Severs, J. Burke.

Whythorne, Thomas. *The Autobiography of Thomas Whythorne*, ed. J. M. Osborne (Oxford, 1961).

Wilkins, D. *Concilia Magnae Britanniae et Hiberniae*, 4 vols (London, 1737).

William of Palerne: an alliterative romance, ed. G. H. V. Bunt (Groningen, 1985).

Wilson, Edward. (ed.) *The Winchester Anthology* (Woodbridge, 1981).

Wilson, H. A. (ed.) *The Pontifical of Magdalen College* Henry Bradshaw Society, 39 (1910).

Withycombe, E. G. *The Oxford Dictionary of English Christian Names*, 2nd edn. (Oxford, 1953).

Woodfield, Charmian. 'Finds from the Free Grammar School at the Whitefriars, Coventry, *c.*1545–*c.*1557/8', *Post Medieval Archaeology*, 15 (1981), pp. 81–159.

Woolgar, C. M. *The Great Household in Late Medieval England* (New Haven and London, 1999).

Wright, A. R. *British Calendar Customs: England*, ed. T. E. Lones, 3 vols, Folk-Lore Society, 97, 102, 106 (1936–40).

Wright, Susan J. 'Confirmation, Catechism and Communion: the Role of the Young in the Post-Reformation Church', *Parish, Church and People: Local Studies in Lay Religion 1350–1750*, ed. Susan J. Wright (London, 1988).

Wright, Thomas. (ed.) *The Book of the Knight of La Tour-Landry*, EETS, os, 33 (1868; revised edn., 1906).

Wright, Thomas. *Anglo-Saxon and Old English Vocabularies*, ed. Richard Paul Wülcker, 2 vols (London, 1884).

Wrigley, E. A., and Schofield, R. S. *The Population History of England 1541–1871* (London, 1981).

The York Plays, ed. Richard Beadle (London, 1982).

Young, John, and Aitken, P. Henderson. *A Catalogue of Manuscripts in the Library of the Hunterian Museum in the University of Glasgow* (Glasgow, 1908).

INDEX

Important places are indexed separately, lesser ones under the historic counties in which they lay.

puberty 328–9
reading 280–3, 285–6, 299
religion 206, 212, 223, 225
sexuality 103–4, 328–33
terminology for 6
violence 182–3, 320
work 71, 307–8, 310, 312–13, 318–19
Bracton, Henry, lawyer 15, 97, 126, 327, 335
brasses, monumental: *see* graves
Bray family 102, 120–1
breast-feeding 58–9, 66
Brereton family 334, 336
Bridget, daughter of Edward IV 42
Bristol (Gloucs.) 142, 145–6, 148, 151, 193, 213, 235
Bruegel, Pieter the Elder, painter 166–7, 170–1, 179
Buckingham, earls and dukes of 19, 34, 108, 119, 291
Buckinghamshire 53, 104, 121, 181, 188, 212, 301; *see also* Eton
bullying 101, 319
burgess tenure 326–7
Burgh, Benedict, author 279, 296
Burgh (Burgo), John: *see* John de Burgh
Byrhtferth, author 6

calendar customs 184–9
Cambridge 77, 190
St John's Hospital 86
Statute of (1388) 183, 311
university and colleges 315
Cambridgeshire 45: *see also* Cambridge, Ely
'camping' 180
Canterbury (Kent)
archbishops: *see* Cranmer, Lanfranc, Morton, Reynolds
cathedral priory 16, 42, 104, 111, 228
convocation of province 219
St Augustine's Abbey 225
Cantilupe family 48
Thomas, bishop and saint 46, 58, 62, 78, 80, 90, 98, 339, 341
Carew families
Richard, of Cornwall 183
of Devon 85, 316–17
of Surrey 37–8, 82
catechism 35, 201, 205
Cato, Distichs of, poem 279, 287, 296, 304

Caxton, William, printer 294–7; mentioned 112, 178, 206, 208–9, 278–82, 285
Cecily, daughter of Edward IV 34, 282
cemeteries 97, 116–20, 123–4, 126
Cessoles, Jacques de, chess author 178, 295, 297
Chandos, Sir John, knight 178
changelings 65–6
chansons de geste 283, 285–6
Chastising of God's Children 267–8
Chaucer, Geoffrey, poet
career of 315
writings of 281
Astrolabe 243, 278
The Canterbury Tales 6, 55, 71, 78, 95, 99–100, 124, 168, 191, 206, 229–30, 266, 282–4, 296–7, 303, 338
Troilus and Criseyde 338
Chauliac, Guy de, medical writer 63, 106, 108
Chelsea, council of (787) 23
Cheshire 334; *see also* Chester
chess 178, 295
Chester 13, 191–2
Chevalere Assigne, romance 55, 290–1
Chichester (Sussex)
bishops: *see* Pecock, Richard of Chichester
cathedral and diocese 218, 226
children and childhood
definitions of 1, 6–7
literature 274–304
other aspects: *see* appropriate words
childwite 332
choristers 226–7; mentioned 79, 116–18, 195, 315, 329; *see also* households (chapels and chapel boys)
Chrétien de Troyes, author 275
chrisom cloth 29, 102, 119
christ-cross row 251–61
Christian names: *see* names
Christopher, saint 233
Church and children 14–35, 200–36, 335–6; mentioned 41, 78, 123, 322, 329
church-going 209–13, 214
churching of women 31–3
churchyards: *see* cemeteries
Cistercian order 225
Clarence, Thomas duke of 57, 285, 329
clocks 69, 339
clothes 60, 73–5, 91
Cnut, king 322